Readings in
Contemporary Psychology

Readings in

Contemporary

Readings in
Contemporary Psychology

Psychology

Edited by Robert E. Lana / Ralph L. Rosnow

Temple University

Holt, Rinehart and Winston, Inc.

New York   Chicago   San Francisco   Atlanta
Dallas   Montreal   Toronto   London   Sydney

Cover: "Manipur" by Victor Vasarely, 1952–1962.

READINGS IN CONTEMPORARY PSYCHOLOGY

Copyright © 1972 by Holt, Rinehart and Winston, Inc.
Library of Congress Catalog Card Number: 76-170638
ISBN: 0-03-084506-8
Printed in the United States of America
34567890 006 9876543

Preface

When each of us were undergraduates, taking the introductory psychology course, we had the feeling that psychology could reveal unique and valuable insights into issues of real and immediate concern. The insights were there, just waiting to be disclosed. Yet these pressing discussions never seemed to take place in the classroom. They never seemed to get beyond the dry fundamentals that enthralled our instructors, never seemed to get at the real bases of behavior that fascinated us.

We have, therefore, tried to select readings for this anthology which will get to that vital aspect of behavior which initially enticed us when we were students. Used in conjunction with the pertinent chapters of the text, *Introduction to Contemporary Psychology,* these readings should provide material of current personal and social concern to today's student.

Because this book is intended to supplement the textbook, the section headings correspond in general to the text chapter titles. In a few instances where there is no text discussion of the general subject matter covered in a particular paper (for example, nonverbal communication), these readings will extend the content of the text.

The articles on the use of psychoactive drugs are clearly relevant to anyone anxious about the growing drug culture that has spread over the Western world. The papers on self-control procedures, nonverbal communication, obedience, and cognitive dissonance illuminate an understanding of our own feelings and behavior. Other readings on the rhetoric of confrontation, violence, racial separateness, and the genetic basis of intelligence deal with some of the most compelling and puzzling problems of contemporary American behavior.

We hope that the vital element of psychology which lured us as undergraduates and still excites and challenges us as professionals is alive for the reader of this volume.

Philadelphia, Pennsylvania
December 1971

Robert E. Lana
Ralph L. Rosnow

Contents

Readings in
Contemporary Psychology

Psychology investigates human behavior by many means. One of these is the study of the specific language of scientific investigation and research. This approach is illustrated in the first article by Fred N. Kerlinger, which makes the distinction between the way that a psychologist deals with the problem of human activity and the common-sense way in which others deal with everyday life situations.

The second reading, an essay by Edward L. Walker, focuses on an issue of primary importance to all research psychologists—their social responsibility and the social utility of their discoveries. "Science cannot proceed as if the individual's roles as scientist and as human being are completely separate," Walker states. "No part of science is categorically free of social values...Intrinsic values are equally applicable to basic and applied research, and social values are applicable to them in the same manner although they differ in remoteness of that applicability." Walker's essay presents a compelling rationale and prescription for socially useful experimentation in the behavioral sciences.

Part I

SCIENTIFIC INQUIRY AND SOCIAL RESPONSIBILITY

To understand any complex human activity we must grasp the language and approach of the individuals who pursue the activity. So it is with understanding science and scientific research. One must know and understand, at least in part, scientific language and the scientific approach to problem-solving.

One of the most confusing things to the student of science is the special way the scientist uses ordinary words. To make matters worse, he invents new words. There are good reasons for this specialized use of language, which will become evident later. Suffice it to say now that we must understand and learn the language of psychological...scientists. When a psychological investigator tells us about his independent and dependent variables we must know what he means. When he tells us that he has randomized his experimental procedures, we must not only know what he means—we must understand why he does what he does.

Similarly, the scientist's approach to the solution of his problems must be clearly understood. It is not so much that this approach is different from the approach of the layman. It *is* different, of course, but it is not strange and esoteric. Quite the contrary. When understood, it will seem natural and almost inevitable that the scientist does what he does. Indeed, we will probably wonder why much more of human thinking and problem-solving is not consciously structured along such lines....

1
Science and the Scientific Approach

Fred N. Kerlinger

SCIENCE AND COMMON SENSE

Whitehead has pointed out that in creative thought common sense is a bad master. "It's [sic] sole criterion for judgment is that the new ideas shall look like the old ones."[1] This is well said. Common sense may often be a bad master for the evaluation of

[1] A. Whitehead, *An Introduction to Mathematics.* New York: Holt, Rinehart and Winston, Inc., 1911, p. 157.

knowledge. But how are science and common sense alike and how are they different? From one viewpoint, science and common sense are alike. This view would say that science is a systematic and controlled extension of common sense, since common sense, as Conant points out, is a series of concepts and conceptual schemes satisfactory for the practical uses of mankind.[2] But these concepts and conceptual schemes may be seriously misleading in modern science—and particularly in psychology and education. It was self-evident to many educators of the last century—it was only common sense—to use punishment as a basic tool of pedagogy. Now we have evidence that this older, common-sense view of motivation may be quite erroneous. Reward seems more effective than punishment in aiding learning.

Science and common sense differ sharply in five ways. These disagreements revolve around the words "systematic" and "controlled." First, the uses of conceptual schemes and theoretical structures are strikingly different. While the man in the street uses "theories" and concepts, he ordinarily does so in a loose fashion. He often blandly accepts fanciful explanations of natural and human phenomena. An illness, for instance, may be thought to be a punishment for sinfulness. An economic depression may be attributed to Jews. The scientist, on the other hand, systematically builds his theoretical structures, tests them for internal consistency, and subjects aspects of them to empirical test. Furthermore, he realizes that the concepts he is using are man-made terms that may or may not exhibit a close relation to reality.

Second, the scientist systematically and empirically tests his theories and hypotheses. The man in the street tests his "hypotheses," too, but he tests them in what might be called a selective fashion.

He often "selects" evidence simply because it is consistent with his hypothesis. Take the stereotype: Negroes are musical. If a person believes this, he can easily "verify" his belief by noting that many Negroes are musicians. Exceptions to the stereotype, the unmusical or tone-deaf Negro, for example, are not perceived. The sophisticated social scientist, knowing this "selection tendency" to be a common psychological phenomenon, carefully guards his research against his own preconceptions and predilections and against selective support of his hypotheses. For one thing, he is not content with armchair exploration of a relation; he must test the relation in the laboratory or in the field. He is not content, for example, with the presumed relations between anxiety and school achievement, between methods of teaching and achievement, between intelligence and creativity, between pupil attitudes and learning. He insists upon systematic, controlled, and empirical testing of these relations.

A third difference lies in the notion of control. In scientific research, control means several things. For the present let it mean that the scientist tries systematically to rule out variables that are possible "causes" of the effects he is studying other than the variables that he has hypothesized to be the "causes." The layman seldom bothers to control his explanations of observed phenomena in a systematic manner. He ordinarily makes little effort to control extraneous sources of influence. He tends to accept those explanations that are in accord with his preconceptions and biases. If he believes that slum conditions produce delinquency, he will tend to disregard the incidence of delinquency in non-slum neighborhoods. The scientist, on the other hand, seeks out and "controls" delinquency incidence in different kinds of neighborhoods. The difference, of course, is profound.

Another difference between science and common sense is perhaps not so sharp. It was said earlier that the scientist is constantly preoccupied with relations among phenomena. So is the layman who invokes common sense for his explanations of phenomena. But the scientist cultivates relations almost for their own sake. More important, he consciously and systematically pursues

[2]J. Conant, *Science and Common Sense.* New Haven: Yale University Press, 1951, pp. 32, 33. A *concept* is a word that expresses an abstraction formed by generalization from particulars. "Aggression" is a concept, an abstraction that expresses a number of particular actions having the similar characteristic of hurting people or objects. A *conceptual scheme* is a set of concepts interrelated by hypothetical and theoretical propositions. (See *ibid.*, pp. 25, 47, 48.) A *construct* is a concept with the additional meaning of having been created or appropriated for special scientific purposes. "Mass," "energy," "hostility," "introversion," and "achievement" are constructs. They might more accurately be called "constructed types" or "constructed classes," classes or sets of objects or events bound together by the possession of common characteristics, characteristics defined by the scientist. The term "variable" will be defined in a later chapter. For now let it mean a symbol or name of a characteristic that takes on different numerical values.

relations. The layman does not do this. His preoccupation with relations is loose, unsystematic, uncontrolled. He often seizes, for example, on the fortuitous occurrence of two phenomena and immediately links them indissolubly as cause and effect.

Take the relation tested in a study by Hurlock.[3] In more recent terminology, this relation might be expressed: Positive reinforcement (reward) produces greater increments of learning than does negative reinforcement (punishment) or no reinforcement. The relation is between reinforcement (or reward and punishment) and learning. Educators and parents of the nineteenth century often assumed that negative reinforcement (punishment) was the more effective agent in learning. Educators and parents of the present often assume that positive reinforcement (reward) is the more effective agent. Both may say that their viewpoints are "only common sense." It is obvious, they may say, that if you reward (or punish) a child he will learn better. The scientist, on the other hand, while he may personally espouse one or the other or neither of these viewpoints, would probably insist on systematic and controlled testing of both (and other) relations, as Hurlock did.

A final difference between common sense and science lies in different explanations of observed phenomena. The scientist, when attempting to explain the relations among observed phenomena, carefully rules out what have been called "metaphysical explanations." A metaphysical explanation is simply a proposition that cannot be tested. To say, for example, that people are poor and starving because God wills it, that studying hard subjects improves the child's moral character, that delinquency is due to lack of moral fiber, that it is wrong to be authoritarian in the classroom, or that the evolving American public school is enhancing democracy is to talk metaphysically.

None of these propositions can be tested; thus they are metaphysical. As such, science is not concerned with them. This does not mean that a scientist would necessarily spurn such statements, rule them out of life, say they are not true, or claim they are meaningless. It simply means that *as a scientist* he is not concerned with them. In short, science is concerned with things that can be publicly observed and tested. If propositions or questions do not contain implications for such public observation and testing, they are not scientific questions.

FOUR METHODS OF KNOWING

Charles Peirce, the great American philosopher, said that there are four general ways of knowing or, as he put it, of fixing belief.[4] The first is the *method of tenacity*. Here men hold firmly to the truth, the truth that they know to be true because they hold firmly to it, because they have always known it to be true. Frequent repetition of such "truths" seems to enhance their validity. If one holds tenaciously to one's beliefs, even in the face of evidence that casts doubt on their validity, one seems to strengthen the beliefs. Recent psychological evidence has shown us that men will often cling to their beliefs in the face of clearly conflicting facts. And they will also infer "new" knowledge, new generalizations, from propositions that may be false.

A second method of knowing or fixing belief is the *method of authority*. This is the method of established belief. If the Bible says it, it is so. If a prominent professor says that modern education is soft and bad, it is so. If a noted physicist says there is a God, it is so. If an idea has the weight of tradition and public sanction behind it, it is so. As Peirce points out, this method is superior to the method of tenacity, because human progress, although slow, can be achieved using the method. Actually, life could not go on without the method of authority. We must take a large body of facts and information on the basis of authority. Thus, it should not be concluded that the method of au-

[3]E. Hurlock, "An Evaluation of Certain Incentives Used in Schoolwork," *Journal of Educational Psychology*, XVI (1925), 145–159.

[4]J. Buchler, ed., *Philosophical Writings of Peirce.* New York: Dover, 1955, chap. 2. In the ensuing discussion, I am taking some liberties with Peirce's original formulation in an attempt to clarify the ideas and to make them more germane to the present work. For a good discussion of the four methods, see M. Cohen and E. Nagel, *An Introduction to Logic and Scientific Method.* New York: Harcourt, 1934, pp. 193–196.

thority is unsound; it is only unsound under certain circumstances.

The *a priori method* is the third way of knowing or fixing belief. (Cohen and Nagel call it the *method of intuition.*) It rests its case for superiority on the assumption that the propositions accepted by the "a priorist" are "agreeable to reason," are self-evident. Note that a priori propositions "agree with reason" and not necessarily with experience. The idea seems to be that men, by free communication and intercourse, can reach the truth because their natural inclinations tend toward truth. The difficulty with this rationalistic position lies in the expression "agree with reason." Whose reason? Suppose two good men, using rational processes, reach different conclusions, as they often do. Which one is right? Is it a matter of taste, as Peirce puts it? If something is self-evident to many men—for instance, that learning hard subjects trains the mind and builds moral character, that American education is inferior to Russian and European education, that women are poor drivers—does this mean it is so? According to the a priori method, it does—it just "stands to reason."

The fourth method is the *method of science.* Peirce says:

> To satisfy our doubts,...therefore, it is necessary that a method should be found by which our beliefs may be determined by nothing human, but by some external permanency—by something upon which our thinking has no effect....The method must be such that the ultimate conclusion of every man shall be the same. Such is the method of science. Its fundamental hypothesis...is this: There are real things, whose characters are entirely independent of our opinions about them...[5]

The scientific approach[6] has one characteristic that no other method of attaining knowledge has: self-correction. There are built-in checks all along the way to scientific knowledge. These checks are so conceived and used that they control and verify

[5]Buchler, *op. cit.*, p. 18.
[6]It should be stated here that the position of this book is that there is no one scientific method as such. Rather, there are a number of methods that scientists can and do use, but it can probably be validly said that there is one scientific approach.

the scientist's activities and conclusions to the end of attaining dependable knowledge outside himself. Even if a hypothesis seems to be supported in an experiment, the scientist will test alternative hypotheses that, if also supported, may cast doubt on the first hypothesis. A scientist does not accept a statement as true, even though the evidence at first looks promising. He insists upon testing it. He also insists that any testing procedure be open to public inspection.

As Peirce says, the checks used in scientific research are anchored as much as possible in reality lying outside the scientist and his personal beliefs, perceptions, biases, values, attitudes, and emotions. Perhaps the best single word to express this is *objectivity*. But, as we shall see later, the scientific approach involves more than this. The point is that more dependable knowledge is attained through science because science ultimately appeals to evidence: propositions are subjected to empirical test. An objection might be raised to the effect that theory, which the scientist uses and exalts, is part of man himself. But, as Polanyi points out, "A theory is something other than myself"[7]; thus a theory helps the scientist to attain greater objectivity. In short, scientists systematically and consciously use the self-corrective aspect of the scientific approach.

SCIENCE AND ITS FUNCTIONS

What is science? This question is not easy to answer. Indeed, no definition of science will be directly attempted. We shall, instead, talk about notions and views of science and then try to explain the functions of science.

Science is a badly misunderstood word. There seem to be three popular stereotypes that impede popular understanding of scientific activity. One of these is the white coat-stethoscope-laboratory stereotype. The scientist seems to be perceived as a peculiar person who works only with facts in laboratories. He uses complicated equipment, does innumerable experiments, and piles up facts

[7]M. Polanyi, *Personal Knowledge.* Chicago: University of Chicago Press, 1958, p. 4.

for the ultimate purpose of improving the lot of mankind. Thus, while he is somewhat of an unimaginative grubber after facts, he is redeemed by his noble motives. And you can believe him when, for example, he tells you that such-and-such a toothpaste is good for you or that you should not smoke cigarettes.

The second stereotype of the scientist is that he is a brilliant individual who thinks, spins complex theories, and generally spends his time in the ivory tower aloof from the world and its problems. The scientist in this stereotype is a rather impractical theorist, even though his thinking and theory occasionally lead to results of practical significance like atomic bombs.

The third stereotype equates science with engineering and technology. The building of bridges, the improvement of automobiles and missiles, the automation of industry, the invention of teaching machines, and the like are thought to be science. The scientist's job, in this conception, is to work at the improvement of man's inventions and artifacts. The scientist himself is conceived to be a sort of highly skilled engineer working to make life smooth and efficient.

These stereotypical notions impede student understanding of science, the activities and thinking of the scientist, and scientific research in general. In short, they unfortunately make the student's task harder than it would otherwise be. Thus they should be cleared away to make room for more adequate notions.

In the scientific world itself there are two broad views of science: the static and the dynamic.[8] The *static view,* the view that seems to influence most laymen and students, is that science is an activity that contributes systematized information to the world. The scientist's job is to discover new facts and to add them to the already existing body of information. In short, science is even conceived to be a body of facts. Science, in this view, is also a way of explaining observed phenomena. The emphasis, then, is on the *present state of knowledge and adding to it,* on the extent of knowledge, and on the present set of laws, theories, hypotheses, and principles.

[8]Conant, *op. cit.,* pp. 23–27.

The *dynamic view,* on the other hand, regards science more as an *activity,* what scientists *do.* The present state of knowledge is important, of course. But it is important mainly because it is a base for further scientific operations, for further scientific theory and research. This has been called a *heuristic view.* The word "heuristic," meaning serving to discover or reveal, was used to describe arguments that were persuasive rather than logically compelling. The word now has the notion of self-discovery connected with it. A heuristic method of teaching, for instance, would be a method that emphasizes students' discovering things for themselves. The heuristic view in science emphasizes theory and interconnected conceptual schemata that are fruitful for further research. A heuristic emphasis is a discovery emphasis.

It is the heuristic aspect of science that distinguishes it in good part from engineering and technology. On the basis of a heuristic hunch, the scientist takes a risky leap. As Polanyi says, "It is the plunge by which we gain a foothold at another shore of reality. On such plunges the scientist has to stake bit by bit his entire professional life."[9] Heuristic may also be called problem-solving, but the emphasis is on imaginative and not routine problem-solving. The heuristic view in science stresses problem-solving rather than facts and bodies of information. Alleged established facts and bodies of information are important to the heuristic scientist because they help lead to further theory, further discovery, and further investigation.

Still avoiding a direct definition of science—but certainly implying one—we now look at the function of science. Here we find two distinct views. The practical man, the non-scientist generally, thinks of science as a discipline or activity aimed at improving things, at making progress. Some scientists, too, take this position. The function of science, in this view, is to make discoveries, to learn facts, to advance knowledge in order to improve things. Branches of science that are clearly and immediately of this character receive wide and strong support. Witness the strong support in the

[9]Polanyi, *op. cit.,* p. 123.

last forty to fifty years of medical research and military research. Recently, perhaps in good part because we have been threatened by alleged Soviet educational supremacy, educational research has been supported. This function of science, to improve man's lot, seems to be supported by most laymen and many scientists. The criterion of practicality is preeminent here. It can be argued (but we will not do so here) that educational research has been and is now dominated by this view.[10]

A very different view of the function of science is well expressed by Braithwaite: "The function of science...is to establish general laws covering the behaviors of the empirical events or objects with which the science in question is concerned, and thereby to enable us to connect together our knowledge of the separately known events, and to make reliable predictions of events as yet unknown."[11] The connection between this view of the function of science and the dynamic-heuristic view discussed earlier is obvious, except that an important element is added: the establishment of general laws — or theory, if you will. If we are to understand modern educational research and its strengths and weaknesses, we must explore the elements of Braithwaite's statement. We do so by considering the aims of science, scientific explanation, and the role and importance of theory.

THE AIMS OF SCIENCE, SCIENTIFIC EXPLANATION, AND THEORY

The basic aim of science is theory. Perhaps less cryptic, the basic aim of science is to find general explanations of natural events. Such general explanations are called theories. Instead of trying to explain each and every separate behavior of children, the scientific psychologist seeks general explanations that encompass and link together many different behaviors. Rather than try to explain children's methods of solving arithmetic

problems, for example, the psychologist seeks general explanations of all kinds of problem-solving. He might call such a general explanation a theory of problem-solving.

This discussion of the basic aim of science as theory may seem strange to the student, especially the student of education, who has probably been inculcated with the notion that human activities have to pay off in practical ways. If we said that the aim of science is the betterment of mankind most readers would quickly read the words and accept them. But the basic aim of science is not the betterment of mankind. It is theory. Unfortunately, this sweeping and really complex statement is not too easy to understand. Still, we must try because it is important.

Other aims of science that have been stated are: explanation, understanding, prediction, and control. If we accept theory as the ultimate aim of science, however, explanation and understanding become simply subaims of the ultimate aim. This is because of the definition and nature of theory:

A theory is a set of interrelated constructs (concepts), definitions, and propositions that presents a systematic view of phenomena by specifying relations among variables, with the purpose of explaining and predicting the phenomena.

This definition says three things. One, a theory is a set of propositions consisting of defined and interrelated constructs. Two, a theory sets out the interrelations among a set of variables (constructs), and in so doing, presents a systematic view of the phenomena described by the variables. Finally, a theory explains phenomena. It does so by specifying what variables are related to what variables and how they are related, thus enabling the researcher to predict from certain variables to certain other variables.

One might, for example, have a theory of school failure. One's variables might be intelligence, verbal and numerical aptitudes, anxiety, social class membership, and motivation. The phenomenon to be explained, of course, is school failure — or, perhaps, more accurately, school achievement. School failure is explained by specified relations between each of the six variables and school fail-

[10]See F. Kerlinger, "Practicality and Educational Research," *School Review*, LXVII (1959), 281–291.
[11]R. Braithwaite, *Scientific Explanation*. Cambridge: Cambridge University Press, 1955, p. 1.

ure, or by combinations of the six variables and school failure. The scientist, successfully using this set of constructs, then, "understands" school failure. He is able to "explain" and, to some extent at least, "predict" school failure.

It is obvious that explanation and prediction can be subsumed under theory. The very nature of a theory lies in its explanation of observed phenomena. Take reinforcement theory in psychology. A simple proposition flowing from this theory is: If a response is rewarded (reinforced) when it occurs, it will tend to be repeated. The psychological scientist who first formulated some such proposition did so as an explanation of the observed repetitious occurrences of responses. *Why* did they occur and reoccur with dependable regularity? Because they were rewarded. This is an explanation, although it may not be a satisfactory explanation to many people. Someone else may ask *why* reward increases the likelihood of a response's occurrence. A full-blown theory would have the explanation. Today, however, there is no really satisfactory answer. All we can say is that, with a high degree of probability, the reinforcement of a response makes the response occur and reoccur. In other words, the propositions of a theory, the statements of relations, constitute the explanation, as far as that theory is concerned, of observed natural phenomena.

Now, about prediction and control. It can be said that scientists do not really have to be concerned with explanation and understanding. Only prediction and control are necessary. Proponents of this point of view would say that the adequacy of a theory is its predictive power. If by using the theory we are able to predict successfully, then the theory is confirmed and this is enough. We need not necessarily look for further underlying explanations. Since we can predict reliably, we can control because control is deducible from prediction.

The prediction view of science has validity. But as far as this book is concerned, prediction is considered to be an aspect of theory. By its very nature, a theory predicts. That is, when from the primitive propositions of a theory we deduce more complex ones, we are in essence "predicting."

When we explain observed phenomena, we are always stating a relation between, say, the class *A* and the class *B*. Scientific explanation boils down to specifying the exact relations between one class of empirical events and another, under certain conditions. We say: If *A*, then *B*, *A* and *B* referring to classes of objects or events. But this *is* prediction, prediction from *A* to *B*. Thus a theoretical explanation implies prediction. And we come back to the idea that theory is the ultimate aim of science. All else flows from theory. This is perhaps what is meant by the expression "There is nothing more practical than a good theory."

It was not intended in the above discussion to discredit or denigrate research that is not specifically and consciously theory-oriented. Much valuable social scientific and educational research is preoccupied with the shorter range goal of finding specific relations; that is, merely to discover a relation is part of science. The ultimately most usable and satisfying relations, however, are those that are the most generalized, those that are tied to other relations in a theory.

The notion of generality is important here. Theories, because they are general, apply widely to many phenomena and to many people in many places. A specific relation, of course, is less widely applicable. If, for example, one finds that test anxiety is related to test performance, this finding, though interesting and important, is less widely applicable and less understood than if one first found the relation in a network of interrelated variables that are parts of a theory. Modest, limited, and specific research aims, then, are good. Theoretical research aims are better because, among other reasons, they are more widely applicable and more general.

SCIENTIFIC RESEARCH—A DEFINITION

Fortunately, it is much easier to define scientific research than it is to define science and theory. It would not be easy, however, to get scientists and researchers to agree on such a definition. Even so, we attempt one here:

Scientific research is systematic, controlled, empirical, and critical investigation of hypothetical propositions about the presumed relations among natural phenomena.

This definition requires little explanation since it is mostly a condensed and formalized statement of much that was said earlier or that will be said soon. Two points need emphasis, however. First, when we say that scientific research is systematic and controlled, we mean, in effect, that scientific investigation is so ordered that investigators can have critical confidence in research outcomes. As we shall see later, this means that the research situation is tightly disciplined. Among the many alternative explanations of a phenomenon, all but one are systematically ruled out. One can thus have greater confidence that a tested relation is as it is than if one had not controlled the situation, had not ruled out alternative possibilities.

Second, scientific investigation is empirical. If the scientist believes something is so, he must somehow or other put his belief to a test outside himself. Subjective belief, in other words, must be checked against objective reality. The scientist must always subject his notions to the court of empirical inquiry and test. That he is hypercritical of the results of his own and others' research results is a truism. Every scientist writing a research report has other scientists reading what he writes while\ he writes it. Though it is easy to err, to exaggerate, to overgeneralize when writing up one's own work, it is not easy to escape the feeling of scientific eyes constantly peering over one's shoulder. Considerable attention will of course be given in subsequent chapters to elaborating and clarifying this definition of scientific research.

THE SCIENTIFIC APPROACH

The scientific approach is a special systematized form of all reflective thinking and inquiry. Dewey, in his famous analysis of reflective thinking, *How We Think*, has given a general paradigm of prob-

lematical inquiry.[12] The present discussion of the scientific approach is based on Dewey's analysis. Dewey's treatment, however, is altered somewhat to suit the scientific framework in which we are working.

Problem-Obstacle-Idea

The scientist will usually experience an obstacle to understanding, a vague unrest about observed and unobserved phenomena, a curiosity as to why something is as it is. His first and most important step is to get the idea out in the open, to express the problem in some reasonably manageable form. Rarely or never will the problem spring full-blown at this stage. He must struggle with it, try it out, live with it. Dewey says, "There is a troubled, perplexed, trying situation, where the difficulty is, as it were, spread throughout the entire situation, infecting it as a whole."[13] Sooner or later, explicitly or implicitly, he states the problem, even if his expression of it is inchoate and tentative. Here he intellectualizes, as Dewey puts it, "what at first is merely an *emotional* quality of the whole situation."[14] In some respects, this is the most difficult and most important part of the whole process. Without some sort of statement of the problem, the scientist can rarely go further and expect his work to be fruitful.

Hypothesis

After intellectualizing the problem, after turning back on experience for possible solutions, after observing relevant phenomena, the scientist may formulate a hypothesis. A hypothesis is a conjectural statement, a tentative proposition, about the relation between two or more observed (sometimes unobservable, especially in psychology and education) phenomena or variables. Our scientist will say, "If such-and-such occurs, then so-and-so results."

[12]J. Dewey, *How We Think*. Boston: Heath, 1933, pp. 106–118.
[13]*Ibid.*, p. 108.
[14]*Ibid.*, p. 109.

Reasoning-Deduction

This step or activity is one that is frequently overlooked or underemphasized. In some respects it is perhaps the most important part of Dewey's contribution to the analysis of reflective thinking. The scientist now deduces the consequences of the hypothesis he has formulated. Conant, in talking about the rise of modern science, says that the new element added in the seventeenth century was the use of deductive reasoning.[15] Here is where experience, knowledge, and perspicuity are important. Often the scientist, when deducing the consequences of a hypothesis he has formulated, will arrive at a problem quite different from the one he started with. On the other hand, he may find that his deductions lead him to believe that the problem cannot be solved with present technical tools. For example, before modern statistics was developed, certain educational research problems were insoluble. It was very difficult, if not impossible, to test two or three interdependent hypotheses at one time. It was next to impossible to test the interactive effect of variables. And we now have reason to believe that certain problems are insoluble unless they are tackled in a multivariate manner. An example of this is teaching methods and their relation to achievement and other variables. It is likely that teaching methods, *per se,* do not differ much if we only study their simple effects. Teaching methods probably work differently under different conditions, with different teachers, and with different pupils.

An example may help us to understand better this reasoning-deduction step. Suppose an investigator becomes intrigued with aggressive behavior. He wonders why people are often aggressive in situations where aggressiveness may not be too appropriate (Problem-Obstacle-Idea). He has noted that aggressive behavior seems to occur when people have experienced difficulties of one kind or another. (Note the vagueness of the problem here.) After thinking for some time, reading the literature for clues, and making further observations, he formulates a hypothesis: Frustration leads to aggression (Hypothesis). He defines "frustration" as prevention from reaching a goal and "aggression" as behavior characterized by physical or verbal attack on other persons or objects.

He may now reason somewhat as follows. If frustration leads to aggression, then we should find a great deal of aggression among children who are in schools that are very restrictive, schools that do not permit children much freedom and self-expression. Similarly, in very difficult social situations, assuming such situations are frustrating, we should expect more aggression than is "usual." Reasoning further, if we give experimental subjects interesting problems to solve and then prevent them from solving the problems, we should predict some kind of aggressive behavior.

Reasoning might, as indicated above, change the problem. We might realize that the initial problem was only a special case of a broader, more fundamental and important problem. We might, for example, have started with a narrower hypothesis: Restrictive school situations lead to negativism in children. Then we can generalize the problem to the form: Frustration leads to aggression. While this is a different form of thinking from that discussed earlier, it is important because of what might almost be called its heuristic quality. Reasoning can help lead to wider, more basic, and thus more significant problems, as well as provide operational (testable) implications of the original hypothesis.

Observation-Test-Experiment

It should be clear to the reader by now that the observation-test-experiment phase is only part of the scientific enterprise. If the problem has been well stated, the hypothesis or hypotheses adequately formulated, and the implications of the hypotheses carefully deduced, this step is almost automatic—assuming that the investigator is technically competent.

The essence of testing a hypothesis is to test the *relation* expressed by the hypothesis. We do not test the variables, as such; we test the relation

[15]Conant, *op. cit.,* p. 46.

between the variables. All observation, all testing, all experimentation is for one large purpose: putting the problem relation to empirical test. To test without knowing at least fairly well what and why one is testing is usually to blunder. Simply to have a vague and poorly stated problem (such as "What effect does the core curriculum have on students?") and then to test students for their achievement in, say, social studies is a very inadequate procedure that can lead only to ignorance and, worse, to misguided information. Similarly, to say one is going to study grouping practices (grouping children by intellectual level, reading level, and the like) of teachers without knowing, really, why one is doing it or without stating a relation between grouping practices and some other variable or variables is research nonsense.

Another point about testing hypotheses is that we do not test a hypothesis directly. As indicated in the previous step on reasoning, we test the deduced implications of the hypothesis. Our hypothesis might be, "Writing remarks on student papers will improve future papers," which was deduced, say, from a broader hypothesis, "Reinforcement of responses leads to an increment in response rate and strength." We are not testing "writing remarks on student papers" nor "the improvement of future papers." We are testing the relation between them.

Dewey emphasized that the temporal sequence of reflective thinking or inquiry is not fixed. We can repeat and re-emphasize what he says in our own framework. The steps of the scientific approach are not neatly fixed. The first step is not neatly completed before the second step begins. Further, we may test before adequately deducing the implications of the hypothesis. The hypothesis itself may seem to need elaboration or refinement

as a result of deducing implications from it.[16]

Let us summarize the so-called scientific approach to inquiry. First there is doubt, a barrier, an indeterminate situation crying out, so to speak, to be made determinate. The scientist experiences vague doubts, emotional disturbance, inchoate ideas. He struggles to formulate the problem, even if inadequately. He studies the literature, scans his own experience and the experience of others. Often he simply has to wait for an inventive leap of the mind. Maybe it will occur; maybe not. With the problem formulated, with the basic question or questions properly asked, the rest is much easier. Then the hypothesis is constructed, after which its implications are deduced, mainly along experimental lines. In this process the original problem, and of course the original hypothesis, may be changed. It may be broadened or narrowed. It may even be abandoned. Lastly, but not finally, the relation expressed by the hypothesis is tested by observation and experimentation. On the basis of the research evidence, the hypothesis is accepted or rejected. This information is then fed back to the original problem and it is kept or altered as dictated by the evidence. Dewey finally pointed out that one phase of the process may be expanded and be of great importance, another may be skimped, and there may be fewer or more steps involved. These things are not important. What is important is the over-all fundamental idea of scientific research as a controlled rational process of reflective inquiry, the interdependent nature of the parts of the process, and the paramount importance of the problem and its statement.

[16]Hypotheses and their expression will often be found inadequate when implications are deduced from them. A frequent difficulty is when a hypothesis is so vague that one deduction is as good as another, that is, the hypothesis may not yield to precise test.

Experimental psychology is a social enterprise. It is an effort to attack problems of behavior in a controlled and rigorous fashion. The goal is the accumulation of data that are reproducible and the development of principles that work. These goals are common to any discipline with scientific aspirations.

Science is a social enterprise. Any effort to examine the problem of experimental psychology and social responsibility must place the problem in a context of the social responsibility of all science. In so doing, it becomes apparent to me that psychology has special problems in the realm of social responsibility that are not shared by other scientific disciplines. This paper is an attempt to explore the problems of social responsibility in an effort to begin the task of the development of a set of guiding principles. Those principles should preserve the integrity of experimental psychology while providing a basis for discussion and decision with respect to particular social realities when psychology is inescapably confronted with them or chooses to respond out of urgent necessity.

Science flourishes to the extent to which it receives social support, and its products may have profound social consequences. I believe that scientists have the responsibility for protecting, encouraging, and guiding social support of their disciplines. Since the products of science may have profound social consequences, I think that the problem of the scientist's responsibilities for the uses to which scientific principles are put requires reexamination.

2
Experimental Psychology and Social Responsibility[1]

Edward L. Walker

THE ROLES OF SCIENTIST AND HUMAN BEING

Some feel that the social responsibility of scientists extends far beyond the realm of the application of principle of science to human affairs. In a recent interview Noam Chomsky (1968) is quoted

[1]Presidential address delivered at the meeting of the Midwestern Psychological Association, Chicago, May 1969.

Reprinted from the *American Psychologist* by permission of the American Psychological Association, vol. 24, 1969, pp. 862–868.

as saying, "I would not criticize a person as a physicist, in Nazi Germany, if he did only physics. But I'd criticize him as a human being. My argument would be that by being complacent and quiescent he's not preventing oppression and destruction."

There are at least two major difficulties with Chomsky's statement. (a) The first is that the roles of scientist and human being may not be as completely disassociatable as Chomsky implies. (b) The second is that the tasks he prescribes for the individual scientist may be physically and psychologically impossible.

While it may be clarifying in some respects to make the distinction between the role as scientist and the role as human being, the difficulty appears to me to arise from the quite unnecessary and invalid assumption that the two roles are in all respects different rather than merely being in some respects different. Specifically, it implies that the scientific enterprise is and should be free of social values. I believe this proposition to be false, and the belief in it to have arisen from false considerations.

There is sometimes confusion between the application of research findings and applied research. The first of these problems is the one that became traumatic for the atomic physicists. Is the individual scientist responsible for the nature of the use that is made of the knowledge he acquires? There is presumably nothing good or bad about knowledge of the structure of the atom. Atomic energy can be used for good purposes (power) and bad purposes (nuclear warfare). Yet individual physicists could not escape a feeling of profound guilt concerning Hiroshima and Nagasaki. The distinction, while useful for some purposes, turned out to be a specious one for individual physicists. Thus the answer the physicist has given us is that the individual scientist does, in fact, share the responsibility for the manner in which his knowledge is used, and physicists have created organizations in response to this problem.

It is often claimed that the criteria of social value are not relevant to basic research as they are to applied and socially relevant research in any discipline. It is implied that basic research is different from applied research in that its values are intrinsic rather than extrinsic. I believe this argument to be specious as well. The intrinsic value of research is independent of the dimension of basic versus applied. An applied problem can possess all of the features of intellectual intrigue of the most esoteric of basic conundrums.

Among the various characteristics that might be used to distinguish between basic and applied research, the functionally significant one may be remoteness of applicability. It is argued that basic research must be protected from close scrutiny because the greatest advances in knowledge frequently arise from research from which the potential applicability of the results is not foreseen or foreseeable. This is a value in the strategy of research in which I believe, yet it has certain limits. The dimension has basic research at one end and at the other end it has research that can be described as applied, relevant, or simply intelligible to the ordinary layman. Applied research is research that offers no mystery to any reasonably intelligent and well-educated individual. He can see how the results may be applied, and he can see the social implications of the results as well as the scientist who was responsible for the acquisition of the knowledge. A basic research study is one that the layman is not able to judge. The judgment must be made by colleagues.

I would argue that in judging the merit of basic research, colleagues have an obligation to evaluate the research in terms of relevance and social need in the broadest sense. The problem is similar to one addressed by Lytton (1863) about a century ago. He said, "In science, address the few, in literature, the many. In science, the few must dictate opinion to the many; in literature, the many, sooner or later, force their opinion on the few." By analogy, the basic research scientist must address himself to his colleagues, the few. The applied scientist, doing relevant research, must address himself to the many as well. And because he must address the many, he is subject to having the opinion of the many forced upon him.

I would argue that basic research enjoys a freedom from accountability in terms of social values that is based on ignorance and is therefore unwarranted. However remote that applicability, I believe that ultimate human usefulness is the primary criterion on which the social support of psychological research should be based. I believe that the individual scientist should take social value into consideration in choosing his problems, and I believe that his colleagues should take social value into consideration in judging the merit of his work. Someone, either the individual scientist or his colleagues, must take the responsibility for assessing the potential social value of the research in question.

Failure to perform this task adequately has led to the charge that experimental psychology too frequently addresses itself to *trivial* problems. I do not think the charge is just. I do, however, believe that the charge is a symptom of two failures on the part of scientific psychology. The first is that we have failed to interpret basic research in terms of social relevance declaring it to be impossible. I would agree that it is difficult, but I would argue that it is necessary. It is the responsibility of the scientist himself or his colleagues, since they are the only ones who understand the research, to perform the task, however difficult it may appear.

The second failure is a disproportionate emphasis on basic research at the expense of applied, or relevant, research. I think this occurs because basic research is not available to public scrutiny and its implications are not clear. It is therefore more comfortable to work on problems where the threat of public controversy is small. If there was more relevant research, there would be less of a tendency to regard basic research as trivial. I think scientific psychologists need to be supported in their basic research, but they also need to be encouraged to tackle the more controversial but more urgent problems.

Finally, it seems reasonable that the physicist can keep his work separate from his daily, nonprofessional life on the grounds that his scientific work involves inanimate matter and that his work is not therefore relevant to human affairs. However, knowledge is a human attribute, and the physicist could not be a physicist if he was not

also human. Thus theoretical physics is a human, social form of behavior whether the immediate object of the theoretical physicist's work is living or nonliving. The inanimate character of his object of study does not make his work asocial in any significant sense. Thus the argument is that the work of a scientist working in physics is a social enterprise because all knowledge is social and of value only because of its social implications.

What *is* true is that the scientist working on non-living matter enjoys a freedom of choice of problem and procedure that is not enjoyed by the scientist whose immediate subject matter is a living organism. Thus, the psychologist has an additional social dimension in his work in that his object of study is usually human. Therefore, he works under a set of varying social proscriptions that affect what he can and cannot do as a scientist. He may not carry out experiments that are obviously harmful to his subject, a proscription he shares with medicine.

In summary, then, I would argue that science cannot proceed as if the individual's roles as scientist and as human being are completely separate. In some respects, they are inseparable. No part of science is categorically free of social values. The scientist shares the responsibility for the uses that are made of his discoveries. Intrinsic values are equally applicable to basic and applied research, and social values are applicable to them in the same manner although they differ in remoteness of that applicability. The social difference between research on atoms and humans is a matter of social restrictions applicable when the object of the research is human but does not imply that one class of object of study makes science a social activity and the other asocial.

THE INDIVIDUAL SCIENTIST AND THE SCIENTIFIC ORGANIZATION

The second major difficulty in Chomsky's position is that, if a man is to be a social activist, it is very difficult for him to be a scientist. If a man is to be a scientist, he has little time and energy for social activism.

The successful scientist is often an individual

who devotes an enormous number of hours to his scientific pursuits. He achieves a high level of scientific productivity by sacrificing a great many activities in which he would otherwise be engaged. He is likely to forego most social activities. He may neglect his family. He may teach sparingly and without substantial preparation. He may avoid involvement in committees and in administrative responsibilities. He attends meetings of scientific societies solely to exchange scientific information. He may do so even though he enjoys social affairs, has great affection for his family, believes in the need and value of teaching, realizes the necessity of administrative activities, and enjoys a party at the meetings as well as the next man. However, he loves science more than any of these, and his single-minded devotion to scientific enterprise is a choice among positively valenced activities. The same man may have deep concerns for social problems and issues, whether they appear to affect his scientific prospects or not. Yet he can no more devote himself to the solution to social problems than he can devote himself to effective university administration. There is only so much time in the day, and that time must be devoted to the scientific problem at hand, if progress is to be made. He cannot *do* science and *promote* science within the limits of his time and energy.

Furthermore, there is not always complete agreement among individual members of a discipline on what should be regarded as oppression that should therefore be opposed. For example, there may be in this audience some individuals who feel that the rabble in the park represented oppression and destruction so redolent of insurrection and threat of assassination that any preventive measures the Chicago police chose to take would be wholly justified. There may also be in this audience some who regard the behavior of the Chicago police as being so oppressive and destructive that very strong opposing action is required.

The only solution that I can see to this problem is for an organization or association of scientific psychologists to act for the individual psychologist. Such an association can determine the majority opinion of its constituency and it could act in the name of the individual scientist who has the will but not the time to devote to social action.

We might then proceed to a brief examination of what kinds of things organizations of scientists have done, what our current problems are, and what an organization of experimental psychologists might undertake to do.

Organized Scientific Psychology and Political and Social Affairs

The involvement of organized scientific psychology in political and social affairs can be contemplated in four aspects. One can review the impact of social forces on the development of psychology as a science on the one hand, and actions of scientific organizations in the realm of social and political action on the other. Both problems can be examined historically, and both can be examined for possible or probable future developments. This is the task that I set for myself in spite of my limited experience as either historian or prophet.

SOCIAL SUPPORT FOR PSYCHOLOGY

Few numbers are required to document the enormous growth of psychology as a science in less than a century. The Midwestern Psychological Association grew from a very small organization in 1926 to its present membership of about 3,500 members today. The American Psychological Association has grown from a small group in 1892 to a membership of over 35,000 in a matter of 77 years. Such growth requires massive social support. That support has come in the form of very rapidly mounting commitments from colleges and universities to staff in psychology, documented in turn by heavy enrollments in psychology from undergraduates and graduate students. The income from salaries of academic psychologists is a very large sum of money. One would have to agree that this constitutes massive social support. When one adds the amount of research support from the various branches of the Federal Government and from private foundations as well as fellowship support for students of psychology, the annual investment in psychology becomes staggering.

In the span of my own academic lifetime there has been a complete change in the forces determining the character of scientific psychology. When I was a graduate student, support came almost exclusively from university budgets. One's choice of problem was almost entirely a matter of individual interest. Now psychology is so heavily subsidized by Federal funds that much of the decision has been removed from the local scene and placed in the hands of a decision-making apparatus located in Washington.

There are, of course, two dangers involved in the present pattern of support for psychology. The remote locus of the decision function now makes it necessary to *sell* research *before* it is accomplished in contrast to the past in which the research was first done and then offered for evaluation by colleagues. Since most graduate students in psychology receive some form of financial support, the psychologist with research money has the graduate students. He who is without research funds is in a very poor competitive position. Thus, we have shifted from a position in which the graduate student tended to work with a scientist whose ideas appealed to the student to a situation in which graduate students, if they wish to be supported, must work with scientists whose ideas appeal to a group in Washington or to some other group with money to give. The support is, of course, welcome. However, I know of no effort that has been made to assess the effects of such a radical shift in the determination of what kind of psychological research may be done and what kind is suppressed because there is no funding agency with a prior interest in that particular kind of problem.

The second problem has to do with the dependence of scientific psychology on the availability of such funds and the dislocations that might occur if they are withdrawn or restricted. We already have seen something of a squeeze in the amount of Federal funds available for fellowships and for research and a profound impact from the change in draft deferment policy. While the squeeze is not yet drastic, it could certainly become so. In a recent speech, Frederick Seitz (1968), President of the National Academy of Sciences and of Rockefeller University, has sounded a warning. He feels that the current crisis is not only a matter of funds but a reaction against scientific research. He feels that the academic community is confronted by an attitude of government "of misgivings and doubt as to the wisdom or need of expenditures for basic science." He thinks that the cause of the growing disenchantment stems from the feeling on the part of government officials that the fruits of basic research are too long delayed and that the scientific part of the academic community "which has enjoyed such generous support from the Federal Government—is largely indifferent to the pressing social problems of the nation."

Thus the massive social support that has been expressed by Federal money in support of psychological research and graduate education turns out to be a mixed blessing. It has restricted the freedom of the individual investigator, warped the pattern of influence of the professor on the student, and created a state of insecurity and instability in the field.

Kenneth S. Pitzer (1968) has warned, "Throughout history, universities have suffered whenever they become tools of political and ideological power." It is to be hoped that history will not repeat itself, but scientific psychology would be remiss if it did nothing in the face of the possibilities inherent in the necessary interinvolvement of the discipline and government.

I am indebted to John Popplestone for a sample of material from the Archives of the History of American Psychology relevant to past social and political involvement of psychology. Let me review a few incidents to give you the flavor of the past.

The good fortune of American psychology is not worldwide. Psychology in the United States showed unusual growth after each of two world wars. Yet psychology in Russia and in Central Europe obviously suffered decline, distortion, or both. The Nazi regime in Germany virtually destroyed the cradle of experimental psychology. Among the documents in the Archives of the History of American Psychology is a bracing letter from Sophie Blumenthal dated July 1966. In it she relates that she had visited the Wundt Institute in Leipzig in 1934 to attend an International Congress. She says that there were but three foreign psychologists there and she was the only Jew. She attended on an "honorary" guest card. The political climate in Central Europe had become extremely inhospitable only 35 years ago.

Sophie Blumenthal's letter also recounts her visit to Bonn in 1960 to attend another International Congress. She says that the participants from Leipzig "were reluctant to participate, even in informal communication" and that they had "absurd conceptions about America." The university in which experimental psychology is generally credited with originating was named the University of Leipzig in 1409. It is now the Karl Marx Institute.

Without further documentation, it should be clear that scientific psychology grows in a climate of positive social and political support and dies in an unfavorable social and political climate. Organized psychology is remiss if it does not do what it can to ensure a favorable political and social climate.

Since it is our task to examine the kinds of social and political actions taken by scientific societies and not make an exhaustive list of them, the Midwestern Psychological Association will serve as an adequate sample. This is especially true, since the MPA has been traditionally oriented to psychology as a science and therefore to experimental psychology.

Thirty years ago the Midwestern Psychological Association passed a resolution urging that the Twelfth International Congress that was scheduled to meet in Vienna in 1941 be moved elsewhere. The resolution offered several reasons for the request. They were: Austria was annexed by Germany on March 11, 1938. "The Nazi dictatorship had subordinated the integrity of science and scientists to a political creed." It had "caused the dismissal of many scientists and scholars." It had "confiscated the passport and available funds of

Sigmund Freud." Germany's official position was described as anti-intellectual and antiscientific. The resolution ended with the statement that "attendance of the International Congress in Vienna could be interpreted at best as a lack of opposition to and at worst an endorsement of the Nazi treatment of science and scientists."

In 1951, Council considered a bid by the city of Louisville, Kentucky, to entertain the annual meeting to be held in 1953. The bid was rejected because the arrangements to be provided for Negro members of the association were intolerable. It was decided to hold the meeting in Chicago instead.

The same Council voted to grant $200 from a meager treasury to CARE to provide for the purchase of books for European and Oriental universities. The grant was eventually divided between the University of Rangoon in Burma and the Free University of Brussels, Belgium. Both of these libraries had been looted during World War II.

Nearly two decades ago, the Board of Trustees of Ohio State University voted that all outside speakers appearing on the campus had to be approved in advance by the President of the University. I have a copy of a letter written by David Grant, then Secretary-Treasurer of the Midwestern Psychological Association, to Professor Harold E. Burtt of Ohio State. It says, in part, "As officers of a responsible scientific society, the...Council...believes that (the) ruling is an unjustified invasion of academic freedom...many of our members would find the ruling so distasteful that they would be unwilling to participate in the Columbus meetings. Therefore...we...voted to cancel our acceptance of the invitation of Ohio State University and to remove our 24th annual meeting from Columbus."

In 1968, Council voted to hold its forty-first annual meeting in Chicago despite events associated with the meeting of the National Democratic Convention in Chicago that had led other scientific and scholarly societies to withdraw from Chicago.

Thus, the Midwestern Psychological Association has a history of using the weapons at hand—the holding of its meetings, or its support for the choice of meeting site for related organizations, or in the form of small contributions from its treasury—in the interest of civil rights, reparation of damage from military action, and in opposition to a political regime that clearly prevented freedom of psychological inquiry. While self-interest cannot be rejected as a motive in these actions, it is clear that the MPA has repeatedly placed itself on record as in favor of freedom of psychological inquiry for all those, whether members of the association or not, who choose to exercise that right and who have been inhibited from doing so by political authorities. The decision to meet in Chicago appears to be a reversal in form.

One might well ask what the Midwestern Psychological Association might have done that it did not do. There can be no exhaustive answer to this question. But one omission does come to mind. I remember almost contemporaneous discussions, when I was a graduate student, of the personal efforts of men such as J.R. Kantor, Kurt Lewin, and Edward C. Tolman to rescue psychological colleagues from Central Europe in the middle and late thirties. They were effective as individuals, and succeeded in saving a number of their colleagues. However, one wonders how much more effective their efforts might have been if organizations such as the Midwestern Psychological Association had joined in a concerted effort to aid scholars to escape with their lives where it was clearly threatened or to escape to a part of the world in which freedom of inquiry was not restricted.

Social and Political Obligations of Experimental Psychology

In a recent speech, excerpts of which appeared in *Science,* Representative Daddario (1968) (D-Conn.) cited an Italian philosopher as saying, "There is nothing more difficult to take in hand, more perilous to conduct, or more uncertain of its success than to take the lead in the introduction of a new order of things." Yet my commitment to talk on this subject has led me to that perilous position. I would like to propose a new order of things for scientific psychology.

I have tried to argue that the new order of things with respect to the involvement of scientific psy-

chology in certain political and social affairs is a task for a formal organization of scientists. The individual scholar must be left to pursue knowledge through individual scientific inquiry, for no organization originates knowledge. Some organizations *must* meet these obligations if we are to survive.

I would like to propose four sets of obligations experimental psychology owes to itself and to society as a whole. They amount to a preliminary formulation of a set of social and political goals, and I believe that an organization of psychologists should use every available means to advance the welfare of scientific psychology within that set of goals.

1. The first is a matter of communication. A convention such as this one provides a means of communication between scientist and scientist. It does not provide communication between scientist and layman. Such communication is an obligation of the profession and means must be developed to accomplish it. In brief, *experimental psychology has the responsibility to interpret its basic research to society as a whole.*

2. The second is the problem posed by the need for social support of experimental psychology. Representative Daddario (1968) sets this problem as a paradox. He says: "science is obviously affected by funding, funding is dependent on public policy, so science must affect public policy. The paradox is that science is characteristically aloof from politicking, feeling that it is in the best interests of the functioning of the scientific method to ignore the exigencies of politics." He also cites the outcome of a meeting that George Wald of Harvard helped to organize in August 1968 at Woods Hole. The problem was to discuss what action could be taken on Federal cutbacks in research support. The meeting seemed to produce the consensus that "the only way for scientists to work effectively for their cause is to become more active politically." I believe, then, that *experimental psychology has the responsibility to encourage its own social support through political action.*

3. The third goal has to do with pressing social

problems. In the public mind, psychology, of all disciplines, should have something to offer that would aid in dealing with them. How can a discipline that has the scientific study of learning as one of its provinces be unable to offer any solution to the problem of educating children in such a manner that they do not turn to violence in the streets and punishment in the courts? How can a discipline that purports to include the scientific study of motivation be unable to provide understanding and control of the will to order the indiscriminate destruction of life that is modern war? Pressing social problems, such as the urban ghetto, police excesses, irrational violence in the name of dissent, racism, and poverty, are clearly matters of the execution of extremely stupid and irrational behavior on the part of intelligent and rational men. If the science of human behavior has too little to offer in the solution to these problems, then we had better reexamine our directions. It is not necessary for experimental psychology to take sides on controversial issues, but it is necessary for experimental psychology to provide the data and principles in terms of which rational solutions can be reached. The third goal is: *Experimental psychology must find a means of stepping up its attack on pressing social problems.*

4. The final goal that I would propose is perhaps the most remote from life in the laboratory, but perhaps the most important of all. Experimental psychology cannot survive in a repressive political atmosphere. It shares this vulnerability with other scientific and scholarly pursuits. However, political ideologies frequently contain dogma that is in direct conflict with the principle of freedom of inquiry with respect to human behavior. Thus there are forms of political milieu in which physics and mathematics can prosper and in which psychology cannot. Thus psychology, of all scientific disciplines, must remain alert to political weather signals and it must act within its power as a political force for freedom of scientific inquiry. Thus my fourth and final goal, and final words of the day are: *Experimental psychology has the responsibility to oppose political climates that would inhibit the progress of free psychological inquiry and to encourage political climates that permit or encourage such progress.*

REFERENCES

Chomsky, N. Quotation in *New York Times,* October 27, 1968.

Daddario, E.Q. Academic science and the federal government. *Science,* 1968, **162,** 1249–1251.

Lytton, E.B. *Caxtoniana: A series of essays on life, literature, and manners.* Edinburgh and London: W. Blackwood and Sons, 1863.

Pitzer, K.S. University integrity. *Science,* 1968, **162,** 228–230.

Seitz, F. Science, government and the university. *Stanford Alumni Almanac,* 1968, **7,** 5–6.

Reading 3 deals with the hazards and mystification in prescribing pharmacological agents which may compound even further the already existing side effects of psychoactive drugs. Norman E. Zinberg and Andrew T. Weil, in the next article, give a popular account of their widely cited research on the behavioral effects of one particular drug, marijuana.

Part II
DRUGS AND THE PSYCHOPHYSIOLOGY OF HUMAN BEHAVIOR

In order to extend the potential market for its product, the pharmaceutical industry, in its communications to physicians, all too often practices mystification (1) in relabeling an increasing number of human and personal problems as medical problems.

In the context of current usage, drugs are medical agents whose function is the solution of medical problems. Only to the extent that interpersonal and other human problems can be construed as medical-psychiatric problems can they be considered appropriate targets for drug treatment. As more and more facets of ordinary human conduct, interactions, and conflicts are considered to be "medical" problems, physicians and, subsequently, patients become convinced that intervention through the medium of psychoactive drugs is desirable or required.

It is apparent that the pharmaceutical industry is redefining and relabeling as medical problems calling for drug intervention a wide range of human behaviors which, in the past, have been viewed as falling within the bounds of the normal trials and tribulations of human existence (2). Much evidence for this position is to be found in the advertisements of drug companies, both in medical journals and in direct mailings to physicians.

A series of examples will be sufficient to illustrate this point. The first involves the potential personal conflict a young woman may experience when first going off to college.

On the inside front cover of one journal (3) an advertisement states: "A Whole New World...of Anxiety"..."to help free her of excessive anxiety... adjunctive Librium." Accompanying the bold print is a full page picture of an attractive, worried looking young woman, standing with an armful of books. In captions surrounding her, the potential problems of a new college student are foretold: "Exposure to new friends and other influences may force her to reevaluate herself and her goals."..."Her newly stimulated intellectual curi-

3
Hazards Implicit in Prescribing Psychoactive Drugs

Henry L. Lennard, Leon J. Epstein, Arnold Bernstein, and Donald C. Ransom

osity may make her more sensitive to and apprehensive about unstable national and world conditions.'' The text suggests that Librium (chlordiazepoxide HCl), together with counseling and reassurance ''can help the anxious student to handle the primary problem and to 'get her back on her feet.' '' Thus, the normal problems and conflicts associated with the status change and personal growth that accompany the college experience are relabeled medical-psychiatric problems, and as such are subject to amelioration through Librium.

Another journal has an advertisement that advises a physician on how he can help deal with such everyday anxieties of childhood as school and dental visits. This advertisement, in the *American Journal of Diseases of Children* (4), portrays a tearful little girl, and in large type appear the words: ''School, the dark, separation, dental visits, 'monsters' ''. On the subsequent page the physician is told in bold print that ''The everyday anxieties of childhood sometimes get out of hand.'' In small print below he reads that ''A child can usually deal with his anxieties. But sometimes the anxieties overpower the child. Then, he needs your help.

''Your help may include Vistaril (hydroxyzine pamoate).''

The advertisement, in effect, presents an oversimplified conception of behavior and behavior change. Potential anxiety engendered by new and different situations is defined as undesirable, as constituting a medical and psychiatric problem which requires the intervention of a physician and, most particularly, intervention through the prescription of a psychoactive drug.

Physicians and parents with low tolerance for anxiety, or those with limited ability to meet the demands of even a temporarily troubled child, are more prone to believe that the child is disturbed and in need of drug treatment.

There is, however, no substantial evidence for the proposition that the prescribed drug does indeed facilitate children's participation in school situations. What is especially disturbing about advertisements such as this is that they tend to enlist the help of physicians to introduce children to a pattern of psychoactive drug use. Paradoxically, such drug use, at a later date, without a physician's prescription, is deplored both by the medical profession and the community at large.

Finally, we come upon a box used to distribute samples of Tofranil (imipramine hydrochloride) to physicians (5). On the box is a picture of an adolescent girl. Above the picture in bold print is the legend, ''Missing, Kathy Miller.'' Below the picture we read, ''$500 reward for information concerning her whereabouts.'' Alongside in white print we read the plea, ''Kathy, please come home!'' Inside the box is a letter entitled, ''Kathy, We love you....Please come home.'' We quote: ''Dear Doctor: For parents, inability to communicate with their children is a significant loss. The ''What did I do wrong?'' lament of the parent may be accompanied by feelings of incapacity, inferiority, guilt and unworthiness. Many may, in fact, be suffering from symptoms of pathological depression. What can Tofranil, imipramine hydrochloride, do for your depressed patient?''

There are multiple levels of mystification in this advertisement. First, the cover suggests that the problem of a runaway child is a medical or psychiatric problem, rather than a human or family problem to be viewed within the larger framework of conflicts between generational outlooks and values. Second, the insert suggests a parent's grief reaction is pathological and characteristic of depression. And third, once having placed the problem into the psychiatric realm the advertisement recommends the use of the antidepressant Tofranil.

This advertisement is only one of many which, as Pillard points out in his testimony before a congressional subcommittee (6), imply ''that antidepressant therapy is indicated in the griefs of everyday life'' and are ''part of a trend to suggest the use, both of antidepressants and tranquilizers, not only for specific mental illness but to soothe life's ordinary woes.''

The contemporary trend of increasing prescription of psychoactive drugs seems to be contributing to the recruitment of more and more persons into a way of life in which the regulation of personal and interpersonal processes is accomplished through the ingestion of drugs. Thus, when a physician prescribes a drug for the control or solution (or both) of personal problems of living, he does more than merely relieve the discomfort caused by the problem. He simultaneously communicates a model for an acceptable and useful way of dealing with personal and interpersonal problems. The implications attaching to this model and its long-term effects are what concern us.

MYSTIFICATION, LABELING, AND DRUG EFFECTS

The descriptions of the effects of psychoactive drugs provided in advertisements and circulars to physicians serve to perpetuate and deepen the mystification that surrounds the use of drugs to alter states of consciousness and regulate behavior. Hence Librium is claimed to "reduce anxiety," Compoz to "calm the nerves," and Elavil to "lift depression." From this frame of reference, specific psychotropic drugs are described as directly altering specific emotional states and effecting specific psychological processes. This paradigm of drug action seems patterned largely after a traditional conception of drug specificity exemplified by Paul Ehrlich's notion of the "magic bullet," wherein a given chemical agent is believed to seek out a specific target in the organism (7). Much contemporary research and theorizing about psychoactive agents (and certainly their application) still appears implicitly to be based upon this model of drug action, despite the fact that sophisticated psychopharmacologists would deny its validity. Although this approach has proved extremely useful in the management of many somatic states and particularly in the control of a wide range of infectious diseases with antibiotics, even within the framework of this conception of specific drug action, it is well established that, with any agent, there is a diffusion of effects, generally referred to as side effects.

Dubos (8) draws attention to some of the disturbances in organismic-ecological relationships resulting from drug use. He concludes that "Even a highly selective drug is likely to react with some structure other than the one for which it has been designed. In other words, absolute lack of toxicity is an impossibility" (8, p. 41).

A more appropriate model of drug action would be that, when any drug is introduced into an individual, it produces a range of systemic alterations in the physiological system of the organism, some of which are desirable effects and others of which may be undesirable effects. The desired effects are conventionally labeled as the main effects and all other changes are labeled as "side effects," regardless of whether they may be positive, negative, uncomfortable, dangerous, or massive.

Drugs are sometimes relabeled when their "side effects" prove to be more interesting than their main effect. The history of psychoactive drugs is replete with such examples. Phenothiazine was initially used as a urinary antiseptic and chlorpromazine was then used to induce artificial hibernation to facilitate anesthesia during surgery, an action Laborit (9) termed "pharmacological lobotomy." Only later were its psychoactive properties identified as its main attribute. The discovery of the "specific" effects of lithium, amphetamines, iproniazid, and others have similar histories (10).

The recognition that "specificity" of drug action is, to quite a considerable extent, a fiction created by such labeling processes should advance our understanding as well as contribute to the process of demystification.

In general, drugs not only affect the organs, functions, and processes to which they are directed, but they alter processes not intended to be so altered. Thus, antibacterial agents frequently change the balance of intestinal environments. Drugs designed to minimize tissue rejection tend to leave the organism less able to deal with viral and bacterial infectious processes.

The nonspecificity of drug action is even more crucial in the case of psychoactive drugs. Drugs designed to change experience or behavior alter not only internal body processes, as revealed by the range of possible side effects, but also affect the complex of psychological and social processes connecting the individual to his physical and human environment.

One may anticipate that the diffusion effect of psychoactive drugs would be extraordinarily broad in the light of their goal of changing human experience or behavior. Unfortunately, equally extraordinary is the extent to which this problem has been oversimplified. The problem is usually dismissed as a problem of "undesirable" but minor side effects. This oversimplification may well be at the root of the neglect of this important issue. Furthermore, while other drugs are available to alleviate unintended physical side effects of psychoactive drugs, the use of a similar strategy to control untoward, nonspecific psychological and social effects will most likely only extend the area of behavioral "fallout." Giving a second drug to counteract an undesirable side effect of a primary drug results in a further diffusion of influence, which all too frequently only extends the problem we are calling attention to. The range of unanticipated experiential and behavioral consequences is increased.

The question that must now bear the most exhaustive scrutiny is the applicability of the medical model of drug action as a rationale for the use of chemical agents to accomplish psychological (as opposed to physiological) alterations. In other words, what is the conceptual justification for the belief that specific chemical agents can be found and utilized for the control and alteration of specific cognitive and emotional states? As Schachter (11) points out, the model of specific drug action does not discriminate between the physiological and the cognitive determinants of emotional states. Research, on the whole, does not support a purely visceral physiological formulation about emotion. On the contrary, as Schachter demonstrates, there is considerable evidence of the role played by cognitive and contextual determinants of emotional states.

Schachter suggests "that a general (rather than specific) pattern of sympathetic discharge is characteristic of emotional states. Given such a state of arousal...one labels, interprets, and identifies this state in terms of the characteristics of the precipitating situation and one's apperceptive mass....Cognitions arising from the immediate situation as interpreted by past experience provide the framework within which one understands and labels one's feelings. It is the cognition that determines whether the state of physiological arousal will be labeled 'anger,' 'joy,' or whatever" (11, p. 139). And, "given a state of physiological arousal for which an individual has no immediate explanation, he will label this state and describe his feelings in terms of the cognitions available to him" (11, p. 167).

The logic of this view is that, however specific the physiological and autonomic effects of a drug may be, the cognitive-psychological effects are exceedingly variable. Within this frame of reference, drugs alone do not trigger such specific affective reactions as fear, anger, depression, joy, and the like. Specificity of psychological effect, following Schachter, hardly ever comes from the drug itself, but comes from the contextual cues surrounding the person whom the drug has "primed." Epinephrine injected in a neutral context, for example, does not induce anger in experimental subjects.

The model appropriate to psychoactive drug effects is more like the following. One takes a drug, thereby introducing specific changes in the body's physiological state. These changes, however, do not trigger specific or uniform psychological or behavioral consequences. A more specific emotional response is then generated both by the social context (the surrounding social and environmental cues) and by one's set (one's past experiences with similarly patterned experience). How one will *label* this inner experience will largely depend upon the nature of the situation and the knowledge of how similar feelings were labeled in the past. Thus, one is cognitively active in the structuring of physiological sensation and in the labeling of inner experience rather than serving as a passing recipient of an effect solely triggered by a biochemical substance (12).

Psychoactive drugs frequently tend to induce

physiological effects which facilitate a range of interpretations of bodily states. It therefore becomes possible to credit the drugs as the source of a specific mood change. The popularity of many over-the-counter "sedatives" and "tranquilizers" may in large measure be due to the ease with which drowsiness, lassitude, and general physiological slowing can be interpreted and labeled as psychic tranquillity. Interestingly enough, a major property of Valium (diazepam), one of the most commonly used minor tranquilizers, is its action as a muscle relaxant (13). Parenthetically, it may also be noted that a major physiological effect of Spanish fly (cantharides), an aphrodisiac, is irritation of the urinary tract. When this drug is given or taken for the purpose of increasing sexual excitement, the recipient of the drug is encouraged to interpret the increased irritability of the urethra and other sensations as a sign of the drug's beneficial effect on the target function.

COSTS OF MYSTIFICATION

When a physician prescribes drugs to a middle-aged woman who is upset about her child's rebellion or who is miserable in an unhappy marriage, or to an elderly man or woman who has been isolated from children and community; or when he prescribes drugs to children who cause trouble in schools, he often only masks the problem. In these instances drugs serve to decrease the anxiety or unhappiness of the individual and, more importantly, decrease the amount of trouble his anxiety, misery, or unhappiness may be causing others. Drugs may thus indeed make it more possible for others to manage or cope with the disturbed or disturbing individual.

The drugs do not, however, reach the sources of the anxiety or misery which may, for example, reside in an unhappy marriage, in the unfortunate position of the elderly in our society, or in the unsuccessful socialization of many youngsters into group settings. In other words, drugs do not remedy the unfavorable social and interpersonal arrangements and personal circumstances which

generate anxiety or unhappiness. Through the creation of chemical barriers, and through diminishing gross social deviance, drugs may actually serve to perpetuate malignant patterns and social arrangements. Were drugs not so readily available, pressure for other solutions and the pursuit of alternative options might be encouraged.

In the giving and taking of drugs, one pays for what one gets. The double entries in this ledger are too often ignored and too easily denied by the youthful user of illegal drugs who thinks that he gets something for nothing, who considers only the immediate sensory experience, the ecstatic "high," and freedom from anxiety, without attending to the personal and group costs exacted. This proposition concerning costs is also strenuously denied by those advocates of "legal" drugs—physicians who casually and consistently prescribe tranquilizers and sedatives. It is part of contemporary medical mythology that drugs somehow do not exact the same price from the user when they are prescribed by a physician and that a patient can get relief from his symptoms and escape from his troubles through psychoactive drugs, provided they are duly prescribed, without paying a cost (14).

One may well ask what costs are involved. Briefly, we see two major kinds: costs at the level of the individual and his personal functioning and experience, and costs at the level of human relatedness in significant social systems within which the drugged person lives.

The first kind range from the multitude of side effects attending drug usage, from the "feeling of being drained"—often reported after amphetamine use to a robot-like sensation frequently noted after phenothiazine ingestion—to the alterations in the body's own self-regulating functions, which are assumed by the drugs ingested.

The second kind is less visible, but potentially even more important. Involved here are fundamental alterations at the level of social interaction and group responsiveness to distressed and deviant behavior. The use of drugs erodes a group's ability to make provisions and develop strategies of human relatedness, which serve to regulate particular kinds of psychological processes of its members, such as anxiety, grief, rage, and other more extreme forms of behavior (15). The regulatory function is delegated to drugs, not to the significant parties in the interpersonal environment. We anticipate that the eventual cost in human group relatedness, of this decision to substitute a drug modality for an interpersonal one, will be a heavy one. The more potent the drug, the more sustained its use, the more likely is there to be an increase in side effects, the unanticipated and unwanted consequences of drug use.

Drug giving and drug taking represent all too brittle and undiscriminating responses, and ultimately, in our view, they will breed only more frustration and more alienation. Changing the human environment is a monumental undertaking. While seeking to change cognitive shapes through chemical means is more convenient and economical, the drug solution has already become another technological Trojan horse.

The ultimate task is to alter the shapes of human relatedness and social arrangements that determine the context and the substance of our existence. To maintain, as do significant groups within the pharmaceutical industry, the medical profession, and the youth culture, that this can be accomplished merely through chemical means is indeed to have fallen victim to mystification.

REFERENCES AND NOTES

1. The concept of "mystification" originally described by Marx has recently been adapted to the study of family dynamics by R.D. Laing and others. For Laing, mystification "entails the substitution of false for true construction of what is being experienced, being done (praxis), or going on (process), and the substitution of false issues for the actual issues" [R.D. Laing, "Mystification, confusion and conflict," in *Intensive Family Therapy*, I. Boszormanyi-Nagy and J. Framo, Eds. (Hoeber Medical Division, New York, 1965)]. It seems to us that the concept of mystification, in the above sense, is applicable to the process by which psychoactive drug action is often presented and defined for those to whom these drugs are administered.

2. We should emphasize that we do not wish to minimize research and clinical observations pointing to the usefulness of psychoactive agents, especially of the major tranquilizers in the management of severe psychiatric disorders. There is, however, an immense difference between psychopharmacological intervention for this patient group with strikingly troublesome symptomatology and the advocacy of the use of psychoactive agents to treat *la condition humaine,* that is, the emotional challenges of daily living.

3. *Journal of the American College Health Association* **17,** No. 5 (June 1969).

4. *American Journal of Diseases of Children* **118,** No. 2 (Aug. 1969).

5. Professional sample, *Geigy Pharmaceutical,* insert dated 15 August 1968.

6. R.C. Pillard, statement before Subcommittee on Monopoly of the Select Committee on Small Business, 30 July 1969 (U.S. Government Printing Office, Washington, D.C., 1969), p. 5408.

7. "If we picture an organism as infected by a certain species of bacterium, it will obviously be easy to effect a cure if substances have been discovered which have an exclusive affinity for these bacteria and act deleteriously or lethally on these and on these alone, while at the same time, they possess no affinity whatever for the normal constituents of the body and cannot therefore have the least harmful, or other effect on that body. Such substances would then be able to exert their final action exclusively on the parasite harboured within the organism, and would represent, so to speak, *magic bullets* which seek their target of their own accord...." — P. Ehrlich's address delivered at the dedication of the Georg-Speyer-Haus, 6 September 1906, in *The Collected Papers of Paul Ehrlich,* F. Himmelweit, Ed. (Pergamon Press, London, 1960), vol. 3.

8. R. Dubos, "On the present limitation of drug research," in *Drugs in Our Society,* P. Talalay, Ed. (Johns Hopkins Press, Baltimore, 1964).

9. H. Laborit and P. Huegenard, *J. Chir.* **67,** 631 (1951).

10. A. Hordern, in *Psychopharmacology,* C.R.B. Joyce, Ed. (Lippincott, Philadelphia, 1968).

11. S. Schachter, in *Psychobiological Approaches to Social Behavior,* P.H. Leiderman and D. Shapiro, Eds. (Stanford Univ. Press, Stanford, California, 1964), pp. 138–173.

12. We are aware of the fact that the validity of this proposition is dose-related.

13. *Medical Newsletter* **11,** No. 20 (3 October 1969), pp. 81–84.

14. We do not wish to minimize the considerable differences between legal and illegal drugs in terms of dose standardization and purity of the chemical compound.

However, we are not addressing ourselves to the issue of physical risks in this paper, though it is an important one.

15. This point is developed in more detail in part IV of our paper "Drug giving and drug taking," given at American College of Neuropsychopharmacology, San Diego, February 1970 (mimeographed).

4
The Effects of Marijuana on Human Beings

Norman E. Zinberg and Andrew T. Weil

Unlike most Bostonians on April 19, 1968, we celebrated Patriots' Day by violating Section 200 of Chapter 94 of the General Laws of the Commonwealth of Massachusetts. The law reads: "A physician or a dentist, in good faith and in the course of his professional practice only, for the alleviation of pain and suffering or for the treatment or alleviation of disease may prescribe, administer, and dispense narcotic drugs...." What we did on the evening of the 19th was to administer marijuana (a narcotic drug under Massachusetts law) to volunteer subjects, not for the alleviation of suffering or disease, but in order to find out what marijuana does to people who smoke it. The legislators of the Bay State had simply not provided a statute to authorize this research.

The event itself, which took place in a pleasant laboratory at the Boston University School of Medicine, was of greater scientific than legal consequence because it was the start of the first human experiments with marijuana ever designed according to modern principles of drug testing. We had received permission to investigate the drug only after a full year of the most frustrating negotiations with Federal agencies and the administrative bureaucracies of two universities (B.U. and Harvard). We were not about to give up when our mid-April deadline came around because of an oversight in state law, even though our lawyer warned us that we might be prosecuted. (Shortly after we began work, he succeeded in extracting a promise of immunity from prosecution from the Attorney General of the Commonwealth, who hinted wryly that the last such request he had received concerned the ill-fated "Titicut Follies"—a film documentary about the state prison for the criminally insane at Bridgewater, Mass.) Nine weeks and some 60 marijuana cigarettes later, we had obtained the first "hard" data on the acute effects of the drug on human beings, and we then began to analyze our results. These were published last December in a long article in the journal Science and have generated considerable discussion.

Our report in Science began: "In the spring of 1968 we conducted a series of pilot experiments on acute marijuana intoxication in human subjects. The study was not undertaken to prove or disprove popularly held convictions about marijuana as an intoxicant, to compare it with other drugs, or to introduce our own opinions. Our concern was simply to collect some long overdue pharmacological data." Nevertheless, the report has given rise to vigorous debate about the harmfulness of marijuana. In both scientific and nonscientific circles our results have been taken to indicate that the "seriousness" of the drug has been overrated. For example, in an editorial, titled "Boston Pot Party," The New Republic wrote: "While pot heads may legitimately ask, 'So what else is new?' the study may have a pacifying influence on parents and officials who fear the drug on the basis of unsubstantiated horror stories. According to the Science report, 'no adverse marijuana reactions occurred in any of our subjects.'" And our experimental findings have already been introduced as evidence in several court challenges to the current harsh laws on possession of marijuana.

Consequently, we feel an obligation to explain what we think is the significance of our study as well as to point out what is and is not known about the effects of marijuana.

It is worth reiterating that very little is reliably known about the effects of marijuana. In studying a drug of this sort there are two ways a researcher can go about getting information: he can ask users of the drug what effects they get from it or he can actually give marijuana to subjects in a laboratory and watch what happens. The trouble with the first kind of information is that it is grossly unreliable. As we have learned more about drugs that affect the mind, it has become all too clear that the pharmacological action of the drug (that is, what a pharmacology text says it should do) is but one of three factors that determine how a given person will react to that drug on a given

occasion. The other factors are called "set" and "setting," and they are at least as important as the drug. Set is the psychologist's term for an individual's expectations of what a drug will do to him; it includes much of what we commonly call "personality." Setting is the total environment—physical and social—in which a drug is taken.

It is quite possible for the combined effects of set and setting to overshadow completely the pharmacological action of a drug. Thus, a barbiturate, which pharmacology texts tell us is a "sedative," can produce stimulation under certain conditions of set and setting. And amphetamine, a "stimulant," can cause sedation under other special circumstances. The vaguer and less predictable are the pharmacological effects of a drug, the greater is the importance of set and setting. Hence the danger of relying on information about marijuana from people who use it. What they say may apply to them, but whether it is pharmacologically accurate and can be applied to other persons is never clear.

Unfortunately, nearly all of the voluminous scientific literature on marijuana consists entirely of this kind of unreliable information. It is a collection of rumor, anecdote, and secondhand accounts. Much of it has been culled from other countries where set and setting are drastically different from set and setting in, say, an American college community. In India, for example, hemp drugs (usually more potent than U.S. marijuana) are in great disrepute and are used only by the lowest socioeconomic classes, often as an escape from the dreariness of everyday life. Observations on these users simply have no relevance to the situation in our country.

This is not to say that experimental laboratory information is always "right," and information from users is always "wrong." In fact, laboratory information has its own problems. The essence of the experimental method is manipulation of the environment so that an observed effect may be ascribed with some confidence to a known cause (in this case the administration of a drug). Consider a simple example. About 9 out of 10 marijuana users we have interviewed (we have now interviewed many hundreds) have told us they are certain marijuana dilates the pupils of their eyes when they are high.

An even higher percentage of law-enforcement agents have told us the same thing. But pupil size depends on other things besides what drug you may happen to have inside you. One obvious determinant is the surrounding illumination: The dimmer the light in a room, the larger are one's pupils. A less obvious factor is the distance at which one's eyes are focused; pupils constrict as part of the eye's accommodation for near vision. Therefore, if a researcher wishes to measure the effect of a drug on pupil size, he is obliged to hold the other factors constant—to *control* them. He must measure the pupils before and after administration of the drug under constant, standard illumination with the eyes focused at a constant, standard distance.

Observations made by users or law-enforcement agents at pot parties are not likely to be this scrupulous. When we finally did the appropriate experiment in Boston, we were not surprised to find that pupil size was not changed at all by marijuana. (Since the lighting at marijuana parties is often dimmer than usual, it is also not surprising that participants commonly have large pupils.)

The curious problem of the experimentalist, however, is that as he controls the laboratory environment more and more carefully, so as to maximize his confidence in ascribing observed effects to known causes, his laboratory becomes less and less like the real world, which is what he set out to study. Indeed, control can proceed to the point that the experimental results are scientifically impeccable, but their relevance to anything in the real world is lost. Then, if someone comes along and says, "So what?"—as happens all too infrequently in science—the experimentalist will be stuck for an answer.

What little laboratory research has been done on marijuana is defective in just this way. Recently a chemical called THC (for tetrahydrocannabinol) has been isolated from marijuana and synthesized. To date, it has not been established that this

chemical is the sole active ingredient of hemp, but it has been so advertised in the scientific literature. In 1967 this drug was given to human beings in a well-designed experiment in the Addiction Research Center in Lexington, Ky. With high doses (probably many times higher than users commonly absorb from marijuana cigarettes) the drug caused psychotic reactions in subjects recruited from a prison population of former opiate addicts. This result was widely interpreted in both scientific and lay journals to mean that marijuana is not such a harmless drug after all—a wholly unjustified conclusion. The only legitimate conclusion is that unusually high doses of a compound that may or may not reproduce the effects of marijuana cause acute psychotic reactions in former opiate addicts. No one spoke up with the "So what?" that was called for.

In our experience, and that of all users we have talked to, true acute psychotic reactions to marijuana are rare to the point of being psychiatric curiosities—at least in persons who have not previously taken hallucinogenic drugs like LSD. This real world observation casts further doubt on the relevance of the findings with THC.

It would seem that the marijuana researcher must steer a middle course between his desire for scientific accuracy and his obligation to make his findings relevant to the world beyond his laboratory. We made a great effort to do this in our Boston University experiments.

One of our first decisions was to administer the drug to subjects in the form of cigarettes. Up to now, most researchers have given the drug in some form to be swallowed. Their argument is that doses are hard to standardize in smoking since different subjects inhale in different ways. In other words, the results are more "scientifically accurate" if the drug is swallowed.

We would agree if we felt the effects of the drug were the same regardless of route of administration. But, in fact, it appears that swallowed marijuana is qualitatively different from smoked marijuana. We have collected massive evidence from interviews suggesting that marijuana causes more powerful, longer-lasting effects when it is eaten, and this does not appear to be due simply to differences in dose. Possibly, components of the plant that are destroyed by the heat of smoking get into the body when the drug reaches the stomach. And since in the real world marijuana is usually smoked, we were willing to risk some inaccuracy in standardizing dose in order to preserve the relevance of our data. We also used doses of marijuana that made users very high in their own judgment; we did not use the very high doses of THC that some researchers have used in the past (as much as 1,000 times the .18 mgm. of THC we estimated subjects received in our experiment as a high dose of marijuana), resulting in florid psychotic or other toxic responses.

In order to minimize variation in the set of our subjects, we used, primarily, a group of nine young men who had never tried marijuana previously; their attitudes toward the drug were explored before the start of testing in an intensive psychiatric interview. (Interviews were repeated six months after the end of the experiment to see whether any of these subjects had "moved up" to other drugs; only two of the nine had tried marijuana subsequently and those on only one occasion each. None had tried any other psychoactive drugs.) The setting of the experiment was as "neutral" as possible. Subjects were made comfortable and secure in a suite of laboratories and offices but no attempt was made to provide them with an enjoyable experience. Interactions with the staff were few and formal, and no subject was permitted to discuss the experiment until he had finished it.

In properly designed research, the number of subjects needed is determined entirely by the kinds of data one wants to collect. For our purposes, nine marijuana-naive subjects were more than sufficient. Each was tested four times. First we held a practice session with tobacco to teach a standardized technique of inhaling and to allow subjects to become familiar with the tests. By instructing the subjects to hold each inhalation for 20 seconds as timed by a stop watch, we achieved

fair standardization of intake. Five volunteers never got past the practice session. Although they had regarded themselves as heavy cigarette smokers, they experienced acute toxic nicotine reactions during this regime of rigorous inhalation. (Indeed, these nicotine reactions were the most impressive physiological responses of the entire experiment.)

Then came three "drug" sessions in which subjects smoked—in random order and at weekly intervals—either high or low doses of marijuana, or inert placebos, prepared from portions of male hemp stalks that contained no pharmacological activity. These sessions were "double-blind"—that is, neither we nor the subjects knew what was being smoked each evening—a precaution against possible contamination of the results by whatever preconceptions we, ourselves, held about marijuana. No previous research with the drug had employed this necessary safeguard.

We also studied a comparison group of eight heavy users of marijuana who were tested only once and only on high doses. (We could not use the double-blind method here because no one has yet found a placebo good enough to fool heavy users.) Interesting differences in the reactions of the two groups showed up; we will discuss them in a moment.

As a result of the care we took in planning these experiments, our results, we think, have more to say about marijuana than those of all earlier studies. Here is what we did, starting on Patriots' Day, 1968.

When we sat down to plan the experiments, we outlined three major areas of investigation. We wanted to clarify the effects of marijuana on the body during a high; we wanted to study psychological performance while under marijuana influence; and we wanted to assess the long-range effects—if any—of heavy marijuana use. Our first tactical decision was to postpone study of the third area simply because accurate measurement of the effects of chronic use of a drug requires far more elaborate procedures and far more time than we had available.

In planning experiments on acute physical effects, we were faced with the problem of not knowing what to look for. Unlike most drugs that affect consciousness, marijuana does not seem to do very much to the body, and we had few clues as to what tests would be likely to pay off. We looked at heart rate because previous studies had consistently found an increase. We studied pupil size because no one had ever done the simple measurement described above. We examined blood-sugar levels because low blood sugar has been invoked as an explanation of the increased appetite users commonly report when they are high. We looked at the whites of the eyes because marijuana allegedly reddens them. And we measured respiratory rate because it is an easily measured vital sign and depression has been reported.

We could have studied other physiological variables (such as level of adrenaline in the blood) but to do so would have been a random approach based on no hypotheses. We feel strongly that mindless experiments of that sort are inconsistent with the principles of good laboratory investigation and that results from such studies merely clutter the scientific literature with facts of obscure significance. Hence our amusement when a biochemist on one of the Harvard committees that got itself into endless muddles over our proposal criticized our experiments for lack of sophistication in that they did not include measuring of "other physiological and biochemical parameters," (Another member of the committee asked why we couldn't do the experiments on rats or pigeons to avoid controversy.)

Our results were clear-cut. Marijuana caused a moderate increase in heart rate, but not enough to make subjects conscious of a rapid pulse, and it reddened whites of eyes. It had no effect on pupil size, blood sugar, or respiratory rate. Possibly the drug has a few other effects on the body (we think it decreases flow of saliva and tears and are about to start new experiments to document these changes), but it is unlikely that other major effects will be found. The significance of this near-absence of physical effects is twofold. First it demonstrates once again the uniqueness of hemp among

psychoactive drugs, most of which strongly affect the body as well as the mind. Thus the mental effects of LSD are accompanied by a panoply of neurological and physiological changes including widely dilated pupils, altered reflexes, abnormal reactions of involuntary muscles, and so forth.

Second, it makes it unlikely that marijuana has any seriously detrimental physical effects in either short-term or long-term usage. The influence of marijuana smoke on the lungs is unknown, but aside from the possibility of local irritation, marijuana has not been accused of having adverse medical effects, even in countries like India and Egypt where government agencies actively campaign against the drug. As recently as 1967, on the basis of no evidence whatever, the American Medical Association told physicians in a statement in its Journal on the hazards of marijuana that "hypoglycemia" (chronic low blood sugar) was a consequence of repeated use of the drug, but our research has undercut that claim. All in all, we think it is fair to say that in terms of medical dangers only, marijuana is a relatively harmless intoxicant.

In approaching the question of psychological effects of the drug, we again had a difficult time deciding what tests to use. The great mystery about marijuana seems to be the enormous discrepancy between its subjective and objective mental effects. Persons who smoke the drug experience great changes in their consciousness, but they seem to have nothing to show for it. Previous researchers have found that if tests are made complicated enough or if doses of the drug are made high enough, subjects will show across-the-board impairments in psychological performance, especially if they are not very familiar with the drug. But these impairments are nonspecific; they are the sort seen with any drug that influences alertness, for example. No one has shown any specific way in which a person, high on marijuana, is different from one who is not.

We used several standard psychological tests and one or two unorthodox ones. The Digit Symbol Substitution Test is a simple test of cognitive function often used on I.Q. tests. Here is an example of the Digit test:

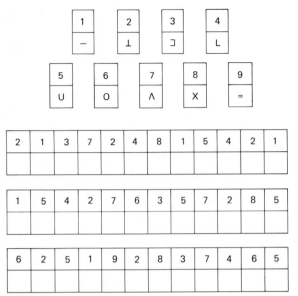

1	2	3	4					
−	⊥	⅃	L					

5	6	7	8	9
∪	O	∧	X	=

2	1	3	7	2	4	8	1	5	4	2	1

1	5	4	2	7	6	3	5	7	2	8	5

6	2	5	1	9	2	8	3	7	4	6	5

FIGURE 4.1
On a signal from the examiner the subject is required to fill as many of the empty spaces as possible with the appropriate symbols (top two lines). The code is always available during the 90-second test.

The Continuous Performance Test measures a subject's capacity for sustained attention. In our study, the subject was placed in a darkened room and directed to watch a small screen upon which six different letters of the alphabet were flashed rapidly and in random order. The subject was instructed to press a button whenever a specified critical letter appeared. Errors of commission and omission were counted over a five-minute period. The test was also done with a strobe light flickering at a distracting rate. Normal subjects make no or nearly no errors on this test either with or without strobe distraction, but sleep deprivation, organic brain disease and certain drugs (like chlorpromazine, an antipsychotic drug) adversely affect performance.

A third standard test we used was the Pursuit Rotor, in which the subject's task is to keep a stylus in contact with a small spot on a moving turntable. It measures muscular coordination and attention. Finally, we collected a "verbal sample" from each subject before and after he smoked the test cigarettes. The subject was left alone in a room with a tape recorder and instructions to describe "an interesting or dramatic experience" in his life until he was stopped. After exactly five minutes he was interrupted and asked how long he thought he had been in the recording room. In this way an estimate of the subject's ability to judge time was also obtained. (After intoxication, time sense was significantly slowed. Some subjects guessed the five-minute period to be as long as 10 or 12 minutes.)

The first three tests were chosen because they are standard tests for specific mental functions we thought might be altered during a marijuana high. The verbal sample was taken because we had a hunch—on the basis of careful interviews with and observations of chronic users—that speech undergoes changes when one is high, and we wanted to see if we were right.

In several ways the results of the psychological tests were surprising. Our first observation was that persons who had never tried marijuana previously had minimal subjective reaction to the drug in our neutral setting—even after smoking high doses that made their hearts beat faster and their eyes turn red. They simply did not get high. By contrast, all the users got high on the same dose, even though many of them thought our setting was extremely negative and were set not to have a pleasant time.

We were struck by the difficulty of recognizing when a subject is high, unless he tells you that he is. As a splendid example of the problem, we should mention that at the end of our study we arranged a demonstration session, in which two of our user subjects volunteered to go through the tests again for the benefit of a party of observers from the Federal Bureau of Narcotics and Dangerous Drugs, the Massachusetts Bureau of Drug Abuse and Drug Control, and several lawyers. Most of the observers had never seen anyone smoke marijuana before. Their universal reaction was extreme disappointment—disappointment that nothing happened. It was not clear what they had expected to happen, but they had expected something. When our subjects continued to behave normally and to go through the tests without difficulty, the observers became restive. "Are you sure they were inhaling right?" one asked. "Are you sure the marijuana is any good?" said another. The subjects, meanwhile, both said they were quite stoned. When asked to rate how high they were on a scale of one to ten, with ten being the highest they had ever been, they rated themselves at eight and nine.

Both groups did exactly the same on the Continuous Performance Test after smoking the drug as before, which led us to conclude that attention as measured by the C.P.T. is unaffected by marijuana. On the Digit Symbol Substitution Test an interesting difference appeared. The naive subjects did worse after smoking, and the degree of impairment was related to the dose smoked: A little made scores go down a little; a lot made scores go down a lot. Here again is the nonspecific effect noted above. But the users improved slightly on the D.S.S.T. when they were high—even though they started out from good baseline scores. They showed a similar improvement in the Pursuit Rotor test. Especially interesting to us was the surprise users expressed on finding how well they could perform when stoned. Most of them were very apprehensive about taking the tests after smoking because they felt so high; some even asked to be excused from them. But when they tried, they were delighted to find they could perform well. This reaction is quite the opposite of the false sense of improvement subjects have under some psychoactive drugs (like alcohol) that actually impair performance.

What do these results mean? Apparently, getting high on marijuana is a much more subtle experience than getting high on alcohol; perhaps it is something that must be learned, so that most persons who take the drug for the first time cannot recognize the changes it causes in their consciousness. This hypothesis is consistent with the evidence that marijuana seems to affect little in the brain besides the highest centers of thought, memory and perception. It has no general stimulating or depressive action on the nervous system (hence the absence of neurological as opposed to psychological changes during a high), no influence on lower centers like those controlling the mechanical aspects of speech and coordination (hence no slurred words or staggering gait). As a result it seems possible to ignore the effects of marijuana on consciousness, to adapt to them, and to control them to a significant degree.

If you pour enough alcohol into a person who has never before had alcohol, he may not have a pleasant time, but at some time he will be unable to ignore the fact that he is intoxicated: he will *feel* that his nervous system is behaving in an abnormal fashion. Not so with marijuana: A first-time smoker can consume enormous amounts and have the physical reactions to the drug without any mental effects at all. As with most intoxicants, as one becomes familiar with alcohol, he can learn to compensate for the drug's adverse effects on performance—but only to a point; alcohol imposes absolute limits on the speed of nervous functioning by its direct pharmacological action. Again, not so with marijuana: Users appear to be able to compensate 100 per cent for the nonspecific adverse effects of ordinary doses of marijuana on ordinary psychological performance (including driving, according to the findings of a soon-to-be published study conducted by the Department of Motor Vehicles of the state of Washington and the University of Washington). A person intoxicated on alcohol, on the other hand, has a hard time acting sober.

Again the question arises: How is a person high on marijuana psychologically different from one who is not? And there is still no answer. In fact, the only way to know someone is high on marijuana is still to have him tell you so.

Our hunch that speech might be an area in which to find a change seems to have paid off, but further experiments must be done before we can spell out the exact nature of the change. We were able to show in our user population that the nature of a verbal sample changed in several important ways after the subjects smoked marijuana. For example, before smoking, in response to the instructions, most subjects told a story about past events. After smoking, the same subjects abandoned narrative format and tended to talk about the present — things going on in their immediate environment. They also tended to become more intimate and to think in free associative patterns rather than according to everyday logic. The imagery they used became less concrete and more dreamlike.

To illustrate this point, here are two excerpts from one subject's verbal sample before and after he smoked marijuana:

> Predrug: "Well, I guess the most interesting event recently that I can think of would have to do with turning my draft card in, which happened Jan. 29, 1968, and — uh — one of the most interesting things to me about handing in my draft card to the Resistance was that I hadn't planned to do so before I did it...."
>
> Postdrug: "...Oh — [clears throat] — you know, the tro-...the trouble is that — uh — the present is more interesting now than events in the past. I mean the idea of sitting here and talking about something that's already happened instead of — uh — you know — instead of happening now — instead of just being now — the present — is kind of ridiculous...."

We are going to pursue these differences in an expanded investigation of language under marijuana influence and also want to search for other possible differences between being straight and being high — particularly in the areas of immediate memory and "secondary perception," that is, what the brain decides to do with incoming sensory information. In the meantime, what can we say about the dangers of marijuana from a psychological standpoint? From our own study and from other studies now in progress, it would seem — in short-term usage only — that usual doses of marijuana do not impair a user's ability to carry out successfully a wide range of tasks of ordinary complexity. But higher than usual doses, especially in novice smokers might be expected to cause performance decrements.

The real debate about the merits or evils of marijuana ought to focus on the long-range psychiatric effects of the drug, if any. This is the main area of controversy because there are still no data at all. We have no information on the subject from our own study, and we regret the continuing lack of any good research on it. What is needed is a decent prospective study of persons — say, medical students — who are setting out to become regular marijuana users matched against a similar group not using the drug. Each group should be followed and tested serially for 5, 10, or more years. If such a study is not organized soon, it may be too late. Marijuana use is becoming so extensive in some sections of the country that within certain age ranges, persons who do not use the drug are so unusual as to constitute what statisticians call a biased sample.

One of the results of not having had any real information on the drug for all these years has been the development of a vicious circle in which administrators of scientific and government institutions feel that marijuana is dangerous. Because it is dangerous, they are reluctant to allow work to be done on it. Because no work is done, people continue to think of it as dangerous.

We hope that our own study has significantly weakened this trend. In view of the ease with which we carried out the tests once they were underway and the lack of harm to any of the participants, we hope that our project will be used as a precedent.

We also hope that state laws obstructing marijuana research will rapidly be amended. For society will never be able to develop an effective and sensible policy on the use and abuse of psychoactive drugs unless it permits the free collection of information on the actual effects — whether harmful or beneficial — these drugs have on the mind.

Anyone attempting research in an area as hotly immersed in controversy as marijuana use knows that he cannot expect his findings to be received with neutrality or scientific objectivity. Nevertheless, even with this in mind we have been surprised at the extent to which we are asked to jump from one experiment concerning a small area of information about marijuana into large political and philosophical questions. We are repeatedly asked, "Should marijuana be legalized?" or, "If it is 'harmless,' do you advocate people trying it?" We don't know the answers. The first question is out of our ken and neither question could be answered until our most important recommendation is implemented. What we proved is that research can be done with this substance. What we recommend is that individuals and institutions in conjunction with the legal authorities do it.

"Personally I do not accept ESP for a moment, because it does not make sense," commented D.O. Hebb, a former president of the American Psychological Association (and a science-fiction fan to boot!)[1]

Extrasensory perception has long been a taboo topic in textbooks. Perhaps we become vulnerable to accusations about own own credibility as scientists unless we reject this idea that people can communicate without the use of recognized sensory channels. McBain reports a typical reaction by a colleague of whom he asked an opinion after informing him that examination of ESP data by mathematicians confirmed the claimed effect unequivocally. "Then I think we should reexamine the basic assumptions of our statistics," the colleague replied.[2]

Whether parapsychology, and ESP in particular, is a valid psychological phenomenon or merely an artifact of the analyses, the concept is one that has aroused heated debate and controversy. The provocative and entertaining papers which follow are by two strong advocates of parapsychology. R.A. McConnell writes an angry recrimination against nonbelievers; Gardner Murphy takes a placid look at some fascinating anecdotal evidence and speculations on what makes a gifted "sensitive."

Is it conceivable that we can communicate by extrasensory channels? The plausibility of this notion is something that each of us can only decide for himself.

[1]D.O. Hebb. "The Role of Neurological Ideas in Psychology," *Journal of Personality*, vol. 20, 1951, p. 45.
[2]W. N. McBain, W. Fox, S. Kimura, M. Nakaniski, and J. Tirado. "Quasi-Sensory Communication: An Investigation Using Semantic Matching and Accentuated Affect," *Journal of Personality and Social Psychology*, vol. 14, 1970, p. 281.

Part III
EXTRASENSORY PERCEPTION— FACT OR FANCY?

5
ESP and Credibility in Science[1]

R.A. McConnell

In discussing extrasensory perception (ESP) before psychology students, it is not uncommon to stress the credulity of the public. Perhaps, instead, we ought to examine the credibility of scientists—including those on both sides of the controversy.

In ESP research whom shall we trust? One can rather easily imagine experimental precautions to keep participating subjects from cheating. But how do we know whether the experimenter is deliberately deceiving us? And in a world where people believe all kinds of nonsense, how can we be sure that the experimenter is not deceiving himself?

Let us suppose that 10 experimenters independently get the same result. Can we accept it? Ten is not a large number. There are about 150,000 names in *American Men of Science*. We may reasonably assume that at least 10,000 of these hold beliefs about the nature of reality that the majority of scientists would regard as wholly without foundation. Thus, on a subject like ESP, where there are no recognized authorities, why should we accept the word of 10 experimenters—or, for that matter, a thousand? Are we not, all of us, creatures of our culture? Is there any way we can be sure that a scientist in any field is as rational as he pretends to be?

Questions concerning the credibility of scientists are rarely asked in our classrooms. I have wondered why. Perhaps it makes us uncomfortable to consider the possibility of incompetence, dishonesty, or mental illness among professional people. Whatever the reason, this is forbidden territory for study.

Once in a long while, these embarrassing ideas do come to the surface. Someone, a little bolder or a little more eccentric than the rest of us, may write an article that slips by the editorial censor. When that happens, we have a chance to learn what people really think.

[1]An invited lecture to the introductory psychology classes at Carnegie-Mellon University, December 18 and 19, 1967.

When I accepted this invitation to talk to you, I was told I could give you an advance reading assignment. I asked that you read an eight-page article on ESP by G.R. Price (1955) that appeared in *Science* together with several letters to the editor (Soal; Rhine; Meehl & Scriven; Bridgman; Price; Rhine, 1956) written in reply to Price. These papers are currently available as part of the Bobbs-Merrill reprint series that is widely used for teaching psychology, and they have thus acquired a quasi-official status as source documents to which the very young may be exposed.

I also suggested that you read an analysis of Price's article (McConnell, 1955) that appeared in the *Journal of Parapsychology* and that was not included in the Bobbs-Merrill series. I hope that most of you have had a chance to study these references, which I shall now discuss briefly.

Price, a chemist by profession, presented a well-supported argument showing that existing experimental evidence constitutes conclusive proof of ESP if one accepts the good faith and sanity of the experimenters. But he went on to say that all of the otherwise convincing evidence for ESP can be easily explained away if one assumes that experimenters, working in collaboration with their witnesses, have intentionally faked their results.

Perhaps the most interesting thing about this unsubstantiated suggestion of fraud is that it was published on the first page of the most influential scientific journal in the United States. I will not say whether Price intended what he wrote as a joke. That is a riddle that I leave to you to answer. The important question is not whether Price took himself seriously, but whether you and I ought to do so.

I believe, as apparently does Price, that all kinds of fraud, even by highly placed scientists, are possible and that it is conceivable that there might be collaboration between two scientists in perpetuating a scientific hoax. Nevertheless, I think that those who accept Price's argument fail to understand two important things about science as a social enterprise.

First, they fail to realize that the way to tell whether a number of scientists are collaborating in a hoax is to consider the intricate web of public and private motivation, belief, and retribution that determines the behavior of professional people in our culture. Price suggested that scientists, university teachers, medical doctors, and intellectually prominent persons who have assisted in the investigation of ESP may have engaged in conscious collusive fraud. Price answered the question of how one might get such people to become willing accomplices by saying: "In recruiting, I would appeal not to desire for fame or material gain but to the noblest motives, arguing that much good to humanity could result from a small deception designed to strengthen religious belief." An experienced lawyer or even a politician would laugh at this explanation of a supposed conspiracy among well-educated and fully engaged members of our society, but evidently quite a few scientists find it plausible.

Second, those scientists who take Price seriously do not understand scientific method. Price suggested that the way to establish the scientific truth of ESP is to carry out a fraudproof experiment. In his words: "What is needed is one completely convincing experiment." He described in specific detail how this might be done by using prominent scientists and stage magicians as witnesses, backed up by motion pictures of the entire proceedings, plus photomicrographs of welded seals, and so on. This is nonsense because it assumes that scientific proof is of the same nature as legal proof. On the contrary, the acceptance of a scientific principle does not, and never can, depend upon the honesty of individual scientists.

I wish I had time to pursue with you the subtle psychological question of the nature of scientific proof and of how the method of science deals with individual experimenter error as well as mass irrationality. Those of you who are especially interested may wish to read a book by T.S. Kuhn (1962) titled *The Structure of Scientific Revolutions*.[2] Here today, I can only say that in my opinion, wittingly or unwittingly, Price's article is a hoax about hoaxes and about the nature of science.

[2]For a condensation of this book see McConnell (1968b).

If you were to ask: "What does it signify that Price successfully placed his article in our most important journal of science?" I would answer as follows: There is a facade of respectability and belief that covers all of the activities of society and makes it possible for men to work together and for society to exist. Most people—including those who are well educated—are unaware of this false front and lose their equilibrium when they are forced by circumstances to penetrate behind it. On the other hand, those of you who are intellectually alienated from our culture understand quite well that this pretense exists. I hope that some day you will also understand why it is necessary and that it is not the contrivance of a group of evil men but reflects what existential philosophers refer to as "the human condition."

This curtain of propriety and convention exists in science also, where it allows us to believe that all is well with our knowledge system. ESP or any other revolutionary discovery may seem to threaten science. From time to time, when such a challenge is offered, the stagehands nervously fumble, the curtain slips, and we see a little of the normally concealed machinery. We get a glimpse of underlying reality, a glimpse of the ignorance and fear that govern the inner affairs of the mind of man. Such was the case when *Science* published Price's critique of ESP. That is why his article is important.

EVIDENCE AND BELIEF

Then, what about ESP? If laboratory scientists lack sophistication about human nature and even about the methodology of science, how do we decide for ourselves whether ESP is real or imaginary, true or false?

Before we try to answer so difficult a question, let us go back to the beginning. I shall give you an operational definition of ESP that you may find a bit confusing. Then I shall describe a test for ESP that I hope will make the matter clear to you.

The definition goes this way: "Extrasensory perception is a response to an unknown event not presented to any known sense." I shall not try to explain it. Instead, let me describe the test.

I have brought with me a deck of ESP cards. These cards have five different kinds of symbols printed on them: a circle, a square, a plus, a star, and wavy lines. Altogether, there are 25 cards, 5 of each kind.

Suppose I shuffle these cards, hide them, and ask you to guess them. By the theory of chance probability, the number you would most often get right is five. Sometimes you would get four or six or seven. Only once in a long while would you get 15 right out of 25. In fact, if you got more than 10 right very often, you would begin to suspect that it was not just good luck. It might even be ESP.

Of course, you could not be sure. It might be luck—or it might be something else. If you look closely at the backs of these cards, sometimes you can see the symbol showing through. Perhaps in this way you recognized some of the cards when I shuffled them. Or again, every time I asked whether you were ready for your next guess, perhaps I gave you a hint without knowing it. Perhaps, unconsciously, I raised the tone of my voice just a little when I came to each star—because I think of stars as being "higher" than the other symbols, or for some other trivial reason.

You can see that there are many subtle ways for information to leak through by sight or by sound. No serious scientist would try to conduct an ESP experiment in this fashion. My only purpose in showing you these cards is to let you know how some of the early tests for ESP were done at Duke University 35 years ago. I regard these cards as a museum piece, although they are a lot of fun and can be used in preliminary testing.

The experiments that are carried out today are often so complex that one cannot evaluate them without advanced training in statistics, physics, and psychology. For this reason, and because the field is too large to describe in one lecture, I have prepared a list of reading materials. Some of these are intended to show the scope of the subject (Heywood, 1964; Langdon-Davies, 1961; McConnell, 1966; Murphy & Dale, 1961); others are experimental reports (Anderson & McConnell,

1961; McConnell & Forwald, 1967a, 1967b, 1968; McConnell, Snowdon, & Powell, 1955; Sinclair, 1962; Soal & Bateman, 1954).

You will notice that I have listed only my own journal articles. For this I offer my apology along with the following explanation. In any frontier field of science there are experimental hazards. If someone questions the soundness of what I recommend to you as evidence, I can probably do a better job of explaining if I have chosen research with which I am most familiar. I also want to convey the idea that there has been a large amount of work done in this field. If you study my papers and cannot find anything wrong with them, you ought to remember that there have been perhaps a hundred other investigators who have found substantial evidence for ESP under controlled experimental conditions.

ESP is a controversial idea in psychology. Nevertheless, the psychologists whom I know personally agree with me on many things. I am sure we agree on what constitutes good quality experimental laboratory research. We also agree that there is a sizable body of high-grade evidence for ESP in the literature.

In 1947 I visited Duke University in North Carolina where a man by the name of Rhine was doing experiments on ESP. I wanted to get acquainted with Rhine and with the people who were working under him. Even more important, I wanted to talk to those faculty members who rejected Rhine's work. I rented a dormitory room, and during four weeks I interviewed everyone I could, beginning with the President of the University and working down to assistant professors in various departments. I shall not have time to describe that adventure, but I will tell you what I was told by one professor of psychology in a private interview.

He said that he was familiar with the experimental literature of ESP and that, in his opinion, if it were anything else *but* ESP, one-tenth of the published evidence would already have established the phenomenon. He also explained that he would not accept ESP himself because, as he put it, he found "a world without ESP a more comfortable place in which to live."

That trip to Duke University was part of a larger investigation that made me decide to leave engineering electronics, in which I had acquired some experience, and to devote my life to the investigation of ESP and related effects.

That was 20 years ago. What has happened in this field since then? Among other things, there has been time to publish 20 more volumes of the *Journal of Parapsychology*. That comes to about 4,000 pages of research. There have been several thousand additional pages in the *Journal of the American Society for Psychical Research* and in the English and Continental journals. You might think that the argument would be settled by now.

Only recently, a brilliant young psychologist, who is here on your campus, gave a lecture on ESP in which he said "I tend to believe the evidence is as good as it is for many of our other psychological phenomena." He also said that "Psychologists will not be interested in ESP until there is a repeatable experiment."

Where my psychologist friends and I disagree, is that I believe that the available evidence for ESP is sufficient to establish its reality beyond all reasonable doubt. My psychologist friends think that the evidence is not yet conclusive. I do not regard this difference of opinion as very important. I am happy to allow anyone the privilege of doubt.

How else does the position of professional psychologists whom I know differ from my own? Perhaps the main difference—the really important difference—lies in our interpretation of the history and methodology of science—in what today we call the philosophy of science.

For one thing, my friends seem to believe that the only good evidence for ESP must come from controlled experimentation in a laboratory. My own belief is that all available evidence must be weighed, taking into account its source and the conditions under which it was gathered.

Perhaps it will clarify the problem if I say that there are only two important kinds of scientific evidence in this world: our own evidence and someone else's. Since most of us are not in a position to gather evidence of ESP, my remarks apply especially to other people's evidence.

The first thing to remember is that, no matter how reputable the scientific journal, someone else's evidence is always suspect. And if the matter is important, we ought to be *aggressively* skeptical about it.

Whether we are listening to a tale of a ghost in a haunted house or reading the tightly edited *Journal of Experimental Psychology*, we have to concern ourselves with two questions: what is the content of the report and what are the competence and motivation of the observer?

What I am suggesting is that our attitude toward *all* supposedly scientific reports must be that of the psychologist in receiving an introspective account from a human subject in a laboratory experiment—for it must be remembered that, as far as the reader is concerned, a journal article by a distant scientist is in some ways even less dependable than what psychologists, often condescendingly, refer to as a "verbal report."

From a study of the history of science, I have come to two conclusions in this connection: (*a*) the evidence presented in scientific journals by professional scientists for all kinds of ordinary phenomena is not as good as commonly supposed, and (*b*) on a controversial subject where the professionals do not agree, the evidence of the layman may have considerable scientific value. As corollaries, I suggest that the textbooks of science are often wrong and that contrary popular opinion is sometimes right. Let us examine these ideas.

STOREHOUSES OF KNOWLEDGE?

Textbooks are the storehouses of man's knowledge. They are presumed to contain all of the things we know to be true. If you are becoming a scientist, you will spend at least 18 years studying from books. It would be not entirely unfair to call most of this training a "brainwashing" process. Nearly everything you learn as factual reality must be accepted upon the word of some recognized authority and not upon your own firsthand experience. It should be a matter of concern to you whether you have been told the truth for those 18 years. Just how bad are the textbooks we use? Let me take an example from the field of geology.

Did you know that until the year 1800 the highest scientific authorities thought that there was no such thing as a meteorite? After all, there are no stones in the sky; so stones cannot fall out of the sky. Only a superstitious person would believe in meteorites.

Many of you are familiar with the work of Lavoisier. He was the founder of modern chemistry. He discovered that burning is the combining of oxygen with other things, and he helped to show that the formula for water is H_2O. He was one of the great scientists of all time.

In 1772 Lavoisier signed a report to the French Academy of Science in which he said he had examined a stone that was believed to have fallen from the sky in a great blaze of light. Lavoisier said in his report that this was just an ordinary stone that had been struck by lightning and had melted partly into glass while lying on the ground.

Eventually, of course, the leaders of science decided that meteorites do come from outer space, and they revised the textbooks accordingly. But in doing so, they forgot to mention that there had ever been any argument about the matter. So here we are, living in the space age, without realizing how hard it is to discover the truth about even a simple thing like meteorites, which can be seen as meteors in the sky on any clear night, and which have been found upon the surface of the earth since the dawn of history.

Even worse, as students, we have no way of estimating how many arguments are still going on in science and how many mistakes—truly serious mistakes—there are in the textbooks from which we study. It is my guess that we can safely believe nearly all of what is said in the physics and chemistry books. But we ought to believe only half of the ideas in the biological sciences—although I am not sure which half. And we should accept as final very little in the social sciences, which try to explain why groups of people behave as they do.

Our subject today is extrasensory perception, which belongs in psychology, one of the biological sciences. ESP is something about which the "authorities" are in error. Most psychology textbooks omit the subject entirely as unworthy of serious attention. But these books are mistaken, because ESP is a real psychological phenomenon.

Of course, I am only giving you my individual opinion about ESP. I do not want you to base your belief upon what I tell you. When you have studied advanced psychology and statistics, and when you come to realize that your professors cannot be expected to teach you everything you wish to know, then I hope you will go to the scientific journals and study the experiments that have been done and decide for yourself.

MENTAL RADIO

I have already discussed the credibility of experts and the errors we find in science textbooks. I would like to turn next to the other half of my thesis, namely, that evidence from a layman may sometimes have scientific value.

Most of you are familiar with the name Upton Sinclair, who was a socialist reformer and a writer active in the first half of the twentieth century. He died in 1968 at the age of 90. In his time he wrote nearly 90 books. One of the best known of these, published in 1906, was called *The Jungle*. It told about the cruel and unsanitary conditions in the processing of beef in the Chicago stock yards. As a result of that book, laws were passed, and today the situation is much improved. In a very real sense, all of us are indebted to this man.

Sinclair discovered that his wife had an unusual amount of what was then known as "psychic ability." (That was before the beginning of the ESP controversy.) After three years of serious experimentation, he wrote a book about it: *Mental Radio* (1962, orig. publ. 1930).

In his experiments, Sinclair, or someone else, would draw a secret picture and ask Mrs. Sinclair to draw another picture to match it. Some of the pairs of pictures are presented in the following examples.[3] The one on the left is always the original picture, and the one on the right is what Mrs. Sinclair got by ESP.

Sometimes the pictures were made as far apart as 40 miles. At other times the target picture was

³Illustrations from *Mental Radio* by Upton Sinclair are reproduced by permission of the publisher, Charles C. Thomas, Springfield, Illinois.

held by Mrs. Sinclair in her hand—without looking, of course—while she concentrated before drawing her matching picture. The degree of success did not seem to depend upon distance.

Let us examine some of the pictures. In Example 5.1 we see an almost perfect ESP response. It is a

EXAMPLE 5.1

knight's helmet. Notice that for every important line in the left-hand picture there is a corresponding line on the right.

Compare that with Example 5.2. Here, the re-

EXAMPLE 5.2

sponse on the right is not quite the same as the target on the left, but the idea is the same.

The next slide is Example 5.3. Sinclair drew a

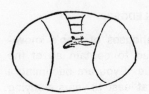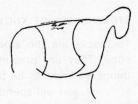

EXAMPLE 5.3

football as a target. Mrs. Sinclair made the drawing on the right, but she thought it was "a baby calf with a belly band." Why did her ESP make this mistake? We cannot be sure, but we think it had something to do with the fact that in her childhood she had known a queer old man who raised calves as parlor pets and dressed them in embroidered belly bands.

Example 5.4 is another instance of the right

EXAMPLE 5.4

shape with a wrong interpretation. Upton Sinclair drew a volcano, and Mrs. Sinclair drew what she called a black beetle. The beetle is upside down. If you turn the example over, you can more easily recognize its antennae and legs.

In Example 5.5 Sinclair drew a fish hook, which turned into two flowers.

EXAMPLE 5.5

Example 5.6 shows a fragmentary response. Sin-

EXAMPLE 5.6

clair drew a balloon. The response on the right is what his wife received by "mental radio." She was not sure what it was, so she wrote beside the picture: "Shines in sunlight, must be metal, a scythe hanging among vines or strings."

Example 5.7 on the left is a swastika. Mrs. Sinclair drew the response on the right. She did not know what it meant, but she wrote beside it, "These things somehow belong together, but won't get together." You can see some of her words which were accidentally included when the

EXAMPLE 5.7

printer made the book. Here is the beginning of "These" and "belong" and "but won't" and "together."

Example 5.8 is a pair of drawings in which a stick man became a skull and crossbones.

EXAMPLE 5.8

Notice that in Example 5.9, Mrs. Sinclair left out some of the stars and added a moon instead.

EXAMPLE 5.9

In Example 5.10 Sinclair drew an umbrella. His

EXAMPLE 5.10

wife responded with this curious picture, which she described in writing beside it as follows: "I feel that it is a snake crawling out of something—vivid feeling of snake, but it looks like a cat's tail." I might mention that she had a special fear of snakes, having grown up on a plantation in a Mississippi swamp.

The last example is the American flag and a response to it that could hardly be called a chance coincidence (Example 5.11).

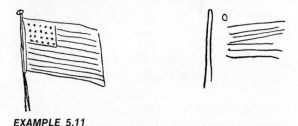

EXAMPLE 5.11

You have seen a selection of 11 pictures out of a total of 290 trials made by Mrs. Sinclair. Perhaps 4 of the 11 would be called direct target hits. The rest are partial hits. Out of the 290 tries, 23% were rated by Upton Sinclair as hits, 53% were partial hits, and 24% were failures.

Of course, before you can be sure that these pictures were made by ESP, many questions must be answered. Because Upton Sinclair and his wife were laymen, you will have to pay particular attention to their competence and motivation. On the other hand, one important feature of Sinclair's book is that you do not have to be a scientist to understand it. Even though you may not have studied statistics and psychology, you can read the book yourself and make up your mind as to its value on the basis of common sense. When you do, I think you will arrive at the same conclusion that many scientists have reached by entirely different kinds of experiments. I think you will decide that extrasensory perception is a reality regardless of the skepticism of the psychological profession.

A MATTER OF INTEREST

I have been told by my friends that psychologists will not be interested in ESP until someone discovers a repeatable experiment. Upton Sinclair repeated his experiments over a period of three years. In London, a mathematician by the name of Soal (Soal & Bateman, 1954) repeated certain card-guessing experiments again and again over a period of six years using two subjects and many different witnesses. What do psychologists mean by a repeatable experiment?

Evidently, they mean an experiment that is "repeatable by prescription." They want a standard experimental procedure that can be described on paper by which any qualified person—or at least some qualified persons—can guarantee to produce ESP upon demand. I must confess that we have not yet reached that stage in ESP research. And, until we do, I can sympathize with my skeptical friends. I can see why they, as busy individuals with other interests, are unwilling to reach a firm position about the reality of ESP.

What I cannot understand is why they say: "Psychologists will not be *interested* in ESP until there is a repeatable experiment."

It is a statement of fact that psychologists are *not* interested in ESP. Recently, I had occasion to examine a number of psychology textbooks. Only one of them mentioned ESP—that book, by Hilgard and Atkinson (1967). After reading the four pages which these authors devote to ESP, I have only two minor critical observations to offer.

The first is that the authors have given too much space to finding fault with unimportant papers. They go back 25 years to a journal article in which they accuse an ESP experimenter of overanalyzing his data. I am sure that comparable examples of weak statistical method could be found in any one of the quantitative journals of the APA—and we would not need to go back a generation in time to do it.

My second comment is that Hilgard and Atkinson may have tended to damage their own scholarly reputations by recommending as a "scholarly review" a book by C.E.M. Hansel (1966) titled *ESP: A Scientific Evaluation*. This book has been reviewed by S.S. Stevens of Harvard, who regards ESP as a Rabelaisian joke and who gave Hansel his unqualified approval. If you like amusing book reviews, I suggest that you read Stevens (1967). I regret that I do not have time here today to document for you the basis of my unfavorable opinion of Hansel's book.[4]

I have wandered over many facets of ESP. I shall

[4]This has since been done. See McConnell (1968a).

now summarize what I think are the most important ideas. Since the scientific study of ESP was begun by the London Society for Psychical Research in 1882, there have been hundreds and perhaps thousands of experiments done with a care typical of the journals of the APA. Many psychologists of high repute admit that the evidence is as good as that for other phenomena that are accepted by their profession.

Surprising though it may seem, most of this research on ESP has been done by people who were not psychologists. From this fact and from the usual psychology textbook treatment of the subject as well as from private discussion, we know that psychologists are *not* interested in ESP. This raises a question — a very mysterious question that I invite you to try to answer: Why are psychologists not interested in ESP?[5]

[5]Those who wish to answer this question might start their odyssey by visiting Clark et al. (1967) and Linder (1967).

REFERENCES

Anderson, M.L., & McConnell, R.A. Fantasy testing for ESP in a fourth and fifth grade class. *Journal of Psychology,* 1961, **52,** 491–503.

Clark, K.E., et al. The scientific and professional aims of psychology. *American Psychologist,* 1967, **22,** 49–76.

Hansel, C.E.M. *ESP: A scientific evaluation.* New York: Scribner's, 1966.

Heywood, R. *ESP: A personal memoir.* New York: Dutton, 1964.

Hilgard, E.R., & Atkinson, R.C. *Introduction to psychology.* New York: Harcourt, Brace & World, 1967.

Kuhn, T.S. *The structure of scientific revolutions* (Vol. II, No. 2, of the *International Encyclopedia of Unified Science*). Chicago: University of Chicago Press, 1962.

Langdon-Davies, J. *On the nature of man.* New York: New American Library Corporation, 1961.

Linder, R. Light one candle. *American Psychologist,* 1967, **22,** 804–805.

McConnell, R.A. Price in *Science. Journal of Parapsychology,* 1955, **19,** 258–261.

McConnell, R.A. ESP research at three levels of method. *Journal of Parapsychology,* 1966, **30,** 195–207.

McConnell, R.A. The ESP scholar. *Contemporary Psychology,* 1968, **13,** 41. (a)

McConnell, R.A. The structure of scientific revolutions: An epitome. *Journal of the American Society for Psychical Research,* 1968, **62,** 321–327. (b)

McConnell, R.A., & Forwald, H. Psychokinetic placement: I. A re-examination of the Forwald-Durham experiment. *Journal of Parapsychology,* 1967, **31,** 51–69. (a)

McConnell, R.A., & Forwald, H. Psychokinetic placement: II. A factorial study of successful and unsuccessful series. *Journal of Parapsychology,* 1967, **31,** 198–213. (b)

McConnell, R.A., & Forwald, H. Psychokinetic placement: III. Cube-releasing devices. *Journal of Parapsychology,* 1968, **32,** 9–38.

McConnell, R.A., Snowdon, R.J., & Powell, K.F. Wishing with dice. *Journal of Experimental Psychology,* 1955, **50,** 269–275.

Murphy, G., & Dale, L.A. *Challenge of psychical research.* New York: Harper, 1961.

Price, G.R. Science and the supernatural. *Science,* 1955, **122,** 359–367.

Sinclair, U. *Mental radio.* Springfield, Ill.: Charles C. Thomas, 1962.

Soal, S.G., & Bateman, F. *Modern experiments in telepathy.* London: Faber & Faber, 1954.

Soal, S.G.; Rhine, J.B.; Meehl, P.E.; & Scriven, M.; Bridgman, P.W.; Price, G.R.; Rhine, J.B. (Letters to the editor in rejoinder to G.R. Price.) *Science,* 1956, **123,** 9–19.

Stevens, S.S. The market for miracles. *Contemporary Psychology,* 1967, **12,** 1–3.

6
The Discovery of Gifted Sensitives[1]

Gardner Murphy

I

In a certain sense the problem that I am going to present to you tonight—the problem of how to find and cultivate good psychic subjects, sensitives, clairvoyants, people with a gift for paranormal communication—is really the beginning and the center of all psychical research. There are practically no abstractions at all about the nature of telepathy or clairvoyance or precognition, or any of the other phenomena of our field, that hold in a blanket fashion without reference to *individuals,* without reference to those who are capable of spontaneous experiences of contact, let us say, with a loved one at a distance who is in trouble; or with an event which has not yet occurred and which could not have been normally inferred.

The first thing we must do is to ask, *Who* had this experience? The Moslems have a fascinating comment on the European's remark that Mohammed had seizures. The Moslem will say, "Yes, there were seizures; but the important thing is *to whom* the seizures came." And in psychical research the important thing is *to whom* the paranormal experiences come.

A few years ago the A.S.P.R. [American Society for Psychical Research] renewed its efforts to try to find out about the unique aspects of the person involved in an experimental or a spontaneous paranormal experience. We found ourselves grossly inadequate to the task, and I personally feel considerable guilt and considerable blindness with reference to this neglect in developing a sophisticated idea of the individual, the gifted person, and what we may learn by recruiting—finding somewhere and somehow—the gifted person and making the most of that man's or that woman's or that child's peculiar and special gift.

In a certain sense, what I am going to tell you tonight is a fairy tale because it is very hard to believe what actually happened in the life histories of many of the most gifted subjects. If we could encounter today phenomena such as those of Mrs.

[1]This paper is based on a lecture given by Dr. Murphy at a meeting of the Society on January 30, 1968.—*Ed.*

Reprinted by permission from the *Journal of the American Society for Psychical Research,* vol. 63, no. 1, 1969, pp. 3–20.

L.E. Piper or of Mrs. Gladys Osborne Leonard from a half century and more ago, psychical research would leap forward as almost no technical study could advance it. I am therefore going to plunge into an account of some of the actual ways in which psychical researchers, particularly British and American, found and studied and tried to cultivate gifted subjects. Unless we actually see this story in its richness, we will wonder why we fail today and what the differences may be, culturally or personally, between the great pioneers such as William James, who could do this, and ourselves, who are unable to do it. Let us be frank about the situation. There is a great deal in the literature of psychical research about the discovery of highly gifted persons, but we have very little today that we can put on the barrelhead and say that it will indeed help us to identify, study, and make the most of such persons.

And so I come to you tonight with the request that you quite earnestly take us all to task and throw at psychical research a doubly enriched challenge. Of course, you may say "All right, you tell us *we* should be doing it—why aren't *you* doing it?" I can only reply that we do not know the error of logic or of the heart, or of both, which accounts for the fact that we have not in recent years effectively found the kinds of people about whom I am going to talk.

II

I am going to begin with the story of Mrs. Leonore E. Piper (19, 23). Mrs. Piper, married and with two little daughters, had paid some visits to mediums of the period in the Boston area. In 1884 she went to a blind medium named J.R. Cocke for medical advice and received some communications from Mr. Cocke's control, who called himself "Finney." Before very long, Mrs. Piper herself began to fall into a swoon-like or trance-like state; some of her utterances had to do with tragedies occurring to people she knew which could later be verified, and some of them had to do with everyday events in

the lives of strangers to whom she was introduced for the purpose of giving sittings.

Now it happened that William James' mother-in-law and sister-in-law had some anonymous sittings in 1885 with this unknown, lonely young woman, and soon thereafter James himself started to sit with Mrs. Piper (9). He was able to establish the fact, first, that there *were* the usual phenomena of suggestibility that were often attributed to psychics in general as identifiably "neuropathic dispositions." For example, there was the fact that a "Frenchman" who called himself Dr. Phinuit—a name so like the "Finney" Mrs. Piper had encountered when sitting with Mr. Cocke—began to give details concerning his life and work. None of these could be verified, nor could Dr. Phinuit speak a word of French, leading the usual skeptical comments to take sharp and clear form: "These are simply the typical phenomena of autosuggestion, of trance dissociation, occurring in an otherwise uninteresting person who, because she was lonely and in need of something exciting in her life, fell into this rather silly antic."

But what has this got to do with the fact that first members of the James family, and then William James himself in a long series of sittings, received extraordinary statements about the family history; about matters so personal that even James, with his extraordinary eagerness and directness, hesitated to put the details down in cold print? It was a long and rich and complex story, indicating that in Mrs. Piper there was at least one individual—one "white crow" in all the array of new mediums—who could rather often give brilliantly successful sittings (9).

This soon led to a long series of incognito sittings, starting in 1887, held under the direction of Richard Hodgson, who had just come to this country from England to be Secretary of the newly-formed A.S.P.R. In these sittings many individuals received veridical communications, though there had been no introduction, and there was no evident way for Mrs. Piper to know anything about their personal lives (6, 7). (Hodgson even had Mrs. Piper and her husband shadowed by private detectives for several weeks to find out whether she could have picked up this extraordinary array of information by normal means.) Over the years there were also several successful series of sittings in England (11, 13).

Some of the material emerging during the Piper sittings could be documented in terms of paranormal contact with distant events—events happening to distant living persons; and some could be documented in terms of telepathic contact with those present, as in the following striking example, which occurred during a sitting held in William James' home in New Hampshire in 1889:

Phinuit: "What are these tickets that you have in your pocket? There are figures on them stamped in red, and they are signed with names underneath."
Sitter: "No, I have nothing of the kind in my pocket."
Comment by sitter: "I had forgotten for the moment that I had, earlier in the day, taken two cheques to be cashed, and had thrust them into my inside pocket, folded up. These cheques were endorsed on the back, as described, and were stamped with large and peculiar red numbers...."
Phinuit: "Who is this funny-footed fellow of yours, the one with the club-feet and the funny shoes?"
Comment by sitter: "Correct. My boy was born with club-feet, and wears machine boots" (11, pp. 572–573).

Many of the Piper sittings, however, were concerned with messages ostensibly from the deceased, as in the case of the long series of communications received from "G.P." (George Pellew) shortly after Pellew's accidental death (7), or in the case of James H. Hyslop's messages from his deceased father, who had lived on a farm in a remote region of rural Ohio (8). In this latter case in particular, it is difficult to see how normal sources of information could have been available to Mrs. Piper.

It might be well to stress at this point that we have no good evidence of a *training process* running through the excellent work of Mrs. Piper; quite the contrary, her mediumistic gifts seemed to appear suddenly, like a bolt from the blue. Nor do we have many examples of the arduous, grilling, and systematic "education" that Mrs. Eileen Garrett underwent at the British College of Psychic Science with Hewat McKenzie (5), both of them being willing to make enormous sacrifices of

time and energy to bring her to the maximal extent of her powers. Actually, we have very few systematic studies on the cultivation of paranormal sensitivity and, as John Beloff has recently pointed out (3), we do not yet know whether there are any specific training techniques which would enable the ordinary person to acquire such sensitivity. Milan Ryzl, the Czech investigator, described a method[2] for creating gifted subjects (21, 22), and he apparently used it successfully, notably with the star subject, Pavel Stepanek. But independent attempts to validate the method have not been successful (see, e.g., 3, pp. 125–126) and one remains doubtful of its general applicability. Thus the question of "training" versus "native gift" (or their interrelations) cannot now be answered, and we must await the results of further research.

To return to Mrs. Piper, how was she "recruited"? She was recruited through the American spiritualist movement. If William James had been afraid to make contact with this type of movement, a very important period in the history of psychical research would have been lost to us. Mrs. Piper went on quietly giving sittings for many years. She never sought any publicity, did not read the published material regarding her work, which was turned out in large quantities, and was even quite vague as to the nature of the research going on and as to the meaning of her own phenomena.

III

At the turn of the century a group of classical scholars in England, including Frederic W.H. Myers, began to think about the kind of evidence that would be contributed if classical material came through a sensitive who knew "small Latin and less Greek"; that is, if scholarly messages were woven into the usual trance communications. They felt that material of this sort would advance our understanding of trance psychology and also plumb the deeper, more serious claims of contact with the deceased. I will give you an illustration:

[2]W.G. Roll (20) has pointed out the similarity of Ryzl's method, which involves the use of hypnosis to develop the clarity of the subject's imagery, to one described more than forty years ago by Gustav Pagenstecher (17) in his monograph on the famous psychometric subject, Senora Maria Reyes de Z. (Mrs. Zierold). However, unlike Ryzl, Pagenstecher did not claim that his method would be useful in developing ESP in the ordinary person.

Mrs. Piper was one of a group of seven automatic writers—persons capable of throwing themselves into a light trance or dissociated state in which the hand moves more or less of its own accord. Both in trance, when she wrote automatically, and as she came out of trance (delivering a few words in the "waking stage" before she was fully returned to this world), she began to give classical references to sources so abstruse that neither the sitters nor the other classical scholars who studied the scripts could identify the material, and frequently believed that she had failed. In point of fact, long strings of quite specific and successful material were delivered both before the death of Myers, and in particular after his death, in very "Myers-like" types of communications (24). In a series of sittings, for example, material was delivered by Mrs. Piper from Ovid's *Metamorphoses,* having to do with the journey to the river Styx and beyond, on the basis of the question, "What does the word *Lethe* suggest to you?" (15, pp. 214–224; 18). Very appropriate classical references were given to the river Lethe—the river of forgetfulness in the underworld—and the related characters with their Greek names coming and going in the midst of this narrative. But the most extraordinary thing about this was that, as time went on, dovetailing quotations from similar classics began to appear in the writings of the other automatists. Communications of this kind came to be known as "cross correspondences," in the sense that interwoven fragments of basic classical messages, quite appropriate as coming from Myers and others in the S.P.R. group of communicators, were produced month after month and indeed year after year by the automatists.

I have already described how Mrs. Piper was recruited. How about the other automatists who were involved in the production of the cross correspondences? How were they recruited? Did someone advertise in the *Atheneum* for them? Were they talked about in the Cambridge lecture halls? Far from it. It started from the fact that the classicists themselves, being well educated and thoughtful men and women, had the opportunity to see at first hand the nature of the trance phenomena of Mrs. Piper, and the thing spread.

For example, Margaret Verrall, the wife of a professor of classics and herself lecturer in classics at Newnham College, Cambridge, gave herself the assignment, at about the turn of the century, of learning how to do automatic writing (31). You will see now why I think this historical record has some relevance to tonight's topic. Mrs. Verrall, an ordinary, thoughtful person with no outstanding psychic gifts that were apparent, sat regularly to see if her hand would move. It finally did, but the curious thing is that it didn't move the way Mrs. Piper's hand moved, in deep trance; in fact, Mrs. Verrall did not go into deep trance. As she herself describes it (31), what usually happened was that one word at a time would drop into her mind and she would write down what she "heard." And before very long, the classical allusions which appeared in Mrs. Verrall's script began to interweave with the messages of Mrs. Piper and the other automatists in the group. Shortly after the death of Myers, Mrs. Holland (Rudyard Kipling's sister) in India began to make references in her automatic script to "5 Selwyn Gardens, Cambridge," Mrs. Verrall's address, a fact unknown to Mrs. Holland. Myers, purporting to communicate through Mrs. Holland, urged that she send her script to Mrs. Verrall. This she did, and the resulting association between these two automatists gave rise to many cross correspondences (10; 24, p. 46).

Before very long, then, a web or texture of communications began to develop which was so rich in classical allusions and so complex in design that people could not help asking the question: "If Myers, having died at the turn of the century, wanted to make his continued existence credible, what would he do?" He might very well plunk little fragments of messages, which could not easily be fitted together, into the minds of different sensitives, some of them classical and some of them non-classical in their education.

IV

In the cross correspondences, the recruitment of subjects was largely a matter of the investigators' courage in becoming their own subjects. And this is a theme of which C.J. Ducasse has often reminded us: the responsibility of all serious investigators to see how far they themselves can go in the expression of the paranormal. This is reminiscent of a principle used in India, for example, in teaching four hundred-odd million people other languages than their own vernacular, many of them wishing, for good economic reasons, to learn English. This principle is "each one teach one"; each person with a little knowledge of the language passes it along to relative, friend, or neighbor. Similarly, a person with a little psychic gift, pushing it with normal common sense, not making a fetish out of it nor becoming unduly excited about it, may through encouragement and support help to develop a similar capacity in others.

A skeptical friend of mine had been reading the cross correspondence material because I had told him that as a civilized person with scientific pretentions he ought to know something about psychical research. He was drowsy that afternoon; he put a pencil between his thumb and finger and dozed off. Then the telephone rang and he was annoyed at being interrupted in his nap. As he answered the phone he looked down at the pad, and on the sheet was written "I hear the bell." He wasn't sure he was going to have anything to do with automatic writing, but in the very midst of this self-induced state it was starting! And very often automatic writing, in one form or another, starts and goes on as far as it is allowed to go. Now, I hasten to agree that it can easily go too far. It can lead a somewhat vulnerable person into developing a form of dissociation which he cannot control. There is some risk. But this is true of a great many things. It is true of drug research, of experimentation with LSD, for example, but we don't stop all research because of the dangers involved.

Now, what I have been saying so far might be called the cultivation of the "in" group; that is to say, not looking upon psychics or sensitives as "those sorts of people out there"—across the East River or on the other side of the Hudson. It is thinking of psychic phenomena as "common human" and belonging in some vestige at least to all human beings and capable of being much more vividly expressed at some times than at others—notably in periods of shock, grief, or alienation—when one may, like Mrs. Piper, be in need of something "out there." And there is also the need for the perfectly normal kind of mutual support which men and women are going to demand if they take up a subject like psychical research which does not chime in well with the *Zeitgeist,* with the dominant mood or thought of the period.

In this connection, it must be pointed out that a good deal has been learned by following prototypes which have been set up in the spontaneously occurring religious experiences of mankind. It is true of India, it is true of the Middle East, it is true of the Catholic and Protestant and Jewish worlds of the west, that wherever the individual has a strong conviction that he is coming nearer the Divine through the cultivation of automatic ways of expression—through speech or writing, or even through dreams—there is likely to be a greater richness and spontaneity in the phenomena than when one takes the hard-boiled point of view that this is science and not religion. The empirical fact is that the disposition to regard these expressions as, in a certain sense, divine has been one of the historical reasons for their effective development.

V

It seems to me that the cultivation of the paranormal gift is not unlike the cultivation of almost any other kind of gift, whether profound or ridiculous—whether learning to play Bach fugues on the piano or learning to wiggle one's ears. It makes no difference so far as the psychology of learning is concerned: it takes motivation, persistence, and a great deal of blind pushing when you just plain don't know how. Suppose I were to tell you, for example, that you can, typically, produce a particular kind of brain wave which you have perhaps only heard of in a vague sort of way. And I say that just as *some* of you could learn to write, if not great, then at least very passable lyric poetry, just so *some* of you could learn to control your brain waves. What do you have to do? You have to have an electronic panel by which the brain waves that are coming all the time from the surface of the brain are magnified and connected to auditory or visual signals (as on a television screen). You look or listen; you see your own brain waves as they are conducted to the screen, or hear the tone that results when your alpha waves are coming. And you try to control them. How do you do this? Well, you simply keep on wishing until it happens, very much as Mrs. Verrall kept on wishing to write automatically, until it finally happened. This sort of thing may be called "self-reinforced" activity. You don't have to give people candy bars to reward them; you don't have to pat them on the shoulder and tell them they are doing a wonderful job. If they are highly motivated to succeed, they will pick up little internal cues from the body, perhaps from the vital organs or the muscles which will begin to tighten in a particular way. Or, instead of controlling your brain waves or wiggling your ears, you might be writing automatically. And you might even write, as Mrs. Verrall did, and as Mrs. Piper did at a different level, some quite interesting and coherent stuff.

Now, it must be stressed that the production of an automatic phenomenon is not in itself important. It is merely a vehicle by means of which the paranormal may or may not be expressed. An automatic script, for example, is no more significant than it would be if I were to tell you that there is a boat drifting by itself near the coast. How good a boat, how useful a boat, how difficult it will be to rescue the crew — we don't know. The question is not whether you can produce an automatism — the chances are that many of you can. The question is whether the automatism becomes a *useful vehicle* for veridical messages. There is a great deal of story-telling in the sphere of automatism. But the material might contain, as Mrs. Verrall's writing did and as Mrs. Piper's writing did over and over again and year after year, messages having to do with distant and not otherwise known events, or having to do with a clear-cut telepathic line of communication with a distant individual, or even having to do with seeming communication between the living and the deceased.

In the perspective of seventy-five years and more of psychical research, most of us, I think, incline toward the view that the motor phenomena, like automatic writing or speech, are in the long run less revealing for most people, most of the time, than the messages that appear at the perceptual level or the cognitive level. These sensory automatisms, as they are called, have to do with *impressions:* you may, as you fall asleep, have an hypnagogic impression, or, as you awake in the morning, an hypnapompic impression. Or, as you wake fitfully in the middle of the night, you may have an experience which is neither quite a dream nor a waking hallucination. These perceptual phenomena or cognitive phenomena have to do with the world of contact with the outer environment, not with motor effects; sometimes they also may be vehicles for the expression of the paranormal. I believe that in the long run we have learned most about the paranormal from the direct psychological study of perceptual and cognitive states, and that the motor phenomena are useful and interesting mostly as secondary indications of what the perceptual and cognitive processes are. At any rate, I will give you my biases and a few concrete cases of veridical sensory automatisms:

Early in the present century two English women, Miss Miles and Miss Ramsden, carried out a series of telepathy tests in which items that Miss Miles concentrated upon during the day appeared in the impressions received by Miss Ramsden (14). For example, when the former selected as "target" *Bishop of Bristol,* the latter recorded as her impression for that day *Bishop Latimer, Archbishop.* The two Miles-Ramsden series of 1905 and 1907 provide a good illustration of the capacity of two people who are in close attunement with each other to develop a type of paranormal sharing. Their results are not of a sort easy to put on a quantitative basis, yet they are so striking that one cannot help feeling that there was real telepathic communication involved.

Another aspect of the problem is highlighted by the experiments of the English writer Hubert Wales, who was skeptical whether successful telepathic communication required any special "attunement" between the persons involved, or concentration on the part of the agent (32). One of Wales' newspaper articles on psychical research had been read by a woman in a photography shop in London, Miss Samuels, who corresponded with Wales and agreed to his suggestion that she should write down her impressions as to what he was doing at different times during the day as he moved around in different areas. Some of Miss Samuels' imagery related rather strikingly to Wales' activities. Wales called this "telepathy without conscious agency" as he was not thinking about Miss Samuels, whom he barely knew, nor concentrating on the events to which her impressions seemed to refer.

Thus, we may have either conscious agency in sending (as in the Miles-Ramsden series), or unconscious agency (as in the Wales experiments); and also unconscious percipiency (as in the case of those to whom spontaneous impressions concerning distant events or persons come unsought). We are led back by cases like these to the notion that perhaps we are dealing with an almost trance-like state, or at least a state of great plasticity, great openness, like the state of creativeness which so many composers and painters have told us about. Here there is no effort to make something new, but rather a capacity to perceive in an unusual way that is not voluntarily controllable. So, in our efforts to recruit, what we are trying to find is a person who is capable of developing that kind of deep relaxation, so often near the sleeping state, in which impressions come, form themselves, and can be remembered and recorded.

VI

I said a minute ago that the perceptual and the cognitive phenomena are usually worth more than the purely motor phenomena. I would like to give an illustration of a fact that we learned in the very beginning, when Myers was formulating his theory of the subliminal self (16)[3], that kind of consciousness which is deeper than consciousness. Myers differentiated here between the motor automa-

tisms and the sensory automatisms, and he gave close attention to the field of sensory automatisms. You have, for example, the almost universal habit among preliterate peoples of using a pool of water, a drop of blood, or some other shimmering, liquid surface which, as you gaze at it, will begin to reflect, glaze over, and seem to show images. The same thing will happen if you use a crystal ball or any other kind of shiny surface. But the interesting thing is that these surface reflections one sees on the crystal ball are not the thing out of which the clairvoyant impression is formed. Typically, what happens as one looks at the ball is that the surface "mists over," becomes foggy, and then an etched image begins to stand out.

Now these crystal visions may have some paranormal content, as in the case of some celebrated subjects that were early studied in this field (4), or they may be nothing more than vehicles for free associations. But why do we have so many people who have monkeyed with automatic writing and so few who have monkeyed with crystal gazing? We laugh at crystal gazing. Perhaps we are a little embarrassed at anything so public as committing ourselves to the utterance of what we see in a surface which mists over and begins to form images. Actually, there are dozens of devices that can be used. And the auditory sphere is probably just as good. The dull, roaring sound one hears when holding a conch shell to the ear will do quite well. All these devices are very rich in offering materials to be restructured. I think that out of every attempt to get people interested in "psychic parlor games," at least a few minutes or a half hour should be given to sensory automatisms, which provide an opportunity to see whether one can get a little bit below the surface impression.

Of course, these phenomena, these sensory and motor automatisms, are fleeting and evanescent. They have to be caught, they have to be trapped; and you have to stay with them. And I would be the first to agree that unless you have considerable self-discipline and considerable sympathy with all kinds of people who will bring all sorts of different human motivations to tests such as these, you will run through a few weeks of work and then the thing will peter out.

[3]See also Myers' *Human Personality* (London: Longmans, Green, 1903), Vol. I, Ch. 6, "Sensory Automatism," and Vol. II, Ch. 8, "Motor Automatism."

VII

Now, I have already spoken about the use of the "stray" medium, Mrs. Piper, and about the use of the "in" group—the investigators themselves becoming the subjects, which was the way many of the great subjects in the early British period came to light. I will now go on to another slightly different angle involving some of these same things, but also something more—the case of two very extraordinary British mediums, Mrs. Willett and Mrs. Osborne Leonard, who were, so to speak, "fair game" for psychical researchers. Mrs. Leonard wrote her autobiography (12) and you can see the "recruitment" process here. You can see how she gave inquirers into psychical phenomena an unusual opportunity to get, through her mediumship, especially clear and vivid communications regarding both the living and the deceased. And with Mrs. Leonard we have something quite similar to what obtained in the case of Mrs. Piper—a willingness to commit herself to "blind" sittings and to experiments scheduled weeks and months in advance. Mrs. Lydia Allison of our A.S.P.R. group arranged for proxy sittings with Mrs. Leonard, and you will find in her book, *Leonard and Soule Experiments* (1), some remarkable examples of the capacity to pluck something interesting out of the midst of a long and complicated context.

The thing that is particularly striking about Mrs. Leonard's work from the point of view of recruitment is the eagerness with which a special elite group of investigators began to gather around her, like bees around clover, filling up her time as far as possible with research sittings. These research sittings differed from Mrs. Leonard's ordinary bereavement-assuaging sittings, which usually had very much less careful recording and documentation and a lower level of scientific importance.

In Mrs. Leonard's case, one may say that the boat was missed by the investigators almost as seriously as it was in Mrs. Piper's case, in the sense that after these long and devoted careers came to an end there was little that emerged in the way of scientific principles. The chief result of all this intensive study was merely a reaffirmation of the reality that William James had pointed out at

the very beginning—the reality of paranormal communication, some of which could very well have been a form of communication with the deceased.

In the case of Mrs. Willett, we have almost the embodiment of a special difficulty that besets psychical research. The more gifted the individual is, the greater the difficulties are in studying this individual at face value. Mrs. Willett, who was quite prominent in British public affairs, went through her life and died without her involvement in psychical research ever being known except to the inner circle of the S.P.R. It was only long after her death that her real name was published. We have a whole series of cultural forces standing in the way, and even G.W. Balfour in his beautiful study of Mrs. Willett's powers (2) never really spelled out the kind of information about her life and achievements which would make possible a systematic scientific study. Thus we have a good deal of evidence by now, on both sides of the Atlantic, that quite a lot of real sensitivity is being excluded from serious study by one or another type of social fear, a fear that perhaps one will be derided or regarded as deranged.

We have a recent example of such difficulties in the case of Bishop Pike who, because of his willingness to report on his sittings with Arthur Ford, has had a good deal of unfavorable publicity. Several newspaper reporters consulted me regarding Bishop Pike's beliefs, on the assumption that their readers would need to know whether this proved that he had had a "nervous breakdown." In other words, we are still at the point where relatively few people have the courage to become publicly identified with investigations which are so open-ended and regarding the meaning of which the public has so much basic doubt.

VIII

To return to the question of finding gifted subjects, how can we tell whether we have recruited successfully or not? The proof of the pudding is in the eating. How do we know that we have found the best? The British have always used the rule,

Try everyone. Let us assume that people who have had one spontaneous experience of telepathy, clairvoyance, or precognition are likely to have more if the same conditions can be established, or if they well up spontaneously within the individual. It may be possible, then, to cull out from those who have had the best spontaneous experiences those most suitable for more intensive studies.

But even without the benefit of spontaneous cases, one may begin with some very simple and unpretentious experiments. One may form a group that meets regularly in which a few elements of sound experimental procedure are developed and some serious consecutive effort over a number of months is maintained. You are likely to find, typically, two or three rather promising people in a group of twenty or so. The problem is very largely one of maintaining the motivation, which in turn is very largely a problem of realizing that wherever there is a little bit of good grain there is bound to be a lot of chaff. It will take a great deal of patience in accumulating, sifting, recording, and ultimately publishing the material before anything very much is going to be learned. The criterion, then, is a rather severe level of scientific interest in the phenomena.

I want to turn now to a different type of recruitment—the recruitment of students as subjects. This can mean elementary school or high school or college students. This has been done a good many times. Gertrude Schmeidler started in with college students in her Harvard studies in 1942 (25, 26), and has continued this work since coming to New York (28). Many other studies of college classes have been carried out in the hope that we might find gifted subjects in this way. I think I ought to add, however, for reasons which need to be looked into closely, that college student groups tested by the use of ESP cards, or any other simple, scorable material, don't usually yield much by way of highly gifted subjects. In all the years that Dr. Schmeidler and many other investigators have been doing college screening of this sort, I have never seen a consistently high-scoring subject pop up.

In this connection, I want to make the point that the atmosphere of college classes, particularly psychology classes, is really basically rigged *against* getting results. With all the falderal, with all the machinery you have to set up to do decently controlled ESP tests, the assumption is, "Oh, if anything should ever happen in this class, what would we *do*? Where would we be if somebody scored 22 out of 25, first crack out of the box, under conditions which we said were watertight? We would have to *explain* for months!" I think this sort of fear lurks in the background. Moreover, I think that college age is the wrong age for good ESP subjects. I think that one does better in early adolescence than in late. I don't know why we don't do more with high school students. I don't know why we don't do more with elementary school students.

Then there is another thing which makes it difficult to do adequate searching and screening of ESP subjects. We don't go quite far enough in providing bins into which to drop good data. Very often experimental results occur that we aren't ready for, and we decide *after the event* to check the data in new ways. One may find, for example, that although there are only the number of direct hits that would be expected by chance, the subject has tended to score on the target just before or just after the one he was aiming at. Now, if one sets up an hypothesis *in advance* that an effect like this is going to occur, then it is quite proper to score it. But to allow oneself a retrospective way of looking at the data, and then treating them as if the hypothesis had been set up to be tested, is not cricket. Odd effects will frequently occur, and all sorts of idiosyncratic and interesting possibilities must be provided for in advance.

If we know, for example, something about the psychology of our subjects, then we can predict the kind of effects they are likely to produce in an ESP test. The best illustration of this that I can think of is Gertrude Schmeidler's studies of the temperament of her subjects in which she undertakes to show, by means of projective tests such as the Rorschach, the kind of scoring patterns that are likely to appear (28, Ch. 7); or better yet, the interactions between members of the subject-agent pairs (27). When he was at Stanford, Charles E. Stuart did similar experiments (30), and both his studies and Schmeidler's studies seem to suggest that a gifted subject is not just a gifted subject as such, but rather that he or she is gifted in terms of communication with a particular person.

When S.G. Soal made his studies of the highly gifted subjects that he used, he found that not all agents were able to send to them (29). He worked, as you will remember, with Basil Shackleton and with Gloria Stewart, and he found that by no means all the people in paired experimental teams succeeded in getting significant results with them. On the contrary, the kind of gift that appeared was the ability of A to communicate with B, or of C to communicate with D. And it is often in the special pairs that the gift lies. We are making a serious psychological error if we fail to realize that the paranormal involves a *relationship* between persons; it is not like a birthmark on the skin, an inseparable part of a unitary individual. Much more, paranormal communication is like a system of communication through tones or paints in which what is meaningful for a particular creator is also meaningful for a particular listener or a particular observer. Some of the things that Beethoven had to say may not mean anything to you, but this is nothing against Beethoven; nor is it anything against your possible enjoyment of Mozart or Bach. In other fields, we all recognize that there are idiosyncrasies and special gifts.

IX

Now, why don't we make the most of this in psychical research? Why don't we constantly try to investigate the *interpersonal* aspects of paranormal phenomena? This can be done in your own private group that meets on alternate Wednesdays to try out some telepathic or clairvoyant exchange; it can be done in the class that you teach, and quite as effectively with little tots as with college students. And right around the corner there may well be other creative possibilities that we haven't even begun to think about. It may be on the "each one teach one" basis that there is a little spark in you or in a member of your family which will generate a fire only if it is provided with appropriate tinder.

I have tried to keep this on the conservative side. I don't say that anyone you recruit is going to develop a Piper type of spectacular phenomena, or a Leonard type. I am saying, however, that there is such a thing as successful recruitment of persons with modest gifts. You can't tell how much is there until you have tried; it takes starting from where you are. It means, for example, taking whatever spontaneous experiences you and your family and friends have had and looking for dyadic relations—that is, person-to-person relations. And it means the hard work of writing down the experiences and keeping systematic records.

Now, I don't want to create the impression that recruiting the subject is a first step unrelated to the next step, which is trying to cultivate the subject's gifts. The more I look at it, the more I am convinced that the recruitment process *in itself* provides a kind of "training." The way in which you listen to the first account of a spontaneous experience—whether you kill the thing by the severity of the treatment you give this account, or whether you encourage it; what you do that will maintain a high scientific level and yet at the same time loosen up and lead on the individual or the pair or the group to communicate—these in themselves may be the first steps in the cultivation process.

Side by side with the cultivation of paranormal powers goes the study of the psychology of learning; practicing; making careful records; watching what you can do now that you couldn't do last week; making note of the dyadic relations between persons in the development of group morale; and, above all, as C.J. Ducasse has often reminded us, developing a capacity to share in the teamwork. This includes a capacity on the part of each man or woman who is interested in psychical research to communicate to others where the real difficulties lie and where the most promising lines for progress seem to be forming. All I can do is to give you a little bit about the historical background, a little bit about the difficulties, and a little bit about the encouragements. But the main job of discovering gifted subjects and making the most of what they can offer to psychical research lies in the hands of people like yourselves who are interested and willing to give the time and energy to carrying out this theme.

REFERENCES

1. Allison, L.W. *Leonard and Soule Experiments.* Boston: Society for Psychic Research, 1929.

2. Balfour, G.W. "A Study of the Psychological Aspects of Mrs. Willett's Mediumship, and of the Statements of the Communicators Concerning Process." *Proc.* S.P.R., Vol. 43, 1935, 41–318.

3. Beloff, J. "Can Paranormal Abilities Be Learned?" *Journal* A.S.P.R., Vol. 61, April, 1967, 120–129.

4. Besterman, T. *Crystal-Gazing.* New Hyde Park, New York: University Books, 1965. (Original ed., London: Rider, 1924.)

5. Garrett, E.J. *Many Voices: The Autobiography of a Medium.* New York: Putnam, 1968.

6. Hodgson, R. "A Record of Observations of Certain Phenomena of Trance." *Proc.* S.P.R., Vol. 8, 1892, 1–167.

7. _____. "A Further Record of Observations of Certain Phenomena of Trance." *Proc.* S.P.R., Vol. 13, 1897–98, 284–582.

8. Hyslop, J.H. "A Further Record of Observations of Certain Trance Phenomena." *Proc.* S.P.R., Vol. 16, 1901, 1–649.

9. James, W. "A Record of Observations of Certain Phenomena of Trance, Part III." *Proc.* S.P.R., Vol. 6, 1889–90, 651–659.

10. Johnson, A. "On the Automatic Writing of Mrs. Holland." *Proc.* S.P.R., Vol. 21, 1908–09, 166–391.

11. Leaf, W. "A Record of Observations of Certain Phenomena of Trance, Part II." *Proc.* S.P.R., Vol. 6, 1889–90, 558–646.

12. Leonard, G.O. *My Life in Two Worlds.* London: Cassell, 1931.

13. Lodge, O. "A Record of Observations of Certain Phenomena of Trance, Part I." *Proc.* S.P.R., Vol. 6, 1889–90, 443–557.

14. Miles, C., and Ramsden, H. "Experiments in Thought-Transference." *Proc.* S.P.R., Vol. 21, 1908–09, 60–93.

15. Murphy, G. *Challenge of Psychical Research.* New York: Harper's, 1961.

16. Myers, F.W.H. "The Subliminal Self." *Proc.* S.P.R., Vol. 7, 1891–92, 298–355; Vol. 8, 1892, 333–404; Vol. 9, 1893–94, 3–128; Vol. 11, 1895, 334–593.

17. Pagenstecher, G. "Past Events Seership. A Study in Psychometry." *Proc.* A.S.P.R., Vol. 16, 1922, 1–136.

18. Piddington, J.G. "Further Experiments with Mrs. Piper in 1908. II. Three Incidents from the Sittings: Lethe; The Sibyl; The Horace Ode Question." *Proc.* S.P.R., Vol. 24, 1910, 86–169.

19. Piper, A.L. *The Life and Work of Mrs. Piper.* London: Kegan Paul, 1929.

20. Roll, W.G. "Pagenstecher's Contribution to Parapsychology." *Journal* A.S.P.R., Vol. 61, July, 1967, 219–240.

21. Ryzl, M. "Training the Psi Faculty by Hypnosis." *Journal* S.P.R., Vol. 41, March, 1962, 234–252.

22. _____. "A Method of Training in ESP." *International Journal of Parapsychology,* Vol. 8, 1966, 501–532.

23. Sage, M. *Mrs. Piper and the Society for Psychical Research.* New York: Scott-Thaw, 1904.

24. Saltmarsh, H.F. *Evidence of Personal Survival from Cross Correspondences.* London: G. Bell, 1939.

25. Schmeidler, G.R. "Predicting Good and Bad Scores in a Clairvoyance Experiment: A Preliminary Report," *Journal* A.S.P.R., Vol. 37, July, 1943, 103–110.

26. _____. "Predicting Good and Bad Scores in a Clairvoyance Experiment: A Final Report," *Journal* A.S.P.R., Vol. 37, October, 1943, 210–221.

27. _____. "Telepathy and Resistance to It." *Journal* A.S.P.R., Vol. 60, July, 1966, 207–209. (Abstract.)

28. Schmeidler, G.R., and McConnell, R.A. *ESP and Personality Patterns.* New Haven: Yale University Press, 1958.

29. Soal, S.G., and Bateman, F. *Modern Experiments in Telepathy.* New Haven: Yale University Press, 1954.

30. Stuart, C.E. "GESP Experiments with the Free Response Method." *Journal of Parapsychology,* Vol. 10, March, 1946, 21–35.

31. Verrall, M. "On a Series of Automatic Writings." *Proc.* S.P.R., Vol. 20, 1906, 1–432.

32. Wales, H. "Report on a Series of Cases of Apparent Thought-Transference without Conscious Agency." *Proc.* S.P.R., Vol. 31, 1920–21, 124–217.

Conditioning can be a part of many kinds of problems as the wide range in subjects of the following papers attests. Conditioning can explain behavior and reinforcement principles and illustrate their wide applicability. The first paper, by I.E. Farber and his colleagues reduces the mysterious effects of what has been called "brainwashing" to some of the more elementary conditioning principles as elaborated in the text. Israel Goldiamond examines a quite different aspect of behavior control— the modification of disordered behavior by the use of self-control procedures. Finally, B.F. Skinner discusses man's ability to control himself from the larger perspective of control of the world about him, arguing that in this way man will ultimately achieve his highest state of well being.

Part IV

APPLICABILITY
OF THE
PRINCIPLES OF
CONDITIONING

7
Brainwashing, Conditioning and DDD (Debility, Dependency, and Dread)

I.E. Farber, Harry F. Harlow, and Louis Jolyon West[1]

Few aspects of Communism have been more puzzling and disturbing to the Western world than the widely publicized collaboration, conversion, and self-denunciation in individuals—communist and noncommunist, innocent and guilty alike—who have suffered Communist imprisonment. Such behavior in persons whose intelligence, integrity, or patriotism can scarcely be doubted has suggested to many a mysterious power or knowledge that enables Communists to manipulate the thoughts and actions of others in a manner ordinarily reserved to characters in the more lurid sorts of science fiction. Accordingly, such terms as "brainwashing," "thought control," "menticide," and so on, have been applied to the process or product of this manipulation. To lend some degree of scientific respectability to such concepts, attempts have been made (e.g., 12, 16) to relate them to the psychiatric implications of Pavlovian conditioning procedures.

While these speculations have an undeniable romantic appeal, more sober analyses (1, 2, 7) of factors influencing the behavior of prisoners under Communist control indicate that they are neither mysterious nor indicative of any unusual amount of psychiatric sophistication on the part of Communists. Indeed, considering the extraordinary degree of control the Communists maintain over the physical and social environments of their prisoners, it is rather surprising that their efforts to indoctrinate and convert have not been more successful. Contrary to the views of some writers in popular media, the record indicates that most American prisoners in Korea, for instance, showed remarkable "sales resistance," even under profound duress.

It is a fact that the Communist Chinese in Korea achieved considerable success in stimulating

[1]This paper is a revision and elaboration of a report for the Study Group on Survival Training, sponsored by the Air Force Personnel and Training Research Center, March, 1956, of which the authors were members. The initial report was prepared by the first two authors, and the research for the revision was supported in part by the United States Air Force under Contract No. AF 41(657)-75 monitored by the Director, Officer Education Research Laboratory, Maxwell Air Force Base, Alabama, with the third author as Chief Investigator. Permission is granted for reproduction, translation, publication, use, and disposal in whole and in part by or for the United States Government.

Reprinted by permission from *Sociometry*, vol. 20, 1957, pp. 271–283.

cooperative behavior in a large number of United Nations prisoners of war through a combination of threats, propaganda, group pressures, and group manipulation. By Segal's criteria, 15 per cent of American army prisoners cooperated unduly. And if it can be considered that it was every man's duty to exercise active resistance to the enemy and his propaganda during the period of captivity, then fully 95 per cent failed to meet the most stringent criteria for commendable behavior (18, 28, p. 80). Nevertheless, the Chinese induced only 21 American prisoners to remain under Communism (13), and it is doubtful whether all these were truly "converted." Most authorities agree that despite occasional lapses the vast majority of American prisoners of war performed well and honorably. As the Secretary of Defense's advisory committee on POW's has reported, "the record seems fine indeed" (30).

In the light of these findings, a complete analysis would concentrate more heavily on the factors that enabled the large majority of POW's to resist in some degree. However, it is not with these phenomena that the present discussion is primarily concerned. Rather, we wish to discuss the basis for the success of techniques whereby false confessions, self-denunciations, and participation in propaganda activities were brought about. The Communists made special efforts to elicit these behaviors in flying personnel, particularly with regard to confessions of participation in bacteriological warfare. After their world-wide propaganda campaign went into high gear with accusations of "germ warfare" in Korea, beginning on February 21, 1952, a vigorous policy of coercive pressure was applied to a large number of American flying personnel captured during the Korean conflict. As a result, a number of flyers from the Air Force and Marine Corps signed false confessions of bacteriological warfare and participated to various extents in enemy propaganda activities. A detailed account of these events may be found elsewhere (24, 28).

The objective intensity of noxious stimulation, injury, disease, malnutrition, deprivation, sleeplessness, fatigue, isolation, and threat suffered by many prisoners for a greater or lesser period was extreme. There were few, if any, who were not subjected to some of these conditions. Accounts of observations and experiments related to these various types of stress are now appearing in the literature in increasing numbers (e.g., 11, 29). The present discussion is concerned with the theoretical analysis of the psychological states and processes resulting from such objective conditions of stress.

DDD

Although the specific components of these states vary in intensity and pattern, in the case of the prisoner of war they contain at least three important elements: debility, dependency, and dread. They refer to the fact that individuals subjected to the kinds of environmental conditions listed above have reduced viability, are helplessly dependent on their captors for the satisfaction of many basic needs, and experience the emotional and motivational reactions of intense fear and anxiety. These components are separable, but it is evident that they also interact. Consequently it seems appropriate as well as convenient to conceive of these states and processes as though they were an entity or syndrome including debility, dependency, and dread, to be referred to as DDD. Among the POW's pressured by the Chinese Communists, the DDD syndrome in its full-blown form constituted a state of discomfort that was well-nigh intolerable.

Debility was induced by semi-starvation, fatigue, and disease. Chronic physical pain was a common feature. Loss of energy and inability to resist minor abuse, combined with the lack of proper facilities for the maintenance of personal hygiene, led to inanition and a sense of terrible weariness and weakness.

Dependency, produced by the prolonged deprivation of many of the factors, such as sleep and food, needed to maintain sanity and life itself, was made more poignant by occasional unpredictable brief respites, reminding the prisoner that it was possible for the captor to relieve the misery if he wished. If an individual was placed in prolonged isolation, as was so often the case with flyers pressed to confess to the bacteriological warfare charges, the deprivation of ordinary social stimulation and relations markedly strengthened the dependency. Although we shall not dwell on this aspect of the situation, the effectiveness of Communist methods was undoubtedly greatly enhanced by their control of the means for satisfying nuclear social needs for recognition, status, communication, and so on. The captors' condemnation and misunderstanding of American social values, in connection with the withdrawal of accustomed social supports, e.g., reliable sources of information and communication with others as a means of testing reality and of appraising moral standards, played a significant part in the dependency relationship (2, 7, 10, 17).

Dread is the most expressive term to indicate the chronic fear the Communists attempted to induce. Fear of death, fear of pain, fear of nonrepatriation, fear of deformity or permanent disability through neglect or inadequate medical treatment, fear of Communist violence against loved ones at home, and even fear of one's own inability to satisfy the demands of insatiable interrogators—these and many other nagging despairs constituted the final component of the DDD syndrome (2).

The interrelations of these factors, carefully contrived and nurtured by the Communists, were of great importance in determining the total effect of DDD. Although there were some individuals who acceded to the demands of their captors fairly early in the game, it is clear that the Chinese realized the importance of preparing the resistant prisoner, through DDD, for the long, drawn-out process designed to bring about the desired goal—complete compliance.

Before considering in greater detail the specific mechanisms underlying the role of DDD in accomplishing this aim, three prefatory comments are in order. First, the present analysis lays no claim to comprehensiveness. It deals with only a few aspects of DDD occurring under certain conditions.

We believe these aspects to be important, but they are not all that is important. In this connection, the present paper may be considered as an elaboration of portions of the comprehensive discussion of Communist "thought reform" by Hinkle and Wolff (7). It is gratifying that our conclusions, arrived at independently and on somewhat more theoretical grounds, are essentially in agreement with theirs.

Second, our use of the terminology of learning theory, broadly conceived, and our use of concepts derived from conditioning, does not imply that we consider learning theory uniquely competent to explain the effects of DDD. On the other hand, we do consider factors influencing behavior in DDD to have something in common with factors affecting behavior in learning situations generally, and, therefore, that it may be worth while attempting to analyze some aspects of behavior associated with DDD in terms of principles of classical and instrumental conditioning. But, as an eminent conditioning theorist has recently noted (20), the view that principles derived from conditioning might apply to more complex behavior does not at all imply that complex behavior can be explained solely in terms of the variables affecting conditioning. In this instance, it is particularly doubtful that the procedures used to influence the behavior of prisoners under Communism derived from the methods of Pavlov, or that the prisoners' reactions are generally understandable in purely Pavlovian terms. On the contrary, to the extent that such concepts apply at all, selective or instrumental (Thorndikean) learning was a more prominent feature than classical (Pavlovian) conditioning. Certainly, only limited aspects of the behavior of prisoners under Communism bear any resemblance to the generalized inhibitory or excitatory states characterizing some of Pavlov's dogs (14).

Finally, we should beware of the "psychologist's error." Although some of the behavior of prisoners under Communism may be susceptible to analysis in terms of learning and conditioning principles, it does not follow that the application of these principles by Communist captors was deliberate and self-conscious. Animal trainers and side-show barkers are often extremely competent manipulators of behavior; this does not mean they are comparative or social psychologists.

DDD, SELF-PERCEPTION, AND THINKING

By providing a radically changed context DDD might be expected to produce new responses that actively compete or interfere with wonted behavior. It may also produce a condition of markedly reduced responsiveness, not unlike the generalized inhibitory states described by Pavlov (14) and Liddell (8), due to the reduced or monotonous stimulation associated with isolation and confinement, or to reduced energy, or to the frustration of previously successful techniques for achieving goals. Whenever individuals show extremely selective responsiveness to only a few situational elements, or become generally unresponsive, there is a disruption of the orderliness, i.e., sequence and arrangement of experienced events, the process underlying time spanning and long-term perspective. By disorganizing the perception of those experiential continuities constituting the self-concept and impoverishing the basis for judging self-consistency, DDD affects one's habitual ways of looking at and dealing with oneself.

This effect, which has elsewhere been related to the collapse of certain ego functions (22), bears an interesting resemblance to some aspects of the postlobotomy syndrome. The latter, too, is characterized by apathy and the disturbance of the self-concept or self-regarding tendency (15). The frequency and degree of flattened affect and self-deprecation in the confessions of prisoners under Communism have probably been overestimated, but to the extent they have occurred, the observed behavior has much in common with that of some brain-damaged individuals.

Closely related to the foregoing consequence of DDD is a disturbance of association and a concreteness of thinking similar to that sometimes seen in schizophrenia. The retention of recent experiences and habit patterns may be impaired,

with consequent regression, i.e., primitivization, in language, thought, and those integretative and mediating symbolic processes essential to reasoning and foresight. Conditioning performance in human subjects is impaired by some kinds of symbolic activity, and conversely, the impoverishment of thinking may increase susceptibility to arbitrary and unsubtle training procedures (cf. 3) leading to relatively automatic and uncritical imitative responses. This susceptibility may be further enhanced by anxiety and emotionality (5, 21, 23).[2]

REINFORCEMENT OF SOCIAL COMMUNICATION

On the assumption that conditioning principles apply in part to the behavior of prisoners of war, it is important to analyze further the nature of the conditioned stimuli and the responses elicited by them. Careful consideration would seem to indicate that the situation contains features both of selective or instrumental learning and of classical conditioning (20). The instrumental (i.e., Thorndikean rather than Pavlovian) aspect is emphasized by the fact that an individual must acquire a particular set of responses in order to bring about a reinforcing state of affairs. It is our thesis that an alleviation in the state of DDD provides the reinforcement for much of the behavior desired by the enemy. In other words, DDD does not, in and of itself, produce the desired behavior. DDD merely provides the occasion for the selective reinforcement of certain modes of response.

The role of DDD in the reinforcement process depends on the fact that it is not constant. Instead, it may be assumed to fluctuate in time, partly as a result of spontaneous psychophysiological processes, and partly as a result of deliberate manipu-

[2]These assumptions do not imply a negative correlation between intelligence and conditioning in normal subjects, nor better conditioning in feeble-minded or brain-damaged subjects than in normal individuals. The empirical evidence does not support any such views. The suggested effect of impoverished thinking relates only to that produced by debility, isolation, and such factors. One may speculate, in this connection, on the relation between this putative effect of DDD and the kinds of hypersuggestibility and automatism reported among primitive peoples suffering from prolonged physical stress and privation. Whether these symptoms result from some state of hyperconditionability is a moot question. Arctic hysteria and latah, for instance, are presumably dissociative and therefore hysteroid in nature (25), and the relation between hysteria and conditioning is as yet uncertain (4, 5, 6). Thus it is not possible at present to identify the effects of DDD with any particular psychiatric state.

lations designed to maintain its intermittent nature (2), thus preventing its fall to a baseline of permanent depression and hopelessness. Those individuals who were reduced to complete apathy undoubtedly represented failures from the point of view of their Communist captors.

At the risk of considerable oversimplification, one may conceive of two consequences of the occasional mitigation of DDD. First is the conditioning of the "expectancy" that DDD will be alleviated. (This constitutes the actual classically conditioned anticipatory goal response.) Relief, whether due to spontaneous factors or deliberate manipulations, is intermittent, temporary, and unpredictable. Far from weakening the expectancy of relief, however, this tends to maintain the expectancy and renders it less susceptible to extinction. In nontechnical terms, this process serves to keep hope alive, permitting some degree of adaptive behavior, and inhibiting self-destructive tendencies, which would frustrate the enemy's purpose.

This aspect of the learning process throws some light on the frequent practice in Communist prisons of having prisoners "punish themselves." Thus, a captive might be instructed to stand or kneel in a certain position until he should decide to cooperate. This emphasis on the self-inflicted nature of the prisoner's punishment, and his ability to mitigate his condition "voluntarily," is clearly calculated to increase the intensity of expectancies of the possibility of relief. At the same time, it is evident that the prisoner's belief that he actually exercises control is delusory, so far as the objective facts are concerned, since the captor may select any behavior he chooses as the condition for relieving a prisoner's distress. The alleviation of DDD at the time of occurrence of the desired behavior leads to the second consequence — the learning of instrumental acts. This is not so difficult to arrange as one might suppose and is certainly not the result of any mysterious power of the manipulator. Very often, the desired behavior is verbal in nature. Verbal behavior is in a general way already strongly conditioned to DDD in all human adults. One learns from infancy to use verbal behavior as a means of relieving or avoiding

many of the components of DDD. And, as the foregoing discussion indicates, the aperiodic and unpredictable nature of the selective reward of particular language responses may be one of its chief strengths. If one may extrapolate from the results of numerous laboratory experiments, this is the very procedure calculated to produce the maximum number of responses and also to make them highly resistant to extinction, even in the absence of rewards (19).

The nature of the rewards used needs no elaboration. Relief of hunger, fatigue, isolation, or pain, even temporarily, serves as an automatic reward. Even the verbal and empty promise of alleviation of DDD leads to appropriate anticipatory goal responses, keeping hope alive. Paradoxically, interrogation, harangues, threats, and contumely may also have a rewarding aspect, so great is the acquired reinforcement value of social communication and speech under conditions of isolation, dependency, and physical debility.

Since the habits of social communication associated with DDD are initially strong, and are further strengthened by selective reinforcement, it is not strange that prisoners often show considerable social responsiveness in the presence of their captors. Despite the impoverishment of the self-concept and primitivization of thinking referred to earlier, prisoners could enjoy in some degree a much needed social relationship in the interrogation and indoctrination situations. It may be hypothesized that some prisoners became the victims of the very socialization process that under ordinary circumstances is regarded as a desirable and, indeed, essential aspect of civilized living. It is of interest in this connection to record the finding of Lifton, who explicitly noted among a group of repatriated prisoners who had most aggressively resisted collaboration with the Communists, a large portion of individuals with significant antisocial tendencies (9). We do not suggest that collaboration and confession by prisoners under Communism are signs of desirable social attitudes. We do suggest that socialization training facilitates the tendency to engage in social communication, even with a recognized enemy, particularly under conditions in which the behavior is reinforced by the satisfaction of powerful drives while at the same time interfering or inhibitory tendencies are markedly reduced.

There are some analogies between the condition of an individual under such circumstances and that of a hypnotized subject. The hypnotized subject also tends to respond automatically, especially to verbal stimuli, to be greatly influenced by the attitude of the hypnotist, and to be highly selective in his social responsiveness. Furthermore, there is general agreement regarding the susceptibility of most normal individuals to hypnosis, except in the case of strong deliberate resistance. Under conditions of DDD, the possibility of resistance over a very long period may be vanishingly small. As soon as resistance appears, the intensity of DDD can be increased, thus at one and the same time punishing resistance and increasing the influence of the reward when relief occurs. It must be remembered that the strengthening effects of rewards—in this instance the alleviation of an intensely unpleasant emotional state—are fundamentally automatic. They occur because of the kind of nervous system we have, and not in any essential way because of the mediation of conscious thought processes.

RETENTION OF PRISON EXPERIENCES AND BEHAVIOR

What is the aftermath of such experiences? The evidence clearly indicates that, except in the case of organic brain damage such as might result from avitaminosis, the behavior of the typical returnee from Communist prisons is "normal," in the special and important sense that he behaves in a manner that would be predicted on the basis of ordinary laws of behavior. There is not the slightest evidence for the necessity of postulating new or unknown factors or conditions. This does not mean the experience of imprisonment leaves no trace. Such a circumstance would in itself be abnormal, i.e., inconsistent with the known principles of behavior. In terms of normative criteria, many ex-prisoners are more than ordinarily anxious, defensive, dependent, suspicious, insecure.

Pressed to explain any possibly discreditable acts, they often exhibit a very considerable degree of hesitancy, vagueness, paramnesia, and rationalization. In a word, they behave exactly as one would expect of any individual required to explain and defend his behavior, many determinants of which he is not aware.

Most returnees remember a great deal of what occurred during their imprisonment. They do not remember everything and may be unable to give a very clear account of their own behavior. Some behavior may appear as strange and inexplicable to the person concerned as to anyone else. The explanation of whatever impairment of memory occurs may be found in the laws of forgetting, deriving from both clinic and laboratory. There is no need to expatiate here on the role of repression in forgetting when the material to be recalled elicits anxiety and guilt. But it may be useful to note briefly some of the factors that would influence retention even in the absence of these emotions.

In an earlier section, it was pointed out that the state of DDD produces responses that actively compete with ordinary responses to environmental stimuli. By the same process, the comforting and familiar stimuli of home and friends are associated with a wholly different set of responses from those produced by DDD. The changed context may actively inhibit recall of the prison experiences. This phenomenon is nothing more than the familiar psychological explanation of forgetting in terms of associative interference.

Among the most important of these competing responses are the affective ones. The returnee simply does not feel as he did as a prisoner. He may be able to talk about how he felt, although this too offers difficulties because our terminology for describing emotional states is woefully inadequate and vague (3), but he does not currently respond affectively in the same way. Similarly, the familiar stimuli of home reinstate different verbal responses, both overt and implicit, that affect recall. The returnee feels different, talks differently, and thinks differently than he did in the former context. Since, like all of us, he is unaware of many of the cues to his former behavior (as well as his current behavior), it is as useless to ask him to explain his earlier reactions as it is to ask a person why he once disliked olives or is for the moment unable to recall the name of an old acquaintance.

The particular reactions and attitudes constituting patriotism, bravery, loyalty, and so on, depend on the appearance of particular cues, symbolic or other. Such qualities are tendencies to respond positively or negatively, in varying degrees and combinations, in the presence of certain combinations of cues. From this point of view, unwonted reactions occurring under DDD do not represent a different attitude; rather, the habitual attitude does not appear because the appropriate cues have been removed. Back home in the presence of adequate cues, the returnee tends to act and feel as he did prior to imprisonment.

Finally, one must consider the effect on retention of the adequacy of the original impression. Occasionally the returnee does not remember much because he did not observe much. The impoverished stimulation, impaired responsiveness, reduced symbolic activity, and disorganization of timespanning characteristic of DDD reduce the clarity and strength of impressions at the time of the original experience, and thus decrease ability to recall.

In the light of all these factors, whose pejorative influence on retention is well known by students of human learning, it is clearly to be expected that the recall of returnees would be something less than complete and wholly accurate as regards their actual prison experiences and behavior.

RESISTANCE TO EFFECTS OF DDD

Despite our opinion that the most undesirable effects of DDD are not necessarily permanent, or, given appropriate social conditions after repatriation, even particularly long-lived, the general picture of DDD presented in the foregoing discussion is rather gloomy. This is in part because we have emphasized its stressful aspects rather than the considerable resources most persons can muster to oppose them. The many environmental, social, and motivational variables that produce resistance

to these effects have not been discussed, but their potency should certainly not be underestimated. As we have observed earlier, the resistance of American prisoners under Communism, in the face of the objective circumstances detailed above, was in most instances notable, and in some nothing less than heroic (2, 24, 28).

It is evident that there are great individual differences in susceptibility to DDD even under conditions in which the level of DDD itself could reasonably be regarded as constant, i.e., not a differential factor. To state the point somewhat differently, there are unquestionably a number of variables, whose values differ from person to person, affecting the degree of resistance to the effects of DDD. The question may then be raised whether the potency of these variables might not be increased in any given individual. We believe they can.

The statement, "Every man has his breaking point," contains a germ of truth, but like other bromides, is liable to misinterpretation. It does not mean the "breaking point" is fixed for any given individual, so that nothing can affect it. Such a view is scientifically indefensible, if not meaningless, since it implies that some kinds of behavior are unlawful, i.e., not affected by variations in any kinds of antecedent conditions. Furthermore, the term "breaking point" is itself misleading. Susceptibility to DDD or any other stressful condition is not an all-or-none affair. We are discussing behavior, and behavior varies in degree and in kind. It may be possible to define "breaking" in the manner that one defines a right or wrong response in arithmetic, but it should be recognized that such a definition would be arbitrary at best and of doubtful conceptual significance. As Biderman has pointed out, a prisoner's physical and moral strength may be sapped by Communist coercive methods to a degree that resistance appears insignificant. But, however feeble his performance, motivation to resist usually persists and shows itself as circumstances permit (2).

It is not the purpose of the present discussion to consider all the possible personal or social variables of which resistance to the effects of DDD may be a function, or indeed to consider any of them in detail. We mention two, not because they are necessarily of particular importance, but because they throw further light on the nature of the DDD state. First, there is the factor of physical health. Other things equal, there is probably a negative relation between degree of physical health and vigor on the one hand and susceptibility to DDD on the other. Debility can be postponed longer, dependency fought against, and the self-concept maintained more easily if bodily well-being obtains. Second, there is the factor of initial or chronic anxiety. No matter what anxiety is due to, the higher the anxiety level, the greater is the possibility of rewarding behavior by its momentary reduction. Contrariwise, a low level of initial anxiety should retard the growth of the "dread" component of DDD, and at least indirectly affect some of its antecedents, e.g., the reactivity to pain (27).

Thus, techniques for promoting health and decreasing anxiety in those who may become prisoners are probably of great importance. Nevertheless, one should not expect factors such as these to block the effects of DDD indefinitely. Physical health, for instance, may be of utmost value over the short haul, e.g., during early interrogation. But on a long-term basis it may be relatively insignificant. Health can be broken down by a determined and informed enemy in a very short time. And although a healthy individual can better resist the effects of debilitating variables, there is no evidence that, once illness and physical debility occur, previously healthy individuals can tolerate this condition better than those who might have become habituated to it. In some cases, indeed, the reverse might obtain.

A somewhat similar reservation may be expressed concerning procedures calculated to reduce initial anxiety, i.e., training individuals to be generally nonanxious. The fear component of DDD, unlike neurotic anxiety or neurotic fears (phobias), is quite realistic for the most part. Realistic fears are not easily extinguishable and, if they were, the desirability of extinguishing such fears is not altogether certain. For instance, fear of punishment for displaying hostility toward one's captors is adaptive. Wolf and Ripley (26) quote one prisoner of the Japanese in World War II in this regard: "I had to make a conscious effort not to resent things because I realized that my bones are brittle."

On the other hand, certain anticipatory fears may be modified through training procedures. Alleviation of unrealistic fears of the unknown (through accurate indoctrination regarding enemy methods) undoubtedly improves the ability of the individual to deal with those fears that are realistic. It may make it possible for him to admit his fear to himself, as a reasonable and expected reaction, thus modifying its influence as a covert force toward compliance. Furthermore, an expectation of the probable psychophysiological effects of stress may rob them of some of their "shock" value. Finally, a certain amount of transfer may be expected from stressful training experiences in which adaptive modalities have been learned, thus permitting the prisoner to conceptualize his current stressful experience in terms of previous (and at least partly successful) transactions under stress.

Still, it would be foolish to disregard the fact that some of the elements of DDD represent a pathological organic state, some consequences of which are probably innately determined. To the extent this is true, one cannot expect to achieve a great degree of prophylactic success in regard to the effects of DDD, any more than one can reasonably expect at the present state of knowledge to prevent some of the undesirable consequences of lobotomy.

Though many of the behavioral consequences of DDD are not innately determined, the conditioning of certain types of responses desired by the enemy may eventually occur, even in the face of superlative resistance. One of the conclusions that may legitimately be drawn from the present analysis of the circumstances of imprisonment under Communism is that, if a prisoner's state of DDD reaches a truly extreme degree of severity (and it cannot now be predicted whose ability to resist will be the most effective in combating DDD), and *if he lives,* he probably cannot be expected to resist indefinitely. This prediction does not require the assumption that Communists have mysterious powers, or that their prisoners are subjected to some strange process of "brainwashing" negating the effects of their previous training and attitudes. It is based, rather, on the assumption that under the physical, social, and emotional conditions of extreme DDD, some degree of ultimate compliance may be considered a natural consequence of the operation of ordinary principles of human behavior.

SUMMARY

Although the behavior of some prisoners under Communism, including collaboration, conversion, and self-denunciation, appears to suggest that Communists are able to "brainwash" their prisoners in a mysterious way, a consideration of the physical, emotional, and social conditions of the prisoner in conjunction with the ordinary principles of human behavior reveals that such behavior may be readily explained. The state of the prisoner may be described in terms of the concepts of debility, dependency, and dread (DDD), and some of the behavioral principles explaining the effects of the DDD state derive from learning and conditioning phenomena.

It is assumed that DDD operates in part to produce a generalized state of hyporesponsiveness, disrupting time-spanning processes and disorganizing the self-concept. Another consequence of DDD is the impairment of symbolic processes, perhaps rendering the prisoner susceptible to relatively simple conditioning techniques. The intermittent nature of DDD leads both to the expectancy of relief (i.e., hope) and to the reinforcement of specific kinds of verbal behavior. The latter effect is facilitated by the fact that social communication is already strongly conditioned to cues such as those produced by DDD, as a result of normal socialization training.

The typical prisoner returnee exhibits no extraordinary peculiarities of memory. The degree of forgetting of prison experiences is such as would be expected as a result of the inhibition of anxiety-producing thoughts (repression), change of situational context during recall, and the inadequacies of original impressions during imprisonment.

Resistance to the undesirable consequences of DDD is a matter of degree and may be modified by such factors as physical health and level of initial anxiety. Nevertheless, factors such as these cannot reasonably be expected to provide more than temporary respite. Through various defenses, a prisoner may postpone the development of extreme DDD for a long time, perhaps indefinitely. But if a prisoner's state of DDD is extreme, and if he lives, he probably cannot resist indefinitely. Far from furnishing proof of the operation of some unnatural process of "brainwashing," this eventuality is a predictable consequence of the operation of laws of normal human behavior.

REFERENCES

1. Bauer, R.A., "Brainwashing—Psychology or Demonology," American Psychological Association Symposium, September, 3, 1956.

2. Biderman, A.D., "Communist Techniques of Coercive Interrogation," Air Force Personnel and Training Research Center Development Report TN-56-132, Lackland Air Force Base, Texas, 1956.

3. Dollard, J., and N.E. Miller, Personality and psychotherapy, New York: McGraw-Hill, 1950.

4. Eysenck, H.J., "Cortical Inhibition, Figural After Effect, and Theory of Personality," Journal of Abnormal and Social Psychology, 1955, 51, 94–106.

5. Farber, I.E., K.W. Spence, and H.P. Bechtoldt, "Emotionality, Introversion-Extraversion, and Conditioning," Midwestern Psychological Association, May 3, 1957.

6. Franks, C.M., "Conditioning and Personality: a Study of Normal and Neurotic Subjects," Journal of Abnormal and Social Psychology, 1956, 52, 143–150.

7. Hinkle, L.E., and H.G. Wolff, "Communist Interrogation and Indoctrination of 'Enemies of the State,'" Archives of Neurology and Psychiatry, 1956, 76, 115–174.

8. Liddell, H.S., "Conditioned Reflex Methods and Experimental Neurosis," in J. McV. Hunt (ed.), Personality and the Behavior Disorders, New York: Ronald, 1944.

9. Lifton, R.J., "Home by Ship: Reaction Patterns of American Prisoners of War Repatriated from North Korea," *American Journal of Psychiatry*, 1954, 110, 732–739.

10. Lifton, R.J. "'Thought Reform' of Western Civilians in Chinese Communist Prisons," *Psychiatry*, 1956, 19, 173–196.

11. Lilly, J.C., "Effects of Physical Restraint and of Reduction of Ordinary Levels of Physical Stimuli on Intact, Healthy Persons," *Group for the Advancement of Psychiatry, Symposium No. 2, Illustrative Strategies for Research on Psychopathology in Mental Health,* New York: GAP Publication Office, 1790 Broadway.

12. Meerloo, J.A.M., "Pavlovian Strategy as a Weapon of Menticide," *American Journal of Psychiatry*, 1954, 110, 809–813.

13. Pasley, V., *21 Stayed,* New York: American Book — Stratford Press, 1955.

14. Pavlov, I.P., *Conditioned Reflexes and Psychiatry,* W. H. Gantt (trans.), New York: International, 1941.

15. Robinson, M.F., and W. Freeman, *Psychosurgery and the Self,* New York: Grune and Stratton, 1954.

16. Santucci, P.S., and G. Winokur, "Brainwashing as a Factor in Psychiatric Illness," *Archives of Neurology and Psychiatry*, 1955, 74, 11–16.

17. Schein, E.H., "The Chinese Indoctrination Program for Prisoners of War," *Psychiatry*, 1956, 19, 149–172.

18. Segal, J. "Factors Related to the Collaboration and Resistance Behavior of U.S. Army PW's in Korea," *Technical Report 33, Human Resources Research Office,* The George Washington University, Washington, D. C., 1956.

19. Skinner, B.F., *Behavior of Organisms,* New York: Appleton-Century, 1938.

20. Spence, K.W., *Behavior Theory and Conditioning,* New Haven, Conn.: Yale University Press, 1956.

21. Spence, K.W., and I.E. Farber, "Conditioning and Extinction as a Function of Anxiety," *Journal of Experimental Psychology*, 1953, 45, 116–119.

22. Strassman, H.D., M.B. Thaler, and E.H. Schein, "A Prisoner of War Syndrome: Apathy as a Reaction to Severe Stress," *American Journal of Psychiatry*, 1956, 112, 998–1003.

23. Taylor, J.A., "The Relationship of Anxiety to the Conditioned Eyelid Response," *Journal of Experimental Psychology*, 1951, 41, 81–92.

24. West, L.J., "U.S. Air Force Prisoners of the Chinese Communists," Group for the Advancement of Psychiatry Symposium on Prisoners of War, Nov. 11, 1956.

25. West, L.J., "Hypnosis and the Dissociative Reactions," *Journal of Clinical and Experimental Hypnosis* (in press).

26. Wolf, S., and H.S. Ripley, "Reactions among Allied Prisoners Subjected to 3 Years of Imprisonment and Torture by Japanese," *American Journal of Psychiatry*, 1947, 104, 180–193.

27. Wolff, H.G., and S. Wolf, *Pain* (3d ed., 1952), New York: Charles C. Thomas, 1952.

28. "Communist Interrogation, Indoctrination and Exploitation of American Military and Civilian Prisoners," *Hearings Before the Permanent Subcommittee on Investigations of the Committee on Government Operations, U.S. Senate, 84th Congress, 2nd Session,* Washington, D.C.: U.S. Government Printing Office, 1956.

29. "Factors Used to Increase the Susceptibility of Individuals to Forceful Indoctrination: Observations and Experiments," *Group for the Advancement of Psychiatry, Symposium No. 3,* New York: GAP Publications Office, 1790 Broadway.

30. "POW: The Fight Continues After the Battle," *Report of the Secretary of Defense's Advisory Committee on Prisoners of War,* Washington, D.C.: U.S. Government Printing Office, 1955.

8

Self-Control Procedures in Personal Behavior Problems[1]

Israel Goldiamond

The present discussion is concerned with the application of self-control procedures to the solution of certain limited behavioral problems.

Often one person comes for help from another because he cannot cope with problems that face him. The appropriate behaviors are not available. The means by which the behavioral deficit can be overcome are varied. Simple instructions often suffice, as when S cannot study because he does not have the assignment. On the other hand, S may not be able to study because he cannot allocate his time appropriately, because he daydreams at his desk, or because he engages in other behaviors which come under the general heading of lack of self-control. In these cases, simple instructions will not remedy the deficit since S himself knows what it is. He has often tried to instruct himself to behave appropriately but with little success. Indeed, the numerous jokes surrounding New Year's resolutions indicate both the prevalence of the problem and the ineffectiveness of its instructional solution, whether imposed by others or by one's self in self-instruction.

The specific behavioral deficit, or presenting problem, is often part of a larger context of deficits. Rather than trying to overcome the presenting deficit directly, the therapist may turn his attention to other, "deeper" behaviors or behavioral deficits. In this case, the presenting problem is considered a symptom, by exactly the same defining operations that make a skin rash a symptom. Here, the dermatologist states that to get rid of the rash he will treat in addition something else, possibly a blood imbalance, rather than only treating the rash itself (Goldiamond, Dyrud, & Miller, 1965). For example, we know of a woman who assumed a fetal posture for three days after an argument with her husband. She was restored to mobility by direct modification of this behavior.

[1]Paper presented at Eastern Psychological Association, April 23, 1965. Written under contract between the Office of the Surgeon General and the Washington School of Psychiatry, DA-49-193-MD-2448. The views expressed herein are those of the author and do not necessarily reflect the views of either contracting agency.

Reprinted with permission of author and publisher: Goldiamond, I. Self-control procedures in personal behavior problems. *Psychological Reports*, 1965, 17, 851–868, M3-V17. (Also available as a separate at $1.00 per copy from Journal.)

It can be argued that a woman who maintains control over her husband by such extreme behaviors is so lacking in more appropriate behaviors that her treatment will require considerably more than the two hours which restored her mobility. This case may be an example of treating a symptom, since behaviors other than the presenting complaint may also require modification. However, the "underlying" problem can still be considered as a behavioral one: in this case, the absence of those behaviors whereby wives normally control their husbands. Yet this general deficit also may be treated directly, as in our research on stuttering where we have, within the laboratory, replaced stuttering by fluent and rapid speech in 30 of 30 cases run thus far (Goldiamond, 1965b). Indeed, one of our stuttering patients, who had been suicidal, became able to read bedtime stories to her children at home, and certain other personal problems at home cleared up because her stuttering cleared up. Some of her other behaviors were accordingly symptomatic of stuttering (Goldiamond, 1965a), as we have defined "symptom."

If there is a danger in premature assignment of behavioral deficits as symptomatic, there is also a danger in premature assumption that the alteration of the presenting problem is the final solution. Further analysis in light of current knowledge will undoubtedly both modify and confirm practice in this area.

Classification of behavior as a problem for treatment or as a symptom may also be an economic or contractual matter. For example, in a marital problem, the presenting complaint may be cleared up in a short period of time, but other problems are sometimes uncovered which may require extensive treatment. At what point is the implicit contract between patient and therapist (cf. Sulzer, 1962) to treat the marital behaviors extended to behaviors in other areas? The answer to this question must depend on the extent to which S can afford the treatment or can afford not to get it, that is, can do without it. It would be nice to have a new car when the present one seems to require extensive repairs, but there may be other considerations such as a piano or a child's education. For going to and from work, minor adjustments may be sufficient. The economy may also be behavioral: is it worth the upset?

The present discussion will be limited to cases where the concern was with a specified behavioral problem. These cases should be interpreted in the context of the foregoing discussion: namely, that the procedures used are not intended to question other more extensive procedures, which may be necessary for other kinds of behavioral deficits.

The discussion will be concerned with self-control (Skinner, 1953) and procedures for its establishment. The procedures to be discussed center around the position that behavior is not an emergent property of an organism or a property solely of its environment but is described by a functional relation between the two. More technically, given a specified behavior B and a specified environmental variable x, a lawful relation can be found, such that $B = f(x)$, under certain empirical constraining conditions c. This implies that when the constraints c are set up, and x is set at a stipulated value, then B will have a stipulated value, given by the value of $B = f(x)$. When E sets x at that value, he will get the B stipulated. This defines the experimental control of behavior which has been demonstrated repeatedly in operant and other laboratories. When S himself sets x at that value, he will get his own B, as stipulated. This defines self-control.

If you want a specified behavior from yourself, set up the conditions which you know will control it. For example, if you cannot get up in the morning by firmly resolving to do so and telling yourself that you must, buy and set an alarm clock. Within this context, the Greek maxim, "Know thyself," translates into "Know thy behaviors, know thy environment, and know the functional relation between the two." Although the relation between an alarm clock and waking up is a simple and familiar one, other relations are neither this simple nor this familiar. There have, however, been developed in laboratories of operant behavior a body of known functional relations between behavior, and programs and other procedures which can alter even more complex behavior systematically. Self-control derived from such research can take at least two forms. One is to instruct S to set up the procedures which change his environment and which thereby bring his behavior under different control. I shall present some cases to this effect. Another form is to train him in the functional analysis of behavior and have him try to determine for himself the procedures which he should apply. This approach will also appear in the following cases.

Inherent in both types of self-control is the problem posed by the tremendous gap between theory and practice. The same theory may dictate numerous alternative methods or solutions, but all may not be equally available, practical, or applicable. The operant paradigm suggests that there are at least 12 different ways to maintain or attenuate behavior (cf. Holz & Azrin, 1963). Which are appropriate to the problem?

One way for selecting effective practical measures is to have S report back to E every week with his results. This hour becomes a session for analysis of data and discussion of changes in procedure. In the laboratory, operant procedures are so arranged that relations between ongoing behavior and its conditions are continuously observed and recorded. Through successes and failures, Es may learn to analyze behavior and conditions and may develop a "feel" for their data, as do other behavioral practitioners in interaction with their subject matter, for example, skilled psychiatrists. Hopefully, such a program of systematic trial and analysis will sensitize S to his own behavior and his own conditions. By training S in control procedures to the extent that these exist and are applicable, we are providing for self-enhancement and self-actualization (Rogers, 1951). Of the individuals who can apply control procedures, S is the one most concerned with his behavior and is most in contact with it, its conditions, and its consequences. Initially E is the consultant, and eventually S becomes his own E. The procedures may be limited to Ss who are intellectually capable of such analysis or who are not otherwise incapacitated. Our Ss were mainly college students. Where systematic training in behavior analysis was used, the sessions started with individual tutorials in behavior analysis, homework assignments from standard texts

(Holland & Skinner, 1961), and readings. Given this intellectual base, we could move on to discussions of the problem in question.

Our first cases were referrals from clinical psychologists who felt that we should work on some of the simpler overt problems, while they tackled their deeper meanings. One of these was a young man who was overweight, and another was a girl who had difficulty studying.

These two problems yielded, for these Ss, to procedures involving *stimulus control*. The program with the young lady started with human engineering of her desk. Since she felt sleepy when she studied, she was told to replace a 40-w lamp with a good one and to turn her desk away from her bed. It was also decided that her desk was to control study behavior. If she wished to write a letter, she should do so but in the dining room; if she wished to read comic books, she should do so but in the kitchen; if she wished to daydream, she should do so but was to go to another room; at her desk she was to engage in her school work and her school work only.

This girl had previously had a course in behavioral analysis and said, "I know what you're up to. You want that desk to assume stimulus control over me. I'm not going to let any piece of wood run my life for me."

"On the contrary," I said, "you *want* that desk to run you. It is you who decides when to put yourself under the control of your desk. It is like having a sharpened knife in a drawer. You decide when to use it; but when you want it, it is ready."

After the first week of the regimen, she came to me and gleefully said, "I spent only ten minutes at my desk this week."

"Did you study there," I asked.

"Yes, I did," she said.

"Good," I said, "let's try to double that next week."

For the next few weeks we did not meet, but she subsequently reported that during the last month of the semester she was able to spend three hours a day at her desk for four weeks in a row, something she had been unable to do previously. When she sat at her desk she studied, and when she did other things she left her desk. The variable maintaining this increase in behavior as the semester drew to an end was apparently the forthcoming final examinations.

With regard to the young man who overate, stimulus control, chaining, and withdrawal of reinforcement were used. The stimulus for overeating is normally not food (Ferster, Levitt, & Nurnberger, 1962). In our culture, food is normally hidden; it is kept in a refrigerator or cupboard. In the cafeteria, where it is in the interests of the management to get people to eat, food is exposed.

The initial strategy for slimming the young man was to bring his eating behavior under the control of food alone, since food is normally not available as a stimulus. He was instructed to eat to his heart's content and not to repress the desire. He was, however, to treat food with the dignity it deserved. Rather than eating while he watched television or while he studied, he was to devote himself to eating when he ate. If he wished to eat a sandwich, he was to put it on a plate and sit down and devote himself exclusively to it. Thus, reinforcing consequences such as watching television or reading would be withdrawn when he engaged in the behaviors of preparing the food, eating, and cleaning up. Responding to the refrigerator in between meals resulted in withdrawal of such consequences, as did going to the refrigerator while watching television. Television, studying, and other stimuli would lose their control of initiating the chain of behaviors and conditions that terminated in eating. Within one week, the young man cut out all eating between meals. "You've taken the fun out of it," he said to me. We then worked on the contents of the meals as well, and he stopped attending sessions. I met him about three months later; he was considerably slimmer and remarked that he needed neither me nor the clinical psychologist to solve his problems. He could handle them himself.

No claim is made that all problems should be treated in this manner, or that the Ss had no other problems. The aim was to alter the specified behavior. We started out with the simplest procedures. Had these not been effective, we would have tried others. Some more complex cases will be presented next.

An interesting aspect of these and other cases as well was the fact that in a very short time Ss ran off by themselves to apply the procedures they had learned. In some cases, I would have preferred more extensive interchange and wondered how clinical psychologists were able to keep Ss coming week after week. Finally, I attributed the tenure of the relationship to what might be called the Scheherazade effect. Scheherazade, as you will recall, became the consort of a king who killed each bedmate after one night, having generalized the infidelity of a previous wife to all women. Scheherazade told him a story on the first night, which was not completed by dawn. The king paroled her for the second night to hear the rest of the story, and having been reinforced, she repeated her behavior. The schedule maintained such behavior for 1001 nights, and the result is known as the *Arabian Nights*.

Few things are more interesting and will sustain behavior better than support for talking about one's self; one is never finished in 50 minutes. Hence, such discussions may maintain therapy sessions and allow the therapist to interact with the patient over an extended period of time. An individual tutorial may serve the same function.

MARITAL CASE 1

The husband in this case was a young man, 29, who was working on his master's degree. His wife was taking my course in behavioral analysis, and they both decided that he should come to see me about their marriage, which both wanted to maintain. The issue, as S told me, was that his wife had committed the "ultimate betrayal" two years ago with S's best friend. Even worse, it was S who had suggested that the friend keep his wife company while he was in the library at night. Since that time, whenever he saw his wife, S screamed at her for hours on end or else was ashamed of himself for having done so and spent hours sulking and brooding. Since the events that led to the "betrayal" were an occasion for bringing home the first lesson on the consequences of behavior, we started from there.

Relation of Behavior to Its Consequences

Early discussions concerned the analysis of behavior in terms of its consequences. S's behavior provided stimuli for his wife's behavior. If he wished his wife to behave differently to him, then he should provide other stimuli than the ones which produced the behaviors he did not like. There was considerable analysis of such interactions. This conceptualization of behavior was apparently new to S, who took detailed notes; I have discovered it to be new to many other Ss as well.

Stimulus Change

Altering the consequences of operant behavior will alter the behavior itself. However, this process may take a considerable amount of time. One of the most rapid ways to change behavior is by altering the conditions under which it usually occurs. This is called *stimulus change* or the effects of novel stimuli. If the novel stimuli are then combined with new behavioral contingencies designed to produce different behavior, these contingencies are apt to generate the new behavior much more rapidly than they would in the presence of the old stimuli.

As part of the program of establishing new stimuli, S was instructed to rearrange the use of rooms and furniture in his house to make it appear considerably different. His wife went one step further and took the occasion to buy herself a new outfit.

Establishment of New Behavior

Since it was impossible for S to converse in a civilized manner with his wife, we discussed a program of going to one evening spot on Monday, another on Tuesday, and another on Wednesday.

"Oh," he said, "you want us to be together. We'll go bowling on Thursday."

"On the contrary," I said, "I am interested in your subjecting yourself to an environment where civilized chit-chat is maintained. Such is not the case at a bowling alley."

I also asked if there were any topic of conversation which once started would maintain itself. He commented on his mother-in-law's crazy ideas about farming. He was then given an index card and instructed to write "farm" on it and to attach a $20 bill to that card. The $20 was to be used to pay the waitress on Thursday, at which point he was to start the "farm" discussion which hopefully would continue into the taxi and home.

Stimulus Control

Since in the absence of yelling at his wife S sulked and since the program was designed to reduce yelling, S's sulking was in danger of increasing. S was instructed to sulk to his heart's content but to do so in a specified place. Whenever he felt like sulking, he was to go into the garage, sit on a special sulking stool, and sulk and mutter over the indignities of life for as long as he wished. When he was through with his sulking, he could leave the garage and join his wife. He was instructed to keep a daily record of such behavior and bring it to each session. The graph is presented in Fig. 8.1. Sulking time had been reported as 7 hours on the preceding day, and, with occasional lapses, it was reported as dropping to less than 30 minutes before disappearing entirely. The reported reversals and drops were occasions for discussions.

Since the bedroom had been the scene of both bickering and occasional lapses, the problem was presented of changing its stimulus value when conjugality was involved. If this could be done consistently, eventually the special stimuli might come to control such behavior. The problem was

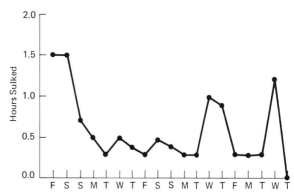

FIGURE 8.1
Graph kept of sulking behavior.

to find a stimulus which could alter the room entirely and would be easy to apply and withdraw. Finally, a yellow night light was put in, was turned on when both felt amorous, and was kept turned off otherwise. This light markedly altered the perceptual configuration of the room.

Records

Daily notes of events were kept in a notebook, as was the graph. S took notes of the discussions with E. These notes were discussed at each weekly session.

One of the notions which S held very strongly was that his wife's behavior stemmed from some inaccessible source within her, and that many of his own behaviors likewise poured out from himself. In this context, the final sharp rise in the sulking curve was discussed. "The whole procedure won't work," he said, "my wife doesn't need me as much as I need her." The psychiatric message was that he had no control over his wife, but I chose to ignore this message in favor of a didactic one on the behavioral definition of needs. He was asked how he knew what his wife's needs were. Was he an amoeba slithering into her tissues and observing tissue needs? Was he a mind reader? After my repeated rejection of subjective definitions of needs, he redefined the problem behaviorally, namely, that his wife behaved a certain way less than he did. He said that stated this way it sounded silly, but I said, "No, it's a problem to you and not silly."

What were these behaviors? They apparently included such dependency behaviors as asking him to do things for her. "When was the last time she asked you to do something for her?" I asked. He replied that the previous day she had asked him to replace a light bulb in the kitchen. Had he done so, I asked. "No," he said. He was then asked to consider the extinction of pigeon behavior and took notes to the effect that, if he wished his wife to act helpless, he should reinforce dependency by doing what she asked.

A discussion on needs and personality ensued. "If by personality all that is meant is my behavior," he said, "then my personality changes from one moment to the next, because my behavior changes," he stated.

"I should hope so," I said.

"Well, what is my true personality, what is the true me?" he asked.

"Do you have a true behavior?" I asked.

He reported this as a viewpoint he had never considered; his previous training had been in terms of being consistent to his self, and of searching for "thine own self (to which he could) be true." He took extensive notes.

The next week he came in and stated: "I did something last week that I have never done before in my life. When I teach in classrooms I am able to manage my students, but when I talk to tradespeople I find I am very timid and allow myself to be cheated. Well, last week my carburetor gave out. I knew if I went to the garage they would make me buy a new one even though I have a one-year's guarantee. I sent my wife down to the garage instead. She is a real scrapper. She came back with a new carburetor. It didn't cost us a cent. Why should I have to be all things to all men? In school I control things, but with tradespeople I don't. So what?"

These weekly sessions continued during ten weeks of the summer term. After the initial training, S was assigned homework along with his wife who was taking the course in behavior analysis. The weekly discussions were centered around behavioral analysis and how it might apply to his problems.

During the course of one of the sessions, S started to talk about his childhood and was summarily cut off.

"Shouldn't I talk about this with a psychologist?" he asked. "Isn't this one of the things that interests you? Doesn't it affect me now?"

"Look," I said, "a bridge with a load limit of three tons opens in 1903. The next day, a farmer drives eighteen tons over it; it cracks. The bridge collapses in 1963. What caused the collapse?"

"The farmer in 1903," he said.

"Wrong," I said. "The bridge collapses in 1963 because of the cracks that day. Had they been filled in the preceding day, it would not have collapsed. Let's discuss the cracks in your marriage."

At the end of the period, there was no sulking in the garage and the partners were able to commune.

MARITAL CASE 2

This case concerned a young couple who had been married almost 10 years; their sexual relations throughout marriage had been limited to about two contacts a year. Both husband and wife ascribed the difficulty to the husband. Both *S*s were professionals, intelligent, were socially well at ease, and highly regarded by their friends and the community. They were Roman Catholic and determined to maintain the marriage, but the wife thought she might be driven into extramarital relations. Both felt that, if only they could get started, the behavior might carry itself.

Husband and wife were seen separately every week, for one hour each. Both were instructed to discuss with me only that which they could discuss with each other, since I would make constant cross reference between the two sessions.

Various procedures were assayed by *S*s, but proved ineffective. Fondling was repulsed. *Playboy* was recommended to initiate amorous activity, but the husband fell asleep reading it. During the lesson on deprivation, the wife stated: "I am at my wit's end as to how to shape his behavior. I don't know what reinforcements I have. The characteristic of good reinforcement is that it can be applied immediately and is immediately consumed. I could withhold supper, but that is not a good reinforcer because I can't turn it off and on. I can't apply deprivation, because that's my problem. I don't know what to do."

The husband was a rising business executive who took evening courses and whose time was so tight that he had to schedule almost every minute of his day. We discussed the possibility of his scheduling his wife in the appointment book for two evenings a week. He thought this might work, but his wife was a bit more dubious. These appointments were kept two weeks in a row, but then lost their control. We then discussed the nature of the control over behavior exerted by discriminative stimuli, of which instructions are one example (Goldiamond, in press). There were differential consequences attached to keeping and not keeping the business appointments, but no differential consequences had been attached to meeting or not meeting appointments with his wife. Hence, the instructions lost their control (Ayllon & Azrin, 1964).

Both *S*s were extremely well-groomed. Their clothing was always in best array. The wife visited the beautician once a week and the husband went to the barber every other week. In the session following the failure of control by the appointment book, the husband suggested that they might attach the opportunity to visit the beautician or barber as consequences to keeping the appointments. In the event that the appointments were not kept, the visits would not be allowed and could be resumed only when the appointments had been kept. His wife also felt that this would be extremely effective.

The next week, both showed up somewhat bedraggled. Thereafter, they were not bedraggled and the appointments were kept for the rest of that semester, at least.

As an incidental effect of the session, *S*s attempted to apply behavioral analysis to other problems as well. They mentioned a staff party which had been held at their home. The behavior of an inefficient secretary was being discussed.

"But you're using aversive control," one of the participants said.

"Well, she has no behaviors that I can reinforce her for," was the answer.

STUDY CASE 1: HANDWRITING

S was a seventeen-year-old high school senior of normal intelligence, who was 28th in a class of 28 and whose handwriting was illegible. He was a referral from a school psychologist.

An example of his early handwriting is given in Fig. 8.2. Lettered lines of translation alternate with cursive lines of handwriting. During the first

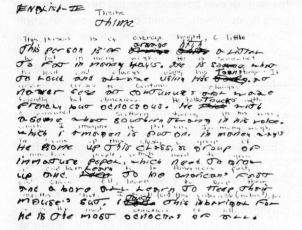

FIGURE 8.2
Sample of initial handwriting; translation appears above line.

session, I asked *S* to sit at my desk and write from dictation. He leaned forward to write but no part of his hand or arm touched paper or desk; the entire force of his shoulder and arm was transmitted to the pencil point, making fine control impossible. Since the primary grades, no one had ever observed his writing behavior; they had, however, criticized its product. I instructed him to keep his arm on the table and to manipulate his pencil from the wrist and fingers. Some simple physics were explained to him. Sheets of onion skin were interlaced with carbon paper, and he was given exercises requiring modulation of force so that he would go through five sheets, four sheets, three sheets, and two sheets. He was instructed to print.

At a later session, his letter size being erratic, he was asked to letter the familiar, "Now is the time..." phrase. Fig. 8.3 presents that initial attempt. The paper is lined, and the writing starts out filling up the space between the lines. The

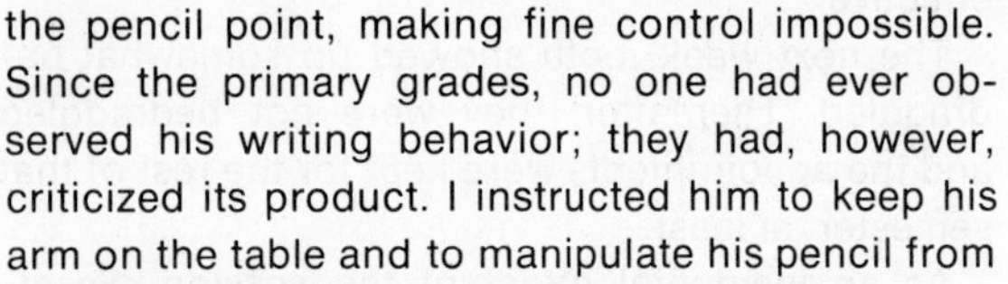

NOW IS TheTime ALL
good menTo comeTo

The a de oF Thair party.

FIGURE 8.3
Stimulus control of ensuing letter size by writing T as capital of same size as preceding letter.

writing becomes smaller and smaller. This tendency can be traced to the letter T. In all cases, T is the same size as the preceding letters, and is also a capital. Since capital letters are followed by small letters, these Ts control the size of the small letters that follow them. The first T in the second line produces a row of smaller letters following it, and the first T in the third line takes off from this size and again cuts down the size of the following letters until the final T produces a tinier Y. S was instructed to write his Ts so that they were larger than the preceding letters. Fig. 8.4 reiterates the control this letter had over the following letters. The letters which follow T are smaller than T, but since T is above the line they stay within the line. The effect has been reversed, demonstrating a causal relation. Incidentally, since T is the second most frequently used letter in English, it is a powerful source of control. In the later session, *S* was instructed to differentiate between capital and small T.

The passage presented is the same as that in

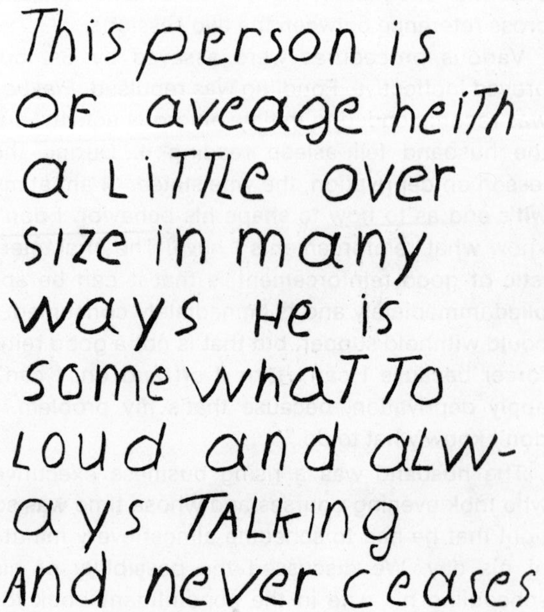

This person is
oF aveage heiTh
a LiTTle over
size in many
ways He is
some whaT To
Loud and alw-
ays TaLking
And never ceases
To TaLk He TaLk

FIGURE 8.4
Reversal of effect by writing T above line.

Fig. 8.2. The change in legibility is evident. The numerous spelling errors are of interest. As long as the writing is undecipherable, spelling errors cannot be noted and corrected.

Many letters contain similar forms. For example, the letters a, b, d, o, p, and q all contain a complete circle of the same size. These circles are modified in letters such as c and e. S was instructed to bring an assortment of buttons to the session and a suitable button was found for him to use for these letters, with other buttons for other letters. He was also instructed in other principles of writing. He practiced at home and brought his material in weekly. After a period of lettering, S was instructed to link his letters in an effort to produce cursive writing.

His handwriting improved markedly during this period, and he rose from 28th in his class to 13th. The undergraduate assistant[2] who worked with him at home paid him money for lines completed and, as long as this procedure was used, S's handwriting was legible and showed evidence of training. When this pay was dropped, the handwriting deteriorated. Although legible handwriting was now contingent upon reinforcement, differential reinforcement alone would not have produced the new behavior. Indeed, without making them contingent upon a program to alter behavior, differential consequences may be ineffective and may result in aversive control, as did the nagging and the poor grades he consistently obtained. Now that S has the new behavior, differential consequences can be applied to maintain it; hopefully, these will be provided by society. The requirement of extrinsic consequences was probably related to difficult conditions at home. He had no desk or work place, and he lived alone with his mother.

Several conclusions can be drawn from this case. One is that observation of the behavior itself may on occasion be far more useful than observation of its end product. Another is that behavior may be controlled by the very stimuli that the behavior itself produces, as in the size of the letters

following T. A third is that merely establishing a behavior will not necessarily maintain it. The consequences which maintain it must be considered, but as a fourth conclusion, these consequences should often be related to a program of behavioral modification. Penalizing his poor writing behavior, as his teachers had done, did not eliminate that behavior. It did, however, bring him in for treatment.

STUDY CASE 2: STUDY PROBLEM

This case involved a junior in college who was being expelled because of his academic record. Inasmuch as I had given him one of his Ds, he came to me for advice. I told him that I would try to get him reinstated, providing he put himself under my control. He agreed and was given a conditional year. S's parents were professionals. Two siblings were at prominent Eastern universities. S was alert, and his IQ tests were within the range of college populations.

S had never actually studied. Accordingly, a self-control regimen for studying was introduced following some of the procedures which were discussed earlier. A daily record was kept of the total number of hours spent in study, for each course and for the total day.

At that time, S studied for an average of six hours a day, but his study hours were not evenly distributed among the various classes. Fig. 8.5 presents the study curves for two different courses. The upper curve depicts minimal studying, except for one peak. [Guess when the test was given!] This fixed interval curve characterizes the behavior of pigeons as well. The lower part of the curve represents the studying pattern for a language class which involved a daily recitation. S studied at regular intervals. These curves so impressed me that I instituted daily quizzes in my classes and was gratified to see the averages rise.

Every week S brought his notebooks, his examinations, and his weekly records for inspection and discussion. Different procedures for keeping notes were developed for each course. In the foreign language, for example, a separate sheet was kept

---

[2] I wish to express my appreciation to Mr. Richard David, then an undergraduate psychology major, who brought S to and from sessions and assisted in them.

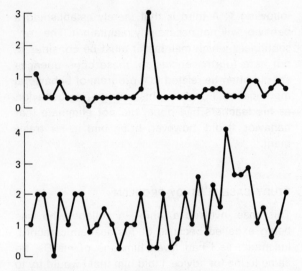

FIGURE 8.5
Daily study charts for class with one examination (upper), and class with daily recitations (lower).

for masculine and feminine nouns and for each verb class. Grammatical classes represent similar ways of treating a word. By putting words of the same grammatical class together, there may be generalization from the changes learned for one word to the changes learned for another. Flash cards which are uniform may not lend themselves to such generalization.

S was taught to outline social science texts. He was asked to be a detective and resurrect the author's outline (where he had one). Red and black ink were used for headings and entries. The outlines were topical rather than sentence outlines. This required restating the sentences in his words, rather than copying them from the book.

In English, we were both at a loss. Several novels were required, and neither one of us knew what should be considered. We used the conventional procedure to find out, namely, the first exam. This told us what the instructor considered to be the terminal behaviors.

At the end of the first semester, S's grades changed from the two Ds and three Es of the preceding semester to two Cs and two Ds. Although this was an improvement, one class was dropped. I was disturbed since I felt that, with this much study and careful outlining, S should have ob-

tained As. A more detailed analysis was then undertaken.

S was taking a course in international trade, for which a knowledge of geography is requisite. He said that he knew his geography quite well and was asked to draw a map of South America. Fig. 8.6 represents the map he drew. Brazil extends from sea to shining sea. The body of water above Venezuela is designated Lake Maracaibo, and Bolivia is north of Peru and abuts on Venezuela.

I asked S what grade he would assign himself for this map, and he looked at it confidently and said, "Oh, 75 per cent or a C." I said that I would give him 20 per cent. Incidentally, in work with other Ss since then who have trouble with history, I have often found that they lack knowledge of geography, and even of map-reading. Accordingly, historical movements become disconnected facts which have to be learned for each case.

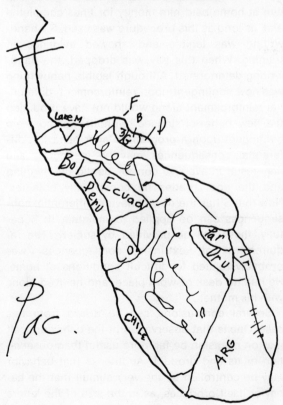

FIGURE 8.6
Map of South America drawn from memory by college junior taking a course in international trade.

This map may be used to exemplify a behavioral definition of stupidity. Many behaviors require other behaviors as prerequisites for their acquisition and maintenance. It is possible that, in one form of stupidity, the prerequisites to the attempted behavior are absent, as well as those discriminative behaviors which differentiate the presence of adequate behaviors from their absence. Stated otherwise, the person we call stupid is lacking certain behaviors but behaves as if he is not so lacking. He does not know to ask. He confidently undertakes assignments and often starts out successfully. However, where the new behaviors require older ones and these are missing, we may obtain the egregious blunders we call stupid. The blunders may be unpredictable to us simply because, in a long sequence, there are too many places in which deficits can occur for us to have come across every one.

These behavioral deficiencies were found in one area after another. Since S was taking courses which had as prerequisites other courses, which he had passed with Ds, he was being required to acquire new behaviors when the prerequisite foundation for them was rather shaky. Accordingly, we "regressed" to the freshman texts in those courses in which he had obtained a D.

But there were deficiencies here, as well. In the economics texts, Humpty-Dumpty was quoted to the effect that words meant what *he* intended them to mean. The point here was that the economist's use of words might differ from their common usage. Humpty-Dumpty appeared in red in S's notes. S knew that Humpty-Dumpty was an egg who fell. I asked why the egg led his paragraph and could obtain no answer. It turned out that S had not read *Alice in Wonderland,* nor any of the childhood classics, nor for that matter *Tom Swift,* nor even comic books. He simply did no home reading as a child.

I had obtained excellent control over S's behavior, but this was like successfully getting someone to work six hours a day copying Chinese letters with a brush, without his ever having learned how to hold a brush or what the significant calligraphic nuances were. I suggested a program of visiting the art galleries, listening to concerts, reading the classics, and otherwise acquiring the behaviors relevant to our cultural heritage.

There are two types of behavioral sequences. In one type of sequence, called the *chaining* sequence, a chain of behavior is maintained by the consequences attached to the last element in the chain. Thus, Lundin (1961) reports a rat who went through various behavioral gyrations, then up five stories and down an elevator. All of these behaviors were maintained by the food he received at the end. In this type of sequence, the order of training is the *reverse* of the chronological order in which the sequence of behavior is performed. The pressing of the lever for food was established first. This was made contingent upon manipulation of the elevator. Then the ride in the elevator was made contingent upon the preceding step and so on. The entire chain was maintained by the food. Thus, if the product of education is not reinforcing, the behaviors which lead to it may not be maintained. Chaining was also exemplified in the weight reduction case, when watching television no longer served as a consequence of going to open the refrigerator.

Another type of sequence, which we shall call the *systematic* sequence, is exemplified in the case of this student. A systematic sequence can be compared to a course or an educational curriculum; the acquisition of one behavior depends upon the *prior* existence of another, just as the acquisition of new knowledge depends upon a grasp of other presupposed knowledge. Thus, in order to learn algebra, we must know how to read. In order to learn to read, a certain degree of socialization must first occur. Such curricula exist not only in academic subjects but are implicit in other types of behavior as well. It is entirely possible, for example, that certain behaviors necessary for marital success presuppose the existence of other interpersonal behaviors, whose acquisition depends upon the existence of yet other behaviors.

Stated otherwise, there are behavioral curricula involved in almost all behaviors. Where the present behavioral deficit exists because an earlier behavior was not acquired, a procedure which attempts to correct the ongoing deficit must consider some of the earlier deficits of which the present one may be an outgrowth. When this is true, in contrast to the first marital case presented, discussion of childhood may be necessary.

The cases presented here have involved different behavioral deficits. Although the content or the topography of these and other behaviors differs, the functional relations of such differing behaviors to their environment may be similar. This may be true not only when the differences are in such categories as marital or academic, both of which involve human behavior, but also where the differences categorize species. Pigeons peck and people talk. Topographically these are different behaviors. However, if the consequences which maintain pecking are scheduled in a certain manner and the (quite different) consequences which maintain speech are scheduled in the same manner, then the differing behaviors of pecking and speech will undergo similar changes in rate. It is upon this functional, or dynamic, similarity in the relation of behavior to its environment that the possibility of the extension of procedures from the laboratory to the clinic rests. It also suggests that problems in the clinic may be used for research in the laboratory.

The cases presented here demonstrate a simple application of certain self-control procedures derived from the laboratory. As was explicitly indicated earlier, they are not intended to supplant or question other more complex procedures (for a more extended analysis see Goldiamond, *et al.,* 1965). However, we are currently examining some of these complex procedures and are discovering that the explicit language of the laboratory may be very useful in analyzing and describing some of the behavioral transactions and changes that go on in other forms of psychotherapy (Goldiamond, Dyrud, & Miller, 1965)[3] Developments in other areas where explicit analysis is utilized may be considered for their relevance to psychotherapy, and psychotherapy, by a reverse lend-lease, may suggest areas for study under more controlled procedures (Goldiamond, in press).

[3]Research being performed under Contracts DA-49-193-MD-2628 and DA-49-193-MD-2448 between the Office of the Surgeon General and the Institute for Behavioral Research and the Washington School of Psychiatry, respectively. These projects involve collaboration between Jarl Dyrud, M.D., Miles Miller, M.D., and the author.

Laboratory research has necessarily been characterized by a simplicity of procedures and concepts, and their extension to the solution of complex human problems requires considerable precaution and careful examination. Nevertheless, these procedures and concepts may provide methods for the analysis and restatement of complex problems in observable and manipulable terms and may thereby assist in the explicit assessment of behavioral change and effectiveness.

The cases presented here involve behavioral problems which could be analyzed by Ss themselves. This training of S to become his own therapist is one of the goals of most branches of psychotherapy. The method used to accomplish this will depend on the state of the art, the nature of the problem, S's past history, and social and other constraints upon S's behavior. In some cases, these factors may dictate a strategy of not instructing S, or not having him define the problem or discover its solution immediately, since such a procedure may disrupt other behaviors and the consequences currently maintaining them.[4] The course of treatment might then be considerably different from any of those discussed here. Other problems and possible procedures could be cited as well. But the cases presented here suggest that, in some areas at least, simple procedures can lead to complex changes.

REFERENCES

Ayllon, T., & Azrin, N.H. Reinforcement and instructions with mental patients. *J. exp. Anal. Behav.,* 1964, 7, 327–331.

Ferster, C.B., Nurnberger, J.I., & Levitt, E.B. The control of eating. *J. Mathetics,* 1962, 1, 87–109.

Goldiamond, I. Justified and unjustified alarm over behavioral control. In O. Milton (Ed.), *Behavior disorders: perspectives and trends.* Philadelphia: Lippincott, 1965. Pp. 237–262. (a)

Goldiamond, I. Stuttering and fluency as manipulable operant response classes. In L. Krasner and L.P. Ulmann (Eds.), *Research in behavior modification.* New York: Holt, Rinehart, & Winston, 1965. Pp. 106–156. (b)

[4]I am indebted to Jarl Dyrud for this observation.

Goldiamond, I. Perception, language, and conceptualization rules. In B. Kleinmuntz (Ed.), *Cognition symposium: problem solving.* New York: Wiley, in press.

Goldiamond, I., Dyrud, J., & Miller, M. Practice as research in professional psychology. *Canad. Psychologist,* 1965, 6a, 110–128.

Holland, J.G., & Skinner, B.F. *The analysis of behavior.* New York: McGraw-Hill, 1961.

Holz, W.C., & Azrin, N.H. A comparison of several procedures for eliminating behavior. *J. exp. Anal. Behav.,* 1963, 6, 399–406.

Lundin, R.W. *Personality: an experimental approach.* New York: Macmillan, 1961.

Rogers, C.B. *Client-centered therapy.* New York: Houghton Mifflin, 1951.

Skinner, B.F. *Science and human behavior.* New York: Macmillan, 1953.

Sulzer, E.S. Reinforcement and the therapeutic contract. *J. consult. Psychol.,* 1962, 9, 271–276.

The second half of the twentieth century may be remembered for its solution of a curious problem. Although Western democracy created the conditions responsible for the rise of modern science, it is now evident that it may never fully profit from that achievement. The so-called "democratic philosophy" of human behavior to which it also gave rise is increasingly in conflict with the application of the methods of science to human affairs. Unless this conflict is somehow resolved, the ultimate goals of democracy may be long deferred.

I

Just as biographers and critics look for external influences to account for the traits and achievements of the men they study, so science ultimately explains behavior in terms of "causes" or conditions which lie beyond the individual himself. As more and more causal relations are demonstrated, a practical corollary becomes difficult to resist: it should be possible to *produce* behavior according to plan simply by arranging the proper conditions. Now, among the specifications which might reasonably be submitted to a behavioral technology are these: Let men be happy, informed, skillful, well behaved and productive.

This immediate practical implication of a science of behavior has a familiar ring, for it recalls the doctrine of human perfectibility of eighteenth- and nineteenth-century humanism. A science of man shares the optimism of that philosophy and supplies striking support for the working faith that men can build a better world and, through it, better men. The support comes just in time, for there has been little optimism of late among those who speak from the traditional point of view. Democracy has become "realistic," and it is only with some embarrassment that one admits today to perfectionistic or utopian thinking.

The earlier temper is worth considering, however. History records many foolish and unworkable schemes for human betterment, but almost all the great changes in our culture which we now regard as worthwhile can be traced to perfectionistic phi-

9
Freedom and the Control of Men

B.F. Skinner

From *The American Scholar* special issue, vol. 25 (Winter 1955–1956), pp. 47–65, used by permission of the author.

losophies. Governmental, religious, educational, economic and social reforms follow a common pattern. Someone believes that a change in a cultural practice—for example, in the rules of evidence in a court of law, in the characterization of man's relation to God, in the way children are taught to read and write, in permitted rates of interest, or in minimal housing standards—will improve the condition of men: by promoting justice, permitting men to seek salvation more effectively, increasing the literacy of a people, checking an inflationary trend, or improving public health and family relations, respectively. The underlying hypothesis is always the same: that a different physical or cultural environment will make a different and better man.

The scientific study of behavior not only justifies the general pattern of such proposals; it promises new and better hypotheses. The earliest cultural practices must have originated in sheer accidents. Those which strengthened the group survived with the group in a sort of natural selection. As soon as men began to propose and carry out changes in practice for the sake of possible consequences, the evolutionary process must have accelerated. The simple practice of making changes must have had survival value. A further acceleration is now to be expected. As laws of behavior are more precisely stated, the changes in the environment required to bring about a given effect may be more clearly specified. Conditions which have been neglected because their effects were slight or unlooked for may be shown to be relevant. New conditions may actually be created, as in the discovery and synthesis of drugs which affect behavior.

This is no time, then, to abandon notions of progress, improvement or, indeed, human perfectibility. The simple fact is that man is able, and now as never before, to lift himself by his own bootstraps. In achieving control of the world of which he is a part, he may learn at last to control himself.

II

Timeworn objections to the planned improvement of cultural practices are already losing much of their force. Marcus Aurelius was probably right in advising his readers to be content with a haphazard amelioration of mankind. "Never hope to realize Plato's republic," he sighed, "...for who can change the opinions of men? And without a change of sentiments what can you make but reluctant slaves and hypocrites?" He was thinking, no doubt, of contemporary patterns of control based upon punishment or the threat of punishment which, as he correctly observed, breed only reluctant slaves of those who submit and hypocrites of those who discover modes of evasion. But we need not share his pessimism, for the opinions of men can be changed. The techniques of indoctrination which were being devised by the early Christian Church at the very time Marcus Aurelius was writing are relevant, as are some of the techniques of psychotherapy and of advertising and public relations. Other methods suggested by recent scientific analyses leave little doubt of the matter.

The study of human behavior also answers the cynical complaint that there is a plain "cussedness" in man which will always thwart efforts to improve him. We are often told that men do not want to be changed, even for the better. Try to help them, and they will outwit you and remain happily wretched. Dostoevsky claimed to see some plan in it. "Out of sheer ingratitude," he complained, or possibly boasted, "man will play you a dirty trick, just to prove that men are still men and not the keys of a piano....And even if you could prove that a man is only a piano key, he would still do something out of sheer perversity—he would create destruction and chaos—just to gain his point....And if all this could in turn be analyzed and prevented by predicting that it would occur, then man would deliberately go mad to prove his point." This is a conceivable neurotic reaction to inept control. A few men may have shown it, and many have enjoyed Dostoevsky's statement because they tend to show it. But that such perversity is a fundamental reaction of the human organism to controlling conditions is sheer nonsense.

So is the objection that we have no way of knowing what changes to make even though we have the necessary techniques. That is one of the great hoaxes of the century—a sort of booby trap left behind in the retreat before the advancing front of science. Scientists themselves have unsuspectingly agreed that there are two kinds of useful propositions about nature—facts and value judgments—and that science must confine itself to "what is," leaving "what ought to be" to others. But with what special sort of wisdom is the nonscientist endowed? Science is only effective knowing, no matter who engages in it. Verbal behavior proves upon analysis to be composed of many different types of utterances, from poetry and exhortation to logic and factual description, but these are not all equally useful in talking about cultural practices. We may classify useful propositions according to the degrees of confidence with which they may be asserted. Sentences about nature range from highly probable "facts" to sheer guesses. In general, future events are less likely to be correctly described than past. When a scientist talks about a projected experiment, for example, he must often resort to statements having only a moderate likelihood of being correct; he calls them hypotheses.

Designing a new cultural pattern is in many ways like designing an experiment. In drawing up a new constitution, outlining a new educational program, modifying a religious doctrine, or setting up a new fiscal policy, many statements must be quite tentative. We cannot be sure that the practices we specify will have the consequences we predict, or that the consequences will reward our efforts. This is in the nature of such proposals. They are not value judgments—they are guesses. To confuse and delay the improvement of cultural practices by quibbling about the word *improve* is itself not a useful practice. Let us agree, to start with, that health is better than illness, wisdom better than ignorance, love better than hate, and productive energy better than neurotic sloth.

Another familiar objection is the "political problem." Though we know what changes to make and how to make them, we still need to control certain relevant conditions, but these have long since fallen into the hands of selfish men who are not going to relinquish them for such pur-

poses. Possibly we shall be permitted to develop areas which at the moment seem unimportant, but at the first signs of success the strong men will move in. This, it is said, has happened to Christianity, democracy and communism. There will always be men who are fundamentally selfish and evil, and in the long run innocent goodness cannot have its way. The only evidence here is historical, and it may be misleading. Because of the way in which physical science developed, history could until very recently have "proved" that the unleashing of the energy of the atom was quite unlikely, if not impossible. Similarly, because of the order in which processes in human behavior have become available for purposes of control, history may seem to prove that power will probably be appropriated for selfish purposes. The first techniques to be discovered fell almost always to strong, selfish men. History led Lord Acton to believe that power corrupts, but he had probably never encountered absolute power, certainly not in all its forms, and had no way of predicting its effect.

An optimistic historian could defend a different conclusion. The principle that if there are not enough men of good will in the world the first step is to create more seems to be gaining recognition. The Marshall Plan (as originally conceived), Point Four, the offer of atomic materials to power-starved countries—these may or may not be wholly new in the history of international relations, but they suggest an increasing awareness of the power of governmental good will. They are proposals to make certain changes in the environments of men for the sake of consequences which should be rewarding for all concerned. They do not exemplify a disinterested generosity, but an interest which is the interest of everyone. We have not yet seen Plato's philosopher-king, and may not want to, but the gap between real and utopian government is closing.

III

But we are not yet in the clear, for a new and unexpected obstacle has arisen. With a world of their own making almost within reach, men of good will have been seized with distaste for their achievement. They have uneasily rejected opportunities to apply the techniques and findings of science in the service of men, and as the import of effective cultural design has come to be understood, many of them have voiced an outright refusal to have any part in it. Science has been challenged before when it has encroached upon institutions already engaged in the control of human behavior; but what are we to make of benevolent men, with no special interests of their own to defend, who nevertheless turn against the very means of reaching long-dreamed-of goals?

What is being rejected, of course, is the scientific conception of man and his place in nature. So long as the findings and methods of science are applied to human affairs only in a sort of remedial patchwork, we may continue to hold any view of human nature we like. But as the use of science increases, we are forced to accept the theoretical structure with which science represents its facts. The difficulty is that this structure is clearly at odds with the traditional democratic conception of man. Every discovery of an event which has a part in shaping a man's behavior seems to leave so much the less to be credited to the man himself; and as such explanations become more and more comprehensive, the contribution which may be claimed by the individual himself appears to approach zero. Man's vaunted creative powers, his original accomplishments in art, science and morals, his capacity to choose and our right to hold him responsible for the consequences of his choice—none of these is conspicuous in this new self-portrait. Man, we once believed, was free to express himself in art, music and literature, to inquire into nature, to seek salvation in his own way. He could initiate action and make spontaneous and capricious changes of course. Under the most extreme duress some sort of choice remained to him. He could resist any effort to control him, though it might cost him his life. But science insists that action is initiated by forces impinging upon the individual, and that caprice is only another name for behavior for which we have not yet found a cause.

In attempting to reconcile these views it is im-portant to note that the traditional democratic conception was not designed as a description in the scientific sense but as a philosophy to be used in setting up and maintaining a governmental process. It arose under historical circumstances and served political purposes apart from which it cannot be properly understood. In rallying men against tyranny it was necessary that the individual be strengthened, that he be taught that he had rights and could govern himself. To give the common man a new conception of his worth, his dignity, and his power to save himself, both here and hereafter, was often the only resource of the revolutionist. When democratic principles were put into practice, the same doctrines were used as a working formula. This is exemplified by the notion of personal responsibility in Anglo-American law. All governments make certain forms of punishment contingent upon certain kinds of acts. In democratic countries these contingencies are expressed by the notion of responsible choice. But the notion may have no meaning under governmental practices formulated in other ways and would certainly have no place in systems which did not use punishment.

The democratic philosophy of human nature is determined by certain political exigencies and techniques, not by the goals of democracy. But exigencies and techniques change; and a conception which is not supported for its accuracy as a likeness—is not, indeed, rooted in fact at all—may be expected to change too. No matter how effective we judge current democratic practices to be, how highly we value them or how long we expect them to survive, they are almost certainly not the *final* form of government. The philosophy of human nature which has been useful in implementing them is also almost certainly not the last word. The ultimate achievement of democracy may be long deferred unless we emphasize the real aims rather than the verbal devices of democratic thinking. A philosophy which has been appropriate to one set of political exigencies will defeat its purpose if, under other circumstances, it prevents us from applying to human affairs the science of man which probably nothing but democracy itself could have produced.

Perhaps the most crucial part of our democratic philosophy to be reconsidered is our attitude toward freedom—or its reciprocal, the control of human behavior. We do not oppose all forms of control because it is "human nature" to do so. The reaction is not characteristic of all men under all conditions of life. It is an attitude which has been carefully engineered, in large part by what we call the "literature" of democracy. With respect to some methods of control (for example, the threat of force), very little engineering is needed, for the techniques or their immediate consequences are objectionable. Society has suppressed these methods by branding them "wrong," "illegal" or "sinful." But to encourage these attitudes toward objectionable forms of control, it has been necessary to disguise the real nature of certain indispensable techniques, the commonest examples of which are education, moral discourse, and persuasion. The actual procedures appear harmless enough. They consist of supplying information, presenting opportunities for action, pointing out logical relationships, appealing to reason or "enlightened understanding," and so on. Through a masterful piece of misrepresentation, the illusion is fostered that these procedures do not involve the control of behavior; at most, they are simply ways of "getting someone to change his mind." But analysis not only reveals the presence of well-defined behavioral processes, it demonstrates a kind of control no less inexorable, though in some ways more acceptable, than the bully's threat of force.

Let us suppose that someone in whom we are interested is acting unwisely—he is careless in the way he deals with his friends, he drives too fast, or he holds his golf club the wrong way. We could probably help him by issuing a series of commands: don't nag, don't drive over sixty, don't hold your club that way. Much less objectionable would be "an appeal to reason." We could show him how people are affected by his treatment of them, how accident rates rise sharply at higher speeds, how a particular grip on the club alters the way the ball is struck and corrects a slice. In doing so we resort to verbal mediating devices which emphasize and support certain "contingencies of reinforcement"—that is, certain relations between behavior and its consequences—which strengthen the behavior we wish to set up. The same consequences would possibly set up the behavior without our help, and they eventually take control no matter which form of help we give. The appeal to reason has certain advantages over the authoritative command. A threat of punishment, no matter how subtle, generates emotional reactions and tendencies to escape or revolt. Perhaps the controllee merely "feels resentment" at being made to act in a given way, but even that is to be avoided. When we "appeal to reason," he "feels freer to do as he pleases." The fact is that we have exerted *less* control than in using a threat; since other conditions may contribute to the result, the effect may be delayed or, possibly in a given instance, lacking. But if we have worked a change in his behavior at all, it is because we have altered relevant environmental conditions, and the processes we have set in motion are just as real and just as inexorable, if not as comprehensive, as in the most authoritative coercion.

"Arranging an opportunity for action" is another example of disguised control. The power of the negative form has already been exposed in the analysis of censorship. Restriction of opportunity is recognized as far from harmless. As Ralph Barton Perry said in an article which appeared in the Spring, 1953, *Pacific Spectator,* "Whoever determines what alternatives shall be made known to man controls what that man shall choose *from.* He is deprived of freedom in proportion as he is denied access to *any* ideas, or is confined to any range of ideas short of the totality of relevant possibilities." But there is a positive side as well. When we present a relevant state of affairs, we increase the likelihood that a given form of behavior will be emitted. To the extent that the probability of action has changed, we have made a definite contribution. The teacher of history controls a student's behavior (or, if the reader prefers, "deprives him of freedom") just as much in *presenting* historical facts as in suppressing them. Other conditions will no doubt affect the student, but the contribution made to his behavior by the presentation of material is fixed and, within its range, irresistible.

The methods of education, moral discourse, and persuasion are acceptable not because they recognize the freedom of the individual or his right to dissent, but because they make only *partial* contributions to the control of his behavior. The freedom they recognize is freedom from a more coercive form of control. The dissent which they tolerate is the possible effect of other determiners of action. Since these sanctioned methods are frequently ineffective, we have been able to convince ourselves that they do not represent control at all. When they show too much strength to permit disguise, we give them other names and suppress them as energetically as we suppress the use of force. Education grown too powerful is rejected as propaganda or "brain-washing," while really effective persuasion is decried as "undue influence," "demagoguery," "sedduction," and so on.

If we are not to rely solely upon accident for the innovations which give rise to cultural evolution, we must accept the fact that some kind of control of human behavior is inevitable. We cannot use good sense in human affairs unless someone engages in the design and construction of environmental conditions which affect the behavior of men. Environmental changes have always been the condition for the improvement of cultural patterns, and we can hardly use the more effective methods of science without making changes on a grander scale. We are all controlled by the world in which we live, and part of that world has been and will be constructed by men. The question is this: Are we to be controlled by accident, by tyrants, or by ourselves in effective cultural design?

The danger of the misuse of power is possibly greater than ever. It is not allayed by disguising the facts. We cannot make wise decisions if we continue to pretend that human behavior is not controlled, or if we refuse to engage in control when valuable results might be forthcoming. Such measures weaken only ourselves, leaving the strength of science to others. The first step in a defense against tyranny is the fullest possible exposure of controlling techniques. A second step has already been taken successfully in restricting the use of physical force. Slowly, and as yet imperfectly, we have worked out an ethical and governmental design in which the strong man is not allowed to use the power deriving from his strength to control his fellow men. He is restrained by a superior force created for that purpose—the ethical pressure of the group, or more explicit religious and governmental measures. We tend to distrust superior forces, as we currently hesitate to relinquish sovereignty in order to set up an international police force. But it is only through such counter-control that we have achieved what we call peace—a condition in which men are not permitted to control each other through force. In other words, control itself must be controlled.

Science has turned up dangerous processes and materials before. To use the facts and techniques of a science of man to the fullest extent without making some monstrous mistake will be difficult and obviously perilous. It is no time for self-deception, emotional indulgence, or the assumption of attitudes which are no longer useful. Man is facing a difficult test. He must keep his head now, or he must start again—a long way back.

V

Those who reject the scientific conception of man must, to be logical, oppose the methods of science as well. The position is often supported by predicting a series of dire consequences which are to follow if science is not checked. A recent book by Joseph Wood Krutch, *The Measure of Man,* is in this vein. Mr. Krutch sees in the growing science of man the threat of an unexampled tyranny over men's minds. If science is permitted to have its way, he insists, "we may never be able really to think again." A controlled culture will, for example, lack some virtue inherent in disorder. We have emerged from chaos through a series of happy accidents, but in an engineered culture it will be "impossible for the unplanned to erupt again." But there is no virtue in the accidental character of an accident, and the diversity which arises from disorder can not only be duplicated by design but vastly extended. The experimental method is superior to simple observation just because it multiplies "accidents" in a systematic coverage of the possibilities. Technology offers many familiar examples. We no longer wait for immunity to disease to develop from a series of accidental exposures, nor do we wait for natural mutations in sheep and cotton to produce better fibers; but we continue to make use of such accidents when they occur, and we certainly do not prevent them. Many of the things we value have emerged from the clash of ignorant armies on darkling plains, but it is not therefore wise to encourage ignorance and darkness.

It is not always disorder itself which we are told we shall miss but certain admirable qualities in men which flourish only in the presence of disorder. A man rises above an unpropitious childhood to a position of eminence, and since we cannot give a plausible account of the action of so complex an environment, we attribute the achievement to some admirable faculty in the man himself. But such "faculties" are suspiciously like the explanatory fictions against which the history of science warns us. We admire Lincoln for rising above a deficient school system, but it was not necessarily something *in him* which permitted him to become an educated man in spite of it. His educational environment was certainly unplanned, but it could nevertheless have made a full contribution to his mature behavior. He was a rare man, but the circumstances of his childhood were rare too. We do not give Franklin Delano Roosevelt the same credit for becoming an educated man with the help of Groton and Harvard, although the same behavioral processes may have been involved. The founding of Groton and Harvard somewhat reduced the possibility that fortuitous combinations of circumstances would erupt to produce other Lincolns. Yet the founders can hardly be condemned for attacking an admirable human quality.

Another predicted consequence of a science of man is an excessive uniformity. We are told that effective control—whether governmental, religious, educational, economic or social—will produce a race of men who differ from each other only through relatively refractory genetic differences. That would probably be bad design, but we must admit that we are not now pursuing another course from choice. In a modern school, for example, there is usually a syllabus which specifies what every student is to learn by the end of each year. This would be flagrant regimentation if anyone expected every student to comply. But some will be poor in particular subjects, others will not study, others will not remember what they have been taught, and diversity is assured. Suppose, however, that we someday possess such effective educational techniques that every student will in fact be put in possession of all the behavior specified in a syllabus. At the end of the year, all students will correctly answer all questions on the final examination and "must all have prizes." Should we reject such a system on the grounds that in making all students excellent it has made them all alike? Advocates of the theory of a special faculty might contend that an important advantage of the present system is that the good student learns *in spite* of a system which is so defective that it is currently producing bad students as well. But if really effective techniques are available, we cannot avoid the problem of design simply by preferring the status quo. At what point should education be deliberately inefficient?

Such predictions of the havoc to be wreaked by the application of science to human affairs are usually made with surprising confidence. They not only show a faith in the orderliness of human behavior; they presuppose an established body of knowledge with the help of which it can be positively asserted that the changes which scientists propose to make will have quite specific results—albeit not the results they foresee. But the predictions made by the critics of science must be held to be equally fallible and subject also to empirical test. We may be sure that many steps in the scientific design of cultural patterns will produce unforeseen consequences. But there is only one way to find out. And the test must be made, for if we cannot advance in the design of cultural patterns with absolute certainty neither can we rest completely confident of the superiority of the status quo.

VI

Apart from their possibly objectionable consequences, scientific methods seem to make no provision for certain admirable qualities and faculties which seem to have flourished in less explicitly planned cultures; hence they are called "degrading" or "lacking in dignity." (Mr. Krutch has called the author's *Walden Two* an "ignoble Utopia.") The conditioned reflex is the current whipping boy. Because conditioned reflexes may be demonstrated in animals, they are spoken of as though they were exclusively subhuman. It is implied, as we have seen, that no behavioral processes are involved in education and moral discourse or, at least, that the processes are exclusively human. But men do show conditioned reflexes (for example, when they are frightened by all instances of the control of human behavior because some instances engender fear), and animals do show processes similar to the human behavior involved in instruction and moral discourse. When Mr. Krutch asserts that "'Conditioning' is achieved by methods which by-pass or, as it were, short-circuit those very reasoning faculties which education proposes to cultivate and exercise," he is making a technical statement which needs a definition of terms and a great deal of supporting evidence.

If such methods are called "ignoble" simply because they leave no room for certain admirable attributes, then perhaps the practice of admiration needs to be examined. We might say that the child whose education has been skillfully planned has been deprived of the right to intellectual heroism. Nothing has been left to be admired in the way he acquires an education. Similarly, we can conceive of moral training which is so adequate to the demands of the culture that men will be good practically automatically, but to that extent they will be deprived of the right to moral heroism, since we seldom admire automatic goodness. Yet if we consider the end of morals rather than certain virtuous means, is not "automatic goodness" a desirable state of affairs? Is it not, for example, the avowed goal of religious education? T.H. Huxley answered the question unambiguously: "If some great power would agree to make me always think what is true and do what is right, on condition of being a sort of clock and wound up every morning before I got out of bed, I should close instantly with the offer." Yet Mr. Krutch quotes this as the scarcely credible point of view of a "protomodern" and seems himself to share T.S. Eliot's contempt for "...systems so perfect / That no one will need to be good."

"Having to be good" is an excellent example of an expendable honorific. It is inseparable from a particular form of ethical and moral control. We distinguish between the things we *have* to do to avoid punishment and those we *want* to do for rewarding consequences. In a culture which did not resort to punishment we should never "have" to do anything except with respect to the punishing contingencies which arise directly in the physical environment. And we are moving toward such a culture, because the neurotic, not to say psychotic, by-products of control through punishment have long since led compassionate men to seek alternative techniques. Recent research has explained some of the objectionable results of punishment and has revealed resources of at least equal power in "positive reinforcement." It is reasonable to look forward to a time when man will seldom "have" to do anything, although he may show interest, energy, imagination and productivity far beyond the level seen under the present system (except for rare eruptions of the unplanned).

What we have to do we do with *effort*. We call it "work." There is no other way to distinguish between exhausting labor and the possibly equally energetic but rewarding activity of play. It is presumably good cultural design to replace the former with the latter. But an adjustment in attitudes is needed. We are much more practiced in admiring the heroic labor of a Hercules than the activity of one who works without having to. In a truly effective educational system the student might not "have to work" at all, but that possibility is likely to be received by the contemporary teacher with an emotion little short of rage.

We cannot reconcile traditional and scientific views by agreeing upon *what* is to be admired or condemned. The question is whether anything is to be so treated. Praise and blame are cultural practices which have been adjuncts of the prevailing system of control in Western democracy. All people do not engage in them for the same purposes or to the same extent, nor, of course, are the same behaviors always classified in the same way as subject to praise or blame. In admiring intellectual and moral heroism and unrewarding labor, and in rejecting a world in which these would be uncommon, we are simply demonstrating our own cultural conditioning. By promoting certain tendencies to admire and censure, the group of which we are a part has arranged for the social reinforcement and punishment needed to assure a high level of intellectual and moral industry. Under other and possibly better controlling systems, the behavior which we now admire would occur, but not under those conditions which make it admirable, and we should have no reason to admire it because the culture would have arranged for its maintenance in other ways.

To those who are stimulated by the glamorous heroism of the battlefield, a peaceful world may not be a better world. Others may reject a world without sorrow, longing or a sense of guilt because the relevance of deeply moving works of art would be lost. To many who have devoted their lives to the struggle to be wise and good, a world without confusion and evil might be an empty thing. A nostalgic concern for the decline of moral heroism has been a dominating theme in the work of Aldous Huxley. In *Brave New World* he could see in the application of science to human affairs only a travesty on the notion of the Good (just as George Orwell, in *1984,* could foresee nothing but horror). In a recent issue of *Esquire,* Huxley has expressed the point this way: "We have had religious revolutions, we have had political, industrial, economic and nationalistic revolutions. All of them, as our descendants will discover, were but ripples in an ocean of conservatism—trivial by comparison with the psychological revolution toward which we are so rapidly moving. *That* will really be a revolution. When it is over, the human race will give no further trouble." (Footnote for the reader of the future: This was not meant as a happy ending. Up to 1956 men had been admired,

if at all, either for causing trouble or alleviating it. Therefore—)

It will be a long time before the world can dispense with heroes and hence with the cultural practice of admiring heroism, but we move in that direction whenever we act to prevent war, famine, pestilence and disaster. It will be a long time before man will never need to submit to punishing environments or engage in exhausting labor, but we move in that direction whenever we make food, shelter, clothing and labor-saving devices more readily available. We may mourn the passing of heroes but not the conditions which make for heroism. We can spare the self-made saint or sage as we spare the laundress on the river's bank struggling against fearful odds to achieve cleanliness.

VII

The two great dangers in modern democratic thinking are illustrated in a paper by former Secretary of State Dean Acheson. "For a long time now," writes Mr. Acheson, "we have gone along with some well-tested principles of conduct: That it was better to tell the truth than falsehoods;...that duties were older than and as fundamental as rights; that, as Justice Holmes put it, the mode by which the inevitable came to pass was effort; that to perpetrate a harm was wrong no matter how many joined in it... and so on....Our institutions are founded on the assumption that most people follow these principles most of the time because they want to, and the institutions work pretty well when this assumption is true. More recently, however, bright people have been fooling with the machinery in the human head and they have discovered quite a lot....Hitler introduced new refinements [as the result of which] a whole people have been utterly confused and corrupted. Unhappily neither the possession of this knowledge nor the desire to use it was confined to Hitler....Others dip from this same devil's cauldron."

The first dangerous notion in this passage is that most people follow democratic principles of conduct "because they want to." This does not account for democracy or any other form of government if we have not explained why people *want* to behave in given ways. Although it is tempting to assume that it is human nature to believe in democratic principles, we must not overlook the "cultural engineering" which produced and continues to maintain democratic practices. If we neglect the conditions which produce democratic *behavior,* it is useless to try to maintain a democratic *form* of government. And we cannot expect to export a democratic form of government successfully if we do not also provide for the cultural practices which will sustain it. Our forebears did not discover the essential nature of man; they evolved a pattern of behavior which worked remarkably well under the circumstances. The "set of principles" expressed in that pattern is not the only true set or necessarily the best. Mr. Acheson has presumably listed the most unassailable items; some of them are probably beyond question, but others—concerning duty and effort—may need revision as the world changes.

The second—and greater—threat to the democracy which Mr. Acheson is defending is his assumption that knowledge is necessarily on the side of evil. All the admirable things he mentions are attributed to the innate goodness of man, all the detestable to "fooling with the machinery in the human head." This is reminiscent of the position, taken by other institutions engaged in the control of men, that certain forms of knowledge are in themselves evil. But how out of place in a democratic philosophy! Have we come this far only to conclude that well-intentioned people cannot study the behavior of men without becoming tyrants or that informed men cannot show good will? Let us for once have strength and good will on the same side.

VIII

Far from being a threat to the tradition of Western democracy, the growth of a science of man is a consistent and probably inevitable part of it. In turning to the external conditions which shape and maintain the behavior of men, while questioning the reality of inner qualities and faculties to which human achievements were once attributed, we turn from the ill-defined and remote to the observable and manipulable. Though it is a painful step, it has far-reaching consequences, for it not only sets higher standards of human welfare but shows us how to meet them. A change in a theory of human nature cannot change the facts. The achievements of man in science, art, literature, music and morals will survive any interpretation we place upon them. The uniqueness of the individual is unchallenged in the scientific view. Man, in short, will remain man. (There will be much to admire for those who are so inclined. Possibly the noblest achievement to which man can aspire, even according to present standards, is to accept himself for what he is, as that is revealed to him by the methods which he devised and tested on a part of the world in which he had only a small personal stake.)

If Western democracy does not lose sight of the aims of humanitarian action, it will welcome the almost fabulous support of its own science of man and will strengthen itself and play an important role in building a better world for everyone. But if it cannot put its "democratic philosophy" into proper historical perspective—if, under the control of attitudes and emotions which it generated for other purposes, it now rejects the help of science—then it must be prepared for defeat. For if we continue to insist that science has nothing to offer but a new and more horrible form of tyranny, we may produce just such a result by allowing the strength of science to fall into the hands of despots. And if, with luck, it were to fall instead to men of good will in other political communities, it would be perhaps a more ignominious defeat; for we should then, through a miscarriage of democratic principles, be forced to leave to others the next step in man's long struggle to control nature and himself.

Leon Festinger's theory of cognitive dissonance, based on the principle of the body's tendency to maintain its equilibrium (homeostasis), has received wide attention. The essence of the theory is the simple assertion that "if a person knows various things that are not psychologically consistent with one another, he will, in a variety of ways, try to make them more consistent."[1] Generally speaking, the term "cognitive dissonance" refers to the psychological state that occurs after someone makes a decision that commits him to a particular alternative. Since commitment to any single alternative logically implies the dissolution of prior commitments to opposing alternatives, it follows that this person would automatically experience the psychological discomfort and uncertainty that comes from accepting one imperfect alternative and thereby rejecting other choices that probably had certain redeeming features of their own. Festinger has postulated that dissonance, because it is a psychologically uncomfortable state, would have the effect of motivating the individual to reduce his cognitive inconsistency and return to a homeostatic state either by changing his behavior or changing his beliefs.

In an extensive review of various homeostatic formulations that have evolved over the past several years in social psychology, R.B. Zajonc summarizes the fundamental tenets of dissonance theory:[2]

1. Cognitive dissonance is a noxious state.

2. In the case of cognitive dissonance the individual attempts to reduce or eliminate it and he acts so as to avoid events that will increase it.

3. In the case of consonance the individual acts so as to avoid dissonance-producing events.

4. The severity or the intensity of cognitive dissonance varies with (a) the importance of the cognitions involved and (b) the relative number of cognitions standing in dissonant relation to one another.

5. The strength of the tendencies enumerated in (2) and (3) is a direct function of the severity of dissonance.

6. Cognitive dissonance can be reduced or eliminated only by (a) adding new cognitions or (b) changing existing ones.

7. Adding new cognitions reduces dissonance if (a) the

[1]L. Festinger, "Cognitive Dissonance, "*Scientific American, 207* (4), 1962, p. 93.
[2]R. B. Zajonc, "Cognitive Theories in Social Psychology," in G. Lindzey and E. Aronson, eds., *The Hand Book of Social Psychology,* Addison-Wesley Publ. Co., vol. 1, 1968, pp. 360–361.

Part V
STRIVING FOR COGNITIVE EQUILIBRIUM AS A SOURCE OF MOTIVATION

new cognitions add weight to one side and thus decrease the proportion of cognitive elements which are in dissonant relation with one another.

8. Changing existing cognitions reduces dissonance if (a) their new content makes them less contradictory with others, or (b) their importance is reduced.

9. If new cognitions cannot be added or the existing ones changed by means of a passive process, behaviors which have cognitive consequences favoring conso-

nance will be recruited. Seeking new information is an example of such behavior.

In the first of the two papers which follow Aronson explores some of the theoretical implications of dissonance theory for the development of values in children and for influencing value-related behavior in adults. In the second, Festinger speculates on the generality of cognitive dissonance as an explanatory principle for infrahuman motivation, concluding that rats and people come to love those things for which they have suffered.

In this presentation I would like to discuss a quite recent approach to the problem of modifying values and behavior. I will be discussing both the formation of values in children (commonly known as socialization) and the modification of value-related behavior in adults.

Let us begin with children. In the process of raising children, most parents are primarily concerned with two basic goals. The first of these is that of preventing the child from performing specific and momentary acts that are destructive, dangerous, and otherwise undesirable—like clobbering his younger brother, spreading blueberry jam on the new drapes, or dashing across a busy street in the midst of traffic. The second is concerned with instilling in the young child a permanent and enduring set of values which will enable him to live in society without breaking too many laws or violating too many cultural mores.

How can parents best achieve these goals? It would be wonderful if we could reason with the child—that is, convince him by rational and persuasive argument why it is not nice to beat up on his younger brother. But, as Aristotle observed 2000 years ago, even many adults cannot be taught by reasonable arguments; this is certainly true when applied to the four-year-old. Less rational techniques must be employed—techniques which involve rewarding or punishing the child. Most child psychologists are in agreement in advocating rewards, both in the form of concrete incentives and in the form of praise and approval, as a means of "reinforcing" desirable behavior. Psychologists generally feel that rewarding desirable behavior is much more effective than punishing undesirable behavior. Thus, they recommend that we should reward Johnny for being kind to his little brother as opposed to punishing him for being unkind to his little brother. But par-

10
Cognitive Dissonance as It Affects Values and Behavior[1]

Elliot Aronson

[1]Excerpted from an address given to the Council for the Advancement of Science Writing in New Brunswick, New Jersey. Portions of this address were published under the title of "Try a Little Dissonance" in the *New York Times Magazine*, Part I, September 11, 1966. The preparation of this paper was supported by a grant from the National Institutes of Health.

ents (even those of us who happen to be psychologists!) are well aware of the fact that punishment or the threat of punishment is often necessary and, when judiciously used, can be an effective means of controlling the behavior of very young children.

Let us take a closer look at threats of punishment as a technique. These threats usually take the form of spankings or denial of priviliges. A reasonable question is one of degree—in order to be most effective, how severe should a threat of punishment be? It stands to reason that if we want to prevent a child from performing a mischievous act, the more severe the threat, the greater the likelihood that he will comply—at least *while the threatening parent is standing there watching him.* And that's the problem: for while severe threats are effective in achieving the first major goal of parents (that of preventing momentary undesirable behavior), they have proved useless in helping the child develop a set of values. For example, child psychologists find that those parents who are most severe in punishing a child's aggressive behavior tend to have children who, although relatively unaggressive in the presence of their parents, are veritable hellions in the schoolyard where their parents are not present to punish them. It is unfortunate that those techniques which are best at preventing momentary infractions are ineffective as a means of imparting basic values. Moreover, of these two goals, it would appear that the latter is the more important, if for no other reason than the fact that it is more efficient—for once a child has developed a set of values, parents (and society) can afford to relax their vigil. If a child has not yet learned to respect the rights of others, we must be continually on our toes, armed with candies or threats, to see to it that Johnny doesn't slug his younger brother or infringe on his rights in other ways. Once the child has developed these values, he will refrain from these behaviors—not because of fear of punishment, but because he wants to. It would certainly be a much more efficient way to run a family (or a society) if we could somehow find a way to imbue young children with complex values; if we could get them to refrain

from slugging their younger brothers because they had come to dislike slugging smaller children.

In the past few years we have been conducting psychological experiments which may have an important bearing on this problem. These experiments have been derived from and inspired by the theory of cognitive dissonance which was proposed by Leon Festinger (1957) and which I have recently revised and extended (Aronson, 1969). Before describing these experiments, let me first present a brief description of the theory. Stated in its simplest form, this theory suggests that when a person simultaneously holds two incompatible ideas (cognitions), dissonance occurs. This creates internal tension. Such tension is unpleasant, and the individual tries to diminish it by reducing the dissonance. This can be done by changing one idea (cognition) or the other to bring them closer together and make them more compatible.

For example, if a person has the cognition that he smokes cigarettes and reads that cigarette smoking leads to lung cancer, he experiences cognitive dissonance. His cognition that he is smoking is dissonant with his cognition that cigarette smoking might cause cancer. He can reduce this dissonance in a number of ways. Perhaps the most direct would be to stop smoking; the cognition that cigarette smoking causes cancer is perfectly compatible (consonant) with *not* smoking. Although this is the most direct way to reduce dissonance, it is not the easiest course of action to take—as many of us have discovered. Consequently, most people attempt to reduce dissonance by working on the other cognition—that is, by making cigarette smoking seem less silly. Perhaps we will try to belittle the evidence linking cigarette smoking to cancer ("Most of the data were gathered on rodents, not people"); or we might associate with other cigarette smokers ("If Sam, Jack, and Harry smoke, then it can't be very dangerous"); or we might smoke filter-tipped cigarettes and delude ourselves with the notion that the filter traps the cancer-producing materials; or we might convince ourselves that smoking is an important and highly pleasurable activity ("I'd rather have a shorter but more enjoyable life than a longer, unenjoyable one''); or we might actually make a virtue out of smoking by developing a romantic, devil-may-care picture of ourselves, flaunting danger by smoking. These behaviors are all acts of ''self-justification'' and, indeed, cognitive dissonance theory is largely concerned with man's attempt to justify his own behavior—to make his actions appear to be reasonable and rational, after the fact. One of the primary ways of reducing dissonance is through this technique, which the psychoanalysts refer to as rationalization.

What does all this have to do with instilling a permanent set of values in young children? Just this: Children are people too; there is every reason to suspect that they experience cognitive dissonance and attempt to reduce it in much the same way that adults do. As mentioned above, in the course of interacting with their children from day to day, parents typically threaten or punish them in order to curtail or prevent them from performing dangerous or undesirable actions. Thus, if a parent came upon his five-year-old in the act of beating up a younger brother, the parent might threaten to punish him in order to get him to stop. The key question is, how do we utilize these situations in order to build a permanent set of values? Let us imagine that each parent has at his disposal a range of punishments from an extremely mild rebuff on the one hand (for example, a stern look) to an extremely severe punishment on the other hand (a very stern look, accompanied by a severe spanking, forcing the child to stand in the corner for two hours, and depriving him of television privileges for a month). As mentioned previously, the more severe the threat, the greater the likelihood that he will stop beating up his little brother at that moment, *while his parent is watching him;* however, he may very well hit his brother again as soon as the parent turns his back.

But suppose instead that the parent threatens him with a very mild punishment—a punishment which was just barely severe enough to get him to stop aggressing at that moment. In either case— under threat of severe punishment or of mild punishment—the child is experiencing dissonance; he

is aware that he is not beating up on his little brother while also aware that he wants to. When the little brother is present, the child has the urge to beat him up and, when he refrains, he asks himself, in effect, ''how come I'm not beating up my little brother?'' Under severe threat he has a ready answer: ''I know damn well why I'm not beating up my little brother. I'm not beating him up because if I do, the giant standing over there (my father) is going to knock the hell out of me, stand me in the corner, and keep me from watching television for a month.'' In effect, the severe threat of punishment has provided the child with justifications for not beating up his brother, *at that moment, while he's being watched.*

But consider the child in the mild threat situation; he experiences dissonance too. He asks himself, in effect, ''How come I'm not beating up my little brother?'' But the difference is that he doesn't have a good answer—because, by definition, the threat, while barely severe enough to get the child to refrain momentarily, is so mild that it does not provide a super-abundance of justification. In effect, the child is *not* doing something he *likes* to do—and while he has some justification, he lacks complete justification. In this situation he continues to experience dissonance. There is no simple way for him to reduce it by blaming his inaction on a severe threat. He must, therefore, find reasons consonant with not hitting his little brother. Much like the cigarette smoker in the earlier example, the child must find a way to justify the fact that he is *not* aggressing against his little brother. The best way is to try to convince himself that he really doesn't like to beat his brother up, that he didn't want to do it in the first place, that beating up little kids is not fun. The less severe the threat, the less the ''external'' justification; the less the external justification, the greater the need for internal justification. Internal justifications are a long step toward the development of a permanent value.

To test this idea, I performed an experiment at the Harvard University nursery school in collaboration with my colleague, Dr. J. Merrill Carlsmith. In our experiment, for ethical reasons, we did not try to change important and basic values like aggression; i.e., we felt that parents might not approve of our changing important values. Instead, we chose a trivial and unimportant aspect of behavior—toy preference. We first asked four and five-year-old children to rate the attractiveness of several toys; then we chose one that a child considered to be quite attractive, and we told him he couldn't play with it. For one-half of the children we threatened mild punishment for transgression—"I would be a little annoyed"; with the other half, we threatened more severe punishment—"I would be very angry. I would have to take all of my toys and go home and never come back again. I would think you were just a baby." After that, we left the room and allowed the children to play with the other toys—and to resist the temptation of playing with the forbidden one. All of the children *did* resist the temptation—none played with the forbidden toy. On returning to the room we remeasured the attractiveness of all of the toys. Our results were both striking and exciting. Those children who underwent a mild threat now found the toy *less* attractive than before. In short, lacking adequate justification for refraining from playing with the toy, they succeeded in convincing themselves that they hadn't played with it *because they didn't really like it.* On the other hand, the toy did *not* become less attractive for those who were severely threatened. These children continued to rate the forbidden toy as highly desirable—indeed, some even found it more desirable than they had before the threat. The children in the severe threat condition had good external reasons for not playing with the toy (the severe threat itself); they therefore had no need to find additional reasons (like that the toy was no longer attractive); consequently, they continued to like the toy.

Our experiment has been repeated successfully and extended by other psychologists at different universities across the United States. The most dramatic of these experiments is one conducted by Dr. Jonathan Freedman (1965) of Stanford University. The exciting aspect of Freedman's study is that he showed that this effect is a long-lasting one. In his experiment, he repeated our procedure with minor changes. The crucial toy was a battery-powered robot which was, by far, the most attractive to all the children. Freedman forbade the children from playing with the mechanical robot, using mild threats for some and severe threats for others.

After some 23 to 64 days had elapsed, different experimenters came to the classroom under totally unrelated circumstances to administer a psychological test. They tested the students in the same room that was used by Freedman—the original toys were rather carelessly strewn about. After each experimenter had administered one test to a child, she told him that she would have to score it and might want to ask him some questions about it later—and while he was waiting, if he wanted to, he could amuse himself by playing with some of the toys lying around.

Freedman's results are consistent with our own. The overwhelming majority of the children who had been mildly threatened weeks earlier *did not* play with this inherently attractive toy; on the other hand, the great majority of the children who had been severely threatened *did,* in fact, play with the toy. In sum, a severe threat was not effective in inhibiting subsequent behavior—but the effect of one *mild* threat succeeded in inhibiting "undesirable" behavior for as long as 64 days! The beauty of this technique is that the child did not come to devalue this behavior (playing with the toy) because some adult told him it was undesirable; rather, he convinced *himself* that it was undesirable.

As I mentioned early in this presentation, the theory of cognitive dissonance is not limited to the area of the socialization of children—it also has a great deal to say about the modification of adult values, attitudes and behavior. I would like to discuss one experimental situation which I feel has important ramifications in this regard. I conducted this experiment in collaboration with Dr. David Mettee at the University of Texas (1968). The experiment is involved with inducing individuals to commit an immoral act or to resist the temptation to commit an immoral act.

Before I describe the experiment, I will present the theoretical rationale behind it. This can be stated in one sentence: All other things being equal, people tend to behave in a manner which is consistent with their self esteem. Thus, if a person is made to feel that he is a decent, worthwhile person, and is subsequently placed in a moral dilemma, he is more likely to behave morally than if he were made to feel that he is worthless as a person. The cognition "I am a decent person" is consistent with decent behavior and inconsistent with immoral behavior. The cognition "I am a worthless person" is consistent with immoral behavior and inconsistent with decent behavior.

In our experiment we attempted to modify a person's self concept (temporarily) in the following manner: College students were asked to fill out a personality inventory. Subsequently, they were given false information about the outcome of this inventory. On an individual basis, each student was given false, prearranged information about the results of this personality test. One third of the students were given positive feedback; specifically, they were told that the test indicated that they were mature, rational, interesting, etc. One third of the students were given negative feedback; they were told that the test indicated that they were relatively immature, irrational, rather shallow, etc. One third of the students were not given any information about the results of the test—they were informed that the inventory had not yet been scored.

Immediately afterwards, the students were scheduled to participate in an experiment which had no apparent relationship to the personality inventory and which was conducted by a different psychologist. As a part of this second experiment, the subjects participated in a game of cards against some of their fellow students. This was a gambling game in which students were allowed to bet money and were told that they could keep whatever money they won. In the course of the game, the subjects were presented with a few opportunities to cheat in a situation where it seemed impossible that they could be detected. The crucial situation was arranged so that if the students were to decide *not* to cheat, they would certainly lose—whereas if they decided to cheat, they would be certain to win a sizable sum of money.

Let me elaborate on this card-playing situation. The game is called "blackjack" (sometimes known as "21"). In this game, each player is dealt as many cards as he needs in an attempt to achieve a face value which totals 21—or to approach a total of 21 without exceeding that score. Thus, a 7, a 4, and a 10 would be a perfect score; likewise, a 5, a 3, a 6, and a 7 would be a winning combination. Since obtaining 21 itself is relatively rare, a score of 19 or 20 is usually sufficient to win. If a player's total exceeds 21, he automatically loses. A player whose cards total 14 or 15 will almost always decide to draw an additional card in the hope of increasing his score without exceeding 21. In the experiment, the subjects were separated from one another and from the experimenter by plywood walls. The cards (and money) were slipped to (and from) the player through a narrow opening at the bottom of his wall. The players were told that the cards would be dealt to them not by a person, but by a mechanical dealing machine. This machine was demonstrated to them. They were informed that the machine had not as yet been perfected and occasionally blundered. Specifically, they were told the mistake the machine might make would be to deal two cards simultaneously instead of one. If this occurred, the subjects were asked to slide the bottom-most card back through the opening since that was not their rightful card.

In the course of the game, the experimenter provided each subject with the opportunity and the temptation to cheat. This was accomplished in the following way: Imagine a player with cards totaling 13. Naturally he requests an additional card. "Whoops," the "machine" blunders and presents the player with two cards. His rightful card is a 10, which would cause him to lose; his illegitimate card is an 8, which would guarantee victory. A subject's decision to keep the illegitimate but winning card was our measure of cheating. In this situation the subjects were led to feel that they could not be detected because of the privacy provided by the booth and because of their belief that the cards were being distributed by an impersonal machine. In actuality, however, the experimenter was able to determine whether or not a person cheated because it was the experimenter who really distributed the cards rather than the machine.

Our results demonstrated that those students who had previously received information designed to raise their self esteem showed little inclination to cheat; i.e., they cheated slightly less frequently than the students in the control condition (who received no prior information about their personalities). On the other hand, those students who had previously received information designed to lower their self esteem cheated more frequently than the students in the control condition. The difference in cheating between the subjects in the two experimental conditions was statistically reliable. It should be noted that, although our procedure caused some discomfort to ⅓ of the subjects, it was only temporary. A complete explanation of the procedure was presented to all subjects at the close of the experiment and whatever discomfort they felt was alleviated.

The results of this experiment are quite provocative, especially when one takes into consideration the fact that one of the unique aspects of this study was the non-specific nature of the self concept manipulation. That is, in the "personality evaluation" that the subjects received, they were not told anything about themselves which would lead them to infer that they were moral-honest or immoral-dishonest people. Rather, as you will recall, they were told things designed to raise or reduce their self esteem in general—concretely, that they were uninteresting and immature people or interesting and mature people. The social implications of these findings would appear to be of some importance. The results suggest that people who have a high opinion of themselves are less prone to perform any activities which are generally dissonant with their opinion. Looking at the other side of this coin, our results indicate that it is easier for a person with a low self concept to commit acts of a criminal nature. Moreover, it may be that the common thread running through the complex variables involved in successful socialization is that of differential development of self esteem. Granted that most children become aware of what behavior is approved (moral) or disapproved (immoral), the development of high self esteem in the individual may be crucial in his choosing a moral rather than an immoral mode of behavior. This discussion is highly speculative, however, and further experimentation is necessary before its validity can be determined.

REFERENCES

Aronson, E. The theory of cognitive dissonance: a current perspective. In L. Berkowitz (Ed.), *Advances in experimental social psychology,* Vol. 4, New York: Academic Press, 1969.

Aronson, E., & Carlsmith, J.M. Effect of the severity of threat on the devaluation of forbidden behavior. *J. abnorm. soc. Psychol.,* 1963, **66,** 584–588.

Aronson, E., & Mettee, D.R. Dishonest behavior as a function of differential levels of induced self-esteem. *J. Pers. soc. Psychol.,* 1968, **9,** 121–127.

Festinger, L. *A theory of cognitive dissonance.* Evanston, Ill.: Row, Peterson, 1957.

Freedman, J.L. Long-term behavioral effects of cognitive dissonance. *J. exp. soc. Psychol.,* 1965, **1,** 145–155.

Some fields of Psychology have for many years been dominated by ideas concerning the importance of rewards in the establishment and maintenance of behavior patterns. So dominant has this notion become, that some of our most ingenious theoretical thinking has been devoted to imagining the existence of rewards in order to explain behavior in situations where, plausibly, no rewards exist. It has been observed, for example, that under some circumstances an organism will persist in voluntarily engaging in behavior which is frustrating or painful. To account for such behavior it has, on occasion, been seriously proposed that the cessation of the frustration or pain is rewarding and thus reinforces the tendency to engage in the behavior.

I want to maintain that this type of explanation is not only unnecessary but also misleading. I certainly do *not* wish to say that rewards are unimportant, but I propose to show that the absence of reward or the existence of inadequate reward produces certain specific consequences which can account for a variety of phenomena which are difficult to deal with if we use our usual conceptions of the role of reward.

Before I proceed, I would like to say that most of the thinking and most of the experimental work which I will present are the result of collaboration between Douglas H. Lawrence and myself. Indeed, whatever you find interesting in what I say you may safely attribute primarily to him.

I will start my discussion in a rather roundabout manner with some remarks which concern themselves primarily with some aspects of the thinking processes of human beings. Human thinking is sometimes a strange mixture of "plausible" and "magical" processes. Let us examine more closely what I mean by this. For example, imagine that a person knows that some event is going to occur, and that the person can do something to prepare himself to cope more adequately with the impending event. Under such circumstances it is very reasonable (perhaps you might even want to

11
The Psychological Effects of Insufficient Rewards

Leon Festinger

Reprinted from the *American Psychologist* by permission of American Psychological Association, vol. 16, 1961, pp. 1–11.

use the word "rational") for the person to do whatever is necessary in preparation for the coming event. Human thinking, however, also works in reverse. Consider a person who goes to a lot of trouble to prepare himself for a future event which might possibly occur. Such a person will subsequently tend to persuade himself that the event is rather likely to occur. There is nothing very plausible or rational about this kind of mental process—rather, it has almost a magical quality about it. Let me illustrate this briefly by describing an experiment recently conducted by Ruby Yaryan (1961).

Under the pretext of investigating the manner in which students study for examinations, she asked subjects to study a list of arbitrary definitions of symbols in preparation for a possible test. Two conditions were experimentally created for the subjects. Half of the subjects were told that, if they actually took the test, this list of definitions of the symbols would be in their possession during the test, and so, all that was necessary in preparation was to familiarize themselves with the list. This was, essentially, an "easy preparation" condition. That is, not much effort was required of the subjects in advance preparation for the test.

The other half of the subjects were told that, if they actually took the test, they would *not* have the list of definitions with them and so it was necessary for them to memorize the symbols and their definitions in preparation for the test. It is clear that this constitutes a much more "effortful preparation" condition. Considerable effort was required of these subjects in advance preparation for the possible test.

It was carefully explained to each subject that not everyone would actually have to take the test. Specifically, they were told that only half of the people in the experiment *would* take the test. It was also carefully explained that the selection of who would, and who would not, have to take the test had already been made in consultation with their teachers (the subjects were all high school girls). Nothing that happened during the experiment would affect whether or not they took the test—this had already been decided in advance for each of them.

After they finished studying the list of definitions, they were asked a number of questions to preserve the fiction that the experiment was concerned with study habits. Each subject was also asked to indicate how likely she thought it was that she, personally, would have to actually take the test. The results show, quite clearly, that subjects in the effortful preparation condition, on the average, thought it was more likely that they would have to take the test than did subjects in the easy preparation condition. In other words, those who were experimentally induced to engage in a lot of preparatory effort, persuaded themselves that the thing they were preparing for would actually occur.

The relevance of this experiment to the problem of the effects of inadequate rewards will become clearer in the following example which illustrates the same psychological process. Consider some person who is strongly attracted to some goal. It is quite reasonable for this person to be willing to expend more effort, or to endure more pain, in order to reach the goal than he would be if he were less attracted. Once more, however, one finds the same process of reasoning in reverse. That is, if a person exerts a great deal of effort, or endures pain, in order to reach some ordinary objective, there is a strong tendency for him to persuade himself that the objective is especially valuable or especially desirable. An experiment conducted by Elliot Aronson and Judson Mills (1959) shows the effect quite nicely.

The subjects in the experiment by Aronson and Mills were college girls who volunteered to join small discussion groups. Each subject, when she appeared for the discussion group, was told that, instead of being put into a new group, she was being considered for inclusion in an ongoing group which had recently lost one of its members. However, the subject was told, because of the group's concern that the replacement be someone who would be able to discuss things freely and openly, the experimenter had agreed to test the replacement before admitting her to the group. Some subjects were then given a very brief and not painful test while others were given a rather extended and embarrassing test. The experimenter then, of course, told each subject that she had done well and was admitted to the group. Thus, there were some subjects who had attained membership in the group easily and some subjects who had endured a painful experience in order to be admitted to the group.

The experimenter then explained to the subject that the discussion was carried on by means of an intercommunication system, each girl being in a separate room. She was brought into her room which contained a microphone and earphones. The experimenter told her that the others had already started and perhaps it would be best for her not to participate in the discussion this time but just to listen. Next meeting, of course, she would participate fully. Speaking into the microphone the experimenter then went through the illusion of introducing her to the three other girls in the group. He then "disconnected" the microphone and gave the subject the earphones to wear. The subject then listened for about 25 minutes to a tape recording of a rather dull and halting discussion. All subjects, of course, heard exactly the same tape recording thinking they were listening to the actual live group discussion.

When the discussion was finished, the experimenter explained to the subject that, after each meeting, each of the girls filled out a "post-meeting reaction form." She was then given a questionnaire to complete which asked a variety of questions concerning how interesting she had found the discussion to be, how much she liked the other members of the group, and other similar questions. The results show, as anticipated, that those subjects who had gone through a painful procedure in order to be admitted to the group thought the discussion was more interesting and liked the other group members better than did those who had gained admission to the group easily. In other words, we see the same process operating here as we noted in the previous experiment. If someone is somehow induced to endure embarrassment in order to achieve something, she then persuades herself that what she has achieved is valuable.

In both of the examples which I have discussed (and one could present many more examples of similar nature) a situation has been produced where the organism has two pieces of information (or cognitions) which do not fit together. In the first example, these two pieces of information were: (a) I have worked hard in preparation for an event. (b) The event is not too likely to occur. In the second example, the two cognitions which did not fit together were: (a) I have endured pain to attain an objective. (b) The objective is not very attractive. This kind of "nonfitting" relationship between two pieces of information may be termed a dissonant relation (Festinger, 1957). The reason, of course, that dissonance exists between these cognitions is that, psychologically, the obverse of one follows from the other. Psychologically, if an objective *is* very attractive, it follows that one would be willing to endure pain to attain it; or if the objective is *not* attractive, it follows that one does *not* endure pain to attain it. This specification of why a given relation between cognitions is dissonant also provides the clues to predicting specifically how the organism will react to the existence of the dissonance. Assuming that the organism will attempt to reduce the dissonance between the cognitions, there are obviously two major classes of ways in which this can be done. He can attempt to persuade himself that the pain which he endured was not really painful or he can attempt to persuade himself that the objective *is* very attractive.

I will not spend any more time than this in general theoretical discussion of the theory of dissonance and the reduction of dissonance. I hope that this small amount of general theoretical discussion will be enough to give context to the specific analysis of the psychological effects of insufficient rewards.

Let us consider in more detail what is suggested by the example of the experiment by Aronson and Mills and by the theory of cognitive dissonance. In that experiment the dissonance which was created was reduced by enhancing the value of the goal. This suggests that organisms may come to like and value things for which they have worked very hard or for which they have suffered. Looking at it from another aspect, one might say that they may come to value activities for which they have been inadequately rewarded. At first glance this may seem to contradict a widely accepted notion in Psychology, namely, that organisms learn to like things for which they *have* been rewarded. In a sense it is contradictory, but not in the sense that it denies the operation of this widely assumed process. It does, however, state that another process also operates which is rather of an opposite character.

Let us analyze the situation with which we are concerned somewhat more carefully and more precisely. We are concerned with the dissonance between two possible cognitions. One of these is a cognition the organism has concerning his behavior, namely, I have voluntarily done something which, all other things being equal, I would avoid doing. The other is a cognition about the environment or about the result of his action, namely, the reward that has been obtained is inadequate. As we mentioned before, this dissonance can be reduced if the organism can persuade himself that he really likes the behavior in which he engaged or if he enhances for himself the value of what he has obtained as a result of his actions.

There is, of course, another way to reduce the dissonance, namely, for the organism to change his behavior. That is, having done something which resulted in an inadequate reward the organism can refuse to perform the action again. This means of reducing the dissonance is undoubtedly the one most frequently employed by organisms. If the organism obtains information which is dissonant with his behavior, he usually modifies his behavior so that it fits better what he knows concerning his environment. Here, however, I am going to consider only situations in which this means of reducing dissonance is not available to the organism. That is, I will consider only situations in which the organism is somehow tricked or seduced into continuing to engage in the activity in spite of the dissonance which is introduced. Under these circumstances we would expect one of the two previously mentioned dissonance reduction mechanisms to be used.

If one thinks for a while about the possible behavioral consequences of such a psychological process as we have described, an explanation suggests itself for the well known finding that resistance to extinction is greater after partial reward than after complete reward.

Before I explain this more adequately, I would like to digress for a moment. Since much of the research on the effects of partial reward has been done on rats, and since the experiments that Lawrence and I have done are also on rats, the question will inevitably arise as to whether or not I really think that rats have cognitions and that rats reduce dissonance the way humans do.

First for the matter of cognitions in rats: All that is meant by cognition is knowledge or information. It seems to me that one can assume that an organism has cognitions or information if one can observe some behavioral difference under different stimulus conditions. If the organism changes his behavior when the environment changes, then obviously he uses information about the environment and, equally obviously, can be said to have cognitions.

Now for the question of whether or not rats reduce dissonance as humans do: Although Lawrence keeps telling me that rats are smarter than humans, I suspect that the rat is a rather stupid organism and does not reduce dissonance nearly as effectively as the human being does. I suspect that the mechanisms available to the rat for dissonance reduction are very limited and that the amount of dissonance which gets effectively reduced is relatively small. Still, I suspect that they *do* reduce dissonance. At any rate, if we find that the theory of dissonance can make valid predictions for rat behavior, this will be evidence that they do, indeed, reduce dissonance.

Now to return to the matter of the increased resistance to extinction following partial reward. Let us examine what occurs, psychologically, during a series of trials on which the behavior of an organism is only occasionally rewarded. Imagine a hungry animal who dashes frantically down some runway and into some so-called "goal box" only to find that there is nothing there. The cognition that he has obtained nothing is dissonant with the cognition that he has expended effort to reach the goal box. If this state of affairs were continually repeated, as we all know, the animal would reduce the dissonance by refusing to go to the goal box, that is, he would change his behavior. But, in a partial reward situation, the animal is tricked into continuing to run to the goal box because an appreciable number of times that he goes there he does find food. But, on each nonrewarded trial dissonance is introduced when the animal finds the goal box empty. The assumed process of dissonance reduction would lead us to expect that, gradually, the animal develops some extra preference either for the activity or for the goal box itself. A comparable animal that was rewarded every time he ran to the goal box would not develop any such extra preference.

Consider the situation, then, when extinction trials begin. In addition to realizing that food is no longer present, the partially rewarded animal also has to overcome his extra preference before he stops going to the goal box. We would thus expect "extinction" to take longer for a partially rewarded animal than for an animal that was always rewarded. The magnitude of the difference should be far greater than just the slight effect which would exist if the 100% animal discovers more rapidly that the situation has changed.

If this explanation is correct, then the greater resistance to extinction following partial reward is a direct consequence of the process of dissonance reduction. This, of course, immediately suggests an extension of this line of reasoning to situations other than those involving partial reward. *Any* procedure which introduces dissonance during the training trials should similarly be expected to increase resistance to extinction since the same kind of dissonance reduction process should operate.

Let us, however, try to be precise about what kinds of procedures would introduce dissonance for an organism during training trials in an experiment. It is, fortunately, possible to define this operationally in a precise manner. Let us imagine that we test an organism in a single choice situation. In the case of a rat, for example, this might be simply an apparatus where, from the starting point the animal can turn either right or left. Let us further imagine that the organism we are testing is quite hungry and that, whichever alternative he chooses, he obtains food. We can, then, vary one at a time a variety of factors to discover what the organism will ordinarily avoid doing. One would, of course, find many such factors which would lead the organism not to choose the alternative with which that factor is associated. Dissonance will be created for the organism if he is somehow tricked into consistently engaging in an activity involving such a factor.

This may sound very involved so let me try to say it again, this time, a bit less abstractly. Imagine that we test rats in a simple left-right choice apparatus and, no matter whether the animal goes left or right, he obtains food. But, imagine that, if he goes left, the animal must swim through water to get to the food but, if he goes right, there is simply a short run down an alley to the food. Let us further imagine that, under such circumstances, the animal will consistently choose to go to the right, that is, he will avoid swimming through water. Armed with this knowledge concerning the behavior of the rat we can then assert the following: if one puts a rat in a situation where we somehow trick the rat into consistently swimming through water, dissonance will have been created.

Remembering what we have already said about the ways in which dissonance can be reduced in this kind of situation (provided that we are successful in tricking the organism into continuing to engage in the activity) we would then arrive at the following statement: any condition which the animal will avoid in the above mentioned test situation will increase resistance to extinction in a nonchoice situation.

Let us look at some of the data which exist which are relevant to this statement. We know that if a hungry rat is put in a situation where he has a choice between a goal box where he is rewarded 100% of the time and a goal box where he is rewarded only part of the time, he will fairly consistently go to the place where he is rewarded 100% of the time. And, of course, we also know that where no choice is involved, partial reward increases resistance to extinction. But there are other variables or conditions which should increase resistance to extinction in a similar manner if our theoretical analysis is correct.

Consider the question of delay of reinforcement. Once more, thinking of our hypothetical test situation, we can be reasonably certain that a rat, if faced with a choice where one alternative led to immediate reward while the other alternative involved an appreciable delay before the rat was allowed to continue to the goal box to obtain food, the rat would rather consistently choose the alternative that led to immediate reward. We should then expect that, in a nonchoice situation, delay of reward should lead to greater resistance to extinction. Existing data show that this is indeed correct. Appreciable delay of reward does lead to greater resistance to extinction. I will briefly review some of the data which exist on delay of reward to give you some idea of the effect which is obtained.

The usual experiment that has been done on extinction following delay of reinforcement compares one condition in which the rats encounter no enforced delay between starting down a runway and obtaining food in the goal box with other conditions in which, on some trials, the rats are detained in a delay chamber before being allowed to proceed to the food. The usual period of delay which has been used has been about 30 seconds. Crum, Brown, and Bitterman (1951) and Scott and Wike (1956) both find that a group of rats delayed on half the trials shows much greater resistance to extinction than a group which was never delayed. In another experiment, Wike and McNemara (1957) ran three groups which differed in the percentage (and of course, number) of trials on which they were delayed. They find that the larger the percentage or number of trials on which the animal experiences delay, the greater is the resistance to extinction. The same kind of result is obtained by Fehrer (1956) who compared rats who were delayed for 20 seconds on *every* trial with ones who were never delayed. She also finds that delay results in increased resistance to extinction.

Before we proceed to other matters, I would like to briefly raise a question concerning one kind of explanation that has frequently, in one form or another, been offered to account for increased resistance to extinction after partial reward. The basis of this kind of explanation, whether it be in terms of expectancy, or conditioning of cues, or any of a number of other varieties, rests in pointing out that there is more similarity between acquisition and extinction for partial reward conditions than for 100% reward conditions. I would like to point out that this type of explanation is clearly not very useful in explaining the increased resistance to extinction after delay of reward. From the point of view of the explanation I am here proposing, however, partial reward and delay of reward clearly involve the same psychological processes.

Let us go on now to examine the matter of work and effort. I am sure it is fairly obvious to all of you now what I want to say about work and effort. If we return to a consideration of our hypothetical test situation we know that, given a choice between an effortless path to food and a path requiring expenditure of effort, the hungry animal will choose the effortless path rather regularly. Hence, in accordance with our analysis concerning dissonance and dissonance reduction, we would expect the requirement of greater effort during acquisition to lead to increased resistance to extinction.

It is surprising that, in spite of the relative consistency of results among the studies which exist in the literature, the effect of effort during acquisition on resistance to extinction has not been generally noted. People have rather tended to note the finding that the greater the effort required during extinction, the faster does extinction occur. But the data are also clear with respect to the effect of effort during acquisition. They show quite clearly that, holding effort during extinction constant, the more effort required during acquisition, the more resistance there is to extinction. The data from one of the more adequately controlled experiments will suffice to illustrate the effect.

Aiken (1957) reports an experiment in which the animal was required to press a panel in order to gain access to food. Some rats were required to exert little effort while others were required to exert considerable effort during training. Half of the animals in each condition were extinguished with the low effort requirement and half with the high effort requirement. Holding effort during extinction constant, the results show clearly that the average number of trials to a criterion of extinction was considerably greater for the high effort acquisition condition than for the low effort acquisition condition. Other experiments in the literature also show this same effect if one examines the data carefully. It should once more be pointed out that any explanation of this effect which depends upon a notion of similarity between acquisition and extinction conditions is clearly inadequate.

One could list many other specific conditions which, analyzed in the same way, would be expected to increase resistance to extinction. I have chosen the three preceding ones to discuss because reasonably good data concerning them exist in the literature. Now, however, I would like to return to a more thorough consideration of the partial reward situation.

I have stated that, on nonrewarded trials in a partial reward situation, dissonance is introduced into the animal's cognition when he realizes that there is no food available. The amount of dissonance can, of course, vary in magnitude. It is important for us to consider the operational variables which will affect the total magnitude of dissonance which is introduced in this manner. This total magnitude of dissonance, of course, will determine how much dissonance reduction occurs through the development of extra preferences (always assuming that the animal does not change his behavior) and hence will determine the resistance to extinction.

In the past, it has generally been assumed that the major operational variable affecting resistance to extinction is the ratio of reward. That is, the smaller the proportion of rewarded trials, the greater the resistance to extinction. However, one might reason that since dissonance is created for the animal on every nonrewarded trial, it seems plausible to suppose that the major operational variable which will affect the resistance to extinction is, rather, the sheer total number of nonrewarded trials which the animal has experienced

rather than the ratio of nonreward. From the data in published experiments it is impossible to assess whether or not this is correct since these two variables are completely confounded in the literature. Experiments on partial reward have always held constant either the number of rewarded trials or else the total number of trials that the animal experiences. It is clear, of course, that when either of these quantities is held constant, the number of nonrewarded trials is perfectly correlated with the ratio of nonreward and so the effects cannot be separated.

It is possible, perhaps, to get some hunch about this, however, from examining the results of experiments which have used rather few training trials. If we are correct, these experiments should show very weak effects of partial reward on resistance to extinction. Sheffield (1949), for example, using a total of 30 trials (only 15 nonrewarded trials) found very small differences between extinction after partial and complete reward. Wilson, Weiss, and Amsel (1955) and also Lewis (1956), replicating the Sheffield experiment almost exactly, also find such small differences that it requires an analysis of covariance to make them appear significant. However, Weinstock (1954), using a similar apparatus, but employing 75 training trials, finds huge and unmistakable differences.

It is unnecessary to belabor the matter by quoting many studies here since it is all a matter of hunch and impression. In general, when one goes through the literature one gets the impression that the experiments which show small effects after partial reward have tended to employ rather few trials. But comparison of this kind between different experiments done by different experimenters is a very shabby business at best since the variation from experimenter to experimenter can be quite large for unknown reasons. The question seemed important enough, however, so that Lawrence and I thought it worthwhile to do a study which could answer the question. The study was carried out through the kind efforts of John Theios. I would like to describe it to you briefly.

The general design of the study is very simple

Reward schedule	Number of unrewarded trials			
	0	16	27	72
33%		24	43	108
50%		31	54	144
67%		48		216
100%	0 54 216			

FIGURE 11.1

Total number of trials after preliminary training in partial reward experiment.

and does not differ in any essential way from the usual study which has been done on the effects of partial reward. The major difference was that we were primarily concerned with seeing the effects of the absolute number of nonrewarded trials and with being able to separate these effects from the effects of ratio of reward. We employed four different conditions of "number of unrewarded trials." Some groups experienced 0 unrewarded trials; some groups of animals experienced a total of 16 unrewarded trials in the apparatus; still other groups experienced a moderate number of unrewarded trials, namely, 27; and finally some groups were run who experienced very many unrewarded trials, namely, 72.

Within these conditions, by varying the total number of trials, different conditions of ratio of reward were set up. Some animals were run with 33% reward, others with 50% reward, and still others with 67% reward. Of course, it was not possible to vary the ratio of reward for animals in the condition of 0 unrewarded trials but the animals were run for varying numbers of trials anyhow. Figure 11.1 shows the total design. The numbers in the cells indicate the total number of trials after preliminary training which the animals in that condition ran. During preliminary training, of course, all groups were rewarded 100% of the time. There were between 11 and 16 animals in each condition. It will be noted that we did not run a condition of 67% reward and 27 unrewarded trials. The reason for this is simple. We ran out of patience and decided this condition was not essential.

It will also be noted that three groups of 0 unre-

warded trials were run so that the total number of trials brackets the entire range for the other groups.

Figure 11.2 shows the results of the experiment. Along the horizontal axis of the figure are indicated the various values of number of unrewarded trials which we employed and along the ordinate are the average number of trials to reach a criterion of extinction. Each circle on the figure represents the results for one of our experimental conditions. The empty circles represent the data for those with the fewest total number of trials. Thus, except for the 0 unrewarded trials conditions, these empty circles represent the data for the 33% reward conditions. Similarly, the dark circles represent the longest number of total trials and hence, for the partial reward groups, represent the 67% reward conditions.

It is clear from an examination of the figure that, holding constant the number of unrewarded trials, there were only slight differences among the different conditions of ratio of reward. On the other hand, the variable of total number of unrewarded trials has a large and significant effect. It would, indeed, seem that in these data the only variable affecting resistance to extinction after partial reward is the number of unrewarded trials. The results of the experiment are hence, quite consistent with the interpretations which we have made from the theory of dissonance.

These data are, of course, encouraging but cer-

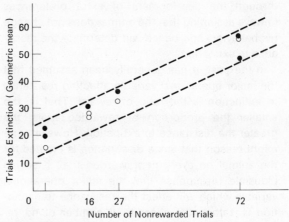

FIGURE 11.2

Number of trials to extinction after partial reward.

tainly not conclusive. It would be nice to be able to have more direct evidence that nonreward tends to result in the development of extra preferences. From the point of view of obtaining such more direct evidence concerning the validity of our theoretical interpretation, the partial reward situation is not very adequate. For one thing, our theoretical analysis states that quite different processes occur, psychologically, on rewarded and on unrewarded trials. In a partial reward situation, however, the animal experiences both kinds of trials and, hence, an attempt to separate the effects of the two kinds of trials is bound to be indirect. And, of course, the possibility always exists that the increased resistance to extinction may depend upon some more or less complicated interaction between rewarded and unrewarded trials.

It would then be desirable to be able to compare pure conditions of reward and nonreward. That is, we could test the theory more adequately if we could compare the resistance to extinction of two groups of animals, one of which had always been rewarded in a given place, and the other of which had *never* been rewarded in that same place. This, of course, presents technical problems of how one manages to induce an animal to consistently go to a place where he never gets rewarded. This problem, however, can be solved by employing a variation of what is, essentially, a delay of reward experiment. With the very able assistance and hard work of Edward Uyeno we proceeded to do a series of such experiments in an attempt to get more direct validation of our theoretical derivations. I would like to describe some of these experiments for you.

The apparatus we used was a runway with two boxes in addition to the starting box. The two boxes were, of course, quite easily distinguishable. We will refer to one of them as the end-box and to the other as the mid-box. From the starting place, the animal was to run through a section of alley to the mid-box and then through another section of alley to the end-box. One group of rats was fed on every trial in the mid-box and also fed on every trial in the end-box. We will refer to this group as the 100% reward condition. Another group of rats was never fed in the mid-box but, instead, was delayed there for the same amount of

time that it took the other to eat its food. These animals then continued to the end-box where they were also fed on every trial. We will refer to this group as the 0% reward condition. The designations of 100% and 0% reward refer, of course, to the reward in the mid-box. Both groups were rewarded on every trial in the end-box and this, of course, is what induced the animals in the 0% reward condition to run consistently to a place where they were never rewarded.

The procedure which was employed in extinction was also somewhat different from the usual procedure in a delay of reward experiment. Because we were interested in comparing the two groups of animals in their willingness to go to the mid-box where one group had always, and the other group had never, been fed, we ran extinction trials only from the starting position to the mid-box. During extinction, of course, no food was present for either condition and after a short period of time in the mid-box the animals were returned to their home cage. Thus, from this experiment we have a better comparison of the effects of reward and of nonreward. Figure 11.3 shows the average running times for the two groups during extinction.

The figure shows the data for the first 30 extinction trials averaged in groups of 3 trials each. It is

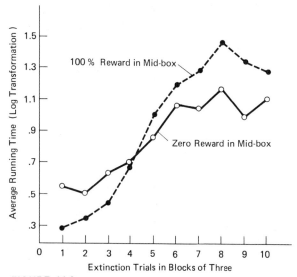

FIGURE 11.3
Running time during extinction in single mid-box experiment.

clear from the figure that there is a very marked difference between the two groups of animals. Those who were always fed in the mid-box start off running quite fast (reflecting their speed of running during acquisition) but slow down very rapidly. Those animals that were never fed in the mid-box start off more slowly (again reflecting their speed of running during acquisition) but they do not show as rapid a rate of extinction. Indeed, between the fourth and fifth blocks of trials the two curves cross over and thereafter the animals run considerably faster to a place where they have never been rewarded than they do to a place where they have always been rewarded.

One may certainly conclude from these data that increased resistance to extinction results from nonreward and that an explanation of the partial reward effect in terms of some interaction between reward and nonreward is not very tenable. Actually, in the experiment I have just described we ran a third group of animals which was rewarded 50% of the time in the mid-box and the results for these animals during extinction fall nicely midway between the two curves in Figure 11.3. The resistance to extinction of those who were never fed in the mid-box is greater than that of either of the other two groups of animals.

At the risk of being terribly repetitious, I would like to remind you at this point of the explanation I am offering for these data. Briefly, dissonance is introduced as a result of the insufficient reward or absence of reward. As long as the organism is prevented from changing his behavior, the dissonance tends to be reduced by developing some extra preference about something in the situation. The existence of this extra preference leads to the stronger inclination to continue running during extinction trials.

If this explanation is correct, however, one should be able to observe the effects of this extra preference even in a situation where all the motivation for food was removed. Indeed, it would seem that this would be a better test of this theoretical explanation. We consequently repeated the experiment I have just described to you with one modification. Three days were allowed to elapse between the end of acquisition and the beginning

of extinction. During these 3 days food was always present in the cages so that by the time the extinction trials started the animals were quite well fed and not hungry. Food remained always available in their cages during the extinction period. In addition, during the 3 intervening days, each animal was placed for periods of time in the end-box without food being available there. In other words, there was an attempt to communicate to the animal that food was no longer available in the apparatus and anyhow the animals were not very motivated for food.

Extinction trials were, of course, run just from the starting box to the mid-box. Three trials were run each day and Figure 11.4 shows the results for the first 10 days of extinction. It is clear from an examination of the figure that the results are very similar to the previous results and are, in a sense, even stronger. Those animals who were always fed in the mid-box start off relatively fast and as extinction trials progress the curve shows steady and rather rapid increase in running time. In short, one obtains a familiar kind of extinction curve for these animals.

The group that was never fed in the mid-box, however, shows a very different pattern of behavior. They start off much more slowly than the

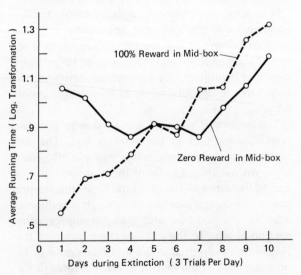

FIGURE 11.4
Running time while satiated during extinction in single mid-box experiment.

other group but, for the first 4 days of extinction, they actually run faster than at the beginning. By the seventh day the two curves have crossed and thereafter the 0% reward group runs faster than the 100% reward group. It is also interesting to note that, for the 0% reward group, through the eighth day, one can see no evidence of any extinction having occurred at all. If one is inclined to do so, one can certainly see in these data some evidence that an extra preference of rather weak strength exists for the animals that were never rewarded in the mid-box.

We were sufficiently encouraged by these results so that we proceeded to perform what I, at least, regarded as a rather ambitious experiment. Before I describe the experiment, let me briefly explain the reasoning which lay behind it. It is plausible to suppose that the extra preference which the organism develops in order to reduce dissonance may be focused on any of a variety of things. Let me explain this by using the experiment I have just described as an illustration. Those animals who were never fed in the mid-box, and thus experienced dissonance, could have developed a liking for the activity of running down the alley to the mid-box, they could have developed a preference for some aspect of the mid-box itself, or they could have developed a preference for any of the things they did or encountered subsequent to leaving the mid-box. Experimentally, of course, there was no control over this.

It occurred to us, in thinking about this, that if the dissonance were reduced, at least to some extent, by developing a preference for something about the *place* where the dissonance was introduced, then it would be possible to show the same effects in a very well controlled experiment. In other words, if the dissonance introduced by absence of reward were reduced, at least in part, by developing some liking for the place where they were not rewarded, then one could compare two groups of animals, both of which experienced the identical amount of dissonance, but who would be expected to develop preferences for different places.

To do this we used the same basic technique as in the previous two experiments I have described

but with an important modification. Instead of one mid-box, two mid-boxes were used. From the starting box the animals went to Mid-box A, from there to Mid-box B, and from there to the end-box where all animals received food on every trial. Two groups of animals were run in this experiment. Group A was delayed in Mid-box A for a period of time and then was allowed to run directly through Mid-box B to the end-box. Group B was allowed to run directly through Mid-box A but was delayed for a period of time in Mid-box B before being allowed to go to the end-box. In other words, both groups of animals had identical experience. The only difference between the groups lay in the particular box in which they were delayed. (All three boxes were, of course, quite distinctive.) For the extinction trials the animals were satiated as in the preceding experiment. For the extinction trials, the animals were run only from Box A to Box B. That is, during extinction the animals were placed directly into Box A, the door was then opened, and when they ran to Box B were removed to their home cage.

Thus, Group A during extinction was running away from the place where they had been delayed, while Group B was running to the place where they had been delayed. If some extra preference had developed for the place where they had been delayed, we would expect Group B to show more resistance to extinction than Group A. In short, during extinction, Group B should behave like the 0% reward groups in the previous experiments. Group A, however, should behave during extinction more like the 100% reward animals in the preceding experiments.

Figure 11.5 shows the data for these two groups of animals for the first 10 days of extinction, three trials having been run on each day. The two curves in the figure must, by now, look very familiar to you. The same result is obtained as in the two previous experiments. The initial difference between the two groups again reflects their previous running speed in that section of the apparatus. During acquisition, Group B ran more hesitantly in the section between the two mid-boxes than did Group A. This difference, of course, still exists at the start of the extinction trials. Thereafter, how-

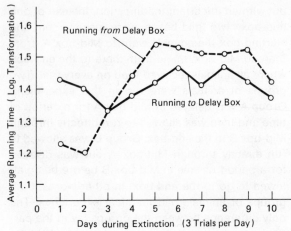

FIGURE 11.5
Running time while satiated during extinction in double mid-box experiment.

ever, Group A, which was running away from its delay box, rapidly increases its running time. Group B, which was running to its delay box, does not increase its time at all and shows no evidence of any extinction during 30 trials. By the fourth day of extinction, the two curves have crossed and thereafter Group B consistently runs faster than Group A.

If one looks carefully at all the data, I think one finds reasonable evidence that insufficient reward does lead to the development of extra preference. This extra preference, at least in the white rat, seems to be of a rather mild nature, but the magnitude of the effect is quite sufficient to account for the increased resistance to extinction after partial reward or after delay of reward.

Let us then briefly examine the implications of these findings and of the theory of dissonance for our traditional conception of how reward functions. It seems clear that the inclination to engage in behavior after extrinsic rewards are removed is not so much a function of past rewards themselves. Rather, and paradoxically, such persistence in behavior is increased by a history of nonrewards or inadequate rewards. I sometimes

like to summarize all this by saying that rats and people come to love things for which they have suffered.

REFERENCES

Aiken, E.G. The effort variable in the acquisition, extinction, and spontaneous recovery of an instrumental response. *J. exp. Psychol.,* 1957, **53,** 47–51.

Aronson, E., & Mills, J. The effect of severity of initiation on liking for a group. *J. abnorm. soc. Psychol.,* 1959, **59,** 177–181.

Crum, J., Brown, W.L., & Bitterman, M.E. The effect of partial and delayed reinforcement on resistance to extinction. *Amer. J. Psychol.,* 1951, **64,** 228–237.

Fehrer, E. Effects of amount of reinforcement and of pre- and postreinforcement delays on learning and extinction. *J. exp. Psychol.,* 1956, **52,** 167–176.

Festinger, L. *A theory of cognitive dissonance.* Evanston, Ill.. Row, Peterson, 1957.

Lewis, D.J. Acquisition, extinction, and spontaneous recovery as a function of percentage of reinforcement and intertrial intervals. *J. exp. Psychol.,* 1956, **51,** 45–53.

Scott, E.D., & Wike, E.L. The effect of partially delayed reinforcement and trial distribution on the extinction of an instrumental response. *Amer. J. Psychol.,* 1956, **69,** 264–268.

Sheffield, V.F. Extinction as a function of partial reinforcement and distribution of practice. *J. exp. Psychol.,* 1949, **39,** 511–526.

Weinstock, S. Resistance to extinction of a running response following partial reinforcement under widely spaced trials. *J. comp. physiol. Psychol.,* 1954, **47,** 318–322.

Wike, E.L., & McNemara, H.J. The effects of percentage of partially delayed reinforcement on the acquisition and extinction of an instrumental response. *J. comp. physiol. Psychol.,* 1957, **50,** 348–351.

Wilson, W., Weiss, E.J., & Amsel, A. Two tests of the Sheffield hypothesis concerning resistance to extinction, partial reinforcement, and distribution of practice. *J. exp. Psychol.,* 1955, **50,** 51–60.

When is the best time to try and teach a child language? Gertrud L. Wyatt answers this question, focusing on the problem of how to program the child to talk. In the next paper, which is also concerned with human communication, Ray L. Birdwhistell considers how some kinds of information—in this case, sexual communication—are transmitted nonverbally from person to person. Finally, R. Allen and Beatrice T. Gardner describe the outcome of a fascinating project they conducted aimed at teaching sign language to a chimpanzee.

Part VI
SOME FUNDAMENTALS OF LANGUAGE AND COMMUNICATION

No one has been able to construct a computer to challenge a mother's ability to teach a child how to talk. If the input (mother's verbal teaching) is correct, the output (the child's mastery of thousands of words and sentences) is fantastic. But just as computers make mistakes as enormous as their achievements, so mothers often snarl up their communications with their children.

Consider the case of Tom and Steve, 4½-year-old twins, who are looking at a picture book with their mother:

Steve: How do the aya-pa go?

Mother: (*who has understood Steve's question*) It takes an elephant 15 years to reach mature size. Elephants are mammals with an enormous appetite.

Steve: (*pointing to a lizard*) How do da-ying go?

Tom: (*echoing*) How do da-ying go?

Mother: What?

Steve: (*angrily*) Da-ying. Da-ying. How do da-ying go?

Mother: (*finally getting the message*) Oh, that thing! That is a prehistoric lizard.

Obviously the communication between mother and the twins had gone wrong somewhere. The boys talked a lot, but most of the time no one could understand them. With the best of intentions, their mother had flooded them with so much information that you might say she had overloaded their systems. The language program she presented did not fit the boys' stage of development, so communication between mother and sons broke down.

Steve and Tom responded quite differently to another language program. A teacher looked at the picture book with them, this time at a picture of a farm.

Teacher: (*slowly and distinctly*) A barn.

Tom: A barn. A big barn.

Teacher: A horse. A horse. Another horse.

Tom: A hort. Anover hort.

Teacher: A hor-se. A horse. Another horse.

Tom: A horse.

Teacher: Yes, Tom. That's right. A horse.

12
In the Beginning Is the Word

Gertrud L. Wyatt

Feeding short words slowly, a few at a time, repeating them often, the teacher presented a much simpler language program to the children, whose discrimination of speech sounds had not progressed beyond the 2-year-old level. The mother had given the twins a language program that had been too complex for them. Her rapid speech and over-sophisticated vocabulary had overloaded the little boys' receiving systems to the point that they had been unable to distinguish and remember single sounds and sequences of sounds.

It was easy enough to explain these facts to the mother and to help her to use a more appropriate language program. First, she was given the basic two rules for successful verbal interaction between adults and children: The adult must find out what words the child understands, and the adult must match his style of speech to that of the child — not the other way around.

Close though it is, the analogy between computers and mother-child interaction eventually breaks down. A child is not a computer into which we simply inset a program. Parents and children contact on many levels — verbal and non-verbal. There is the sensory-motor level, the linguistic level and the level of feelings. Love, trust, acceptance or rejection, anger and fear will color the choice of words and the interpretation of those words.

It is a fact that without careful and continuous programing, no child, however well endowed physically and mentally, would learn language efficiently. Fortunately, most adults have a built-in aptitude for teaching children their first language. Parents and children all over the world play "games of mutual imitation," as Jean Piaget, the famous Swiss psychologist, called them. Such games with their endless repetitions are hugely enjoyed by adults and child alike. Anyone interested in understanding how children acquire skills can observe the process easily enough. "Communication watching" can be indulged in at the beach, in the supermarket, in a kitchen where a mother and her children are having a meal together. The communication watcher will soon find out that parents of all social classes and levels of education can be excellent or poor language programers, that their individual style of talking with their children may either facilitate the child's language development or inhibit it. As one psychologist said, it is not so much what the parents *are* but what they do that counts.

An observation, made in a London taxicab, illustrates this point. Getting from one railroad station to another I had to share a cab with a grandmother and a young mother with two children, a girl of 7 months and a boy of 2 years, standing at the window. While the mother cuddled the baby, the grandmother acted as the boy's language teacher, talking to him almost constantly.

Grandmother: Look, Johnny, look. We are riding in a taxi. We are going home in a taxi. See the taximan. Taximan. See the taximan.

Johnny: (looking out the window) Taximan. Taximan.

Grandmother: Yes, Johnny, taximan. We are riding in a taxi. Look, Johnny (*pointing to the fountains at Trafalgar Square*). Look! Water! Water (*aside to mother*) He wouldn't know what a fountain is.

Johnny: Water. Water.

Baby: (starts to babble) Oohahwooaah.

Grandmother: (looking at the baby, echoes) Oohahwooaah.

This grandmother was being an excellent language teacher. Using simple words and short phrases, she provided the boy with labels for his experiences, thus giving him "verbal input." She did not need to study linguistics to know that it was wiser to teach him the word "water" rather than the less common one "fountain." Johnny repeated his grandmother's words again and again. Articulating the sounds he heard and connecting them with their meanings, he stored the words and their sounds in his memory, ready for "verbal output" when needed. Thus, he learned the two vital skills of "decoding" (understanding the meaning of words spoken by others) and "encoding" (putting his own images and ideas into words.)

During the episode in the taxicab, it was particularly striking to observe that the grandmother repeated the child's words and phrases much more often than the boy repeated hers. Psychologists, analyzing the language development of some children between 18 and 30 months, found that mothers repeated the children's words about three times as often as the children imitated their mothers' words.

Grandmother not only imitated the boy's words, but when the baby began to babble a string of sounds, she also imitated the sounds.

Another vignette, this one of 4-year-old Lisa and her mother who are looking at a picture together demonstrates the variety of communication skills parents teach in a seemingly artless and casual way.

Lisa: (*pointing to the picture*) This is my cat.

Mother: Where is the cat?

Lisa: Up a tree. He wouldn't come home for his supper. The daddy cat wasn't home?

Mother: He wasn't home?

Lisa: No, he runned up a tree.

Mother: Oh, he ran up a tree!

Lisa: (*turns the page and looks at another picture*) Look at the man. He is writing on the thing.

Mother: That's a typewriter. He is writing on the typewriter.

Lisa: (*losing interest*) I am hot (*she puts the book on the floor*).

Mother: If you are through, put the book away.

Lisa: (*pointing to bookcase*) Over here?

Mother: Yes, over there. Put it on the middle shelf.

Lisa: (*touching the middle shelf*) This one?

Mother: That's right. You are a good girl.

We should not hesitate to call this an ideal teaching-learning situation. In about five minutes the mother not only taught Lisa words and their meanings as well as correct patterns of grammar, she also brought Lisa's attention to fine differences between words: "over here" versus "over there" or the "middle" shelf. Thus the mother was teaching not only sounds, words and sentence patterns, but also concepts, similarities and dissimilarities, all indispensable to the development of thinking. And there was even more to it: mother and child shared the joys of learning and of communicating.

If we wish to teach a child, we must respect him and his feelings. Parents who are preoccupied with other people or things may brush aside a child and communication may break down completely, as happened in the following situation.

Mrs. Brown, 4-year-old Cathy, 2-year-old Bobby, and a friend of Mrs. Brown's were at the beach together. The two women were sunning themselves and chatting when Bobby came up from the water with a stone that he offered to his mother. "Okay," said Mrs. Brown, taking the stone and putting it down on the sand. Bobby walked away, but immediately returned with another stone. With some annoyance she said: "Okay, okay, go down to the water!" Bobby picked up his stone and seemed about to throw it. "Don't throw it, don't throw it, get down to the water," called his mother sharply.

Bobby obeyed. He stood at the water's edge for a moment, then he caught sight of his sister Cathy who was running toward the mother. He ran after her, smiling and pointing at his mother.

Cathy flopped down in the sand near her mother and said "Will you help me build a castle?" The mother and Cathy were already building in the sand when Bobby reached them. Pointing at the sand structure, he called excitedly, "Whatisit? Whatisit, Mommy?" His mother took a piece of tissue paper and wiped his nose. She did not answer his question. Suddenly Bobby smashed the sand castle with his foot. Cathy cried out and the mother said angrily to Bobby, "Why did you do that? Get down to the water, I say!" As Bobby made no move to go, she took him by the arm and pushed him toward the water. Bobby turned around and moved to the other woman, saying, "Dat's a boat, is it? Dat's a boat, is it?" The other woman did not hear him. His voice was drowned out by the radio she had turned on.

The mother had continually rejected Bobby. She did not respond to his requests for information, she disregarded his offerings, she seemed to take no pleasure in the child and her tone of voice in talking to him was always angry. When she played with Cathy, she had excluded Bobby even to the point of not answering his question about what they were making. Bobby had shown his frustration in various ways, all of them nonverbal, finally smashing his sister's sand castle.

In programing a child's language, timing is of great importance. A parent who insists on giving information at a time when the child is either unable or unwilling to listen, will not help the child in learning language. During a fireworks display, the following exchange between a father and his 3-year-old daughter was heard. The little girl, wiggling in her father's arms, kept saying, "I want to go, I want to go!"

The father assured her, "There won't be any more loud bangs!" But the fireworks and the bangs continued. The father exclaimed; "Isn't that a pretty one! Swoosh! Swish! Swoosh! Clap your hands, clap!"

The little girl remained silent, moving in her father's arms with increasing restlessness. "There goes another one," continued the father. "Isn't that pretty! Say Swoosh! Swoosh! Swoosh!"

The child, getting more and more agitated, finally started crying. "I want to go home! I want to go home!"

The father's interest in the fireworks had blinded him to the child's distress. His naive attempts at making her talk were useless. Trying to defend herself against an overwhelming experience, the child had tuned out, excluding the messages from her father as well as the explosions of the fireworks.

Some children communicate superbly even though their linguistic skills may be quite faulty, while others master the English language but refrain from communicating. These vital differences tell us much about the child's feelings about himself and about the world around him. Watching a group of third-graders during a period of language training, we become aware of how wide these differences can be.

The teacher, working with a group of six children, had given them a large sheet of wrapping paper and some crayons. The children sat on the floor around the paper and the teacher said: "Now, each boy and girl can draw his own world. Draw whatever you think of, whatever you would like to have in your own world. Draw anything you want. Draw the way you feel and let's talk about it afterwards!"

Nicky, Jerry and Josh sat on one side of the paper: Ann, Sue and Dan on the other. The chil-dren immediately went to work. Ann, Sue and Dan stayed on their side of the paper. While they worked they talked to themselves, to each other, or to the teacher. Jerry, a black boy, and Josh, a white one, were the obvious leaders of the group. Josh moved over to the narrow side of the paper and drew an enormous skyscraper over most of the paper. Jerry, on his side, drew a huge mountain spitting fire and flames all around. As each boy claimed more and more territory, their drawings began to overlap. The two boys talked, shouted, laughed, pushed each other around. As Jerry's volcano spat fire over Josh's building, Josh drew Superman and his airplane on top of Jerry's mountain.

There was total communication between the two: "My fire get him, you watch out, you big house! Oh no, my Superman is coming! Bzzzzzz! Bzzzz! Pshsh! Watch out! Here he goes! No, he ain't! I get you a superwoman! That's what you get. Here is a superwoman." When the teacher asked them about "their world," Josh and Jerry answered together, using the "we" form, "We have a fight. We have a volcano and a superman. It's great!"

With all the excitement generated by Josh and Jerry, little attention had been paid to Nicky. Nicky had mapped out a small corner of the paper, drawing a line around it. Behind this protective barrier he had drawn a conventional little house and a stiff little tree. He did not speak and nobody spoke to him. The teacher turned to Nicky and asked him to tell her something about his world and what he felt about it. Nicky, sitting on the floor, pulled away from the drawing until his back reached the wall behind him. In a whisper he said, "A tree. A house."

It would be wrong to assume that Nicky's language training had been neglected. The teacher reported that Nicky was able to write elaborate stories, demonstrating a excellent command of language for his age. This fearful child had learned all the necessary skills, but transforming language into living speech, reaching out to others to communicate with them, was impossible for him.

Jerry and Josh communicated their feelings,

their ideas, their fantasies, through their bodies, their tone of voice, their laughter, their drawings as well as their words. Their vocabulary was limited, their grammar often incorrect and their spelling impressionistic, but all this could be learned. Nicky, however, needed a form of therapeutic communication with a trained helper over a long period of time. Only through such small group therapy can Nicky, and children like him, find the courage to relate to others and discover the joys of communicating.

Watching children like these teaches us that the job of parents is infinitely more delicate and more complex than that of programing a computer. Machines have been put to good use, recently, to teach college students the accent and grammar of a foreign language. Communication between students and faculty, however, or between parents and children, asks for sincerity of thoughts and feelings, and for degrees of mutual understanding and adaptation which transcend all machines and their programs.

13
The Tertiary Sexual Characteristics of Man: A Fundamental in Human Communication

Ray L. Birdwhistell

Zoologists and biologists have over the years accumulated archives of data which attest to the complex ordering animal gender display, courtship and mating behavior. Until recently, the implications of much of this data has been obscured by the governing assumption that this behavior was, while intricate and obviously patterned, essentially a mechanical and instinctual response to a genetically based program. There has been, however, an increasing realization that intra-gender and inter-gender behavior throughout the animal kingdom is not simply a response to instinctual mechanisms but is shaped, structured and released, both by the ontogenetic experiences of the participating organisms and by the patterned circumstances of the surround. Behavioral scientists focussing upon human behavior have been forced to relinquish the ethnocentric assumption that human gender and sexual behavior was qualitatively different from that of other animals. Many have conceded that culture, a human invention, is not interpreted profitably as a device for curbing and ordering "animalistic," "brutal," "beastial" or instinctual appetites. The elaborate regulation of fish, bird and mammalian courtship and mating behavior has been of particular interest to sociologists and anthropologists. That this interest has not been more productive seems to me to be at least in part a function of a confusion in the ordering of gender-centered behavior. In the discussion to follow, utilizing certain insights derived from communicational analysis, I wish to focus upon one aspect of gender-related interactional behavior—that of gender identification and response.

Biologists have long been aware that the clear demarcation between the production of ova and of spermatazoa in organisms of a bi-sexual species is not necessarily accompanied by any comparable moiety in the distribution of secondary sexual characteristics. In some species there is such extreme gender-linked dimorphism that only the

Ray L. Birdwhistell, "Masculinity and Femininity as Display," *Kinesics and Context: Essays on Body Motion Communication* (Philadelphia: University of Pennsylvania Press, 1970), pp. 39–40; also from Ray L. Birdwhistell, *Kinesics and Context,* Copyright © Ray L. Birdwhistell, 1971, published by Penguin Books Ltd. This article is a slight abridgement of an address before the American Association for the Advancement of Science, Montreal, Canada, 1964.

specialist in the particular species can recognize that males and females are conspecial. At the other extreme, some species are so uni-morphic that near-surgical techniques are required to determine the gender of isolated individuals. By and large, researchers concerned with human behavior have assumed that in relatively unimorphic species there were subtle differences in the perceptible taxonomy of males and females which were easily recognizable by conspecifics even if difficult to detect by humans. However, it would be difficult for any reader, conversant with Lorenz's description of the difficulties involved the mating of greylag geese, (4) to maintain the fiction that gender differences are at all apparent to the membership of a uni-morphic species. There is humor and a certain pathos in the situation when two greylag males meet and each acts as though the other were a member of the opposite sex. Only the reproductive rate of greylags gives us confidence that even a goose can solve such a problem.

The social biologist, Peter Klopfer, has pointed out that, even with the incomplete evidence now at hand, it would be possible to establish a spectrum of species rated by the extent of their sexual dimorphism. (5) Insofar as I have been able to determine no such list has been prepared. However, by establishing an ideal typical gamut with an uni-morphic species at one end and an extreme of dimorphy at the other it has been possible to make a tentative placement of Homo sapiens on this scale. Obviously, the position of any particular species on this scale is a function of both the number of species chosen and of the special characteristics of the selected species. When, however, the secondary sexual characteristics themselves are stressed, (whether visibly, audibly or olfactorily perceptible,) man seems far closer to the uni-morphic end of the spectrum than heretofore suspected.

Physical anthropologists have long pointed out that if such anatomical markers as differential bone structure or the distribution of body hair are used, the measurement of human population reveals no bi-modal curve in the distribution of secondary sexual characteristics. Most authorities agree that instead of a single curve shaped ⌒⌒ ,

we find two overlapping bell curves: ⌒⌒. "Masculinity" and "femininity" in aural sound production seems to be distributed in a similar manner following puberty. There is as yet no evidence that there is a significant difference in the olfactible chemicals released by human males and females. This may be a function of the crudity of our available measuring instruments, but at the present, odor does not seem to function as a gender marker for humans.

The case for the relative unimorphy or the weak dimorphy of Homo sapiens should not be overstressed for the purposes of this argument. The upright position of humans obviously makes for clear visibility of differential mammary development and for the easy display of the genitalia. These may provide sufficient signals in themselves. However, certain pieces of data permit us to discount these as definitive of gender in and of themselves. First, we have long been aware that children do not, even in societies as preoccupied with these organs as is ours, immediately note the gender definitional qualities of either the external genitalia or the differential mammary development. I doubt seriously that this represents some psychological denial function in the child's perception of his universe. The near universality of the G-string or other clothing protecting, obscuring or hiding the genital region, even in societies with minimal shame or embarrassment about genital display, would tend to rule out a primary importance of genitalia display for gender identification. Furthermore, the fact that the more prominent breasts of females or the less prominent breasts of males do not seem to have universal sexual stimulus value would seem to support our deemphasis upon mammary dimorphism as gender identifiers. Needless to say, however, until we have more systematic knowledge about clothing and other cosmetological devices we are not going to be able to settle this particular question. There is no reason to make the apriori assumption that uncovered breasts are more or less obvious than covered ones (except of course, to those trained to make these distinctions). It seems permissible to procede in our discussion while holding this aspect of human di-morphy open for future investigation.

My work in kinesics (the study of human body motion communication) leads me to postulate that man and probably a number of other weakly dimorphic species necessarily organize much of gender display and recognition at the level of position, movement and expression. It seems methodologically useful to me to distinguish between *primary* sexual characteristics which relate to the physiology of the production of fertile ova or spermatazoa, the *secondary* sexual characteristics which are anatomic in nature and the *tertiary* sexual characteristics which are patterned social behavioral in form. These latter are learned and are situationally produced.

Let me hasten to say that the terms, "primary," "secondary" and "tertiary" imply no functional priorities. There seems plenty of reason to believe that these levels are mutually inter-influencing. Patterned social behavior seems to be required to permit the necessary physiological functioning prerequisite to successful and fertile mating. (6) And, we have at least anecdotal evidence and clinical reports that certain of the secondary sexual characteristics respond both to the physiological underlog and to the social behavioral surround. However, as are all inter-level emergent mechanisms, this is complex. I can only hope that premature rationalization of this by reductionistic explication, by assignment to a catch basin called "psycho-somatic" or by cultural determinism will not foreclose against multi-level investigation.

I have worked with informants from seven different societies. It has been clear from their responses that not only could native informants distinguish male movement from female movement (and the items of what was regarded as "masculine" and "feminine" varied from society to society) but they easily detected different degrees of accentuation or diminution of such movement depending upon the situation. In all of these societies (Chinese, middle and upper class London British, Kutenai, Shushwap, Hopi, Parisian French and American) both male and female informants distinguished not only typically male communicational behavior from typically female communicational behavior but, when the opportunity presented itself, distinguished "feminine" males and "masculine" females. This is not to say that any informant could make a complete and explicit list of "masculine" or "feminine" behaviors. However, each culture did have stereotypes which could be acted out or roughly described. That the behavior abstracted by the informants did not always coincide with the observable reactions to the general range of scientifically abstractable gender-identifying behavior should not come as a surprise to any field worker who has tried to elicit micro-cultural behavior from native informants. One comment should be included here before we turn for examples to the body motion communicational system most intensively studied, the American. Informants from all of these societies either volunteered or without hesitation responded that young children matured into these behaviors and that as people got older they gave up or matured out of them. As might be expected, both the propedeutic period and the duration of the active gender display varied from society to society. Furthermore, while most informants agreed that in their particular society some individuals learned how to accentuate or obscure these signals, informants from all of these societies interpreted the differences as instinctually and biologically based.

I have no data which would permit me to assess the relative emphasis American culture places upon gender display and recognition as compared to other societies. However it is quite clear that within American society class and regional variations occur—not so much in the signals themselves as in the relative youth of the expectable incorporation of such messages, the duration and situationality of their performance and of the accentuation of these as contrasted to other identification signals discussed elsewhere. (7) Limitations of time preclude the presentation of these local and class differences here.

For the purpose of illustration, I should like to present a few of the most easily recognizable American gender identification signals. Two are derived from the analysis of posture, one from "facial expression." Subject to exact measurement are the male-female differences in intra-femoral angle and arm body angle. American females, when sending gender signals and/or as a reciprocal to male gender signals bring the legs together, at times to the point that the upper legs cross, either in a full leg cross *with feet still together,* the lateral aspects of the two feet parallel to each other, or in standing knee over knee. In contrast, the American male position is one in which the intrafemoral index ranges up to a ten or fifteen degree angle. Comparably, the American female gender presentation arm position involves the proximation of the upper arms to the trunk while the male in gender presentation moves the arms some five to ten degrees away from the body. In movement, the female may present the entire body from neck to ankles as a moving whole, whereas the male moves the arms independent of the trunk. The male may subtly wag his hips with a slight right and left presentation with a movement which involves a twist at the base of the thorasic cage and at the ankles.

Another body position involved in gender presentation is made possible by the flexibility of the pelvic spinal complex. In gender identification the American male tends to carry his pelvis rolled slightly back as contrasted with the female anterior roll. If the range of pelvic positioning is depicted as ⌣ , the female position can be depicted as ⌣ , the male as ⌣ . As males and females grow older or in pathology over or underemphasize gender messages, the male and female position can become almost indistinguishable, or become bizarrely inappropriate.

One more example may be sufficient for our point. Lid and eye behavior are often referred to by informants as masculine or feminine. However, only careful observation and measurement reveal that the structural components of circumorbital behavior related to the prohibition of male lid closure with a movement of the position of the eyeballs while the lids are closed. Comparably, the communicative convention prescribes that unless accompanying signals indicate sleepiness or distress, males should close and open their lids in a relatively continuous movement. Let me stress again that these positions, movements and expressions are culturally coded — that what is masculine in one culture is feminine in another.

I have presented the examples above with a hes-itation occasioned by past experience. Inevitably have such examples been interpreted as the messages males and females send to each other when they wish consciously or unconsciously to invite coitus. Let me say it simply and firmly: *No position, expression or movement ever carries meaning in and of itself.* It is true that in certain contexts gender display, appropriately responded to, is an essential element in the complex interchange between humans preliminary to courtship, to coitus and, even, to mating. However, the identical behavior inappropriately presented may have the opposite function; it may prevent the development of the interaction that might culminate in a more intimate interpersonal exchange. (8) For example, a prematurely presenting male may define a situation in such a manner that the female cannot respond without considerable role sacrifice. Thus, the male can prevent coitus and, even, courtship from occurring by presenting in a manner which defines his action as insufficiently directed to the receiving female. The so-called "sexy" female can by inappropriate gender display effectively protect herself against intimate heterosexual involvement. The male who sends "feminine" or pubescent and awkward "masculine" display signals may in one context be signalling to a male, in another he de-genderizes his female respondent by returning a message appropriate to female-female interaction than a male-female interaction. Furthermore, while it is not at all difficult to detect in context the message sent by either a male or a female which reads "I wish to be considered a homo-sexual," we have been able to isolate no message, masculine or feminine which is in itself an indicant of homosexuality or heterosexuality when such sexuality is measured by active genital participation.

For the sociologist and the anthropologist, a more important aspect of the possibility of decoding the given society's gender display and recognition system is that such a code provides him with a tool for more adequately studying the division of labor as operant in the day to day life of a community. Social role and status theory has been very useful at one level of social investigation. However, when the researcher seeks to relate such theory to problems of social learning, to personality and character development, or to the solution of individual and social problems, he all too often is prevented from testing high level generalizations in the crucible of behavior. Gender identity and relationship is only one of a range of nodal points coded into the communicational system. Kinesic and linguistic research has demonstrated, at least for American society, that such nodal behavior never stands alone—it is always modified by other identification signals and by the structured nature of the context of the occurrence of the behavior. In these complex but decodable behaviors lies the proof that gender behavior is not limited to a sexual response and that sexual behavior is not always *either* genital or uncompleted genital behavior.

In the discussion thus far an attempt has been made to demonstrate the methodological rectitude and convenience of ordering gender-related phenomena into primary, secondary and tertiary characteristics. Tertiary sexual behavior has been described as learned and patterned communicative behavior which is identificatory behavior in the American body motion communication system have been presented with the fiat that gender display or response is not necessarily sexually provocative or responsive and is probably never exclusively genital in nature. The paper was introduced with a discussion of the relatively weak di-morphy in the human secondary sexual characteristics structure. Until more animal societies are studied *qua* societies and until the nature of the range of possibilities for differential structuralization of the division of labor has been investigated in these animal societies, we cannot make any final appraisal of the cross-speciational import of unimorphy or dimorphy as a base line for social interaction. However, we are in a position to postulate that for human society at least, the weak dimorphy creates an opportunity for the development of intricate and flexible tertiary sexual characteristics which can be variably exploited as nodal points in the division of labor.

Finally, in a society like ours, with its complex division of labor and with the rapid change in social role as related to gender, we should not be surprised to find that the youth have considerable difficulty in learning appropriate intra- and inter-gender messages. Nor should we be surprised to find that in such a society that messages about sex and gender can become a preoccupation. Children who become confused about the meaning of gender messages can become adults with difficulty in comprehending the relationship between the male and the female roles in a changing society. Only the fact that children can learn in spite of parental teaching protects us from a situation in which accumulating discrepancy could destroy the necessary conditions for appropriate mating. There is no evidence for the popular statement that men in Western European society are becoming "weaker" or that women are becoming "stronger"—there is considerable evidence that both are confused in their communication with each other about such matters.

REFERENCES

1. Bateson, Gregory. *Naven* A survey of the problems suggested by a composite picture of a New Guinea tribe drawn from three points of view. Cambridge, England, 1936.

2. Mead, Margaret. While Mead has demonstrated her interest in a wide range of publications in animal behavior over the past 30 years possibly the best summary can be seen in *Continuities in Cultural Evolution* Terry Lectures; New Haven and London, Yale University Press 1964. Of special historical relevance to this whole problem is her Male and Female, 3rd edition (New York. William Morrow and Co.), 1953.

3. *Group Processes* (5 Vols. 1954, 1955, 1956, 1957 and 1958) (ed.) Bertram Schaffner, Josiah Macy, Jr., *Foundation,* New York.

4. Lorenz, Konrad. "The Role of Aggression in Group Formation" *Group Processes,* Transactions of the 4th Conference, 1957 pp. 181 ff.

5. Personal Communication, Philadelphia, 1954. *See* Klopfer discussion of the information of dimorphy in his *Behavioral Aspects of Ecology* (Englewood Cliffs, New Jersey, Prentice Hall), 1962, pp. 136–137.

6. For a detailed cogent discussion for biologically appropriate and inappropriate context for mating, Calhoun, John B. "The Ecology and Sociology of the Norway Rat," Public Health Service 1008. (Washington, D.C.: U.S. Government Printing Office), 1963.

7. Birdwhistell, Ray L. "Paralanguage: 25 Years After Sapir," in *Lectures on Experimental Psychiatry,* Henry W. Brosin, ed. (Pittsburgh: University of Pittsburgh Press), 1961.

_____. "Communication as a Multi-Channel System" *International Encyclopedia of the Social Sciences* (in press).

8. Scheflen, Albert E. "Quasi Sexual Behavior in Psychotherapy" (paper to be published).

The extent to which another species might be able to use human language is a classical problem in comparative psychology. One approach to this problem is to consider the nature of language, the processes of learning, the neural mechanisms of learning and of language, and the genetic basis of these mechanisms, and then, while recognizing certain gaps in what is known about these factors, to attempt to arrive at an answer by dint of careful scholarship (1). An alternative approach is to try to teach a form of human language to an animal. We chose the latter alternative and, in June 1966, began training an infant female chimpanzee, named Washoe, to use the gestural language of the deaf. Within the first 22 months of training it became evident that we had been correct in at least one major aspect of method, the use of a gestural language. Additional aspects of method have evolved in the course of the project. These and some implications of our early results can now be described in a way that may be useful in other studies of communicative behavior. Accordingly, in this article we discuss the considerations which led us to use the chimpanzee as a subject and American Sign Language (the language used by the deaf in North America) as a medium of communication; describe the general methods of training as they were initially conceived and as they developed in the course of the project; and summarize those results that could be reported with some degree of confidence by the end of the first phase of the project.

PRELIMINARY CONSIDERATIONS

The Chimpanzee as a Subject

Some discussion of the chimpanzee as an experimental subject is in order because this species is relatively uncommon in the psychological laboratory. Whether or not the chimpanzee is the most intelligent animal after man can be disputed; the

14
Teaching Sign Language to a Chimpanzee

R. Allen Gardner and Beatrice T. Gardner

Reprinted with slight abridgement from *Science*, vol. 165, August 15, 1969, pp. 664–672. Copyright 1969 by the American Association for the Advancement of Science.

gorilla, the orangutan, and even the dolphin have their loyal partisans in this debate. Nevertheless, it is generally conceded that chimpanzees are highly intelligent, and that members of this species might be intelligent enough for our purposes. Of equal or greater importance is their sociability and their capacity for forming strong attachments to human beings. We want to emphasize this trait of sociability; it seems highly likely that it is essential for the development of language in human beings, and it was a primary consideration in our choice of a chimpanzee as a subject.

Affectionate as chimpanzees are, they are still wild animals, and this is a serious disadvantage. Most psychologists are accustomed to working with animals that have been chosen, and sometimes bred, for docility and adaptability to laboratory procedures. The difficulties presented by the wild nature of an experimental animal must not be underestimated. Chimpanzees are also very strong animals; a full-grown specimen is likely to weigh more than 120 pounds (55 kilograms) and is estimated to be from three to five times as strong as a man, pound-for-pound. Coupled with the wildness, this great strength presents serious difficulties for a procedure that requires interaction at close quarters with a free-living animal. We have always had to reckon with the likelihood that at some point Washoe's physical maturity will make this procedure prohibitively dangerous.

A more serious disadvantage is that human speech sounds are unsuitable as a medium of communication for the chimpanzee. The vocal apparatus of the chimpanzee is very different from that of man (2). More important, the vocal behavior of the chimpanzee is very different from that of man. Chimpanzees do make many different sounds, but generally vocalization occurs in situations of high excitement and tends to be specific to the exciting situations. Undisturbed, chimpanzees are usually silent. Thus, it is unlikely that a chimpanzee could be trained to make refined use of its vocalizations. Moreover, the intensive work of Hayes and Hayes (3) with the chimpanzee Viki indicates that a vocal language is not appropriate for this species. The Hayeses used modern, sophisticated, psychological methods and seem to have spared no effort to teach Viki to make speech sounds. Yet in 6 years Viki learned only four sounds that approximated English words (4).

Use of the hands, however, is a prominent feature of chimpanzee behavior; manipulatory mechanical problems are their forte. More to the point, even caged, laboratory chimpanzees develop begging and similar gestures spontaneously (5), while individuals that have had extensive contact with human beings have displayed an even wider variety of communicative gestures (6). In our choice of sign language we were influenced more by the behavioral evidence that this medium of communication was appropriate to the species than by anatomical evidence of structural similarity between the hands of chimpanzees and of men. The Hayeses point out that human tools and mechanical devices are constructed to fit the human hand, yet chimpanzees have little difficulty in using these devices with great skill. Nevertheless, they seem unable to adapt their vocalizations to approximate human speech.

Psychologists who work extensively with the instrumental conditioning of animals become sensitive to the need to use responses that are suited to the species they wish to study. Lever-pressing in rats is not an arbitrary response invented by Skinner to confound the mentalists; it is a type of response commonly made by rats when they are first placed in a Skinner box. The exquisite control of instrumental behavior by schedules of reward is achieved only if the original responses are well chosen. We chose a language based on gestures because we reasoned that gestures for the chimpanzee should be analogous to bar-pressing for rats, key-pecking for pigeons, and babbling for humans.

American Sign Language

Two systems of manual communication are used by the deaf. One system is the manual alphabet, or finger spelling, in which configurations of the hand correspond to letters of the alphabet. In this system the words of a spoken language, such as English, can be spelled out manually. The other system, sign language, consists of a set of manual configurations and gestures that correspond to particular words or concepts. Unlike finger spelling, which is the direct encoding of a spoken language, sign languages have their own rules of usage. Word-for-sign translation between a spoken language and a sign language yields results that are similar to those of word-for-word translation between two spoken languages: the translation is often passable, though awkward, but it can also be ambiguous or quite nonsensical. Also, there are national and regional variations in sign languages that are comparable to those of spoken languages.

We chose for this project the American Sign Language (ASL), which, with certain regional variations, is used by the deaf in North America. This particular sign language has recently been the subject of formal analysis (7). The ASL can be compared to pictograph writing in which some symbols are quite arbitrary and some are quite representational or iconic, but all are arbitrary to some degree. For example, in ASL the sign for "always" is made by holding the hand in a fist, index finger extended (the pointing hand), while rotating the arm at the elbow. This is clearly an arbitrary representation of the concept "always." The sign for "flower," however, is highly iconic; it is made by holding the fingers of one hand extended, all five fingertips touching (the tapered hand), and touching the fingertips first to one nostril then to the other, as if sniffing a flower. While this is an iconic sign for "flower," it is only one of a number of conventions by which the concept "flower" could be iconically represented; it is thus arbitrary to some degree. Undoubtedly, many of the signs of ASL that seem quite arbitrary today once had an iconic origin that was lost through years of stylized usage. Thus, the signs of ASL are neither uniformly arbitrary nor uniformly iconic; rather the degree of abstraction varies from sign to sign over a wide range. This would seem to be a useful property of ASL for our research.

The literate deaf typically use a combination of ASL and finger spelling; for purposes of this project we have avoided the use of finger spelling as much as possible. A great range of expression is possible within the limits of ASL. We soon found that a good way to practice signing among ourselves was to render familiar songs and poetry into signs; as far as we can judge, there is no message that cannot be rendered faithfully (apart from the usual problems of translation from one language to another). Technical terms and proper names are a problem when first introduced, but within any community of signers it is easy to agree on a convention for any commonly used term. For example, among ourselves we do not finger-spell the words *psychologist* and *psychology,* but render them as "think doctor" and "think science." Or, among users of ASL, "California" can be finger-spelled but is commonly rendered as "golden playland." (Incidentally, the sign for "gold" is made by plucking at the earlobe with thumb and forefinger, indicating an earring—another example of an iconic sign that is at the same time arbitrary and stylized.)

The fact that ASL is in current use by human beings is an additional advantage. The early linguistic environment of the deaf children of deaf parents is in some respects similar to the linguistic environment that we could provide for an experimental subject. This should permit some comparative evaluation of Washoe's eventual level of competence. For example, in discussing Washoe's early performance with deaf parents we have been told that many of her variants of standard signs are similar to the baby-talk variants commonly observed when human children sign.

Washoe

Having decided on a species and a medium of communication, our next concern was to obtain an experimental subject. It is altogether possible that there is some critical early age for the acquisition of this type of behavior. On the other hand, newborn chimpanzees tend to be quite helpless and vegetative. They are also considerably less hardy than older infants. Nevertheless, we reasoned that the dangers of starting too late were much greater than the dangers of starting too early, and we sought the youngest infant we could get. Newborn laboratory chimpanzees are very scarce, and we found that the youngest laboratory infant we could get would be about 2 years old at the time we planned to start the project. It seemed preferable to obtain a wild-caught infant. Wild-caught infants are usually at least 8 to 10 months old before they are available for research. This is because infants rarely reach the United States before they are 5 months old, and to this age must be added 1 or 2 months before final purchase and 2 or 3 months for quarantine and other medical services.

We named our chimpanzee Washoe for Washoe County, the home of the University of Nevada. Her exact age will never be known, but from her weight and dentition we estimated her age to be between 8 and 14 months at the end of June 1966, when she first arrived at our laboratory. (Her dentition has continued to agree with this initial estimate, but her weight has increased rather more than would be expected.) This is very young for a chimpanzee. The best available information indicates that infants are completely dependent until the age of 2 years and semi-dependent until the age of 4; the first signs of sexual maturity (for example, menstruation, sexual swelling) begin to appear at about 8 years, and full adult growth is reached between the ages of 12 and 16 (8). As for the complete lifespan, captive specimens have survived for well over 40 years. Washoe was indeed very young when she arrived; she did not have her first canines or molars, her hand-eye coordination was rudimentary, she had only begun to crawl about, and she slept a great deal. Apart from making friends with her and adapting her to the daily routine, we could accomplish little during the first few months.

Laboratory Conditions

At the outset we were quite sure that Washoe could learn to make various signs in order to obtain food, drink, and other things. For the project to be a success, we felt that something more must be developed. We wanted Washoe not only to ask for objects but to answer questions about them and also to ask us questions. We wanted to develop behavior that could be described as conversation. With this in mind, we attempted to provide Washoe with an environment that might be conducive to this sort of behavior. Confinement was to be minimal, about the same as that of human infants. Her human companions were to be friends and playmates as well as providers and protectors, and they were to introduce a great many games and activities that would be likely to result in maximum interaction with Washoe.

In practice, such an environment is readily achieved with a chimpanzee; bonds of warm affection have always been established between Washoe and her several human companions. We have enjoyed the interaction almost as much as Washoe has, within the limits of human endurance. A number of human companions have been enlisted to participate in the project and relieve each other at intervals, so that at least one person would be with Washoe during all her waking hours. At first we feared that such frequent changes would be disturbing, but Washoe seemed to adapt very well to this procedure. Apparently it is possible to provide an infant chimpanzee with affection on a shift basis.

All of Washoe's human companions have been required to master ASL and to use it extensively in her presence, in association with interesting activities and events and also in a general way, as one chatters at a human infant in the course of the day. The ASL has been used almost exclusively, although occasional finger spelling has been permitted. From time to time, of course, there are lapses into spoken English, as when medical personnel must examine Washoe. At one time, we considered an alternative procedure in which we would sign and speak English to Washoe simultaneously, thus giving her an additional source of informative cues. We rejected this procedure, reasoning that, if she should come to understand speech sooner or more easily than ASL, then she might not pay sufficient attention to our gestures. Another alternative, that of speaking English among ourselves and signing to Washoe, was also rejected. We reasoned that this would make it seem that big chimps talk and only little chimps sign, which might give signing an undesirable social status.

The environment we are describing is not a silent one. The human beings can vocalize in many ways, laughing and making sounds of pleasure and displeasure. Whistles and drums are sounded in a variety of imitation games, and hands are clapped for attention. The rule is that all meaningful sounds, whether vocalized or not, must be sounds that a chimpanzee can imitate.

TRAINING METHODS

Imitation

The imitativeness of apes is proverbial, and rightly so. Those who have worked closely with chimpanzees have frequently remarked on their readiness to engage in visually guided imitation. Consider the following typical comment of Yerkes (9): "Chim and Panzee would imitate many of my acts, but never have I heard them imitate a sound and rarely make a sound peculiarly their own in response to mine. As previously stated, their imitative tendency is as remarkable for its specialization and limitations as for its strength. It seems to be controlled chiefly by visual stimuli. Things which are seen tend to be imitated or reproduced. What is heard is not reproduced. Obviously an animal which lacks the tendency to reinstate auditory stimuli—in other words to imitate sounds—cannot reasonably be expected to talk. The human infant exhibits this tendency to a remarkable degree. So also does the parrot. If the imitative tendency of the parrot could be coupled with the quality of intelligence of the chimpanzee, the latter undoubtedly could speak."

In the course of their work with Viki, the Hayeses devised a game in which Viki would imitate various actions on hearing the command "Do this" (10). Once established, this was an effective means of training Viki to perform actions that could be visually guided. The same method should be admirably suited to training a chimpanzee to use sign language; accordingly we have directed much effort toward establishing a version of the "Do this" game with Washoe. Getting Washoe to imitate us was not difficult, for she did so quite

spontaneously, but getting her to imitate on command has been another matter altogether. It was not until the 16th month of the project that we achieved any degree of control over Washoe's imitation of gestures. Eventually we got to a point where she would imitate a simple gesture, such as pulling at her ears, or a series of such gestures—first we make a gesture, then she imitates, then we make a second gesture, she imitates the second gesture, and so on—for the reward of being tickled. Up to this writing, however, imitation of this sort has not been an important method for introducing new signs into Washoe's vocabulary.

As a method of prompting, we have been able to use imitation extensively to increase the frequency and refine the form of signs. Washoe sometimes fails to use a new sign in an appropriate situation, or uses another, incorrect sign. At such times we can make the correct sign to Washoe, repeating the performance until she makes the sign herself. (With more stable signs, more indirect forms of prompting can be used—for example, pointing at, or touching, Washoe's hand or a part of her body that should be involved in the sign; making the sign for "sign," which is equivalent to saying "Speak up"; or asking a question in signs, such as "What do you want?" or "What is it?") Again, with new signs, and often with old signs as well, Washoe can lapse into what we refer to as poor "diction." Of course, a great deal of slurring and a wide range of variants are permitted in ASL as in any spoken language. In any event, Washoe's diction has frequently been improved by the simple device of repeating, in exaggeratedly correct form, the sign she has just made, until she repeats it herself in more correct form. On the whole, she has responded quite well to prompting, but there are strict limits to its use with a wild animal—one that is probably quite spoiled, besides. Pressed too hard, Washoe can become completely diverted from her original object; she may ask for something entirely different, run away, go into a tantrum, or even bite her tutor.

Chimpanzees also imitate, after some delay, and this delayed imitation can be quite elaborate (10). The following is a typical example of Washoe's delayed imitation. From the beginning of the project she was bathed regularly and according to a standard routine. Also, from her 2nd month with us, she always had dolls to play with. One day, during the 10th month of the project, she bathed one of her dolls in the way we usually bathed her. She filled her little bathtub with water, dunked the doll in the tub, then took it out and dried it with a towel. She has repeated the entire performance, or parts of it, many times since, sometimes also soaping the doll.

This is a type of imitation that may be very important in the acquisition of language by human children, and many of our procedures with Washoe were devised to capitalize on it. Routine activities—feeding, dressing, bathing, and so on—have been highly ritualized, with appropriate signs figuring prominently in the rituals. Many games have been invented which can be accompanied by appropriate signs. Objects and activities have been named as often as possible, especially when Washoe seemed to be paying particular attention to them. New objects and new examples of familiar objects, including pictures, have been continually brought to her attention, together with the appropriate signs. She likes to ride in automobiles, and a ride in an automobile, including the preparations for a ride, provides a wealth of sights that can be accompanied by signs. A good destination for a ride is a home or the university nursery school, both well stocked with props for language lessons.

The general principle should be clear: Washoe has been exposed to a wide variety of activities and objects, together with their appropriate signs, in the hope that she would come to associate the signs with their referents and later make the signs herself. We have reason to believe that she has come to understand a large vocabulary of signs. This was expected, since a number of chimpanzees have acquired extensive understanding vocabularies of spoken words, and there is evidence that even dogs can acquire a sizable understanding vocabulary of spoken words (11). The understanding vocabulary that Washoe has acquired, however, consists of signs that a chimpanzee can imitate.

Some of Washoe's signs seem to have been originally acquired by delayed imitation. A good example is the sign for "toothbrush." A part of the daily routine has been to brush her teeth after every meal. When this routine was first introduced Washoe generally resisted it. She gradually came to submit with less and less fuss, and after many months she would even help or sometimes brush her teeth herself. Usually, having finished her meal, Washoe would try to leave her highchair; we would restrain her, signing "First, toothbrushing, then you can go." One day, in the 10th month of the project, Washoe was visiting the Gardner home and found her way into the bathroom. She climbed up on the counter, looked at our mug full of toothbrushes, and signed "toothbrush." At the time, we believed that Washoe understood this sign but we had not seen her use it. She had no reason to ask for the toothbrushes, because they were well within her reach, and it is most unlikely that she was asking to have her teeth brushed. This was our first observation, and one of the clearest examples, of behavior in which Washoe seemed to name an object or an event for no obvious motive other than communication.

Following this observation, the toothbrushing routine at mealtime was altered. First, imitative prompting was introduced. Then as the sign became more reliable, her rinsing-mug and toothbrush were displayed prominently until she made the sign. By the 14th month she was making the "toothbrush" sign at the end of meals with little or no prompting; in fact she has called for her toothbrush in a peremptory fashion when its appearance at the end of a meal was delayed. The "toothbrush" sign is not merely a response cued by the end of a meal; Washoe retained her ability to name toothbrushes when they were shown to her at other times.

The sign for "flower" may also have been acquired by delayed imitation. From her first summer with us, Washoe showed a great interest in flowers, and we took advantage of this by providing many flowers and pictures of flowers accompanied by the appropriate sign. Then one day in the 15th month she made the sign, spontaneously, while she and a companion were walking toward a flower garden. As in the case of "toothbrush," we believed that she understood the sign at this time, but we had made no attempt to elicit it from her except by making it ourselves in appropriate situations. Again, after the first observation, we proceeded to elicit this sign as often as possible by a variety of methods, most frequently by showing her a flower and giving it to her if she made the sign for it. Eventually the sign became very reliable and could be elicited by a variety of flowers and pictures of flowers.

It is difficult to decide which signs were acquired by the method of delayed imitation. The first appearance of these signs is likely to be sudden and unexpected; it is possible that some inadvertent movement of Washoe's has been interpreted as meaningful by one of her devoted companions. If the first observer were kept from reporting the observation and from making any direct attempts to elicit the sign again, then it might be possible to obtain independent verification. Quite understandably, we have been more interested in raising the frequency of new signs than in evaluating any particular method of training.

Babbling

Because the Hayeses were attempting to teach Viki to speak English, they were interested in babbling, and during the first year of their project they were encouraged by the number and variety of spontaneous vocalizations that Viki made. But, in time, Viki's spontaneous vocalizations decreased further and further to the point where the Hayeses felt that there was almost no vocal babbling from which to shape spoken language. In planning this project we expected a great deal of manual "babbling," but during the early months we observed very little behavior of this kind. In the course of the project, however, there has been a great increase in manual babbling. We have been particularly encouraged by the increase in movements that involve touching parts of the head and body, since these are important components of many signs. Also, more and more frequently, when Washoe has been unable to get something that she wants, she has burst into a flurry of random flourishes and arm-waving.

We have encouraged Washoe's babbling by our responsiveness; clapping, smiling, and repeating the gesture much as you might repeat "goo goo" to a human infant. If the babbled gesture has resembled a sign in ASL, we have made the correct form of the sign and have attempted to engage in some appropriate activity. The sign for "funny" was probably acquired in this way. It first appeared as a spontaneous babble that lent itself readily to a simple imitation game—first Washoe signed "funny," then we did, then she did, and so on. We would laugh and smile during the interchanges that she initiated, and initiate the game ourselves when something funny happened. Eventually Washoe came to use the "funny" sign spontaneously in roughly appropriate situations.

Closely related to babbling are some gestures that seem to have appeared independently of any deliberate training on our part, and that resemble signs so closely that we could incorporate them into Washoe's repertoire with little or no modification. Almost from the first she had a begging gesture—an extension of her open hand, palm up, toward one of us. She made this gesture in situations in which she wanted aid and in situations in which we were holding some object that she wanted. The ASL signs for "give me" and "come" are very similar to this, except that they involve a prominent beckoning movement. Gradually Washoe came to incorporate a beckoning wrist movement into her use of this sign. In Table 13.1 we refer to this sign as "come-gimme." As Washoe has come to use it, the sign is not simply a modification of the original begging gesture. For example, very commonly she reaches forward with one hand (palm up) while she gestures with the other hand (palm down) held near her head. (The result resembles a classic fencing posture.)

Another sign of this type is the sign for "hurry," which, so far, Washoe has always made by shaking her open hand vigorously at the wrist. This first appeared as an impatient flourish following some request that she had made in signs; for example, after making the "open" sign before a door. The correct ASL for "hurry" is very close, and we began to use it often, ourselves, in appropriate contexts. We believe that Washoe has come to use this sign in a meaningful way, because she has frequently used it when she, herself, is in a hurry—for example, when rushing to her nursery chair.

Instrumental conditioning

It seems intuitively unreasonable that the acquisition of language by human beings could be strictly a matter of reiterated instrumental conditioning—that a child acquires language after the fashion of a rat that is conditioned, first, to press a lever for food in the presence of one stimulus, then to turn a wheel in the presence of another stimulus, and so on until a large repertoire of discriminated responses is acquired. Nevertheless, the so-called "trick vocabulary" of early childhood is probably acquired in this way, and this may be a critical stage in the acquisition of language by children. In any case, a minimal objective of this project was to teach Washoe as many signs as possible by whatever procedures we could enlist. Thus, we have not hesitated to use conventional procedures of instrumental conditioning.

Anyone who becomes familiar with young chimpanzees soon learns about their passion for being tickled. There is no doubt that tickling is the most effective reward that we have used with Washoe. In the early months, when we would pause in our tickling, Washoe would indicate that she wanted more tickling by taking our hands and placing them against her ribs or around her neck. The meaning of these gestures was unmistakable, but since we were not studying our human ability to interpret her chimpanzee gestures, we decided to shape an arbitrary response that she could use to ask for more tickling. We noted that, when being tickled, she tended to bring her arms together to cover the place being tickled. The result was a very crude approximation of the ASL sign for "more" (see Table 14.1). Thus, we would stop tickling and then pull Washoe's arms away from her body. When we released her arms and threatened to resume tickling, she tended to bring her hands together again. If she brought them back together, we would tickle her again. From time to time we would stop tickling and wait for her to put her

hands together by herself. At first, any approximation to the "more" sign, however crude, was rewarded. Later, we required closer approximations and introduced imitative prompting. Soon, a very good version of the "more" sign could be obtained, but it was quite specific to the tickling situation.

In the 6th month of the project we were able to get "more" signs for a new game that consisted of pushing Washoe across the floor in a laundry basket. In this case we did not use the shaping procedure but, from the start, used imitative prompting to elicit the "more" sign. Soon after the "more" sign became spontaneous and reliable in the laundry-basket game, it began to appear as a request for more swinging (by the arms)—again, after first being elicited with imitative prompting. From this point on, Washoe transferred the "more" sign to all activities, including feeding. The transfer was usually spontaneous, occurring when there was some pause in a desired activity or when some object was removed. Often we ourselves were not sure that Washoe wanted "more" until she signed to us.

The sign for "open" had a similar history. When Washoe wanted to get through a door, she tended to hold up both hands and pound on the door with her palms or her knuckles. This is the beginnning position for the "open" sign (see Table 14.1). By waiting for her to place her hands on the door and then lift them, and also by imitative prompting, we were able to shape a good approximation of the "open" sign, and would reward this by opening the door. Originally she was trained to make this sign for three particular doors that she used every day. Washoe transferred this sign to all doors; then to containers such as the refrigerator, cupboards, drawers, briefcases, boxes, and jars; and eventually—an invention of Washoe's—she used it to ask us to turn on water faucets.

In the case of "more" and "open" we followed the conventional laboratory procedure of waiting for Washoe to make some response that could be shaped into the sign we wished her to acquire. We soon found that this was not necessary; Washoe could acquire signs that were first elicited by our holding her hands, forming them into the desired

TABLE 14.1
Signs used reliably by chimpanzee Washoe within 22 months of the beginning of training. The signs are listed in the order of their original appearance in her repertoire (see text for the criterion of reliability and for the method of assigning the date of original appearance).

Signs	Description	Context
Come-gimme	Beckoning motion, with wrist or knuckles as pivot.	Sign made to persons or animals, also for objects out of reach. Often combined: "come tickle," "gimme sweet," etc.
More	Fingertips are brought together, usually overhead. (Correct ASL form: tips of the tapered hand touch repeatedly.)	When asking for continuation or repetition of activities such as swinging or tickling, for second helpings of food, etc. Also used to ask for repetition of some performance, such as a somersault.
Up	Arm extends upward, and index finger may also point up.	Wants a lift to reach objects such as grapes on vine, or leaves; or wants to be placed on someone's shoulders; or wants to leave potty-chair.
Sweet	Index or index and second fingers touch tip of wagging tongue. (Correct ASL form: index and second fingers extended side by side.)	For dessert; used spontaneously at end of meal. Also, when asking for candy.
Open	Flat hands are placed side by side, palms down, then drawn apart while rotated to palms up.	At door of house, room, car, refrigerator, or cupboard; on containers such as jars; and on faucets.
Tickle	The index finger of one hand is drawn across the back of the other hand (Related to ASL "touch.")	For tickling or for chasing games.
Go	Opposite of "come-gimme."	While walking hand-in-hand or riding on someone's shoulders. Washoe usually indicates the direction desired.
Out	Curved hand grasps tapered hand; then tapered hand is withdrawn upward.	When passing through doorways; until recently, used for both "in" and "out." Also, when asking to be taken outdoors.
Hurry	Open hand is shaken at the wrist. (Correct ASL form: index and second fingers extended side by side.)	Often follows signs such as "come-gimme," "out," "open," and "go," particularly if there is a delay before Washoe is obeyed. Also, used while watching her meal being prepared.
Hear-listen	Index finger touches ear.	For loud or strange sounds: bells, car horns, sonic booms, etc. Also, for asking someone to hold a watch to her ear.
Tooth-brush	Index finger is used as brush, to rub front teeth.	When Washoe has finished her meal, or at other times when shown a toothbrush.
Drink	Thumb is extended from fisted hand and touches mouth.	For water, formula, soda pop, etc. For soda pop, often combined with "sweet."
Hurt	Extended index fingers are jabbed toward each other. Can be used to indicate location of pain.	To indicate cuts and bruises on herself or on others. Can be elicited by red stains on a person's skin or by tears in clothing.
Sorry	Fisted hand clasps and unclasps at shoulder. (Correct ASL form: fisted hand is rubbed over heart with circular motion.)	After biting someone, or when someone has been hurt in another way (not necessarily by Washoe). When told to apologize for mischief.
Funny	Tip of index finger presses nose, and Washoe snorts. (Correct ASL form: index and second fingers used; no snort.)	When soliciting interaction play, and during games. Occasionally, when being pursued after mischief.
Please	Open hand is drawn across chest. (Correct ASL form: fingertips used, and circular motion.)	When asking for objects and activities. Frequently combined: "Please go," "Out, please," "Please drink."
Food-eat	Several fingers of one hand are placed in mouth. (Correct ASL form: fingertips of tapered hand touch mouth repeatedly.)	During meals and preparation of meals.
Flower	Tip of index finger touches one or both nostrils. (Correct ASL form: tips of tapered hand touch first one nostril, then the other.)	For flowers.
Cover-blanket	Draws one hand toward self over the back of the other.	At bedtime or naptime, and, on cold days, when Washoe wants to be taken out.
Dog	Repeated slapping on thigh.	For dogs and for barking.
You	Index finger points at a person's chest.	Indicates successive turns in games. Also used in response to questions such as "Who tickle?" "Who brush?"

Table 14.1 (Cont'd)

Signs	Description	Context
Napkin-bib	Fingertips wipe the mouth region.	For bib, for washcloth, and for Kleenex.
In	Opposite of "out."	Wants to go indoors, or wants someone to join her indoors.
Brush	The fisted hand rubs the back of the open hand several times. (Adapted from ASL "polish.")	For hairbrush, and when asking for brushing.
Hat	Palm pats top of head.	For hats and caps.
I-me	Index finger points at, or touches, chest.	Indicates Washoe's turn, when she and a companion share food, drink, etc. Also used in phrases, such as "I drink." and in reply to questions such as "Who tickle?" (Washoe: "you"); "Who I tickle?" (Washoe: "Me.")
Shoes	The fisted hands are held side by side and strike down on shoes or floor. (Correct ASL form: the sides of the fisted hands strike against each other.)	For shoes and boots.
Smell	Palm is held before nose and moved slightly upward several times.	For scented objects: tobacco, perfume, sage, etc.
Pants	Palms of the flat hands are drawn up against the body toward waist.	For diapers, rubber pants, trousers.
Clothes	Fingertips brush down the chest.	For Washoe's jacket, nightgown, and shirts; also for our clothing.
Cat	Thumb and index finger grasp cheek hair near side of mouth and are drawn outward (representing cat's whiskers).	For cats.
Key	Palm of one hand is repeatedly touched with the index finger of the other (Correct ASL form: crooked index finger is rotated against palm.)	Used for keys and locks and to ask us to unlock a door.
Baby	One forearm is placed in the crook of the other, as if cradling a baby.	For dolls, including animal dolls such as a toy horse and duck.
Clean	The open palm of one hand is passed over the open palm of the other.	Used when Washoe is washing, or being washed, or when a companion is washing hands or some other object. Also used for "soap."

configuration, and then putting them through the desired movement. Since this procedure of guidance is usually much more practical than waiting for a spontaneous approximation to occur at a favorable moment, we have used it much more frequently.

RESULTS

Vocabulary

In the early stages of the project we were able to keep fairly complete records of Washoe's daily signing behavior. But, as the amount of signing behavior and the number of signs to be monitored increased, our initial attempts to obtain exhaustive records became prohibitively cumbersome. During the 16th month we settled on the following procedure. When a new sign was introduced we waited until it had been reported by three different observers as having occurred in an appropriate context and spontaneously (that is, with no prompting other than a question such as "What is it?" or "What do you want?"). The sign was then added to a checklist in which its occurrence, form, context, and the kind of prompting required were recorded. Two such checklists were filled out each day, one for the first half of the day and one for the second half. For a criterion of acquisition we chose a reported frequency of at least one appropriate and spontaneous occurrence each day over a period of 15 consecutive days.

In Table 14.1 we have listed 30 signs that met this criterion by the end of the 22nd month of the project. In addition, we have listed four signs ("dog," "smell," "me," and "clean") that we judged to be stable, despite the fact that they had not met the stringent criterion before the end of the 22nd month. These additional signs had, nevertheless, been reported to occur appropriately and spontaneously on more than half of the days in a period of 30 consecutive days. An indication of the variety of signs that Washoe used in the course of a day is given by the following data: during the 22nd month of the study, 28 of the 34 signs listed were reported on at least 20 days, and the smallest number of different signs reported for a single day was 23, with a median of 29 (*12*).

The order in which these signs first appeared in Washoe's repertoire is also given in Table 1. We considered the first appearance to be the date on which three different observers reported appropriate and spontaneous occurrences. By this criterion, 4 new signs first appeared during the first 7 months, 9 new signs during the next 7 months, and 21 new signs during the next 7 months. We chose the 21st month rather than the 22nd month as the cutoff for this tabulation so that no signs would be included that do not appear in Table 14.1. Clearly, if Washoe's rate of acquisition continues to accelerate, we will have to assess her vocabulary on the basis of sampling procedures. We are now in the process of developing procedures that could be used to make periodic tests of Washoe's performance on samples of her repertoire. However, now that there is evidence that a chimpanzee can acquire a vocabulary of more than 30 signs, the exact number of signs in her current vocabulary is less significant than the order of magnitude—50, 100, 200 signs, or more— that might eventually be achieved.

Differentiation

In Table 14.1, column 1, we list English equivalents for each of Washoe's signs. It must be understood that this equivalence is only approximate, because equivalence between English and ASL, as between any two human languages, is only approximate, and because Washoe's usage does differ from that of standard ASL. To some extent her usage is indi-

cated in the column labeled "Context" in Table 14.1, but the definition of any given sign must always depend upon her total vocabulary, and this has been continually changing. When she had very few signs for specific things, Washoe used the "more" sign for a wide class of requests. Our only restriction was that we discouraged the use of "more" for first requests. As she acquired signs for specific requests, her use of "more" declined until, at the time of this writing, she was using this sign mainly to ask for repetition of some action that she could not name, such as a somersault. Perhaps the best English equivalent would be "do it again." Still, it seemed preferable to list the English equivalent for the ASL sign rather than its current referent for Washoe, since further refinements in her usage may be achieved at a later date.

The differentiation of the signs for "flower" and "smell" provides a further illustration of usage depending upon size of vocabulary. As the "flower" sign became more frequent, we noted that it occurred in several inappropriate contexts that all seemed to include odors; for example, Washoe would make the "flower" sign when opening a tobacco pouch or when entering a kitchen filled with cooking odors. Taking our cue from this, we introduced the "smell" sign by passive shaping and imitative prompting. Gradually Washoe came to make the appropriate distinction between "flower" contexts and "smell" contexts in her signing, although "flower" (in the single-nostril form) (see Table 14.1) has continued to occur as a common error in "smell" contexts.

Transfer

In general, when introducing new signs we have used a very specific referent for the initial training—a particular door for "open," a particular hat for "hat." Early in the project we were concerned about the possibility that signs might become inseparable from their first referents. So far, however, there has been no problem of this kind: Washoe has always been able to transfer her signs spontaneously to new members of each class of referents. We have already described the transfer of "more" and "open." The sign for "flower" is a particularly good example of transfer, because flowers occur in so many varieties, indoors, outdoors, and in pictures, yet Washoe uses the same sign for all. It is fortunate that she has responded well to pictures of objects. In the case of "dog" and "cat" this has proved to be important because live dogs and cats can be too exciting, and we have had to use pictures to elicit most of the "dog" and "cat" signs. It is noteworthy that Washoe has transferred the "dog" sign to the sound of barking by an unseen dog.

The acquisition and transfer of the sign for "key" illustrates a further point. A great many cupboards and doors in Washoe's quarters have been kept secure by small padlocks that can all be opened by the same simple key. Because she was immature and awkward, Washoe had great difficulty in learning to use these keys and locks. Because we wanted her to improve her manual dexterity, we let her practice with these keys until she could open the locks quite easily (then we had to hide the keys). Washoe soon transferred this skill to all manner of locks and keys, including ignition keys. At the same time, we taught her the sign for "key," using the original padlock keys as a referent. Washoe came to use this sign both to name keys that were presented to her and to ask for the keys to various locks when no key was in sight. She readily transferred the sign to all varieties of keys and locks.

Now, if an animal can transfer a skill learned with a certain key and lock to new types of key and lock, it should not be surprising that the same animal can learn to use an arbitrary response to name and ask for a certain key and then transfer that sign to new types of keys. Certainly, the relationship between the use of a key and the opening of locks is as arbitrary as the relationship between the sign for "key" and its many referents. Viewed in this way, the general phenomenon of transfer of training and the specifically linguistic phenomenon of labeling become very similar, and the problems that these phenomena pose for modern learning theory should require similar solutions. We do not mean to imply that the problem of labeling is less complex than has generally been supposed; rather, we are suggesting that the problem of transfer of training requires an equally sophisticated treatment.

Combinations

During the phase of the project covered by this article we made no deliberate attempts to elicit combinations or phrases, although we may have responded more readily to strings of two or more signs than to single signs. As far as we can judge, Washoe's early use of signs in strings was spontaneous. Almost as soon as she had eight or ten signs in her repertoire, she began to use them two and three at a time. As her repertoire increased, her tendency to produce strings of two or more signs also increased, to the point where this has become a common mode of signing for her. We, of course, usually signed to her in combinations, but if Washoe's use of combinations has been imitative, then it must be a generalized sort of imitation, since she has invented a number of combinations, such as "gimme tickle" (before we had ever asked her to tickle us), and "open food drink" (for the refrigerator—we have always called it the "cold box").

Four signs—"please," "come-gimme," "hurry," and "more"—used with one or more other signs, account for the largest share of Washoe's early combinations. In general, these four signs have functioned as emphasizers, as in "please open hurry" and "gimme drink please."

Until recently, five additional signs—"go," "out," "in," "open," and "hear-listen"—accounted for most of the remaining combinations. Typical examples of combinations using these four are, "go in" or "go out" (when at some distance from a door), "go sweet" (for being carried to a raspberry bush), "open flower" (to be let through the gate to a flower garden), "open key" (for a locked door), "listen eat" (at the sound of an alarm clock signaling mealtime), and "listen dog" (at the sound of barking by an unseen dog). All but the first and last of these six examples were inventions of Washoe's. Combinations of this type tend to amplify the meaning of the single signs used. Sometimes, however, the function of these five signs has been about the same as that of the emphasizers, as in "open out" (when standing in front of a door).

Toward the end of the period covered in this article we were able to introduce the pronouns "I-me" and "you," so that combinations that resemble short sentences have begun to appear.

CONCLUDING OBSERVATIONS

From time to time we have been asked questions such as, "Do you think that Washoe has language?" or "At what point will you be able to say that Washoe has language?" We find it very difficult to respond to these questions because they are altogether foreign to the spirit of our research. They imply a distinction between one class of communicative behavior that can be called language and another class that cannot. This in turn implies a well-established theory that could provide the distinction. If our objectives had required such a theory, we would certainly not have been able to begin this project as early as we did.

In the first phase of the project we were able to verify the hypothesis that sign language is an appropriate medium of two-way communication for the chimpanzee. Washoe's intellectual immaturity, the continuing acceleration of her progress, the fact that her signs do not remain specific to their original referents but are transferred spontaneously to new referents, and the emergence of rudimentary combinations all suggest that significantly more can be accomplished by Washoe during the subsequent phases of this project. As we proceed, the problems of these subsequent phases will be chiefly concerned with the technical business of measurement. We are now developing a procedure for testing Washoe's ability to name objects. In this procedure, an object or a picture of an object is placed in a box with a window. An observer, who does not know what is in the box, asks Washoe what she sees through the window. At present, this method is limited to items that fit in the box; a more ingenious method will have to be devised for other items. In particular, the ability to combine and recombine signs must be tested. Here, a great deal depends upon

reaching a stage at which Washoe produces an extended series of signs in answer to questions. Our hope is that Washoe can be brought to the point where she describes events and situations to an observer who has no other source of information.

At an earlier time we would have been more cautious about suggesting that a chimpanzee might be able to produce extended utterances to communicate information. We believe now that it is the writers—who would predict just what it is that no chimpanzee will ever do—who must proceed with caution. Washoe's accomplishments will probably be exceeded by another chimpanzee, because it is unlikely that the conditions of training have been optimal in this first attempt. Theories of language that depend upon the identification of aspects of language that are exclusively human must remain tentative until a considerably larger body of intensive research with other species becomes available.

REFERENCES AND NOTES

1. See, for example. E.H. Lenneberg, *Biological Foundations of Language* (Wiley, New York, 1967).

2. A.L. Bryan, *Curr. Anthropol.* **4,** 297 (1963).

3. K.J. Hayes and C. Hayes, *Proc. Amer. Phil. Soc.* **95,** 105 (1951).

4. K.J. Hayes, personal communication. Dr. Hayes also informed us that Viki used a few additional sounds which, while not resembling English words, were used for specific requests.

5. R.M. Yerkes, *Chimpanzees* (Yale Univ. Press, New Haven, 1943).

6. K.J. Hayes and C. Hayes, in *The Non-Human Primates and Human Evolution*, J.A. Gavan, Ed. (Wayne Univ. Press, Detroit, 1955), p. 110; W.N. Kellogg and L.A. Kellogg, *The Ape and the Child* (Hafner, New York, 1967; originally published by McGraw-Hill, New York, 1933); W.N. Kellogg, *Science* **162,** 423 (1968).

7. W.C. Stokoe, D. Casterline, C.G. Croneberg, *A Dictionary of American Sign Language* (Gallaudet College Press, Washington, D.C., 1965); E.A. McCall, thesis, University of Iowa (1965).

8. J. Goodall, in *Primate Behavior,* I. DeVore, Ed. (Holt, Rinehart & Winston, New York, 1965), p. 425; A.J. Riopelle and C.M. Rogers, in *Behavior of Nonhuman Primates,* A.M. Schrier, H.F. Harlow, F. Stollnitz, Eds. (Academic Press, New York, 1965), p. 449.

9. R.M. Yerkes and B.W. Learned, *Chimpanzee Intelligence and Its Vocal Expression* (William & Wilkins, Baltimore, 1925), p. 53.

10. K.J. Hayes and C. Hayes, *J. Comp. Physiol. Psychol.* **45,** 450 (1952).

11. C.J. Warden and L.H. Warner, *Quart. Rev. Biol.* **3,** 1 (1928).

12. The development of Washoe's vocabulary of signs is being recorded on motion-picture film. At the time of this writing, 30 of the 34 signs listed in Table 1 are on film.

13. The research described in this article has been supported by National Institute of Mental Health grants MH-12154 and MH-34953 (Research Scientist Development Award to B.T. Gardner) and by National Science Foundation grant GB-7432. We acknowledge a great debt to the personnel of the Aeromedical Research Laboratory, Holloman Air Force Base, whose support and expert assistance effectively absorbed all of the many difficulties attendant upon the acquisition of a wild-caught chimpanzee. We are also grateful to Dr. Frances L. Fitz-Gerald of the Yerkes Regional Primate Research Center for detailed advice on the care of an infant chimpanzee. Drs. Emanual Berger of Reno, Nevada, and D.B. Olsen of the University of Nevada have served as medical consultants, and we are grateful to them for giving so generously of their time and medical skills. The faculty of the Sarah Hamilton Fleischmann School of Home Economics, University of Nevada, has generously allowed us to use the facilities of their experimental nursery school on weekends and holidays.

The profile of Arthur Jensen, whose controversial views on the genetic basis of intelligence were discussed in the text, is presented in the first reading by science writer Lee Edson. The article is illuminating not only because it presents the critical arguments on both sides of this heated controversy in layman's language but also because, in bringing to the surface the emotional undertones surrounding "Jensenism," it captures some of the temper of our times.

The important study by Doris R. Entwisle and Ellen Greenberger records some solid information which may guide current programs aimed at the early education of disadvantaged children. While it has been assumed that educational and reading problems are largely predicated on prior language deficits, there is surprisingly little documentation of this assumption. Based on measures of form class of word association responses of inner-city children in Baltimore, Maryland, the study shows that in spite of an early spurt in syntactic development, black first-graders give responses that are less mature in terms of semantic content than their white counterparts, and that in the case of verbs and adverbs this immaturity may persist at least to the fifth grade. The implication of this finding that semantic structures are different for black and white children at the time they enter public school is that the verbal cues in primers and basic readers which we use to teach elementary schoolers may be entirely inappropriate for black inner-city children.

Part VII
CONTROVERSIAL ISSUES IN LEARNING CAPACITY

15
Jensenism, *n.* the Theory that IQ Is Largely Determined by the Genes

Lee Edson

For most of the last 10 years Prof. Arthur Robert Jensen of the University of California, one of the nation's leading educational psychologists, has lived the generally quiet, cloistered existence of a scholar, burying himself with statistics, standards and students. If the Free Speech Movement, the People's Park confrontation or any of the other well-publicized blowoffs of Berkeley student unrest penetrated the Education Building on the west corner of the campus (where such egg-yolk institutions as Agricultural Extension, Life Sciences and Home Economics are clustered), it was hard to tell it from Jensen. A tall, almost somber figure, addicted to dark attire, he strode through the corridors with aloof dignity. He seldom cracked a smile, fraternized with colleagues or engaged in small talk. He was a very involved, very serious professor's professor who had no time for hanky-panky and insisted on keeping himself free of the academic maelstrom. "It's incredible," a colleague once remarked after leaving his office, "Jensen is so absorbed he doesn't realize he's on top of a volcano."

Then on Feb. 15 [1969] the volcano erupted. The Harvard Educational Review, a 30-year-old scholarly journal published by Harvard graduate students, came out with an article by Jensen entitled: "How Much Can We Boost I.Q. and Scholastic Achievement?" The detailed scientific paper, the longest ever printed in the review, begins with an appraisal of the alleged failure of compensatory education programs such as Head Start, a project to help preschool ghetto youngsters overcome years of cultural deprivation in order to catch up with middle-class youngsters in school readiness. The article goes on to state that these programs seek, in effect, to raise children's academic achievement by increasing their I.Q.'s. Jensen then examines the entire concept of the I.Q.: "what makes it vary from one individual to another; what can change it, and by what amount." In the process he says that Negroes as a group—as opposed to any single individual Negro—test out poorly compared with whites or Orientals on that aspect of general intelligence that involves abstract reasoning and problem-solving. And he adds that this ability (which he equates with the ability measured by I.Q. tests) is largely inherited, a matter of genes and brain structure, and therefore no amount of compensatory education or forced exposure to culture is going to improve it substantially.

Jensen emphasizes in his article, that the "particular constellation of abilities we call 'intelligence,' and which we can measure by means of 'intelligence' tests," is only a part of the whole spectrum of human abilities—and that it "has been singled out from the total galaxy of mental abilities as being especially important in our society mainly because of the nature of our traditional system of formal education and the occupational structure with which it is coordinated." He points out that, "as far as we know, the full range of human talents is represented in all the major races of man." But such statements did little to lessen the impact of the article's conclusions about I.Q. and race. The magazine had hardly hit the academic mailboxes when a sound truck manned by members of the Students for a Democratic Society roared through the Berkeley campus, blaring: "Fight racism. Fire Jensen." Jensen's normally sparse scholarly mail grew fat with hate literature. He was accused of being a fascist, a white supremacist, of having black ancestry and hating it. He received postcards emblazoned with the Nazi swastika; one had a single handscrawled word: "Death." A group of aroused left-wing students invaded his classroom and he had to lecture in secret locations; crank callers engaged him on the phone, and he was forced to summon the Berkeley campus security forces to protect his files from being raided. At night the lights burned bright in his office to discourage looters. One fearful assistant quit her job.

In the academic and political worlds the furor has become ever more intense. Not since Darwin's theory of evolution, as one writer put it, has so much fiery discussion and violent opposition been generated over a treastise. A Congressman put all 123 pages of the article into the Congressional Record, and segregationists took to citing the ar-

ticle in court as the word of science. Lengthy reviews of the article were printed almost everywhere in intellectual circles. At Columbia University's Teachers College the article became required reading in some classes, and at the University of Minnesota a psychology professor, in as irrelevant a reaction as one could find, offered $100 to anyone who could predict a man's intelligence by looking at his features.

At the University of California a number of Jensen's professional colleagues sought to have him censured, and he was in effect summoned before a specially organized symposium which at first had the tone of a modern witch trial—perhaps the first time in recent academic history that a professor has had to defend a scholarly paper before his assembled colleagues and the videotape cameras. Since then word has filtered down that the article was distributed as "must reading" by Daniel Patrick Moynihan to members of the Nixon Cabinet. An educator in San Juan was forced to resign when he quoted Jensen in a talk opposing Negro violence. And The Wall Street Journal started to speak of "Jensenism" (though one colleague informed Jensen that he should "wait till they print it in lower case before you think you've made it").

The extent to which some critics have gone in denigrating Jensen was illustrated by a paper distributed by a University of California psychologist, John G. Hurst. It cited a study which found that among 24 leading psychologists, the 12 who generally favored environment over heredity were radical and liberal in their political point of view and largely included people who had come from poor environments and worked their way up; whereas the other half, those who believed in heredity, were conservative in politics and came from the conservative middle class. Hurst argued that Jensen fits the latter category. This attempt to establish Jensen's guilt by association helps point up the problem social scientists have in dealing with uncomfortable findings in an emotionally charged social environment.

The affair has caused the 45-year-old, mild-mannered Jensen some severely trying moments.

A contract he held with the Berkeley Unified School District to evaluate the effect of busing and integration in the city has been canceled. His home life, according to his wife, Barbara, hasn't been the same since the article appeared. "Our house in Orinda was turned into a mad office," she says. "I bought a special IBM typewriter to answer the bushel of letters, and we still have files marked "kookie mail" where we throw all the threats and nasty remarks." Friends with a sick sense of humor inquire whether the Jensens are taking out double-indemnity insurance. "We always remember what happened to that professor at San Francisco State," Barbara Jensen says with a shudder. (Prof. John Bunzel's car was smeared with paint and he narrowly escaped injury from a bomb placed outside his office door. He was attacked by radical students as a symbol of establishment liberalism.) A lesser impact, she adds with a quick smile, is on the family dog, a Rhodesian ridgeback who seems to growl more fiercely than ever at male visitors to the Jensen home. "However, it may be genetic," she says, "since the Boers used to train these dogs to like women and attack men."

This reaction to Jensen's views—amounting to a kind of intellectual overkill—is a measure of the deep tensions that run through the heart of American life today. The nature vs. nurture controversy is an old one, and most observers agree that Jensen has added little that is new. Yet the attacks on him have been vicious, notwithstanding the fact that he is not an ideal target. He has no connection with the South and no history of racial intolerance which the enemy might seize upon. He opposes segregation and declares himself to be a political liberal or—"at worst"—a moderate. A registered Democrat (a colleague calls him an "unconcerned Democrat"), he voted for Eugene McCarthy in the primary and later switched to Nixon in the Presidential election because "I felt that Humphrey was just giving us more of the same Johnson bankrupt policy."

As a leading educational psychologist and a former Guggenheim Fellow, Jensen's academic credentials are impeccable. In addition to his professorship in Berkeley, he holds degrees from three universities and is one of the founding fathers of Berkeley's prestigious Institute of Human Learning. He maintains membership and some high posts in the leading psychological and educational research organizations and has written a book and more than 90 scientific papers in education and educational psychology.

Many of his co-professionals find it unforgivable that a man with this formidable background should rock the boat. They blame him, in the words of columnist Joseph Alsop, for "speaking the unspeakable" and "mentioning the unmentionable." In the early days of psychological testing, educators spoke freely of the hereditary base of intelligence, just as they spoke of the inherited maladaptive traits of the Jukes and Kallikaks over six generations, but in recent times, as Federal funds have poured into the education of preschool slum children, educators have kept silent on such themes. Many of the critics are traumatized by the memory of the Nazi genocidal insanity and lash out at anyone who hints of racial differences. "The incredible consequences that arose from Nazi theory," says a professor, "makes every liberal with historical memory blind to any opinions in this area."

But there is more to it than that. The liberal egalitarian point of view is tied up with the romantic anthropological wish that all races should be equal—that all men should be born with a kind of *tabula rasa*—a clean slate on which everyone can write his own destiny. This notion of the unlimited plasticity of the human brain is pervasive in social science circles and in Government position papers; on the wall of one university researcher I found a sign reading: "We're all different—sorry about that." "Scientists drop their cool on this one," says a prominent educational psychologist. "They don't want people to be different in the area of intelligence, and attempts made to find differences are quickly put down. The ascendancy of the sociologist, anthropologist and psychologist over educational theory has blocked any consideration of nonenvironmental forces as contributing to the spread of ability throughout the population. One Harvard anthropologist wrote a 700-page book on the origin of the races but left out all information on brain differences. To these people there is only one race—Homosapiens—and that's that. Jensen scrapes a raw nerve when he keeps using science's own statistics against an entrenched point of view, and they can't stand it."

Jensen says his case is based, "not on a single definitive study but on a preponderance of evidence pointing in a single direction, like the theory of evolution." Geneticists have long agreed, for instance, that intelligence has a genetic base. Studies of matings between cousins of normal I.Q. reveal that they produce larger numbers of retarded offspring than are produced in nonfamily, random matings. The link between retardation and heredity is very direct.

Jensen's most telling argument, he believes, and the easiest to grasp, proceeds from studies of identical twins—siblings whose genetic inheritance is precisely the same, since they have developed from a single fertilized egg. Psychologist Sir Cyril Burt and geneticist J.A. Shields studied 100 pairs of identical twins in England who were reared apart from each other. It was found that the separated twins were, on the average, only six points apart in I.Q. By contrast, any two people in the total population, chosen at random, will be on the average 18 points apart. Nonidentical siblings reared in the same household are on the average 12 I.Q. points apart.

"If you look at studies of adopted children," Jensen says, "you find that their intelligence relates more closely to their natural parents than to their adoptive parents. And if you add this to 100 other twin and kinship studies over the last 25 years over four continents and a wide range of environmental conditions, you have a strong body of evidence for the heritability of I.Q. In short, the closer people are related, the more similar are their I.Q.'s."

The second line of evidence of the heritability of intelligence, Jensen says, comes from the studies of the relationship between intelligence and socioeconomic status dating back to the work of Alfred Binet 70 years ago. We know that people in the upper classes generally have higher I.Q.'s than those in lower classes. Some people like to read an environmental cause into this. But, in fact,

studies indicate otherwise. Regardless of the social class in which an adopted child is reared, for example, the child's I.Q. will correlate better with that of his natural parents than that of his adoptive parents. If a child's natural parents have high I.Q.'s, it is most likely that he will also have a high I.Q. even if he is raised by low-I.Q., lower-class adoptive parents. The environment is not the deciding factor.

How does all this evidence tie up with racial differences? "First," Jensen says, "it should be noted that race is not an abstract Platonic essence—it is actually a 'breeding population,' as the geneticists term it; the population is not closed, but there is a well-known probability of greater mating within this population than outside it. As a result, the frequency of genes for white skin or dark skin differs in the different groups. It is true that there are extremely few if any Negroes of pure African descent in the United States today; but this doesn't change the genetic analysis of a particular population or affect the opportunity to study it by methods that have worked in other genetic fields."

Social scientists have been studying racial differences for many years, Jensen says, citing some 400 major studies. "All of them point out—unhappily perhaps—that in the standard distribution of I.Q. throughout the population the Negro is 15 points lower than the white. Only 3 per cent of the Negro population exceed an I.Q. of 115; in the white population 16 per cent exceed 115. In the white population 1 per cent exceed 140; a sixth of that exceed 140 in the Negro population. A similar percentage prevails at the lower end of the distribution. In fact it may even be worse in the retarded area. A long-term study by researchers at Johns Hopkins, conducted in one rural county of Maryland, showed that 31 per cent of the Negro males tested between the ages of 40 and 44 were mentally retarded—that is, they had I.Q.'s under 70. This was true of only 1.5 per cent of the tested white males of the same age."

Jensen asks: "Is this genetic in origin or caused by environment? I think it must be genetic to a very large extent. When you control samples of white and black population for social class differences, you still have major differences in I.Q. between them—from 15 points on the average to 11 points over the various social classes. In other words, across the same occupational category and income bracket, you still find this striking fact—children of Negroes in the highest income class of our society will average lower in I.Q. than white children of the lowest class; this is backed up by a great deal of data, including that obtained in studies conducted by the Federal Government. You couldn't predict such results from purely environmental theory, and it would be highly improbable to assume that the entire influence was due to subtle factors of early prenatal and postnatal environment. It is more likely—though speculative of course—that Negroes brought here as slaves were selected for docility and strength rather than mental ability, and that through selective mating the mental qualities never had a chance to flourish.

"In the famous Coleman study, the American Indians come out lower on all environmental indices than do American Negroes; yet the Indians score higher on I.Q. and scholastic achievement. So do disadvantaged children of the island of Taiwan. In fact, they do as well as children of white middle-class parents in the United States.

"Remember—we're talking of populations here, not of individuals. There are Negro geniuses, and certainly many greatly talented figures among Negroes, and race should not stand in the way of hiring, promotions or providing awards. But in large groups, one is compelled to say that on the basis of these studies improved environment is not likely to change the fundamental intelligence of large groups of individuals to a substantial extent—no matter how romantic the environmentalists want to be."

Jensen grants that some extremely deprived children can have their I.Q.'s raised by markedly changing their environment. He mentions the classic and dramatic case of Isabel, studied by Kingsley Davis of the University of California. An illegitimate child, she was reared for her first six years in a dark attic by a deaf-mute mother. When found, she was unable to speak, and tests showed

that she had an idiot's mentality. But in two years in a good home with lots of attention her mental age jumped up to the average of her age group, and she could perform normally in school. But, as Jensen points out, her I.Q. didn't increase further than this average value. "You can boost an I.Q. in an enriched environment, but once its genetic potential is achieved—once the threshold environment capacity is reached—you cannot improve I.Q. any further. I am afraid there is nothing you can do to create an Einstein without the right kind of genes."

Against this skein of evidence the more rational critics of Jensen in anthropology, sociology and psychology have retaliated with a barrage of their own evidence and argument, picking their targets in virtually every aspect of the Jensen case. The I.Q. test, on which Jensen relies for a good deal of his data, has, for instance, come under probably the severest attack in the last few years. New York and Washington, anticipating pressure from minority groups, withdrew I.Q. testing from their school systems some years ago, but as a result of the Jensen article, the momentum of antipathy to testing has increased. This year, under pressure from Negro groups, the Los Angeles City Council voted to eliminate I.Q. tests from the early grades of the public school system; in Philadelphia, a similar change is being considered. One of the ironies of this movement is that the uneasiness that I.Q. testing generates among ethnic groups is shared by ardent right wingers such as the Birchites, who regard such testing as an instrument for Big Government brainwashing.

Many social scientists who once accepted I.Q. tests as predictive tools of school success and never thought more about it now slip into silence and leave the field to those who question whether there is even a definable quantity known as "g" or general intelligence separate from interaction with environment. Some in fact argue that I.Q. tests are culturally unfair—loaded with factual material that only certain groups in our society could know or respond to.

Then there are those who attack the reliability of the tests on other grounds. In the case of the highly tested Sirhan Sirhan, for instance, his first test score was 89, and a second test score some months later was 109. Did his intelligence increase or was there something wrong with the tests? Teacher expectations are also said to contribute to scores. An experiment performed by Harvard's Robert Rosenthal and Lenore Jacobson showed that if the teacher persuaded a random group of subjects to believe they were superior, they actually did better than a group not told anything. "If all this is so," the argument runs, "then intelligence tests tell us nothing. They're even dangerous because they lead one to believe that mental ability is fixed at birth and nothing can be done about it."

Jensen is not convinced, "I am afraid," he says, "that the long history of the I.Q. test cannot be overcome by these recent bursts of criticism. The reliability of the Stanford-Binet test is 95 per cent, with a 5 per cent error, due to such things as the subject's not being up to par when he took the test. This test is more reliable than TB diagnosis based on chest X-rays.

"I.Q. predicts scholastic performance better than any single factor or personality trait. The higher the I.Q., the higher the performance. Below 75 he will not get a high-school education (though he might get a diploma), and below 90 it is doubtful. A good I.Q. is necessary for school success, and this in turn stands at the heart of our technological civilization, which in its simplest terms depends on the ability to manipulate symbols and reason abstractly from them. Not all people with high I.Q.'s succeed in school or in life, of course; other qualities are also needed. The I.Q., however, as a thermometer, explains why children differ in school, and there is no better measure, when used properly, to indicate the factors involved in these differences.

"As for the argument that the I.Q. is culturally unfair, psychologists have tested children in a variety of cultures and have eliminated as many items that relate to one culture and not to another as they can. While you probably can't make an entirely culture-fair test, we do find that in these spe-cially devised, cross-culture tests, Negro youngsters score lower on abstract questions.

"As to teacher expectations, I am afraid that too much publicity in the popular press has been given to the book by Rosenthal and Jacobson, 'Pygmalion in the Classroom.' As a study, it is not regarded highly by professionals. Drs. Robert L. Thorndike and Richard Snow, for example, two psychologists who reviewed the book recently, state categorically that the book does nothing to raise standards of educational research. 'If there is such a bias as teacher expectation, the authors have not demonstrated it,' says Thorndike, and Snow adds that 'by publishing prematurely and inadequately they have performed a disservice to teachers and schools, to users and developers of mental tests, and perhaps worst of all to parents and children whose newly gained expectation may not prove quite so self-fulfilling.'"

Critics: Bruno Bettelheim and Benjamin Bloom argue that environment does have an effect on children's I.Q.'s, citing studies in Israel. They found that deprived Oriental Jewish youngsters from the desert raised in the kibbutzim showed higher I.Q.'s than those raised by their parents. And what about the Army qualification tests which showed that the scores of draftees in World War II were higher than those in World War I? Wasn't this caused by the general improvement in education—an environmental factor?

Jensen: "Bloom's and Bettelheim's argument would be more convincing if Negroes were to be raised in kibbutzim (as Bettleheim suggested recently to Congress) to see whether they improved greatly. In any case some deprived youngsters would get adequate nutrition and possibly the right adult models to identify with. This is a study worth pursuing. But as it stands conclusions drawn from the Israeli work are rather wishful.

"Social scientists who raise the environmentalist flag over the Army Alpha tests are also drawing too much from the data. After all, an Army Alpha test is not an I.Q. test; it is a knowledge test. The Army wanted mainly to know what the draftees knew, and thus the test correlates highly with the number of years of schooling. Moreover, to clinch this argument, a national survey in Scotland in which all the youngsters were given the I.Q. test a generation apart shows that the gain was a mere two to four points."

Critics: Could the I.Q. be determined at a very early stage of life, before or soon after birth, when it might be affected by a lack of proper nutrition? Perhaps many Negroes are short-changed in intelligence because of inadequate diets.

Jensen: "Nutrition is undoubtedly important in early development. But one would have to prove malnutrition in a majority of Negro youngsters who have taken the I.Q. tests. Herbert Birch of Albert Einstein Medical School, one of the leading researchers in this area, says he cannot find malnutrition in marked degree in Harlem and had to go for his studies of deprivation to Mexico and other Latin-American countries. The Indian youngsters, who came out higher on the I.Q. tests than the Negro, are much more malnourished than American Negro youngsters. So are the children of the poorest untouchables in India, but they got approximately the same I.Q. scores as the Negro youngsters in California public schools.

"I am in favor of studies of early environment, particularly the prenatal environment, and I have been analyzing data from California school children in this regard. I am studying two groups of half-brothers and half-sisters. The brother and sister live in the same home, so the environment is a common factor. However, they have different parentage. The members of one group have the same fathers but different mothers. Those of the second group have the same mother. The question is, are the children with different mothers less alike in I.Q. than those with the same mother. In other words, will the difference in their prenatal environments affect their I.Q.'s? I think the answer could help reduce the heredity-environment uncertainty, at least insofar as the prenatal aspect of environment is concerned."

Critics: The argument has been raised in the Harvard Educational Review and elsewhere that you cannot separate black genes from white genes, so how can you tell which produce high or low intelligence?

Jensen: "That is a silly question. There are no 'black' genes or 'white' genes; there are intelligence genes, which are found in populations in different proportions, somewhat like the distribution of blood types. The number of intelligence genes seems to be lower, over-all, in the black population than in the white.

"As to the effect of racial mixing, nobody has yet performed experiments that reveal its relative effect on I.Q. If the racial mixture weren't there, it is possible that the I.Q. difference between blacks and whites would be even greater. I think such studies should be done to lay this uncertainty to rest once and for all."

Critics: Even if the evidence suggests a genetic difference in racial intelligence distribution, is science really in a position to separate experimentally the effects of environment from heredity? Surely the factors are too complex, our tools too imprecise, and it would take generations to work out the interactions.

(The National Academy of Sciences underscored this viewpoint in their reaction to William Shockley, the Nobel physicist, who called for research into the genetic aspects of Negro intelligence. The academy declared that "there is no scientific basis for the statement that there are or are not substantial hereditary differences in intelligence between Negro and white populations. In the absence of some unforeseen way of equalizing all aspects of environment, answers to this question can hardly be more than reasonable guesses.")

Jensen: "This is true of a good deal of science. Take air turbulence for instance—my engineering friends tell me that we don't really know all the factors in it, and we have no precise law of turbulence, but engineers design many devices to take it into account.

"I think we can set up experiments to decrease the heredity-environment uncertainties. I referred earlier to Bettelheim's suggestion—place disadvantaged Negro children in kibbutzlike setups and see what happens. I think this is preferable to throwing money into the entire school system, hoping for the best. I believe science is capable of creating techniques to cut through the complexities, if given a chance. Social scientists should be scientists, not ideologists."

Critics: Isn't it terrible and self-defeating to make people think they can never break the bonds of their genes? Why raise the specter of invisible disadvantage to an already disadvantaged group? Right now the Negro is coming into his own. Why allow others to use a weapon against him at such a critical time in history when he needs everything to give him a sense of uplift?

Jensen: "I don't think one gets uplift from hiding from truths. Social scientists are annoyed because I am showing them that they must be loyal either to their science or their longings."

Thus the flames of this bloody social-moral-scientific debate leap ever higher, and Jensen has begun to take on the aspect of a professorial Joan of Arc. His square jaw seems more stubbornly set, and his deep-set eyes flash with the light of battle. In the cause (if one can call it that) he takes time off from a busy program to write his critics long, well-argued rebuttals. Though inherently a reticent person, he accepts interview sessions on popular television shows such as an upcoming David Susskind show. He has turned down offers that obviously are directed toward intellectually tarring and feathering him, but he says he is willing to match wits with opponents who will debate the subject without overtones of circus and politics.

One of Jensen's strongest characteristics, according to friends and colleagues, is his single-minded intensity and his extraordinary capacity for work. A friend recalls the day when Jensen left a building and took a seat in his car, his mind caught up in a problem. He waited there some minutes before it occurred to him he was supposed to be driving the car. As is often true of men given to such mental absorptions, Jensen's breaks for relaxation occasionally have a weird, childlike aspect. His wife recalls that he was once so overcome with joy after leaving a theater that he broke into a jog and skipped down the street, flapping his arms like a modern day Icarus trying to reach the sun. A police car pulled up and Jensen had to explain that nothing was wrong. Jensen says he was inspired by Nureyev, the Russian dancer, who followed a similar routine once when he was overcome by the tall buildings in New York. "Moving one's arms," Jensen says thoughtfully, "helps the sense of momentum."

Jensen has always been dominated by an ascetic approach to life though he has somewhat mellowed in recent years. He still doesn't smoke and seldom drinks. An old friend claims that as a young man Jensen didn't even use after-shave lotion because it seemed impure. Yet Jensen seems always to have been captivated by men of power and charisma. He was terribly attracted to Norman Thomas because of his great magical skill as an orator; and he once became so intrigued with Gandhi that he wanted to run off to India to write a book about him. For one six-month period he was an avowed vegetarian—possibly under the influence of another of his god-heroes, Bernard Shaw.

Arthur Jensen (known as Bob to his family) was born in San Diego, the only son of a Minnesotan of Danish stock who owned a lumber supply business. He recalls that his mother, who is now 80, traveled by stage coach. One of his earliest memories is of the neighborhood magic shows he used to organize. He himself gave free mind-reading performances, a bit of small-boy fraud that depended upon exchange of secret signals.

Friends recall that Jensen grew up a loner. As a teenager he became enamored of orchestra conductors and wanted to become one. Working day and night, he achieved his ambition at the tender age of 13, when he took the baton of the Bonham Brothers Band, a private orchestra of 100 pieces that played at Sunday night church gatherings.

Although in time Jensen concluded that he could not become a great conductor—"I couldn't quite believe in my own infallibility"—over the years he has continued to worship the orchestra conductor, and every chance he gets he tries to crash rehearsals. On one occasion he was thrown out of a rehearsal by Pierre Monteux, though

Jensen says he felt better about it when he learned that Otto Klemperer once suffered the same fate.

"Conductors are great brains," says Jensen, his eyes flashing. "They believe in themselves and they're marvelously undemocratic about art. The great conductor has a clear picture of what he wants and how to get it. He internalizes everything and the orchestra follows him like a slave if it's convinced he's touched with genius. The conductor uses all of himself; the scientist uses only part."

Today Jensen still works up musical scores as though readying himself for the call. He reads and remembers virtually everything he reads about his heroes and their music. In London he won a B.B.C. contest by identifying Sibelius's Fifth from hearing just the last two notes.

Jensen's interest in psychology may have been a natural consequence of his fascination with powerful and awe-inspiring individuals. He recalls that an aunt gave him a book on I.Q. when he was in high school, and from that moment on he haunted the San Diego Public Library, reading such works as the great John B. Watson's book on behaviorism and trying to find out why people are different from one another.

In 1942 he enrolled at Berkeley, majoring in psychology, larded with such hard sciences as physiology and biology. After graduation he returned to San Diego and accepted a teaching appointment at Hoover High School while he continued on for a masters degree at San Diego State College. Then he served a brief stint in the Social Welfare Department of the city interviewing applicants for old-age assistance.

In 1952 Jensen enrolled at Columbia University for his Ph.D. in psychology and then went on to the University of Maryland, where he did a comparative personality study of three types of adolescents—delinquent aggressive boys, nondelinquent aggressive boys and "shrinking violets." The boys were asked to respond to a series of pictures. Jensen found some relationship between aggression and sex (as others had found before him), particularly in the delinquent boys, and he pub-

lished these and related findings in 1961 in his first book, written with Dr. Percival M. Symonds of Columbia and entitled: "From Adolescent to Adult."

Jensen moved on to the University of London, where he came under the influence of Prof. Hans Eysenck, a pioneer in behavior therapy, or as he describes it, "the application of Pavlov to neuroses." Jensen was impressed with Eysenck's efforts to find objective, quantitative approaches to psychological testing.

In 1958 he accepted an appointment in Berkeley as assistant professor and devoted himself to his current interest—the relationship between behavior and intelligence. At Berkeley he met a black-haired, vivacious girl named Barbara De-Larme; the daughter of an airline pilot, she was studying psychology. Barbara describes the courtship very simply: "Bob's approach to women is like his approach to everything else: direct and candid. He stared at me for two weeks, followed me to the laboratory and proposed, and I accepted. What else could I do?" They were married in 1960.

Jensen concentrated at first on individual differences in verbal learning in college students, but in 1962 he became interested in testing children. He developed a series of tests which could be used in any language, directed at discovering how fast children learn. He tested Mexican-American youngsters and then went on to test Negro and white children in Oakland, Richmond and other Bay Area cities. He found that he was measuring two different sets of learning abilities—what he now calls Level 1, associative learning, and Level 2, conceptual learning and problem-solving ability. The first ability involves simply the retention of input and the capacity to repeat it; the second involves the student's ability to manipulate and transform material.

For example, one of Jensen's Level 1 tests is made up of a series of pictures of common objects (or the objects themselves in miniature) which the child is asked to recall by name after they're shown one by one and removed from sight. Negroes and whites who may differ in I.Q. by as much as 20 points score equally on this test. In a Level 2 test, the examiner groups the different objects in categories—say, furniture, animals, clothing and food. Then he mixes them again and they are presented in random order, one at a time. After the child has seen all the objects again, he is asked to name as many as he can remember. This is done a number of times. The white children catch on and soon recall the objects by their categories; they call them off in groups and thus remember more individual objects. The Negro children by and large don't do this, or they group the objects on a functional basis; they relate apples and horses for instance. They fail to make use of the group concept as a memory device, but call off the objects more or less in the order they saw them, and they don't remember as many.

In the first and second grades there is no signifant difference in the amount of recall or in the amount of "clustering" as it is called, but in the fourth and fifth grades the difference appears and Negro children in general start to fall behind white children as the conceptual material gets more difficult. In short, Jensen concludes that Level 1 ability is distributed about equally in all races while Level 2 is distributed unevenly. Jensen contends that for Level 2 abilities to develop requires not merely learning ability but also certain inherited neural structures in the brain. "Without them, the learning of abstract concepts doesn't develop," he says.

Jensen drew this conclusion slowly. In the tests themselves, he made sure that the children knew the names of each object and each category. He also investigated the role of motivation and found that both Negro and white children do better when well motivated but not enough better to change the scores significantly. (Oriental children, incidentally, stay the same; they are apparently already motivated to do their best.)

Jensen found that scores on the category lists correlated with I.Q. differences among the youngsters. He concluded that Level 2 is "pretty much what we mean by I.Q.

Then Jensen reviewed all the published papers dealing with genetic differences. He found Burt's

study on twins and was amazed at the lack of attention given to it by social scientists in America.

Even major geneticists had not heard of it—largely, Jenson believes, because of the built-in environmental bias which had led most social scientists in the field to forgo their usual examination of opposing studies.

Jensen's first paper on the heritability of intelligence was published by the National Academy of Sciences in 1967; in it he expressed the belief that 80 per cent of the variability in intelligence could be attributed to inheritance, the other 20 per cent to environment. He did point out that this estimate was based on tests in Europe and North America and could not be generalized to other populations, and he is amused today by those critics who cannot bring themselves to believe in the figures but refuse to examine the test data. Jensen gave a talk on the subject in San Diego suggesting how educational policy might be geared to this finding through schools catering to diversity of mental ability rather than to sameness and returned to Berkeley to find himself headlined: "UC Prof Urges Diverse School for Minorities." He didn't know it then, but the article inspired a confidential memo circulated in Berkeley educational circles hinting that Jensen was "racist."

In April, 1968, Donald Moore, then editor of the Harvard Educational Review, invited Jensen to write an article based on his report in San Diego. The editors outlined the article, and Jensen wrote it, as is his custom, in longhand on airplanes. He says several geneticists had a chance to review his draft and concurred with his basic analysis, if not with all his conclusions. His opening sentence ("Compensatory education has been tried and apparently has failed"), which caused a storm all its own, was put in, Jensen says, because he learned from a high-school English teacher always to start an article with a strong statement.

The editors cut some 15 pages from the original manuscript, and though Jensen says he never saw galley proofs, he admits to being pleased with the final results, even though there were some printing errors in text and figures. The editors then sent a copy of the article to The Boston Globe, whose reporter telephoned Jensen to check it out. By an odd coincidence, George Jones of U.S. News and World Report was in Jensen's office when Jensen took the call from Boston. Jones immediately sensed a good story, and the result was an interview in the magazine which unleashed some of the torrent of controversy.

The Harvard editors, taken aback by the storm they had raised, reacted at first in a confused manner. For one thing, they refused to send out reprints of the article, even to Jensen. He had to reprint the article himself, paying the costs out of his own pocket. A protest was lodged with Harvard President Nathan Pusey by University of Buffalo psychologists, and reprints became available. Then a comedy of errors developed over who said what and did what to whom. The review editor, for example, insisted he'd never asked Jensen for material on racial differences, but apologized when Jensen waved aloft his letter outlining the article.

While the furor over his article continues to mount, Jensen has been giving some thought to the practical implications of his findings. His own visits to schools in the Bay Area and elsewhere have convinced him that educational policy requires a complete overhaul. "Everywhere I saw children failing to learn at all," he says. "In New York City children in the 12th grade are at the sixth-grade level. In one classroom in Berkeley I found a group of Negro youngsters who were going to class but not learning to read; I tested them and found that they did as well on the test as did white youngsters doing well in school in another neighborhood. What happened? I think that teachers reward only signs of conceptual brightness but not things learned by rote. So without a sense of satisfaction these youngsters get turned off on school. Both sets should be rewarded."

Children arrive in first grade lacking intellectual readiness, Jensen says. "It is important for a child to have a perception of his own growing mastery and to see himself approach a goal. If the child doesn't get this, he fails to get reinforcement and he responds by failure to learn. I once tried to teach my daughter Roberta how to play chess when she was 5 because I heard that the great Capablanca learned it at 4.

"Some psychologists say that the child can learn anything if he or she has each prerequisite step under control. I don't quite believe this. In the case of chess we started with simple categories like black and white and then worked up to the names and moves of the pieces. She found it was fun—learning is fun, and kids do it naturally—and she quickly learned how each piece moved, but she couldn't put it all together in a game. She made bad moves; it wasn't fun any longer, and she turned off. So I learned 5 was too young for her. Her capacity was not yet developed. So I finally dropped it and taught her how to play checkers. At 6 she went back to chess and now plays reasonably well.

"Our schools ignore this simple lesson. Intellectual activity is not simply a function of prior experience; it is prior experience plus maturation of the brain. An average child of 5 cannot draw a diamond; it takes a child of 7 to accomplish it. A 4-year-old can copy a square but cannot copy a square which has a diagonal in it. The long and short of it is this: you don't teach before the organism is ready, or what is learned will be learned with inferior mechanisms to the detriment of the individual in later life. Teachers need to recognize readiness and adapt their teaching to differences among children and not, as they do now, teach everyone with the same program and the same sequencing of materials."

In effect, Jensen says, the school system must set up a diversity of programs that match the abilities and readiness of youngsters. "Some children will be happiest and most productive learning by rote alone. Others, who have conceptual abilities, should be in classes where they can make the best use of them. If this results in a racial imbalance in classes, so be it. You don't do a service for the child who has a mental age of 5 if you treat him as though he were 7."

In his article, Jensen emphasizes this concern for individual differences: "Whenever we select a person for some special educational purpose, whether for special instruction in a grade-school class for children with learning problems, or for a 'gifted' class with an advanced curriculum...we are selecting an *individual*....It is unjust to allow the mere fact of an individual's racial or social background to affect the treatment accorded to him. All persons rightfully must be regarded on the basis of their individual qualities and merits, and all social, educational, and economic institutions must have built into them the mechanisms for insuring and maximizing the treatment of persons according to their individual behavior."

Jensen acknowledges, however, that "whether we like it or not," our educational system serves to sort out children to assume different levels in the occupational hierarchy. Intelligence tests and academic performance have become occupational screening devices. But since I.Q. "is not the whole of human abilities," Jensen says, "there may be some fallacy and some danger in making it the *sine qua non* of fitness to play a productive role in modern society." He suggests that such hiring requirements may be irrelevant for many jobs, and that they should be re-examined. Educational programs to train people to meet the actual requirements of a given job, he says, may be more worthwhile than efforts to raise I.Q.'s or academic performance.

As a professor, Jensen still operates from the cool objectivity (he hopes) of the university, but he is closer to the great social debates than ever before. With racial alienation rising, his ordeal, one realizes, is only beginning, as it is for the rest of America.

There appear to be wide differences in "educability" of children of similar IQ drawn from different social classes or different subcultural groups.[3] Individual differences in cognitive style may depend, to a degree as yet unappreciated, upon the individual's subcultural milieu. The data that this paper presents on differences in semantic systems and differences in linguistic development between subcultural groups directly address the cognitive style-educability problem.

A survey of word associations of black and white elementary school children has revealed, contrary to expectation, that slum children are apparently more advanced linguistically than suburban children in the *first grade* in terms of paradigmatic responses.[4] Paradigmatic responses are those with form class matching that of the stimulus; they are by far the most frequent kind of adult response. To "table," for instance, adults respond "chair," "leg," "furniture," etc. Very young children do *not* give responses with similar substitution properties, i.e., response words that could replace the stimulus word in a sentence. They tend to give syntagmatic responses ("table—break, table—red"), responses that follow (or precede) the stimulus word in a sentence. Paradigmatic responses increase markedly between kindergarten and fifth grade, and within age strata their prevalence is correlated positively with IQ. They are one index of linguistic development. White first-grade slum children of average IQ resemble gifted (IQ 130) suburban children; black first-graders of average IQ who live in the inner-city lag behind inner-city white first-graders in paradig-

[1]This research was performed pursuant to a grant from the Office of Education, U.S. Department of Health, Education, and Welfare to the Center for the Study of the Social Organization of Schools and the Learning Process, The Johns Hopkins University. Some earlier data-gathering for this research was supported by the National Institute of Child Health and Development, Grant No. HD 00921-05 to Doris R. Entwisle.

[2]We are grateful to Dr. Orlando Furno, Director of Research, Baltimore City Public Schools for arranging for this research and to the staff and students in Schools 1, 6, 10, 17, 19, 22, 23, and 114 for their help.

[3]See Arthur R. Jensen "Social Class, Race and Genetics: Implications for Education." *American Educational Research Journal*, 5 (January, 1968), pp. 1–42.

[4]See Doris R. Entwisle, *Word Associations of Young Children*, Baltimore: The Johns Hopkins Press, 1966; also "Developmental Sociolinguistics: Inner City Children." *American Journal of Sociology*, 74 (July, 1968), pp. 37–49.

16
Racial Differences in the Language of Grade School Children[1, 2]

Doris R. Entwisle and Ellen Greenberger

Reprinted by permission from *Sociology of Education*, vol. 42, no. 3, Summer 1969, pp. 238–250.

matic responses, but they are *ahead* of white sub-urban first-graders of average IQ.

Using paradigmatic response rate as a measure, one finds that there is relative superiority of the white over the black disadvantaged child when both are raised in the inner-city, but the black slum child excels the white suburban child. The superiority is short-lived, however, for by third grade suburban children have surpassed the inner-city children.

What cultural influences within the family and/or community could produce the patterns observed? Why, for instance, with IQ held constant across groups, are first-grade white children advanced in paradigmatic response rates compared to first-grade black children when both have been raised in the inner-city? A more revealing index than paradigmatic rate may be the actual distribution of responses given. What responses, for instance, do white and black children give? If few responses are given in common, the implication is that the same (stimulus) word means different things to children of different groups. The main issue to which this paper addresses itself is the congruence between distributions of associations of white and black children. As will be shown, the associative patterns differ much more between the two groups than the paradigmatic-rate index would suggest. Many linguists suppose that the urban American Negro has a significantly different dialect from that of his white neighbor, possibly because of historical development of the Negro vernacular from Creole roots.[5] It is not the intention of this paper to provide evidence on that issue. Rather this report concerns *cognitive* aspects of language and the linguistic resources of various groups. Differences in word associations presumably reflect differences in semantic structure between white and black children and could develop apart from, or in addition to, dialect differences, especially in segregated environments. That this may be one consequence of segregation is suggested by recent evidence that black college

students have different associative patterns from white college students.[6]

To what matters are word associations relevant? Appropriate word associations are directly related to word recognition,[7] to acquisition of syntax,[8] to problem solving,[9] and especially to reading.[10] Word associations that are "different" reduce both speed and comprehension of reading, and interfere, perhaps on these grounds, with efficiency of taking multiple choice tests.[11] Word associations, then, are a means of describing cultural differences in language and thinking and a source of differences in performance on cognitive tasks.

Many reading primers and language workbooks are designed to capitalize upon high frequency words and the associations between these words assumed to exist in the language habits of the "average" child. Lately efforts have been directed toward making story themes more appropriate for children of different cultural and socioeconomic backgrounds, but as far as we know, no systematic notice has been taken of differing verbal habits or of differences in semantics among cultural groups that could affect the teaching of basic language skills in the elementary school. One hindrance to research on semantics is that there is neither a theoretical basis from which to begin, nor even consensus concerning the range of phenomena for which a theory should be constructed.[12] Different semantic structures may be an important component of differences in educability among SES groups. To profit from instruction

[5]This is described by William A. Stewart in "Urban Negro Speech: Sociolinguistic Factors Affecting English Teaching," in Roger W. Shuy (ed.), *Social Dialects and Language Learning*, Champaign, Illinois: National Council of Teachers of English, 1964.

[6]See Leon H. Belcher and Joel T. Campbell, "An Exploratory Study of Word Associations of Negro College Students," *Psychological Reports*, in press.
[7]This is widely documented. See for example William M. O'Neil, "The Effect of Verbal Association in Tachistoscopic Recognition," *Australian Journal of Psychology*, 5 (June, 1953), pp. 42–45; Richard O. Rouse and J. Scott Vernis, "The Effect of Associative Connections on the Recognition of Flashed Words," *Journal of Verbal Learning and Verbal Behavior*, 1 (January, 1963), pp. 300–303.
[8]Roger Brown and Jean Berko, "Word Association and the Acquisition of Grammar," *Child Development*, 31 (March, 1960), pp. 1–14.
[9]Paul E. Johnson, "Associative Meaning of Concepts in Physics," *Journal of Educational Psychology*, 55 (April, 1964), pp. 84–88.
[10]Siegmar Muehl, "The Effects of Visual Discrimination PreTraining on Learning to Read a Vocabulary List in Kindergarten Children," *Journal of Educational Psychology*, 4 (August, 1960), pp. 218–221.
[11]S. Jay Samuels, "Effect of Experimentally Learned Word Associations on the Acquisition of Reading Responses," *Journal of Educational Psychology*, 57 (April, 1966), pp. 159–163.
[12]For a broad description of this problem see George A. Miller, "Psycholinguistic Approaches to the Study of Communication," in David L. Arm (ed.), *Journeys in Science: Small Steps—Great Strides*, Albuquerque: The University of New Mexico Press, 1967.

TABLE 16.1
Design of subjects in Sample

	White children				Black children				
	White interviewer		Black interviewer		Black interviewer		White Interviewer		Grand totals
Subjects	Med. IQ	Low IQ	Med. IQ	Low IQ	Med. IQ	Low IQ	Med. IQ	Low IQ	
Kindergarten:									
Number of children	—	20	—	20	—	20	—	20	80
Average IQ*	—	—	—	—	—	—	—	—	
First Grade:									
Number of children	20	20	17	20	20	20	9	20	146
Average IQ	100.1	79.5	99.4	80.1	98.7	79.9	97.6	79.9	
Third Grade:									
Number of children	20	20	19	20	20	20	20	16	155
Average IQ	99.7	80.8	100.3	80.5	99.9	80.6	99.6	81.1	
Fifth Grade:									
Number of children	20	20	20	20	20	20	20	20	160
Average IQ	99.7	80.3	99.8	80.6	99.5	80.7	99.6	80.5	
Total	—	—	—	—	—	—	—	—	541

*No IQ data available for kindergarten children.

TABLE 16.2
Racial composition of schools sampled

School	Non-white	White	Total
1	207	3	210
6	1	460	461
10	60	449	509
19 and A	1447	0	1447
22	155	620	775
23	0	394	394
114	447	18	465

the learner must bring many skills to the classroom; a semantic system congruent with that of the teacher or the text-book authors may be one crucial "skill." Since associations can be shaped by training[13]—experimentally learned word associations have been shown to facilitate acquisition of reading responses—the findings presented in the following section should have practical application. One of us (Entwisle) is presently developing some classroom procedures derived from this evidence.

METHOD

Both the sample design and the procedure for data collection have been reported completely elsewhere and will be reviewed here briefly.[14]

Data were gathered from children in Baltimore City, Maryland, who resided within census tracts in the downtown area with the lowest median family incomes (as low as $2400) in the city. Since elementary schools in the downtown area are very racially imbalanced, to procure children whose living conditions were similar, schools with one racial group predominating were balanced by nearby schools (within 3 or 4 blocks) with the other group predominant.

Tables 16.1 and 16.2 illustrate the sample design and show the racial composition of the schools. Black and white children of average IQ (95–105)

[13]Samuels, *op. cit.*

[14]Entwisle, *op. cit.*

and low IQ (85 or below) were identified through the use of school records. (For the most part, IQs for third- and fifth-grade children were based on their Kuhlmann-Anderson scores obtained in the second and fourth grades, respectively. First-grade children were given the Primary Mental Abilities [PMA] test upon school entrance; their IQs were based on four subtests, omitting the motor subtest.)

The entire design for grades 1, 3, and 5 was replicated four times (see Table 16.1): white interviewers with white children, black interviewers with white children, white interviewers with black children, and black interviewers with black children. Racial groups were equivalent in terms of IQ and grade. Interviewers were all middle-class with some college training. The interviewing procedure was on an individual basis; care was taken to keep the atmosphere game-like and pleasant.

Eighty (40 white and 40 black) kindergarten children also were interviewed; some comparative data will be reported for them. Since they could not be selected on IQ (no tests were given to them), both age and racial comparisons involving them are not as easy to interpret as similar comparisons of older children. We infer from data on first-grade children in the same schools attended by the kindergartners that the white kindergarten children in our sample probably have a mean IQ about 76 and the black kindergarten children have a mean IQ somewhat lower, around 70. Nevertheless, because of these limitations, the main data cited in this article are for grades 1, 3, and 5.

The ninety-six stimulus words represent the several form classes (nouns, adjectives, verbs, pronouns, adverbs). Nouns, adjectives, and verbs are stratified on frequency: there are eight high frequency (over 1,000), eight medium frequency (500–999), and eight low frequency (499 or less) of each according to the Thorndike-Lorge J-count. Although other form classes do not permit a frequency division (since there are not enough words), eight words of each kind were included as stimulus words. Each child in the sample responded to the entire list of 96 stimulus words; after classification (in terms of frequency and

type), these responses provide the basis for the results reported here.

Earlier (1961–63) another study using the same procedures was carried out in the suburbs of Baltimore; that study provides comparable data for white middle-class and blue collar children.[15] IQ strata were formed in the same way. The middle-class youngsters were drawn from schools in a good residential area just north of the city line (median annual income of $9200, average years of schooling of father, 14.1, estimated from 1960 Census data), and the blue collar youngsters were drawn from schools located in a highly industrialized area along the Chesapeake Bay just east of the city (median annual income of $6200, average years of schooling of father, 9.7, estimated from 1960 Census data).

One might question the reliability of associates. For example, if two separate groups of suburban children were interviewed, to what extent would their associates be the same?[16] Is variation within groups as large as the variation noted here between groups? The reliability of associates (shown by way of internal consistency when groups are broken down by sex) is high, especially for associates that occur at rates of 10% or more; moreover, there is considerable correspondence for words with rates below 10%. In no case for suburban first-graders is a word occurring at or above a rate of 10% not consistent for boys and girls; many others below that rate are consistent. (Most of the differences pointed to in this paper are based on "frequent" responses.) This consistency between sexes composing a larger sample occurs even though sex differences in word associations are well-documented—"pants" is a more frequent response to "long" for boys than for girls, for instance. Reliability, then, is high and suggests that racial differences would hold up if the same individuals were re-interviewed.

[15]*Ibid.*
[16]Reliabilities of over .90 are reported for associations over all form classes by Murray Tillman and Charlotte L. Williams, "Associative Characteristics of Selected Form Classes for Children Varying in Age and Intelligence," presented at AERA meetings, February, 1968.

TABLE 16.3
Percentages of paradigmatic responses (inner city children, Baltimore City, Maryland, 1965–66; suburban children, Baltimore County, Maryland, 1961–63).

| Stimulus Word | Inner city children | | | | Suburban children (all white) | | | |
| | White | | Black | | Middle class | | Blue collar | |
	Med. IQ	Low IQ	Med. IQ	Low IQ	High IQ	Low IQ	Med. IQ	Low IQ
First grade								
Nouns	57.5	62.8	57.2	51.6	66.8	65.1	59.0	59.7
Adjectives	45.9	34.0	38.9	24.3	45.7	29.3	30.1	21.7
Verbs	26.0	23.3	20.2	22.3	22.4	21.1	18.7	19.2
Adverbs	26.9	15.0	15.9	12.2	30.9	15.5	16.4	8.8
Pronouns	45.6	32.2	37.5	31.0	43.0	30.2	27.0	19.1
Third grade								
Nouns	77.1	70.5	72.5	63.7	74.8	71.8	73.1	70.7
Adjectives	69.1	64.2	63.6	55.0	74.2	71.4	73.3	62.8
Verbs	38.1	34.7	38.6	31.3	57.1	47.4	49.9	35.5
Adverbs	40.6	39.6	35.0	30.3	63.0	50.2	49.1	42.7
Pronouns	69.7	64.0	70.0	60.9	64.6	67.3	64.8	64.6

RESULTS

The Syntactic-Paradigmatic Shift

First-grade black slum children have lower paradigmatic response rates than white slum children, but they have *higher* rates than white suburban children. Pronouns and adjectives are the two classes that show the largest changes around this age; the medium-IQ inner city black child *exceeds* the medium-IQ white suburban child (whether middle-class or blue collar) in paradigmatic rates for pronouns (37% vs. 30% and 27%) and for adjectives (39% vs. 29% and 30%). Low-IQ blue collar children (there are no low-IQ middle-class children in the sample) are surpassed by low-IQ black slum children in paradigmatic rates for adjectives (24% vs. 22%) and for pronouns (31% vs. 19%). The medium-IQ inner-city black first-grader is far ahead of the medium-IQ white suburban child for adjectives (39% vs. about 30% for both middle-class and blue collar). Verbs would be expected to show small differences because paradigmatic rates for verbs are still low for all groups at this age—verbs show changes later—but the slum child compares favorably on verbs across both IQ levels. By third grade, however, the favorable position of the slum child has been erased; suburban children lead on all paradigmatic measures. (See Table 16.3.)

The next question concerns the syntactic-paradigmatic shift. Considerable data support the fact that word associations evolve through a syntagmatic-paradigmatic phase.[17] A response word which normally follows a stimulus word syntactically (go—home) is replaced by a response word that is a substitute for the stimulus word (go—went) as children grow older. With some subcultural groups whose pace of linguistic development is slowed, namely the Amish, syntagmatic responses disappear relatively slowly.[18] A rough

[17]See Doris R. Entwisle, Daniel F. Forsyth, and Rolf Muuss, "The Syntactic-Paradigmatic Shift in Children's Word Association," *Journal of Verbal Learning and Verbal Behavior*, 3 (1964), pp. 19–29.
[18]Doris R. Entwisle, "Developmental Sociolinguistics: A Comparative Study in Four Subcultural Settings," *Sociometry*, 29 No. 1 (March, 1966), pp. 67–84.

TABLE 16.4
Syntactic responses in per cents

Slum children		Verbs Adverbs	Nouns Verbs	Adjectives Nouns
Kindergarten	White	6.5	21.1	46.5
	Black	3.8	12.4	55.3
First grade	White	7.5	15.5	34.0
	Black	7.5	14.7	35.0
Suburban children (combined middle class and blue collar, all white)*				
First grade		7.3	18.9	44.1
Third grade		8.6	13.6	18.3

*Differences in the IQ composition of the inner city and suburban groups are ignored. Since this favors the suburban group, one would expect the shift to occur sooner rather than later in the suburban children. Blue collar and middle class differences are negligible; suburban data are combined.

measure of the number of syntactic responses can be obtained by tabulating nouns in response to adjectives, verbs in response to nouns, and adverbs in response to verbs. (These form classes frequently are manifest in these orders in sentences.)

The data in Table 16.4 reveal that there are negligible differences between white and black first-graders for these three categories of syntagmatic responses. (The kindergarten difference probably reflects an IQ effect more than a racial effect, but is consistent with the finding that delay in the shift implies a slower rate of development.) In comparing inner-city children with suburban children, in every instance slum first-graders are ahead of suburban first-graders. For example, nouns responded to with verbs generally decrease between first and third grade (part of the syntactic-paradigmatic shift) and both white and Negro slum children are more advanced than the suburban children on this measure at the first grade level. Thus, slum children of both racial groups appear to be further along the path of the syntactic-paradigmatic shift but about equal with respect to one another. (One should bear in mind that the average IQ of the suburban children is at least 10 points higher.) The shift away from syntagmatic responses, then, in black and white slum children

is about the same, but the paradigmatic response rate is higher in the white children.

Numbers of Different Responses[19]

Blacks consistently give more different responses than whites to the same stimulus. The increased variability of response is most apparent at first grade where in 67 out of 96 possible comparisons (96 stimulus words) blacks exceed whites. Furthermore, it is for words of *highest* frequency that the difference is most noticeable. (See Table 16.5.) In some ways the number of different responses and paradigmatic rates are complementary, but in a certain sense they are not. For example, to the stimulus word "table," *54* white first-graders and *52* Negro first-graders respond with a noun, but *10* more different nouns are given by Negro children (80 children in each group). This finding pervades words of all form classes. Low level of commonality (low total percentage of responses accounted for by primary, secondary, and tertiary associates) in other groups has pointed to

[19]Complete data are given in Doris R. Entwisle and Ellen Greenberger, "Differences in the Language of Negro and White Grade-School Children," Center for the Study of the Social Organization of Schools, The Johns Hopkins University (May, 1968).

TABLE 16.5

Number of different responses (out of 640) by form-class frequency groups (IQ composition of black and white groups is equivalent)

Form-class	First grade		Third grade		Fifth grade	
	Black	**White**	**Black**	**White**	**Black**	**White**
Nouns						
High frequency	407	367	280	249	191	179
Med. frequency	408	365	260	248	163	156
Low frequency	464	457	359	340	222	187
Adjectives						
High frequency	419	343	208	176	102	89
Med. frequency	397	380	255	263	186	179
Low frequency	428	396	277	273	152	160
Verbs						
High frequency	447	438	363	311	235	194
Med. frequency	511	495	462	435	354	355
Low frequency	511	505	450	442	338	348
Adverbs	517	487	388	385	297	286
Pronouns	394	377	220	235	156	137
Miscellaneous	457	421	312	315	231	220

(a) less mature individuals or (b) less educated individuals.[20]

Semantic Systems

The most interesting racial differences are those between semantic systems. If a stimulus word elicits an entirely different set of associations in white children from those it elicits in black children, the stimulus word can be considered to mean two different things. Tabulations of the three most frequent responses for each stimulus word suggest that there may be *wide* differences in meaning for the same words.[21] Racial differences are greatest for the youngest children. For example, the word "color" yields "blue," "book," and "yellow" for white kindergarten children as the three most frequent responses. *None* of these is present for Negro kindergartners; their three high frequency responses are "crayon," "coloring book," and "tolor," Similarly, while black and white first-graders' responses look more alike than

[20]Mark R. Rosenzweig, "Word Associations of French Workmen: Comparisons with Associations of French Students and American Workmen and Students," *Journal of Verbal Learning and Verbal Behavior*, 3 (February, 1964), pp. 57–69.
[21]Entwisle and Greenberger, *op. cit.*

kindergartners', there are still rather remarkable differences between them. Comparisons in terms of specific responses are difficult to make because the data are so voluminous, but two facts are outstanding:

(1) The number of nonsense or klang responses (an immature kind of response) is far greater in the black first-graders. *Using only the three most frequent responses* to the 24 adjectives, and emphasizing that adjectives are rather well developed by first grade, we note among black first-graders "mack," "bark," "mard," "nigh," "bong," "bean," "teasant," "mo," "mour," "bristy," plus some other words that are difficult to classify unambiguously but which are probably also nonsense or klang (like "hour" as a response to "sour"). Comparable responses made by white first-graders include only "hong." In other words, the 24 adjectives are, with one or two exceptions, already well on the way to being incorporated into the semantic systems of white children, but black youngsters are giving *as high frequency responses* a minimum of 11 nonsense responses to these 24 adjectives at first grade. The reader will see the same patterns if he examines high-frequency responses to nouns ("sheep" yields "heap"), to adverbs ("mently" and "bently" are given to "gently"), to verbs ("bad," "fad," and

"mad" are given to "add"). Even for pronouns, where responses of both racial groups consist almost exclusively of other pronouns, black children give "mit," "hen," "bus," and "must" while all responses of white children seem to be standard English.

(2) Even when primary responses are identical as between blacks and whites, as for instance "hot" in response to "cold," the frequency of response for Negro children is markedly lower (34% vs. 13%). This comparison is made more readily among third-graders' responses, because by then convergence toward a single high-frequency response has proceeded rather far. For eight high-frequency adjectives the strength of the primary response in white children ranges from 46% to 71%, whereas for Negro children the corresponding figures are 34% to 58%.

Do slum groups differ in semantics from suburban children? Again, comparisons in terms of specific responses are awkward, but the overall impression is that white slum children possess semantic systems that overlap considerably with those of the (white) suburban children at first grade. The differences already noted between disadvantaged white and black first graders also separate the black slum child from the suburban child.

At third grade there are more synonyms given by suburban children. This is consistent with their greater production of paradigmatic responses, but it also seems to reflect a much more mature kind of semantic structure. For example, to the high-frequency verb "tell" suburban children respond "ask" (11%), and "talk" (8%); white slum children respond "me" (12%) and "told" (9%); and black slum children respond "well" (9%) and "talk" (8%).

Differences between Negro and white responses to "black" are particularly interesting. No responses that pertain to human beings are given by white children, whereas black children respond "child," "girls," "hand," "man," and even "yes" to the stimulus word "black." Along the same lines, the most frequent response among black third-graders to "sour" is "still good" (25%); this response never occurs for white suburban children.

These particular responses suggest a great deal about the self-concepts and life styles of black youngsters.

All responses given ten or more times by any race-grade group were compared across groups, but were found to add little information to that already given.

DISCUSSION

Analyses of word association responses suggest that inner-city black children are slightly behind inner-city white children in evolution of word-association responses along a syntagmatic-paradigmatic continuum when both are of the same measured IQ. In the development of paradigmatic responses and in the shift away from syntactic responses, the two groups do not differ greatly. The relative position of the two groups in the general population, however, is not generally as favorable as our results suggest, because all comparisons are made with IQ held constant and overall a greater proportion of blacks have lower IQs in the population at large.[22] Our own estimate of unselected first-graders suggests a group difference of at least 6–10 IQ points. The data from kindergarten children unselected on IQ suggest that the typical inner city black child is probably rather far behind the typical white child in linguistic development at the time of school entrance.

The significance of large differences in semantic structures between black and white disadvantaged children is not simply the lagging paradigmatic rates for blacks. It is the kindergarten children whose reading readiness and other verbal behaviors are being shaped for beginning reading instruction in the first grade, and yet at this grade level almost no responses were held in common by the two racial groups. (As mentioned, the kindergarten groups are not matched on IQ, so differences owing to IQ, expected to be large at this

[22]A.M. Shuey, *The Testing of Negro Intelligence* (2nd edition), New York: Social Science Press, 1966. A difference in average IQ of 10 points favoring whites over blacks is documented. Other differences with Jewish or Oriental children deviating from the general mean in a positive direction are also well known. When one generalizes to the population as a whole, these group differences must be taken into account.

age, add to the racial differences.) We suspect that differences in semantics may be of overriding importance, because by our measures suburban children are also behind the average-IQ inner-city child at first grade, whereas by third grade the suburban children have advanced tremendously. The inner-city black children have semantic systems overlapping more with white systems by third grade than at first grade, but even for groups of matched IQ, many responses, and particularly the strengths of responses, are still widely different. Moreover, it is these inner-city black children who are least well served by the educational system.

The first-to-third grade decline in the relative position of disadvantaged children compared to suburban children obviously parallels success, or lack of success, in engaging children with the educational system and the failure of inner-city children to become literate early in their school career. One can only speculate about the practical effects of the different semantic systems. (For words like "never" that are evolving over the elementary school period, "always" is the response of 14% of white suburban children, 8% of white slum children, and only 2% of Negro slum children. And, whereas white suburban children give "listen" as the primary response to "obey," this response is not among the first three responses for either white or Negro slum children.) It seems clear that the semantics being acquired by the young suburban child in his early school career are *not* being acquired by the inner-city child.

One can only wonder how much these differing semantic systems becloud not only current research but also the educational task. If paired associates (PA) are used to study developmental learning processes but no account is taken of the differing associative and semantic properties of the PA words, then the learning processes described may be as much a function of group differences in semantics as of anything else.

The data reported here present just a suggestion of what the actual problem must be. The "average" child in the first grade probably recognizes almost 24,000 basic and derivative words.[23] If we

take the conservative view that the disadvantaged child's vocabulary is constricted to 12,000 words (it may actually be expanded), then we have sampled only about 1% of it. Also, we have not touched on morphology, syntax, or phonology, also known to be deficient in disadvantaged groups. In kindergarten and first grade it appears that word meanings, and therefore the cognitive role of words, is vastly different for the black and the white child. It also appears that whereas suburban children are making orderly progress toward expanding their semantic systems to imbed less frequent words over the elementary school years, inner-city children are making little or no progress toward use of language that is conceptually more elaborate than that with which they started school ("Maintain" produces "can," "retain," and "begin" for suburban third-graders, but "no response" is the most frequent response in both white and Negro slum children; "seldom" gives "often" [7.5%] and "always" [5%] in suburban third-graders but gives "sell" and "no response" as the two most frequent associates in both white and Negro slum-dwellers.)

Remedies are not obvious. Aside from what occurs in the motivational and affective domains, and we do not wish to discuss this here although we acknowledge its possibly overriding importance, it is clear that over the early school years the suburban child is engaged in rapid linguistic development on several fronts. The disadvantaged child, from what appears to be a more favored initial position, seems to decelerate his rate of language development.

Several kinds of action suggest themselves. First, specific training with word associates in the form of oral group drills like those featured in some pre-school curricula[24] may have value in enriching and consolidating associative structures. We are in the process of developing a classroom game that may help meet this need. Second, if more data on the actual vocabularies of disadvantaged children were available, revised primers

[23]See George A. Miller, *Language and Communication*, New York: McGraw-Hill, 1951.

[24]Such a curriculum is described in Carl Bereiter, Siegfried Engleman, Jean Osborn, and Philip A. Reidford, "An Academically Oriented Pre-School for Culturally Deprived Children," in Fred Hechinger (ed.), *Pre-School Education Today*, New York: Doubleday, 1966.

based on their response strengths and semantic structures could be prepared. It is important to emphasize here that eventually the aim is for children to acquire standard English, and although revised primers might seem opposed to that, in fact we do not believe they would be. Instead, they would increase the chances that the first and second grader might "crack the code" and experience more success in beginning reading. It would be a simple step to shape his reading toward standard English after he had once become skillful at it. An alternate approach being tried, apparently with great success, is to encourage children to invent their own reading material.[25] Third, and perhaps most important, further racial integration of both children and teachers probably would be the most effective solution. As long as groups are separated, semantic systems that are disjunct can flourish. The natural needs of day-to-day communication would produce congruent associative distributions if more racial mixing was present in the schools and *both* groups might change rather than having the entire burden of change placed upon one group.

[25]Lyman Huff, personal communication. Also see Alton Packer, "Sylvia Aston-Warner's Methods Tried in Four U.S. Cities," presented at AERA meetings, Los Angeles, California, February, 1969.

Whether a person is mentally healthy or mentally ill can depend, according to Abraham H. Maslow, on the intrinsic nature of human beings. In striving to define human health, the psychologist deals with the ethics of science and a natural system of values for people.

J.P. Scott discusses his own and other's research on critical periods of life, potent mediating influence in normal development. For humans and animals alike, these critical periods determine the direction of social, intellectual, and emotional development.

Part VIII
HEALTHY BEHAVIOR —MEANING AND DEVELOPMENT

There is now emerging over the horizon a new conception of human sickness and of human health, a psychology that I find so thrilling and so full of wonderful possibilities that I yield to the temptation to present it publicly even before it is checked and confirmed, and before it can be called reliable scientific knowledge.

The basic assumptions of this point of view are:

1. We have, each of us, an essential biologically based inner nature, which is to some degree "natural," intrinsic, given, and, in a certain limited sense, unchangeable, or, at least, unchanging.

2. Each person's inner nature is in part unique to himself and in part species-wide.

3. It is possible to study this inner nature scientifically and to discover what it is like — (not *invent — discover*).

4. This inner nature, as much as we know of it so far, seems not to be intrinsically evil, but rather either neutral or positively "good." What we call evil behavior appears most often to be a secondary reaction to frustration of this intrinsic nature.

5. Since this inner nature is good or neutral rather than bad, it is best to bring it out and to encourage it rather than to suppress it. If it is permitted to guide our life, we grow healthy, fruitful, and happy.

6. If this essential core of the person is denied or suppressed, he gets sick sometimes in obvious ways, sometimes in subtle ways, sometimes immediately, sometimes later.

7. This inner nature is not strong and overpowering and unmistakable like the instincts of animals. It is weak and delicate and subtle and easily overcome by habit, cultural pressure, and wrong attitudes toward it.

8. Even though weak, it rarely disappears in the normal person—perhaps not even in the sick person. Even though denied, it persists underground forever pressing for actualization.

9. Somehow, these conclusions must all be articulated with the necessity of discipline, deprivation, frustration, pain, and tragedy. To the extent that these experiences reveal and foster and fulfill our inner nature, to that extent they are desirable experiences.

Observe that if these assumptions are proven

17
Toward a Psychology of Health

Abraham H. Maslow

Reprinted by permission from *Toward a Psychology of Being* by Abraham H. Maslow © 1968 by Litton Educational Publishing, Inc. Published by Van Nostrand Reinhold Company, Chapter 1, pp. 3–8.

true, they promise a scientific ethics, a natural value system, a court of ultimate appeal for the determination of good and bad, of right and wrong. The more we learn about man's natural tendencies, the easier it will be to tell him how to be good, how to be happy, how to be fruitful, how to respect himself, how to love, how to fulfill his highest potentialities. This amounts to automatic solution of many of the personality problems of the future. The thing to do seems to be to find out what *you* are *really* like inside, deep down, as a member of the human species and as a particular individual.

The study of such healthy people can teach us much about our own mistakes, our shortcomings, the proper directions in which to grow. Every age but ours has had its model, its ideal. All of these have been given up by our culture; the saint, the hero, the gentleman, the knight, the mystic. About all we have left is the well-adjusted man without problems, a very pale and doubtful substitute. Perhaps we shall soon be able to use as our guide and model the fully growing and self-fulfilling human being, the one in whom all his potentialities are coming to full development, the one whose inner nature expresses itself freely, rather than being warped, suppressed, or denied.

The serious thing for each person to recognize vividly and poignantly, each for himself, is that every falling away from species-virtue, every crime against one's own nature, every evil act, *every one without exception records itself* in our unconscious and makes us despise ourselves. Karen Horney had a good word to describe this unconscious perceiving and remembering; she said it "registers." If we do something we are ashamed of, it "registers" to our discredit, and if we do something honest or fine or good, it "registers" to our credit. The net results ultimately are either one or the other—either we respect and accept ourselves or we despise ourselves and feel contemptible, worthless, and unlovable. Theologians used to use the word "*accidie*" to describe the sin of failing to do with one's life all that one knows one could do.

This point of view in no way denies the usual Freudian picture. But it does add to it and supplement it. To oversimplify the matter somewhat, it is as if Freud supplied to us the sick half of psychology and we must now fill it out with the healthy half. Perhaps this health psychology will give us more possibility for controlling and improving our lives and for making ourselves better people. Perhaps this will be more fruitful than asking "how to get *unsick*."

How can we encourage free development? What are the best educational conditions for it? Sexual? Economic? Political? What kind of world do we need for such people to grow in? What kind of world will such people create? Sick people are made by a sick culture; healthy people are made possible by a healthy culture. But it is just as true that sick individuals make their culture more sick and that healthy individuals make their culture more healthy. Improving individual health is one approach to making a better world. To express it in another way, encouragement of personal growth is a real possibility; cure of actual neurotic symptoms is far less possible without outside help. It is relatively easy to try deliberately to make oneself a more honest man; it is very difficult to try to cure one's own compulsions or obsessions.

The classical approach to personality problems considers them to be problems in an undesirable sense. Struggle, conflict, guilt, bad conscience, anxiety, depression, frustration, tension, shame, self-punishment, feeling of inferiority or unworthiness—they all cause psychic pain, they disturb efficiency of performance, and they are uncontrollable. They are therefore automatically regarded as sick and undesirable and they get "cured" away as soon as possible.

But all of these symptoms are found also in healthy people, or in people who are growing toward health. Supposing you *should* feel guilty and don't? Supposing you have attained a nice stabilization of forces and you *are* adjusted? Perhaps adjustment and stabilization, while good because it cuts your pain, is also bad because development toward a higher ideal ceases?

Erich Fromm, in a very important book (50), attacked the classical Freudian notion of a superego because this concept was entirely authoritarian and relativistic. That is to say, your superego or your conscience was supposed by Freud to be primarily the internalization of the wishes, demands, and ideals of the father and mother, whoever they happen to be. But supposing they are criminals? Then what kind of conscience do you have? Or supposing you have a rigid moralizing father who hates fun? Or a psychopath? This conscience exists—Freud was right. We do get our ideals largely from such early figures and not from Sunday School books read later in life. But there is also another element in conscience, or, if you like, another kind of conscience, which we all have either weakly or strongly. And this is the "intrinsic conscience." This is based upon the unconscious and preconscious perception of our own nature, of our own destiny, or our own capacities, of our own "call" in life. It insists that we be true to our inner nature and that we do not deny it out of weakness or for advantage or for any other reason. He who belies his talent, the born painter who sells stockings instead, the intelligent man who lives a stupid life, the man who sees the truth and keeps his mouth shut, the coward who gives up his manliness, all these people perceive in a deep way that they have done wrong to themselves and despise themselves for it. Out of this self-punishment may come only neurosis, but there may equally well come renewed courage, righteous indignation, increased self-respect, because of thereafter doing the right thing; in a word, growth and improvement can come through pain and conflict.

In essence I am deliberately rejecting our present easy distinction between sickness and health, at least as far as surface symptoms are concerned. Does sickness mean having symptoms? I maintain now that sickness might consist of *not* having symptoms when you should. Does health mean being symptom-free? I deny it. Which of the Nazis at Auschwitz or Dachau were healthy? Those with stricken conscience or those with a nice, clear, happy conscience? Was it possible for a profoundly human person not to feel conflict, suffering, depression, rage, etc?

In a word if you tell me you have a personality problem I am not certain until I know you better whether to say "Good!" or "I'm sorry." It depends on the reasons. And these, it seems, may be bad reasons, or they may be good reasons.

An example is the changing attitude of psychol-ogists toward popularity, toward adjustment, even toward delinquency. Popular with whom? Perhaps it is better for a youngster to be *unpopular* with the neighboring snobs or with the local country club set. Adjusted to what? To a bad culture? To a dominating parent? What shall we think of a well-adjusted slave? A well-adjusted prisoner? Even the behavior problem boy is being looked upon with new tolerance. *Why* is he delinquent? Most often it is for sick reasons. But occasionally it is for good reasons and the boy is simply resisting exploitation, domination, neglect, contempt, and trampling upon.

Clearly what will be called personality problems depends on who is doing the calling. The slave owner? The dictator? The patriarchal father? The husband who wants his wife to remain a child? It seems quite clear that personality problems may sometimes be loud protests against the crushing of one's psychological bones, of one's true inner nature. What is sick then is *not* to protest while this crime is being committed. And I am sorry to report my impression that most people do not protest under such treatment. They take it and pay years later, in neurotic and psychosomatic symptoms of various kinds, or perhaps in some cases never become aware that they are sick, that they have missed true happiness, true fulfillment of promise, a rich emotional life, and a serene, fruitful old age, that they have never known how wonderful it is to be creative, to react aesthetically, to find life thrilling.

The question of desirable grief and pain or the necessity for it must also be faced. Is growth and self-fulfillment possible at all without pain and grief and sorrow and turmoil? If these are to some extent necessary and unavoidable, then to what extent? If grief and pain are sometimes necessary for growth of the person, then we must learn not to protect people from them automatically as if they were always bad. Sometimes they may be good and desirable in view of the ultimate good consequences. Not allowing people to go through their pain, and protecting them from it, may turn out to be a kind of overprotection, which in turn implies a certain lack of respect for the integrity and the intrinsic nature and the future development of the individual.

18
Critical Periods in Behavioral Development

J.P. Scott

A number of years ago I was given a female lamb taken from its mother at birth. My wife and I raised it on the bottle for the first 10 days of life and then placed it out in the pasture with a small flock of domestic sheep. As might have been expected from folklore, the lamb became attached to people and followed the persons who fed it. More surprisingly, the lamb remained independent of the rest of the flock when we restored it to the pasture. Three years later it was still following an independent grazing pattern. In addition, when it was mated and had lambs of its own it became a very indifferent mother, allowing its offspring to nurse but showing no concern when the lamb moved away with the other members of the flock (1).

Since following the flock is such a universal characteristic of normal sheep, I was impressed by the extensive and permanent modification of this behavior that resulted from a brief early experience. The results suggested that Freud was right concerning the importance of early experience, and pointed toward the existence of critical periods in behavioral development. As I soon discovered, there is considerable evidence that a critical period for determining early social relationships is a widespread phenomenon in vertebrates; such a critical period had long been known in ants (2).

The theory of critical periods is not a new one in either biology or psychology. It was strongly stated by Stockard in 1921, in connection with his experiments on the induction of monstrosities in fish embryos, although he gave credit to Dareste for originating the basic idea 30 years earlier (3). In experimenting with the effects of various inorganic chemicals upon the development of *Fundulus* eggs, Stockard at first thought one-eyed monsters were specifically caused by the magnesium ion. Further experiments showed him that almost any chemical would produce the same effect, provided it was applied at the proper time during development. These experiments and those of Child (4) and his students established the fact that the most rapidly growing tissues in an embryo

Reprinted by permission from *Science*, vol. 138, 1962, pp. 949–958. Copyright 1962 by the American Association for the Advancement of Science.

are the most sensitive to any change in conditions, thus accounting for the specificity of effects at particular times.

Meanwhile Freud had attempted to explain the origin of neuroses in human patients as the result of early experience and had implied that certain periods in the life of an infant are times of particular sensitivity. In 1935, Lorenz (5) emphasized the importance of critical periods for the formation of primary social bonds (imprinting) in birds, remarking on their similarity to critical periods in the development of the embryo, and McGraw soon afterward (6) pointed out the existence of critical periods for optimal learning of motor skills in the human infant.

Since then, the phenomenon of critical periods has excited the imagination of a large group of experimenters interested in human and animal development. In describing this fast-moving scientific field, I shall point out some of the most significant current developments. More detailed information is available in some excellent recent reviews (7, 8).

To begin with, three major kinds of critical-period phenomena have been discovered. These involve optimal periods for learning, for infantile stimulation, and for the formation of basic social relationships. The last of these has been established as a widespread phenomenon in the animal kingdom and consequently receives major attention in this article.

PERIODS ARE BASED ON PROCESSES

In the dog, the development of behavior may be divided into several natural periods marked off by important changes in social relationships (Table 18.1). Only a few other species have been studied in sufficient detail for making adequate comparisons, but enough data have been accumulated to show that similar periods can be identified in other mammals and in birds (9, 10). I originally expected to find that the course of postnatal development, like that of embryonic development, would be essentially similar in all vertebrates, and that while

the periods might be extended or shortened, the same pattern of development would be evident in all (11). However, comparison of only two species, man and the dog, shows that the periods can actually occur in reverse order, and that there is an astonishing degree of flexibility in behavioral development (12).

This leads to the conclusion that the important aspect of each developmental period is not time sequence but the fact that each represents a major developmental process. Thus, the neonatal period is chiefly characterized by the process of neonatal nutrition—nursing in mammals and parental feeding in many birds. The transition period is characterized by the process of transition to adult methods of nutrition and locomotion and the appearance of adult patterns of social behavior, at least in immature form. The period of socialization is the period in which primary social bonds are formed. If we consider processes alone, it is apparent that they are not completely dependent on each other and that they can therefore be arranged in different orders. It is also apparent that certain of these processes persist beyond the periods characterized by them. For example, a mammal usually retains throughout life the ability to suck which characterizes the neonatal period, although in most cases this ability is little used.

PROCESS OF PRIMARY SOCIALIZATION

Since one of the first acts of a young mammal is to nurse, and since food rewards are known to modify the behavior of adult animals, it once seemed logical to suppose that the process of forming a social attachment begins with food rewards and develops as an acquired drive. However, the experimental evidence does not support this extreme viewpoint. Brodbeck reared a group of puppies during the critical period of socialization, feeding half of them by hand and the other half by machine, but giving all of them the same degree of human contact (13). He found that the two sets of puppies became equally attached to people. This result was later confirmed by Stanley and his co-workers (14), who found that the only difference in response between the machine-fed and the hand-fed puppies was that the latter yelped more when they saw the experimenter. Elliot and King (*15*) fed all their puppies by hand but overfed one group and underfed another. The hungry puppies became more rapidly attached to the handlers. We can conclude that, in the dog, food rewards per se are not necessary for the process of socialization, but that hunger will speed it up.

Fisher (*16*) reared fox terrier puppies in isolation boxes through the entire socialization period. The puppies were fed mechanically (thus, food was entirely eliminated as a factor in the experiment), but they were removed from the boxes for regular contacts with the experimenter. One group of puppies was always rewarded by kind social treatment. A second group was sometimes rewarded and sometimes punished, but in a purely random way. Still a third group was always punished for any positive approach to the experimenter. The puppies that were both rewarded and punished showed most attraction and dependency behavior with respect to the experimenter, and the puppies that were always punished showed the least. After the treatment was discontinued, all the puppies began coming toward the experimenter, and the differences rapidly disappeared. This leads to the surprising conclusion that the process of socialization is not inhibited by punishment and may even be speeded up by it.

At approximately 3 weeks of age—that is, at the beginning of the period of socialization—young puppies begin to bark or whine when isolated or placed in strange places. Elliot and Scott (*17*) showed that the reaction to isolation in a strange place reaches a peak at 6 to 7 weeks of age, approximately the midpoint of the critical period, and begins to decline thereafter. Scott, Deshaies, and Morris (*18*) found that separating young puppies overnight from their mother and litter mates in a strange pen for 20 hours per day produced a strong emotional reaction and speeded up the process of socialization to human handlers. All this evidence indicates that any sort of strong emotion, whether hunger, fear, pain, or loneliness, will speed up the process of socialization. No ex-

periments have been carried out to determine the effects of pleasant types of emotion, such as might be aroused by play and handling, but these were probably a factor in Brodbeck's experiment with machine-fed puppies.

The results of these experiments on dogs agree with evidence from other species. While they were going on, Harlow (*19*) was performing his famous experiments with rhesus monkeys isolated at birth and supplied with dummy "mothers." When given the choice between a comfortable cloth-covered mother without a nipple and an uncomfortable mother made of wire screening but equipped with a functional nursing bottle, the young rhesus monkeys definitely preferred the cloth-covered models from which they had received no food rewards. Harlow concluded that the acquired-drive theory of the origin of social attachment could be discarded.

Later, Igel and Calvin (*20*) performed a similar but more elaborate experiment with puppies. These animals had more opportunity to choose, being provided with four kinds of mother models: comfortable and uncomfortable, each type with and without nipples. Like rhesus monkeys, the puppies preferred the comfortable "mother" but usually chose one with a nipple. Thus, it appears that food rewards do contribute something to the social relationship, although they do not form its prime basis.

Since then Harlow (*21*) has raised to maturity the monkeys raised on dummy mothers, has mated them, and has observed their behavior toward their own young. They become uniformly poor mothers, neglecting their offspring and often punishing them when they cry. In spite of such rejection, the young rhesus infants desperately crawl toward their mothers and give every evidence of becoming attached to them, although perhaps not as strongly as in the normal relationship. Here again punishment does not inhibit the formation of a social bond.

The hypothesis that the primary social bond originates through food rewards had already been shown to be invalid in the precocial birds, many of which form attachments prior to the time when they begin to feed. Lorenz (*5*) was the first to point out the significance of this phenomenon, which he called "imprinting." He also stated that it differed from conditioning, primarily in that it was very rapid and apparently irreversible. However, rapid formation and great persistence are also characteristic of many conditioned responses and other learned behavior. Fabricius (22) pointed out that no sharp line can be drawn between imprinting and conditioning, and Collias (23) concluded that imprinting is a form of learned behavior that is self-reinforcing.

The process of imprinting in young ducklings and chicks has since been experimentally analyzed in much detail, with results that invariably confirm the conclusion that it takes place without any obvious external rewards or reinforcement. Hess (24) found that if he caused young ducklings to follow a model over varying distances or over hurdles, the ducklings which had to make the greater effort became more strongly imprinted. He also found that the drug meprobamate and its congener carisoprodol, which are muscle relaxants as well as tranquilizers, greatly reduce imprinting if given during the critical period. James

(25) found that chicks would become attached to an object illuminated by a flickering light, even though they were not allowed to follow, and Gray (26) later showed that they will become attached to a motionless object illuminated by a steady light and viewed from an isolation box. It is therefore apparent that chicks can become imprinted without following, although muscular tension may still be important.

Guiton (27) found that chicks allowed to follow a model in a group become less strongly imprinted than chicks exposed singly, and he attributed the results to the greater fear shown by the isolated chicks. Recently, Pitz and Ross (28) subjected young chicks following a model to a loud sound and found that this increased the speed with which they formed a social bond. Hess (29) (with the apparatus shown in Fig. 18.1) has given a mild electric shock to chicks following a model and finds that this also increases the strength of imprinting. Instead of avoiding the model, the distressed chick runs after it more closely.

We may conclude that these young birds become attached to any object to which they are

TABLE 18.1
Periods of development in the puppy and song sparrow. The six periods of development described by Nice (10) for the song sparrow correspond to the first four periods in the puppy, as indicated in the table. The young of the two species are born or hatched in an immature state, require intensive parental care and feeding, and go through much the same stages before becoming independent. Development is much more rapid in the bird than in the puppy, although small mammals such as mice mature at about the same rate as birds.

Puppy			Song sparrow		
Name of period	Length of period (weeks)	Initial event	Name of period	Length of period (days)	Initial event
I. Neonatal	0-2	Birth, nursing	Stage 1 (nestling)	0-4	Hatching, gaping
II. Transition	2-3	Eyes open	Stage 2	5-6	Eyes open
III. Socialization	3-10	Startle to sound	Stage 3	7-9	Cowering—first fear reactions
			Stage 4 (fledgling)	10-16	Leaving nest—first flight
			Stage 5	17-28	Full flight
IV. Juvenile	10-	Final weaning	Stage 6 (juvenile)	29-	Independent feeding

Figure 18.1
Hess's apparatus for measuring the following response in ducklings and chicks. A decoy revolves on a circular path, the young duckling staying nearby. Other revolving objects may be substituted for the decoy, which is wired for sound. The following response is a major positive timing mechanism that initiates the critical period for imprinting; it is also an indicator that an attachment has been formed. [From a photo by E. H. Hess]

long exposed during the critical period, even when their contact is only visual. We may also conclude that the speed of formation of a social bond is dependent upon the degree of emotional arousal, irrespective of the nature of that arousal. Whether attachment is the result of the emotion itself or of the reduction of emotion as the chick or duckling approaches the model is still a matter of conjecture (*30*).

The basic timing mechanisms for developmental periods are obviously the biological processes of growth and differentiation, usually called maturation. For various reasons, these are not precisely correlated with age from birth or hatching. For example, birds often retain newly formed eggs in their bodies overnight, thus incubating them for several hours before laying. By chilling duck eggs just before placing them in an incubator (thus killing all embryos except those in the earliest stages of development) Gottlieb (*31*) was able to time the age of ducklings from the onset of incubation rather than from hatching and found that variation in the timing for the critical period was much reduced. No such exact timing studies have been made in mammals, but I have estimated that there is at least a week's variation in development among puppies at 3 weeks of age, and the variation among human infants must be considerably greater (*32*).

Another approach to the problem is to try to identify the actual mechanisms which open and

close a period. Since an important part of forming a primary social relationship appears to be emotional arousal while the young animal is in contact with another, it is obvious that the critical period for socialization could be timed by the appearance of behavioral mechanisms which maintain or prevent contact, and this indeed is the case. There are demonstrable positive mechanisms, varying from species to species, which bring young animals close to other members of their kind: the clinging response of young rhesus monkeys; the following response of chicks, ducklings, and lambs and other herd animals; the social investigation, tail wagging, and playful fighting of puppies; and the visual investigation and smiling of the human infant (*33*). These are, of course, accompanied by interacting responses from adult and immature members of the species: holding and clasping by primate mothers, brooding of mother hens and other birds, calling by mother sheep, investigation and play on the part of other young puppies, and the various supporting and nurturing activities of human mothers.

If contact and emotional arousal result in social attachment, there must be negative mechanisms which prevent such attachment once the critical period is past. Perhaps the most widespread of these is the development of a fear response which causes the young animal to immediately leave the vicinity of a stranger and hence avoid contact. This developing fear response is found in young chicks (*7*), ducklings (*22, 34*), dogs (*35;* Fig. 18.2), rhesus monkeys (*36*), and in many other birds and mammals. Even in children there is a period between the ages of 5 and 12 months in which there is a mounting fear of strangers (*37*), sometimes called "8-months anxiety" (*38*). As already pointed out, there is a time in development when certain fear responses actually facilitate imprinting, but, as they grow stronger, the escape reaction follows so quickly that it prevents contact altogether.

Another sort of negative mechanism is the rejection of strange young by adult sheep, goats, and many other herd animals (*39*). In these species the mothers become strongly attached to the young within a few hours after birth and refuse to accept

FIGURE 18.2

Puppy reacting to leash training, according to its experience during the critical period. Reaction of a puppy that had had contact only with other dogs prior to the end of the critical period. This puppy shows an extreme fear reaction and refuses to follow. Courtesy of Dr. H. F. Harlow, University of Wisconsin Regional Primate Research Center.

strangers thereafter (Fig. 18.3). This indicates that the rapid formation of emotional bonds is not limited to young animals.

These timing mechanisms all depend primarily on the development of social behavior patterns, but both sensory and motor development can also influence timing. For example, a very immature animal cannot maintain contact by following, and in slowly developing altricial birds such as jackdaws and doves (*5, 40*), the period of imprinting comes much later than it does in the precocial species. In the human infant the process of social-

ization begins before the adult motor patterns develop, but contact is maintained by visual exploration and by the smiling response to human faces (*33*). Thus, understanding the process of socialization and its timing mechanisms in any particular species requires a systematic study of the development of the various capacities which affect the time of onset and the duration of the critical period. These include sensory, motor, and learning capacities as well as the ability to perform essential patterns of social behavior.

The fact that emotional arousal is so strongly

FIGURE 18.3
Rejection by a mother goat of a kid not her own. The behavior of adults terminates the critical period for primary socialization in sheep and goats. Immediately after giving birth the mother will accept any young kid, but within a few hours she will reject any strange kid that approaches. [*From a photo by A.U. Moore*]

connected with the process of primary socialization suggests that the capacity to produce emotional reactions may also govern the time of onset of a critical period. Figure 18.4 summarizes the results of a study of emotional development in the dog during the critical period. If puppies are kept in large fields, totally isolated from people, fear and escape responses toward human beings very nearly reach a maximum by the time the puppies are 14 weeks old—a finding that fixes the upper limit of the period of socialization (*35*). On the other hand, the peak of the emotional response to isolation in a strange place occurs when puppies are approximately 6 to 7 weeks old, as does the peak of the heart-rate response to handling. At this age, such emotional arousal actually contributes to the strength of the social bond. Fuller (*41*) was unable to condition the heart-rate response consistently until puppies were 5 weeks old. This indicates that one of the factors that brings the

critical period to a close may be the developing ability of the young puppy to associate fear responses with particular stimuli.

All this suggests that if the development of the escape response to strangers could be held in check, the critical period might be extended indefinitely. Raising puppies in small isolation boxes during the critical period inhibits the development of the escape response, but they still show obvious signs of fear when they are first removed from their cages. Fuller (*42*) reports some success in socializing these older pups by overcoming their fear responses, either by careful handling or through the use of tranquilizing drugs.

Fear responses thus have the dual effect of facilitating the formation of the social bond during the critical period (along with other emotions) and of bringing the period to a close. This is understandable because the type of fear which terminates the critical period is a developing fear of strange animals. In the early part of the critical period the escape reaction is either lacking or is momentary and weak. At the close of the period it is strong enough to prevent contact altogether.

FORMATION OF AFFECTIONAL BONDS IN ADULT LIFE

Until recently, most investigators have concentrated their attention on the critical period for primary socialization or imprinting and few have gone on to study similar phenomena in later development. This field of investigation is just beginning to open up, though many related facts have long been known. For example, many birds form strong pair bonds which are maintained as long as both members survive. In studying the development of various types of social bonds in different species of ducks, Schutz (*43*) finds that, while attachments to particular individuals may be formed in the early critical period from 12 to 17 hours after hatching, the critical period for the attachment to the species may not come until sometime later, in some cases as late as 30 days after hatching, and the attachment to a particular member of the opposite sex, or the pair bond, does not come until

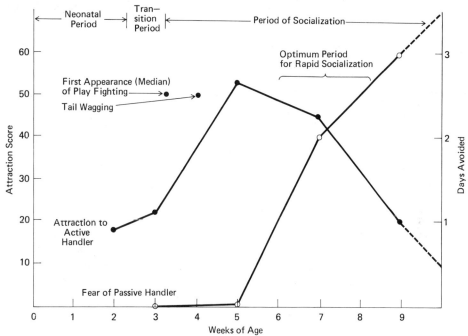

FIGURE 18.4

Timing mechanisms for the critical period in puppies. The period is initiated by positive behavior mechanisms, such as playful fighting, which result in attraction to a strange individual, and it is brought to a close by the development of a fear response which causes the attraction to decline. The optimum period for rapid and permanent socialization comes shortly after the appearance of prolonged avoidance reactions.

the age of 5 months or so. Schutz also finds that female mallards cannot be sexually imprinted with respect to other species but always mate with other mallards no matter what their earliest experience has been. A similar phenomenon is reported by Warriner (44), who finds that male pigeons prefer to mate with birds whose color is similar to that of the parents who reared them, whether of the same or another color from themselves, but females show no preference.

Certain species of mammals, such as foxes (45), form long-lasting mating bonds. It is possible that the violence of the sexual emotions contributes to the formation of the adult bond, just as other sorts of emotional arousal are important to the primary socialization of the infant. Klopfer (46) has suggested that the rapid formation of the social bond in a mother goat toward her kid is the result of the high degree of emotional arousal which accompanies the birth of the offspring.

In short, it seems likely that the formation of a social attachment through contact and emotional arousal is a process that may take place throughout life, and that although it may take place more slowly outside of certain critical periods, the capacity for such an attachment is never completely lost.

At this point it may be remarked that, in attempting to analyze the development of affection and social bonds objectively, scientists have often tried to simplify the problem by postulating various unitary, unromantic, and sometimes unesthetic explanations. One of these was the "acquired drive" hypothesis—that children love you because you feed them. Taking a more moderate view Harlow (19) has emphasized "contact comfort" as a major variable—that the young monkey begins to love its mother because she feels warm and comfortable—but that a number of other factors are involved. As this article indicates, evidence is accumulating that there is a much less specific, although equally unromantic, general mechanism involved—that given any kind of emotional arousal a young animal will become attached to any individual or object with which it is in contact for a sufficiently long time. The necessary arousal would, of course, include various specific kinds of emotions associated with food rewards and contact comfort.

It should not be surprising that many kinds of emotional reactions contribute to a social relationship. The surprising thing is that emotions which we normally consider aversive should produce the same effect as those which appear to be rewarding. This apparent paradox is partially resolved by evidence that the positive effect of unpleasant emotions is normally limited to early infancy by the development of escape reactions.

Nevertheless, this concept leads to the somewhat alarming conclusion that an animal (and perhaps a person) of any age, exposed to certain individuals or physical surroundings for any length of time, will inevitably become attached to them, the rapidity of the process being governed by the degree of emotional arousal associated with them. I need not dwell on the consequences for human behavior, if this conclusion should apply to our species as well as to other animals, except to point out that it provides an explanation of certain well-known clinical observations such as the development by neglected children of strong affection for cruel and abusive parents, and the various peculiar affectional relationships that develop between prisoners and jailors, slaves and masters, and so on. Perhaps the general adaptive nature of this mechanism is that since the survival of any member of a highly social species depends upon the rapid development of social relationships, a mechanism has evolved which makes it almost impossible to inhibit the formation of social bonds.

CRITICAL PERIODS OF LEARNING

Unlike the process of socialization, the phenomenon of critical periods of learning was first noticed in children rather than in lower animals. McGraw's (47) famous experiment with the twins Johnny and Jimmy was a deliberate attempt to modify behavioral development by giving one of a pair of identical twins special early training. The result varied according to the activity involved. The onset of walking, for example, was not affected by previous practice or help. Other activities, however, could be greatly speeded up—notably roller skating, in which the favored twin became adept almost as soon as he could walk. In other activities performance was actually made worse by early practice, simply because of the formation of unskillful habits. McGraw (6) concluded that there are critical periods for learning which vary from activity to activity; for each kind of coordinated muscular activity there is an optimum period for rapid and skillful learning.

In an experiment with rats, Hebb (48) used the technique of providing young animals with many opportunities for spontaneous learning rather than formal training. Pet rats raised in the rich environment of a home performed much better on learning tasks than rats reared in barren laboratory cages. Since then, other experimenters (49) have standardized the "rich" environment as a large cage including many objects and playthings and have gotten similar effects.

Forgays (see 50) finds that the age at which the maximum effect is produced is limited to the period from approximately 20 to 30 days of age, immediately after weaning. A similar experience in adult life produces no effect. In rats, at any rate, the critical period of learning seems to coincide with the critical period of primary socialization, and it may be that the two are in some way related. Candland and Campbell (51) find that fearful behavior in response to a strange situation begins to increase in rats between 20 and 30 days after birth, and Bernstein (52) showed earlier that discrimination learning could be improved by gentle handling beginning at 20 days. It may well be that the development of fear limits the capacity for future learning as well as the formation of social relationships.

In addition to these studies on motor learning and problem solving, there are many experiments demonstrating the existence of critical periods for the learning of social behavior patterns. It has long been known that many kinds of birds do not develop the characteristic songs of their species if they are reared apart from their own kind (53). More recently, Thorpe (54) discovered a critical period for this effect in the chaffinch. If isolated at 3 or 4 days of age, a young male chaffinch produces an incomplete song, but if he hears adults singing, as a fledgling 2 or 3 weeks old or in early juvenile life before he sings himself, he will the next year produce the song characteristic of the species, even if he has been kept in isolation. In nature, the fine details of the song are added at the time of competition over territory, within a period of 2 or 3 weeks, when the bird is about a year old. At this time it learns the songs of two or three of its neighbors, and never learns any others in subsequent years. The critical period for song learning is thus a relatively long one, but it is definitely over by the time the bird is a year old. There is no obvious explanation for its ending at this particular time, but it is possible that learning a complete song pattern in some way interferes with further learning.

King and Gurney (55) found that adult mice reared in groups during youth fought more readily than animals isolated at 20 days of age. Later experiments showed that most of the effect was produced in a 10-day period just after weaning, and that similar experience as adults produced little or no effect (56). Thus, there appears to be a critical period for learning to fight through social experience, and this experience need be no more than contact through a wire. In this case the effect is probably produced by association with other mice before the fear response has been completely developed. Similarly, Fisher (16) and Fuller (57) inhibited the development of attacking behavior in fox terriers by raising them in isolation through the critical period for socialization. The animals would fight back somewhat ineffectually if attacked, but did not initiate conflicts. Tinbergen (58) found a critical period in dogs for learning territorial boundaries, coinciding with sexual maturity.

The results of corresponding experiments on sexual behavior vary from species to species. In mice, rearing in isolation produced no effects (59). Beach (60) found that male rats reared with either females or males were actually slower to respond to sexual behavior than isolated males, and he suggested that habits of playful fighting established by the group-reared animals interfered with sexual behavior later on. In guinea pigs, contact with other young animals improves sexual performance (61).

On the other hand, young chimpanzees (62) reared apart from their kind can only be mated with experienced animals. Harlow (21) discovered that his rhesus infants reared on dummy mothers did not develop normal patterns of sexual behavior, and he was able to obtain matings only by exposing females to experienced males (Fig. 5). Normal behavior can be developed by allowing 20-minute daily play periods with other young monkeys, but if rhesus infants are reared apart from all other monkeys beyond the period when they spontaneously play with their fellows, patterns of both sexual and maternal behavior fail to develop normally. These results suggest that play has an important role in developing adult patterns of social behavior in these primates, and that the decline of play behavior sets the upper limit of the critical period during which normal adult behavior may be developed.

Such great changes in the social environment rarely occur in humans even by accident, but Money, Hampson, and Hampson (63) have studied the development of hermaphroditic children who have been reared as one sex and then changed to the other. They find that if this occurs before 2½ years of age, very little emotional disturbance results. Thus, there is a critical period for learning the sex role, this capacity persisting unchanged up to a point in development which roughly corresponds to the age when children begin to use and understand language. Perhaps more important, this is the age when children first begin to take an interest in, and play with, members of their own age group.

It is difficult to find a common factor in these critical periods for learning. In some species, such as rats, mice, dogs, and sheep, certain critical pe-

FIGURE 18.5
Through play behavior during a critical period young rhesus monkeys develop the capacity for adult sexual behavior. The two at right exhibit an approximation of the adult posture. It is almost impossible to mate monkeys raised with cloth "mothers" without an opportunity for play with other infants. [H.F. Harlow]

riods for learning coincide with the period for primary socialization and seem to be similarly brought to a close by the development of fear reactions. Other critical periods, in chaffinches and dogs, coincide with the formation of adult mating bonds. However, the critical period for sexual learning in the rhesus monkey comes later than that for primary socialization (*64*), as do critical periods for various kinds of learning in human beings.

Part of this apparent inconsistency arises from our ignorance regarding timing mechanisms. One such mechanism must be the development of learning capacities, and we have evidence in dogs (*65*), rhesus monkeys (*66*), and human infants (*12*) that learning capacities change during development, sometimes in a stepwise fashion. One element in these capacities is the ability to learn things which facilitate subsequent learning.

It is equally possible, however, to "learn not to learn," and such a negative learning set may act to bring the critical period to a close. At this point, we can only state a provisional general hypothesis: that the critical period for any specific sort of learning is that time when maximum capacities—sensory, motor, and motivational, as well as psychological ones—are first present.

CRITICAL PERIODS FOR EARLY STIMULATION

Experiments to determine the effects of early stimulation have been mainly performed on infant mice and rats, which are usually weaned at about 21 days at the earliest, and have been concerned with the effect of stimulation during this pre-weaning period. All investigators beginning with Levine (*67*) and Schaefer (*68*), agree that rats handled during the first week or 10 days of life have a lessened tendency to urinate and defecate in a strange "open field" situation, learn avoidance behavior more readily, and survive longer when deprived of food and water. In short, early stimulation produces an animal that is less timorous, learns more quickly, and is more vigorous. Levine found that the effect could be obtained by a variety of stimuli, including electric shock and mechanical shaking as well as handling. This ruled out learned behavior as an explanation of the effect, and Levine, Alpert, and Lewis (*69*) discovered that animals handled in the early period showed a much earlier maturation of the adrenocortical response to stress. Levine interpreted these results as indicating that the laboratory environment did not provide sufficient stimulation for the proper development of the hormonal systems of the animals. This interpretation is in agreement with Richter's finding (70) that laboratory rats are quite deficient in adrenocortical response as compared with the wild variety. Schaefer, Weingarten, and Towne (71) have duplicated Levine's results by the use of cold alone, and have suggested temperature as a possible unitary mechanism. However, their findings are not necessarily in disagreement with those of Levine, as the hormonal stress response can be elicited by a variety of stimuli, and temperature may simply be another of the many kinds of stimuli which produce the effect.

According to Thompson and Schaefer (72) the earlier the stimulation the greater the effect. If the hormonal mechanism is the chief phenomenon involved, we can say that there is a critical period during the first week or 10 days of life, since the adrenal response in any case matures and becomes fixed by 16 days of age.

Denenberg (73) takes a somewhat different approach, pointing out that there should be optimal levels of stimulation, so that either very weak or very strong stimulation would produce poor results. He suggests that there are different critical periods for the effect of early stimulation, depending on the intensity of stimulation and the kind of later behavior measured. Working within the critical first 10 days, Denenberg found that the best avoidance learning was produced by stimulation in the second half of the period, whereas the best survival rates were produced by stimulation in the first half. Weight was approximately equally affected, except that there was little effect in the first 3 days (74).

Analyzing the effect on avoidance learning, Denenberg (75) and his associates found that both unhandled controls and rats handled for the first 20 days performed poorly, the former because they were too emotional and the latter because they were too calm to react quickly. An intermediate amount of emotional response produces the best learning, and this can be produced by handling only in the first 10 days of life; handling during the second 10 days has a lesser effect. No handling produces too much emotionality, and handling for 20 days results in too little. Irrespec-

tive of the effect on learning, the data lead to the important conclusion that emotional stimulation during a critical period early in life can lead to the reduction of emotional responses in later life.

More precisely, there appear to be two critical periods revealed by research on early stimulation of rats, one based on a physiological process (the development of the adrenal cortical stress mechanism) and extending to 16 days of age at the latest, the other based on a psychological process (the reduction of fear through familiarity) (51), beginning about 17 days when the eyes first open and extending to 30 days. The effects of handling during these two periods are additive, and many experiments based on arbitrary time rather than developmental periods undoubtedly include both.

The deleterious effects of excessive stimulation in the life of the infant may also be interpreted as a traumatic emotional experience. Bowlby (76), in studying a group of juvenile thieves, found that a large proportion of them had been separated from their mothers in early infancy, and he postulated that this traumatic emotional experience had affected their later behavior. Since this conclusion was based on retrospective information, he and his coworkers have since studied the primary symptoms of separation and have described in detail the emotional reactions of infants sent to hospitals, and thus separated from their mothers (77). Schaffer (78) found a difference in reaction to separation before 7 months and separation afterward. Both sets of infants were disturbed, but they were disturbed in different ways. Infants show increasingly severe emotional reactions to adoption from 3 through 12 months of age (33). It seems logical to place the beginning of the critical period for maximum emotional disturbance at approximately 7 months—at the end of the critical period for primary socialization, which Gray (79) places at approximately 6 weeks to 6 months. Infants whose social relationships have been thoroughly established and whose fear responses toward strangers have been fully developed are much more likely to be upset by changes than infants in which these relationships and responses have not yet been developed.

However, not all apparently "traumatic" early experiences have such a lasting effect. Experimental work shows that young animals have a considerable capacity to recover from unpleasant emotions experienced in a limited period in early life (80), and that what is traumatic in one species may not be in another. While young rats become calmer after infantile stimulation, young mice subjected to excessive auditory stimulation later become more emotional (81). At this point it is appropriate to point out that critical periods are not necessarily involved in every kind of early experience. Raising young chimpanzees in the dark produces degeneration of the retina, but this is a long and gradual process (82).

Another approach to the problem is to stimulate emotional responses in mothers and observe the effect on the offspring. Thompson (83) and other authors (84) have shown that the offspring of rats made fearful while pregnant are more likely to be overemotional in the open-field situation than the offspring of animals not so stimulated. Since any direct influence of maternal behavior was ruled out by cross-fostering experiments, it seems likely that the result is produced by modification of the adrenocortical stress mechanism—in this case, by secretion of maternal hormones acting on the embryo rather than by stimulation after the birth of the young animal itself. No precise critical period for the effect has been established, but it is probably confined to the latter part of pregnancy. Similar effects have been obtained in mice (85), and if such effects can be demonstrated in other mammals, the implications for prenatal care in human beings are obvious.

It is interesting to note that, whereas shocking the mother both before and after parturition has the effect of increasing emotional responses in the young, the emotional responses of young rats are *decreased* when the treatment is applied directly to them. The explanation of this contradiction must await direct experiments on the endocrine system.

GENERAL THEORY OF CRITICAL PERIODS

There are at least two ways in which experience during critical periods may act on behavioral development. The critical period for primary socialization constitutes a turning point. Experience during a short period early in life determines which shall be the close relatives of the young animal, and this, in turn, leads the animal to develop in one of two directions—the normal one in which it becomes attached to and mates with a member of its own species or an abnormal one, in which it becomes attached to a different species with consequent disrupting effects upon sexual and other social relationships with members of its own kind.

The concept of a turning point applies equally well to most examples of critical periods for learning. Up to a certain point in development a chaffinch can learn several varieties of song, but once it has learned one of them it no longer has a choice. Similarly, the human infant can learn either sex role up to a certain age, but once it has learned one or the other, changing over becomes increasingly difficult. What is learned at particular points limits and interferes with subsequent learning, and Schneirla and Rosenblatt (86) have suggested that there are critical stages of learning—that what has been learned at a particular time in development may be critical for whatever follows.

A second sort of action during a critical period consists of a nonspecific stimulus producing an irrevocable result, not modifiable in subsequent development. Thus, almost any sort of stimulus has the effect of modifying the development of the endocrine stress mechanism of young rats in early infancy.

Is there any underlying common principle? Each of these effects has its counterpart in embryonic development. Up to a certain point a cell taken from an amphibian embryo and transplanted to a new location will develop in accordance with its new environment. Beyond this turning point it develops in accordance with its previous location. Some cells retain a degree of lability, but none retain the breadth of choice they had before. Similarly, specific injuries produced by nonspecific causes are also found in embryonic development: damage to an embryonic optic vesicle results in a defective eye, no matter what sort of chemical produces the injury. It is obvious that the similarity between this case and the critical period for early stimulation can be accounted for by the single common process of growth, occurring relatively late in development in the case of the endocrine stress mechanism and much earlier in the development of the eye. The effects are nonspecific because of the fact that growth can be modified in only very limited ways, by being either slowed down or speeded up.

Both growth and behavioral differentiation are based on organizing processes. This suggests a general principle of organization: that once a system becomes organized, whether it is the cells of the embryo that are multiplying and differentiating or the behavior patterns of a young animal that are becoming organized through learning, it becomes progressively more difficult to reorganize the system. That is, organization inhibits reorganization. Further, organization can be strongly modified only when active processes of organization are going on, and this accounts for critical periods of development.

CONCLUSION

The concept of critical periods is a highly important one for human and animal welfare. Once the dangers and potential benefits for each period of life are known, it should be possible to avoid the former and take advantage of the latter.

The discovery of critical periods immediately focuses attention on the developmental processes which cause them. As these processes become understood, it is increasingly possible to deliberately modify critical periods and their results. For example, since the development of fear responses limits the period of primary socialization, we can deliberately extend the period by reducing fear reactions, either by psychological methods or by the use of tranquilizing drugs. Or, if it seems desirable, we can increase the degree of dependency of a child or pet animal by purposely increasing his emotional reactions during the critical period. Again, if infantile stimulation is desirable, parents can be taught to provide it in appropriate amounts at the proper time.

Some data suggest that for each behavioral and physiological phenomenon there is a different critical period in development. If this were literally true, the process of development, complicated by individual variability, would be so complex that the concept of critical periods would serve little useful purpose. Some sort of order can be obtained by dealing with different classes of behavioral phenomena. For example, it can be stated that the period in life in which each new social relationship is initiated is a critical one for the determination of that relationship. Furthermore, there is evidence that critical-period effects are more common early in life than they are later on, and that the critical period for primary socialization is also critical for other effects, such as the attachment to particular places (87), and may overlap with a critical period for the formation of basic food habits (88).

We may expect to find that the periods in which actual physiological damage through environmental stimulation is possible will turn out to be similarly specific and concentrated in early life.

A great deal of needed information regarding the optimum periods for acquiring motor and intellectual skills is still lacking. These skills are based not merely on age but on the relative rate of maturation of various organs. Any attempt to teach a child or animal at too early a period of development may result in his learning bad habits, or simply in his learning "not to learn," either of which results may greatly handicap him in later life. In the long run, this line of experimental work should lead to greater realization of the capacities possessed by human beings, both through avoidance of damaging experiences and through correction of damage from unavoidable accidents (89).

REFERENCES AND NOTES

1. J.P. Scott, *Comp. Psychol. Monogr.* **18,** 1 (1945).

2. A.M. Fielde, *Biol. Bull.* **7,** 227 (1904).

3. C.R. Stockard, *Am. J. Anat.* **28,** 115 (1921).

4. C.M. Child, *Patterns and Problems of Development* (Univ. of Chicago Press, Chicago, 1941).

5. K. Lorenz, *J. Ornithol,* **83,** 137, 289 (1935).

6. M.B. McGraw, in *Manual of Child Psychology,* L.C. Carmichael, Ed. (Wiley, New York, 1946), pp. 332–369.

7. E.H. Hess, in *Nebraska Symposium on Motivation* (Univ. of Nebraska Press, Lincoln, 1959), pp. 44–77.

8. H. Moltz, *Psychol. Bull.* **57,** 291 (1960); J.L. Gewirtz, in *Determinants of Infant Behaviour,* B.M. Foss, Ed. (Methuen, London, 1961), pp. 213–299.

9. J.P. Scott, in *Social Behavior and Organization in Vertebrates,* W, Etkin, Ed. (Univ. of Chicago Press, Chicago, in press).

10. M.M. Nice, *Trans. Linnaean Soc. N.Y.* **6,** 1 (1943).

11. J.P. Scott and M.V. Marston, *J. Genet. Psychol.* **77,** 25 (1950).

12. J.P. Scott, *Child Develop. Monogr.,* in press.

13. A.J. Brodbeck, *Bull. Ecol. Soc. Am.* **35,** 73 (1954).

14. W.C. Stanley, private communication (1962).

15. O. Elliot and J.A. King, *Psychol. Repts.* **6,** 391 (1960).

16. A.E. Fisher, thesis, Pennsylvania State Univ. (1955).

17. O. Elliot and J.P. Scott, *J. Genet. Psychol.* **99,** 3 (1961).

18. J.P. Scott, D. Deshaies, D.D. Morris, "Effect of emotional arousal on primary socialization in the dog," address to the New York State Branch of the American Psychiatric Association, 11 Nov. 1961.

19. H. Harlow, *Am. Psychologist* **13,** 673 (1958).

20. G.J. Igel and A.D. Calvin, *J. Comp. Physiol. Psychol.* **53,** 302 (1960).

21. H.F. Harlow and M.K. Harlow, personal communication (1962).

22. E. Fabricius, *Acta Zool. Fennica* **68,** 1 (1951).

23. N. Collias, in *Roots of Behavior,* E.L. Bliss, Ed. (Harper, New York, 1962), pp. 264–273.

24. E.H. Hess, *Ann. N.Y. Acad. Sci.* **67,** 724 (1957); in *Drugs and Behavior,* L. Uhr and J.G. Miller, Eds. (Wiley, New York, 1960), pp. 268–271.

25. H. James, *Can. J. Psychol.* **13,** 59 (1959).

26. P.H. Gray, *Science* **132,** 1834 (1960).

27. P. Guiton, *Animal Behavior* **9,** 167 (1961).

28. G.F. Pitz and R.B. Ross, *J. Comp. Physiol. Psychol.* **54,** 602 (1961).

29. E.H. Hess, "Influence of early experience on behavior," paper presented before the American Psychiatric Association, New York State Divisional Meeting, 1961.

30. H. Moltz, L. Rosenblum, N. Halikas, *J. Comp. Physiol. Psychol.* **52,** 240 (1959).

31. G. Gottlieb, *ibid.* **54,** 422 (1961).

32. J.P. Scott, *Psychosomat. Med.* **20,** 42 (1958).

33. B.M. Caldwell, *Am. Psychol.* **16,** 377 (1961).

34. R.A. Hinde, W.H. Thorpe, M.A. Vince, *Behaviour* **9,** 214 (1956).

35. D.G. Freedman, J.A. King. O. Elliot, *Science* **133,** 1016 (1961).

36. H.F. Harlow and R.R. Zimmermann, *ibid.* **130,** 421 (1959).

37. D.G. Freedman, *J. Child Psychol. Psychiat.* **1961,** 242 (1961).

38. R.A. Spitz, *Intern. J. Psychoanalysis* **31,** 138 (1950).

39. N.E. Collias, *Ecology* **37,** 228 (1956).

40. W. Craig, *J. Animal Behavior* **4,** 121 (1914).

41. J. L. Fuller and A. Christake, *Federation Proc.* **18,** 49 (1959).

42. J.L. Fuller, private communication.

43. F. Schutz, private communication.

44. C.C. Warriner, thesis, Univ. of Oklahoma (1960).

45. R.K. Enders, *Sociometry* **8,** 53–55 (1945).

46. P.H. Klopfer, *Behavioral Aspects of Ecology* (Prentice-Hall, New York, in press).

47. M.B. McGraw, *Growth: a Study of Johnny and Jimmy* (Appleton-Century, New York, 1935).

48. D.O. Hebb, *Am. Psychologist* **2,** 306 (1947).

49. D.G. Forgays and J.W. Forgays, *J. Comp. Physiol. Psychol.* **45,** 322 (1952).

50. D.G. Forgays, "The importance of experience at specific times in the development of an organism," address before the Eastern Psychological Association (1962).

51. D.K. Candland and B.A. Campbell, private communication (1962).

52. L. Bernstein, *J. Comp. Physiol. Psychol.* **50,** 162 (1957).

53. W.E.D. Scott, *Science* **14,** 522 (1901).

54. W.H. Thorpe, in *Current Problems in Animal Behaviour,* W.H. Thorpe and O.L. Zangwill, Eds. (Cambridge Univ. Press, Cambridge, 1961).

55. J.A. King and N.L. Gurney, *J. Comp. Physiol. Psychol.* **47,** 326 (1954).

56. J.A. King, *J. Genet. Psychol.* **90,** 151 (1957).

57. J.L. Fuller, "Proceedings, International Psychiatric Congress, Montreal," in press.

58. N. Tinbergen, *The Study of Instinct* (Oxford Univ. Press, Oxford, 1951).

59. J.A. King, *J. Genet. Psychol.* **88,** 223 (1956).

60. F.A. Beach, *ibid.* **60,** 121 (1942).

61. E.S. Valenstein, W. Riss, W.C. Young, *J. Comp. Physiol. Psychol.* **47,** 162 (1954).

62. H. Nissen, *Symposium on Sexual Behavior in Mammals, Amherst, Mass.* (1954), pp. 204–227.

63. J. Money, J.G. Hampson, J.L. Hampson, *Arch. Neurol. Psychiat.* **77,** 333 (1957).

64. H. Harlow, in *Determinants of Infant Behaviour,* B.M. Foss, Ed. (Wiley, New York, 1961), pp. 75–97.

65. J.L. Fuller, C.A. Easler, E.M. Banks, *Am. J. Physiol.* **160,** 462 (1950); A.C. Cornwell and J.L. Fuller, *J. Comp. Physiol. Psychol.* **54,** 13 (1961).

66. H.F. Harlow, M.K. Harlow, R.R. Rueping, W.A. Mason, *J. Comp. Physiol. Psychol.* **53,** 113 (1960).

67. S. Levine, J.A. Chevalier, S.J. Korchin, *J. Personality* **24,** 475 (1956).

68. T. Schaefer, thesis, Univ. of Chicago (1957).

69. S. Levine, M. Alpert, G.W. Lewis, *Science* **126,** 1347 (1957).

70. C.P. Richter, *Am. J. Human Genet.* **4,** 273, (1952).

71. T. Schaefer, Jr., F.S. Weingarten, J.C. Towne, *Science* **135,** 41 (1962).

72. W.R. Thompson and T. Schaefer, in *Functions of Varied Experience,* D.W. Fiske and S.R. Maddi, Eds. (Dorsey, Homewood, Ill., 1961), pp. 81–105.

73. V.H. Denenberg, in *The Behaviour of Domestic Animals,* E.S.E. Hafez, Ed. (Bailliere, Tindall and Cox, London), 109–138.

74. _____, *J. Comp. Physiol. Psychol.,* in press.

75. _____ and G.G. Karas, *Psychol. Repts.* **7,** 313 (1960).

76. J. Bowlby, *Intern. J. Psychoanalysis* **25, 19,** 107 (1944).

77. C.M. Heinicke, *Human Relations* **9,** 105 (1956).

78. H.R. Schaffer, *Brit. J. Med. Psychol.* **31,** 174 (1950).

79. P.H. Gray, *J. Psychol.* **46,** 155 (1958).

80. M.W. Kahn, *J. Genet. Psychol.* **79,** 117 (1951). A. Baron, K.H. Brookshire, R.A. Littman, *J. Comp. Physiol. Psychol.* **50,** 530 (1957).

81. G. Lindzey, D.T. Lykken, H.D. Winston, *J. Abnormal Soc. Psychol.* **61,** 7 (1960).

82. A.H. Riesen, in *Functions of Varied Experience,* D.W. Fiske and S.R. Maddi, Eds. (Dorsey, Homewood, Ill., 1961), pp. 57–80.

83. W.R. Thompson, *Science* **125,** 698 (1957).

84. C.H. Hockman, *J. Comp. Physiol. Psychol.* **54,** 679 (1961); R. Ader and M.L. Belfer, *Psychol. Repts.* **10,** 711 (1962).

85. K. Keeley, *Science* **135,** 44 (1962).

86. T.C. Schneirla and J.S. Rosenblatt, *Am. J. Orthopsychiat.* **31,** 223 (1960).

87. W.H. Thorpe, *Learning and Instinct in Animals* (Methuen, London, 1956).

88. E.H. Hess, in *Roots of Behavior,* E.L. Bliss, Ed. (Harper, New York, 1962), pp. 254–263.

89. Part of the research described in this article was supported by a Public Health Service research grant (No. M-4481) from the National Institute of Mental Health.

What is "mental illness"? Is it truly a disease with specific psychological symptoms of a type similar to the biological symptoms of physical illness? Or is this just a way of characterizing certain kinds of unusual—and often unacceptable—behavior?

Albert Ellis reviews some of the arguments on both sides of this intriguing question. He concludes that the labeling process itself is not necessarily harmful, even in view of some negative social ramifications, but that careful definition of this term and others like it could lead to scientific and meaningful use of these terms without value judgment for the individuals so labeled.

Responding to this argument, Thomas Szasz concludes that the rules of society determine whether or not one is labeled "mentally ill." He declares that the word "sickness" allows a person to whom the label is attached to act differently from others around him.

Part IX
MENTAL ILLNESS— DISEASE OR EPITHET?

19
Should Some People Be Labeled Mentally Ill?

Albert Ellis

For the last two decades there has been increasing objection by a number of psychologists and sociologists (as well as an even greater number of nonprofessional writers) to labeling certain people as "mentally ill" or "emotionally sick." Thus, Szasz (1961, 1966) has vigorously alleged that the concept of mental illness "now functions merely as a convenient myth." Mowrer (1960) has contended that behavior disorders are manifestations of personal irresponsibility and sin rather than of disease. Whitaker and Malone (1953), as well as many other experiential and existential psychotherapists, have held that emotional disturbance is a rather meaningless term because practically all therapists are just about as sick as their patients. Keniston (1966) and a number of sociological writers have insisted that individual psychodynamics are not nearly as important as has commonly been assumed in the creation of human alienation and insecurity, but that our technological society itself lays the groundwork for the growing estrangement of young people and, to one degree or another, makes us all emotionally aberrant.

The question of whether some individuals are especially "mentally ill" and should be clearly labeled so is of profound importance, since it affects decision making in the areas of hospitalization, imprisonment, psychotherapy in the community, vocational training and placement, educational advancement, and many other aspects of modern life. Siegel (1966) has recently reported that high school students who are hospitalized for emotional disturbance or who undertake psychotherapy without hospitalization, are frequently held to be poor risks for higher education and are consequently refused admittance to college. Obviously, labeling a person "mentally ill" has more than theoretical import.

To my knowledge, no dispassionate discussion of both sides of this question has yet been published. I shall, therefore, try to list the main disadvantages and advantages of labeling certain

Reprinted with slight abridgement from the *Journal of Consulting Psychology* by permission of the American Psychological Association, vol. 31, 1967, pp. 435–446.

people "mentally ill," so that psychologists in general and psychotherapists in particular may be better able to see and cope with this problem. The main issues that have recently been raised in connection with diagnosing individuals as "emotionally sick" involve (a) social discrimination against the "mentally ill," (b) self-denigration by disturbed people, (c) moral responsibility and "mental illness," (d) prophylaxis and treatment of aberrant individuals, (e) social progress and emotional disturbance, and (f) scientific attitude and advancement in regard to labeling people "mentally ill."

SOCIAL DISCRIMINATION AGAINST THE "MENTALLY ILL"

There are several discriminatory practices which seem to be inevitably connected with labeling an individual as neurotic, psychotic, or emotionally disturbed. When so diagnosed, either officially or semiofficially, he is often discriminated against in some practical ways—is refused jobs, kept out of schools, rejected as a love or marriage partner, etc. This discrimination is entirely unjust in many cases, since the sick individual is not given a chance to prove that he can succeed vocationally, educationally, or otherwise. In some instances, a person who behaves unconventionally or idiosyncratically may be adjudged psychotic and may be forcibly hospitalized. Consequently, his—and everyone else's—freedom of speech may be restricted by his incarceration or threat thereof. Siebert (1967) has noted in this connection:

> The thing that has pained me for so long is that, while Americans will go to extreme lengths to protect a person's right to speak, there is really very little freedom in this country to express all of one's thoughts. I talked to many, many people in mental hospitals who were placed there because they revealed some personal thoughts to a relative or to a psychiatrist. Few citizens realize how easy it is to lock up a person who has "undesirable" thoughts [p. 11].

Practically all psychological labels today are inexact. What is more, they keep changing from diagnostician to diagnostician and from decade to decade. Thus, most of the patients whom Freud called neurotic would today be designated as borderline psychotic or schizophrenic reaction. Yet, once a person is psychiatrically labeled, he is treated as if that label were indubitably correct and as if it accurately describes his behavior. His remaining inside or outside of a mental institution, being employed or unemployed, or remaining married or unmarried may depend on the particular kind of labeling done by a given psychologist or psychiatrist who is in a certain mood at a special time and place.

Labeling some people as emotionally disturbed tends to set up a caste system, with consequent social discriminations. In most communities of our society, so-called healthy individuals are socially favored over the "mentally sick." But in some groups—Bohemian, hippie, criminal, or drug-taking groups—the reverse may be true, and the sick individual may be considered "in" and may be favored over the "square."

As an escapee from a New York mental hospital points out (Anonymous, 1966), individuals who commit clearly illegal acts, such as trespassing on others' property and refusing to support their wives, may be discriminated against once they are judged to be "mentally ill" by not being held morally responsible for their acts and not being given a stipulated prison term for committing these acts, but, instead, being indefinitely committed to a mental institution. These individuals are thus deprived of their moral (or immoral) choices and of being held accountable for such choices.

Our psychiatric terminology itself, as Davidson (1958) and Menninger (1965) indicate, is highly pejorative. Referring to people with behavior problems by such designations as "anal character," "sadistic," "castrating," "infantile," "psychopathic," and "schizophrenic" hardly helps their states of mind and adds grave doubts to the attitudes of life insurance companies, social clubs, officer groups, and other organizations about their eligibility. Nor, as Menninger (1965) points out,

> is the patient, or ex-patient, the only sufferer from this situation. An entire family can be hurt by the diag-

nostic label attached to one of its members, because of the various implications such labels have in the minds of the various groups of people with whom that family comes in contact [p. 45].

With the very best intentions, then, psychologists and psychiatrists who are instrumental in labeling individuals as "mentally ill" may unwittingly subject these individuals to a variety of social and legal discriminations and may seriously interfere with their civil and their human rights. And not all psychiatric intentions are the very best! Redlich and Freedman (1966), while favoring involuntary commitment of psychotics in many instances, admit that "Certainly, commitments in many cases are entirely rational acts; however, in some cases there is evidence that psychiatrists and other involved persons are motivated, in part, by counteraggression toward very provocative patients [p. 780]." So, quite apart from the contention of groups helping ex-mental patients (during the last two decades) that many Americans have been and still are being railroaded by their relatives into institutions when they are not truly disturbed, there seems to be considerable evidence that commitment procedures leave much to be desired and that various discriminatory mistakes are made in this connection.

There is, however, another side to the story. Some individuals in our society, whatever we choose to call them, are clearly unfit to live unattended in the community—as even Szasz (1966) admits. Many of them should, perhaps, best be placed in regular prisons, even though today that solution is hardly ideal! Others, such as those who have committed no crimes but are obviously on the brink of harming themselves and/or other people, can hardly be incarcerated in jail, nor can they even properly be given determinate sentences in a mental hospital. If their behavior is sufficiently aberrant, they may well have to be placed in some kind of protective custody for an indeterminate period, and what better place do we have for this kind of treatment than a mental institution?

The main point here is that labeling an individual as "mentally ill," and thereby being enabled to send him for therapy either in a suitable institu-tion or as an involuntary patient in his own community, frequently subjects him to unfair legal and social discrimination. Nonetheless, many other people, and sometimes this individual himself, may be unfairly discriminated against if this kind of procedure is not in some way followed. Take, for example, the case of a suicidal individual. Morgenstern (1966) states:

Since suicide is not only irrational—it punishes oneself for rage directed at others—but is also irrevocable, the psychiatrist and society have the human obligation to force reconsideration. All of us are at times tempted to do the irrational and the irrevocable, and I would doubt that, having been stopped, we were ungrateful [p. 4].

The seriously disturbed person, in other words, may well be unfairly discriminating against himself, even to the point of irrevocably harming himself in some major ways. Is it not, therefore, fair under these conditions to judge him ill and forcibly restrain him from his self-sabotaging, even at the expense of possibly discriminating against him in other ways?

Granted that this question may have no utterly agreed-upon, clear-cut answer, here is another that warrants asking: Assuming that legal and social discriminations may accrue to the individual who is labeled "mentally ill," is it not sometimes necessary to discriminate against him in this manner in order to prevent him from needlessly harming others? Mrs. Hyman Brett (1966), in a letter to the New York Times following its publication of Szasz' article, "Mental Illness is a Myth" (1966), puts this question in more detail:

What about the freedom and the liberties of the relatives of the mentally ill person who consistently refuses care? At the same time that we refuse to tamper with the mentally ill person's freedom are we not tampering with theirs? By returning the mentally ill member to his family we are chaining his relations to a life of dread, despondency, and frustration. When we allow the neurotic or psychotic the freedom to reject care we are allowing him at the same time another very special freedom: the freedom to drive his family over the border line into the realm of mental illness, too. For though his condition may not be a danger to society, it is a very grave and definite threat to the emotional stability of the members of his family [p. 4].

Mrs. Brett may exaggerate here, since family members of a "mentally ill" individual may, at least to some extent, choose whether or not to be unduly influenced by his illness. Her general point, however, seems to have some validity. For in giving a highly disturbed person his full civil rights, we may easily impinge upon those of others whom he may incessantly annoy, frustrate, maim, and even kill, his behavior ranging from playing his radio very loudly all night to mowing down some of his neighbors with a machine gun. Just as the protection of the civil rights of Jews or Negroes does not extend to their rights to libel, injure, or slay non-Jews and non-Negroes, so may the civil rights of highly idiosyncratic individuals have to be curtailed when they infringe upon the similar rights of not-so-idiosyncratic others.

SELF-DENIGRATION BY DISTURBED PEOPLE

Perhaps the most pernicious aspect of a person's being labeled "mentally ill" is that he not only tends to be denigrated by other members of his social group, including even the professionals who diagnose him, but also that he almost always accepts their estimations of himself and makes them his own. This is exceptionally unfair and pernicious; even if he can unmistakably be shown to be disturbed, he is obviously not entirely responsible for being so, but has been born and/or reared to be sick and is not to be condemned for his state of being.

It is true that an individual, unless he is in a state of complete breakdown, is somewhat responsible for his acts, since he performed or caused them and usually has some degree of choice in doing or not doing them. Not every psychotic murders, and under the Old McNaughten rule there was some justification for our courts holding certain disturbed people responsible for their crimes, as long as it could be shown that they were aware of what

they were doing when they committed these crimes and that they had some choice in their commission. There is no reason, however, why even thieves and murderers have to be condemned in toto or held to be worthless persons for their misdeeds. They are, like all of us, intrinsically fallible humans and to demand that they (or we) be infallible is unrealistic. They, moreover, are much different from and greater than their performances, and although we can legitimately measure and evaluate an individual's *products,* there is no way—as Hartman (1959, 1962) has shown—of accurately assessing his *self.* Finally, when we do assess a person as a whole for his performances, we inevitably make it impossible for him to have self-respect; for as soon as he does something wrong, which, being fallible, he soon must, we label *him* as bad and, thereby, strongly imply that as a bad *person* he has no other choice than to keep doing wrong acts again and again (Ellis, 1962).

This is what frequently happens when we pejoratively label an individual "mentally ill." Instead of indicating to him that some of his *behavior* is inefficient or mistaken, we insist that *he* is psychotic or sick, whereupon he logically concludes that he is probably unable to do anything efficiently or right, gives in to his illness, and keeps perpetuating ineffectual behavior that he actually has the ability to change or stop. To the degree that he feels denigrated by the label of "mental illness," he is likely to feel hopeless about acting in anything but a sick manner and likely to continue to act in a negative manner that is congruent with this label. Self-deprecation, as practically all psychologists and professionals agree, is one of the main causes of disturbed behavior. Labeling an individual as emotionally ill or schizophrenic often tends to exacerbate this cause.

It must be admitted, on the other hand, that people in our society are predisposed to condemn themselves in toto when they perceive that their performances are wrong or ineffective and that one of the best ways to help them to ameliorate or stop their self-denigration is to show them that they are basically immature or sick. They then are likely to conclude either that they are not truly responsible for their misdeeds or that even though they are responsible, they are not to be blamed or condemned. It is perhaps a sad commentary on our society that the only individuals who are not consigned to everlasting Hell for their sins are little children and sick adults, but the fact is that we do largely exonerate "mentally ill" people for their misdeeds and forgive them their sins. Until society's attitudes in this respect significantly change, labeling a person "ill" has distinct advantages (as well as disadvantages) in minimizing his self-denigration.

MORAL RESPONSIBILITY AND "MENTAL ILLNESS"

Mowrer (1960) and Szasz (1961, 1966) have persuasively argued that if we cavalierly and indiscriminately label an individual "mentally ill," we are thereby glossing over the fact that he is still responsible for a good deal of his behavior, that it is quite possible for him to change his performances for the better, and that (in Mowrer's terms) he is not likely to improve his condition until he fully acknowledges his sins and actively sets about making reparations and correcting them. By focusing on the illness of certain individuals, these writers would contend, we give them rationalizations for being the way they are and fail to teach them how to modify their self-destructive and immoral deeds.

Ellis (1962), Glasser (1965), Morgenstern (1966), and various other psychotherapists have recently emphasized the point that people are personally responsible for the social consequences of their behavior and that unless they admit that they can largely control their own destinies, in spite of the strong parental and societal conditioning factors that existed during their childhood, they are not likely to change their ineffectual behavior. As Morgenstern (1966) points out, labeling a person as "mentally ill" and involuntarily committing him to a mental institution frequently "reinforces the immature wish to avoid this responsibility, by blaming the illness for failure to achieve desired goals [p. 4]."

As usual, however, there is another side to the story. Ausubel (1961) heartily concurs with Mowrer that "personality disorders...can be most fruitfully conceptualized as products of moral conflict, confusion, and aberration [p. 70]," but he seriously questions the notion that these disorders are basically a reflection of sin; he demonstrates that most immoral behavior is committed by individuals who would never be designated as ill or disturbed and that many people who display disordered behavior are not particularly sinful or guilty. Moreover, Ausubel points out that not all "mentally sick" persons are truly responsible for their behavior:

It is just as unreasonable to hold an individual responsible for symptoms of behavior disorder as to deem him accountable for symptoms of physical illness. He is no more culpable for his inability to cope with socio-psychological stress than he would be for his inability to resist the spread of infectious organisms. In those instances where warranted guilt feelings *do* contribute to personality disorder, the patient is accountable for the misdeeds underlying his guilt, but is hardly responsible for the symptoms brought on by the guilt feelings or for unlawful acts committed during his illness....Lastly, even if it were true that all personality disorder is a reflection of sin and that people are accountable for their behavioral symptoms, it would still be unnecessary to deny that these symptoms are manifestations of disease. Illness is no less real because the victim happens to be culpable for his illness. A glutton with hypertensive heart disease undoubtedly aggravates his condition by overeating and is culpable in part for the often fatal symptoms of his disease, but what reasonable person would claim that for this reason he is not really ill [pp. 71–72]?

PROPHYLAXIS AND TREATMENT OF ABERRANT INDIVIDUALS

In several important ways labeling an individual as "mentally ill" may interfere with the treatment of any behavior problem he may display and may hinder the prevention of emotional disorder. For example:

1. Calling a person "mentally sick" frequently enhances his feelings of shame about his "illness," so that he defensively refuses to admit that

he has serious behavior problems and therefore does not seek help with these problems.

2. A person who is set apart as being emotionally aberrant may become so resentful of this kind of segregation that he may refuse to acknowledge his "persecutors'" efforts to help him and may get into hostile encounters with them and others that only serve to increase his living handicaps.

3. In many instances, the "mentally ill" individual is forcibly incarcerated in an institution where he is kept from doing many things he enjoys and where his condition may become aggravated rather than improved.

4. Labeling a person as psychotic may easily imply, to himself and those who may be able to help him, that he is hopeless and that little can be done to get him to change his behavior. As Menninger (1965) indicates, psychological treatment today is carried out by many people in addition to psychologists and psychiatrists, and the cooperation of family members is often urgently needed. "Schizophrenia" and "mental illness" are such impressive labels that they induce many people to feel that only highly trained professionals, if indeed anyone, can work with sick people and to ignore the fact that less trained individuals can often be specifically shown how to help troubled humans.

5. By being encouraged to label other people as sick, many of us fail to consider adequately our own problem areas. If we are not seen as being totally ill, we easily assume that we have few or no shortcomings; when we can easily label others as neurotic or psychotic we tend to assume that we are not in the least in such a class. By an all-or-none labeling technique, we tend to gloss over our own correctable deficiencies.

6. Labeling individuals as "mentally ill" often bars them from various social, vocational, and educational situations where they would best learn how to help themselves. It sometimes interferes with adequate research into treatment, while focusing on more precise research into diagnosing or labeling. It consumes psychological and psychiatric manpower which might better go into treatment.

7. If people have close relatives who are labeled psychotic, they sometimes become so afraid of going insane themselves that they actually bring on symptoms of disturbance and begin to define themselves as "mentally ill."

On the other side of the ledger, if we have a clear-cut concept of "mental disease" and if we unequivocally refer to certain kinds of behavior as neurotic or psychotic, many benefits in preventing and treating "emotional disturbance" are likely to accrue. For instance:

1. If needlessly self-defeating and overly hostile behavior does exist and is to be fought and minimized, the individual who exhibits it has to acknowledge (a) that it exists and (b) that he is to some degree responsible for its existence and, hence, can change it. This is what we really mean when we say that an individual is "mentally ill"— that he has symptoms of mental malfunctioning or illness. More operationally stated, he thinks, emotes, and acts irrationally and can usually uncondemningly acknowledge and change his acts. If this, without any moralistic overtones, is the definition of "mental illness," then it can distinctly help the afflicted individual to accept himself while he is ill and to work at changing for the better.

2. When an individual fully accepts the fact that he is emotionally disturbed, he often starts to improve (Redlich & Freedman, 1966). Why? Because (a) to some extent he knows why he is behaving ineffectively; (b) he can begin to define in more detail exactly what his sickness consists of and what he is doing to cause and maintain it; (c) he may accept his symptoms with more equanimity and tend to be less guilty about creating them; (d) he may be much more inclined to seek professional help, just as he would if he were physically ill.

3. By accepting the concept of "mental illness," a person can often accept and help others who are neurotic or psychotic. I have seen many parents with highly disturbed children who, after learning that their child's peculiar behavior is the result of a deep-seated disturbance which is biologically as well as environmentally rooted, became enormously less guilty and were able to sympatheti-

cally accept their child and do their best to help him ameliorate his symptoms.

4. There is an essential honesty about the full acceptance of states of "emotional illness" that is itself often curative. In the last analysis, almost all neurosis and psychosis consists of some fundamental self-dishonesty (Glasser, 1965; London, 1964; Mowrer, 1960, 1964) or some self-deceptive defense that one raises against one's perfectionistic and grandiose leanings (A. Freud, 1948; S. Freud, 1963). When, therefore, one fully faces the fact that one is "mentally ill," that this is not a pleasant way to be, and that one is partially responsible for being so, one becomes at that very point more honest with oneself and begins to get a little better.

5. Accepting the fact that he is emotionally sick may give an individual an incentive to improve his lot. Most confirmed homosexuals in our society utterly refuse to admit that their homosexuality is a symptom of disturbance (Benson, 1965; Wicker, 1966[1]). They mightily inveigh against clinicians such as Adler (1917), Bieber et al. (1962), and Ellis (1965a), who insist that they are sick. As a result, relatively few mixed homosexuals come for psychotherapy, and of those who do come only a handful work to change their basic personality structure and to become heterosexually interested and capable. At the same time, many phobiacs admit their disturbance, come for therapy, and are significantly helped (Redlich & Freedman, 1966; Wolpe, 1958). This is not to say that all those who accept the idea of their being "mentally ill" work hard at becoming better. Far from it! But their chances are often improved, compared to those who insist that they are no more disturbed than is anyone else.

6. Psychotherapists are often more effective when they face the fact that their patients are "mentally ill." When they look upon these patients as merely having behavior problems, they work moderately hard with them and often become disillusioned at the poor results obtained. When they acknowledge that their patients often have basic, deep-seated emotional disorders, they know they are in for a long hard pull, work with greater vigor, expect many setbacks and limited successes, and take a realistic rather than an over-optimistic or over-pessimistic therapeutic view.

7. Whether we like it or not, it sometimes seems to be necessary for some individuals to be adjudged "mentally ill" and even to be forcibly incarcerated, if they are to be treated effectively. A dramatic case in point is the recent one of the Texas resident, Charles Whitman, who killed 16 innocent bystanders shortly after he had gone for one interview with a psychiatrist and failed to return for further treatment, although he was found to be potentially homicidal. Redlich and Freedman (1966) remark:

> As therapeutic interventions increase in intensity and scope, we more frequently encounter the question of a person impulsively leaving treatment when there appears to be a good chance that he could further improve his status and diminish his self-destructive behavior. Without some element of restraint, such a person might not have received therapeutic help at all. Nonetheless, it is probably best, both for society and for therapy of the patient, that coercion be restricted to the minimum necessary for the protection of life [p. 782].

Redlich and Freedman note how difficult it often is, as in the case of James Forrestal, Secretary of the Navy, who committed suicide while under psychiatric observation in a naval hospital, to adequately supervise persons of high position and eminence who are seriously disturbed. While their book was going through the press, Hotchner's (1966) *Papa Hemingway* appeared. According to Hotchner, Hemingway, because of his literary genius, was treated with unusual leniency by psychiatrists at the Mayo Clinic, and the day after he returned home from the Clinic he shot and killed himself. There is little doubt in Hotchner's mind that Hemingway might have lived for many more years if he had been honestly adjudged "mentally ill" and had been involuntarily treated.

8. If the facts of "mental illness" are forthrightly faced and it is recognized that numerous individ-

[1]R. Wicker. Statement made on the Larry Glick Show, radio station WMEX, Boston, January 8, 1966.

uals in our population are predisposed, for biosocial reasons, to be severely disturbed, educational prophylaxis will tend to be stressed. For if none of us is truly sick, just because all humans have some problems of adjustment, it seems futile to teach people the principles of mental hygiene, methods of sound thinking about themselves, and ways of coping with reality. But if it is accepted that all of us are a bit "touched" and that some of us are more so, greater efforts toward prevention of "mental illness" may become the rule.

9. If the concept of emotional disturbance is admitted, proper surveillance of predisposed individuals can be instituted for preventive, protective, and curative reasons. Thus, if a child or adolescent is known to have tendencies toward severe illness, he can be specifically watched to see when these are breaking out. He can be kept out of situations where he may inflict damage on others, can at times be placed in protective custody to safeguard himself and others, and can be regularly treated to minimize his sick tendencies. In this respect, I recall a patient who was referred to me by a psychologist almost 20 years ago because, although he was only moderately disturbed, his twin brother had just been institutionalized with a diagnosis of paranoid schizophrenia. I saw this patient steadily for a couple of years and since that time have been seeing him a few times a year. I believe that it is largely as a result of my treating him and seeing him through a number of incipient crises during these years that he has been helped to remain only moderately ineffective and never to be in danger of a serious break, although in my opinion he is clearly a borderline schizophrenic. Similarly, other incipient psychotics can, if recognized early enough, be helped to remain perennially incipient and prevented from overtly breaking down.

SOCIAL PROGRESS AND EMOTIONAL DISTURBANCE

If we label people who display various adjustment problems or idiosyncratic ways of living as "mentally ill," we may impede social progress in various ways. Many of the world's great statesmen, innovators, and creative artists have been "crackpots" who might well have been diagnosed as neurotic or psychotic and whose contributions to the world could have been (and in some cases actually were) sadly curtailed because of such labels. Thus, Dorothea Dix, who helped reform our mental hospital procedures, was opposed because she was deemed a "screwball," and Richard Wagner had difficulty getting some of his works performed because he was considered a "madman." In our own way, highly qualified people may not be elected to public office because of their unconventional and "crackpotty" views. Diplomats may not take with sufficient seriousness the statements of the Hitlers of the world because these leaders are seen as maniacs. Notable inventions may go unused because their inventors are considered "crazy."

Actually, an individual's aberrant or peculiar characteristics may have distinct advantages as well as disadvantages. Rank (1945, 1958) held that what is normally called neurosis is a creative process that may lead to beneficial and exciting aesthetic productions, and several other writers have noted the creative aspects of some psychotic states, but once an idiosyncratic individual in our society is labeled "mentally ill," it is assumed that his illness is wholly pernicious and that it must quickly be interrupted and abolished.

The very concept of illness or disease, as applied to emotional malfunctioning, may be socially retrogressive, since it limits thinking in this area. As Albee (1966), Rieff (1966), and several other students of mental health have recently shown, the medical or disease model of human disorder is restrictive and misleading, in that it implies that the afflicted individual has a specific handicap caused by a concrete organism or event and that his troubles can fairly easily be diagnosed and cured, as is the case in many physical disorders. Actually, what has been called "mental illness" appears to have multifarious causative factors and appears to be interrelated with the individual's entire existence and his global philosophy of life. It is therefore best understood and attacked on a philosophical, sociological, and psychological level rather than a narrow medical level, and those who practice psychotherapy (in itself a bad word because of its medical origins and implications) would aid their patients (another medical term!) in particular and the art of mental healing (!!) in general if they forgot about the illness or disease aspects of ineffectual behavior and focused in a more global way on the causes and amelioration of such behavior.

Viewing disorganized thought, emotion, and action as "mental illness" may again limit social and psychotherapeutic progress by supporting the concomitant view that only psychiatrists and other physicians are truly equipped to treat the emotionally disturbed, when, actually, some of the best theoreticians and practitioners in the field have been psychologists, social workers, marriage counselors, clergymen, and various other kinds of nonmedical workers. Social progress is at present probably being seriously hampered in the field of mental health by professional opposition to nonprofessionals, such as intelligent housewives and college students, who have been found to be quite helpful with sick individuals but who have often been kept from doing very much in this respect because their patients are designated as being "mentally ill" (Ellis, 1966).

As usual, much can be said in opposition to the view that diagnosing people as "emotionally sick" tends to hinder social and therapeutic progress. First, there is no good evidence to support Rank's (1945, 1958), view that neurosis is a creative process and that it should be cherished if artists and their public are to continue to make great progress. Nor is there any reason to believe that many of the outstanding innovators of the past and present would not be ignored and opposed by their contemporaries even if the latter could not call them "mentally ill" or "crazy."

As for the concept of "mental disease" aiding social reaction and blocking therapeutic progress, Menninger (1965) points out that modern medicine is not atomistic but holistic and that good physicians see disease in a broad, almost nonmedical

(in the old sense of the term) way. He quotes Virchow, "Disease is nothing but life under altered conditions," and Engel, "Disease corresponds to failures or disturbances in the growth, development, functions, and adjustments of the organism as a whole or of any of its systems," (Menninger, 1965, p. 460) to show that the medical model of "mental illness' that Albee (1966) so severely criticizes is not longer typical of modern psychiatrists.

Ausubel (1961, p. 70) contends that to label personality disorder as disease not only would not hinder social and therapeutic progress but that the Szasz-Mowrer view of the "myth of mental illness" would "turn back the psychiatric clock twenty-five hundred years." The most significant and perhaps the only real advance registered by mankind in evolving a rational and humane method of handling behavioral aberrations has been in substituting a concept of disease for the demonological and retributional doctrines regarding their nature and etiology that flourished until comparatively recent times. Conceptualized as illness, the symptoms of personality disorders can be interpreted in the light of underlying stresses and resistances, both genic and environmental, and can be evaluated in relation to specifiable quantitative and qualitative norms of appropriately adaptive behavior, both cross-culturally and within a particular cultural context. It would behoove us, therefore, before we abandon the concept of mental illness and return to the medieval doctrine of unexpiated sin or adopt Szasz' ambiguous criterion of difficulty in ethical choice and responsibility, to subject the foregoing proposition to careful and detailed study.

Ausubel (1961, p. 69) also points out that labeling individuals with aberrant behavior "mentally ill" does not preclude nonmedical personnel from helping these individuals, since "an impressively large number of recognized diseases are legally treated today by both medical and nonmedical specialists (e.g., diseases of the mouth, face, jaws, teeth, eyes, and feet)." Consequently, even if we maintain the concept of "mental illness," we can justifiably allow and encourage all kinds of professionals and nonprofessionals to treat the ill.

SCIENTIFIC ADVANCEMENT AND THE LABEL OF "MENTAL ILLNESS"

There would seem to be several impediments to the use of the scientific method and to the advancement of science when we label individuals "mentally ill." For one thing, this kind of labeling leads to over-categorization and higher-order abstracting, which obscures scientific thought and leads to countless human misunderstandings (Korzybski, 1933, 1951). To say that an individual is bad because his *behavior* is poor is to fabricate a sadly overgeneralized and invariably false description of him, as it is most unlikely that *all* his behavior—past, present, and future—was, is, or will be poor. Similarly, to label a person as a genius is to describe loosely and inaccurately, because it is likely that (at most!) he displays certain aspects of genius in only some of his productions—even if his name is Leonardo da Vinci; it is most probable that in many or most of the other aspects of his life, for example, his playing pingpong, making love, and cooking a soufflé, he is far from displaying many aspects of genius (Ellis, 1965b).

This kind of overgeneralizing distorts reality and causes the unrealistic (and often unfair) condemnation or deification of a human as a whole for relatively isolated parts or aspects of his functioning. Just as an individual's good deeds do not prove that he, on the whole, is a genius, so his bizarre or dysfunctional acts fail to show that he is totally "mentally ill" or incompetent. Designating him in this manner may, therefore, lead to misapprehension and misunderstanding of his sick and healthy behavior.

Labels of all kinds promote close-mindedness rather than open-minded, experimental, scientific attitudes. Calling an individual "mentally ill" tends to put him in a niche, from whence his removal may never be considered. It encourages us to diagnose an individual's condition and then to forget about it because it has been neatly categorized, to rigidify our thinking in the field of mental health itself, and to help us forget that the patient's "illness" is more of a hypothesis than a well-established fact.

Szasz (1961) has contended that the concept of "mental illness" is antithetical to science because it is demonological in nature, in that it follows the lines of religious myths in general and the belief in witchcraft in particular and because it uses a reified abstraction, "a deformity of personality," to account causally for disordered behavior and human disharmony. Many other writers, such as Ellis (1950) and LaPiere (1960), have held that the Freudian terms, in which most forms of emotional disturbance are put today (e.g., "weak ego" and "punishing superego"), are reifications that have no actual substance behind them and are hence mythical and misleading entities. The entire field of "mental health" appears to be replete with these kinds of myths.

While some of these objections to the diagnosis of "mental disease" are important (and others seem to be trivial), there is much to be said in favor of the notion that categorizations of this sort are, when carefully made, reasonably accurate and quite helpful to the cause of scientific advancement. Arguments in this connection include the following:

1. Although it is inaccurate to state that the individual in our culture who is usually labeled "mentally ill" is a much different kind of person from the healthy individual, or that he exhibits entirely aberrant behavior, or that he is a bad or lower kind of person because he sometimes behaves oddly, the fact remains that there is almost always some significant difference between the actions of this ill individual and those of another who is well. What is more, the existing difference is one that can usually (if not always) be detected by a trained observer, is fairly consistently evident, and leads to definite behavior of a self-defeating or antisocial nature. If the individual with aberrant behavior is not in any way to be labeled "mentally ill," neurotic, psychotic, or something similar, the peculiarity, undesirability, and improvability of his behavior is likely to be overlooked, some segment of

reality will thereby be denied, and the essence of science—observation and classification—will be rejected.

2. There is considerable and ever-increasing scientific evidence to show that although the term "mental illness" itself is vague, the major characteristics which are subsumed under its rubric, such as compulsion, oversuspiciousness, phobia, depression, and intense rage, do exist and have observable ideational and physiological correlates. Thus, feelings of depression are usually accompanied by the individual's belief that "When I do the wrong thing, I am no good and will probably always remain worthless," and "If significant people in my life do not approve of me, I can't approve of myself." These feelings are, in addition, frequently accompanied by fatigue, poor appetite, insensitivity to stimulation, ineffective performance, etc. Objectively, therefore, some individuals can be described as being consistently depressed and in that sense, at least, may be thought of as being "mentally ill."

3. Some kind of general factor of emotional distress appears to exist in certain individuals, since they are observed to display various major symptoms (e.g., hostility, anxiety, and depression), while other individuals are practically symptom free. Thousands of years of observation would seem to attest to the existence of this general factor, as many of the descriptions of peculiar people in past centuries are amazingly similar to modern clinical descriptions. Recently, moreover, a great deal of evidence has accumulated which tends to show that people who display severe behavior problems are to some degree biologically different from others (Chess, Thomas, & Birch, 1965; Greenfield & Lewis, 1965; Redlich & Freedman, 1966) and that they can be reliably selected from the general population (Joint Commission on Mental Illness and Health, 1961). To ignore this evidence of "mental illness" would seem to be highly unrealistic; to acknowledge it would be to accept people as they truly are.

4. Although all self-defeating human behavior may well have elements of social learning and may be best understood, as Szasz contends, by being studied in a sociological context and in the light of social deviance, the fact remains that the individual himself contributes significantly to what he accepts or rejects from his culture and, at times, may therefore be justifiably deemed sick or disordered. Anyone of us, as Messer (1966) observes, may be neurotically influenced by dramatic television commercials which convince us that we have acid indigestion when we experience abdominal discomfort. Few of us would conclude, however, that the discomfort represents a demon tearing away the lining of our stomachs and that unless the pain stops we must cut ourselves open to get at this demon. Those few, who gratuitously add their own distorted perceptions and thoughts to their socially imbibed neurotic ideas, may justifiably be diagnosed as psychotic, even though some of their notions (e.g., that demons could exist) are partially derived from their cultures.

5. Although we may concede Szasz' (1961) points that what we usually call "mental illness" is largely an expression of man's struggle with the problem of how he should live and that human relations are inherently fraught with difficulties, Ausubel (1961) demonstrates that,

there is no valid reason why a particular symptom cannot both reflect a problem in living *and* constitute a manifestation of disease....Some individuals, either because of the magnitude of the stress involved, or because of genically or environmentally induced susceptibility to ordinary degrees of stress, respond to the problems of living with behavior that is either seriously distorted or sufficiently unadaptive to prevent normal interpersonal relations and vocational functioning. The latter outcome—gross deviation from a designated range of desirable behavior variability— conforms to the generally understood meaning of mental illness [p. 71].

Discussion

It would appear that there are important disadvantages as well as advantages in labeling people "mentally ill." Many of the disadvantages result from our tendency to include in the terms "mental illness," "neurosis," and "psychosis" not only a description of the fact that the afflicted individual behaves self-defeatingly and inappropriate to his social group, but also the evaluative element that he is bad, inferior, or worthless for so behaving. If this evaluative element were not gratuitously added, the term "mental illness," even though an abstraction that is not too precise, might have descriptive, diagnostic, and therapeutic usefulness. It is a kind of shorthand term which can be used to describe the usual and fairly consistent state of a person who keeps driving himself to act ineffectually and bizarrely.

Thus, instead of saying, "He is mentally ill," we could say, "He is a human being who at the present time is behaving in a self-defeating and/or needlessly antisocial manner and who will most probably continue to do so in the future, and, although he is partially creating or causing (and in this sense is responsible for) his aberrant behavior, he is still not to be condemned for creating it but is to be helped to overcome it." This second statement is more precise, accurate, and helpful than the first one, but it is often impractical to spell it out in this detail. It is, therefore, legitimate to use the first statement, "He is mentally ill," as long as we clearly understand that it means the longer version.

A good solution, then, to the problem of labeling an individual "mentally ill" is to change the evaluative attitude which gives the term "mental illness" a prejorative tone and to educate all of us, including professionals, to accept "emotionally sick" human beings without condemnation, punishment, or needless restriction. This, to some degree, has already occurred, since the attitude that most of us take toward disturbed people today is much less negative than that taken by most people a century or more ago; much, however, remains to be accomplished in this respect.

Meanwhile, what is to be done? For psychologists, psychiatrists, psychiatric social workers, and other professionals, the following conclusions are in order:

1. The term "mental illness," or some similar label, is likely to be around for some time, even though continuing efforts can be made to change current psychological usage.

2. An individual who is "mentally ill" may be more operationally defined as a person who, with some consistency, behaves in dysfunctional ways in *certain aspects* of his life, but who is rarely *totally* "disturbed" or uncontrolled.

3. It is highly dangerous to evaluate a "mentally ill" person as you would evaluate his acts or performances. If he is sufficiently psychotic, he may not even be responsible for his acts. If he is less disturbed, he may be responsible but not justifiably condemnable for his deeds, since they are only a part or an aspect of him, and to excoriate him in toto for these deeds is to make an unwarranted and usually harmful overgeneralization about him.

4. Although most "mentally ill" individuals perform bizarre and unconventional acts, not all people who perform such acts are sick or ill. Neurosis or psychosis exists not because of an individual's deeds, but because of the overly anxious, compulsive, rigid, or unrealistic manner in which he keeps performing them.

5. Most "mentally ill" individuals are variable from day to day and changeable from one period of their lives to another. The fact that they act inappropriately today does not mean that their behavior was equally dysfunctional yesterday nor that it will be so tomorrow. Such people usually have considerable capacities for growth and can change radically for the better (as well as for the worse).

6. People, no matter how "mentally ill" they may be, are always human. We owe them the same kind of general respect that we owe to all human beings, namely, giving them the rights to survive, to be as happy as possible in their handicapped conditions, to be helped to function as well as possible and to develop their potentials, and to be protected from needlessly harming themselves and others.

If these approaches to individuals with severe emotional problems are kept solidly in the forefront of our consciousness and are actualized in our relationships with them, the question of whether to label them as "mentally ill" may well become academic.

REFERENCES

Adler, A. The homosexual problem. *Alienist & Neurologist,* 1917, **38,** 285.

Albee, G. In B. Saper (Chm.), Caste versus competence in the field of mental health. Symposium presented at the meeting of the New York State Psychological Association, New York, May 1966.

Anonymous. Letter. *New York Times Magazine,* July 3, 1966, 33.

Ausubel, D.P. Personality disorder *is* disease. *American Psychologist,* 1961, **16,** 69–74.

Benson, O. *In defense of homosexuality.* New York: Julian Press, 1965.

Bieber, I., Dain, H.J., Dince, P.R., Drellich, M.G., Grand, H.G., Gundlach, R.H., Kremer, M.W., Rifkin, A.H., Wilbur, C.B., & Bieber, T.B. *Homosexuality.* New York: Basic Books, 1962.

Brett, Mrs. Hyman. Letter. *New York Times Magazine,* July 3, 1966, 33.

Chess, S., Thomas, A., & Birch, H.G. *Your child is a person.* New York: Viking Press, 1965.

Davidson, H. Dr. Whatsisname. *Mental Hospitals,* 1958, **9,** 8.

Ellis, A. *An introduction to the scientific principles of psychoanalysis.* Provincetown, Mass.: Journal Press, 1950.

Ellis, A. *Reason and emotion in psychotherapy.* New York: Lyle Stuart, 1962.

Ellis, A. *Homosexuality: Its causes and cure.* New York: Lyle Stuart, 1965. (a)

Ellis, A. Showing the patient that he is not a worthless individual. *Voices,* 1965, **1**(2), 74–77.(b)

Ellis, A. Should nonprofessionals be trained to do psychotherapy? *Newsletter of the Division of Clinical Psychology of the American Psychological Association,* 1966, **19**(2), 10–11.

Freud, A. *The ego and the mechanisms of defense.* New York: International Universities Press, 1948.

Freud, S. *Collected papers.* New York: Collier Books, 1963.

Glasser, W. *Reality therapy.* New York: Harper & Row, 1965.

Greenfield, N.S., & Lewis, W.C. *Psychoanalysis and current biological thought.* Madison: University of Wisconsin Press, 1965.

Hartman, R.S. *The measurement of value.* Crotonville, N.Y.: General Electric Company, 1959.

Hartman, R.S. *The individual in management.* Chicago: Nationwide Insurance Company, 1962.

Hotchner, A.E. *Papa Hemingway.* New York: Random House, 1966.

Joint Commission on Mental Illness and Health. *Action for mental health.* New York: Basic Books, 1961.

Keniston, K. *The uncommitted.* New York: Harcourt, Brace & World, 1966.

Korzybski, A. *Science and sanity.* Lancaster, Pa.: Lancaster Press, 1933.

Korzybski, A. The role of language in the perceptual process. In R.R. Blake & G.V. Ramsey (Eds.), *Perception.* New York: Ronald Press, 1951. Pp. 170–205.

LaPiere, R. *The Freudian ethic.* London: Allen & Unwin, 1960.

London, P. *Modes and morals of psychotherapy.* New York: Holt, Rinehart, & Winston, 1964.

Menninger, K. *The vital balance.* New York: Viking Press, 1965.

Messer, A.A. Letter. *New York Times Magazine,* July 3, 1966, 33.

Morgenstern, F.V. Letter. *New York Times Magazine,* July 3, 1966, 4.

Mowrer, O.H. "Sin," the lesser of two evils. *American Psychologist,* 1960, **15,** 301–304.

Mowrer, O.H. *The new group therapy.* Princeton: Van Nostrand, 1964.

Rank, O. *Will therapy and truth and reality.* New York: Knopf, 1945.

Rank, O. *Beyond psychology.* New York: Dover Publications, 1958.

Redlich, F.C., & Freedman, D.X. *The theory and practice of psychiatry.* New York: Basic Books, 1966.

Reiff, R. In B. Saper (Chm.), Caste versus competence in the field of mental health. Symposium presented at the meeting of the New York State Psychological Association, New York, May 1966.

Siebert, A. *Are you my friend?* Portland: Author, 1967.

Siegel, M. Statement. *New York Times,* January 9, 1966, 11.

Szasz, T.S. *The myth of mental illness.* New York: Hoeber, 1961; Dell, 1967.

Szasz, T.S. Mental illness is a myth. *New York Times Magazine,* June 12, 1966, 7–13.

Whitaker, C.A., & Malone, T.A. *Roots of psychotherapy.* New York: McGraw-Hill, 1953.

Wolpe, J. *Psychotherapy of reciprocal inhibition.* Stanford: Stanford University Press, 1958.

"What's the use of their having names," the Gnat said, "if they won't answer them?"

"No use to *them,*" said Alice; "but it's useful to the people that name them, I suppose. If not, why do things have names at all?"

Lewis Carroll ([1865] 1946, p. 182)

When we say that someone has or suffers from a mental illness, we assert a logically highly dubious proposition. It is virtually impossible to ascertain whether this proposition is true or false, because of the wide range of meaning that may be assigned to the term "mental illness." In the face of such logical opacity, what is required, of course, is clarification. The clarification of poorly defined terms or obscure concepts is mainly a problem for logical analysis. Such an analysis of the concept of mental illness was presented previously (Szasz, 1960a). While this usually suffices for concepts used in the physical sciences, in the social sciences further analyses in terms of sociohistorical and ethical considerations may prove useful or even indispensable. The aim of this essay, accordingly, is to undertake a clarification of the concept of mental illness by examining its hidden or inexplicit historical antecedents and ethical implications.

USES OF LANGUAGE

According to linguists and logicians, language has three main functions: to transmit information, to induce mood, and to promote action (Reichenbach, 1947). While the details of the functions of language (or communication) need not concern us here, it should be noted that conceptual clarity is required only for the cognitive or information transmitting use of language. Lack of clarity may be no handicap in using language to influence people. Indeed, it might even be helpful. Since the social sciences, psychiatry among them, are concerned precisely with this phenomenon—

20
The Uses of Naming and the Origin of the Myth of Mental Illness

Thomas S. Szasz

Reprinted from the *American Psychologist,* 1961, vol. 16, pp. 59–65, by permission of the American Psychological Association.

namely, with how people influence each other—the so-called promotive use of language is a significant part of the observational data that they endeavor to describe and explain. A major source of difficulty in such undertakings is that the social sciences themselves use everyday language which is often logically obscure or ambiguous and which lends itself readily to promotive rather than cognitive usage. Thus, psychiatric or sociologic descriptions and explanations may themselves present a barrier to recognizing and comprehending the very phenomena which they allegedly seek to elucidate, because in their formulations they frequently offer promotive statements in the guise of cognitive assertions. Or, to put it more simply, psychiatrists often *prescribe* conduct, while claiming merely to *describe* it. The phenomenon of calling someone "sick"—bodily, physically, mentally, emotionally, or in any other way—constitutes an excellent example of the promotive use of language. This claim will be buttressed by evidence. If successful, this analysis should provide further epistemological clarification of the concept of mental illness.

The rules of the game of society determine whether it is good or bad for a person to be called "sick." A remarkable bit of psychological insight into the fact that the word "sickness" is merely a *name* for some permissible moves in a game, rather than for the state of being disabled, is to be found in Samuel Butler's inspired little book, *Erewhon* ([1872] 1954). There, Butler described an imaginary society in which "sickness" was punished like "crime" is in our culture, whereas "criminality" was treated like "illness."

Without reviewing the details of the social history of illness, the sick role, and related variables, let us merely note that during the latter half of the nineteenth century—that is, when so-called modern neurology and psychiatry originated—the rules of the game of living were such that if a person was disabled, there was an advantage to his being called "sick." It might be said, therefore, that physicians had two basic choices. One was to classify (or rename) all who were disabled (in whatever way) as "sick," to "cash in" on the instrumental use of this symbol and thus improve the lot of these people. The other was, or would have been, to make the rules themselves clear and then extend the humane treatment accorded to the "sick" to other members of society. This would have involved expanding, so to speak, man's humanity to man. As is well known, the first alternative was invariably adopted by physicians. Moreover, this choice is still constantly made whenever this problem, which appears in many guises, arises. Preferring to use the word "sick" (or some other word) promotively, rather than making the rules of the game explicit and perhaps altering them, seems to be generally regarded as the easier of the two choices. This fact seems to be attributable to its consonance with the Christian ethic, which places much greater emphasis on charitableness than on truthfulness or scientific clarity. I shall try to demonstrate the social consequence of each of these choices and indicate the basis for my preference of the latter.

More specifically, the decision which faced the pioneer neuropsychiatrists—Charcot, Janet, Bernheim, Kraepelin, Freud, and others—was what to label persons exhibiting disability by means of certain so-called neuromuscular and sensory symptoms? Should they be called physically ill, malingerers, hysterics, mentally ill, or perhaps something else? On the whole, the pre-Charcotian predilection was to label all those not demonstrably physically ill "malingerers." One of Charcot's alleged discoveries was not a "discovery" at all, however, but consisted rather in promoting the relabeling of these persons as "hysterics" (Freud [1893] 1948; Guillain, 1959). It is this process of relabeling that will occupy our attention in this study.

TWO CONVERSIONS: MALINGERERS TO HYSTERICS—JEWS TO CHRISTIANS

The maneuver of renaming is insidious because it has certain, at least consciously, undesired consequences. There are many similarities between it and religious conversion. This thesis will be illustrated by taking the social game of anti-Semitism as an example. In Europe in Freud's day, anti-Semitism amounted to the following rule: To be a Jew was a disability in that it made life more difficult in various ways. For a Christian (particularly a Roman Catholic in Austria-Hungary), life was easier, all other things being equal. Hence, there is a compelling analogy between being sick, with say a congenital hip injury, or chronic peptic ulcer, or a chronic low grade infection, on the one hand, and being Jewish on the other. Conversely, there was a similarity between being Catholic and being healthy. If Jews desired to improve their status, they had two choices. These were the same choices that Charcot and Freud had when they faced the problem of malingering and hysteria! First, there was the option of being renamed and reclassified. This, of course, must be taken quite literally. Jews could adopt German names instead of their Jewish ones, and they could also be reclassified as Christians. That is, they could be converted. This process involved being placed in a group (Christian) in which, in a sense, they did not belong. Conversion of this kind constitutes a sort of socially accepted form of lying. People *agree* to call something by a name which, in one sense, is a false denoter. This is done in full awareness of the cognitive falsity of the new semantics for the instrumental purpose of insuring a better life for the renamed. I submit that when "malingerers" were renamed "hysterics"—to secure for them the rights and privileges of the "sick"—what was accomplished was essentially similar to the restoring of the full range of human rights to the disenfranchised Jews by promoting their conversion to Catholicism (Szasz, 1956).

It is important to note that only the instrumental use of language was involved here. The cognitive proposition underlying the rules—namely, that Jews are inferior to Christians, or that "malingerers" are inferior to "patients"—remained unaltered! This is very different from explicitly adopting a Jeffersonian kind of humanism—however idealistic—according to which all men have the same rights and dignities, irrespective of their religions or disabilities. If we were to classify human beings—instead of their disembodied disabilities—into classes, according to which some would have more rights and opportunities than others (I am speaking here of legal rules, not of physical abilities to perform), then I think most physicians would hesitate to make any distinctions whatever. As matters still stand, however, certain disabilities are much more honorable—and hence more socially useful—than others. In other words, although society no longer recognizes aristocracies of birth, at least not in the forms in which these were honored in medieval monarchies, there are today aristocracies of illness. A residual paralysis from poliomyelitis, for example, ranks with the nobility; chronic peptic ulcer is on the level of the bourgeoisie; schizophrenia is slavery.

The rules of anti-Semitism having been what they were in, say, Austria-Hungary, Jews had the option of converting to Christianity. I have commented on how this worked. Presently, I shall trace its consequences beyond this initial stage. The second basic choice whereby the game of life could be altered was by immigrating, especially to America. This meant, in essence, to leave the field of current action, hoping that the new life—the new game—would not be played by the same rules, but by rules more favorable to the subject. The process of immigration has its exact analog in the psychiatric situation: It is for the physician (psychiatrist) to decide that the sufferer should be better treated, *not because he is sick, but because he is human!* But this means that the physician leaves his social role as doctor and adopts another role. Now this, in fact, happened to Freud and psychoanalysis, but it came about in a very complicated and confused manner. For, it has become clear that psychoanalysis—not only in theory but even more in actual practice—has little in common with medicine (Szasz, 1959a, 1959b). Hence, a new social role was created. Freud and the psychoanalysts who followed him immigrated, as it were, by leaving medicine behind, and by engaging in a new life, that is psychotherapy. But the new life, as it usually happens, was built partly after the image of the old. Instead of building a "New England," Freud built a "New Medicine." The similarities between the old and the new, however, were slight except in *name*.

As a result of the ways in which psychoanalysis, and modern dynamic psychiatries in general, originated and developed, it came to pass that the psychiatric study of problems in human living became incorporated into medicine, much as converted Jews were incorporated into the social body of Austria-Hungary. This maneuver may be paraphrased as follows: "Psychoanalysis *is* a part of medicine because it deals with mental health and illness." The convert corollary of this statement is: "Psychoanalysis *should* be a part of medicine because this will be good for psychoanalysts." (By analogy: "Jews *are* citizens of Austria-Hungary because they speak German, which is the official language of the country." And its corollary: "Jews *should* be considered citizens of the country because it will be good for them.")

This method of solving the problem of the disenfranchisement of psychoanalytic psychology (among the sciences)—or of the Jews—makes it impossible to take advantage of a solution which is scientifically more accurate and socially more promising. It may be paraphrased as follows: "Psychoanalysis, which clearly differs in many ways from other branches of medicine, *may be regarded* as a part of it because its subject matter is relevant to the broad idea of human abilities and disabilities." The covert implication of this statement is that psychoanalysts *do not* plead for the special privileges bestowed on the physician by Western European and American societies. Rather, it is as though they had said: "Psychoanalysis is a form of scientific activity, composed of an abstract or theoretical part and an applied or therapeutic part. As such, its primary aspiration is not the improvement of the social role of its practitioners. Its aims are, rather, first, increasing and improving the sum total of scientific knowledge concerning man as a social being, and second, helping certain persons by means of a special method (for influencing people), known as 'psychoanalytic treatment'." The Jewish-Gentile analogy to this would run as follows: "Jews, while different from Gentiles—e.g., in language, religion, physical appearance, etc.—nevertheless may be regarded as citizens of Austria-Hungary because they do in fact constitute a part of its social body." The corollary of this would be to state that: "We, as Jews, do not claim the special privileges which are usually bestowed on citizens in contrast to foreigners. On the contrary, we are also opposed to discriminations against, say, Czechs and Rumanians." The latter position, while equalizing the differences between Jews and Gentiles at one stroke, creates new differences between them with the next. This, I submit, is the reason why it has been avoided in all situations in which the participants' purpose does not lie chiefly in enlarging cognitive horizons but lies rather in the immediate) improvement of human conditions.

Problem of Reconversion

Adopting the first alternative, that is, naming all disabilities "illness," left the underlying rules of the game unaltered and thus invited the participants to continue playing by the old rules, whenever possible. Specifically, the renaming of "malingering" as "hysteria" left untouched the basic rule that some disabilities could be treated with kindness, and others with hostility (by physicians and others). This maneuver was simply a trick to provide an advantage for certain participants in the game who had been previously handicapped. Similarly, the conversion of Jews recodified the correctness, as it were, of the premise and rule that it was a "good" thing for members of an in-group to discriminate against, and debase, members of certain out-groups. The conversion, once again, is merely a trick or maneuver whereby members of the out-group became converted into members of the in-group.

Such a maneuver, it seems to me, invites its converse. In other words, two can play at this game of "conversion" as well as one. For each step of "conversion," there is a corresponding step of "reconversion." This has occurred in both the Jew-Gentile relationship in Europe and in the relationship of psychiatry to medicine. Each of these processes has been facilitated, or so I submit, by earlier social changes which have not only left the basic rules of discrimination unaltered, but covertly strengthened them—and the beliefs they embodied—by the very attempts to evade them. In so describing the "return of the old rules" I am speaking, of course, of the same sort of occurrence which Freud subsumed under the expression "return of the repressed." The former emphasizes the rule-following aspects of behavior (Peters, 1958), and the fate of inexplicit rules; the latter focuses on the tendency of old patterns of human relationships to reappear in new forms, especially when the most significant past relationships drop out of awareness.

One of the things that happened in medicine and psychiatry in regard to the so-called problem of mental illness during the past half-century could be briefly summarized as follows. Human disabilities previously called "malingering" (or "sin," or by still other names) were renamed "mental illnesses." This was done in part to give the bearers of these names a new citizenship, so to speak, in the land of the "sick." And for a while, perhaps, this maneuver worked. But soon, people bearing the names of mental illnesses—much like Jews with certain distinguishing German names or physical characteristics—began to reacquire their former ill repute. And so it has come to pass that the new label "mental illness"—and all its variants—has in everyday language come to mean much the same thing as had been denoted by the previously abandoned words of denigration. This is not to say that in the context of some psychoanalytic writings certain terms, such as "hysteria" or "schizophrenia," do not have a more precise, technical meaning. They do, and to that extent have a limited scientific (cognitive) usefulness. More often than not, however, these terms are used, even by psychiatrists and psychoanalysts, only for their instrumental-promotive effect. When used in this way, as for instance when it is asserted that "Mr. A. is mentally ill," what is meant is

some thing such as this: "Do not pay any attention to what Mr. A. says," or "Do not take Mr. A. seriously," or "I suggest that you deprive Mr. A. of his civil liberties," and so forth (Szasz, 1958a, 1958c). If the person so labeled is a fellow psychiatrist, psychologist, or psychoanalyst, then the assertion means: "Dr. A. is all wrong," or "Dr. A. is a poor psychotherapist, do not send him any patients," and so forth. The expression "mental illness," as a convenient term of derogation, denigration, or thinly veiled attack, has thus been woven into the very fabric of everyday life. Indeed, even psychoanalysts have been unable to resist adopting this usage.

This thesis may be illustrated by considering Ernest Jones' (1953–57), otherwise surely most praiseworthy, biography of Freud, and some of the reactions to it. In a recent essay, Fromm (1958) decried what he considered to be Jones' unjust attack on Ferenczi and Rank as "mentally ill." The gist of Fromm's thesis was that they were healthy mentally (whatever he meant by that), but that Jones called them "sick" only to impugn their stature. Fromm went even further by implying that it was not Ferenczi and Rank who were "sick," but rather Freud and Jones. It is curious that although Fromm must have been well aware of this derogatory use of the expression "mental illness," he did not consider the possibility that this notion is devoid of a clear cognitive meaning, and that its main function might be precisely such an instrumental one. This game of psychiatric name calling tends to go on and on, with new players aspiring to the status of power of being able to denigrate and injure others by such linguistic exhortation.

It is consistent with this view that not only did Freud, Jones, and others use the expression "mental illness" to depreciate and injure others (particularly fellow professionals), but they also used its converse, "mental health," to promote the good fortune of those whom they liked and respected. For example, Freud failed to find any signs of "mental illness" in the American psychiatrist, Frink, whom he analyzed, although the latter had apparently behaved in a socially disordered manner before his analysis and "passed through a psychotic phase" during it.[1] The same was true for Freud's earlier relationship with Ferenczi, when, for example, the latter showed disappointment over Freud's reluctance to confide in him *all* of his (i.e., Freud's) dreams, while the two spent their vacations together (Jones, 1955, pp. 82–84). The point I wish to make is that Freud (and others after him) tended to view those whom he considered talented and promising spokesmen for his new science as "mentally healthy," irrespective of other indications which might conflict with this appraisal. In this usage, the old rules of the game according to which "mental illness" is but a form of imitating illness or malingering are evident. In brief, then, "mental illness" is considered to be a bit of nasty behavior, the purpose of which is to antagonize those toward whom it is directed.

In this connection, Eisendorfer's (1959) recent review of the policies governing admission for training to the New York Psychoanalytic Institute is pertinent. He stated that candidates diagnosed as having "perversions" or "overt psychopathology" are *automatically* excluded from acceptance. He did not specify the definition of perversion or psychopathology that was used. This

makes for a convenient arrangement for the admissions committee, but provides no help for those wishing to ascertain the actual practices described. It is worth noting, too, that inasmuch as analytic training organizations have adopted this openly antipsychopathology attitude, it may not be a coincidence that their applicants present them with a facade of normality! At the same time, this allegedly pseudonormal attitude of present-day candidates seems to be resented by many analysts.[2] The possible connections between the currently prevalent psychoanalytic position toward the candidate's so-called psychopathology and his facade of normality are, curiously, never drawn in discussions of this subject.

For a final illustration of the contemporary usage of "mental illness," we may consider a portion of *Time* magazine's recent (June 23, 1958) commentary on Taft's (1958) biography of Rank. It read, in part, as follows:

> In Rank's later years his behavior was more appropriate to the role of patient than of therapist. He went through one emotional crisis after another (diagnosed by famed Freud Biographer Ernest Jones as a mild manic-depressive psychosis), even suffered artist's and writer's block—a symptom that analysts claim to relieve most effectively. One thing certain from Biographer Taft's candid pages: in the post-Freud patter of the cocktail hour, Otto Rank was "sick, sick, sick" (p. 68).

Surely, in this context the word "sick" is used very differently than it is when the patient develops in his later life, say, generalized arteriosclerosis or coronary heart disease. Thus, the expression "mental illness," and the phenomena to which it refers, has, since the early days of psychoanalysis,

---

[1]In this connection, see Jones' (1957) following comments concerning the Frink affair:

"This year brought Freud a keen personal disappointment, second only to that concerning Rank. Frink of New York had resumed his analysis in Vienna in April, 1922, continuing until February, 1923, and Freud had formed the very highest opinion of him. He was, so Freud maintained, by far *the ablest American he had come across, the only one from whose gifts he expected something* [italics added]. Frink had passed through a psychotic phase during his analysis—he had indeed to have a male nurse with him for a time—but Freud considered he had quite overcome it, and *he counted on his being the leading analyst in America* [italics added]. Unfortunately, on returning to New York Frink behaved very arrogantly to the older analysts, particularly Brill, telling everyone how out of date they were. Frink's second marriage, which had caused so much scandal and on which high hopes of happiness had been set, had proved a failure, and his wife was suing for a divorce. That, together with the quarrels just mentioned, must have precipitated another attack. Frink wrote to me in November, 1923, that for reasons of ill health he had to give up his work for the Journal and also his private practice. In the following summer he was a patient in the Phipps Psychiatric Institute, and he never recovered his sanity. He died in the Chapel Hill Mental Hospital in North Carolina some ten years later" (pp. 105–106).

The Frink affair, I think, might be paradigmatic of many later—and now current—problems of *psychoanalytic training*. I refer to the disposition training analysts seem to have to see mental health in those of their candidates of whom they approve. This is especially true for those training analysts who have proselytizing tendencies; they will be disposed to think well of those candidates whom they consider worthy disciples. Contrariwise, training candidates whom their analysts dislike—or with whom they find themselves in serious disagreement—are in danger of being found mentally unhealthy, requiring prolonged or repeated analyses. Needless to say, I am not implying that this is the *only* criterion used for assessing "psychopathology" in training analyses. I only wish to point out a significant bias inherent in the present organization of the psychoanalytic training system. I have examined this problem in greater detail in my two papers on this subject (Szasz, 1958b, 1960b).

[2]According to Eisendorfer (1959): "Such factors as overt psychopathology, perversions, homosexuality, and antisocial psychopathic acting out automatically eliminate the candidate" (p. 376). Barely one paragraph later he noted that "A not uncommon characteristic of a considerable number of candidates (about ten per cent) is a facade of normality" (p. 377); adding that "A dogged determination to present himself as being normal, more often than not, serves as veneer to conceal chronic pathology" (p. 377). Apparently Eisendorfer did not regard these two requirements—namely, presenting *no* overt psychopathology on the one hand, and presenting *no* facade of normality on the other—as mutually contradictory. But what else is left for the candidate to present, except, of course, having precisely the "right kind of psychopathology" (my formulation). Eisendorfer's statements offer rather clear evidence that psychoanalytic training organizations use the notion of psychopathology, and the process of *naming*, to promote their particular ends, rather than to communicate verifiable observations.

traversed a full cycle. Like "malingering," then, "mental illness" now denotes behavior considered unpleasant and socially deviant by the user of the label. There is a parallel between this turn of events and the recrudescence of anti-Semitism in Central Europe that began after the first World War. The period during which the life of the Jews by means of religious and social conversion was greatly improved was soon followed by another during which the semantic and social changes were reconverted, as it were, into their original form. Thus, certain people who bore German names and professed to believe in the Christian religion were—under the Nazi laws (rules)—once again treated as though they were Jews, and further, as though persecuting Jews was the "right" thing to do. The rule which stated that hostility to members of out-groups (Jewish or otherwise) was a social "good"—in other words, that it was the sign by which (German) patriotism was to be recognized—could be readapted to the new conditions with a minimum of effort. All this was inherent, as I suggested, in the fact that these rules—which in a way constitute the rules of a primitive sort of patriotism everywhere—were never challenged by those who sought to improve their lot in life by semantic and religious conversion. Indeed, it is well known that many converted European Jews became identified with their aggressors, which is to say that they continued to play by their rules. Thus, not only was this type of conversion not a successful revolt against anti-Semitism, but it was a covert way of pouring oil on the fires of this sort of social orientation. Accordingly, anti-Semitism was not given up by the in-group, and all that had happened was that some Jews removed themselves from the group of the "hated" and enlisted themselves in the group of "haters." I do not cite these facts to dwell on the recent history of European Jews, and can only hope that the events depicted will not distract the reader from the primary purpose of this analysis, which is the clarification of the vicissitudes of the notion of mental illness.

The events sketched above are paralleled by the following developments in the history of medical psychology. The psychiatrists of the late nine-teenth and early twentieth century—that is, the former "alienists"—were distinctly depreciated by their medical colleagues. They were medical outcasts. Contrast this with the public image and social role of the mid-twentieth century psychiatrist (in the United States of America) whose prestige often outranks that of other physicians. He has become a kind of supertherapist. But this is not all. He has joined with his medical colleagues in enthusiastic "togetherness" and has become a leader in proclaiming his "loyalty" to medicine. And how is this loyalty demonstrated? By an aggressively depreciating posture vis-à-vis psychologists and other nonmedical psychotherapists. But it is evident that such a trend is bound to be corrupting to the scientific-technical integrity of psychiatry. Movement in this direction, moreover, is inimical to another trend, namely to that which would further professional integrity by ever-increasing professional competence (Szasz, 1959a).

CONVERSION, RELABELING, AND THE PROBLEM OF PROFESSIONAL INTEGRITY

Summing up this analysis, it is possible to identify a parallel development in the Nazi reclassification of formerly Jewish Christians to the status of (persecutable) Jews on the one hand, and in the contemporary trend to interpret the notion of "mental illness" (which was created in an effort to improve the lot of those designated as "malingerers") as meaning nothing but a derogation of the subject who is so named, on the other hand. Similarly, when "hysteria" was taken out of the large group called "malingering," what happened was only that some members of the latter group were promoted to a higher status. The notion of malingering, and all it implied, was retained—just as, during periods when conversion from Judaism to Christianity was encouraged, the social operations of anti-Semitism continued unabated.

Even today there are those who expect human betterment for all types of suffering to come via the path of labeling everything "illness." This position would correspond to the conversion of *all* Jews to Christianity, or, in a larger sense, to the abolition of all out-groups by their open adherence to the values and behavior of the dominant in-group. But what could this accomplish—even if it were feasible—so long as those basic rules of conduct which include the positive valuation of human destructiveness toward certain out-groups (e.g., minorities, "criminals," etc.) are retained unaltered? It would seem to me that under such conditions the rules would tend to be implemented essentially as before, although changes in semantic usage may make it *appear* as though great progress had been made. I think it behooves all physicians, psychologists, social scientists—and, for that matter, the intelligent layman as well—to examine carefully the precise nature of the present status of our scientific (as well as everyday) attitudes toward problems of so-called mental illness. This is not to gainsay the progress that has been made in our science since the days of Charcot, much of it through the efforts of Freud and psychoanalysis. Yet, in this very progress—based as it has been in large part on an adventitious acquisition of positive values through a partly misleading professional association with the practice of medicine—may lie the seeds of its destruction! In order to secure the scientific advances that have been made in our field, I believe we could do no better than to recast our knowledge in a psychosocial, linguistic, and ethical framework. This would entail a re-emphasis of the differences, rather than the similarities, between man the social being and man the mammal. It would also result in abandoning the persistent attempts to convert psychologists and sociologists to biologists (physicians) or physicists, and they themselves would no longer need to aspire to these roles. The integrity of the science of man as social being thus requires—just as does the integrity of the individual—a forthright recognition of its historical origins together with an accurate assessment of its individual unique characteristics and potentialities. It is in this way, and not by imitating the greatness of the older, more securely established sciences, that the psychosocial disciplines must establish their rightful place among the sciences.

REFERENCES

Butler, S. *Erewhon.* (Originally published 1872) Harmondsworth, Middlesex: Penguin Books, 1954.

Carroll, L. *Alice in wonderland and through the looking glass.* (Originally published 1865, 1872) New York: Grosset & Dunlap, 1946.

Eisendorfer, A. The selection of candidates applying for psychoanalytic training. *Psychoanal. Quart.,* 1959, **28,** 374–378.

Freud, S. Charcot. (Originally published 1893) In, *Collected papers.* Vol. 1. London: Hogarth, 1948. Pp. 9–23.

Fromm, E. Freud, friends and feuds: I. Scientism or fanaticism? *Saturday Rev.,* 1958, June 14, 11.

Guillain, G. *J.M. Charcot, 1825–1893: His life— his work.* (Trans. by Pearce Bailey) New York: Hoeber, 1959.

Jones, E. *The life and work of Sigmund Freud.* Vols. I–III. New York: Basic Books, 1953, 1955, 1957.

Peters, R.S. *The concept of motivation.* London: Routledge & Kegan Paul, 1958.

Reichenbach, H. *Elements of symbolic logic.* New York: Macmillan, 1947.

Szasz, T.S. Malingering: "Diagnosis" or social condemnation? *AMA Arch. Neurol. Psychiat.,* 1956, **76,** 432–443.

Szasz, T.S. Psychiatry, ethics, and the criminal law, *Columbia Law Rev.,* 1958, **58,** 183–198. (a)

Szasz, T.S. Psychoanalytic training: A socio-psychological analysis of its history and present status, *Int. J. Psycho-Anal.,* 1958, **39,** 598–613. (b)

Szasz, T.S. Politics and mental health: Some remarks apropos of the case of Mr. Ezra Pound, *Amer. J. Psychiat.,* 1958, **115,** 508–511. (c)

Szasz, T.S. Psychiatry, psychotherapy, and psychology. *AMA Arch. gen. Psychiat.,* 1959, **1,** 455–463. (a)

Szasz, T.S. Psychoanalysis and medicine. In M. Levitt (Ed.), *Readings in psychoanalytic psychology.* New York: Appleton-Century-Crofts, 1959. Pp. 355–374. (b)

Szasz, T.S. The myth of mental illness. *Amer. Psychologist,* 1960, **15,** 113–118. (a)

Szasz, T.S. Three problems in contemporary psychoanalytic training. *AMA Arch. gen. Psychiat.,* 1960, **3,** 82–94. (b)

Taft, J. *Otto Rank.* New York: Julian, 1958.

The rhetoric of confrontation politics has become a new tool for social influence on university campuses throughout the nation. In the first paper that follows, Herbert W. Simons contrasts the use of this pattern of persuasion among militants and moderates, pointing out some of the factors that make it a particularly potent tactic under some conditions but rather weak at other times.

The morass of political propaganda that bombards us every two years may be merely another form of confrontation rhetoric. Bernard Rubin in his book, *Political Television,* has probed the dramatic reshaping of elections (and indeed of the presidency itself) by this contemporary medium that lets us confront history face-to-face in the comfort of our own living rooms. The second reading, an excerpt from Rubin's book, outlines some of the scenario of the 1964 presidential campaign, presenting a fascinating documentary of how the mass media were used by major political parties in their attempts to sway majority public opinion to their sides.

Part X
ON THE USE AND MISUSE OF POLITICAL CONFRONTATION AND PROPAGANDA

To those who would plot campus rebellions, Professor John R. Searle (1968) has provided a formula. Somewhat facetiously, he labels it a "foolproof scenario."

> *Stage One*—Pick any issue on which the administration cannot give in and which is related to a Sacred Topic—the First Amendment, race, the war. Demonstrate, violating as many rules as possible, to assure punishment.
>
> *Stage Two*—Make the university authorities the target of the protest (if they opposed an anti-war sit-in, they must be for the war). The number of demonstrators will grow, and TV will pick the leaders and dignify the uproar.
>
> *Stage Three*—Force the administration to call the police. There will be widespread revulsion; sympathetic professors will become active in the protest, and opposition to it will collapse. The original issue will have been forgotten, but the president will probably be fired, the faculty set to bickering and the campus closed. The forces of 'progress' will have triumphed.

The pattern Searle describes is referred to these days as confrontation, a term which in other contexts, has much more peaceful connotations. In a generic sense, confrontation denotes any act which challenges the ideas or intentions of another. A conference participant is confronted by inconsistencies in his reasoning; a defendant by eyewitness testimony; a husband by lipstick on his collar. Broadly speaking, confrontation is practiced by college presidents as well as by students, by the politically entrenched as well as by the politically homeless, by moderates as well as by militants. Increasingly, however, the meaning assigned the term has been restricted to a special type of challenge employed by student protestors, black power advocates, anti-war agitators and other militant types. Even as used here, in its more militant sense, the term embraces a wide spectrum of rhetorical aims, tactics and styles.

My purpose in this paper is not to render value judgments. Rather, it is to indicate, in theoretical

21
Confrontation as a Pattern of Persuasion in University Settings

Herbert W. Simons

Reprinted by permission from the *Central States Speech Journal*, Fall 1969, pp. 163–169.

terms, what confrontation is and how it works, particularly in university settings. Toward those ends, I should like to defend two propositions.

(1) Confrontation is a rhetorical form of militancy, designed to influence or supplant institutions from the outside by engaging their representatives in a drama of self-exposure.

(2) Although confrontation is particularly workable in university settings, it is not nearly so foolproof a scenario as Searle indicated.

I

Returning to the first proposition, it seems quite clear that confrontation is a form of organized collective behavior, designed to reform or transform institutions, but employed by those who are either denied access to participation in intra-institutional deliberations or who are unwilling to rely exclusively on such vehicles for decision-making to accomplish their ends. Within institutions, individuals may effect change by forwarding recommendations to superiors, rising to positions of authority themselves, participating in problem-solving conferences, debating their respective claims in deliberative bodies, etc. In the restricted sense in which I am using the term, confrontation is clearly not an internal process although it may well be designed to lead to confrontations of a different sort within institutions. Its closest cousins within institutions are politicking and bargaining, power tactics designed to wrest changes through promises of reward and threats of punishment.

Individuals may reform or transform institutions from the outside in a variety of ways. The movement for black equality runs the gamut from the sweet reasonableness of a Roy Wilkins to the revolutionary fervor of an Eldridge Cleaver. Who are the confronters? In what sense are their acts rhetorical? In what sense are they militant?

Like those who employ socially sanctioned means of persuasion, practitioners of confrontation generally seek to attain their objectives collectively by joining social movements. As militants, however, confronters differ sharply from moderates in

terms of both goals and strategy. Dressed in the garb of respectability, the rhetoric of moderacy inveighs against social mores but always in the value language of the social order. In textbook terms, it adapts to the listener's needs, wants and values; speaks his language, adjusts to his frame of reference, builds an atmosphere free from fear or threat. Roy Wilkins (1964) exemplified the approach when he argued that "the prime, continuing racial policy looking toward eradication of inequities must be one of winning friends and influencing people among the white majority."

Rhetoricians should recognize moderacy as the pattern of persuasion which they characteristically prescribe. It should therefore be of considerable interest that a contrasting pattern of rhetoric may also be effective. Whereas moderates assume or pretend to assume an ultimate identity of interests between the movement and the larger structure, militants act on the assumption of a fundamental clash of interests. Whereas moderates seek to pull people together, militants tend to polarize differences. Whereas moderates assume the sufficiency of rational deliberations, militants assume the necessity of supplementing arguments with displays of power. Whereas moderates employ rhetoric as an alternative to force, militants use rhetoric as an expression, an instrument and an act of force. Whereas moderates seek changes in attitudes as a means for securing action, militants attempt to change the actions of their primary targets without necessarily seeking a change in their attitudes.

In common with other militants, the confronter seeks to impose change by *acting upon* social institutions from a position of *power*. Not all pressure tactics are confrontational, however. The distinction rests on the extent to which pressure is direct or symbolic. Strikes, violence, boycotts, destruction of property are generally not confrontational. The California grape boycott, for example, may have symbolic overtones but it is primarily a form of direct punishment. By contrast, the burning of a draft card at a rally involves some property damage but it is primarily a symbolic act, an act which carries a message. Confronters may threaten, harass, cajole, disrupt, provoke, intimidate, coerce. But they do so rhetorically.

The foregoing analysis raises the central questions of this paper. If confrontation is not a direct form of punishment, what, then, is its weaponry? If confrontation is rhetorical but flies in the face of prescribed rhetorical canons, how, then does it persuade? The answers to both questions may be derived, in part, by examining sources of vulnerability in the targets of confrontation.

Confrontation works best against those institutions which have the following in common: (1) they are publicly committed to unfulfilled and frequently unfillable standards of conduct and attainment; (2) they can neither tolerate nor suppress violations of behavioral norms.

It should not be surprising that the public and quasi-public institutions of so-called liberal democracies are most susceptible to confrontation. Or that the Democratic Party is more vulnerable than the Republican Party, the "socially responsible" corporation more vulnerable than the self-serving corporation, the "progressive" university more vulnerable than the "conservative" one. Institutions which are unabashedly tyrannical may suppress unsanctioned forms of dissent. Institutions which come near to achieving their publicly stated objectives provide little reason for such dissent. But institutions whose facades are more impressive than their interiors provide the grounds for confrontation and are ill-equipped to counter it.

The problem for most "liberal" institutions is not simply that they profess liberal ideals. It is that these ideals are incompatible with other organizational objectives which, although less publicly affirmed, are nevertheless just as pressing. However Christian its Christian Ethic, the church must answer to the less noble demands of its parishioners. However responsible its doctrine of social responsibility, the business corporation must make money. However democratic the Democratic Party's ideals, its officials must pay homage to the bosses and large contributors who constitute its power elite. Norman Mailer (1968, p. 96) has written of a "schizophrenia on which America is built...a modest ranch-house life with Draconian military adventures; a land of opportunity where a white culture sits upon a black; a horizontal community of Christian love and a vertical hierarchy of churches—the cross was well designed; a politics of principle and a politics of property, a land of family, a land of illicit heat..." and so on.

It is generally a gap between conditions and expectations on which confrontation builds its power base and attracts sympathizers from within the institution. Frequently it is a symbolic edifice at which the confronter fires his most penetrating broadsides; a monument to pleasure amidst poverty at Columbia, a segregated school or lunch-counter in the Deep South, the Pentagon, an institute for defense analysis, a helicopter plant, etc. At other times it is a symbol of authority such as a university president or a symbolic issue such as the firing of a controversial professor.

The verbal rhetoric of confrontation is a curious mixture of sound argument and exhortation. Building on a careful exposé of the institution's hypocrisies, the leadership offers oversimplified "if-only" beliefs about solutions.[1] Oftentimes, the leader sounds much like a religious demagogue urging a redemptive crusade against a large and powerful, but not invincible devil.

Confrontational rhetoric is by no means confined to verbal discourse. In full view of the TV cameras,[2] the confronter joins with others in a deliberate violation of the institution's written and unwritten code of conduct, fastening on those taboos which symbolize the institution's false ideals and inequitable practices. The sit-in, the seizure of a building, the heckling of a speaker, the desecration of the flag are forms of "body rhetoric"[3] which carry a message: we will no longer adhere to your standards of conduct for they mask your own hypocrisies; we are so fed up with those hypocrisies that we are willing to suffer

[1]For a fuller discussion of these "generalized beliefs," see Neil J. Smelser, *A Theory of Collective Behavior* (New York, 1962), pp. 79–130.
[2]For discussions of the important role of the TV camera, see Searle, pp. 12–13; Eli A. Rubenstein, "Paradoxes of Student Protests," *American Psychologist*, XXIV (February 1969), 133–141.
[3]See Leland M. Griffin's use of the term. "The Rhetorical Structure of the 'New Left Movement': Part I," *Quarterly Journal of Speech*, L (April 1964), 113–135.

or die for the cause; this is only the beginning; we are united and will not stop until our demands are met; defy us and you will suffer even more.

The confrontative act presents the liberal institutions representatives with a king-sized dilemma. Suppression of the confrontation may belie the institution's appearance of liberalism and feed the flames of protest. This the authorities recognize. But they also know that the confronters are a minority, frequently an unpopular minority, and that they are already interfering, if only in a small way, with the business of the institution. To permit violations of the code is to brook other violations and to undermine the offices of authority in the institution. To yield to demands is even more self-destructive. And so, after promising a fair hearing and pleading in vain for a return to its standards of reason, decorum and civility, the institution acts to check or suppress the violations and punish the violators, frequently breaking its own rules in the process.

Institutional authorities may temporarily contain the confrontation but, in doing so, they "complete the rhetorical act" by revealing their own ugliness. It is in this sense that confrontation engages the enemy as actor in a drama of self-exposure. As Scott and Smith (1969, p. 8) have described it:

> The use of force to get students out of halls consecrated to university administration, or out of holes dedicated to construction projects seems to confirm the radical analysis that the establishment serves itself rather than justice. In this sense, the confronter who prompts violence in the language or behavior of another has found his collaborator. "Show us how ugly you really are," he says, and the enemy with dogs and cattle prods, or police billies and mace complies. How can administrators ignore the insurgency of those committed to jamming the machinery of whatever enterprise is supposed to be on-going? Those who would confront have learned a brutal art, practiced sometimes awkwardly and sometimes skillfully, which demands response. But that art may provoke the response that confirms its presuppositions, gratifies the adherents of those presuppositions, and turns the power-enforced victory of the establishment into a symbolic victory for its opponents.

If the institution is fortunate, its defeat is only symbolic. More often than not, however, the first confrontation *is* only the beginning. Suppressive actions by the institution transform the focus of the cause by providing more concrete targets and additional supporters. Emboldened, the movement chips away at chinks in the institution's armor. Pressure from within adds to the erosion of its social fabric—that delicate web of largely unquestioned loyalties, identifications, modes of conduct and friendship ties on which any structure is dependent. Minimally, then, the institution or its representatives are delegitimatized. In extreme circumstances, it is brought down.

II

Universities seem particularly susceptible to confrontation for a number of reasons, some of which only need mentioning. First, they are highly likely to attract protesters. Second, they are geographically centralized, providing an arena for easy communication among protesters. Third, they are our "ultraliberal" institutions, necessarily committed in public to the search for truth and to democratic processes of deliberation. Fourth and fifth, they are unable to fulfill those ideals and are ill-equipped to handle unsanctioned forms of protest.

The modern university is a curious combination of organizational models. By way of one tradition, universities have been construed as collegial assemblies in which those dedicated to scholarship hired administrators to do their dirty work. A more realistic picture is that of a clash between two competing models: a federal model of faculty bodies which make policy and an executive which acts upon it; another model of a corporate hierarchy which generously consults with its underlings but is only beholden to its trustees.

Where do students enter the picture? In the most repressive sense, they are non-people, products ground out by the institution upon payment by parents or the state. Not much prettier is the view of the student as consumer who, still outside the system, comes on his own to have his brain lubricated. More in keeping with the modern day stereotype, the student is a citizen but a second-class citizen, not quite responsible enough to participate fully in the decision-making process yet numerically powerful enough to make trouble.

The conflict among models creates inevitable friction within the institution and renders it ill-equipped to deal with protest once it arises. Adherence to the federal model requires that decisions be made slowly and deliberately by persons who can devote little time to collegial matters. Simultaneous adherence to the hierarchial model means that some decisions will inevitably be imposed from above and will thus belie the image of democratic decision-making. Finally, disenfranchisement of students provides a festering sore around which students and sympathetic faculty members may be mobilized.

Add to that the many hypocrisies of which most universities appear guilty: the public concern for students and the private and frequently conflicting concern for personal gain; the public dedication to quality and the private interest in profit-making; the public devotion to disinterested humanism and the private devotion to fulfilling the training and research demands of business corporations and government agencies. Protesters at Universities are not lacking for issues.

Still, confrontation is not nearly so foolproof a scenario as Searle described, even at universities. The following are some of the problems which student militants themselves confront.

(1) Confrontation is effective with those vulnerable to power but it creates backlash effects among those not as vulnerable. These persons may bring their own power to bear upon the institution.[4]

Persons vulnerable to pressure tactics are the leaders of public and quasi-public institutions, especially those obliged by dint of their institution's public image to apply "high-minded" standards in dealing with protest. Most persons, however, have little or nothing to lose by publicly voicing their self-concerns. Those not directly connected with universities may fear student demonstrations but they can escape their effects. As they perceive their social norms to be violated, they are likely to form counter-movements which affect the institution directly or compel other agencies on which the institution is dependent to take punitive action. Pressure to call out the National Guard in Wisconsin, special legislation against student demonstrators in several states, cutbacks in alumni contributions at a number of universities, support given to Ronald Reagan's hawkish treatment of protestors in California—these are but a few examples of the backlash effect.

(2) The targets of confrontation are not static entities. Reinforced by outside pressures, they are capable of bringing their own pressure to bear upon the protestors. Herbert Marcuse (1965) has labelled one form of that power "repressive tolerance." The university or other institution may steal the movement's thunder by anticipating its demands and acting upon some of them, by appointing a commission to "study the problem," or by co-opting movement personnel. In that the heart of their case against confrontation rests on the claim that they are free and open consultative bodies,[5] universities are particularly likely to grant students greater participation in the decision-making process. Actions of this kind place those after bigger game in the none too enviable position of having to condemn as palliatives the very actions for which they have been pressing.

At the same time that they engage in acts of repressive tolerance, universities are likely to increase suppressive actions, backed up by moral claims. Confrontational tactics have never been very popular, even within university communities. According to a survey conducted by the Bureau of Applied Research, while 51 per cent of the faculty and 58 per cent of the students were for the goals of the Columbia demonstration, only 10 per cent of the faculty and 19 per cent of the students sup-

[4]For a more detailed conceptualization of the distinction between "power-vulnerables" and "power-invulnerables," see Herbert W. Simons, "Patterns of Persuasion in the Civil Rights Struggle," *Today's Speech,* XV (February 1967), 25–27.

[5]See for example, George F. Kennan, "Rebels Without a Program," *New York Times Magazine,* January 21, 1968, pp. 1–4.

ported the tactics (Barton, 1968). Militant confrontation has been attacked as a weapon which denies freedom in the name of freedom, as an imposition by a minority upon the rights of a majority and, of course, as an obstruction to the normal life of the university. It is on these grounds that universities may well follow the lead of Father Hesburgh (1969) of Notre Dame in promising speedy action against demonstrators. If all other arguments fail, university administrators may argue that unless the university disciplines itself, it will be exposed to the greater wrath of the community.

(3) Frequently more injurious to the life of a militant protest movement than external forces are the sources of fragmentation within the movement itself.

Within any movement—and particularly those student movements which value participatory democracy—competing factions inevitably develop over questions of value, strategy, tactics or implementation. Purists and pragmatists clash over the merits of compromise. Academics and activists debate the necessity of long-range planning. Others enter the movement with vested interests or personal grievances.

Ideological differences among the followers of a movement are also apt to be reflected among its leadership. In addition, any movement requires somewhat incompatible leadership types: theoreticians, agitators and propagandists who launch the movement, political and bureaucratic types who carry it forward, those vested with positions of legitimate authority, those charismatic figures with special followings, those who have special competencies and those who have special sources of funds or influence outside the movement.

Finally, there may well be friction between any one leader and his following. Having aroused their supporters, the leaders of a militant movement sometimes become victims of their own creation, Dantons and Robespierres who can no longer contain energies within prescribed limits or guarantee their own tenure. With greater frequency, these same leaders may justly complain that their followers are apathetic. Membership in a movement offers few inducements to render sustained and disciplined effort. Members may feel the need to participate in decision-making, to "put down" leaders or other followers, to obstruct meetings by socializing or to disobey directives; worse yet, they may refuse to work at all. Faced with inertia or opposition, the leader may easily antagonize his followers by demands for directed action.

Although I have deliberately left the task of evaluating the ethics of confrontation to others,[6] I should like to emphasize before closing that confrontation comes in many forms and serves a variety of ends. Those who place a single judgment on all confrontation frequently overlook the fact that it may be peaceful or violent, conspiratorial or largely spontaneous, in service of an unselfish end or brutishly self-serving, used without prior recourse to normal channels or employed as a last resort. The early civil rights sit-ins were non-violent protests by clean-cut Bible-wielding types acting in the name of love. Their rhetorical armament is in sharp contrast with the militant symbols of black power: the raised fist and the "honkie" epithets, the in-group jargon and the barely veiled threats of retaliative violence. Similar diversity characterizes the student protests. The recent sleep-in at Penn bears little resemblance to the take-over at Columbia. Those who have heckled outside speakers or disrupted classrooms or destroyed college property might well be differentiated from those who have caused only minimal interference with university life.

[6]For an excellent discussion of these issues, see Franklyn S. Haiman, "The Rhetoric of the Streets: Some Legal and Ethical Considerations," *Quarterly Journal of Speech*. LIII (April 1967), 99–114.

REFERENCES

Barton, A.H. *The Columbia Crisis: Campus, Veterans and the Ghetto* (New York, 1968).

Hesburgh, T.M. "Letter to Notre Dame Students," reprinted in *Philadelphia Bulletin,* March 3, 1969, p. 12.

Mailer, N. "Miami Beach and Chicago," *Harper's Magazine,* November, 1968, Vol. 237.

Scott, R.L., and Smith, D.K. "The Rhetoric of Confrontation." *Quarterly Journal of Speech,* February, 1969, Vol. 55.

Searle, J.R., "A Foolproof Scenario for Student Revolts," *New York Times Magazine,* December 29, 1968.

Wilkins, R. "What Now?—One Negro Leader's Answer," *New York Times Magazine,* August 16, 1964.

22
The Best and the Worst of Times

Bernard Rubin

TELEVISION ENTERPRISE: THE CRISIS FACTOR

During a Presidential campaign, the television industry, largely through the enterprise of the networks, performs several major functions. First, there is the function of following the candidates around the country and arranging for the appropriate coverage of their activities and pronouncements. That function attracts the most attention in that it has to do with the overt processes of political solicitation, by the specific candidates, for specific offices of government.

Television's second function—covering the general news at home and abroad—is often as consequential to the election as are the speeches and other traditional trappings. During the 1964 campaign period, this second major element of television work often provided the public with more important election stories than the activities and speeches of the candidates themselves could provide.

There appears to be a strong connection between specific electioneering every four years, and the actions taken by individuals and groups anxious to impress the public or to force governmental change on matters of domestic importance. Governor Wallace's 1964 "candidacy" in several Democratic presidential primaries was one example. Likewise, the results on November's election night were not the only targets of those who were pressuring for or against civil rights, for or against extremist groups, or for or against "morality."

A general election stirs society to reshape itself more quickly, in part because a mood of agitation is inherent in the specific political contest. Emphasis is constantly on problem-raising and problem-solving. No matter which way the election goes, the citizenry tends to associate the word "election" with the idea of reform. The seeds of change sown by rival candidates—particularly by challengers anxious to expose the abuses of the incumbent group—take root and flower during election years. Elections are societal crises!

From *Political Television* by Bernard Rubin. © 1967 by Wadsworth Publishing Company, Inc., Belmont, California 94002.
Reprinted by permission of the publisher.

Our conclusion is by no means a novel one. The point is simply that a people accepting television almost as a political staff of life should also be aware of its potential side effects; without belaboring the power of television to cover and display events so vividly, it is possible to foresee a normal timetable of agitation, specifically set to election crises, that tells us when the public is to be stirred up as few publics, before television, could have been stirred up.

RACIAL VIOLENCE

We had a long, hot summer in 1964. In major cities across the land social disturbances over racial issues ranged from peaceful picketing to bloody riots. In mid-July, ugly rioting took place in New York City's black ghettos—Harlem and the Bedford-Stuyvesant section of Brooklyn. Rochester, New York, had a full-scale race riot.

In August, a six-week search by federal agents and forces produced grisly results in Mississippi. The bodies of young civil rights workers Andrew Goodman (20 years old), Michael Schwerner (24 years old), and James Chaney (21 years old) were found buried in a cattle-pond dam. Goodman and Schwerner were two white boys from New York who had set out to promote Negro voter registration. Chaney was a local Negro who worked with them, in and about their base in the town of Philadelphia. Evidence uncovered pointed to the strong possibility that the three were brutally murdered by white racists.

The Ku Klux Klan was growing; in Biloxi, Mississippi, three Negro children became the first of their race to desegregate Mississippi public schools below the college level (mid-August); in Paterson and Elizabeth, New Jersey, Negro youths rioted on three successive nights (mid-August); in the Chicago suburb of Dixmoor, 70 persons were arrested after a two-day racial outbreak caused by a liquor store proprietor's accusations against a Negro woman (mid-August). He accused her of stealing a bottle of gin.

On September 26, a report to the President on the racial disturbances in nine cities over the country was made public by the Federal Bureau of Investigation. Item number 10 of the "Conclusions" (about what caused the troubles and what aggravated the situations in cities as far apart as New York City and Seaside, Oregon) was as follows:

10. The arrival of large numbers of reporters and television cameras at the riots provided an opportunity for self-seeking individuals to publicize wild charges on television and radio and in the press. These circumstances provided additional incitement to the rioters and served to attract others to the scene.[1]

KEEPING RACIAL TENSION DOWN

A Suggestion, a Meeting, and Communique

Barry Goldwater, at a news conference on July 20, urged that the "tension that exists" over civil rights be excluded from the campaign. "I don't want to see any words of mine or anyone connected with me touch anything off." That same day, Johnson asked Congress for an additional 13 million dollars to implement the civil rights law.

That Goldwater suggestion about removing tension was connected to the thought that he and the President might join together in opposing further racial inflammation. The two men met in the White House on July 24 for 16 minutes. When Goldwater left, he avoided reporters and photographers and made no personal statement. A cryptic communique, agreed to by both men, was made available. "The President met with Senator Goldwater and reviewed the steps he had taken to avoid the incitement of racial tensions. Senator Goldwater expressed his opinion, which was that racial tension should be avoided. Both agree on this position."

A Televised News Conference

Perhaps Goldwater was a victim of "one-upsmanship." Two hours prior to his appointment with

[1]"Text of F.B.I. Report to President on Summer Riots in 9 Cities over Country," *New York Times*, September 27, 1964; for another view on background to riots, see Ralph Ellison, "Harlem Is Nowhere," *Harper's Magazine* (August 1964), pp. 53–57.

Goldwater, the President had held a televised press conference. According to *Newsweek,* the President had had his press secretary, George Reedy, "plant" a question with Edward T. Folliard of the *Washington Post.* Folliard asked whether Johnson was going to have a "pact" with Goldwater to take the civil rights issue out of the campaign. Johnson replied:

I believe that all men and women are entitled to equal opportunities, so that they can be judged according to their merits and not according to some artificial barrier. Now, to the extent that Senator Goldwater differs from these views, or the Republican Party differs, there will, of course, be discussion. I propose to discuss and debate the hard and difficult issues...on the assumption that the American people are willing to listen, and are intelligent and are unafraid....If Senator Goldwater and his advisors and his followers will follow the same course that I intend to follow, and that I expect the Democratic Party to follow, which is a course of rebutting and rebuking bigots and those who seek to excite and exploit tensions, then it will be most welcome [and] a very fine contribution to our political life in America.[2]

ISSUES BANDIED ABOUT DURING THE CAMPAIGN

Precious little orderly debate occurred after the campaign opened, following Labor Day. There was a great deal that could have been argued through, but most of the topics were raised and analyzed in polemical manner. Pugnacity was a more noticeable trait than sagacity in the candidates. Once Johnson began on his "President of all the people" theme and Goldwater began his fundamentalist emotionalizing, almost all hopes for enlightening public debate on the issues were dashed.

The President's strategy was to *ignore* Goldwater. Certainly, the Rooseveltian disciple Johnson was well aware of how studiously FDR had ignored Thomas E. Dewey in the campaign of 1944. On the other side, Goldwater's natural bent toward emo-

tionalism and exaggeration increased when he found Johnson unwilling to take the bait and argue with him directly. Thus, each man talked his way through his own version of the 1964 race without unduly bothering the other.

After a few weeks of touring in September, Johnson became certain that he had analyzed the fighting tactics of his opponent. Goldwater's inability to inject any great surge of enthusiasm into the ranks of his followers was surprising. In time, it became apparent to all that he was making grave mistakes. The very directional appeal for Southern support and the related loss of almost all of the Negro vote across the nation was one. As others followed, it was explained that Goldwater was an honest man who said exactly what he thought. Theodore White says that a "vast incoherence" was observable in the Goldwater effort.

The campaign in September had begun in confusion; a speech on crime in peaceful St. Petersburg, Florida, whose retired elderly wanted to hear about Social Security...; a speech scoring Johnson's antipoverty program in stricken West Virginia; an anti-reapportionment stand in under-represented Atlanta; a swift and unsatisfactory reference to TVA...in Tennessee.[3]

Goldwater soon complained that he was misunderstood. Sometimes he *was* misunderstood, or misquoted, or maligned; but most of the time he was losing potential votes because he was *understood.* Richard Rovere, writing for publication on November 1, 1964, expressed the opinion that Goldwater's views about domestic politics were "pre-industrial" and his views on foreign policy, "preatomic."[4]

Despite the platitudinous character of the campaign, Rovere suggests that we, as a people, got a clear picture on a clear choice. That is true, but how abundantly beneficial it would have been if Johnson had been shaken out of his father-image role and really forced to answer his challenger on the subjects of foreign policy (China, the bomb, NATO), war policy (Vietnam), economic questions, Medicare, Social Security changes, and the like. All these topics were cited by the candidates,

[2]For Goldwater proposals, see "Goldwater Asks Truce on Rights," *New York Times* (International edition, Paris), July 21, 1964; for President's news conference statements, see "Civil Rights: The White House Meeting," *Newsweek* (August 3, 1964), p. 15.

[3]Theodore H. White, *The Making of the President, 1964,* p. 335.
[4]Richard H. Rovere, *The Goldwater Caper,* p. 167.

but a careful study of the daily reports on the speeches indicates that Goldwater and Miller failed to "draw blood" with their arguments. For the Republican nominees, the only absolutely sure-fire oratorical line was an allusion to the Bobby Baker scandal.

CAMPAIGNERS' CHARACTERISTICS AND SIGNIFICANT CAMPAIGN EVENTS

Aside from the major Johnson television appearance on October 18 to discuss leadership changes in the Soviet Union, the President did not bother to exert himself before the cameras during the 1964 campaign. He and his advisors reasoned that the campaign's more than ample television coverage of Johnson wading into crowds of admirers and giving short talks, or shouting out to crowds along a parade route, "Come on now, let's all go to the speakin'," was more valuable than formal television appearances.

Mrs. Johnson, on October 6, began an eight-state, 1,800-mile, 48-speech tour of the South in support of her husband's candidacy. Her staff and her daughter Lynda accompanied her on a whistle-stop jaunt unique in American history. Television went along, and at every stop, the cameras ground out her adventures as she stressed the national implications of the election as seen by a gracious Southern "Lady Bird."

Between October 7 and October 13, the President managed to appear before hundreds of thousands of persons in 15 states and to millions via the press coverage he attracted. The next three days were filled with events of immediate and long-range political consequence. Of immediate attention was the personal tragedy of Walter W. Jenkins, special assistant to the President. It was revealed, on October 14, that he had been arrested by Washington police on a morals charge involving what were described as "disorderly [indecent] gestures." This sad story was widely played up in the press, and many commentators on politics remarked that, if Goldwater wanted to, he could take political advantage of this personal disaster striking at the inner chambers of the White House, However, FBI and other reports convinced Goldwater that the tragedy was one that troubled the Jenkins family to a greater extent that it implicated the Administration. It was made clear that national security was not violated. To his credit, the Republican nominee did not play up the affair. Had he chosen to, especially in an era of electronic mass communications, the results might have utterly destroyed Jenkins while winning voters to the Republican ticket. Barry Goldwater displayed admirable restraint in this instance.

President Johnson was much distressed by the news of the Jenkins difficulties. The two men had worked together for some time. It was said that the President was visibly shaken when his advisor's breakdown was brought to his attention. Still, he went on and campaigned even more vigorously. One speculates that Lyndon Johnson took renewed confidence from the subsequent warm receptions he received on his tours.

Goldwater was less familiar with crowds, not an extraordinary crowd-pleaser at rallies of his supporters (except when he called out the name of Bobby Baker), and less than spectacular as a television personality. Only when he appeared on purchased time to discuss the meaning of his campaign with a few well-chosen representatives of the public did he shine. In a living room setting, Goldwater was at ease and cogent; in the rally situation, he disappointed followers by not striking those resounding blows they were expecting and by repeating so much of his material from place to place that his remarks fell flat with those who had heard them before. He did not have that charismatic quality that is the mark of most successful politicians. William Miller, his running mate, drew more enthusiastic receptions with his quick, sharp, angry, and satiric interpretations of the Administration in Washington. The success of the vice-presidential nominee as a bantam contender drew cheers from hopeful Republicans of the right wing, but it did not attract new voters to the ticket.

The candidates traveled extensively. By the midpoint between Labor Day and election day, Johnson had gone some 15,000 miles and made 20 appearances; Goldwater had gone some 20,000 miles and stopped 67 times.[5] The President alternated between White House duties and campaign obligations. At home or on the road, his publicity was excellent. After all, the nature of most of the campaigning allowed him the freedom for speeches that were a mixture of Andrew Jackson and modern evangelism. Then again, when he was in Washington, his duties as President attracted much attention—he saw to it that they did.

It could well be that, by the midpoint of the campaign, Goldwater could not have won the election. Perhaps a slashing attack on his opponents, couched in specifics, could have taken Goldwater off the downgrade. But Johnson chose to be general, and Goldwater did not seem able to do what he most needed to do. Incredible as it was, the Republican nominee, on October 6, told 350 editors and publishers of United Press International, at their annual conference, that he would not discuss "nit-picking issues" or offer solutions to specific problems. Neither, he said, would he tailor his remarks to the area of the country in which he campaigned. "I don't have any desire or particular interest in getting down to what will make this particular district or that particular district respond to me."[6]

He should have developed such interests, if the barometer of editorial press support was meaningful. By the middle of October, *Editor and Publisher* noted that, since its editorial-support poll had begun in 1932, Johnson was the first Democratic presidential candidate ever to have a majority of the decided newspapers in his favor.[7]

GOLDWATER ON TELEVISION

A study of the itinerary of the Republican nominees shows that Goldwater appeared frequently on television. A good guide is provided by surveying the press releases of the Republican National Committee, which announced those appearances or contained the texts of the programs.

September 14—Goldwater's television debut of the campaign; a five-minute message (2:25–2:30 P.M., Eastern Daylight Time) on why the Administration "does not understand the nature of the threats to the peace, the nature of the enemy who threatens the peace...."

September 18—The first half-hour television program, carried nationwide by more than 200 CBS stations (9:30–10 P.M., EDT). "Peace for you, for your children—and my children. Peace with honor and Justice. Lasting, permanent peace....That is my goal, my prayer, and my pledge to you."

September 22—An appearance with Dwight Eisenhower entitled "Conversation at Gettysburg—Dwight D. Eisenhower and Barry Goldwater." (9:30–10 P.M., EDT; NBC.) At the conclusion of the program, actor Raymond Massey appealed for money to sustain Goldwater's television appearances. He said, "If you agree with me that the Goldwater story needs to be told, put your money where your heart is—send a check to T.V. for Goldwater-Miller, Box 80, Los Angeles 51, California....Support the Goldwater crusade. In Your Heart, You Know He's Right. Thank You."

October 2—Announcement by the Republican National Committee that at least five 30-minute, nationwide telecasts featuring the Senator would highlight the final month of the campaign. (October 6, 9:30–10 P.M., EDT—NBC network; October 13, 9:30–10 P.M.—NBC network; October 20, October 29, and November 2, all beginning at 9:30 P.M., EDT).

October 6—Half-hour address (9:30–10 P.M., EDT) over more than 180 stations of the NBC Network. The Senator answered questions on "America Asks Barry Goldwater." A member of Teamsters local #399, 37 years old and the father of two children, asked about the nominee's tax-reduction proposal; an executive secretary from Tulsa, Oklahoma, asked about the seeming rift between China and Russia. Goldwater replied, in part, "Just keep this in mind: No matter who wins that fight, we're still fighting Communists as our enemy in this world." Other questioners posed inquiries about Cuba; the desirability of a stronger stand towards Communists; Social Security; foreign aid programs; and antipoverty programs. Goldwater ended the session, which originated in the NBC studios in Washington, D.C., by stressing the public's

[5]Harold Faber, editor, *The Road to the White House*, p. 217.
[6]Warren Weaver, Jr., "Goldwater Maps Ideological Drive." *New York Times*, October 7, 1964.
[7]"Johnson Picks Up Fresh Support in Endorsements by Newspapers." *New York Times*, October 17, 1964.

right to get "straight answers, honest answers, and answers now before November 3rd." He jibed at Johnson for refusing "to debate me before the nationwide audience" and suggested that the refusal could be explained in two ways—"through fear of facing up to these issues or through contempt for the good sense of the American people, and for their right to know where candidates for offices of public trust really stand."

October 7—Announcement by the Republican National Committee that 30 nationwide, five-minute telecasts covering nine top issues would feature Goldwater, "CBS will carry 17..., NBC will broadcast 11, and ABC will air two of them," Dean Burch said.

October 9—Richard Nixon appeared before and after Goldwater's address to discuss "The Real Job of the Presidency." Nixon expounded on the upsurge of Goldwater sentiment he found all over the country. He said, "People are beginning to listen. They're beginning to think, and, most important, they're beginning to learn the truth." Also, "...I'm sure that when you finish listening to him, you will say: here's a reasonable man, here's a calm man, here is a patriotic man. Above all, here is a great American who will make a great President."

Among other points, Goldwater, in his address, stressed his reasons for going into different sections of the country and, seemingly, speaking in an unorthodox manner. "I have gone into the heart of Appalachia...and there I have deliberately attacked this administration's phony war on poverty....I will not attempt to buy the votes of the American people....I will not treat any of you as just so many special interests....I will not appeal to you as if you were simply pocketbooks...surrounded on all sides by self-serving concerns."

October 13—Senator Goldwater was interviewed by NBC correspondent Ron Nessen. Nessen asked Goldwater, at one point, what had hurt him the most. The reply—"Well, I think the repetition of the outright lie I am trigger happy has hurt me more than anything." Nessen asked later whether Goldwater expected some sort of a "big break" before the election or whether "the current trend" would take him over 50 per cent! Goldwater commented, "I think we have had our big break, and, I think we are now moving up. The break would be no one specific thing—just a combination of things that a campaigner likes to see happen in a campaign."

October 23—A "TV Brunch With Barry" on the NBC network (11:30–12:00 noon, EDT). Six women were featured with the candidate. They included the widow of a pilot shot down in Vietnam (he had sent letters revealing the use of obsolete equipment); a 68-year-old woman entirely dependent on Social Security; a housewife concerned about rising costs of living; a mother of three children, concerned about the school-bussing issue; a physician's wife worried about crime; a corporation lawyer to discuss women holding important jobs in business and government.

October 20—Nationwide address on "Morality and Government" over the CBS network, 9:30–10 P.M., EDT.

October 21—Nationwide address on "Soviet Shift and U.S. Policy" over the ABC network, 10:30–11 P.M., EDT.

October 22—Nationwide address on "The Free Society" over the ABC network, 10–10:30 P.M., EDT. Here are two of the key paragraphs from his talk.

Where government presumes to control equality, forgetting that in its essential areas it lies with God's province and the laws of nature, there can only be conformity. Government must consider and treat all men equal in the areas of law and civic order. Otherwise, and in no other area, can it *make* men equal....

Our aim, as I understand it, is neither to establish a segregated society nor to establish an integrated society. It is to preserve a *free* society.

October 28—Announcement that a special five-minute *radio* "Goldwater Report" would be carried on more than 300 stations of the Mutual Broadcasting System, from October 28 through the Monday preceding Election day.

October 31—A campaign rally speech, from Columbia Township Auditorium, Columbia, S.C., was carried by 87 TV stations in 14 Southern and Southwestern states (7:30–8:30 P.M., Eastern Standard Time). Goldwater asked, "Don't you want a President who, above all, respects the Constitution—who respects the independence of other branches of government, and the rights of our sovereign states? Don't you want a President who opposes the forced bussing of children from their normal neighborhood schools—who opposes the principle of forced integration as well as forced segregation?"

November 1—Actor Ronald Reagan delivered an address entitled "A Time for Choosing" in support of the Senator (5 P.M., EST) on the NBC television and radio networks.

November 2—Election-eve campaign appearances of Goldwater and Miller and their families, CBS-TV Network, 9:30–10:00 P.M., EST.[8]

DEMOCRATIC TV COMMERCIALS AND A REPUBLICAN MORALITY FILM

Both parties hired advertising agencies to handle their advertising on television. Doyle, Dane, Bernbach, Inc., took on the Democrats' account, and Erwin Wasey, Ruthrauff & Ryan, Inc., a subsidiary of the Interpublic Group of Companies, Inc., worked for the Republicans.

It was announced that the Democratic ads would concentrate on the general theme, "take the record of this Administration to the American people." Twenty-second, one-minute, and five-minute "spots" were prepared for television. The Democratic National Committee reportedly had a budget of about $4 million for advertising, almost all of which was earmarked for television. Network television was to account for $1.7 million of that budget, with the remainder of the broadcast fund set aside for those television "spot" presentations.

The Republican National Committee, it was alleged, had about $4.8 million set aside to advertise their national candidates. All but $200,000 was assigned to national television. According to Erwin Wasey, the Republican advertisements were to cover issues of foreign policy, morality, and peace.

We have just surveyed the program developed by the Republicans for the display of Goldwater and Miller on half-hour and hour-long programs. The Democratic Party did similar organizing for the President and Hubert Humphrey. Both National Committees planned programs right through to election day.[9]

By-products of the over-all preparations were highly controversial. The Democrats took the lead on the controversy front on September 7, when one of their campaign "spots" interrupted NBC-TV's *Monday Night at the Movies* showing of "David and Bathsheba." In the course of the one-minute film, a little girl with windblown hair was seen picking daisies in a sun-swept field. The child starts to pick the petals of one daisy, and as she plucks each petal, she counts, "One, two,..." Behind her, the sound track provides a male voice counting the numbers backwards, from ten to zero. The man counts with "doom-filled cadence." When he intones, "Zero," there is a screen-filling scene of an atomic explosion. Then the voice of the President is heard saying, "These are the stakes. To make a world in which all of God's children can live, or go into the dark. We must either love each other, or we must die." The doom-voiced announcer picks up the thread at this point and urges viewers to vote for President Johnson on November 3—"The stakes are too high for you to stay home."

It is not surprising that the Republicans were up in arms after viewing the film. Three weeks after the first showing, Goldwater said, "The homes of America are horrified and the intelligence of Americans is insulted by weird television advertising by which this Administration threatens the end of the world unless all-wise Lyndon is given the nation for his very own." Prior to the Goldwater blast, Hubert Humphrey had already expressed his opinion that the commercial was "unfortunate."[10]

Dean Burch issued a statement on October 15, attacking the Democratic Party for a campaign based upon "slanted, biased, and fraudulent propaganda which is unparalleled in American political

[8]The author thanks the Republican National Committee, and especially its news editor (at headquarters during the campaign), Mr. James L. McKenna, for providing him with a complete file of the Committee's news releases on the Goldwater television effort. The following news releases are referred to in the text. "Present Administration Doesn't Understand Threats to Peace, Sen. Goldwater Says in First GOP Television Message" (September 14, 1964); "First Nationwide Television Address...by Senator Barry Goldwater" (September 19, 1964); "America Asks Barry Goldwater" (October 6, 1964); "Senator Goldwater to Speak to Nation Five Times for Half Hour on Television during Last Month of GOP Presidential Campaign" (October 2, 1964); "30 Five-Minute Telecasts...Discussing Issues to be Presented on Nationwide TV..." (October 7, 1964); "Dick Nixon to Appear on TV...with Senator Goldwater..." (October 8, 1964); "The Real Job of the Presidency..." (October 10, 1964); "Interview...by Ron Nessen of NBC..." (October 13, 1964); "6 Women Who Will Join Sen. Goldwater for 'TV Brunch with Barry...'" (October 16, 1964); "Nationwide TV Address on 'Morality and Government' over the CBS Network..." (October 20, 1965); "Nationwide TV Address on 'Soviet Shift and U.S. Policy...'" (October 21, 1964); "Nationwide TV Address on 'The Free Society'..." (October 22, 1964); "5-Minute 'Goldwater Report'..." (October 28, 1964); "Campaign Speech at the Columbia Township Auditorium, Columbia, S.C...." (October 31, 1964); "Ronald Reagan's Address Supporting Sen. Goldwater..." (October 31, 1964); "Election Eve Campaign Appearances..." (November 2, 1964).

[9]Leonard Sloane, "Advertising: Democrats, G.O.P. Woo Voters," *New York Times*, September 27, 1964.
[10]Pete Hamill, "When the Client Is a Candidate," *New York Times Magazine*, October 25, 1964.

history." He did not aim solely at the aforementioned commercial. He was just as angered by the one that took off on a "Goldwaterism" occasioned by the Republican candidate's travails in New England early in the year. Goldwater had blurted out, "Sometimes I think this country would be better off if we could just saw off the Eastern seaboard and let it float out to sea." A television "spot" was prepared for the Democrats, showing a representation of the continental United States being sawed apart at about the Mississippi River. As the film displayed the Eastern seaboard floating off, the Goldwater sentiment was repeated by the announcer. Still another "spot" concentrated on a campaign poster showing Rockefeller's face and name. It called to viewers' minds, in no uncertain imagery, the San Francisco convention. The poster toppled onto a littered floor, and the announcer's voice said, "Remember him? Governor Rockefeller. He said Barry Goldwater's positions can spell disaster for the [Republican] party and for the country.[11] Other such inventive "spots" were presented during September and October.

Burch complained about the Democrats' offerings to Charles Taft, chairman of the Fair Campaign Practice Committee. Among other things, the Republican National Chairman said:

> We feel sure that these tactics will do the President more damage than good, but Senator Goldwater has no desire to benefit from a public revulsion. The dignity of democracy must not be permitted to suffer unduly in the heat of a political campaign.
> The fear and scare technique is not new in politics. But its use in the extreme sense to avoid an honest discussion of the issues should not be tolerated.[12]

Representative Charles A. Halleck, the House Republican minority leader, protested from the floor of that august legislative chamber on September 15. He asked his colleagues, "If the Democrats will stoop to these tactics to win an election what can the country expect next?[13]

The next time the issue was raised, the Republicans were the offenders! One of Barry Goldwater's cardinal causes was furthering *morality*. To bring that cause to the American people, a half-hour documentary film was prepared for the Republican Party. It was designed to show how President Johnson was leading a society that was morally decaying; a group called the Mothers for a Moral America sponsored the film. When it was brought to the National Broadcasting Company, the officials of that network debated whether it could be screened without extensive editing. The film, entitled "Choice," was narrated by Raymond Massey. To show the need for a more moral America, it contained many scenes of *immorality*.

One staged portion had a speeding Lincoln Continental racing across the screen, with beer cans being tossed out of the driver's window from time to time. It was an obvious allusion to news reports of the previous Easter that the President had been drinking beer while driving his car near the LBJ ranch. The President was not mentioned by name. Other scenes showed violence and looting in city streets; gyrations of young people doing the "twist" with frenzy; shots of a young girl in a topless bathing suit being peered at by young men; "montages of pornographic magazines and book covers"; "the marquees of 'nudie' theaters"; shots of Billie Sol Estes, the legally loose Texas financier; and pictures of Robert G. (Bobby) Baker.

When Senator Goldwater saw the film, he urged the party to withdraw it and cancel bookings. He called it "racist" on the grounds that certain of its scenes dealing with Negroes and whites did not win his approval.[14]

The advertising campaigns of the Democratic and Republican Parties, to the degree that they included these overtly propagandistic offerings, should give all Americans cause for worry. There is no doubt that advertising men can so distort elections with their "creativity" that all semblance of rationality can be lost. In 1964, the campaign

[11]*Ibid.*
[12]News release, "GOP Chairman Files Official Protest about Democrats' Commercial with Fair Campaign Practices Committee," Republican National Committee, Washington, D.C., September 15, 1964.
[13]News release, "Representative Halleck Reports He Has Received Protests Deploring Democrats' Campaign Commercial," Office of Representative Charles Halleck, Washington, D.C., September 15, 1964.

[14]For commentary on "morality" and on the film, see Nan Robertson, "G.O.P. Film Depicts 'Moral Decay,'" *New York Times*, October 21, 1964; William Buckley, Jr., "The Campaign, the Film and Morality," *Boston Globe*, November 2, 1964; Richard L. Strout, "Morality Issue Gets New Impetus," *Christian Science Monitor*, October 16, 1964; Charles Mohr, "Campaign Issues—V," *New York Times*, October 29, 1964.

opened a Pandora's box, and out poured the hit-them-below-the-belt productions that demean democratic standards. In that campaign both major parties appear to have erred seriously. In politics, as in sports, it is not always whether you win or lose that counts; most important is how you play with peoples' emotions and sensibilities and capacities to reason. One hopes that the bad experiences of 1964 will lead to reforms. However, there is nothing presently on the horizon that gives the critical observer any cause for optimism.

POLLSTERS' CONCLUSIONS

Politicians find great sport in decrying the significance of public opinion polls. A favored theme in campaign speeches lampoons anyone who would rely on such polls. Popular election decisions are made at the ballot boxes, say contenders, not upon questionnaires.

For all that, it is difficult to find a political office seeker who does not diligently follow polling results that bear upon his campaign or upon the opposition's. When polling results appear adverse to a politician's chances, he ignores any public mention of them or makes known his haughty indifference to such surveys. If polling results show that he leads, he cheerfully accepts indications of the will of the people, even if he takes the precaution of emphasizing to his supporters that there is truth in the old adage "There's many a slip between the cup and the lip." When polls show a strong leaning to his cause, he feels it necessary to urge his people to do more work. Few political savants can forget the historical importance of that race in 1948, when the polls predicted a Dewey victory, and the populace selected Truman.

In 1964, both major parties relied upon polls to a greater extent than was admitted publicly. However, the *core* campaign leaders were loathe to equate reliance upon polls with confidence in polls because, among other things, politicians still had too much to learn about the net effects of television. They could not decide whether, for example, last-minute effects of television work could throw even the most reliable polls for a loop.

The major polling organizations, from Labor Day of 1964 on, consistently revealed that Johnson was leading Goldwater nationally. On July 23, the Gallup poll gave the President a 7-to-3 lead. When Goldwater was given the edge, it was often restricted to estimates of Southern thinking—as was the case in the Gallup poll of August 7, which held that Goldwater had the support of 51 per cent of the Dixie electorate, while his rival had 40 per cent.

Pollster Samuel Lubell was reported as saying that, as of mid-August, one of every seven persons who had voted Democratic in 1960 had shifted to Goldwater, while Johnson had picked up the support of one of every five individuals who had voted Republican four years before. By early September, *The New York Times* reported, "George C. Gallup puts the ratio at 68 to 32 in Mr. Johnson's favor; the survey of Elmo Roper finds it 67–28 with 5 per cent undecided; and Louis Harris...reports Mr. Johnson leading 62 to 38." A Gallup survey made public on October 18 gave Johnson 64 per cent and Goldwater 29 per cent, with 7 per cent cited as undecided. The final Gallup organization poll results forecast a Johnson sweep, with the President credited with 64 per cent of the popular vote to Goldwater's 36 per cent. Louis Harris, in his nationwide poll, offered the same conclusion. Samuel Lubell predicted a "Johnson landslide."[15]

THE VOTERS TURN OUT: TELEVISION REPORTS

When a hard-fought political campaign nears its conclusion and the electorate is preparing for the day when ballots will decide arguments, television functions in two ways to serve the people: getting out the vote and reporting results.

The Get-Out-the-Vote Promotions

Television performs a vital get-out-the-vote service with its drives to remind voters of their responsi-

[15]See the following news items: "Gallup Poll—Johnson 7, Goldwater 3," *New York Herald Tribune*, July 23, 1964; George Gallup, "Goldwater Leads Johnson in South," *New York Herald Tribune*, August 7, 1964; "Voter Shifts Found to Favor Johnson," *New York Times*, August 19, 1964; Earl Mazo, "If the Polls Are Right," *New York Times*, September 11, 1964; George Gallup, "LBJ Tops Barry by 64%–29%," *Boston Globe*, October 18, 1964; George Gallup, "Personal Appeal Dips in Campaign," *Boston Globe*, October 25, 1964; Earl Mazo, "A Johnson Landslide Predicted in the Final Polls," *New York Times*, November 3, 1964.

bility in a democracy. Unlike the newspaper and magazine industries, which have no statutory obligations, the television industry is expected by the Federal Communications Commission to provide such public service announcements as a condition for maintaining their licenses in good standing. In recent years, heavy reliance has been placed upon television to get people trooping to the polling booths. The industry, acting in association with private public-spirited and nonpartisan organizations such as the American Heritage Foundation and the Advertising Council, has prepared promotional campaigns that consist of one-minute, 30-second, and 20-second films designed to remind people to register and vote.[16] Individual television stations and networks are also active in preparing and presenting other promotional material to stimulate voting.

Reporting Election Returns

Network election service

A heartening development in a highly competitive business took place in early June of 1964, when it was announced that the Network Election Service (NES) had been created by the three television networks, acting in conjunction with the Associated Press. NES was designed to streamline and speed up reporting of the returns. A three-man board was established to direct the combined operation. Each network had one director on the board—the AP was a nonvoting member. It was estimated that the organization would have the news supplied by some 100,000 reporters, who would feed reports into headquarters in the 50 states and in Washington, D.C. The 51 centers would, in turn, send returns to a television-industry tabulating complex in New York City. From the New York City complex, each network and the AP would feed its own vote-reporting organizations. Shortly after the establishment of NES, the United Press International organization joined. NES concentration was planned for the presiden-

tial contest and for gubernatorial and senatorial races at the state level.

The television audiences benefited because the major effect of the pool was to eliminate differences in incomplete vote results during the counting. At each stage, identical figures would be supplied to the television networks and to the press associations. Most of the expense for the pool coverage was carried by the networks, but the press associations also provided substantial funds.

The individual networks and press associations each reserved the right to predict the winner of any race, basing the prediction upon its own calculations and projections. Thus the door was left open for claims of superiority in news reporting.[17]

Reporting the late returns

Because of time-zone differences that enabled voters in the Middle West and West to go to the polls after polling booths in the East had closed, there was some concern that network predictions about voting results could lead to voter reactions from citizens who had not yet cast their ballots. On November 1, Dean Burch, the Republican National Chairman, asked the networks not to *slant* "the import of early returns in Tuesday's elections as happened in 1960." He went on:

> In 1960, the TV industry performed a distinct disservice with the inaccurate interpretation of the early results....
>
> The entire nation was misinformed. From almost the very outset it was made to appear that Sen. Kennedy was substantially ahead and that he would score a landslide victory....
>
> At no time did the TV computer-prediction apparatus indicate that the election would be decided in a photo-finish. In fact, Mr. Nixon was repeatedly abused and ridiculed by TV commentators [for] not conceding early in the evening....
>
> This was the poorest kind of reporting. And who can tell whether or not the false impressions given

[16]William A. Glaser, "Television and Voting Turnout," *Public Opinion Quarterly*, Vol. 29, No. 1 (Spring 1965), p. 73.

[17]"NETS, AP Pool Forces for Nov. 3 Elections," *Radio-Television Daily*, Vol. 94, No. 112 (June 10, 1964); "UPI Joins Election Pool Coverage Plan," *Radio-Television Daily*, Vol. 94, No. 114 (June 12, 1964); Jack Gould, "1000,000 To Gather Election Returns," *New York Times*, June 10, 1964; "TV Pool: New Core of U.S. Election Coverage," *Broadcasting* (June 15, 1964), pp. 78, 80.

the nation by TV commentators and TV pollsters did not influence some of the voters in the Middle West and West who had not yet voted.[18]

We have precious little scientific evidence to affirm or deny the Burch allegations. It is too early to sound the alarm bells or the all-clear signals. It is possible that, in a future election, voters under the influence of election news broadcasts could swing a Presidential election one way or another by voting late (in California, for example). As voters become more aware of the power of late returns, they *could* act accordingly, although in 1964, it appears that they did not.

Gladys and Kurt Lang, in a paper presented at the 1965 Annual Conference of the American Association for Public Opinion Research and entitled "Ballots and Broadcasts: The Impact of Expectations and Election Day Perceptions on Voting Behavior," found little by way of startling voter shifts. They concentrated primarily on a sample of 364 registered voters in the East Bay area of California. From their study, we learn that reports of the Johnson sweep that were given early on election day "were sufficiently unambiguous to dispel most doubts." As for late-election-day slack, or the reduced motivation to vote, they reported, "Our data indicate that neither the broadcasts nor the perceptions they induced were influential in causing the abstentions." Finally, they observed, "Our study found clear-cut broadcast-induced slack only in the case of one single Goldwater supporter, who as a result of what he heard lost all interest in voting."[19] The Lang study of a small group of California voters is valuable but was obviously not intended to be a definitive study of the larger problem.

As a footnote to the problem, it should be noted that the Columbia Broadcasting System announced on October 20 that, in order to allay any criticism, it had instructed its staff not to declare a winner in the Johnson-Goldwater race until one or

the other had achieved, clearly, the necessary majority of 270 electoral votes. Fred W. Friendly, president of CBS News, said, "We will speak of 'indicated winners,' 'apparent winners' or 'probable winners' until both our analysis of the vote and the vote itself leave no doubt of the result."[20]

Network variations

Each of the networks touted the virtues of its own procedures for reporting returns swiftly and accurately. CBS had what it called "vote profile analysis." VPA was a system of carefully analyzing selected voting precincts in each state with the objective of setting up political "models." Each model consisted of between 32 and 60 well-chosen precincts. The precincts chosen formed a cross section of the electorate. An enormous amount of data about the precincts was programmed into computers "which compare the actual statewide vote in previous elections with the total vote from the model precincts in those same elections. The model as a whole must accurately reflect the political behavior of the state, and research goes on until it does." Ethnic, age, education, and status data are also fed into the computers. Altogether, CBS prepared 108 Vote Profile Analyses—"49 for the Presidential contest, plus 25 Gubernatorial and 34 Senatorial elections." Regional and national reports, combined with the sagacity of the network's experienced reporters, filled out the VPA picture. CBS worked with the Louis Harris political research team and the International Business Machine organization to accomplish its objectives.[21]

The American Broadcasting Corporation boasted about the twin Burroughs B 5500 computers that it had installed in its New York City studios to analyze "nationwide voting patterns on November 3, and provide the network with an advance look at the outcome of the 1964 Presidential Election."

ABC developed a scheme similar to the VPA by feeding "volumes of historical data from past elections" into the computers and comparing the data with the "latest information from national public

[18]News release, "GOP Chairman Asks TV Networks Not To 'Slant' Early Returns as in '60," Republican National Committee, Washington, D.C., November 1, 1964.
[19]Gladys Engel Lang and Kurt Lang, "Ballots and Broadcasts: The Impact of Expectations and Election Day Perceptions on Voting Behavior," paper presented at the 1965 annual conference of the American Association for Public Opinion Research, May 14, 1965.

[20]Jack Gould, "CBS Will Delay Forecasts Nov. 3," *New York Times*, October 21, 1964.
[21]*Vote Profile Analysis: A New Tool for Election Night Reporting*, Brochure prepared by the Columbia Broadcasting System, 1964, 11 pages.

opinion polls being collected by Oliver Quayle Associates."[22]

The National Broadcasting Company worked in conjunction with Radio Corporation of America, its parent company, to put together a computer system for election-day reporting. It, too, was similar to the CBS effort. NBC had what it labeled its "Electronic Vote Analysis System."

All in all, it was estimated that the networks expended about 7 million dollars to cover the story of election day.[23]

THE BIG STORY OF ANOTHER BEGINNING

Human beings love a story that has a clear beginning, a good plot, and a definite conclusion that leads them on to another story. The presidential election of 1964 was such a story. After much public controversy and personal soul-searching, the voter stepped into the voting booth. By pulling on plungers of an electric voting machine or by filling out his paper ballot and casting it into a box, he declared his views and defended his heritage.

When all the votes were counted, the result was as indicated by the pollsters—a Johnson victory by a substantial margin. The President garnered 43,-126,218 votes (61 per cent) to overwhelm Goldwater, whose candidacy was approved by 27,-174,898 voters (38.5 per cent). The electoral-college vote was 486 to 52. Goldwater carried (by .04 per cent) his own home state of Arizona and five states of the Deep South—Mississippi, Alabama, Georgia, Louisiana, and South Carolina—by decisive margins.

On November 4, 1964, even before the dust settled, the campaigns for Congress of 1966 and for the Presidency of 1968 were beginning, however faintly, to take shape. Even for a Republican party battered by the returns of the previous day, there would be another chance.

Lessons and suggestions

The presidential campaigns are too long. Six weeks of active soliciting by candidates, aided and abetted by the mass media, would be reasonable. Campaigning would certainly tend to be more educational and less tedious for the public. Nominees would find the process more attractive if they were not forced to wear themselves out both physically and mentally. Interparty debate would probably be less repetitious and more profound if office seekers and campaign managers did not have to concentrate so much on *lasting out* the campaign. A Gallup poll taken after election day of 1964 found that there was much public criticism of the whole process of selecting a President of the United States. Objections were widespread on "mudslinging" and on the length of the campaign. A majority opinion, it was reported, supported the idea of having the candidates restrict most of their efforts to television and radio appearances in lieu of traditional approaches.[24]

Some major reform is necessary to offset the financial problem that faces aspirants to all public offices in this country. On the eve of election day 1964, *Broadcasting* magazine compiled an estimate of the television and radio costs of the election from the convention days through to November 3. That estimate, based on information supplied by "unofficial but authoritative sources," did not include production costs or the millions of dollars spent on the primary campaigns. Amazingly, it was found that costs had jumped almost three times above the 1960 expenditures—from $14.2 million in 1960 to the record total of approximately $40 million in 1964. Half of the 1964 total was for the presidential contest, and half was part of the television and radio campaigning for state and local candidates.[25]

Perhaps it is time for us to think seriously about establishing two national presidential primaries, to be held under the same general regulations that have been developed for the general election in November. Each party's candidates would thereby avoid the tiresome business of jumping from state

[22]News release, News Bureau, *Burroughs Corporation*, Detroit, Michigan, n.d.; see also, news release, "Politics 1964," American Broadcasting Company, October 15, 1964.

[23]"Fast Count, Accurate Calls and It's Over," *Broadcasting* (November 9, 1964), pp. 38–39; also, Edwin H. James, "The Trouble $2,475,000 Can Buy," *Television*, Vol. 21, No. 12 (December 1964), pp. 72–73.

[24]"Gallup Poll Finds Most Voters Would Be Happier with Shorter Campaigns," *Boston Sunday Globe*, November 22, 1964.

[25]"Campaign Radio-TV $40 million," *Broadcasting* (November 2, 1964), p. 23.

primary to state primary. This idea may have serious flaws, however, and the proposal should be argued at length. There are virtues to the present system. The principal one is that it stresses the importance of local and regional reactions to the candidates. Again, the present arrangement allows the arguments of the contenders to mature over a period of time.

It is conceivable that there would be no loss to democracy if the federal government, in conjunction with the networks, provided an established amount of program time for the nominees selected by the conventions—so many hour-long programs, so many half-hour programs, and so on. Of course, since such a scheme should be a product of Congressional legislation, the major political parties would have to see the benefits to be derived.

The Federal Communications Commission, in conjunction with other appropriate federal agencies, should regulate the advertising material prepared for the campaign, to the sole end that the more distressing products of 1964 do not become historical precedents for even worse preparations. It must be emphasized here that this suggestion is not intended as an opening wedge for censorship. There are limits to public endurance, however, and fearmongering must be curbed before it increases.

If the two major parties and the minor parties were required to hold their conventions during the last week in August and the first week in September, we would have less tiresome campaigns. Under that arrangement, active campaigning would not begin until the third week of September. The idea of a six-week campaign would be made practical. No one would be allowed a head start.

These suggestions and others that have been made by serious students are lessons taken from recent experience.

TELEVISION, EDUCATION, AND POLITICS

Civic responsibility does not increase in proportion to the quantity of television programming on political subjects; it increases only in proportion to the quality and the pertinence of the presentations.

We are on the verge of a television environment that will lead future observers to comment that we conducted politics in a rather primitive fashion. Commentators of decades yet to come will probably resolve that the pattern of today and of the recent past was far too disorganized and freewheeling. They will note that, when network television first flowered, the political trend was to highlight the novelty and the powers of the medium, with insufficient attention paid to the necessity for restraint.

We can now just see the beginnings of global television made possible by satellite communications systems. Let us hope that we do not suffer from mass communications. Above all, we are required, if our free society is to continue and to prosper, to exert ourselves to keep ahead of the machinery that science produces.

The first paper, by Gordon W. Allport, explores in depth—theoretically and empirically—the question, How can we reduce prejudice? By considering the paradoxical relationship between religious orientation and prejudice, Allport's fascinating findings may lead to one simple answer: Enlarge the population of intrinsically oriented churchgoers.

Thomas F. Pettigrew's article examines the complex social and psychological ramifications of the choice between separatism and integration. Shall Americans of the future live racially separate or together? Pettigrew's vital question and its answer strike at the very core of some of the serious ailments afflicting contemporary American society.

Part XI
TOWARD A RESOLUTION OF INTERGROUP CONFLICTS

23
The Religious Context of Prejudice

Gordon W. Allport

Two contrary sets of threads are woven into the fabric of all religion—the warp of brotherhood and the woof of bigotry. I am not speaking of religion in any ideal sense, but, rather, of religion-in-the-round as it actually exists historically, culturally, and in the lives of individual men and women, the great majority of whom (in our land) profess some religious affilation and belief. Taken in-the-round, there is something about religion that makes for prejudice, and something about it that unmakes prejudice. It is this paradoxical situation that I wish to explore here.

It is a well-established fact in social science that, on the average, churchgoers in our country harbor more racial, ethnic, and religious prejudice than do nonchurchgoers. Needless to say, this fact is both surprising and distressing to thoughtful religionists. Many public opinion surveys, as well as intensive investigations establish this finding [Adorno et al., 1950; Rokeach, 1960; Allport and Kramer, 1946; Williams, Jr., 1964; Stouffer, 1955]. The finding is always the same: it is secularism and not religion that is interwoven with tolerance. In S.A. Stouffer's words, "More churchgoers are intolerant of...nonconformity...than nonchurchgoers." And this relationship holds when "education, age, region, and type of community also are taken into account" [Stouffer, 1955, p. 147].

Although we do not know whether this correlation holds for other lands, or for past centuries, we can assume that it does. At least we know that most persecutions and inquisitions of the past, especially the vicious and shameful, have occurred within religious contexts.

One can become immediately defensive and argue that today, as in the past, many (perhaps most) battlers for civil rights, for social justice, for tolerance and equi-mindedness—in short, for brotherhood—have been religiously motivated and fortified by religious doctrine. The array of such spiritual heroes is long; it would include Christ himself and many followers: Tertullian, Pope Gelasius the First, Raymond Lully, who dared oppose

Reprinted by permission from *The Graduate Journal,* vol. 7, 1966, pp. 115–130. This reading was first presented at the First Edward F. Gallahue Conference on World Religions, Princeton Theological Seminary, Fall 1964.

both the Crusades and the rising Inquisition, Cardinal Cusa, Sebastian Castellio, Schwenkfeld and the Irenicists; and, in this country, Roger Williams, John Woolman, and modern figures such as Father John La Farge, Martin Luther King, and an expanding army of religiously motivated workers for civil rights. Ghandi, a non-Christian, was also religiously motivated. It is further possible to point to recent pronouncements from nearly every major religious body stating in golden words its stand for racial justice and brotherhood.

All this evidence is convincing; but it does not cancel the fact that members of Christian churches in this country are, on the average, more bigoted than nonchurchgoers. Since the evidence on both sides is incontestable, we are surely confronted with a paradoxical situation which requires careful analysis in order to unravel the contrary sets of threads.

The needed analysis can follow three lines of inspection, corresponding to the three religious contexts which seem to me to contain the seeds of bigotry:

1. The theological context
2. The sociocultural context
3. The personal-psychological context

WHAT IS PREJUDICE?

Before entering upon our analysis it is well to pause for a moment to ask what we mean by prejudice. At what point do our justifiable predilections, beliefs, and convictions spill over into prejudice?

The clearest answer, I think, comes from Thomistic philosophy which defines prejudice very simply as "thinking ill of others without sufficient warrant." Such is a definition of "prejudice against," what Spinoza calls "hate prejudice." There is, of course, a condition of "thinking *well* of others without sufficient warrant" (as we sometimes do concerning our own children)—Spinoza's "love prejudice."

By this definition of hate prejudice (the type that

concerns us here), we identify two ingredients: a negative feeling or attitude, and a failure of rationality. A particularly ugly example is the illogic of the Ku Klux Klan rabble rouser who justified the killing of Negro children in Birmingham on the grounds that if one kills rattlesnakes one doesn't care whether they are old rattlers or young. Or take a person who was once cheated by a Jew and thereupon turns anti-Semite. Here, also, is a clear case of "insufficient warrant." Sometimes the situation is subtler, as with the rabbi who had vigorously fought against the McCarthy concept of guilt by association, but who judged Kennedy unfit to be President on the basis of a medieval papal encyclical.

Here we should recall that in many regions of human life we learn through harsh experience not to think or act without sufficient warrant. Our scientific work, our family budgets, our jobs, our health require a measured calculation of warranted cause-and-effect relationships. But in other regions of our life there is little if any objective monitoring of our activities or beliefs. Religion is one such region; our view of our fellow man is another. Both of these contexts of living are particularly prone to unwarranted assumptions.

A more recent attempt to define prejudice proceeds in a different way. It takes off from certain ideal values affirmed by our democratic society. It declares that prejudice is a departure from three different sets of ideal norms. Since prejudice is ordinarily a matter of gross and unwarranted overgeneralization, it departs from the norm of *rationality* (just as the Thomistic definition says). Since prejudice often leads to segregation, discrimination, and denial of rights, it is a departure from the norm of *justice*. And, finally, since it entails contempt, rejection, or condescension, it is a departure from the norm of *human-heartedness* [cf. Schuman, 1963]. This three-fold definition somewhat amplifies the Thomistic, but is not inconsistent with it.

I am not saying that it is always possible to ticket a given state of mind as clearly prejudiced or unprejudiced. As in all of our mental life, there are borderline conditions. My argument is simply that there are attitudes that are unwarranted, unjust, and insensitive; and that these attitudes may all be, in varying degrees and for varying reasons, interlocked with their possessor's religious life.

The Theological Context

We now come to the theological context of prejudice. Although I have little competence in the field I venture to suggest that, while plentiful supports for brotherhood are found in nearly all systems of theology, these systems also contain three invitations to bigotry. In the past all three have led to prejudice, injustice, outrage, and inquisition. Even today the peril exists, although it is greatly lessened.

First, the doctrine of *revelation* has led, and can still lead, a religion to claim exclusive possession of final truth concerning the destiny and end of man, as well as sole authority and means for interpreting that end. Held rigidly, this position regards the teaching of other religious and philosophical formulations as a threat to human salvation. Saint Augustine declared that where truth is known men have not the right to err. Within the Protestant tradition heresy was for a long time a capital crime. Menno Simons [1550], the Anabaptist, reinterpreted Saint Paul's injunction to "judge nothing before the time, until the Lord shall come." It meant, he said, "none may judge unless he have the Judging Word on his side."

The General Court of Massachusetts decreed in 1647 that "No Jesuit or spiritual or ecclesiastical person (as they are termed), ordained by a pope of the see of Rome, shall henceforth come into Massachusetts. Any person not freeing himself of suspicion shall be jailed, then banished. If taken a second time he shall be put to death." If the law has not been repealed, 3200 Catholic clergy in Massachusetts are there illegally.[1]

Most theologians today, of course, take a far softer position, agreeing in effect with Bishop Lessslie Newbigin [1955] who writes, "We must claim absoluteness and finality for Christ and His finished work; but that very claim forbids us to claim

absoluteness and finality for our understanding of it." Firm faith in revelation is not incompatible with tentativeness and tolerance in our attempts to interpret this faith to mankind. From the practical point of view, this leniency is not different from the "fallibilism" of Charles Peirce and John Dewey, who held that the best society is one that remains open and encourages all men to search with equal freedom for satisfying truths.

Whatever the reasons may be, persecutions deriving from rigid interpretations of divine revelation have largely vanished. Today's religious wars—and we still have them—between Moslem and Hindu, between Buddhist and Catholic, are largely due to traditional economic and ethnic hostilities wearing convenient religious tags.

The second theological goad to bigotry (likewise more common in the past than in the present) is the doctrine of *election*. The frenzied battle-cry of the Crusades, *Deus vult,* the more recent *Gott mit uns,* the very concepts of God's chosen people, of God's country, have all conferred sanctions for persecution and cruelty. The infidel is accurst; so, too, the black children of Ham. In speaking to the Jews, Saint Chrysostom said, "God hates you." The doctrine of election divides the ins from the outs with surgical precision. Since God is for the ins, the outs must be excluded from privileges, and, in extreme cases, eliminated by sword or by fire.

Such divinely sanctioned ethnocentrism is decreasing; ecumenism, its polar opposite, is in ascendance. It seems that the principal active residue of prejudice based on the doctrine of election is the racial bigotry of South Africa and our own South, where we find lingering doctrinal justification for keeping the descendants of Ham in the position of drawers of water and hewers of wood.

The third and last theological peril has by now virtually disappeared. I speak of *theocracy*—the view that a monarch rules by divine right, that the Church is a legitimate guide for civil government; or that a legal code (perhaps based, as in early New England, on the Ten Commandments), being divinely ordained, is inviolable on the pain of fierce punishment or death. No theological idea has caused so much persecution and suffering in

[1]This and similar instances of theologically induced intolerance are presented in G.W. Allport, *Religion and Prejudice, The Crane Review*, 2: 1–10, 1959. See also Gustavus Myers, *History of Bigotry in the United States*, New York, Random House, 1943.

both the Old World and the New as have the various versions of theocracy. By virtue of its control over civil government, ecclesiastical whims based on doctrines of revelation and election could be translated into immediate and cruel sanctions.

Theocracy, we now know, disappeared soon after this country adopted the First Amendment to its Constitution, guaranteeing religious liberty and the separation of church and state. Historians have claimed that this achievement is America's principal contribution to civilization [Pfeffer, 1960].

What I have been saying is that, for all its stress on compassion, theology itself has been far from blameless. It has encouraged bigotry in thought, in word, and in deed. At the same time this particular context of prejudice, prominent in the past, has undergone marked relaxation, and may be destined to vanish.

The Sociocultural Context

Since the average churchgoer has only vague intimations of theology, it seems farfetched to search for the roots of his prejudices in their theological context—especially since, as we have seen, the pathogenic elements in theology are disappearing. But if theological influences in daily life are diminishing, sociocultural influences in religion are increasing. What are the sociocultural factors in religion that predispose the churchgoer to prejudice?

If we stand off and look at our contemporary social edifice, we note that without doubt religion is one of its pillars; but, also, that a parallel pillar is built of the clichés of secular prejudice. Where would our social structure be if most people didn't believe in "my country right or wrong," in the superiority of Western culture, in the prevailing social stratification and earmarks of status, in the moral superiority of people with ambition over people without ambition—which means, in effect, in the moral superiority of privileged over unprivileged classes—in the evils of miscegenation, in the backwardness of immigrants, and in the undesirability of deviants? Secular prejudice is a pillar of a functioning society.

Now pillars must be well matched. Religion, therefore, finds itself peculiarly tailored to the na-

tionalistic, class, and ethnic cleavages and outlooks that sustain the prevailing social order. It is a conservative agent, rather than an agent of change. A striking instance is the extent to which German Catholicism capitulated to the political and cultural demands of Nazi pressure [cf. Lewy, 1964; Zahn, 1962].

The phenomenon is also clearly visible at the parish level. By and large every congregation is an assemblage of like-minded people, each congregation representing the ethnic, class, and racial cleavages of society, over and above denominational cleavages. Churches exclude Jews, and synagogues exclude Christians. Protestants and Catholics keep apart in their religious subcommunities. Negro churches are peculiarly isolated in tradition and in function [Washington, 1964]. Sects affirm values held by the less-educated working classes; churches foster congenial middle-class values. The fact that many parishioners leave their group when Negroes or other deviants are admitted shows that, for them, ethnic and class values hold priority over religious values. Church membership for them is primarily of sociocultural significance, a matter of class and caste—a support for their own ethnocentrism.

Here we find a key to our riddle. The reason churchgoers on the average are more prejudiced than nonchurchgoers is not because religion instills prejudice. It is rather that a large number of people, by virtue of their psychological make-up, require for their economy of living both prejudice and religion. Some, for example, are tormented by self-doubt and insecurity. Prejudice enhances their self-esteem; religion provides them a tailored security. Others are guilt-ridden; prejudice provides a scapegoat, and religion, relief. Still others live in fear of failure. Prejudice provides an explanation in terms of menacing outgroups; religion promises a heavenly, if not terrestrial, reward. Thus, for many individuals, the functional significance of prejudice and religion is identical. One does not cause the other; rather both satisfy the same psychological needs. Multitudes of churchgoers, perhaps especially in times of social anomie and crisis, embrace both supports.

According to this line of reasoning, we assume

that nonchurchgoers, on the whole, have less psychological need for prejudice and for religion. Their philosophy of life, whatever it is, seems self-contained, requiring no direct reliance on these two common social supports.

Here, then, in broadest outline, is an explanation for the troublesome correlation we find between churchgoing and bigotry. We need, however, to look much more closely at both data and theory in order to sharpen our understanding of the religious context of prejudice.

First, we must remind ourselves that there are churchgoers *and* churchgoers. Today 63 percent of the population claims formal religious affiliation, a figure far larger than in earlier decades. Also, we recall the common poll finding that as many as 96 percent of the American people say they believe in God. Religion seems to be neither dead nor dying.

But here we need to draw an immediate distinction between two polar types of religious affiliation, as Will Herberg [1955] and Gerhard Lenski [1961] have done. Some religious groups and many individuals stress the sociocultural factor in membership. The result is a "communal" type of affiliation. For example, many Jewish congregations and Negro Protestant groups provide an important communal service quite apart from their specifically religious functions. Herberg and Lenski both argue that Americans are turning increasingly to their religious groups for the satisfaction of the communal identification and need to belong. Paradoxically, it can be said that Americans are becoming more religious while at the same time they are becoming more secular.

In *all* religious groups we find parishioners whose interests are primarily communal. Affiliation is in fashion; it provides status for some, a gossip center for others, a meeting place for the lonely, entertainment for the disengaged, and even a good way to sell insurance. One study reports that 80 percent of members indicated they are more concerned about a comfortable life on earth than about other-worldly considerations, and 54 percent admit that their religious beliefs do not have any effect on the way they conduct their daily affairs. [Raub, 1964, p. 15].

The type opposite to "communal" is "associational" which includes those members whose involvement is primarily for purposes of religious fellowship. Comparing these types revealing differences emerge. To give one example: Lenski finds that among Detroit Catholics whose communal involvement is high and whose associational involvement low, 59 percent favor segregated schools; whereas among Catholics whose associational involvement is high and whose communal involvement low, only 27 percent favor segregated schools—a difference of thirty-two percentage points between the religiously oriented and the communally oriented churchgoers. A significant trend in the same direction is found also among Detroit Protestants [Lenski, 1961, p. 173].

Thus, we see that one type of churchgoer tends to be prejudiced; another type relatively unprejudiced. To my mind, it is precisely here that we find the analytic tool we need to solve our problem. Soon I shall return to this mode of analysis and to several relevant supporting researches.

Meanwhile, let me say that a sociological or historical scholar could point to many additional relationships between religion as a cultural institution and prejudice. For one thing, almost every religious group has been a target for hostility. The fierce anti-Catholicism in the United States during the nineteenth century was certainly in large part a mask for the workingman's resentments against the flood of immigration from Ireland, and later from Italy and other Catholic countries. Not only was there vague uneasiness about the curious folkways of these foreigners, there was growing fear of the power of the cities where they settled. Rural nativism focused upon ecclesiastical visibility as a target, likewise upon the Jew who was also an identifiable foreigner.

A different line of sociological interest deals with the ideological differences among Protestant, Catholic, and Jew; and sometimes between Negro and white churches. Lenski, for example, argues that the communications networks, being relatively limited to the adherents of the same faith, facilitate the development and transmission of distinctive political and economic norms and outlooks [Lenski, 1961, p. 303]. In short, religious groups favor provincialism and a compartmentalization of living. Since immigration has virtually ceased, the socioreligious community is becoming a substitute for ethnic groupings, and we must accordingly expect many of the prejudices formerly supported in ethnic terms to be sustained in socioreligious communities. The drift he sees is toward a more compartmentalized society where the heightened sense of religious group loyalty will lead to a lessened sense of responsibility toward those outside. Lenski's research establishes the fact that there are appreciable differences (independent of social class) that mark the political and social attitudes of the major religious groups and affect their images of one another. The Jews, for example, turn out to be the least critical of other groups, but at the same time to suffer the severest criticism from them.

Virtually all of the studies of religion and social conflict are focused on the demographic level. That is to say, trends are found to be true of certain groups taken as a whole. The spirit of capitalism, says Max Weber, is built into Protestantism and not into Catholicism. Negro religion is, by and large, a religion of protection and protest; Jews, having most to lose through violations of the First Amendment, are its strongest supporters. Churches guard middle-class values, sects, working-class values [e.g., Lee and Marty, 1964].

All such analyses are, of course, useful as background to the study of the religious context of prejudice. And, yet, I feel that they fail to reach the heart of the matter. They focus upon religion as a sociocultural phenomenon, that is to say in its communal aspects, and overlook its place in the personal life. Both religion and prejudice are intensely personal states of mind. To understand their inherent relationships (whether positive or negative) we have to examine the psychological composition of individual people.

The Personal-Psychological Context

There are, as we have observed, churchgoers *and* churchgoers. Now what is the simplest possible distinction between them? Well, some attend frequently and regularly, some only on occasion or rarely. Offhand, this distinction may seem to be purely demographic—the "regulars" versus the "irregulars." But, in reality, the process of forming the habit of regular attendance, or the state of mind that lets weather, circumstance, and mood determine attendance clearly depends on personal motives and attitudes. True, there is a tendency for Protestants to attend less regularly than Catholics, although much more regularly than Jews. In Detroit among self-styled Protestants, 30 percent go to church every Sunday, 20 percent between one and three times a month, 30 percent only occasionally, 14 never [Lenski, 1961, p. 35]. But, for our purposes, the important consideration is that each major religious group has its nuclear and its marginal members in terms of attendance. The outer fringe of the marginal groups consists of those who attend exceedingly rarely—as someone has said, only thrice in a lifetime: once when they were hatched; again when matched; and, finally, when dispatched.

Now, many investigations have shown that regular and frequent church attenders harbor, by and large, less ethnic and racial hostility than do members who are casual about their attendance. An illustrative study is one made by E.L. Streuning [1957] whose data come from nearly 900 faculty members in a large Midwestern university. Besides obtaining scores on a prejudice scale, he learned what their habits were regarding church attendance. Almost a third never attended church at all, and they had a low prejudice score (14.7). Many attended once a month, and, for these, the average prejudice score nearly doubled (25). This finding immediately confirms our earlier statement that nonchurchgoers are less prejudiced than churchgoers—or at least than casual churchgoers. The prejudice scores of those attending once, twice, or three times a month were also high. For weekly attenders, the score fell, and it continued to fall rapidly for those whose attendance ranged from five to eleven or more times a month. For the last group (eleven or more a month), the average score of 11.7 was significantly lower even than for the nonattenders. In these data we clearly perceive what is called a curvilinear relation: nonattenders and frequent attenders having low prejudice scores; intermediate attenders, high.

This evidence fits well with Lenski's distinction between communal and associational religion. Frequent attendance is not required to maintain nominal membership or to derive the benefits of communal contact. On the other hand, a religiously motivated person who seeks spiritual association is drawn with greater regularity and frequency to the church's fellowship. An imposing array of studies supports this finding and interpretation [Holtzman, 1956; Kelly, Ferson, and Holtzman, 1958; Friedrichs, 1959; Tumin, 1958; Williams, Jr., 1964].

The lives of many marginal attenders, it seems, are regulated in a fitful way by what we may call "religious tokenism." A token of churchmanship is all they need—an occasional anchorage against the gusts of fate. Tokenism, while superficial, may be fiercely important. Its devotees may incline to see in the Supreme Court ruling against prescribed prayers in public schools a menacing threat. Religion resides in a symbol. One Southern politician complained that while the Supreme Court ushered Negroes into the public schools it ushered God out—as though God dwells in a token.

While the data on frequency of church attendance and its relation to prejudice are revealing, they do not tell us directly about the nature of the personal religious sentiment that provides the context for prejudice, nor about the nature of the contrary sentiment that engenders tolerance, fair play, and humane regard.

To take this additional step, we borrow from axiology the concepts of *extrinsic* value and *intrinsic* value. The distinction helps us to separate churchgoers whose communal type of membership supports and serves other (nonreligious) ends from those for whom religion is an end in itself—a final, not instrumental, good.

The distinction clearly overlaps with that drawn by Father Joseph Fichter [1954] in his study of the urban Catholic parish. What he calls the "marginal" and "modal" parishioner corresponds fairly well to our extrinsic type. What he calls the "nuclear" parishioner—who orients his life wholly by the full doctrine of the Church—is essentially our intrinsic type. For our purposes, it is important to note that Father Fichter assigns only 10 percent to the intrinsic or nuclear group. Unless I am mistaken, the ratio is roughly what we would find in the average congregation of any Christian (and perhaps Jewish) parish.

Every minister knows and laments the preponderance of the extrinsic type. Some such parishioners find self-expression in managing investments, arranging flowers, running bazaars, in simply avoiding loneliness. They have no true association with the religious function of the Church. Others do, to varying degrees, accept the spiritual ministry, but remain dabblers because their connections are determined exclusively by mood or by crisis. Many extrinsics do, of course, have religious needs, but they feel no obligation to attend church regularly nor to integrate religion into their way of life. Lenski, we have seen, regards compartmentalization as the chief mark of religion today. It is something for an occasional Sunday morning, for High Holy Days, or for moments of crisis. Since its function is to serve other needs, we call it an extrinsic value in the personal life.

While most extrinsics are casual and peripheral churchgoers, a few are ideological extremists. With equal fervor, they embrace some political nostrum along with the tenets of some religious (usually fundamentalist) sect. In such cases religious extremism is found to be ancillary to a prejudiced philosophy of life. I am thinking here of the right-wing groups whose ardent desire is to escape from the complexities of modern life. They do not seek so much to preserve the *status quo* as to return to a former, simple small-town or agrarian way of life where individual achievement and responsibility are the only virtues. God has an important role in this ideology as a dispenser of rewards for individual achievement. Modern life threatens this idyll; immigrants threaten it; Negroes, Jews, Catholics are seen as menacing. Extreme right ideology invariably harbors this sort of bigotry; and its supporting religion justifies and rationalizes the prejudice, often through the selection of congenial scriptural passages.

The same phenomenon is seen, though less often, in ideologies of the extreme left. Ralph Roy has pointed to cases of clergy who justify hatred of the wealthy, expropriation, and extreme left-wing policies by one-sided scriptural interpretations.[2]

Thus, while there are several varieties of extrinsic religious orientation, we may say they all point to a type of religion that is strictly utilitarian: useful for the self in granting safety, social standing, solace, and endorsement for one's chosen way of life. As such, it provides a congenial soil for all forms of prejudice, whether racial, national, political, or religious. Since extrinsic religion predominates among churchgoers we have an explanation for our riddle.

By contrast, the intrinsic form of the religious sentiment regards faith as a supreme value in its own right. It is oriented toward a unification of being, takes seriously the commandment of brotherhood, and strives to transcend all self-centered needs. Dogma is tempered with humility, and in keeping with the biblical injunction the possessor withholds judgment until the day of the harvest. A religious sentiment of this sort floods the whole life with motivation and meaning. Religion is no longer limited to single segments of self-interest.[3]

While many of the intrinsically religious are pietists and express their religion chiefly by being good neighbors, others are of a militant stripe. Were not Saint Francis, John Wesley, Mahatma Gandhi—was not Christ himself—intrinsically religious; and were they not all zealous beyond the bounds of moderation? Yes, there are intrinsic as well as extrinsic zealots. We can usually distinguish between them: the latter group having ulterior motives of personal or political advantage; the former being fired only by a conviction that the kingdom of God should be realized on earth.

AN EMPIRICAL APPROACH

Up to now we have been speaking chiefly in theoretical terms concerning the religious context of prejudice. And I have been moving the argument closer and closer toward a psychological analysis of the situation, with the claim that in the last analysis both prejudice and religion are subjective formations within the personal life. One of these formations of religion (the extrinsic) is entirely compatible with prejudice; the other (intrinsic) rules out enmity, contempt, and bigotry.

With the proposition stated in this way, an empiricist will ask, "Can we not test it? After all, you have simply stated an hypothesis at the speculative level. Do not all hypotheses need empirical verification before they can be accepted?"

In a series of investigations, my students and I have undertaken this very task. There is not time to describe the studies in detail. Essentially, they consist of using two questionnaires with assorted groups of churchgoers. One undertakes—and I apologize for the audacity—to determine to what extent a given parishioner holds an extrinsic or an intrinsic view of his religion. As an example, a person who agrees with the following propositions would receive scores indicating an *extrinsic* orientation:

> The purpose of prayer is to secure a happy and peaceful life.
> The Church is most important as a place to formulate good social relationships.

A person would be credited with an *intrinsic* orientation if he subscribed to such statements as the following:

> I try hard to carry my religion over into all my other dealings in life.
> Quite often I have been keenly aware of the presence of God or the Divine Being.

There are twenty-one items in the scale, which enables us to locate each subject on a continuum from consistently extrinsic to consistently intrinsic. There are also a number of subjects who

[2]R.L. Roy, *Conflict from the Communist Left and the Radical Right, Religion and Social Conflict*, pp. 55–68.
[3]For further discussion of the extrinsic and intrinsic types see G.W. Allport, *Behavioral Science, Religion, and Mental Health, Journal of Religion and Health*, 2: 187–97, 1963; also, *Personality and Social Encounter* (Boston: Beacon Press, 1960), Chapter 16; also, *The Nature of Prejudice* (Reading, Mass.: Addison-Wesley, 1954), Chapter 23.

are inconsistent in the sense that they endorse any and all propositions favorable to religion, even though these propositions are contradictory to one another.

A second questionnaire consists of a valid measure of prejudice.[4] It deals primarily with the extent to which the subject favors discriminatory practices and segregation.

In brief, the findings, not yet published, support the hypothesis that the extrinsic religious orientation in personality is indeed the context of prejudice. The intrinsic orientation is the matrix of tolerance. An additional interesting finding is that those subjects who are inconsistent who grasp at any and all statements favorable to religion, regardless of their logical consistency, are the most prejudiced of all. Thus, it seems that the religious context for bigotry lies both in the extrinsic and in the muddle-headed types of religious sentiment. Only the consistent intrinsic type (a small minority) escapes [Allport and Ross, 1967].

It is clear that these investigations, still in progress, tend to confirm demographic and sociological studies that we have also reviewed. Further, I believe, they are compatible with our theological analysis, since it is clear that communal and extrinsic religion can draw strong support from the doctrines of revelation, election, and theocracy, which, as we have seen, provide the theological context of prejudice, so far as such exists.

We can hope that this convergence of theological, sociological, and psychological analysis will lead to a further co-operation between behavioral and religious disciplines. We can also hope that our findings, when understood by clergy and laity, may lead to a decrease in bigotry and to an enhancement of charity in modern religious life.

If I were asked what practical applications ensue from this analysis, I would, of course, say that to reduce prejudice we need to enlarge the population of intrinsically religious people. There is no simple formula, for each personality is unique and is stubbornly resistant to change. Yet, precisely

here lies the pastor's task, his opportunity, and his challenge.

REFERENCES

Adorno, T.W. et al., *The Authoritarian Personality,* New York: Harper & Bros., 1950.

Allport, G.W., & Kramer, B.M., "Some Roots of Prejudice," *Journal of Psychology,* 1946, Vol. 22, pp. 9–39.

Allport, G.W., & Ross, J.M., "Personal Religious Orientation and Prejudice," *Journal of Personality and Social Psychology,* 1967, Vol. 5, pp. 432–443.

Fichter, J.H., S.J., *Social Relations in the Urban Parish,* Chicago: University of Chicago Press, 1954.

Friedrichs, R.W., "Christians and Residential Exclusion: An Empirical Study of a Northern Dilemma," *Journal of Social Issues,* 1959, Vol. 15, pp. 14–23.

Herberg, W., *Protestant, Catholic, Jew,* Garden City, L.I.: Doubleday, 1955.

Holtzman, W.H., "Attitudes of College Men Toward Non-Segregation in Texas Schools," *Public Opinion Quarterly,* 1956, Vol. 2, pp. 559–569.

Kelly, J.G., Ferson, J.E., & Holtzman, W.H., "The Measurement of Attitudes Toward the Negro in the South," *Journal of Social Psychology,* 1958, Vol. 48, pp. 305–317.

Lee, R., & Marty, M.E., eds., *Religion and Social Conflict,* New York: Oxford University Press, 1964.

Lenski, G.E., *The Religious Factor,* Garden City, L.I.: Doubleday, 1961.

Lewy, G., *The Catholic Church and Nazi Germany,* New York: McGraw-Hill, 1964.

Newbigin, L., "The Quest for Unity Through Religion," *Journal of Religion,* 1955, Vol. 35, pp. 17–33.

Pfeffer, L., "Freedom and Separation: America's Contribution to Civilization," *Journal of Church and State,* 1960, Vol. 2, pp. 100–111.

Raub, E., ed., *Religious Conflict in America,* Garden City, L.I.: Doubleday, 1964.

Rokeach, M., *The Open and Closed Mind,* New York: Basic Books, 1960.

Schuman, H., "Sympathetic Identification with the Un-

---

[4]Devised by J.S. Harding and Howard Schuman, in preparation.

derdog," *Public Opinion Quarterly,* 1963, Vol. 27, pp. 230–241.

Simons, M., *A Foundation and Plain Instruction of the Saving Doctrine of Christ, on the Ban: Questions and Answers,* 1550 (Transl. by I.D. Rupp, Lancaster, Pa.: Elias Barr, 1863).

Stouffer, S.A., *Communism, Conformity, and Civil Liberties,* Garden City, L.I.: Doubleday, 1955.

Streuning, E.L., *The Dimensions, Distributions and Correlates of Authoritarianism in a Midwestern University Faculty Population,* unpublished doctoral dissertation, Purdue University, 1957.

Tumin, M.M., *Desegregation,* Princeton: Princeton University Press, 1958.

Washington, J.R., *Black Religion,* Boston: Beacon Press, 1964.

Williams, Jr., R.M., *Strangers Next Door: Ethnic Relations in American Communities,* Englewood Cliffs: Prentice-Hall, 1964.

Zahn, G.C., *German Catholics and Hitler's Wars,* New York: Sheed and Ward, 1962.

24
Racially Separate or Together?[1]

Thomas F. Pettigrew

Reprinted from *Journal of Social Issues*, vol. 25, 1969, pp. 43–69.

America has had an almost perpetual racial crisis for a generation. But the last third of the twentieth century has begun on a new note, a change of rhetoric and a confusion over goals. Widespread rioting is just one expression of this note. The nation hesitates; it seems to have lost its confidence that the problem can be solved; it seems unsure as to even the direction in which a solution lies. In too simple terms, yet in the style of the fashionable rhetoric, the question has become: Shall Americans of the future live racially separate or together?

This new mood is best understood when viewed within the eventful sweep of recent years. Ever since World War I, when war orders combined with the curtailment of immigration to encourage massive migration to industrial centers, Negro Americans have been undergoing rapid change as a people. The latest product of this dramatic transformation from southern peasant to northern urbanite is a second- and third-generation northern-born youth. Indeed, over half of Negro Americans alive today are below twenty-two years of age. The most significant fact about this "newest new Negro" is that he is relatively released from the principal social controls recognized by his parents and grandparents, from the restraints of an extended kinship system, a conservative religion and an acceptance of the inevitability of white supremacy.

Consider the experience of the twenty-year-old Negro youth today. He was born in 1948; he was an impressionable six years old when the highest court in the land decreed against *de jure* public school segregation; he was only nine years old at the time of the Little Rock, Arkansas desegregation confrontation; he was twelve years old when the student-organized sit-ins began at segregated lunch counters throughout the South; and he was fifteen when the dramatic March-on-Washington took place and seventeen when the climatic Selma march occurred. He has literally witnessed during

[1]This paper was the author's presidential address to the Society for the Psychological Study of Social Issues, delivered at the annual convention of the American Psychological Association in San Francisco, California on September 1, 1968. Its preparation was facilitated by Contract No. OEC 1-6-061774-1887 of the United States Office of Education.

his short life the initial dismantling of the formal structure of white supremacy. Conventional wisdom holds that such an experience should lead to a highly satisfied generation of young Negro Americans. Newspaper headlines and social psychological theory tell us precisely the opposite is closer to the truth.

RELATIVE DEPRIVATION THEORY...

The past three decades of Negro American history constitute an almost classic case for relative deprivation theory (Pettigrew, 1964, 1967). Mass unrest has reoccurred throughout history after long periods of improvement followed by abrupt periods of reversal (Davies, 1962). This pattern derives from four revolt-stirring conditions triggered by long-term improvements: (a) living conditions of the dominant group typically advance faster than those of the subordinate group; (b) the aspirations of the subordinate group climb far more rapidly than actual changes; (c) status inconsistencies among subordinate group members increase sharply; and (d) a broadening of comparative reference groups occurs for the subordinate group (Pettigrew, 1967).

Each of these four conditions typifies the Negro American situation today (Geschwender, 1964; Pettigrew, 1964, 1967). (a) Though the past few decades have witnessed the most rapid gains in Negro American history, these gains have generally not kept pace with those of white America during these same prosperous years. (b) Public opinion surveys document the swiftly rising aspirations of Negro Americans, especially since 1954. Moreover, (c) status inconsistency has been increasing among Negroes, particularly among the young whose educational level typically exceeds the low status employment offered them. Finally, (d) Negro Americans have greatly expanded their relevant reference groups in recent years; affluent referents in the richest country on earth are now routinely adopted as the appropriate standard with which to judge one's condition. The second component of unrest involving a sudden reversal has been supplied, too, by the Vietnam War. Little

wonder, then, that America's racial crisis reached the combustible point in the late sixties.

The young Negro surveys the current scene and observes correctly that the benefits of recent racial advances have disproportionately accrued to the expanding middle class, leaving further behind the urban lower class. While the middle-class segment of Negro America has expanded from roughly five to twenty-five per cent of the group since 1940,[2] the vast majority of Negroes remain poor. Raised on the proposition that racial integration is the basic solution to racial injustice, the young Negro's doubts grow as opportunities open for the skilled while the daily lives of the unskilled go largely unaffected. Accustomed to a rapid pace of events, many Negro youth wonder if integration will ever be possible in an America where the depth of white resistance to racial change becomes painfully more evident: the equivocation of the 1964 Democratic Party Convention when faced with the challenge of the Mississippi Freedom Democratic Party; the Selma bridge brutality; the summary rejection by the 1966 Congress of anti-discrimination legislation for housing; the repressive reaction to riots from the Chicago Mayor's advocacy of police state methods to the New Jersey Governor's suspension of the Bill of Rights in Plainfield; and, finally, the wanton assassinations within ten weeks of two leading symbols of the integration movement. These events cumulated to create understandable doubts as to whether Dr. Martin Luther King's famous dream of equality could ever be achieved.

SHIFT IN MILITANT STANCE AND RHETORIC...

It is tempting to project this process further, as many mass media accounts unhesitantly have done, and suggest that all of Negro America has undergone this vast disillusionment, that Negroes now overwhelmingly reject racial integration for

[2]These figures derive from three gross estimates of "middle class" status: $6,000 or more annual family income, high school graduation or white-collar occupation. Thus, in 1961 roughly a fifth of Negro families received in excess of $6,000 (a percentage that now must approach a fourth even in constant dollars), in 1960 22 per cent of Negroes over 24 years of age had completed high school, and in 1966 21 per cent of employed Negroes held white-collar occupations.

separatist goals. As we shall note shortly, this is emphatically not the case. Nevertheless, the militant stance and rhetoric *have* shifted, and many whites find considerable encouragement in this new Negro mood. Indeed, strictly separatist solutions for the black ghettos of urban America have been most elaborately and enthusiastically advanced not by Negroes at all but by such white writers as newspaper columnist Joseph Alsop (1967a, 1967b) and W.H. Ferry (1968) of the Center for the Study of Democratic Institutions.[3] Nor should we confuse "black power" ideas as such with separatism, since there are numerous variants of this developing ideology, only a few of which portray a racially-separate United States as the desirable end-state. As a presumed intervening stage, black separatism is more concerned with group pride and "local control," more a retreat from whites than an attempt to dominate them. This contrasts with the traditional attempts at racial supremacy of white segregationists. Black separatism and white separatism present the danger that they might well congeal to perpetuate a racially-separate nation; but they are otherwise somewhat different phenomena as a cursory examination of their basic assumptions readily reveals.

Separatist Assumptions

White segregationists, North and South, base their position upon three bedrock assumptions. First, they maintain that separation benefits both races in that each feels awkward and uncomfortable in the midst of the other (Armstrong and Gregor, 1964). Whites and Negroes are happiest and most relaxed when in the company of "their own kind." We shall call this "*the comfortable assumption*."

The second assumption of white segregationists is blatantly racist. The underlying reality of the nation's racial problem, they unashamedly maintain, is that Negroes are inherently inferior to Caucasians. The findings of both social and biological

[3]See, too, replies to Alsop by Schwartz *et al.* (1967, 1968). Alsop eagerly calls for giving up the effort to integrate schools racially in order to put all efforts into achieving separate but improved schools in the ghetto. Ferry goes further and advocates "black colonies" be formally established in American central cities, complete with treaties enacted with the federal government. Black militants, in sharp contrast, complain of being in a colonial status now but do not endorse it as a desired state of affairs.

science place in serious jeopardy every argument put forward for "*the racial inferiority assumption,*" and an ever-decreasing minority of white Americans subscribe to it (Pettigrew, 1964). Yet it remains the essential substrata of white segregationist thinking; racial contact must be avoided, according to this reasoning, if white standards are not to be diluted. Thus, Negro attendance at a predominantly white school may benefit the Negro children, but it is deemed by segregationists as inevitably harmful to white children.[4]

The third assumption flows from this presumption of white racial superiority. Since contact can never be mutually beneficial, it will inevitably lead to racial conflict. The White Citizens' Councils in the deep South, for example, stoutly insist that they are opposed to violence and favor racial separation as the primary means of maintaining racial harmony. As long as Negroes "know their place," as long as white supremacy remains unchallenged, "*the racial conflict assumption*" contends strife will be at a minimum.

Coming from the opposite direction, black separatists fundamentally base their position upon three parallel assumptions. They agree with "*the comfortable assumption*" that both whites and Negroes are more at ease when separated from each other. Some of this agreement stems from the harsh fact that Negroes have borne the heavier burden of desegregation and have entered previously all-white institutions where open hostility is sometimes explicitly practiced by segregationist whites in order to discourage the process. Yet some of this agreement stems, too, from more subtle situations. The demands by a few black student organizations on interracial campuses for all-black facilities have been predicated on "*the comfortable assumption.*"

A second assumption focuses directly upon white racism. Supported by the chief conclusion of the National Advisory Commission on Civil Disorders (1968), black separatists label white racism as a central problem which so-called "white liberals" should confine their energies to eradicating. "*The white-liberals-must-eradicate-white-racism-*

[4]Analysis specifically directed on this point shows this contention not to be true for predominantly-white classrooms as contrasted with comparable all-white classrooms (U.S. Commission on Civil Rights, 1967; Vol. I, 160).

assumption" underlies two further contentions: namely, that "white liberals" should stay out of the ghetto save as their money and expertise are explicitly requested, and that it is no longer the job of black militants to confront and absorb the abuse of white racists.

The third assumption is the most basic of all, and is in tacit agreement with the segregationist notion that interracial contact as it now occurs makes only for conflict. Interaction between Negro and white Americans, it is held, can never be truly equal and mutually beneficial until Negroes gain personal and group autonomy, self-respect and power. *"The autonomy-before-contact assumption"* often underlies a two-step theory of how to achieve meaningful integration: the first step requires separation so that Negroes can regroup, unify and gain a positive self-image and identity; only when this is achieved can the second step of real integration take place. Ron Karenga, a black militant leader in Los Angeles, states the idea forcefully: "We're not for isolation, but interdependence. But we can't become interdependent unless we have something to offer. We can live with whites interdependently once we have black power" (Calame, 1968).

Each of these ideological assumptions deserves examination in light of social psychological theory and findings.

Social Psychological Considerations of Separatist Assumptions

The comfortable assumption

There can be no denying the reality of initial discomfort and ill-ease for many Negro and white Americans when they encounter each other in new situations. This reality is so vivid and generally recognized that both black and white separatists employ it as a key fact in their thinking, though they do not analyze its nature and origins.

The social science literature is replete with examples of the phenomenon. Kohn and Williams (1956), for instance, studied New York State facilities unaccustomed to Negro patronage. Negro researchers would enter a tavern, seek service and later record their experiences, while white re-

searchers would observe the same situation and record their impressions for comparison. Typically the first reaction of waitresses and bartenders was embarrassment and discomfort; they turned to the owner or others in authority for guidance. When this was unavailable, the slightest behavioral cue from anyone in the situation was utilized as a gauge of what was expected of them. And if there were no such cues, confusion often continued until somehow the tense situation had been structured. Needless to add, the tension was at least as great for the potential Negro patron.

Other examples arise from small group and summer camp research. Irwin Katz (1964) has described the initial awkwardness in biracial task groups in the laboratory; white partners usually assumed an aggressive, imperious role, Negro partners a passive role. Similarly, Yarrow (1958) found initial tension and keen sensitivity among many Negro children in an interracial summer camp, much of which centered around fears of rejection by white campers. Not all Negroes and whites, of course, manifest this discomfort. Furthermore, such tension does not continue to pervade a truly integrated situation. Katz noted that once Negroes were cast in assertive roles behavior in his small groups became more equalitarian and this improvement generalized to new situations. Yarrow, too, observed a sharp decline in Negro anxiety and sensitivity which occurred after two weeks of successful integration at the summer camp. Similar increments in cross-racial acceptance and reductions in tension have been noted in new interracial situations in department stores (Harding and Hogrefe, 1952; Saenger and Gilbert, 1950), the merchant marine (Brothy, 1946), the armed forces (Stouffer *et al.,* 1949), public housing (Deutsch and Collins, 1951; Jahoda and West, 1951; Wilner *et al.,* 1955; and Works, 1961), and even among the Philadelphia police (Kephart, 1957).

CONTACT EFFECTS LIMITED TO THE SITUATION

This is not to say that new interracial situations invariably lead to acceptance. As we shall note, the *conditions* of the interracial contact are crucial. Moreover, even under optimal conditions, the cross-racial acceptance generated by contact is typically limited to the particular situation. Thus, white steelworkers learn to work easily with Negroes as co-workers and vote for them as union officers; but this acceptance does not carry over to attitudes and action concerning interracial housing (Reitzes, 1953). A segregated society restricts the generalization effects of even truly integrated situations; and at times like the present when race assumes such overwhelming salience, the racial tension of the larger society may poison previously successful interracial settings.

Acquaintance and similarity theory helps to sort out the underlying process. Newcomb states the fundamental tenet as follows:

> Insofar as persons have similar attitudes toward things of importance to both or all of them, and discover that this is so, they have shared attitudes; under most conditions the experience of sharing such attitudes is rewarding, and thus provides a basis for mutual attraction (Newcomb *et al.,* 1965)

Rokeach has applied these notions to American race relations with some surprising results. He maintains that white American rejection of Negro Americans is motivated less by racism than by assumed belief and value differences. In other words, whites generally perceive Negroes as holding contrasting beliefs, and it is this perception and not race *per se* that leads to rejection. Indeed, a variety of subjects have supported Rokeach's ideas by typically accepting in a social situation a Negro with similar beliefs to their own over a white with different beliefs (Rokeach *et al.,* 1960; Rokeach and Mezei, 1966; Smith *et al.,* 1967; Stein, 1966; and Stein *et al.,* 1965).

Additional work specifies the phenomenon more precisely. Triandis and Davis (1965) have shown that the relative importance of belief and race factors in attraction is a joint function of the interpersonal realm in question and personality. Belief similarity is most critical in more formal matters of general personal evaluation and social acceptance, where racial norms are ambiguously defined. Race is most critical in intimate matters of marriage and neighborhood, where racial norms are explicitly defined. For interpersonal realms of intermediate intimacy, such as friendship, both belief and race considerations appear important. Moreover, there are wide individual differences in the application of belief similarity and race, especially in contact realms of intermediate intimacy.[5]

ISOLATION'S NEGATIVE EFFECTS

Seen in the light of this work, racial isolation has two negative effects both of which operate to make optimal interracial contact difficult to achieve and initially tense. First, isolation prevents each group from learning of the common beliefs and values they do in fact share. Consequently, Negroes and whites kept apart come to view each other as so different that belief dissimilarity typically combines with racial considerations to cause each race to reject contact with the other. Second, isolation leads in time to the evolution of genuine differences in beliefs and values, again making interracial contact in the future less likely.

A number of pointed findings of social psychological research support this extrapolation of interpersonal attraction theory. Stein *et al.* (1965) noted that relatively racially-isolated ninth-graders in California assumed an undescribed Negro teenager to be similar to a Negro teen-ager who is described as being quite different from themselves. Smith *et al.* (1967) found that belief similarity relative to racial similarity was more critical in desegregated settings, less critical in segregated settings. And the U.S. Commission on Civil Rights (1967), in its study of *Racial Isolation in the Public Schools,* found that both Negro and white adults who as children had attended interracial schools were more likely today to live in an interracial neighborhood and hold more positive racial attitudes than comparable adults who had known

---

[5]This resolution of the earlier Triandis (1961) and Rokeach (1961) controversy takes on added weight when the data from studies favorable to the Rokeach position are examined carefully. That different interpersonal realms lead to varying belief-race weightings is borne out by Table 4 in Stein *et al.* (1965); that intensely prejudiced subjects, particularly in environments where racist norms even extend into less intimate realms, will act on race primarily is shown by one sample of whites in the deep South of Smith *et al.* (1967).

only segregated schools. Or put negatively, those Americans of both races who experienced only segregated education are more likely to reflect separatist behavior and attitudes as adults.

Racial separatism, then, is a cumulative process. It feeds upon itself and leads its victims to prefer continued separation. In an open-choice situation in Louisville, Kentucky, Negro children were far more likely to select predominantly white high schools if they were currently attending predominantly white junior high schools.[6] From these data, the U.S. Commission on Civil Rights concluded: "The inference is strong that Negro high school students prefer biracial education only if they have experienced it before. If a Negro student has not received his formative education in biracial schools, the chances are he will not choose to enter one in his more mature school years" (U.S. Commission on Civil Rights, 1963).

Similarly, Negro adult products of segregated schools, the Civil Rights Commission (1967) finds, are more likely to believe that interracial schools "create hardships for Negro children" and less likely to send their children to desegregated schools than Negro products of biracial schools. Note that those who most fear discomfort in biracial settings are precisely those who have experienced such situations least. If desegregation actually resulted in perpetual and debilitating tension, as separatists blithely assume, it seems unlikely that children already in the situation would willingly opt for more, or that adults who have had considerable interracial contact as children would willingly submit themselves to biracial neighborhoods and their children to biracial schools.

A SOCIAL COST ANALYSIS IS NEEDED

A social cost analysis is needed. The question becomes: What price comfort? Racially homogeneous settings are often more comfortable for members of both races, though this seems to be especially true at the start of the contact and does not seem to be so debilitating that those in the situation typically wish to return to segregated living. Those who remain in racial isolation, both Negro and white, find themselves increasingly less equipped to compete in an interracial world. Lobotomized patients are more comfortable, too, but they are impaired for life.

There is nothing inevitable, then, about the tension that characterizes many initial interracial encounters in the United States. Rather it is the direct result of the racial separation that has traditionally characterized our society. In short, separation is the cause, not the remedy, for interracial awkwardness.

The Assumptions of Racial Inferiority and White-Liberals-Must-Eradicate-White-Racism

The second set of separatist assumptions raises related issues. Indeed, both of these assumptions also afford classical cases of self-fulfilling prophecies. Treat a people as inferior, force them to play subservient roles,[7] keep them essentially separate and the products will necessarily support the initial racist notions. Likewise, assume whites are unalterably racist, curtail Negro efforts to confront racism directly, separate from whites further, and the result will surely be continued, if not heightened, racism.

The core of racist attitudes, the assumption of innate racial inferiority, has been under sharp attack from social science for over three decades.[8] Partly because of this work, white American attitudes have undergone massive change over these years. For example, while only two out of five white Americans regarded Negroes as their intellectual equals in 1942, almost four out of five did by 1956—including a substantial majority of white Southerners (Hyman and Sheatsley, 1956; 1964).

[6]For twelve junior highs, the Spearman-Brown rank order correlation between the white junior high percentage and the percentage of Negroes choosing predominantly-white high schools is +.82 (corrected for ties)—significant at better than the one per cent level of confidence.

[7]For a role analysis interpretation of racial interactions in the United States, see Pettigrew (1964).
[8]One of the first significant efforts in this direction was the classic intelligence study by Klineberg (1935). For a summary of current scientific work relevant to racist claims in health, intelligence and crime, see Pettigrew (1964).

Yet a sizable minority of white Americans, perhaps still as large as a fifth, persist in harboring racist attitudes in their most vulgar and naive form. This is an important fact in a time of polarization such as the present, for this minority becomes the vocal right anchor in the nation's social judgment process.

Racist assumptions are not only nourished by separatism but in turn rationalize separatism. Equal-status contact is avoided because of the racist stigma branded upon Negro Americans by three centuries of slavery and segregation. Yet changes are evident in social distance attitudes, too. Between 1942 and 1963, the percentage of white Americans who favored racially desegregated schools rose from 30 to 63; and those with no objections to a Negro neighbor from 35 to 63 (Hyman and Sheatsley, 1964; Sheatsley, 1965). Nor has this trend abated during the recent five years of increasing polarization—a period which the mass media misinterpreted with the vague label of "backlash."[9] The most dramatic shifts have occurred in the South; the proportion of white Southern parents who stated that they would not object to having their children attend classes with "a few" Negro children rose from only 38 per cent in 1963 to 62 per cent by 1965 (American Institute of Public Opinion, 1965). Consistently favorable shifts also characterized white opinion in the North. Here, a school with "a few" Negro children was declared objectionable by 87 per cent of white parents in 1963, by 91 per cent in 1965; a school where the student body was one-half Negro was acceptable to 56 per cent in 1963, to 65 per cent in 1965; and a school with a majority of Negro students found no objection among 31 per cent in 1963, among 37 per cent in 1965. Similar changes are evident in white attitudes in other realms and in more current surveys, though shifts in attitudes toward intimate contact have remained limited.

This slow but steady erosion of racist and separatist attitudes among white Americans has occurred during years of confrontation and change.

[9]The incorrect interpretation of present white animosities toward the Negro as a "backlash" is a classic case of the ecological fallacy; see Pettigrew (1966).

To be sure, the process has been too slow to keep pace with the Negro's rising aspirations for full justice and complete eradication of racism. Yet this relentless trend parallelling the drive for integration should not be overlooked.

IN A PERIOD OF CONFRONTATION...

Thus, in a period of confrontation, dramatic events can stimulate surprisingly sharp shifts in a short period of time. Consider the attitudes of white Texans before and after the tragic assassination of Martin Luther King, Jr., the riots that followed his murder, and the issuance of the forthright Report of the National Advisory Commission on Civil Disorders (1968). Table 24.1 shows the data collected prior to the assassination in November 1967 and February 1968 and following the assassination in May 1968.

Observe the especially large change in the four realms of relatively formal contact—desegregation in busses, jobs, restaurants and hotels; the moderate change in realms of relatively informal contact—the desegregation of schools and churches; and the lack of significant change in realms of intimate contact—desegregation of social gatherings, housing, swimming pools, house parties and college dormitories. Despite the ceiling effect, approval increased greatest for those items already most approved. One is reminded of the Triandis and Davis (1965) breakdown of racial realms by degree of intimacy. The attitude change also varied among different types of white Texans; the young and the middle class shifted positively the most, again despite ceiling effects.[10] The tentative generalization growing out of these data is: In times of confrontation, dramatic events can achieve positive attitude changes among those whites and in those realms least subject to separatist norms.

[10]That the post-King murder data do not reflect merely temporary shifts is demonstrated by further data collected in Texas in August of 1968. Similar to these results was an overall shift of approximately five per cent toward favoring the racial desegregation of public schools noted among white Texans between two surveys taken immediately before and after the 1957 crisis in Little Rock. And, once again, the most positive shifts were noted among the young and the middle-class (Riley and Pettigrew, 1968).

TABLE 24.1
*Per cent of white Texans who approve**

Area of Desegregation	November 1967	February 1968	May 1968	May − Nov. + Feb. / 2 Change
Same busses	65.6	66.6	75.6	+9.5
Same jobs	68.5	70.7	77.3	+7.7
Same restaurants	60.7	62.5	69.2	+7.6
Same hotels	55.2	55.4	62.5	+7.2
Same schools	57.1	60.4	64.3	+5.6
Teach your child	53.1	53.6	57.7	+4.4
Same churches	61.5	62.9	66.2	+4.0
Same social gatherings	42.1	42.4	45.3	+3.1
Live next door	34.2	36.2	36.8	+1.6
Same swimming pools	35.1	30.9	34.2	+1.2
Same house party	29.4	30.0	30.3	+0.6
College roommate of your child	21.4	21.5	21.4	−0.1

*These results are taken from R.T. Riley and T.F. Pettigrew, "Dramatic events and racial attitude change." Unpublished paper. Harvard University, August 1968. The data are from probability samples of white Texans drawn and interviewed by Belden Associates of Dallas, Texas specifically for the U.S. Office of Education Contract No. OEC 1-6-061-774-1887 to Harvard University.

CONTACT STUDIES...

The most solid social psychological evidence of racial attitude change comes from the contact studies. Repeated research in a variety of newly desegregated situations discovered that the attitudes of both whites and Negroes toward each other markedly improved. Thus, after the hiring of Negroes as department store clerks in New York City, one investigation noted growing acceptance of the practice among the white clerks (Harding and Hogrefe, 1952) and another noted rapid acceptance among white customers (Saenger and Gilbert, 1950). And a series of studies concentrating on public housing residents found similar results (Deutsch and Collins, 1951; Jahoda and West, 1951; Wilner *et al.*, 1955; and Works, 1961), as did studies on servicemen (Stouffer *et al.*, 1949; MacKenzie, 1948), the merchant marine (Brophy, 1946), government workers (MacKenzie, 1948), the police (Kephart, 1957), students (MacKenzie, 1948), and general small town populations (Williams, 1964). Some of these results can be interpreted not as the result of contact, but as an indication that more tolerant white Americans seek contact with Negro Americans. A number of the investigations, however, restrict this self-selection factor, making the effects of the new contact itself

the only explanation of the significant alterations in attitudes and behavior.

A major study by Deutsch and Collins (1951) illustrates this important literature. These investigators took ingenious advantage of a made-to-order natural experiment. In accordance with state law, two public housing projects in New York City were desegregated; in all cases, apartment assignments were made irrespective of race or personal preference. In two comparable projects in Newark, the two races were assigned to separate buildings. Striking differences were found between the attitudes toward Negroes of randomly selected white housewifes in the desegregated and segregated developments. The desegregated women held their Negro neighbors in higher esteem and were considerably more in favor of interracial housing (75 per cent to 25 per cent). When asked to name the chief faults of Negroes, they mentioned such personal problems as feelings of inferiority and oversensitivity; the segregated women listed such group stereotypes as troublemaking, rowdy and dangerous.

As discussed earlier, however, improvements in social distance attitudes are often limited to the immediate contact situation itself. Yet basic racist stereotypes are often affected, too. One white housewife in an interracial development put it bluntly: "Living with them my ideas have changed altogether. They're just people...they're not any different." Commented another: "I've really come to like it. I see they're just as human as we are" (Deutsch and Collins, 1951). And a Negro officer on an interracial ship off Korea summed it up candidly: "After a while you start thinking of whites as people."

ON A NATIONAL SCALE

Recent surveys bear out these contact findings on a national scale. Hyman and Sheatsley (1964) found that the most extensive racial attitude changes among whites have occurred where extensive desegregation of public facilities had already taken place.[11] And data from the Equal Educational Opportunity Survey—popularly known as "the Coleman Report"—indicate that white students who attend public schools with Negroes are the least likely to prefer all-white classrooms and all-white "close friends"; and this effect is strongest among those who began their interracial schooling in the early grades (Coleman et al., 1966, 333). Recall, too, the similar findings of the U.S. Commission on Civil Rights (1967) for both Negro and white adults who had attended biracial schools as children.

Not all intergroup contact, of course, leads to increased acceptance; sometimes it only makes matters worse. Gordon Allport (1954), in his intensive review of this research concluded that four characteristics of the contact situation are of the utmost importance. Prejudice is lessened when the two groups: (a) possess equal status in the situation, (b) seek common goals, (c) are cooperatively dependent upon each other, and (d) interact with the positive support of authorities, laws or custom. Reviewing the same work, Kenneth Clark (1953) came to similar conclusions, and correctly predicted one year prior to the Supreme Court ruling against de jure public school segregation that the process would be successful only to the extent that authorities publicly backed and rigorously enforced the new policy.

The Allport statement of contact conditions is actually an application of the broader theory of interpersonal attraction. All four of his conditions maximize the likelihood of shared values and beliefs being evinced and mutually perceived. Rokeach's belief similarity factor is apparently, then, a key agent in the effects of optimal contact. Thus, following the Triandis and Davis (1965) findings, we would anticipate the attitude alterations achieved by intergroup contact, at least initially, to be greatest for formal realms and least for intimate realms—as with the changes wrought in white Texan attitudes by the dramatic events of early spring 1968.

Accordingly, from this social psychological perspective, the black separatist assumption that "white liberals" should eliminate white racism is an impossible and quixotic hope. One can readily appreciate the militants' desire to avoid further abuse from white racists; but their model for change is woefully inadequate. White liberals can attack racist attitudes publicly, conduct research on racist assertions, set the stage for confrontation. But with all the will in the world they cannot accomplish by themselves the needed Negro push, the dramatic events, the actual interracial contact which has gnawed away at racist beliefs for a generation. A century ago the fiery and perceptive Frederick Douglass (1962; 366–367) phrased the issue pointedly:

I have found in my experience that the way to break down an unreasonable custom is to contradict it in practice. To be sure in pursuing this course I have had to contend not merely with the white race but with the black. The one has condemned me for my presumption in daring to associate with it and the other for pushing myself where it takes it for granted I am not wanted.

[11]This is, of course, a two-way causal relationship. Not only does desegregation erode racist attitudes, but desegregation tends to come first to areas where white attitudes are least racist to begin with. The Hyman-Sheatsley (1964) finding cited, however, specifically highlights the former phenomenon: "In those parts of the South where some measure of school integration has taken place official action has *preceded* public sentiment, and public sentiment has then attempted to accommodate itself to the new situation."

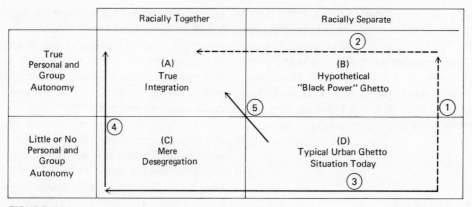

FIGURE 24.1
*Schematic Diagram of Autonomy and Contact-separation**

*The author is indebted to Professor Karl Deutsch, of Harvard University, for several stimulating discussions out of which came this diagram. Dotted lines denote hypothetical paths, solid lines actual paths.

The Assumptions of Racial Conflict and Autonomy-Before-Contact

History reveals that white separatists are correct when they contend that racial change creates conflict, that if only the traditions of white supremacy were to go unchallenged racial harmony might be restored. One of the quietest periods in American racial history, 1895–1915, for example, witnessed the construction of the massive system of institutional racism as it is known today—the nadir of Negro American history as Rayford Logan (1957) calls it. The price of those two decades of relative peace is still being paid by the nation. Even were it possible in the late twentieth century, then, to gain racial calm by inaction, America could not afford the enormous cost.

But if inaction is clearly impossible, the types of action called for are not so clear. Black separatists believe that efforts to further interracial contact should be abandoned or at least delayed until greater personal and group autonomy is achieved by Negroes. This is the other side of the same coin that leaves the struggle against attitudinal racism completely in the hands of "white liberals." And it runs a similar danger. Racism is reflected not only in attitudes but more importantly in institutionalized arrangements that operate to restrict Negro choice. Both forms of racism are fostered by seg-

regation, and both have to be confronted directly by Negroes. Withdrawal into the ghetto, psychologically tempting as it may be for many, essentially gives up the fight to alter the racially-discriminatory operations of the nation's chief institutions.

The issues involved are highlighted in the schematic diagram shown in Figure 24.1. By varying contact-separation and an ideologically vague concept of "autonomy," four cells emerge that represent various possibilities under discussion. Cell "A" true integration, refers to institutionalized biracial situations where there is cross-racial friendship, racial interdependence, and a strong measure of personal autonomy (and group autonomy, too, if group is defined biracially). Such situations do exist in America today, but they are rare imbattled islands in a sea of conflict. Cell "B" represents the autonomous "black power" ghetto, relatively independent of the larger society and with a far more viable existence than commonly the case now. This is an ideologically-derived hypothetical situation, for no such urban ghettos exist today. Cell "C" stands for merely desegregated situations. Often misnamed as "integrated," these institutionalized biracial settings include both races but little cross-racial acceptance and often patronizing legacies of white supremacy. Cell "D" represents today's typical Negro scene—

the highly separate urban ghetto with little or no personal or group autonomy.

TO GET FROM "D" TO "A"...

Save for white separatists, observers of diverse persuasions agree that the achievement of true integration (cell "A") should be the ideal and ultimate goal. But there are, broadly speaking, three contrasting ways of getting there from the typical current situation (cell "D"). The black separatist assumes only one route is possible: from the depressed ghetto today to the hypothetical ghetto of tomorrow and then, perhaps, on to true integration (lines numbered 1 and 2 on Figure 24.1). The desegregationist assumes precisely the opposite route: from the present-day ghetto to mere desegregation and then, hopefully, on to true integration (lines numbered 3 and 4 in Figure 24.1). But there is a third, more direct route right across the diagonal from the current ghetto to true integration (line 5 in Figure 24.1). Experience to date combines with a number of social psychological considerations to favor the last of these possibilities.

The black separatist route has a surprising appeal for an untested theory; besides those whites who welcome any alternative to integration, it seems to appeal to cultural pluralists, white and black, to militant black leaders searching for a new direction to vent the ghetto's rage and despair, and to Negroes who just wish to withdraw as far away from whites as possible. Yet on reflection, the argument involves the perverse notion that the way to bring two groups together is to separate them further. One is reminded of the detrimental consequences of isolation in economics, through "closed markets," and in genetics, through "genetic drift." In social psychology, isolation between two contiguous groups generally leads to: (a) diverse value development, (b) reduced intergroup communication, (c) uncorrected perceptual distortions of each other, and (d) the growth of vested interests within both groups for continued separation. American race relations already suffer from each of these conditions; and the proposal for further separation even if a gilded ghetto were possible, aims to exacerbate them further.

NO ACCESS TO THE TAX BASE...

Without pursuing the many economic and political difficulties inherent in the insulated ghetto conception, suffice it to mention the meager resources immediately available in the ghetto for the task. Recognizing this limitation, black separatists call for massive federal aid with no strings attached. But this requires a national consensus. Some separatists scoff at the direct path to integration (line 5 in Figure 1) as idealistic dreaming, then turn and casually assume the same racist society that resists integration will unhesitatingly pour a significant portion of its treasure exclusively into ghetto efforts. Put differently, "local control" without access to the necessary tax base is not control. This raises the political limitations to the black separatist route. The Irish-American model of entering the mainstream through the political system is often cited as appropriate to black separatism—but is it really? Faster than any other immigrant group save Jewish-Americans, the Irish have assimilated via the direct diagonal of Figure 24.1. Forced to remain in ghettos at first, the Irish did not settle for "local control" but strove to win city hall itself. Boston's legendary James Michael Curley won "Irish power" not by becoming mayor of the South Boston ghetto, but by becoming mayor of the entire city. There are serious problems with immigrant analogies for Negroes, since immigrants never suffered from slavery and legalized segregation. But to the extent an analogy is appropriate, Mayor Carl Stokes of Cleveland and Mayor Richard Hatcher of Gary are far closer to the Irish-American model than are black separatists.

FATE CONTROL...

A critical part of black separatist thinking centers on the psychological concept of "fate control"—more familiar to psychologists as Rotter's (1966) internal control of reinforcement variable. "Until we control our own destinies, our own schools and areas," goes the argument, "blacks cannot possibly achieve the vital sense of fate control." And Coleman Report (Coleman *et al.,* 1966) data are cited to show that fate control is a critical correlate of Negro school achievement. But no mention is made of the additional fact that levels of fate control among Negro children were found by Coleman to be significantly higher in interracial than in all-Negro schools. Black separatists brush this important finding aside on the grounds that all-Negro schools today are not what they envision for the future. Yet the fact remains that interracial schools appear to be facilitating the growth of fate control among Negro students now, while the ideological contention that it can be developed as well or better in uniracial schools remains an untested and hypothetical assertion.

Despite the problems, black separatists feel their route (lines 1 and 2 in Figure 24.1) is the only way to true integration in part because they regard the indirect desegregation path (lines 3 and 4 in Figure 24.1) as an affront to their dignity. One need only know the blatantly hostile and subtly rejecting racial acts that typify some interracial situations to know to what this repudiation of non-autonomous desegregation refers (Cell "C" in Figure 24.1; Chessler, 1967). But it is conceptually and practically useful to make a clear distinction between true integration (Cell "A" in Figure 24.1) and mere desegregation (Cell "'C" in Figure 24.1). The U.S. Commission on Civil Rights (1967), in reanalyzing Coleman's data, found this distinction provided the tool for separating empirically between effective and ineffective biracial schools where whites form the majority, Negro student achievement, college aspirations, and sense of fate control proved to be highest in truly integrated schools when these schools are independently defined as biracial institutions characterized by no racial tension and widespread cross-racial friendship. Merely desegregated schools, defined as biracial institutions, typified by racial tension and little cross-racial friendship have scant benefits over segregated schools.

ALLPORT CONDITIONS FOR OPTIMAL CONTACT

This civil rights commission finding reflects the Allport (1954) conditions for optimal contact. Truly integrated institutions afford the type of equal-status, common goal, interdependent and authority-sanctioned contact that maximizes cross-racial acceptance and Rokeach's belief similarity.[12] They apparently also maximize the positive and minimize the negative factors which Katz (1964, 1967) has carefully isolated as important for Negro performance in biracial task groups. And they also seem to increase the opportunity for beneficial cross-racial evaluations which may well be critical mediators of the effects of biracial schools (Pettigrew, 1967). Experimental research following up these leads is now called for to detail the precise social psychological processes operating in the truly integrated situation (Pettigrew, 1968).

The desegregation route (lines 3 and 4 in Figure 24.1) has been successfully navigated, though the black separatist contention that Negroes bear the principal burden for this effort is undoubtedly true. Those southern institutions that have attained integration, for example, have typically gone this indirect path. So it is not as hypothetical as the black separatist path, but it is hardly to be preferred over the direct integrationist route (line 5 in Figure 24.1).

THE SELF-FULFILLING PROPHECY...

So why not the direct route? The standard answer is that it is impossible, that demographic trends and white resistance make it out of the question in our time. The self-fulfilling prophecy threatens once more. Secretary of Health, Education and

[12]Another white observer enthusiastic about black separatism even denies that the contact studies' conclusions are applicable to the classroom and other institutions which do not produce "continual and extensive equal-status contact under more or less enforced conditions of intimacy." Stember (1968) selectively cites the public housing and armed forces contact investigations to support his point; but he has to omit the many studies from less intimate realms which reached the same conclusions—such as those conducted in schools (Pettigrew, 1968), employment situations (Harding and Hogrefe, 1952; Kephart, 1957; and MacKenzie, 1948; and Williams, 1964), and even one involving brief clerk and customer contact (Saenger and Gilbert, 1950).

Welfare, Wilbur Cohen, insists integration will not come in this generation—hardly a reassuring assertion from the chief of the federal department with primary responsibility for furthering the process.[13] The Secretary adopts the Alsop separatist argument and opts for programs exclusively within the ghetto, a position that makes extensive integration unlikely even a generation hence. One is reminded of the defenders of slavery who in the 1850's attacked the Abolitionists as unrealistic dreamers and insisted slavery was so deeply entrenched that efforts should be limited to making it into a benign institution.

If the nation acts on the speculations of Cohen, Alsop and Ferry, then, they will probably be proven correct in their pessimistic projections. For what better way to prevent racial change than to act on the presumption that it is impossible?

URBAN RACIAL DEMOGRAPHY...

The belief that integration is impossible is based on some harsh facts of urban racial demography. Between 1950 and 1960, the average annual increment of Negro population in the central cities of the United States was 320,000; from 1960 to 1966 the estimated annual growth climbed to 400,000. In the suburbs, however, the average annual growth of the Negro population has declined from 60,000 between 1950 and 1960 to an estimated 33,000 between 1960 and 1966. In other words, it would require about thirteen times the present trend in suburban Negro growth just to maintain the sprawling central city ghettos at their present size. In the nation's largest metropolitan areas, then, the trend is forcefully pushing in the direction of ever-increasing separatism.

But these bleak data are not the whole picture. In the first place, they refer especially to the very largest of the metropolitan areas—to New York City, Chicago, Los Angeles, Philadelphia, Detroit,

[13]Consistent with the thesis of this paper, a number of leading black separatists attacked the Cohen statement. For example, Bryant Rollins, separatist spokesman in Boston, called Cohen's statement "a cop-out" and described it as typical of "white bureaucratic racists who don't want to do anything" (Jordan, 1968).

Washington, D.C. and Baltimore. Most Negro Americans, however, do not live in these places, but reside in areas where racial integration is in fact possible in the short run were a good faith attempt to be made. The Harlems and Wattses, especially during this period of urban riots, have blinded some analysts into thinking of the entire Negro population as residing in such ghettos. Put differently, there are more Berkeleys and White Plainses—small enough for school integration to be effectively achieved—than there are New York Cities.

In the second place, the presumed impossibility of reversing the central city racial trends are based on anti-metropolitan assumptions. Without metropolitan cooperation, central cities—and many suburbs, too—will find their racial problems insoluble. So need we assume such cooperation impossible? Effective state and federal incentives are being proposed, and a few established, to further this cooperation. Moreover, some large Negro ghettos are already extending into the suburbs (e.g., Pittsburgh and soon in Chicago); the first tentative metropolitan schemes to aid racial integration are emerging (e.g., Boston, Hartford, and Rochester); and several major metropolitan areas have even consolidated (e.g., Miami-Dade County and Nashville-Davidson County). Once the issue is looked at in metropolitan terms, its dimensions become more manageable. Negro Americans are found in America's metropolitan areas in almost the same ratio as white Americans; about two-thirds of each group resides in these 212 regions, so that on a metropolitan basis Negroes are not significantly more metropolitan than their one-ninth proportion in the nation as a whole.

Policy Implications

Much of the policy confusion seems to derive from the assumption that since *complete* integration in the biggest cities will not be possible in the near future, present efforts toward opening integration opportunities for both Negro and white Americans are premature. This thinking obscures two fundamental issues. First, the democratic objective is not total racial integration and the elimination of the ghetto; the idea is simply to provide an honest choice between separation and integration. This separation side of the choice is available today; it is integration that is closed to Negroes who would choose it. The long-term goal is not a complete obliteration of cultural pluralism, of distinctive Negro ghettos, but rather the transformation of these ghettos from today's racial prisons to tomorrow's ethnic areas of choice. Life within ghettos can never be fully satisfactory as long as there are Negroes who reside within them only because discrimination requires them to.

Second, the integrationist alternative will not become a reality as long as we disparage it, as long as we abandon it to future generations. Exclusive attention to within-ghetto enrichment programs is almost certain, to use Kenneth Clark's pointed word, to "embalm" the ghetto, to seal it in even further from the rest of the nation (making line 2 in Figure 24.1 less likely yet). This danger explains the recent interest of conservative whites in exclusive ghetto enrichment programs. The bribe is straight-forward: "Stop rioting and stop demanding integration, and we'll minimally support separatist programs within the ghetto." Even black separatists are understandably ambivalent about such offers, as they come from sources long identified with opposition to all racial change. Should the bargain be struck, however, American race relations will be dealt still another serious blow.

WHAT IS POSSIBLE...

The outlines of the situation, then, are these: (a) widespread integration is possible everywhere in the United States save in the largest central cities; (b) it will not come unless present trends are reversed and considerable resources are provided for the process; (c) big central cities will continue to have significant Negro concentrations even with successful metropolitan dispersal; (d) large Negro ghettos are presently in need of intensive enrichment; and (e) some ghetto enrichment programs run the clear and present danger of embalming the ghetto further.

Given this situation and the social psychological considerations of this paper, the overall strategy needed must contain the following elements:

(a) A major effort toward racial integration must be mounted in order to provide genuine choice to all Negro Americans in all realms of life. This effort should envisage by the late 1970's complete attainment of the goal in smaller communities and cities and a halting of separatist trends in major central cities with a movement toward metropolitan cooperation.

(b) A simultaneous effort is required to enrich the vast central city ghettos of the nation, to change them structurally, and to make life in them more viable. In order to avoid embalming them, however, strict criteria must be applied to proposed enrichment programs to insure that they are productive for later dispersal and integration. Restructuring the economics of the ghetto, especially the development of urban cooperatives, is a classic example of productive enrichment. The building of enormous public housing developments within the ghetto presents a good illustration of counterproductive enrichment. Some programs, such as the decentralization of huge public school systems or the encouragement of Negro business ownership, can be either productive or counterproductive depending upon how they are focused. A Bundy Decentralization Plan of many homogeneous school districts for New York City is clearly counterproductive for later integration; a Regents Plan of a relatively small number of heterogeneous school districts for New York City could well be productive. Likewise, Negro entrepreneurs encouraged to open small shops and expected to prosper with an all-Negro clientele are not only counterproductive but are probably committing economic suicide. Negro businessmen encouraged to pool resources to establish somewhat larger operations and to appeal to white as well as Negro customers on major traffic arteries in and out of the ghetto could be productive.

A MIXED INTEGRATION-ENRICHMENT STRATEGY

In short, a mixed integration-enrichment strategy is called for that contains safeguards that the enrichment will not impede integration. Recent survey results strongly suggest that such a mixed strategy would meet with widespread Negro approval. On the basis of their extensive 1968 survey of Negro residents in fifteen major cities, Campbell and Schuman (1968, 5) conclude:

> Separatism appeals to from five to eighteen per cent of the Negro sample, depending on the question, with the largest appeal involving black ownership of stores and black administration of schools in Negro neighborhoods, and the smallest appeal the rejection of whites as friends or in other informal contacts. Even on questions having the largest appeal, however, more than three-quarters of the Negro sample indicate a clear preference for integration. Moreover, the reasons given by respondents for their choices suggest that the desire for integration is not simply a practical wish for better material facilities, but represents a commitment to principles of nondiscrimination and racial harmony.

Young men prove to be the most forthright separatists, but even here the separatist percentages for males sixteen to nineteen years of age ranged only from eleven to twenty-eight per cent. An interesting interaction between type of separatism and educational level of the respondent appears in the Campbell and Schuman (1968, 19) data. Among the twenty-to-thirty-nine-year-olds, college graduates tended to be the more separatist in those realms where their training gives them a vested interest in competition-free positions — Negro-owned stores for Negro neighborhoods and Negro teachers in mostly-Negro schools; while the poorly educated were most likely to believe that whites should be discouraged from taking part in civil rights organizations and to agree that "Negroes should have nothing to do with whites if they can help it" and that "there should be a separate black nation here."

NEGROES WANT BOTH INTEGRATION AND BLACK IDENTITY

But if separatism draws little favorable response even in the most politicized ghettos, positive aspects of cultural pluralism attract wide interest.

For example, forty-two per cent endorse the statement that "Negro school children should study an African language." And this interest seems rather general across age, sex and education categories. Campbell and Schuman (1968, 6) regard this as evidence of a broadly-supported attempt "...to emphasize black consciousness *without* rejection of whites...A substantial number of Negroes want *both* integration and black identity."[14] Or in the terms of this paper, they prefer cell "A" in Figure 24.1 — "true integration."

The Campbell and Schuman data indicate little if any change from the pro-integration results of earlier Negro surveys (Brink and Harris, 1964; 1967). And they are consistent with the results of recent surveys in Detroit, Miami, New York City, and other cities (Meyer, 1967, 1968; and Center for Urban Education, 1968). Data from Bedford-Stuyvesant in Brooklyn are especially significant, for here separatist ideology and a full-scale enrichment program are in full view. Yet when asked if they would prefer to live on a block with people of the same race or of every race, eighty per cent of the Negro respondents chose an interracial block (Center for Urban Education, 1968). Interestingly, the largest Negro segment choosing integration — eighty-eight per cent — consisted of residents of public housing where a modest amount of interracial tenancy still prevails.

A final study from Watts links these surveys to the analysis of this paper. Ransford (1968) found that Negro willingness to use violence was closely and positively related to a sense of powerlessness, feelings of racial dissatisfaction and limited contact with whites. Respondents who indicated that they had no social contact with white people, "like going to the movies together or visiting each other's homes," were significantly more likely to feel powerless and express racial dissatisfaction as well as to report greater willingness to use violence. The personal, group and national costs of racial separatism are great.

[14]This is not a new position for Negro Americans, for their dominant response to Marcus Garvey's movement in the 1920's was essentially the same. Garvey stressed black beauty and pride in Africa and mounted a mass movement in the urban ghettos of the day, but his "back to Africa" separatist appeals were largely ignored.

A Final Word...

Racially separate or together? Our social psychological examination of separatist assumptions leads to one imperative: the attainment of a viable, democratic America, free from personal and institutional racism, requires extensive racial integration in all realms of life. To prescribe more separation because of discomfort, racism, conflict or autonomy needs is like getting drunk again to cure a hangover. The nation's binge of *apartheid* must not be exacerbated but alleviated.

REFERENCES

Allport, G.W. *The nature of prejudice.* Cambridge, Mass.: Addison-Wesley, 1954.

Alsop, J. No more nonsense about ghetto education! *The New Republic,* July 22, 1967, **157,** 18–23. (a)

Alsop, J. Ghetto education. *The New Republic,* November 18, 1967, **157,** 18–23. (b)

American Institute of Public Opinion, press release, May 22, 1965.

Armstrong, Clairette P. and Gregor, A.J. Integrated schools and Negro character development: some considerations of the possible effects. *Psychiatry,* 1964, **27,** 69–72.

Brink, W. and Harris, L. *The Negro revolution in America.* New York: Simon and Schuster, 1964.

Brink, W. and Harris, L. *Black and white: a study of U.S. racial attitudes today.* New York: Simon and Schuster, 1967.

Brophy, I.N. The luxury of anti-Negro prejudice. *Public Opinion Quarterly,* 1946, **9,** 456–466.

Calame, B.E. A west coast militant talks tough but helps avert racial trouble. *The Wall Street Journal,* July 26, 1968, **172,** (1), 15.

Campbell, A. and Schuman, H. Racial attitudes in fifteen American cities. In The National Advisory Commission on Civil Disorders, *Supplemental studies.* Washington, D.C.: U.S. Government Printing Office, 1968.

Center for Urban Education. Survey of the residents of Bedford-Stuyvesant. Unpublished paper, 1968.

Chessler, M. *In their own words.* Atlanta, Ga.: Southern Regional Council, 1967.

Clark, K.B. Desegregation: an appraisal of the evidence. *Journal of Social Issues,* 1953, **9,** 1–76.

Coleman, J.S., Campbell, E.Q., Hobson, C.J., McPartland, J., Mood, A.M., Weinfeld, F.D. and York, R.L. *Equality of educational opportunity.* Washington, D.C.: U.S. Government Printing Office, 1966.

Davies, J.C. Toward a theory of revolution. *American Sociological Review,* 1962, **27,** 5–19.

Deutsch, M. and Collins, Mary. *Interracial housing: a psychological evaluation of a social experiment.* Minneapolis: University of Minnesota Press, 1951.

Douglass, F. *Life and times of Frederick Douglass: the complete autobiography.* New York: Collier Books, 1962 (original edition in 1892).

Ferry, W.H. Black colonies: a modest proposal. *The Center Magazine,* January 1968, **1,** 74–76.

Geschwender, J.A. Social structure and the Negro revolt: an examination of some hypotheses. *Social Forces,* 1964, **43,** 248–256.

Harding, J. and Hogrefe, R. Attitudes of white department store employees toward Negro co-workers. *Journal of Social Issues,* 1952, **8,** 18–28.

Hyman, H.H. and Sheatsley, P.B. Attitudes toward desegregation. *Scientific American,* December 1956, **195,** 35–39.

Hyman, H.H. and Sheatsley, P.B. Attitudes toward desegregation. *Scientific American,* July 1964, **211,** 16–23.

Jahoda, Marie and West, Patricia. Race relations in public housing. *Journal of Social Issues,* 1951, **7,** 132–139.

Jordan, R.A. Go-slow integration draws retorts. *The Boston Globe,* August 8, 1968, **194,** 2.

Katz, I. Review of evidence relating to effects of desegregation on the performance of Negroes. *American Psychologist,* 1964, **19,** 381–399.

Katz, I. The socialization of competence motivation in minority group children. In D. Levine (Ed.), *Nebraska symposium on motivation, 1967.* Lincoln: University of Nebraska Press, 1967.

Kephart, W.M. *Racial factors and urban law enforcement.* Philadelphia: University of Pennsylvania Press, 1957.

Klineberg, O. *Negro intelligence and selective migration.* New York: Columbia University Press, 1935.

Kohn, M.L. and Williams, R.M., Jr. Situational patterning in intergroup relations. *American Sociological Review,* 1956, **21,** 164–174.

Logan, R.W. *The Negro in the United States: a brief history.* Princeton, N.J.: Van Nostrand, 1957.

MacKenzie, Barbara. The importance of contact in determining attitudes toward Negroes. *Journal of Abnormal and Social Psychology,* 1948, **43,** 417–441.

Meyer, P. *A survey of attitudes of Detroit Negroes after the riot of 1967.* Detroit, Mich.: Detroit Urban League, in press.

Meyer, P. *Miami Negroes: a study in depth.* Miami, Florida: *The Miami Herald,* 1968.

National Advisory Commission on Civil Disorders. *Report.* Washington, D.C.: U.S. Printing Office, 1968.

Newcomb, T.M., Turner, R.H. and Converse, P.E. *Social psychology: the study of human interaction.* New York: Holt, Rinehart and Winston, 1965.

Pettigrew, T.F. *A profile of the Negro American.* Princeton, N.J.: Van Nostrand, 1964.

Pettigrew, T.F. Parallel and distinctive changes in anti-Semitic and anti-Negro attitudes. In C.H. Stember (Ed.), *Jews in the mind of America.* New York: Basic Books, 1966.

Pettigrew, T.F. Social evaluation theory: convergences and applications. In D. Levine (Ed.), *Nebraska symposium on motivation, 1967.* Lincoln: University of Nebraska Press, 1967.

Pettigrew, T.F. Race and equal educational opportunity. *Harvard Educational Review,* 1968, **38,** 66–76.

Ransford, H.E. Isolation, powerlessness, and violence: a study of attitudes and participation in the Watts riot. *American Journal of Sociology,* 1968, **73,** 581–591.

Reitzes, D.C. The role of organizational structures: union versus neighborhood in a tension situation. *Journal of Social Issues,* 1953, **9,** 37–44.

Riley, R. and Pettigrew, T.F. Dramatic events and racial attitude change. Unpublished paper, Harvard University, 1968.

Rokeach, M. Belief versus race as determinants of social distance: comment on Triandis' paper. *Journal of Abnormal and Social Psychology,* 1961, **62,** 187–188.

Rokeach, M., Smith, Patricia W. and Evans, R.I. Two kinds of prejudice or one? In M. Rokeach (Ed.), *The open and closed mind.* New York: Basic Books, 1960.

Rokeach, M. and Mezei, L. Race and shared belief as factors in social choice. *Science,* 1966, **151,** 167–172.

Rotter, J.B. Internal versus external control of reinforcement. *Psychological Monographs,* 1966, **80,** Whole no. 609.

Saenger, G. and Gilbert, Emily. Customer reactions to the integration of Negro sales personnel. *International Journal of Opinion and Attitude Research,* 1950, **4,** 57–76.

Schwartz, R., Pettigrew, T. and Smith, M. Fake panaceas for ghetto education. *The New Republic,* September 23, 1967, **157,** 16–19.

Schwartz, R., Pettigrew, T. and Smith, M. Is desegregation impractical? *The New Republic,,* January 6, 1968, **157,** 27–29.

Sheatsley, P.B. White attitudes toward the Negro. In T. Parsons and K.B. Clark (Eds.), *The Negro American.* Boston: Houghton Mifflin, 1966.

Smith, Carole R., Williams, L. and Willis, R.H. Race, sex and belief as determinants of friendship acceptance. *Journal of Personality and Social Psychology,* 1967, **5,** 127–137.

Stein, D.D. The influence of belief systems on interpersonal preference. *Psychological Monographs,* 1966, **80,** Whole no. 616.

Stein, D.D., Hardyck, Jane A. and Smith, M.B. Race *and* belief: an open and shut case. *Journal of Personality and Social Psychology,* 1965, **1,** 281–290.

Stember, C.H. Evaluating effects of the integrated classroom. *The Urban Review,* June 1968, **2,** (3–4), 30–31.

Stouffer, S.A., Suchman, E.A., DeVinney, L.C., Star, Shirley A. and Williams, R.M., Jr. *Studies in social psychology in World War II,* Vol. I, *The American soldier: adjustment during army life.* Princeton, N.J.: Princeton University Press, 1949.

Triandis, H.C. A note on Rokeach's theory of prejudice. *Journal of Abnormal and Social Psychology,* 1961, **62,** 184–186.

Triandis, H.C. and Davis, E.E. Race and belief as determinants of behavioral intentions. *Journal of Personality and Social Psychology,* 1965, **2,** 715–725.

United States Commission on Civil Rights. *Civil rights USA: public schools, southern states, 1962.* Washington, D.C.: U.S. Government Printing Office, 1963.

United States Commission on Civil Rights. *Racial isolation in the public schools.* Vols. I and II. Washington, D.C.: U.S. Government Printing Office, 1967.

Williams, R.M., Jr. *Strangers next door: ethnic relations in American communities.* Englewood Cliffs, N.J.: Prentice-Hall, 1964.

Wilner, D.M., Walkley, Rosabelle and Cook, S.W. *Human relations in interracial housing: a study of the contact hypothesis.* Minneapolis: University of Minnesota Press, 1955.

Works, E. The prejudice-interaction hypothesis from the point of view of the Negro minority group. *American Journal of Sociology,* 1961, **67,** 47–52.

Yarrow, Marian R. (Ed.) Interpersonal dynamics in a desegregation process. *Journal of Social Issues,* 1958, **14,** (1), 3–63.

Environmental psychology is defined as the scientific study of the psychological dynamics involved in the interaction of man with his contemporary physical environment. This recently developed problem area shows promise of providing new and sensitive insights about human behavior.[1] An example is the paper by Norum, Russo, and Sommer, which describes two experiments on the ecology of seating arrangements in the classroom. This research is part of a more extensive series of studies by Sommer on human territoriality.

The second paper, by Stanley Milgram, deals with the question of blind submission to authority. Milgram's research on this topic has aroused considerable interest and controversy, both from the standpoint of ethical implications of the chosen experimental task and from the disturbing conclusions we can draw from his findings.

[1]For a recent discussion of environmental psychology studies *see* K.H. Craik, Environmental Psychology," in *New Directions in Psychology 4,* (New York:) Holt, Rinehart and Winston, Inc., 1970, pp. 1–121.

Part XII
EXPLORATIONS IN HUMAN TERRITORIALITY AND BLIND OBEDIENCE

25
Seating Patterns and Group Task

Gary A. Norum, Nancy Jo Russo, and Robert Sommer[1]

Reprinted from *Psychology in the Schools,* Vol. IV, no. 3, July 1967, pp. 276–280.

Very little is known about the ecology of participation within classrooms. The origins of the fixed-row classroom are obscure, going back as it does for centuries, and it seems likely that it was adopted because it reduced interaction and communication between people in the rows and focused their attention on the front of the room. Such an outcome is desirable from the standpoint of a "sit-and-learn" philosophy, but as early as 1900, John Dewey criticized the fixed-row arrangement as antagonistic to the philosophy of experimentalism. Much has been written, for example, about the advantages of horseshoe or semicircular arrangements, but there are few studies to buttress these recommendations. A recent study using college students (Sommer, in press) showed that in a horseshoe arrangement, those students in visual contact with the instructor participated more than those at the sides, while in the straight-row arrangement, those students in the center participated more than those at the sides of the rows. Both of these findings were in accord with the principle that visual contact between people facilitates interaction and communication. Educators have an obligation to learn the connection between classroom layout and learning, as well as codifying these principles so that they can be used in teacher education and in-service training. According to Otto (1955) the systematic evaluation of classroom desks by Pinnell (1954) opened up a new approach to classroom usage by focusing directly on student usage. Previous studies had been concerned with elements of light reflection, posture, color, and normative surveys of current practice. Sanders (1958), who compared teaching programs in conventional classrooms to those with "work-center furniture" which include a number of different pieces but only half as many individual desks as there are students, emphasized the role of educational philosophy in determining the usage of classroom layout. He found that teachers and administrators were remarkably in-

[1]This study represents an M.A. thesis by Gary A. Norum, a senior honors thesis by Nancy Jo Russo, and was supported in part by a grant from the U.S. Office of Education.

sensitive to the connection between the physical environment and educational program, rarely taking advantage of innovative furniture arrangements. Portable chairs, he found, rarely moved from the fixed-row arrangement.

The present study is an attempt to learn how children and college students would arrange themselves when asked to perform tasks involving different interpersonal relationships—cooperative, competitive, and co-acting activities. No attempt was made to use normal school tasks, since we were interested in the ecology of the different interpersonal relationships. The goal of the work is to develop principles of small group ecology so they can be used in the design and layout of classrooms that must contain a variety of activities, some taking place at different times in the day, and some taking place at the same time. This study, although one in a series of investigations of small group ecology (Sommer, 1959, 1961, 1962, 1965) is only one small step toward understanding the classroom as a man-environment system.

STUDY I

Method

The seating arrangements of randomly chosen pairs of pre-school and elementary school children were observed under the following experimental conditions—cooperation, where two children worked together; competition, where two children worked competitively; and co-action, where two children worked individually. Study I was conducted at a children's pre-school on successive days, co-action tasks the first day, cooperative the second, and competitive the third. The sixteen children enrolled at the pre-school were used each day. No child was used twice in the same condition and no pair was used twice in separate conditions. The sessions took place in a large side room (13' x 20'), which contained a table 66'' x 30'' surrounded by six chairs, two at each side, and one at each end. In the co-action condition, two children at a time were asked if they would like to play a game (consisting of a Lego board and six blocks)[2] and were then requested to enter the ad-

[2]Lego is a brand name for a children's game consisting of a small board on which plastic blocks of various sizes can be attached.

joining room, sit down at the table, and make the design they liked best. They were told to work separately and that anyone making a design would receive a tootsie roll for a prize. After the pair sat down, their seating position was recorded. When the children finished, E went into the room and gave them their reward. The chairs were replaced after each session and the table orientation to the door was changed by 90° after each fourth pair. The cooperating sessions were held the following day, with the procedure the same, except that each pair was given a single Lego board, and the children were told to work together to make the design they both liked, so they could win a prize consisting of a package of two lollipops. For the competitive condition the next day, the children were told that this was a contest to see which of them would make the best design and the winner would receive a large tootsie roll—only the best design would win. The winners were to be announced after everyone had a turn. At the end of the day, the children were told that all the designs were done so well that everyone would receive a prize.

In the second phase of the study, 74 like-sex pairs of children from Grades 4–6 (ages 9–12) in a local public school were given the same co-acting, cooperating, and competing instructions, but because the sample was drawn from a public school, it was decided to substitute praise for candy as a reinforcer. Again, the children were asked to sit around a rectangular table (60'' x 30'') surrounded by six chairs, two to a side and one at each end. The three types of instructions were given in random order, and the sessions took place over two days. On the second day, before the session began, each pair was asked casually, "Have you heard about the game yet?" The answer was always in the negative, probably due to the formation of friendship patterns within the classrooms rather than between classrooms, since the students were drawn from four classrooms on the first day and four other classrooms on the second day.

Results

On the basis of previous work on small group ecology, it is possible to rank arrangements of pairs in terms of psychological closeness (Sommer, 1959, 1965). The most intimate arrangement is side-by-side seating, followed by corner seating, opposite seating, and distant (catty-corner) seating. For statistical treatment of our data, arbitrary

TABLE 25.1
Mean closeness score in each condition

	Cooperating	Competing	Co-acting
Preschool Children	2.00	2.71	3.38
Grade School Children	1.35	2.22	2.56

ranks from 1 to 4 were assigned to these arrangements — side seating receiving a rank of 1, corner seating a rank of 2, opposite seating a rank of 3, and distant seating a rank of 4. Average closeness scores could then be computed; the lower the mean, the closer the seating arrangement. Instead of saying that in the co-acting group, 12% sat across from one another, 25% sat corner-to-corner, and 63% sat in a distant arrangement, an overall mean could be computed (see Table 25.1) and an F test made permitting overall comparison of the groups.[3]

The analysis of variance showed a clear relationship ($p < .01$) in both the preschool and public school groups between the task set and the closeness of the seating arrangement. Pairs in the co-operating groups tended to sit side-by-side, in a corner arrangement during competition, and in a catty-corner arrangement in the co-acting condition. Very few children sat directly across from one another, a widely used arrangement in studies with adults, second only in popularity to corner seating. Sex also influenced closeness ($p < .05$) with girls making more use than boys of side-by-side seating.

STUDY II

Method

Since the previous study used children with a specific task, it was thought that another study using adults with a different task was warranted. It seemed necessary to see if our results had been produced solely by the specific task (attaching plastic blocks to a board) that was involved. The subjects in Study II were 20

male and 27 female undergraduates in introductory psychology classes at the University of California at Davis. The goal was to learn how the perceived interpersonal relationship between S and a decoy, a student of the same sex as S already seated in the room, would affect where S would sit. The decoys were all volunteers from the same classes as the Ss and were seated in the room before the S entered. The decoy did not know which experimental condition was being used at any time. In the competitive condition the Ss were told, "You will be doing competitive problem-solving, and you will be competing individually against one other person. You will be working at the same tasks, but you will be competing against each other. Your performance will be scored on the basis of speed and quality....." The Ss in the cooperative condition were told, "You will be doing cooperative problem-solving and you will be working as a team with one other person. You will both be working together at the same tasks...." Nothing was specified about the nature of the task, but only that S's partner or opponent had already arrived and was waiting in the experimental room. The room contained a large rectangular table with four chairs at each side and one chair at the head and foot, respectively. The decoy always occupied the same chair, one from the end along the side of the table. After the S had taken a seat, the experimenter entered the room, recorded the S's seating position and then explained the purpose of the experiment. The S was then interviewed as to why he sat where he did and asked to refrain from talking about the experiment to other students.

Results

The perceived relationship of cooperation or competition had a marked effect on seating patterns. In the cooperative condition, 13 Ss sat on the same side of the table as the decoy and 11 sat opposite. In the competitive condition, only 4 Ss sat on the same side as the decoy and 19 sat opposite ($\chi^2 = 6.88$, $p < .01$). There was also a non-

[3]In addition, all comparisons were statistically analyzed by Chi square tests using separate categories (side-by-side seating, corner seating, etc.). The results in every case paralleled those using the analysis of variance test.

significant trend for females in both conditions to make greater use of side-by-side seating.

DISCUSSION

The results indicate that the perceived interpersonal relationship between individuals affects how they arrange themselves spatially. It is noteworthy that this occurs with preschool children as well as college students. It would seem that the functional requirements of different task sets are learned early in life. These different arrangements were chosen voluntarily by the students who were provided with a *choice.* In most classrooms using the straight-row layout, there is very little opportunity for choosing spatial arrangements suited to an individual activity. The work-center approach described by Otto (1955), which involves a variety of furniture, including round tables, upholstered furniture, and movable bookcases, as well as reducing to one-half the number of individual desks required, seems a more satisfactory design solution. The approach is based on the assumption that only a portion of the class needs to engage in mass writing activities at any single time, but even when this is necessary, some students can use tables. However, even a work-center approach that provides teachers with many options of classroom layout does not guarantee that the options will be exercised. Both Rolfe (1961) and Sanders (1958) emphasized the need to instruct teachers and administrators in the best ways to use classroom layout in terms of educational objectives. Nor can we say that pupils who are placed in arrangements they would not choose voluntarily (e.g., side-by-side seating in a competitive task) will not be able to perform effectively. It is a well-documented fact that people are remarkably adaptable to different environmental conditions. Leavitt (1951) placed people in various communication networks — straight-row, star-shaped, circular, etc., and found that the different networks influenced the style of problem-solving and member satisfaction, but not the time it took to solve the problems. Intellectual honesty requires researchers to consider the null hypothesis that classroom layout, within wide limits, has no discernible effect on educational programming and activities. Considering the research accumulated to date, this is not an untenable position. Nonetheless we regard it as a premature and unduly pessimistic view of the possibilities for environmental programming in the classroom field, since systematic research into classroom layout from the standpoint of pupil behavior is a relatively recent development.

REFERENCES

Leavitt, H.J. Some effects of certain communication patterns in group performance. *Journal of Abnormal and Social Psychology,* 1951, *46,* 38–50.

Otto, H.J. An experiment with elementary school classroom seating and equipment. *Texas School Board Journal,* 1955, *2,* 3–6.

Pinnell, L.K. *Functionality of elementary school desks.* Bureau of Laboratory Schools Publication No. 5. Austin: University of Texas, 1954.

Rolfe, H.C. Observable differences in space use of learning situations in small and large classrooms. Unpublished Ed.D. thesis, University of California at Berkeley, 1961.

Sanders, D.C. *Innovations in elementary school classroom seating.* Bureau of Laboratory Schools Publication No. 10. Austin: University of Texas, 1958.

Sommer, R. Studies in personal space. *Sociometry,* 1959, *22,* 247–260.

Sommer, R. Leadership and group geography. *Sociometry,* 1961, *24,* 99–110.

Sommer, R. The distance for comfortable conversation. *Sociometry,* 1962, *25,* 111–116.

Sommer, R. Further studies of small group ecology. *Sociometry,* 1965, *28,* 337–348.

Sommer, R. Classroom ecology. *Journal of Applied Behavioral Science,* in press.

The situation in which one agent commands another to hurt a third turns up time and again as a significant theme in human relations. It is powerfully expressed in the story of Abraham, who is commanded by God to kill his son. It is no accident that Kierkegaard, seeking to orient his thought to the central themes of human experience, chose Abraham's conflict as the springboard to his philosophy.

War too moves forward on the triad of an authority which commands a person to destroy the enemy, and perhaps all organized hostility may be viewed as a theme and variation on the three elements of authority, executant, and victim.[2] We describe an experimental program, recently concluded at Yale University, in which a particular expression of this conflict is studied by experimental means.

In its most general form the problem may be defined thus: if X tells Y to hurt Z, under what conditions will Y carry out the command of X and under what conditions will he refuse. In the more limited form possible in laboratory research, the question becomes: if an experimenter tells a subject to hurt another person, under what conditions will the subject go along with this instruction, and under what conditions will he refuse to obey. The laboratory problem is not so much a dilution of the general statement as one concrete expression of the many particular forms this question may assume.

One aim of the research was to study behavior in a strong situation of deep consequence to the

[1]This research was supported by two grants from the National Science Foundation: NSF G-17916 and NSF G-24152. Exploratory studies carried out in 1960 were financed by a grant from the Higgins Funds of Yale University. I am grateful to John T. Williams, James J. McDonough, and Emil Elges for the important part they played in the project. Thanks are due also to Alan Elms, James Miller, Taketo Murata, and Stephen Stier for their aid as graduate assistants. My wife, Sasha, performed many valuable services. Finally, I owe a profound debt to the many persons in New Haven and Bridgeport who served as subjects.
[2]Consider, for example, J.P. Scott's analysis of war in his monograph on aggression:

'...while the actions of key individuals in a war may be explained in terms of direct stimulation to aggression, vast numbers of other people are involved simply by being part of an organized society.

'...For example, at the beginning of World War I an Austrian archduke was assassinated in Sarajevo. A few days later soldiers from all over Europe were marching toward each other, not because they were stimulated by the archduke's misfortune, but because they had been trained to obey orders.' (Slightly rearranged from Scott (1958), *Aggression,* p. 103.)

26
Some Conditions of Obedience and Disobedience to Authority

Stanley Milgram[1]

Reprinted with slight abridgement from *Human Relations* vol. 18, 1965, pp. 57–75.

participants, for the psychological forces operative in powerful and lifelike forms of the conflict may not be brought into play under diluted conditions.

This approach meant, first, that we had a special obligation to protect the welfare and dignity of the persons who took part in the study; subjects were, of necessity, placed in a difficult predicament, and steps had to be taken to ensure their wellbeing before they were discharged from the laboratory. Toward this end, a careful, post-experimental treatment was devised and has been carried through for subjects in all conditions.[3]

TERMINOLOGY

If Y follows the command of X we shall say that he has obeyed X; if he fails to carry out the command of X, we shall say that he has disobeyed X. The terms to obey and to disobey, as used here, refer to the subject's overt action only, and carry no implication for the motive or experiential states accompanying the action.[4]

[3]It consisted of an extended discussion with the experimenter and, of equal importance, a friendly reconciliation with the victim. It is made clear that the victim did not receive painful electric shocks. After the completion of the experimental series, subjects were sent a detailed report of the results and full purposes of the experimental program. A formal assessment of this procedure points to its overall effectiveness. Of the subjects, 83·7 per cent indicated that they were glad to have taken part in the study; 15·1 per cent reported neutral feelings; and 1·3 per cent stated that they were sorry to have participated. A large number of subjects spontaneously requested that they be used in further experimentation. Four-fifths of the subjects felt that more experiments of this sort should be carried out, and 74 per cent indicated that they had learned something of personal importance as a result of being in the study. Furthermore, a university psychiatrist, experienced in outpatient treatment, interviewed a sample of experimental subjects with the aim of uncovering possible injurious effects resulting from participation. No such effects were in evidence. Indeed, subjects typically felt that their participation was instructive and enriching. A more detailed discussion of this question can be found in Milgram (1964).

[4]To obey and to disobey are not the only terms one could use in describing the critical action of Y. One could say that Y is cooperating with X, or displays conformity with regard to X's commands. However, cooperation suggests that X agrees with Y's ends, and understands the relationship between his own behavior and the attainment of those ends. (But the experimental procedure, and, in particular, the experimenter's command that the subject shock the victim even in the absence of a response from the victim, preclude such understanding.) Moreover, cooperation implies status parity for the co-acting agents, and neglects the asymmetrical, dominance-subordination element prominent in the laboratory relationship between experimenter and subject. Conformity has been used in other important contexts in social psychology, and most frequently refers to imitating the judgements or actions of others when no explicit requirement for imitation has been made. Furthermore, in the present study there are two sources of social pressure: pressure from the experimenter issuing the commands, and pressure from the victim to stop the punishment. It is the pitting of a common man (the victim) against an authority (the experimenter) that is the distinctive feature of the conflict. At a point in the experiment the victim demands that he be let free. The exprimenter insists that the subject continue to administer shocks. Which act of the subject can be interpreted as conformity? The subject may conform to the wishes of his peer or to the wishes of the experimenter, and conformity in one direction

To be sure, the everyday use of the word obedience is not entirely free from complexities. It refers to action within widely varying situations, and connotes diverse motives within those situations: a child's obedience differs from a soldier's obedience, or the love, honor, and obey of the marriage vow. However, a consistent behavioral relationship is indicated in most uses of the term: in the act of obeying, a person does what another person tells him to do. Y obeys X if he carries out the prescription for action which X has addressed to him; the term suggests, moreover, that some form of dominance-subordination, or hierarchical element, is part of the situation in which the transaction between X and Y occurs.

A subject who complies with the entire series of experimental commands will be termed an obedient subject; one who at any point in the command series defies the experimenter will be called a disobedient or defiant subject. As used in this report, the terms refer only to the subject's performance in the experiment, and do not necessarily imply a general personality disposition to submit to or reject authority.

SUBJECT POPULATION

The subjects used in all experimental conditions were male adults, residing in the greater New Haven and Bridgeport areas, aged 20 to 50 years, and engaged in a wide variety of occupations. Each experimental condition described in this report employed 40 fresh subjects and was carefully balanced for age and occupational types. The occupational composition for each experiment was: workers, skilled and unskilled: 40 per cent; white collar, sales, business: 40 per cent; professionals: 20 per cent. The occupations were inter-

means the absence of conformity in the other. Thus the word has no useful reference in this setting, for the dual and conflicting social pressures cancel out its meaning.

In the final analysis, the linguistic symbol representing the subject's action must take its meaning from the concrete context in which that action occurs; and there is probably no word in everyday language that covers the experimental situation exactly, without omissions or irrelevant connotations. It is partly for convenience, therefore, that the terms obey and disobey are used to describe the subject's actions. At the same time, our use of the words is highly congruent with dictionary meaning.

sected with three age categories (subjects in 20s, 30s, and 40s, assigned to each condition in the proportions of 20, 40, and 40 per cent respectively).

The General Laboratory Procedure[5]

The focus of the study concerns the amount of electric shock a subject is willing to administer to another person when ordered by an experimenter to give the 'victim' increasingly more severe punishment. The act of administering shock is set in the context of a learning experiment, ostensibly designed to study the effect of punishment on memory. Aside from the experimenter, one naïve subject and one accomplice perform in each session. On arrival each subject is paid $4.50. After a general talk by the experimenter, telling how little scientists know about the effect of punishment on memory, subjects are informed that one member of the pair will serve as teacher and one as learner. A rigged drawing is held so that the naïve subject is always the teacher, and the accomplice becomes the learner. The learner is taken to an adjacent room and strapped into an 'electric chair.'

The naïve subject is told that it is his task to teach the learner a list of paired associates, to test him on the list, and to administer punishment whenever the learner errs in the test. Punishment takes the form of electric shock, delivered to the learner by means of a shock generator controlled by the naïve subject. The teacher is instructed to increase the intensity of electric shock one step on the generator on each error. The learner, according to plan, provides many wrong answers, so that before long the naïve subject must give him the strongest shock on the generator. Increases in shock level are met by increasingly insistent demands from the learner that the experiment be stopped because of the growing discomfort to him. However, in clear terms the experimenter orders the teacher to continue with the procedure in disregard of the learner's protests. *Thus, the*

naïve subject must resolve a conflict between two mutually incompatible demands from the social field. He may continue to follow the orders of the experimenter and shock the learner with increasing severity, or he may refuse to follow the orders of the experimenter and heed the learner's pleas. The experimenter's authority operates not in a free field, but against ever-mounting countervailing pressures from the person being punished.

A few technical points need to be considered before the findings of the study are described. For the purpose of delivering shock, a simulated shock generator is used, with 30 clearly marked voltage levels that range from 15 to 450 volts (and each activated by one of 30 individual lever switches set in a horizontal line). The naïve subject is given a sample shock of 45 volts to convince him of the authenticity of the instrument. The generator bears verbal designations that range from 'Slight Shock' to 'Danger: Severe Shock.'

The responses of the victim are standardized on tape, and each protest is coordinated to a particular voltage level on the shock generator. Starting with 75 volts the learner begins to grunt and moan. At 150 volts he demands to be let out of the experiment. At 180 volts he cries out that he can no longer stand the pain. At 300 volts he refuses to provide any more answers to the memory test, insisting that he is no longer a participant in the experiment and must be freed. In response to this last tactic, the experimenter instructs the naïve subject to treat the absence of an answer as equivalent to a wrong answer, and to follow the usual shock procedure. The experimenter reinforces his demand with the statement: 'You have no other choice, you must go on!' (This imperative is used whenever the naïve subject tries to break off the experiment.) If the subject refuses to give the next higher level of shock, the experiment is considered at an end. A quantitative value is assigned to the subject's performance based on the maximum intensity shock he administered before breaking off. Thus any subject's score may range from zero (for a subject unwilling to administer the first shock level) to 30 (for a subject who proceeds to the highest voltage level on the board). For any particular subject and for any particular experi-

[5]A more detailed account of the laboratory procedure can be found in Milgram (1963). A similar and independently evolved experimental procedure, employing a shock generator, victim, and learning task, was reported by Buss (1961). Buss used the technique for studying aggression, not obedience, and did not make use of the fundamental measure employed in the present study: break-off points. His investigation promises to be a useful complement to the present research.

mental condition the degree to which participants have followed the experimenter's orders may be specified with a numerical value, corresponding to the metric on the shock generator.

This laboratory situation gives us a framework in which to study the subject's reactions to the principal conflict of the experiment. Again, this conflict is between the experimenter's demands that he continue to administer the electric shock, and the learner's demands, which become increasingly more insistent, that the experiment be stopped. The crux of the study is to vary systematically the factors believed to alter the degree of obedience to the experimental commands, to learn under what conditions submission to authority is most probable, and under what conditions defiance is brought to the fore.

PILOT STUDIES

Pilot studies for the present research were completed in the winter of 1960; they differed from the regular experiments in a few details: for one, the victim was placed behind a silvered glass, with the light balance on the glass such that the victim could be dimly perceived by the subject (Milgram, 1961).

Though essentially qualitative in treatment, these studies pointed to several significant features of the experimental situation. At first no vocal feedback was used from the victim. It was thought that the verbal and voltage designations on the control panel would create sufficient pressure to curtail the subject's obedience. However, this was not the case. In the absence of protests from the learner, virtually all subjects, once commanded, went blithely to the end of the board, seemingly indifferent to the verbal designations ('Extreme Shock' and 'Danger: Severe Shock'). This deprived us of an adequate basis for scaling obedient tendencies. A force had to be introduced that would strengthen the subject's resistance to the experimenter's commands, and reveal individual differences in terms of a distribution of break-off points.

This force took the form of protests from the victim. Initially, mild protests were used, but proved inadequate. Subsequently, more vehement protests were inserted into the experimental procedure. To our consternation, even the strongest protests from the victim did not prevent all subjects from administering the harshest punishment ordered by the experimenter; but the protests did lower the mean maximum shock somewhat and created some spread in the subject's performance; therefore, the victim's cries were standardized on tape and incorporated into the regular experimental procedure.

The situation did more than highlight the technical difficulties of finding a workable experimental procedure: it indicated that subjects would obey authority to a greater extent than we had supposed. It also pointed to the importance of feedback from the victim in controlling the subject's behavior.

One further aspect of the pilot study was that subjects frequently averted their eyes from the person they were shocking, often turning their heads in an awkward and conspicuous manner. One subject explained: 'I didn't want to see the consequences of what I had done.' Observers wrote:

> ...subjects showed a reluctance to look at the victim, whom they could see through the glass in front of them. When this fact was brought to their attention they indicated that it caused them discomfort to see the victim in agony. We note, however, that although the subject refuses to look at the victim, he continues to administer shocks.

This suggested that the salience of the victim may have, in some degree, regulated the subject's performance. If, in obeying the experimenter, the subject found it necessary to avoid scrutiny of the victim, would the converse be true? If the victim were rendered increasingly more salient to the subject, would obedience diminish? The first set of regular experiments was designed to answer this question.

IMMEDIACY OF THE VICTIM

This series consisted of four experimental conditions. In each condition the victim was brought 'psychologically' closer to the subject giving him shocks.

In the first condition (Remote Feedback) the victim was placed in another room and could not be heard or seen by the subject, except that, at 300 volts, he pounded on the wall in protest. After 315 volts he no longer answered or was heard from.

The second condition (Voice Feedback) was identical to the first except that voice protests were introduced. As in the first condition the victim was placed in an adjacent room, but his complaints could be heard clearly through a door left slightly ajar, and through the walls of the laboratory.[6]

The third experimental condition (Proximity) was similar to the second, except that the victim was now placed in the same room as the subject, and 1½ feet from him. Thus he was visible as well as audible, and voice cues were provided.

The fourth, and final, condition of this series (Touch-Proximity) was identical to the third, with this exception: the victim received a shock only when his hand rested on a shockplate. At the 150-volt level the victim again demanded to be let free and, in this condition, refused to place his hand on the shockplate. The experimenter ordered the naïve subject to force the victim's hand onto the plate. Thus obedience in this condition required that the subject have physical contact with the victim in order to give him punishment beyond the 150-volt level.

Forty adult subjects were studied in each condition. The data revealed that obedience was significantly reduced as the victim was rendered more immediate to the subject. The mean maximum shock for the conditions is shown in *Figure 26.1*.

Expressed in terms of the proportion of obedient to defiant subjects, the findings are that 34 per cent of the subjects defied the experimenter in the Remote condition, 37.5 per cent in Voice Feedback, 60 per cent in Proximity, and 70 per cent in Touch-Proximity.

How are we to account for this effect? A first conjecture might be that as the victim was brought closer the subject became more aware of the in-

[6]It is difficult to convey on the printed page the full tenor of the victim's responses, for we have no adequate notation for vocal intensity, timing, and general qualities of delivery. Yet these features are crucial to producing the effect of an increasingly severe reaction to mounting voltage levels. (They can be communicated fully only by sending interested parties the recorded tapes.) In general terms, however, the victim indicates no discomfort until the 75-volt shock is administered, at which time there is a light grunt in response to the punishment. Similar reactions follow the 90- and 105-volt shocks, and at 120 volts the victim shouts to the experimenter that the shocks are becoming painful. Painful groans are heard on administration of the 135-volt shock, and at 150 volts the victim cries out, 'Experimenter, get me out of here! I won't be in the experiment any more! I refuse to go on!' Cries of this type continue with generally rising intensity, so that at 180 volts the victim cries out, 'I can't stand the pain,' and by 270 volts his response to the shock is definitely an agonized scream. Throughout, he insists that he be let out of the experiment. At 300 volts the victim shouts in desperation that he will no longer provide answers to the memory test; and at 315 volts, after a violent scream, he reaffirms with vehemence that he is no longer a participant. From this point on, he provides no answers, but shrieks in agony whenever a shock is administered; this continues through 450 volts. Of course, many subjects will have broken off before this point.

A revised and stronger set of protests was used in all experiments outside the Proximity series. Naturally, new baseline measures were established for all comparisons using the new set of protests.

There is overwhelming evidence that the great majority of subjects, both obedient and defiant, accepted the victims' reactions as genuine. The evidence takes the form of: (a) tension created in the subjects (see discussion of tension); (b) scores on 'estimated pain' scales filled out by subjects immediately after the experiment; (c) subjects' accounts of their feelings in post-experimental interviews; and (d) quantifiable responses to questionnaires distributed to subjects several months after their participation in the experiments. This matter will be treated fully in a forthcoming monograph.

(The procedure in all experimental conditions was to have the naïve subject announce the voltage level before administering each shock, so that—independently of the victim's responses—he was continually reminded of delivering punishment of ever-increasing severity.)

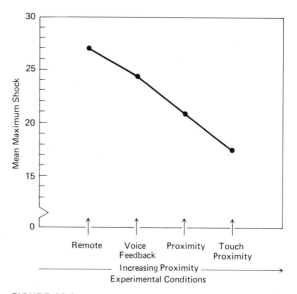

FIGURE 26.1
Mean Maxima in Proximity Series

tensity of his suffering and regulated his behavior accordingly. This makes sense, but our evidence does not support the interpretation. There are no consistent differences in the attributed level of pain across the four conditions (i.e. the amount of pain experienced by the victim as estimated by the subject and expressed on a 14-point scale). But it is easy to speculate about alternative mechanisms:

Empathic Cues

In the Remote and to a lesser extent the Voice Feedback condition, the victim's suffering possesses an abstract, remote quality for the subject. He is aware, but only in a conceptual sense, that his actions cause pain to another person; the fact is apprehended, but not felt. The phenomenon is common enough. The bombardier can reasonably suppose that his weapons will inflict suffering and death, yet this knowledge is divested of affect, and does not move him to a felt, emotional response to the suffering resulting from his actions. Similar observations have been made in wartime. It is possible that the visual cues associated with the victim's suffering trigger empathic responses in the subject and provide him with a more complete grasp of the victim's experience. Or it is possible that the empathic responses are themselves unpleasant, possessing drive properties which cause the subject to terminate the arousal situation. Diminishing obedience, then, would be explained by the enrichment of empathic cues in the successive experimental conditions.

Denial and Narrowing of the Cognitive Field

The Remote condition allows a narrowing of the cognitive field so that the victim is put out of mind. The subject no longer considers the act of depressing a lever relevant to moral judgement, for it is no longer associated with the victim's suffering. When the victim is close it is more difficult to exclude him phenomenologically. He necessarily intrudes on the subject's awareness since he is continuously visible. In the Remote conditions his existence and reactions are made known only after the shock has been administered. The auditory feedback is sporadic and discontinuous. In

the Proximity conditions his inclusion in the immediate visual field renders him a continuously salient element for the subject. The mechanism of denial can no longer be brought into play. One subject in the Remote condition said: 'It's funny how you really begin to forget that there's a guy out there, even though you can hear him. For a long time I just concentrated on pressing the switches and reading the words.'

Reciprocal Fields

If in the Proximity condition the subject is in an improved position to observe the victim, the reverse is also true. The actions of the subject now come under proximal scrutiny by the victim. Possibly, it is easier to harm a person when he is unable to observe our actions than when he can see what we are doing. His surveillance of the action directed against him may give rise to shame, or guilt, which may then serve to curtail the action. Many expressions of language refer to the discomfort or inhibitions that arise in face-to-face confrontation. It is often said that it is easier to criticize a man 'behind his back' than to 'attack him to his face.' If we are in the process of lying to a person it is reputedly difficult to 'stare him in the eye.' We 'turn away from others in shame' or in 'embarrassment' and this action serves to reduce our discomfort. The manifest function of allowing the victim of a firing squad to be blindfolded is to make the occasion less stressful for him, but it may also serve a latent function of reducing the stress of the executioner. In short, in the Proximity conditions, the subject may sense that he has become more salient in the victim's field of awareness. Possibly he becomes more self-conscious, embarrassed, and inhibited in his punishment of the victim.

Phenomenal Unity of Act

In the Remote conditions it is more difficult for the subject to gain a sense of *relatedness* between his own actions and the consequences of these actions for the victim. There is a physical and spatial separation of the act and its consequences. The subject depresses a lever in one room, and protests and cries are heard from another. The two events are in correlation, yet they lack a compelling phenomenological unity. The structure of a meaningful act—*I am hurting a man*—breaks down because of the spatial arrangements, in a manner somewhat analogous to the disappearance of phi phenomena when the blinking lights are spaced too far apart. The unity is more fully achieved in the Proximity conditions as the victim is brought closer to the action that causes him pain. It is rendered complete in Touch-Proximity.

Incipient Group Formation

Placing the victim in another room not only takes him further from the subject, but the subject and the experimenter are drawn relatively closer. There is incipient group formation between the experimenter and the subject, from which the victim is excluded. The wall between the victim and the others deprives him of an intimacy which the experimenter and subject feel. In the Remote condition, the victim is truly an outsider, who stands alone, physically and psychologically.

When the victim is placed close to the subject, it becomes easier to form an alliance with him against the experimenter. Subjects no longer have to face the experimenter alone. They have an ally who is close at hand and eager to collaborate in a revolt against the experimenter. Thus, the changing set of spatial relations leads to a potentially shifting set of alliances over the several experimental conditions.

Acquired Behavior Dispositions

It is commonly observed that laboratory mice will rarely fight with their litter mates. Scott (1958) explains this in terms of passive inhibition. He writes: 'By doing nothing under...circumstances [the animal] learns to do nothing, and this may be spoken of as passive inhibition...this principle has great importance in teaching an individual to be peaceful, for it means that he can learn not to fight simply by not fighting.' Similarly, we may learn not to harm others simply by not harming them in everyday life. Yet this learning occurs in a context of proximal relations with others, and may not be

generalized to that situation in which the person is physically removed from us. Or possibly, in the past, aggressive actions against others who were physically close resulted in retaliatory punishment which extinguished the original form of response. In contrast, aggression against others at a distance may have only sporadically led to retaliation. Thus the organism learns that it is safer to be aggressive toward others at a distance, and precarious to be so when the parties are within arm's reach. Through a pattern of rewards and punishments, he acquires a disposition to avoid aggression at close quarters, a disposition which does not extend to harming others at a distance. And this may account for experimental findings in the remote and proximal experiments.

Proximity as a variable in psychological research has received far less attention than it deserves. If men were sessile it would be easy to understand this neglect. But we move about; our spatial relations shift from one situation to the next, and the fact that we are near or remote may have a powerful effect on the psychological processes that mediate our behavior toward others. In the present situation, as the victim is brought closer to the man ordered to give him shocks, increasing numbers of subjects break off the experiment, refusing to obey. The concrete, visible, and proximal presence of the victim acts in an important way to counteract the experimenter's power and to generate disobedience.[7]

CLOSENESS OF AUTHORITY

If the spatial relationship of the subject and victim is relevant to the degree of obedience, would not the relationship of subject to experimenter also play a part?

There are reasons to feel that, on arrival, the

---

[7]Admittedly, the terms *proximity, immediacy, closeness*, and *salience-of-the-victim* are used in a loose sense, and the experiments themselves represent a very coarse treatment of the variable. Further experiments are needed to refine the notion and tease out such diverse factors as spatial distance, visibility, audibility, barrier interposition, etc.

The Proximity and Touch-Proximity experiments were the only conditions where we were unable to use taped feedback from the victim. Instead, the victim was trained to respond in these conditions as he had in Experiment 2 (which employed taped feedback). Some improvement is possible here, for it should be technically feasible to do a proximity series using taped feedback.

subject is oriented primarily to the experimenter rather than to the victim. He has come to the laboratory to fit into the structure that the experimenter—not the victim—would provide. He has come less to understand his behavior than to *reveal* that behavior to a competent scientist, and he is willing to display himself as the scientist's purposes require. Most subjects seem quite concerned about the appearance they are making before the experimenter, and one could argue that this preoccupation in a relatively new and strange setting makes the subject somewhat insensitive to the triadic nature of the social situation. In other words, the subject is so concerned about the show he is putting on for the experimenter that influences from other parts of the social field do not receive as much weight as they ordinarily would. This overdetermined orientation to the experimenter would account for the relative insensitivity of the subject to the victim, and would also lead us to believe that alterations in the relationship between subject and experimenter would have important consequences for obedience.

In a series of experiments we varied the physical closeness and degree of surveillance of the experimenter. In one condition the experimenter sat just a few feet away from the subject. In a second condition, after giving initial instructions, the experimenter left the laboratory and gave his orders by telephone; in still a third condition the experimenter was never seen, providing instructions by means of a tape recording activated when the subjects entered the laboratory.

Obedience dropped sharply as the experimenter was physically removed from the laboratory. The number of obedient subjects in the first condition (Experimenter Present) was almost three times as great as in the second, where the experimenter gave his orders by telephone. Twenty-six subjects were fully obedient in the first condition, and only 9 in the second....Subjects seemed able to take a far stronger stand against the experimenter when they did not have to encounter him face to face, and the experimenter's power over the subject was severely curtailed.[8]

[8]The third condition also led to significantly lower obedience than this first situation, in which the experimenter was present, but it contains technical difficulties that require extensive discussion.

Moreover, when the experimenter was absent, subjects displayed an interesting form of behavior that had not occurred under his surveillance. Though continuing with the experiment, several subjects administered lower shocks than were required and never informed the experimenter of their deviation from the correct procedure. (Unknown to the subjects, shock levels were automatically recorded by an Esterline-Angus event recorder wired directly into the shock generator; the instrument provided us with an objective record of the subjects' performance.) Indeed, in telephone conversations some subjects specifically assured the experimenter that they were raising the shock level according to instruction, whereas in fact they were repeatedly using the lowest shock on the board. This form of behavior is particularly interesting: although these subjects acted in a way that clearly undermined the avowed purposes of the experiment, they found it easier to handle the conflict in this manner than to precipitate an open break with authority.

Other conditions were completed in which the experimenter was absent during the first segment of the experiment, but reappeared at the point that the subject definitely refused to give higher shocks when commanded by telephone. Although he had exhausted his power via telephone, the experimenter could frequently force further obedience when he reappeared in the laboratory.

Experiments in this series show that the physical *presence* of an authority is an important force contributing to the subject's obedience or defiance. Taken together with the first experimental series on the proximity of the victim, it would appear that something akin to fields of force, diminishing in effectiveness with increasing psychological distance from their source, have a controlling effect on the subject's performance. As the victim is brought closer, the subject finds it harder to administer shocks to him. When the victim's position is held constant relative to the subject, and the authority is made more remote, the subject finds it easier to break off the experiment. This effect is substantial in both cases, but manipulation of the experimenter's position yielded the more powerful results. Obedience to destructive commands is highly dependent on the proximal relations between authority and subject.

TENSIONS

The description of final scores does not fully convey the character of the subjects' performance, and it would be useful to interrupt our reporting of quantitative relationships to remark on the subjects' general reaction to the situation.

One might suppose that a subject would simply break off or continue as his conscience and temperament dictated. Yet this is very far from what happened. There were powerful reactions of tension and emotional strain in a substantial proportion of the participants. Persons were observed to sweat, tremble, stutter, bite their lips, and groan as they found themselves increasingly implicated in the experimental conflict. Some sense of the subjects' mood can be gotten from a transcript of their remarks at break-off point. Here are the remarks of two defiant subjects:

Is he banging?...Is he hurt out there? Well, I don't want to be responsible for anything that happens to him. No, I can't go on with it. I don't know whether he's all right or not. I mean he may have a heart condition or something; I wouldn't feel right doing it. He's banging for help. He's evidently in trouble or he wouldn't bang...I don't see any sense to this—to knocking him out or something. I just can't see it.

(Subject refuses to administer shocks)
[*Subject 0108*]

The man is banging. He wants to get out...I'm sorry. If the man wants to get out I'd just as soon stop...I don't want to administer any more [extremely excited]...I will gladly refund the check, but I will not harm this man...I'm sorry, I will not give him any more if he obviously wants to get out. There is no money in the world that will make me hurt another individual. [*Subject 010X*]

And here is a transcript from an obedient subject.

He began the experiment calmly, but became increasingly tense as the experiment proceeded. After administering the 150-volt shock, he began to address the experimenter in agitated tones:

150 volts delivered. You want me to keep going?
165 volts delivered. That guy is hollering in there. There's a lot of them here. He's liable to have heart condition. You want me to go?
180 volts delivered. He can't stand it! I'm not going to kill that man in there! You hear him hollering? He's hollering. He can't stand it. What if something happens to him?...I'm not going to get that man sick in there. He's hollering in there. You know what I mean? I mean I refuse to take responsibility. He's getting hurt in there. He's in there hollering. Too many left here. Geez, if he gets them wrong. There's too many of them left. I mean who is going to take responsibility if anything happens to that gentleman?
[*The experimenter accepts responsibility.*] All right.
195 volts delivered. You see he's hollering. Hear that. Gee, I don't know. [*The experimenter says: 'The experiment requires that you go on.'*]—I know it does, sir, but I mean—hugh—he don't know what he's in for. He's up to 195 volts.
210 volts delivered
225 volts delivered
240 volts delivered. Aw, no. You mean I've got to keep going up with the scale? No sir. I'm not going to kill that man! I'm not going to give him 450 volts! [*The experimenter says: 'The experiment requires that you go on.'*]—I know it does, but that man is hollering in there, sir...

Despite his numerous, agitated objections, which were constant accompaniments to his actions, the subject unfailingly obeyed the experimenter, proceeding to the highest shock level on the generator. He displayed a curious dissociation between word and action. Although at the verbal level he had resolved not to go on, his actions were fully in accord with the experimenter's commands. This subject did not want to shock the victim, and he found it an extremely disagreeable task, but he was unable to invent a response that would free him from E's authority. Many subjects cannot find the specific verbal formula that would enable them to reject the role assigned to them by the experimenter. Perhaps our culture does not provide adequate models for disobedience.

One puzzling sign of tension was the regular occurrence of nervous laughing fits. In the first four conditions 71 of the 160 subjects showed definite signs of nervous laughter and smiling. The laughter seemed entirely out of place, even bizarre. Full-blown, uncontrollable seizures were observed for 15 of these subjects. On one occasion we observed a seizure so violently convulsive that it was necessary to call a halt to the experiment. In the post-experimental interviews subjects took pains to point out that they were not sadistic types and that the laughter did not mean they enjoyed shocking the victim.

In the interview following the experiment subjects were asked to indicate on a 14-point scale just how nervous or tense they felt at the point of maximum tension (*Figure 26.2*). The scale ranged from 'Not at all tense and nervous' to 'Extremely tense and nervous.' Self-reports of this sort are of limited precision, and at best provide only a rough indication of the subject's emotional response. Still, taking the reports for what they are worth, it can be seen that the distribution of responses spans the entire range of the scale, with the majority of subjects concentrated at the center and upper extreme. A further breakdown showed that

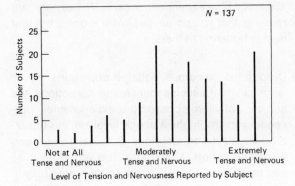

FIGURE 26.2
Level of Tension and Nervousness

obedient subjects reported themselves as having been slightly more tense and nervous than the defiant subjects at the point of maximum tension.

How is the occurrence of tension to be interpreted? First, it points to the presence of conflict. If a tendency to comply with authority were the only psychological force operating in the situation, all subjects would have continued to the end and there would have been no tension. Tension, it is assumed, results from the simultaneous presence of two or more incompatible response tendencies (Miller, 1944). If sympathetic concern for the victim were the exclusive force, all subjects would have calmly defied the experimenter. Instead, there were both obedient and defiant outcomes, frequently accompanied by extreme tension. A conflict develops between the deeply ingrained disposition not to harm others and the equally compelling tendency to obey others who are in authority. The subject is quickly drawn into a dilemma of a deeply dynamic character, and the presence of high tension points to the considerable strength of each of the antagonistic vectors.

Moreover, tension defines the strength of the aversive state from which the subject is unable to escape through disobedience. When a person is uncomfortable, tense, or stressed, he tries to take some action that will allow him to terminate this unpleasant state. Thus tension may serve as a drive that leads to escape behavior. But in the present situation, even where tension is extreme, many subjects are unable to perform the response that will bring about relief. Therefore there must be a competing drive, tendency, or inhibition that precludes activation of the disobedient response. The strength of this inhibiting factor must be of greater magnitude than the stress experienced, else the terminating act would occur. Every evidence of extreme tension is at the same time an indication of the strength of the forces that keep the subject in the situation.

Finally, tension may be taken as evidence of the reality of the situations for the subjects. Normal subjects do not tremble and sweat unless they are implicated in a deep and genuinely felt predicament.

BACKGROUND AUTHORITY

In psychophysics, animal learning, and other branches of psychology, the fact that measures are obtained at one institution rather than another is irrelevant to the interpretation of the findings, so long as the technical facilities for measurement are adequate and the operations are carried out with competence.

But it cannot be assumed that this holds true for the present study. The effectiveness of the experimenter's commands may depend in an important way on the larger institutional context in which they are issued. The experiments described thus far were conducted at Yale University, an organization which most subjects regarded with respect and sometimes awe. In post-experimental interviews several participants remarked that the locale and sponsorship of the study gave them confidence in the integrity, competence, and benign purposes of the personnel; many indicated that they would not have shocked the learner if the experiments had been done elsewhere.

This issue of background authority seemed to us important for an interpretation of the results that had been obtained thus far; moreover it is highly relevant to any comprehensive theory of human obedience. Consider, for example, how closely our compliance with the imperatives of others is tied to particular institutions and locales in our day-to-day activities. On request, we expose our throats to a man with a razor blade in the barber shop, but would not do so in a shoe store; in the latter setting we willingly follow the clerk's request to stand in our stockinged feet, but resist the command in a bank. In the laboratory of a great university, subjects may comply with a set of commands that would be resisted if given elsewhere. *One must always question the relationship of obedience to a person's sense of the context in which he is operating.*

To explore the problem we moved our apparatus to an office building in industrial Bridgeport and replicated experimental conditions, without any visible tie to the university.

Bridgeport subjects were invited to the experiment through a mail circular similar to the one used in the Yale study, with appropriate changes in letterhead, etc. As in the earlier study, subjects were paid $4.50 for coming to the laboratory. The same age and occupational distributions used at Yale, and the identical personnel, were employed.

The purpose in relocating in Bridgeport was to assure a complete dissociation from Yale, and in this regard we were fully successful. On the surface, the study appeared to be conducted by RESEARCH ASSOCIATES OF BRIDGEPORT, an organization of unknown character (the title had been concocted exclusively for use in this study).

The experiments were conducted in a three-room office suite in a somewhat run-down commercial building located in the downtown shopping area. The laboratory was sparsely furnished, though clean, and marginally respectable in appearance. When subjects inquired about professional affiliations, they were informed only that we were a private firm conducting research for industry.

Some subjects displayed skepticism concerning the motives of the Bridgeport experimenter. One gentleman gave us a written account of the thoughts he experienced at the control board:

...Should I quit this damn test? Maybe he passed out? What dopes we were not to check up on this deal. How do we know that these guys are legit? No furniture, bare walls, no telephone. We could of called the Police up or the Better Business Bureau. I learned a lesson tonight. How do I know that Mr. Williams [the experimenter] is telling the truth...I wish I knew how many volts a person could take before lapsing into unconsciousness...

[*Subject 2414*]

Another subject stated:

I questioned on my arrival my own judgment [about coming]. I had doubts as to the legitimacy of the operation and the consequences of participation. I felt it was a heartless way to conduct memory or learning processes on human beings and certainly dangerous without the presence of a medical doctor.

[*Subject 2440 V*]

There was no noticeable reduction in tension for the Bridgeport subjects. And the subjects' estimation of the amount of pain felt by the victim was slightly, though not significantly, higher than in the Yale study.

A failure to obtain complete obedience in Bridgeport would indicate that the extreme compliance found in New Haven subjects was tied closely to the background authority of Yale University; if a large proportion of the subjects remained fully obedient, very different conclusions would be called for.

As it turned out, the level of obedience in Bridgeport, although somewhat reduced, was not significantly lower than that obtained at Yale. A large proportion of the Bridgeport subjects were fully obedient to the experimenter's commands (48 per cent of the Bridgeport subjects delivered the maximum shock *vs.* 65 per cent in the corresponding condition at Yale).

How are these findings to be interpreted? It is possible that if commands of a potentially harmful or destructive sort are to be perceived as legitimate they must occur within some sort of institutional structure. But it is clear from the study that it need not be a particularly reputable or distinguished institution. The Bridgeport experiments were conducted by an unimpressive firm lacking any credentials; the laboratory was set up in a respectable office building with title listed in the building directory. Beyond that, there was no evidence of benevolence or competence. It is possible that the *category* of institution, judged according to its professed function, rather than its qualitative position within that category, wins our compliance. Persons deposit money in elegant, but also in seedy-looking banks, without giving much thought to the differences in security they offer. Similarly, our subjects may consider one laboratory to be as competent as another, so long as it *is* a scientific laboratory.

It would be valuable to study the subjects' performance in other contexts which go even further than the Bridgeport study in denying institutional support to the experimenter. It is possible that, beyond a certain point, obedience disappears completely. But that point had not been reached in the Bridgeport office: almost half the subjects obeyed the experimenter fully.

FURTHER EXPERIMENTS

We may mention briefly some additional experiments undertaken in the Yale series. A considerable amount of obedience and defiance in everyday life occurs in connexion with groups. And we had reason to feel in the light of many group studies already done in psychology that group forces would have a profound effect on reactions to authority. A series of experiments was run to examine these effects. In all cases only one naïve subject was studied per hour, but he performed in the midst of actors who, unknown to him, were employed by the experimenter. In one experiment (Groups for Disobedience) two actors broke off in the middle of the experiment. When this happened 90 per cent of the subjects followed suit and defied the experimenter. In another condition the actors followed the orders obediently; this strengthened the experimenter's power only slightly. In still a third experiment the job of pushing the switch to shock the learner was given to one of the actors, while the naïve subject performed a subsidiary act. We wanted to see how the teacher would respond if he were involved in the situation but did not actually give the shocks. In this situation only three subjects out of forty broke off. In a final group experiment the subjects themselves determined the shock level they were going to use. Two actors suggested higher and higher shock levels; some subjects insisted, despite group pressure, that the shock level be kept low; others followed along with the group.

Further experiments were completed using women as subjects, as well as a set dealing with the effects of dual, unsanctioned, and conflicting authority. A final experiment concerned the personal relationship between victim and subject. These will have to be described elsewhere, lest the present report be extended to monographic length.

It goes without saying that future research can

proceed in many different directions. What kinds of response from the victim are most effective in causing disobedience in the subject? Perhaps passive resistance is more effective than vehement protest. What conditions of entry into an authority system lead to greater or lesser obedience? What is the effect of anonymity and masking on the subject's behavior? What conditions lead to the subject's perception of responsibility for his own actions? Each of these could be a major research topic in itself, and can readily be incorporated into the general experimental procedure described here.

LEVELS OF OBEDIENCE AND DEFIANCE

One general finding that merits attention is the high level of obedience manifested in the experimental situation. Subjects often expressed deep disapproval of shocking a man in the face of his objections, and others denounced it as senseless and stupid. Yet many subjects complied even while they protested. The proportion of obedient subjects greatly exceeded the expectations of the experimenter and his colleagues. At the outset, we had conjectured that subjects would not, in general, go above the level of 'Strong Shock'. In practice, many subjects were willing to administer the most extreme shocks available when commanded by the experimenter. For some subjects the experiment provides an occasion for aggressive release. And for others it demonstrates the extent to which obedient dispositions are deeply ingrained, and are engaged irrespective of their consequences for others. Yet this is not the whole story. Somehow, the subject becomes implicated in a situation from which he cannot disengage himself.

The departure of the experimental results from intelligent expectation, to some extent, has been formalized. The procedure was to describe the experimental situation in concrete detail to a group of competent persons, and to ask them to predict the performance of 100 hypothetical subjects. For purposes of indicating the distribution of break-off points judges were provided with a diagram of the shock generator, and recorded their predictions before being informed of the actual results. Judges typically underestimated the amount of obedience demonstrated by subjects.

In *Figure 26.3*, we compare the predictions of forty psychiatrists at a leading medical school with the actual performance of subjects in the experiment. The psychiatrists predicted that most subjects would not go beyond the tenth shock level (150 volts; at this point the victim makes his first explicit demand to be freed). They further predicted that by the twentieth shock level (300 volts; the victim refuses to answer) 3·73 per cent of the subjects would still be obedient; and that only a little over one-tenth of one per cent of the subjects would administer the highest shock on the board. But, as the graph indicates, the obtained behavior was very different. Sixty-two per cent of the subjects obeyed the experimenter's commands fully. Between expectation and occurrence there is a whopping discrepancy.

Why did the psychiatrists underestimate the level of obedience? Possibly, because their predictions were based on an inadequate conception of the determinants of human action, a conception that focuses on motives *in vacuo*. This orientation may be entirely adequate for the repair of bruised impulses as revealed on the psychiatrist's couch, but as soon as our interest turns to action in larger settings, attention must be paid to the situations in

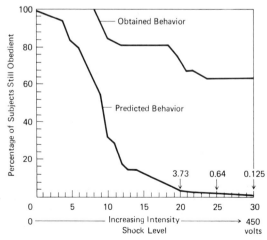

FIGURE 26.3
Predicted and Obtained Behavior in Voice Feedback

which motives are expressed. A situation exerts an important press on the individual. It exercises constraints and may provide push. In certain circumstances it is not so much the kind of person a man is, as the kind of situation in which he is placed, that determines his actions.

Many people, not knowing much about the experiment, claim that subjects who go to the end of the board are sadistic. Nothing could be more foolish as an overall characterization of these persons. It is like saying that a person thrown into a swift-flowing stream is necessarily a fast swimmer, or that he has great stamina because he moves so rapidly relative to the bank. The context of action must always be considered. The individual, upon entering the laboratory, becomes integrated into a situation that carries its own momentum. The subject's problem then is how to become disengaged from a situation which is moving in an altogether ugly direction.

The fact that disengagement is so difficult testifies to the potency of the forces that keep the subject at the control board. Are these forces to be conceptualized as individual motives and expressed in the language of personality dynamics, or are they to be seen as the effects of social structure and pressures arising from the situational field?

A full understanding of the subject's action will, I feel, require that both perspectives be adopted. The person brings to the laboratory enduring dispositions toward authority and aggression, and at the same time he becomes enmeshed in a social structure that is no less an objective fact of the case. From the standpoint of personality theory one may ask: What mechanisms of personality enable a person to transfer responsibility to authority? What are the motives underlying obedient and disobedient performance? Does orientation to authority lead to a short-circuiting of the shame-guilt system? What cognitive and emotional defenses are brought into play in the case of obedient and defiant subjects?

The present experiments are not, however, directed toward an exploration of the motives engaged when the subject obeys the experimenter's commands. Instead, they examine the situational variables responsible for the elicitation of obedience. Elsewhere, we have attempted to spell out some of the structural properties of the experimental situation that account for high obedience, and this analysis need not be repeated here (Milgram, 1963). The experimental variations themselves represent our attempt to probe that structure, by systematically changing it and noting the consequences for behavior. It is clear that some situations produce greater compliance with the experimenter's commands than others. However, this does not necessarily imply an increase or decrease in the strength of any single definable motive. Situations producing the greatest obedience could do so by triggering the most powerful, yet perhaps the most idiosyncratic, of motives in each subject confronted by the setting. Or they may simply recruit a greater number and variety of motives in their service. But whatever the motives involved—and it is far from certain that they can ever be known—action may be studied as a direct function of the situation in which it occurs. This has been the approach of the present study, where we sought to plot behavioral regularities against manipulated properties of the social field. Ultimately, social psychology would like to have a compelling *theory of situations* which will, first, present a language in terms of which situations can be defined; proceed to a typology of situations; and then point to the manner in which definable properties of situations are transformed into psychological forces in the individual.[9]

POSTSCRIPT

Almost a thousand adults were individually studied in the obedience research, and there were many specific conclusions regarding the variables that control obedience and disobedience to authority. Some of these have been discussed briefly in the preceding sections, and more detailed reports will be released subsequently.

There are now some other generalizations I should like to make, which do not derive in any

[9]My thanks to Professor Howard Leventhal of Yale for strengthening the writing in this paragraph.

strictly logical fashion from the experiments as carried out, but which, I feel, ought to be made. They are formulations of an intuitive sort that have been forced on me by observation of many subjects responding to the pressures of authority. The assertions represent a painful alteration in my own thinking; and since they were acquired only under the repeated impact of direct observation, I have no illusion that they will be generally accepted by persons who have not had the same experience.

With numbing regularity good people were seen to knuckle under the demands of authority and perform actions that were callous and severe. Men who are in everyday life responsible and decent were seduced by the trappings of authority, by the control of their perceptions, and by the uncritical acceptance of the experimenter's definition of the situation, into performing harsh acts.

What is the limit of such obedience? At many points we attempted to establish a boundary. Cries from the victim were inserted; not good enough. The victim claimed heart trouble; subjects still shocked him on command. The victim pleaded that he be let free, and his answers no longer registered on the signal box; subjects continued to shock him. At the outset we had not conceived that such drastic procedures would be needed to generate disobedience, and each step was added only as the ineffectiveness of the earlier techniques became clear. The final effort to establish a limit was the Touch-Proximity condition. But the very first subject in this condition subdued the victim on command, and proceeded to the highest shock level. A quarter of the subjects in this condition performed similarly.

The results, as seen and felt in the laboratory, are to this author disturbing. They raise the possibility that human nature, or—more specifically—the kind of character produced in American democratic society, cannot be counted on to insulate its citizens from brutality and inhumane treatment at the direction of malevolent authority. A substantial proportion of people do what they are told to do, irrespective of the content of the act and without limitations of conscience, so long as they perceive that the command comes from a legitimate authority. If in this study an anonymous experimenter could successfully command adults to subdue a fifty-year-old man, and force on him painful electric shocks against his protests, one can only wonder what government, with its vastly greater authority and prestige, can command of its subjects. There is, of course, the extremely important question of whether malevolent political institutions could or would arise in American society. The present research contributes nothing to this issue.

In an article titled 'The Dangers of Obedience', Harold J. Laski wrote:

'...civilization means, above all, an unwillingness to inflict unnecessary pain. Within the ambit of that definition, those of us who heedlessly accept the commands of authority cannot yet claim to be civilized men.

'...Our business, if we desire to live a life, not utterly devoid of meaning and significance, is to accept nothing which contradicts our basic experience merely because it comes to us from tradition or convention or authority. It may well be that we shall be wrong; but our self-expression is thwarted at the root unless the certainties we are asked to accept coincide with the certainties we experience. That is why the condition of freedom in any state is always a widespread and consistent skepticism of the canons upon which power insists.'

REFERENCES

Buss, Arnold H. (1961). *The psychology of aggression.* New York and London: John Wiley.

Kierkegaard, S. (1843). *Fear and trembling.* English edition, Princeton: Princeton University Press, 1941.

Laski, Harold J. (1929). The dangers of obedience. *Harper's Monthly Magazine* **159,** June, 1–10.

Milgram, S. (1961). Dynamics of obedience: experiments in social psychology. Mimeographed report, *National Science Foundation,* January 25.

Milgram, S. (1963). Behavioral study of obedience. *J. abnorm. soc. Psychol.* **67,** 371–8.

Milgram, S. (1964). Issues in the study of obedience: a reply to Baumrind. *Amer. Psychol.* **19**, 848–52.

Miller, N.E. (1944). Experimental studies of conflict. In J. McV. Hunt (Ed.), *Personality and the behavior disorders*. New York: Ronald Press.

Scott, J.P. (1958). *Aggression*. Chicago: University of Chicago Press.

In this incredible era in which Western society has achieved a level of technological efficiency that enables us to kill and destroy masses of people with relative ease, one of the most disturbing questions facing us is how to prevent human aggression from threatening man's survival. Marshall F. Gilula and David N. Daniels explore the plausible roots of human aggression and the principal maladaptive consequences of violence in this technological age. Is violence unique to this time and place? No, but aggression is multidetermined, and at least some aspect of it may indeed be inherent in man. This native capacity for violent aggression, the authors argue, keeps us from adapting to our environment. Our failure to recognize that our anachronistic, violent style of coping with problems may ultimately destroy us all. This is the major obstacle in the way of removing violence from our society.

Violence threatens our very being, but a no less disquieting problem is the fantastic growth in population around the world. John B. Calhoun is perhaps best known to psychologists for his dramatic studies of population density and social pathology. In a now-classic study in which a population of laboratory rats was allowed to increase in density in a confined space, Calhoun discovered that the animals developed acutely pathological patterns of behavior. As the population grew, increasingly more female rats began to exhibit a typically male aggressiveness outside the sheltered living space; greater numbers of these females lost the capacity for nest-building; and fewer matured into adulthood with normal pregnancies. At the maximum attained density, few of the weaker males survived; and among those that did, there was a marked loss in the potentiality for engaging in normal reproduction and aggression.[1] In his provocative essay, Calhoun speculates on the frightening implications for future generations of analagous increases in human population.

[1] J.B. Calhoun, "Population Density and Social Pathology," *Scientific American*, vol. 206, no. 2, 1962, pp. 139–148; J.B. Calhoun, "Control of Population: Numbers," URBSDOC Report 157, Unit for Research on Behavioral Systems (Bethesda, Maryland: National Institute of Mental Health), January 21, 1970.

Part XIII

VIOLENCE AND OVERPOPULATION— TWO URGENT CONCERNS

The need is not really for more brains, the need is now for a gentler, a more tolerant people than those who won for us against the ice, the tiger, and the bear (1).

> Violence waits in the dusty sunlight of a tenement yard and in the shadows of a distraught mind. Violence draws nearer in the shouts of a protest march and in ghetto rumblings. Violence erupts from Mace-sprinkled billy clubs and a homemade Molotov cocktail. Violence of war explodes the peace it promises to bring. Hourly reports of violence bring numbness, shock, confusion, sorrow. We live in a violent world (2).

Violence surrounds us, and we must try to understand it in the hopes of finding alternatives that will meet today's demand for change. Do we benefit from violence? Or is violence losing whatever adaptive value it may once have had? We present two theses. (i) Violence can best be understood in the context of adaptation. Violence is part of a struggle to resolve stressful and threatening events—a struggle to adapt. (ii) Adaptive alternatives to violence are needed in this technological era because the survival value of violent aggression is diminishing rapidly.

The shock of Robert F. Kennedy's death prompted the formation of a committee on violence (3) in the Department of Psychiatry, Stanford University School of Medicine. We committee members reviewed the literature on violence and then interpreted this literature from the point of view of psychiatrists and psychologists. We discussed our readings in seminars and sought answers to our questions about violence. This article presents a synthesis of our group's findings and observations and reflects our view of adaptation theory as a unifying principle in human behavior.

We define pertinent terms and describe the adaptation process before we examine violence as it relates to individual coping behavior and collective survival. We then describe three theories of aggression and relate them to adaptation. Next,

27
Violence and Man's Struggle to Adapt

Marshall F. Gilula and David N. Daniels

we discuss relevant examples of violence as attempted coping behavior and factors that foster violence and illustrate the urgent need for other ways of expressing aggression. Finally, we consider the changing nature of adaptation and suggest ways of coping with violence.

DEFINITION OF TERMS

Two groups of terms require definition: (i) aggression and violence; and (ii) adaptation, adjustment, and coping. We found that these terms have quite different meanings for different disciplines.

We here define aggression (4, 5) as the entire spectrum of assertive, intrusive, and attacking behaviors. Aggression thus includes both overt and covert attacks, such defamatory acts as sarcasm, self-directed attacks, and dominance behavior. We extend aggression to include such assertive behaviors as forceful and determined attempts to master a task or accomplish an act. We choose a broad definition of aggression rather than a restrictive one because relations between the underlying physiological mechanisms and the social correlates of dominant, assertive, and violent behavior are still poorly understood. Hence, our definition encompasses but is broader than the definition of aggression in animals that is used in experimental biology (6, 7), which says that an animal acts aggressively when he inflicts, attempts to inflict, or threatens to inflict damage upon another animal. Violence (4) is destructive aggression and involves inflicting physical damage on persons or property (since property is so often symbolically equated with the self). Violent inflicting of damage is often intense, uncontrolled, excessive, furious, sudden, or seemingly purposeless. Furthermore, violence may be collective or individual, intentional or unintentional, apparently just or unjust.

By adaptation we mean the behavioral and biological fit between the species and the environment resulting from the process of natural selection (8, 9). In man, adaptation increasingly involves modifying the environment as well. Here we want to stress that behavior, especially group-living behavior in higher social species like man, is a crucial element in natural selection (10). Adaptive behaviors are those that enhance species survival and, in most instances, individual survival. In contrast, we define adjustment as behavior of a group or individual that temporarily enhances the way we fit with the immediate situation. By definition, adjustment is often a passive rather than active process and does not result in an enduring alteration of behavior structure or patterns (4, 11). In fact, adjustment may have biologically maladaptive consequences in the long run. In addition, rapid environmental change or extraordinary environmental circumstances may render formerly adaptive behaviors largely maladaptive (10), that is, behaviors appropriate to past environmental conditions can work against survival in "new" or unusual environments.

We define coping as the continuing and usually successful struggle to accomplish tasks and goals with adaptive consequences. Put another way: "Behavior may be considered to serve coping functions when it increases the likelihood (from a specified vantage point with respect to a specified time unit) that a task will be accomplished according to standards that are tolerable both to the individual and to the group in which he lives" (12). Whereas each specific sequence of task-oriented behaviors may or may not have adaptive value, coping taken as a whole is an adaptive rather than adjustive human process.

DEFINITION OF HUMAN ADAPTATION

Every culture prescribes the range of coping behaviors available to its people, but within this range individual adaptive behavior is forged and tested in times of stress. Stressful or new situations paradoxically offer us both the danger of failure and the opportunity for learning. Stress can be dangerous when it overwhelms the individual or group. Either the situation itself or unpleasant feelings about the situation (including massive anxiety) may block our usual resources and prevent problem solving, and aggressive reactions that are both indiscriminate and protective may occur. We may show primitive forms of behavior: passive adjustment, withdrawal, falsely blaming others, indiscriminate rage, violence, or confusion.

Alternately, stressful events provide a constructive challenge and expanded opportunity for learning. In a stressful situation that is not overwhelming, we seek information helpful in dealing with the situation and try to apply this information (13). From information seeking and subsequent exploratory behavior come not only greater use of information and eventual mastery of new situations, but also a sense of heightened self-awareness, enhanced coping skills, and personal growth.

A number of commonly occurring stressful life situations that may challenge and develop our coping skills have been recognized (13). These are associated with the transitions in life and include adolescence, separation from parents, and marriage. Other challenging transitions involve cultural stresses, such as war and the threat of war; rapid technological change; and physical events, such as drought, earthquakes, and famine. These transition points in life are important because they provide opportunity for learning and developing more sophisticated ways of coping with problems.

We have marvelous adaptive abilities for coping with varying, even extreme, situations. These abilities result from cultural evolution interacting with our biological evolution. Culturally we survive through complex communal living. Through our living groups we obtain satisfaction, develop identity, and find meaning to life. Basic social values are of special cultural importance, for they determine the limits of acceptable behavior, especially during times of stress. Biologically we are uniquely endowed for complex communal living. Such biological characteristics as aggression, the upright posture, prehension, speech, prolonged infancy and maturation, and profound development of the brain—all favor and allow for rich, dynamic, and complex living. Development of the cerebral hemispheres has played an especially important role in adaptation, for the cerebrum constitutes the biological basis of higher intelli-

gence, self-awareness, complex language, and flexibility (8).

Thus through the interaction of biological evolution and cultural evolution, we have the equipment for adapting to and molding diverse environments. But this ability to adapt by manipulating the environment is now our cause for greatest concern, for in changing the environment, man changes the conditions necessary for his survival. We now are seeing an unprecedented acceleration of various man-made changes which call for accompanying changes in man, changes which we are having difficulty in making. While biological change is extremely slow, cultural change theoretically occurs at least every generation, although some aspects of culture (such as technology) change faster than others (for example, beliefs and customs). The term "generation gap" not only describes how we today view the battle of the generations but also alludes to the speed of cultural change and how people have trouble keeping pace. Living in the electronic age, we watch televised accounts of preagricultural-age violence and feel our industrial-age mentality straining to cope with the environment.

Since survival results from the long-range adaptiveness of our behavior, knowledge of adaptive mechanisms is important for understanding the role of violence in human behavior and survival. In the section that follows we shall relate three theories of aggression to adaptation.

ADAPTATION AND THEORIES OF AGGRESSION

Aggression has helped man survive. Aggression in man—including behaviors that are assertive, intrusive, and dominant as well as violent—is fundamental and adaptive. Violence is not a result of aggresssion but simply a form of aggression. Nor is all violence necessarily motivated by destructive aggression. For instance, in the sadistic behavior of sexual assaults, violence is evoked in part by sexual motives. In other instances, violence can occur accidentally or without conscious intent, as in many auto accidents. Currently there are three main views of aggression—all involving adaptation—but each suggests a different solution to the problem of violent behavior. Broadly labeled, these theories are (i) the biological-instinctual theory, (ii) the frustration theory, and (iii) the social-learning theory.

1) *The biological-instinctual theory* (14–16) holds that aggressive behavior, including violence, is an intrinsic component of man resulting from natural selection: Man is naturally aggressive. It is hard to imagine the survival of man without aggressiveness, namely because aggression is an element of all purposeful behavior and, in many cases, provides the drive for a particular action. This theory says that aggression includes a wide variety of behaviors, many of which are constructive and essential to an active existence. Stimulus-seeking behavior (for example, curiosity or the need to have something happen) is certainly at least as important a facet of human behavior as avoidance behavior and need-satisfaction. Seeking the novel and unexpected provides much of life's color and excitement. Aggression can supply much of the force and power for man's creative potential.

Psychiatric and psychoanalytic case studies are one source of evidence supporting this theory (14–17). Examples range from individuals with destructive antisocial behavior who express violent aggression directly and often impulsively, to cases of depression and suicide in which violent aggression is turned against the self, and to seriously inhibited persons for whom the expression of aggression, even in the form of assertion, is blocked almost entirely. Psychiatrists and other mental-health professionals describe many disordered behaviors as stemming from ramifications and distortions of the aggressive drive (14).

Animal studies (6, 15, 18) (including primate field studies), studies of brain-damaged humans, and male-female comparisons provide behavioral, anatomical, and hormonal data illustrating the human predisposition to aggression. Among non-human mammals, intraspecies violence occurs less frequently than with humans (7). When violent aggressive behaviors do occur among members of the same species, they serve the valuable func-tions of spacing the population over the available land and maintaining a dominance order among the group members. Uncontrolled aggression in animals generally occurs only under conditions of overcrowding. Aggression in humans, even in the form of violence, has had similar adaptive value historically.

The biological-instinctual theory suggests that since aggression is inevitable, effective controls upon its expression are necessary, and reduction of violence depends upon providing constructive channels for expressing aggression.

2) *The frustration theory* (19) states that aggressive behavior comes from interfering with ongoing purposeful activity. A person feels frustrated when a violation of his hopes or expectations occurs, and he then tries to solve the problem by behaving aggressively. Frustrations can take various forms: threats to life, thwarting of basic needs, and personal insults. This theory often equates aggression with destructive or damaging violent behavior. Major factors influencing aggressive responses to frustration are the nature of the frustration, previous experience, available alternatives for reaction (aggression is by no means the only response to frustration), the person's maturity, and the preceding events or feelings. Even boredom may provoke an aggressive response. As a response to frustration, aggression is often viewed as a learned rather than an innate behavior. According to this theory, frustration-evoked aggression aims at removing obstacles to our goals; hence the frustration theory also ties in with adaptation. The aggressive response to frustration often is a form of coping behavior that may have not only adjustive but also long-range consequences.

The frustration theory suggests that control or reduction of violence requires reducing existing frustrations as well as encouraging constructive redirection of aggressive responses to frustration. This reduction includes removing or improving frustrating environmental factors that stand between personal needs and environmental demands. Such factors include violation of human rights, economic deprivation, and various social stresses.

3) *The social-learning theory* (20) states that

aggressive behavior results from child-rearing practices and other forms of socialization. Documentation comes from sociological and anthropological studies and from observing social learning in children. Aggressive behavior can be acquired merely by watching and learning—often by imitation—and does not require frustration. Aggressive behaviors rewarded by a particular culture or subculture usually reflect the basic values and adaptive behaviors of the group. In American culture, where achievement, self-reliance, and individual self-interest are valued highly, we also find a relatively high emphasis on military glory, a relatively high incidence of personal crime, and a society characterized by a relatively high degree of bellicosity. Similar patterns occur in other cultures. From this theory we infer that as long as a nation values and accepts violence as an effective coping strategy, violent behavior will continue.

The social-learning theory of aggression suggests that control and reduction of violence require changes in cultural traditions, child-rearing practices, and parental examples. Parents who violently punish children for violent acts are teaching their children how and in what circumstances violence can be performed with impunity. Other changes in cultural traditions would emphasize prevention rather than punishment of violent acts and, equally important, would emphasize human rights and group effort rather than excessive and isolated self-reliance. The first step toward making the changes that will reduce violence is to examine our values. We must decide which values foster violence and then begin the difficult job of altering basic values.

In reality, the three theories of aggression are interrelated. Proclivities for social learning and for frustration often have a biological determinant. For example, the biology of sex influences the learning of courting behavior. Regarding violence, from these theories of aggression we see that the many expressions of violence include man's inherent aggression, aggressive responses to thwarted goals, and behavior patterns imitatively learned within the cultural setting. All three theories of aggression and violence fit into the adaptation-coping explanation. Violence is an attempt to cope with stressful situations and to resolve intolerable conflicts. Violence may have short-run adjustive value, even when the long-run adaptive consequences may in fact be adverse. It is the sometimes conflicting natures of adjustment and adaptation that are confusing and insufficiently appreciated. In some instances violence emerges when other more constructive coping strategies have failed. In other instances violence is used to enhance survival. Our species apparently has overabsorbed violence into our cultures as a survival technique. Children and adolescents have learned well the accepted violent behaviors of their elders.

All three theories help us understand violent behavior and hence suggest potential ways of reducing violence. In the following sections we consider current examples of violence from the persepective of those factors in our society that foster violence and from the standpoint of how these examples reflect the changing nature of adaptation.

PHENOMENON OF PRESIDENTIAL ASSASSINATION

Assassination is not an isolated historical quirk, eluding comprehension or analysis. The event is usually overdetermined by multiple but equally important factors: personal qualities of the assassin, a fatalistic posture assumed by the victim, and such factors in the social environment as political stereotypes, murder sanctions, and the symbolic nature of high offices.

Although assassination can strike down anyone, we have restricted our examination to assassination of presidents in America (21) by studying the personal qualities of "successful" assassins and of others who almost succeeded. Of the eight assassination attempts on American presidents, four have been successful. The following facts emerge. (i) All the assassination attempts were made with guns, all but one with pistols. (ii) All the assassins were shorter and weighed less than average men of the period. (iii) All the assassins were young adult Caucasian males. (iv) All the assassination attempts but one were made by individuals who were seriously disturbed or even paranoid schizophrenics (22). The exception was the final attempt of two Puerto Rican nationalists to kill President Harry S Truman. The successful assassins, for the most part, were mentally unbalanced and had persecutory and grandiose delusions.

Assassination provides a method for instantly satisfying a need for personal importance. The delusional assassin very probably had a fantasy that once the act was committed, an outcry of favorable opinion and acclaim would vindicate what he had done. In most of the instances of attempted or successful assassination, escape plans were inadequate or nonexistent.

The life pattern of most of the assassins included extreme resentment toward others—a resentment aggravated by a long history of isolation and loneliness. Often the isolation stemmed from poor and inconsistent relations with parents and others early in life, which resulted in most of the assassins having resentment and mistrust of parental figures. Their resentment toward parental figures might have included the President (political symbol of parenthood) as the head of the federal government. In response to imagined unfair treatment from others and a distortion of his own inadequacies, the assassin turned his anger on the chief of state.

Typically the assassin had struggled for importance, success, and manliness, but had failed. At the time of the attempted presidential assassination, the assassin was on a downward life course. Haunted by resentment and failure and plagued with disordered thinking and distortions of reality, the assassin took action. Shooting the President was thus an attempt to resolve conflicts with which he apparently could not otherwise cope. Providing an alternate outlet for his violent dissatisfaction would be one way of preventing the potential assassin from killing. Perhaps the ombudsman (public complaint receiver) system would allow the would-be assassin to voice his grievances against his intended victim, thereby lessening his pent-up frustrations and reducing the likelihood that he would kill.

Our discussion of another important determinant of assassination—the victim's fatalistic attitude—is not restricted to presidential assassinations. The fatalistic thinking and actions of several assassination victims are reflected in their strong disinclination toward taking precautionary measures despite recognizing the existence of violent impulses in others toward presidents and presidential candidates. Robert Kennedy stated a view that he shared with Abraham Lincoln, Martin Luther King, Jr., and John F. Kennedy: "There's no sense in worrying about those things. If they want you, they can get you" (23). This attitude often leads to dangerous negligence that is an exaggerated form of denying that one is actually afraid of physical harm. Lincoln has been described as "downright reckless" (24) about personal safety. Robert Kennedy was quoted as saying, "I'll tell you one thing: If I'm President, you won't find me riding around in any of those awful [bullet-proof] cars" (23). The fatalistic attitude illustrated by statements like this is encouraged by our tradition of expecting physical courage in our leaders. Men who repeatedly and publicly proclaim their vulnerability may be unwittingly encouraging assassination by offering an invitation to the delusional, grandiose, and isolated person who dreams of accomplishing at least one important and publicly recognized act in his life. "Mixing with the people" is firmly embedded in the American political tradition, but it is also an accomplice to assassination. One way to cope with this problem would be legislation to restrict the contact and exposure of a President with crowds when his presence has been announced in advance.

MASS MEDIA AND VIOLENCE

Television could be one of our most powerful tools for dealing with today's violence. It could provide education and encourage, if not induce, desired culture modification. Unfortunately, it does little of either today, perhaps because the harmful effects of televised violence have been glossed over. However, all the mass media do little to discourage and much to encourage violence in America. The Ugly American as a national stereotype is rapidly being displaced in the eyes of the world by the Violent American, his brother of late.

This stereotype is fostered by the media but is sustained by the violent acts of some of our citizens. Armed with shotgun, ignorance, frustrations, or hunger, this Violent American can be seen today throughout our society. We are not all violent Americans, but mass media are giving us the violence we seem to want.

What effect do the mass media have (25)? All of us are probably affected by the media to some degree, but most research has focused on children, since an immature and developing mind is usually less capable of discrimination when responding to a given stimulus. One comprehensive review (26) described short-term effects that include the child's emotional reactions to what he views, reads, and hears. Long-term effects, what the child actually learns as a result of his exposure, may include vocabulary, factual information, belief systems, and such altered personality characteristics as increased aggressiveness. No one selects all the media materials available, nor does anyone absorb or retain the selected materials consistently or completely. Prior information, differing needs, and quality of life adjustment also help to filter the child's processing of the offered materials. Mass media effects also depend somewhat on the applicability of the learned material to the child's own life situation.

Similarly, as shown by another researcher (27), frustration, the anger evoked by it, the overall situation, the apparent severity and justification of the violence viewed in a film—all relate to whether or not children use these aggressive responses.

A large study in Great Britain (28) showed that certain portrayals of violence are more disturbing to children than others. Unusual motives, settings, and weapons are more disturbing than stereotyped violence. For example, knives or daggers are more upsetting than guns or fist fights. Similarly, seeing violence or disasters in newsreels bothered children more than dramatized violence.

Another study (29) found that the average American child from 3 through 16 years old spends more of his waking hours watching television than attending school. First-graders spend 40 percent and sixth-graders spend 80 percent of their viewing time watching "adult" programs, with Westerns and situation comedies being most popular. By the eighth grade, children favor crime programs.

Can we justifiably say that the media teach violence? Television teaches more than vocabulary and factual information to the impressionable young viewer, who learns by identification and social imitation. Learning theorists have shown that children readily mimic the aggressive behavior of adults and that the degree of imitation is comparable whether the behavior is live or televised. In another study (30) nursery school children watched a film of adults aggressively hitting an inflatable plastic figure, a Bobo doll. Later these and other children were first mildly frustrated and then led individually into a room in which they found the Bobo doll and other materials not shown in the film. Those who had seen the film imitated precisely the film's physical and verbal aggression and made more aggressive use of other toys, such as guns, that had not been in the film. Film-watchers showed twice as much aggressiveness as those who had not seen the film.

These children were all from a "normal" nursery school population, and all showed some effect. This finding seriously questions the claim that such violence is learned only by deviant individuals. The findings apply equally to real, fictional, and fantasy violence. The impact on children observing aggressive behavior has been further corroborated in experiments in which live models, cartoons, and play materials were used. The idea that watching television satisfactorily releases pent-up aggressions (the catharsis theory) loses credibility in the face of these data from social-learning experiments. Watching dramatized violence may actually lead to subsequent aggressive behavior.

A tendency toward repeating certain behaviors viewed in the media clearly exists. The mass media teach the alphabet of violence, but whether or not the actual performance of violent behaviors occurs depends on personality, subcultural values, and other factors. The research to date indicates that the learning of violence must be distinguished from the performance of it. One fear we have is that restraints and taboos against violent behavior may diminish as the result of observing prohibited behavior being condoned and rewarded on the screen. Violence depicts a way of life; it is disguised by a cloak of history or locale and becomes acceptable. We are never taught "in this School for Violence that violence in itself is something reprehensible" (31).

Even with the portrayed violence, the screen environment may be more desirable than the viewer's actual environment. In the culturally deprived American household the underfed, underoccupied, undereducated person may be an apt pupil of the school for violence. Such pupils more readily accept as real a violent world made of movies, newsprint, comic books, and video. The blurred line between fiction and reality grows fainter when there is nothing for dinner. Ghetto violence is one way of at least temporarily adjusting to intolerable personal frustrations and an unbearable environment.

Given the effectiveness of the mass media in achieving culture modification, we should determine whether the content of the media produces desirable or undesirable modification. How frequently is violent content offered in our media? According to a 1951 New Zealand study (32), 70 American films had roughly twice as much violence per film as did 30 films from other countries. A 1954 study of network television programs (33) found an actual doubling from one year to the next in the number of acts or threats of violence, with much of the increase occurring during children's viewing hours. These studies were all conducted before the documentary and news depiction of violence became common, and thus these studies dealt essentially with fictional violence. More recent studies reflect the same trends, however. A New York *Times* headline from July 1968, reads "85 Killings Shown in 85½ TV Hours on the 3 Networks" (34).

Thus the media's repetitive, staccato beat of violence and the evidence of its impact upon the most impressionable members of our society show that violence is valued, wanted, enjoyed. In teaching that violence is a good quick way to get things done, television and other media teach that violence is adaptive behavior.

Part of the tragedy is that the mass media could effectively promote adaptive behaviors like nonviolent protest and other alternatives to violence. The communications personnel and we consumers alike share the responsibility for seeing that our mass media develop their own constructive educational potential. At the very least, violence in the media must be reduced. The statement is hackneyed, the conclusion is not.

MENTAL ILLNESS, VIOLENCE, AND HOMICIDE

What is the relationship between mental illness and violence (35)? Generally the stereotype of the mentally ill person as a potentially dangerous criminal is not valid. The act of homicide often raises the question of psychosis, but only a relatively few psychotic individuals are potential murderers. The stereotype is kept alive, however, by the sensationalist news coverage of the few homicides committed by psychotics.

Mental illness does not usually predispose one to commit violent acts toward others. The patient with severe mental illness (psychosis) is frequently so preoccupied with himself and so disorganized that he is more likely to commit suicide than homicide. A main exception is the fairly well-organized paranoid patient with persecutory delusions concerning one or more particular individuals, intense hostility and mistrust for others, and a pervasive tendency to blame his troubles on the world. However, this type of mentally disordered person constitutes a small minority and does not greatly increase the low incidence of violent acts committed by those identified as mentally ill. In fact, several comparative studies indicate that patients discharged from mental hospitals have an arrest rate considerably lower than that of the general population. In a Connecticut state mental hospital (36) the felony arrest rate was 4.2 per 1000 patients, whereas among the general population it was 27 per 1000. Compared to an arrest rate of 491 per

100,000 among the general population, New York state mental hospitals (37) reported a figure of 122 per 100,000 for male patients discharged during 1947. Ten thousand patients were studied. One state-wide survey of Maryland psychiatric hospitals (38) showed that the mentally ill are involved in criminal behavior about as often as the general population.

Since mental illness of itself is not predictive of violence or homicide, we must look for other predisposing conditions. Predicting specifically who will murder is difficult because over 90 percent of the murders committed are not premeditated and 80 per cent involve an acquaintance or family member (39). One often demonstrated factor related to homicide is the excessive use of alcohol (40). Overindulgence in alcohol has been cited as one feature of the "pre-assaultive state" (40). Persons who are preassaultive usually show some combination of the following five factors: (i) difficulty enjoying leisure time often associated with the heavy use of alcohol; (ii) frequent clashes with close friends, spouse, and others; (iii) history of many fistfights and evidence of past violence (such as scars) reflecting difficulty with impulse control; (iv) fondness for guns and knives; and (v) being relatively young, usually under 45 years old. Comparing homicide rates for males and females universally indicates that a potential murderer is more often male than female. This difference reflects more frequent use of guns and knives ("male" weapons) for murdering as well as sex differences in expressing aggression.

Case histories of homicide reveal repeatedly that a person uses murder as a means of conflict resolution in an unbearable situation for which he can find no other solution. Predisposing factors for homicide include alcoholism, subcultural norms accepting violence as a means of settling conflict, a setting in which the individual experiences intolerable frustration or attack, helplessness resulting from the unavailability of or the inability to perceive alternative actions, intense emotions, and distortion of reality (perhaps even to the point where reality disappears because of personality disintegration). In the instance of blind rage, a person sometimes murders without realizing what he is doing.

The act of homicide may be viewed as attempted coping behavior. Homicide eliminates the immediate problem at a time when there seems to be no future or when the future seems unimportant, and the long-range consequences of the act are not considered. Put another way, homicide has adjustive rather than adaptive value.

FIREARMS CONTROL AND VIOLENCE

Violence by firearms has recently caused great concern (41, 42). The question of whether there is a gun problem is complicated by regional variations in both the actual incidence and the reporting of crime and multiple psychosocial variables, such as individual "choice" of homicide, population density, age, race, socioeconomic status, religion, and law-enforcement effectiveness.

Even so, the following statistics (39, 43) estimating the involvement of guns in various forms of violence in America indicate that a problem does exist. In 1967 firearms caused approximately 21,500 deaths—approximately 7,700 murders, 11,000 suicides, and 2,800 accidental deaths. In addition, there were also about 55,000 cases of aggravated assault by gun and 71,000 cases of armed robbery by gun. Between 1960 and 1967, firearms were used in 96 percent (that is, 394) of 411 murders of police officers. More than 100,000 nonfatal injuries were caused by firearms during 1966. A study in Chicago (44) in which assaults with guns were compared to those with knives shows many more equally serious assaults with knives than with guns; but more of the gun assaults were fatal. Another study (27) convincingly shows that the mere presence of a gun serves as a stimulus to aggression, that is, "The finger pulls the trigger, but the trigger may also be pulling the finger." The number of guns owned by citizens is unknown, but estimates run from 50 to 200 million (39). In 1967 approximately 4,585,000 firearms were sold in the United States, of which 1,208,000 were imports (43). Lately, data from a 1963 World Health Organization survey of 16 developed countries (39) give America an overwhelming lead in death rates for both homicide and suicide by firearms.

These data speak for themselves. What they do not show are the steady increases in all categories for gun-related mortality cited during the past few years. Firearms sales increased by 132 percent between 1963 and 1967.

Responsibility for legal restrictions on guns has generally been left to the states. Consequently, regulations on the sale of guns vary greatly. The lack of uniform laws and the ability (until recently) to buy guns in one state and transport them to another state have made it difficult to compare accurately the gun laws of different states. Even the so-called strict gun laws may not possess sufficient strength to reduce gun killings significantly.

Until 1968 there were only two federal laws of note (45). The National Firearms Act of 1934 imposes a tax on the transfer of certain fully automatic weapons and sawed-off shotguns. The Federal Firearms Act of 1938 requires a license for interstate sale of firearms and prohibits interstate shipment of guns to convicted felons, fugitives, and certain other persons. Two bills passed in 1968 go somewhat further but do not include firearm registration (41). The Omnibus Crime Control and Safe Streets Act restricts interstate and foreign commerce in hand guns. The Gun Control Act also adds mail-order sale of rifles and shotguns to this restriction and prohibits over-the-counter sales to out-of-state residents, juveniles, convicted felons, drug users, mental defectives, and patients committed to mental hospitals.

Although the data do not provide an ironclad indictment against weak, inconsistent legislation, we believe that they make a convincing argument. What is more, more than two-thirds of the American people continue to favor stronger gun-control legislation (42). Even the frightening regularity of assassination has not resulted in strong legislation (that is, legislation requiring registration of guns and owners). How then can we account for the successful opposition to strong gun legislation?

Diverse groups comprise the one-third or less of

Americans who do not favor stricter gun control laws. The most visible opposition group is the large (about 1 million members), well-organized National Rifle Association (NRA). With an immense operating budget (approximately $5.7 million in 1967), the NRA is an especially effective "gun lobby" (46). Another group, the Black Panthers, sees arms as necessary for survival. Eldridge Cleaver, Defense Minister of the Black Panthers, wrote, "We are going to keep our guns to protect ourselves from the pigs [police]" (47). Protection is also the issue in Dearborn, Michigan, where housewives are arming against the potential rioter and looter who might "invade" Dearborn from Detroit. Tragic escalation continues around the interplay of urban and suburban action and reaction.

Arguments opposing gun legislation can be divided into five overlapping categories.

1) Gun control would cause the loss of rights and possessions. This argument takes various forms: Restrictive legislation is an effort to disarm American sportsmen and law-abiding citizens; legislation would result in the loss of the so-called basic American freedom, "the right of the people to keep and bear arms"; and maintaining an armed citizenry ensures the protection of American liberties, especially against tyrannies from the political right or left. A common fear is that gun laws could lead from registration to discrimination and finally to confiscation of all firearms.

Our traditional frontier and rural ways of life are disappearing, and with this change has come a decrease in our traditional freedom and individualism. For many opposing gun legislation, the actual and potential loss of a way of life and its prized symbol—the gun—make gun legislation a concern basic to the adaptiveness of our society. These opponents assume that restrictions on the "right to bear arms" endanger our way of life.

2) Guns represent protection from dangers. The gun is seen as providing personal protection from and a means of coping with life-threatening dangers and destructive evil forces, be they criminals, drug addicts, rapists, communists, other subversives, mental patients, rioters, police, or racists. The NRA promotes this coping strategy in its official publication, The American Rifleman (48). A

monthly NRA column, "The Armed Citizen," states that "law-enforcement officers cannot at all times be where they are needed to protect life or property in danger of serious violation. In many such instances, the citizen has no choice but to defend himself with a gun" (48). The power of this argument depends upon a person's feelings of helplessness and mistrust in the face of danger.

Many people in urban areas or changing neighborhoods fear the rising crime rate and the breakdown of law and order. However, there is no documentation that an armed citizenry provides greater individual or group protection than an unarmed citizenry. On the contrary, the potential danger of such individual armed protection in our congested urban society includes harm to innocent bystanders, accidental shootings, and the increased likelihood of impulsive violence, which already accounts for over 90 percent of homicides in America.

3) Crime is reduced by punishment and not by gun control. Several forms of this argument state that gun-control legislation simply is not an effective way of reducing crime and violence: (i) Guns don't kill people, people kill people; (ii) when guns are outlawed, only outlaws will have guns (because they steal them anyway); (iii) crime is not associated with guns but with such social factors as population density, population composition, economic status, and strength of police; and (iv) effective enforcement of present laws has not been tried.

Using stronger and even cruel punishment to cope with gun-using criminals has to date not been proven as an effective deterrent, and its use, we believe, is morally indefensible. The "crime and punishment" thesis ignores data showing that more than three out of four homicides and two out of three criminal assaults occur among family and friends, that is, most murders are committed by "law-abiding citizens." In addition, criminals can and do purchase weapons from legal sources.

4) A gun represents strength and manliness. Gun literature usually implies this argument. Acts of heroism and bravery are associated with gun usage. Members of the NRA receive distinguished fighting medals. Pictures and advertisements reflect manliness and imply that gun usage means "standing up for your rights."

Guns may serve as a source of power, pride, and independence (the "equalizer"—for feelings of inferiority or inadequacy) and as the symbol of manliness and potency. Guns can and do represent these qualities in our culture, even to a pathological degree for some of us.

5) Guns provide recreation and support the economy. Arguments here portray citizens as being restricted from and deprived of healthy outdoor life, the hobby of gun collecting, family recreation, and the fellowship associated with hunting and target shooting. For example, an article in *The American Rifleman* entitled "Happiness is a Warm Gun" (49) depicts a close father-son relationship based on shooting. Additionally, gun sales and fees are held to be important economic factors supporting hunting states and conservation programs.

These arguments indicate that the issue of gun legislation is pragmatic, ideological, psychological, and economic, and is not based upon sound empirical data. The fervor of the arguments accurately reflects the deep emotional attachments at stake. Indeed, the specific content of proposed gun laws often seems irrelevant. Tragically, the arguments confuse ideology with issues of violence that must be solved. If strictly pragmatic issues of protection were involved, better police protection and increased communication with the feared group or groups should diminish the fear.

Finally, we have found that the "statistics game" is often played by both sides of this particular controversy. By presenting selected statistics and invalid inferences, both sides have obscured the more important goals of reducing gun killings and violence.

Yet, on balance, data document the need for strong and more uniform firearms legislation. We know of no single issue concerning violence that reflects more clearly the changing nature of adaptation. Challenges of the complex urban society in which we live cannot be met with old frontier means of survival—every man protecting himself with his own gun. Yet, gun legislation is no panacea. While reflecting America's desire for action, focusing or relying on legislation alone tends to obscure basic issues of violence and how we persist in using both individual and collective violence as a means of resolving conflict.

COLLECTIVE AND SANCTIONED VIOLENCE

An additional dilemma is that killing is neither legally nor socially defined as an unequivocally criminal act. The existence of capital punishment and war gives qualified sanction to violence as a means of resolving conflict. Both the general public and their leaders always seem to be able to justify any violence perpetrated on their fellow man. Thus in practice the legitimacy of violence is arbitrary and depends more on the will of powerful men than on moral, ethical, or humane considerations. In a sense, all sanctioned violence is collective, since it has group social approval. Certainly the existence of sanctioned violence abrades the concept of law and order.

We desperately need research on the psychological processes that permit an individual or group to view some violence as good (and presumably adaptive) and other forms of violence as bad (and presumably maladaptive). Although the history of violence in man is polymorphous, there likely are psychological mechanisms common to all cultures and times. For instance, the psychology of sanctioned violence everywhere depends on attributing evil motives to the "outsiders." Then because "they" are violent (evil), "we" *have* to be violent, or (twisted even further) because "they" are violent, it is *good* for "us" to be violent.

Thus people who have seen sanctioned violence being committed in the name of law, order, justice, moral obligation, and duty come to use violence themselves as a "just" means of solving their own problems. The people are acting as their government's representatives have acted—if the cause is just, the grievance real, then unlimited power and force can be used.

Nowhere do we better find this thinking reflected than in the actions of rioters (50). Study of the 1967 Detroit uprising (51) showed that the rioters (young, better educated men who had experienced frustration of their rising expectations) viewed violence against the "system" as justified. Not surprisingly, their views of what justifies violence differed greatly from those of the law enforcers and of the middle-aged black citizens. To the rioters violence was a means of accomplishing goals seemingly not attainable by nonviolent means. Their belief in the power of violence is understandable. Civil disorders are serving in part as a catalyst for change and an instrument of achievement. Some uprising participants reported that violence provided a sense of manliness and strength. But do these supposed gains outweigh the damage of escalations of counterviolence and potential suppression? At least the hypothesis that violence purifies, enhances manliness, and strengthens identity is subject to empirical study.

The results of social-psychiatric field investigations like those in Detroit and at Brandeis University's Lemberg Center for the Study of Violence are useful steps toward understanding the psychological processes and conditions evoking collective violence. For instance, a Lemberg report (52) cited four socio-psychological antecedents to ghetto uprisings: (i) a severe conflict of values between dominant and minority groups; (ii) a "hostile belief system" held by the aggrieved group, based considerably on reality; (iii) a failure of communication between the aggrieved and dominant groups; and (iv) a failure in social control resulting from either overcontrol or undercontrol. In short, these studies show that psychiatrists and psychologists can and must help to resolve the crisis of violence through field studies, facilitating communication between opposing groups, and making recommendations for social change.

But what of war? Behavioral scientists have grasped at all sorts of explanations for this species' warring behavior. Perhaps even this attempt to explain war is a cause of war; our ability to justify any form of violence is part of man's magnificent cerebral endowment. Many causes of war have been suggested: contiguity, habituation, social learning, predation, psychological defenses (for example, rationalization, blaming, denial, counterphobic tendencies among others), the host of fears associated with the human condition, territoriality and power, intolerable frustration, biologically rooted aggressive instincts, and sadism (53–55). One wonders whether the mere distance and speed with which we kill are factors rendering meaningless the signals of submission that other animals use to halt violent encounters (54). Often we literally no longer have to touch the results of our violence. The impersonal factor shows up in another way. Since war is an activity between organized nation states rather than angry individuals, decisions producing war often are made in a calculated manner by those who do not participate directly in any personal acts of violence.

The evidence of history is that war proves everything and nothing. An adequate analysis of the Vietnam war and of the myriad of other wars dotting history is far too great a task for this discussion, despite the relevance of war to the current crisis of violence (55).

Although preventive measures are difficult to administer in the face of the contradicting sanctioned and unsanctioned violence, there are remedies to violence, and we have discussed some of them. More effort could be expended trying to understand the all-important relation between the excessive use of alcohol and homicide. Disseminating currently available information on how to identify a potential murderer will help. Despite Americans' conflicting feelings about guns, there is a gun-death problem today, and more effective and uniform gun legislation can keep guns out of the hands of those who are likely to act impulsively. The mass media can play an increasingly responsible and educational role, while reducing the amount of violence for violence's sake. Many positive potentials of the media have not yet been tapped. Citizen complaint agencies can be established, of which one possibility might be homicide prevention centers along the lines of the suicide prevention centers. Frustrated minority groups will become less frustrated when they are not blocked from responsible participation and self-determination. Peaceful resolution of conflict (56) such as

nonviolent protest and negotiation, reducing the amount of sanctioned violence, encouraging a shared sense of humanity, and moving toward rehabilitation rather than retribution in dealing with crime—all these are promising directions. Violence must be studied scientifically so that human behavior can be sustained by knowledge.

CHANGING NATURE OF HUMAN ADAPTATION: SOME SPECULATIONS

Violence is unique to no particular region, nation, or time (55). Centuries ago man survived primarily as a nomadic hunter relying on violent aggression for both food and protection. Even when becoming agricultural and sedentary, man struggled against nature, and survival still required violent aggression, especially for maintaining territory when food was scarce.

Then in a moment of evolution man's energies suddenly produced the age of technology. Instead of adapting mainly by way of biological evolution, we are now increasingly subject to the effects and demands of cultural evolution. Instead of having to adapt to our environment, we now can adapt our environment to our needs. Despite this potential emancipation from biological evolution, we retain the adaptive mechanisms derived from a long history of mammalian and primate evolution, including our primitive forms of aggression, our violence, bellicosity, and inclination to fight in a time of emergency. Where these mechanisms once responded more to physical stress, they now must respond more to social, cultural, and psychological stresses, and the response does not always produce adaptive results. Where violent aggressive behavior once served to maintain the human species in times of danger, it now threatens our continued existence.

In this new era, culture changes so rapidly that even time has assumed another dimension—the dimension of acceleration. Looking to the past becomes less relevant for discerning the future.

In the current rapidly expanding technological era, many once useful modes of adaptation are transformed into threats to survival. Territorial exclusivity is becoming obsolete in an economy of abundance. Vast weapons, communication, and transportation networks shrink the world to living-room size and expand our own backyard to encompass a "global village." Yet war and exclusivity continue. Our exploitation of natural resources becomes maladaptive. Unlimited reproduction, once adaptive for advancing the survival of the species, now produces the overcrowded conditions similar to those that lead to destructive and violent behavior in laboratory experiments with other species.

The rate at which we change our environment now apparently exceeds our capacity for adapting to the changes we make. Technological advances alter our physical and social environments, which in turn demand different adaptive strategies and a reshaping of culture. The accelerated civilization of technology is crowded, complex, ambiguous, uncertain. To cope with it, we must become capable of restructuring knowledge of our current situation and then applying new information adaptively. Several factors give us reason to hope that we can succeed.

1) Our social organization and intellectual abilities give us vast potential for coping. Knowledge and technology can be harnessed to serve goals determined by man. Automation makes possible the economics of abundance, but only our cultural values can make abundance a reality for all people. Medicine permits us to control life, but we have not yet seen fit to use this power to determine the limits of population. The technologies of communication and travel shrink the world, but man has not yet expanded the horizon of exclusion. We can learn to unite in goals that transcend exclusivity and direct cultural evolution in accordance with adaptive values and wisdom. The past need not be master of our future.

2) Violence can be understood and controlled. The crisis is one of violence, not of aggression, and it is violence that we must replace. Aggression in the service of adaptation can build and create rather than destroy. The several theories of aggression and current issues of violence suggest many complementary ways of controlling and redirecting aggression. We have suggested some in this article. Furthermore, our brief review of theory and issues points to many possibilities for multi-dimensional research—an approach that we believe is needed rather than "one note" studies or presentations.

3) Greater attention can be focused on both social change and adaptation processes. Cultural lag in the technological era produces not stability but a repetitive game of "catch up" characterized by one major social crisis after another and by behaviors that are too often only adjustive in that they bring relief of immediate problems while doing little to provide long-range solutions. Expanding our knowledge of the processes of social change and understanding resistance to change are of highest priority. Unforeseen change produces intolerable stress, anxiety, and increased resistance to rational change. These reactions inhibit solution-seeking behavior; evoke feelings of mistrust, loss, and helplessness; and lead to attacks on the apparent agents of change. We must develop the ability to foresee crises and actively meet them. We must dwell more on our strengths, assets, and potential as the really challenging frontier.

CONCLUSION

The current examples of violence and the factors encouraging it reflect our vacillation between the anachronistic culture of violence and the perplexing culture of constant change. We feel alienated and experience social disruption. Current demands for change are potentially dangerous because change activates a tendency to return to older, formerly effective, coping behaviors. Social disruption caused by change tends to increase violence as a means of coping at a time when violence is becoming a great danger to our survival.

America's current crises of violence make it difficult for us to cope with our changing world. Today's challenge, the crisis of violence, is really the crisis of man. This crisis is especially difficult because violence, a once useful but now increasingly maladaptive coping strategy, seems to be firmly rooted in human behavior patterns. We conquer the elements and yet end up facing our own image. Adaptation to a changing world rests on how effectively we can understand, channel, and redirect our aggressive energies. Then man can close his era of violence.

REFERENCES AND NOTES

1. L. Eiseley, *The Immense Journey* (Random House, New York, 1946).

2. D.N. Daniels, M.F. Gilula, F.M. Ochberg, Eds., *Violence and the Struggle for Existence* (Little, Brown, Boston, in press).

3. Dr. T. Bittker, C. Boelkins, Dr. P. Bourne, Dr. D.N. Daniels (co-chairman); Dr. J.C. Gillin, Dr. M.F. Gilula, Dr. G.D. Gulevich, Dr. B. Hamburg, Dr. J. Heiser, Dr. F. Ilfeld, Dr. M. Jackman, Dr. P.H. Leiderman, Dr. F.T. Melges, Dr. R. Metzner, Dr. F.M. Ochberg (co-chairman); Dr. J. Rosenthal, Dr. W.T. Roth, Dr. A. Siegel, Dr. G.F. Solomon, Dr. R. Stillman, Dr. R. Taylor, Dr. J. Tinklenberg, Dr. Edison Trickett, and Dr. A. Weisz.

4. *Webster's Third New International Dictionary* (Merriam, Springfield, Mass., 1966).

5. J. Gould and W.L. Kolb, *A Dictionary of the Social Sciences* (Free Press, New York, 1964); L.E. Hinsie and R.J. Campbell, *Psychiatric Dictionary* (Oxford Univ. Press, ed. 3, New York, 1960).

6. R.C. Boelkins and J. Heiser, "Biological aspects of aggression," in *Violence and the Struggle for Existence,* D.N. Daniels, M.F. Gilula, F.M. Ochberg, Eds. (Little, Brown, Boston, in press).

7. *The Natural History of Aggression,* J.D. Carthy and F.J. Ebling, Eds. (Academic Press, New York, 1964).

8. Th. Dobzhansky, *Mankind Evolving* (Yale Univ. Press, New Haven, 1962).

9. G.G. Simpson, "The study of evolution: Methods and present states of theory," in *Behavior and Evolution,* A. Roe and G.G. Simpson, Eds. (Yale Univ. Press, New Haven, 1958).

10. D.A. Hamburg, "Emotions in the perspective of human evolution," in *Expression of the Emotions in Man,* P.D. Knapp, Ed. (International Universities Press, New York, 1963).

11. C. Kluckhohn, "The limitations of adaptation and adjustment as concepts for understanding cultural behavior," in *Adaptation,* J. Romano, Ed. (Cornell Univ. Press, Ithaca, New York, 1949).

12. E. Silber, D.A. Hamburg, G.V. Coelho, E.B. Murphey, M. Rosenberg, L.I. Pearlin, *Arch Gen. Psychiat.* **5,** 354 (1961).

13. D.A. Hamburg and J.E. Adams, *ibid.* **17,** 277 (1967).

14. O. Fenichel, *The Psychoanalytic Theory of Neurosis* (Norton, New York, 1945).

15. K. Lorenz, *On Aggression* (Harcourt, Brace and World, New York, 1966).

16. A. Storr, *Human Aggression* (Atheneum, New York, 1968).

17. G.F. Solomon, "Case studies in violence," in *Violence and the Struggle for Existence,* D.N. Daniels, M.F. Gilula, F.M. Ochberg, Eds. (Little, Brown, Boston, in press).

18. J.P. Scott, *Aggression* (Univ. of Chicago Press, Chicago, 1958).

19. L. Berkowitz, *Aggression: A Social-Psychological Analysis* (McGraw-Hill, New York, 1962); J. Dollard, L.W. Doob, N.E. Miller, O.H. Mowrer, R.R. Sears, *Frustration and Aggression* (Yale Univ. Press, New Haven, 1939).

20. A. Bandura and R.H. Walters, *Social Learning and Personality Development* (Holt, Rinehart, & Winston, New York, 1963); F. Ilfeld, "Environmental theories of aggression," in *Violence and the Struggle for Existence,* D.N. Daniels, M.F. Gilula, F.M. Ochberg, Eds. (Little, Brown, Boston, in press); M.E. Wolfgang and F. Ferracuti, *The Sub-Culture of Violence* (Barnes and Noble, New York, 1967).

21. R. Taylor and A. Weisz, "The phenomenon of assassination," in *Violence and the Struggle for Existence,* D.N. Daniels, M.F. Gilula, F.M. Ochberg, Eds. (Little, Brown, Boston, in press).

22. L.Z. Freedman, *Postgrad. Med.* **37,** 650 (1965); D.W. Hastings, *J. Lancet* **85,** 93 (1965); *ibid.,* p. 157; *ibid.,* p. 189; *ibid.,* p. 294.

23. "It's Russian roulette every day, said Bobby," San Francisco *Examiner* (6 June 1968).

24. J. Cottrel, *Anatomy of an Assassination* (Muller, London, 1966).

25. A.E. Siegel, "Mass media and violence," in *Violence and the Struggle for Existence,* D.N. Daniels, M.F. Gilula, F.M. Ochberg, Eds. (Little, Brown, Boston, in press); O.N.

Larsen, Ed., *Violence and the Mass Media* (Harper and Row, New York, 1968).

26. E.A. Maccoby, "Effects of the mass media," in *Review of Child Development Research,* L.W. Hoffman and M.L. Hoffman, Eds. (Russell Sage Foundation, New York, 1964).

27. L. Berkowitz, *Psychol. Today* 2 (No. 4), 18 (1968).

28. H.T. Himmelweit, A.N. Oppenheim, P. Vince, *Television and the Child* (Oxford Univ. Press, New York, 1958).

29. W. Schramm, J. Lyle, E.B. Parker, *Television in the Lives of Our Children* (Stanford Univ. Press, Stanford, Calif., 1961).

30. A. Bandura, D. Ross, S. Ross, *J. Abnorm. Soc. Psychol.* **63,** 575 (1961); *ibid.* **66,** 3 (1963).

31. F. Wertham, *A Sign for Cain* (Macmillan, New York, 1966).

32. G. Mirams, *Quart. Film Radio Television* 6, 1 (1951).

33. Purdue Opinion Panel, *Four Years of New York Television* (National Association of Educational Broadcasters, Urbana, Ill., 1954).

34. Associated Press report of 25 July 1968; *Christian Science Monitor* article; New York *Times* (29 July 1968).

35. G.D. Gulevich and P. Bourne, "Mental illness and violence," in *Violence and the Struggle for Existence,* in D.N. Daniels, M.F. Gilula, F.M. Ochberg, Eds. (Little, Brown, Boston, in press).

36. L.H. Cohen and H. Freeman, *Conn. State Med. J.* **9,** 697 (1945).

37. H. Brill and B. Malzberg, *Mental Hospital Service (APA) Suppl. No. 153* (August 1962).

38. J.R. Rappaport and G. Lassen, *Amer. J. Psychiat.* **121,** 776 (1964).

39. C. Bakal, *No [sic] Right to Bear Arms* (Paperback Library, New York, 1968).

40. C.A. deLeon, "Threatened homicide—A medical emergency," *J. Nat. Med. Assoc.* **53,** 467 (1961).

41. J.C. Gillin and F.M. Ochberg, "Firearms control and violence," in *Violence and the Struggle for Existence,* D.N. Daniels, M.F. Gilula, F.M. Ochberg, Eds. (Little, Brown, Boston, in press).

42. D.N. Daniels, E.J. Trickett, J.R. Tinklenberg, J.M. Jackman, "The gun law controversy: Issues, arguments, and speculations concerning gun legislation," *Violence and the Struggle for Existence,* in D.N. Daniels, M.F. Gilula, F.M. Ochberg, Eds. (Little, Brown, Boston, in press).

43. Criminal Division, U.S. Department of Justice, *Firearms Facts* (16 June 1968); based in large part on the Federal Bureau of Investigation, *Uniform Crime Reports* (1967) (U.S. Government Printing Office, Washington, D.C., 1968).

44. F. Zimring, *"Is Gun Control Likely To Reduce Violent Killings?"* (Center for Studies in Criminal Justice, Univ. of Chicago Law School, Chicago, 1968).

45. *Congressional Quarterly,* "King's murder, riots spark demands for gun controls" (12 April 1968), pp. 805–815.

46. R. Harris, *The New Yorker* **44** (20 April 1968), p. 56.

47. E. Cleaver, *Ramparts* **7** (15 June 1968), p. 17.

48. *Amer. Rifleman* **116** (Nos. 2–5) (1968), various writings.

49. W.W. Herlihy, *ibid.* **116** (No. 5), 21 (1968).

50. T.E. Bittker, "The choice of collective violence in intergroup conflict," in *Violence and the Struggle for Existence,* D.N. Daniels, M.F. Gilula, F.M. Ochberg, Eds. (Little, Brown, Boston, in press).

51. P. Lowinger, E.D. Luby, R. Mendelsohn, C. Darrow, *"Case study of the Detroit uprising: The troops and the leaders"* (Department of Psychiatry, Wayne State Univ. School of Medicine, and the Lafayette Clinic, Detroit, 1968); C. Darrow and P. Lowinger, "The Detroit uprising: A psychosocial study," in *Science and Psychoanalysis, Dissent,* J.H. Masserman, Ed. (Grune and Stratton, New York, 1968), vol. 13.

52. J. Spiegel, *Psychiat. Opinion* **5** (No. 3), **6** (1968).

53. J.D. Frank, *Sanity and Survival: Psychological Aspects of War and Peace* (Random House, New York, 1967); I. Ziferstein, *Amer. J. Orthopsychiat.* **37,** 457 (1967).

54. D. Freeman, "Human aggression in anthropological perspective," in *The Natural History of Aggression,* J.D. Carthy and F.J. Ebling, Eds. (Academic Press, New York, 1964).

55. L.F. Richardson, *Statistics of Deadly Quarrels* (Boxwood Press, Pittsburgh, 1960).

56. F. Ilfeld and R. Metzner, "Alternatives to violence: Strategies for coping with social conflict," in *Violence and the Struggle for Existence,* D.N. Daniels, M.F. Gilula, F. M. Ochberg, Eds. (Little, Brown, Boston, in press).

57. We thank Dr. D.A. Hamburg and Dr. A. Siegel for their review and critique of this paper and M. Shapiro, C. DiMaria, and R. Franklin for their contributions in preparing this manuscript.

Today I wish to share with you a few ideas that may be relevant to the human condition as man rushes forward into what Sir Julian Huxley[1] calls "the human crisis" of passing through "the great transition" envisioned by Professor Kenneth Boulding[2] into a "post-civilized" society where striving becomes a combination of power with goodness. As I have pursued my studies of animal behavior...in the laboratory, field and forest, I have kept wondering if the lives of these simpler creatures are giving us a message we can ignore only with peril.

...Two passages from the book *From Utopia to Nightmare*[3] serve as a text for my theme today:

> In the midst of old countries disappearing and new ones coming to birth, few men have paused to notice that a familiar and cherished nation, unique in offering honorary citizenship to all humanity, is in danger of quietly fading from the map. That country is Utopia....During this century there has been an unequalled production of imaginary societies....But the significant fact is this. A decreasing percentage of the imaginary worlds are utopias. An increasing percentage are nightmares. The 'dystopia' or 'inverted utopia' or 'anti-utopia'...was a minor satiric fringe of the utopian output in the 19th century. It promises to become the dominant type today, if it has not already achieved statistical preponderance. I believe man once lived in utopia but does no longer, and that he is always trying to return. The name of the first utopia was Eden. I do not care whether one conceives of Eden as a tract of real estate or a purely metaphysical garden. It may never have existed 'in time'. But however conceived, it is a part of our heritage. We want to go back. The flaming swords of angels bar the way. So we must create another garden, a new Eden.

Man's entire evolutionary history, back through his earliest mammalian ancestors at least—to some 130 million years ago—forms part of his garden of Eden. So our task today becomes that of

[1]Julian Huxley, *The Human Crisis* (Seattle: University of Washington Press, 1963) 88 pp.
[2]Kenneth E. Boulding, *The Meaning of the Twentieth Century: The Great Transition* (New York: Harper and Row, 1964) 199 pp.
[3]Chad Walsh, *From Utopia to Nightmare* (New York: Harper, 1962) 191 pp.

28
A Glance into the Garden

John B. Calhoun

Reprinted with permission and with slight abridgement from *Three Papers on Human Ecology*, Mills College Assembly Series, 1965–1966, Oakland, California, Mills College, 1966, pp. 19–36.

TABLE 28.1
The increase in the numbers of man on earth

Date*	Population in millions	Years required to double
13,743 B.C.	12.5	7,939
5,804 B.C.	25	3,943
1,861 B.C.	50	1,958
96.9 A.D.	100	971.5
1,068.4 A.D.	200	482.6
1,551 A.D.	400	239.6
1,790.6 A.D.	800	118.9
1,909.6 A.D.	1,600	59.1
1,968.6 A.D.	3,200	29.3
1,997.9 A.D.	6,400	14.5
2,012.5 A.D.	12,800	—

*Dates calculated from Equation (11) in von Foerster[4]

looking into these earlier gardens to see what impress they made upon man before his Promethean experience. But before doing so it will be well to look at the course of change in the numbers of man over the surface of the earth; for it is this that makes it imperative in our time to grasp for any insights into the nature of man and the world about him.

For a long time it has been recognized that it has taken a shorter time to add the last million persons to the world population than it did the million prior to it. Von Foerster[4] and his colleagues re-examined this trend of increase on the basis of the best estimates of world population from the time of Christ to 1958. They developed an equation describing population growth over this period of time and speculated that the same type of growth, which is quite different from all other animals, has persisted for a long time over the course of the human lineage. When I examined their equation, a very interesting relationship appeared: Each doubling of the population requires half the time as that of the immediately prior doubling. Table 28.1, with projections back before the time of Christ and into the future, presents this doubling time process as revealed by the von Foerster equation. Continuation of this process into the near future produces some remarkable contrasts between times past and future.

[4]Heinz von Foerster, Patricia M. Mora, and Lawrence W. Amiot, "Doomsday: Friday, 13 November, A.D. 2026," *Science,* 132: 1291–1295 (1960)

Individuals born in 1960 may live to see the world population double twice: a change comparable to that which spanned the entire Old Testament period of cultural evolution. And when I speak of change I also refer to the fact that the change in complexity of culture is roughly proportional to the change in world population. Let us look at this problem in round numbers. From Table 28.1 it can be seen that there were two doublings of the population in the 6,000 years before the birth of Christ. Likewise it may be seen that starting from now two doublings may be anticipated in 54 years. Now, just for the sake of argument, let us give mankind the benefit of doubt and temper this population explosion to the point that it will take a century for two more doublings of the population to take place. Even with this slowing down of population increase as much change will have taken place in the near future during one year as took 60 years during the six millennia before Christ. As we emerge into the near future each year of our life will be equivalent to an entire life-span of Old Testament man in so far as the amount of cultural change that will be experienced. In terms of cultural change a gulf of generations must separate the early experience of parents with that impinging on their offspring.

This increasing rate of change in both population size and complexity of culture, along with the unpredictability of the changes it will impose on man's life, is viewed by many modern writers[5-11] as *the* threat to man. The dystopian writers[3] wonder whether man has the capability to adjust so rapidly with vision. So drastic appears the challenge to adjustment than von Foerster[4] and his colleagues have, not facetiously, designated Doomsday as Friday, the 13th of November, 2026. Implied in their study is the conclusion that a critical point in man's evolution will occur when the rate of change in his numbers and the complexity of his society is such that both double within a period of time equal to the minimum number of years possible between generations. This period can be taken as something slightly longer than the number of years to the average age of puberty. For our purposes this period may be assumed to be about 15 years. This breaking point comes at around a world population of 12 billion. As one looks at the dynamics of human population growth, even with the likely impact on it of family planning for fewer births, it is difficult to see how a stable population on this flickering light in the sky, which is this earth of ours, can be attained at less than about four times its present numbers. The time of its attainment may be delayed for a few years, until about a century from now. But what is a century in the two million years since the genus *Homo* emerged? It is but one per cent of the time of all civilization. It is but the time in which our grandchildren may see the last faint rays of vision and hope sputter and fade away forever.

With this prologue let us turn to the garden of 130 million years ago. There through the undergrowth scurried those diminutive shrew-like animals to whom we trace our ancestry. Take five coins, five quarters, and there in the palm of your hand you have the mass of one of these creatures whose legacy we can view all about us. We can view it because their garden still surrounds us. It is now the grassland or the forest where today the ecological counterpart of those long-gone creatures are replaced by others like the white-footed mouse (*Peromyscus*), the red-backed mouse (*Clethrionomys*), and the harvest mouse (*Reithrodontomys*). Like their counterparts of earlier times they are faced with the necessity of searching for morsels of food scattered widely through the habitat. In recording where such animals respond to objects like food we are essentially asking them the question: "How do you use your environment?" When we so question a number of animals a typical answer, or pattern, emerges despite individual idiosyncracies, as shown in Figure 28.1

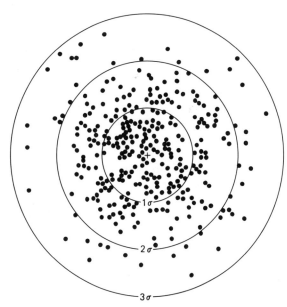

FIGURE 28.1
The pattern of distribution of responses by a rodent about its home, shown as a plus mark in the center of a field of dots, places where responses occurred. Normally 38% of all responses are included within a 1σ radius of the home site, 86% within a 2σ radius and 99% within a 3σ radius. Sigma is a measure of distance. (This figure appeared originally in an article titled, "The Role of Space in Animal Sociology," to be included in a special 1966 issue of the Journal of the Society for the Psychological Study of Social Issues.)

[5]Max Ways, "The Era of Radical Change," *Fortune*, 70:113–115, 210, 215–216 (1964)

[6]Arie Querido, "Population Problems and Mental Health," pp. 29–39 of Henry P. David (ed.), *Population and Mental Health* (New York: Springer, 1964) 181 pp.

[7]E.E. Krapf, "Social Changes in the Genesis of Mental Disorder and Health," pp. 97–103 of Hnery P. David (ed.), *Population and Mental Health* (New York: Springer, 1964) 181 pp.

[8]Nathan W. Ackerman, "Adolescent Struggle as Protest," pp. 81–93 of S.M. Farber, P. Mustacchi, and R.H.L. Wilson (eds.), *The Family's Search for Survival* (New York: McGraw-Hill, 1965) 210 pp.

[9]Arthur G. Nikelly, "The Psychologic Problems of Democratization," *American Journal of Psychotherapy*, 18(1):52–58 (1964)

[10]Donald N. Michael, *The Next Generation: The Prospects Ahead for the Youth of Today and Tomorrow* (New York: Random House, 1963) 218 pp.

[11]James K. Feibleman, "Biological Adaptation and Mental Illness," *International Journal of Social Psychiatry*, 9(2):94–103(1963)

Here, the plus mark in the center represents the site of the animal's home, and each dot is a place where it stops and responds to some object. You will note that the number of responses within comparable small areas declines as you look further away from the home site. This means that when an animal utilizes those resources nearest its home fairly effectively without over-utilizing them, it must be making quite inefficient use of resources toward the periphery of its range. But one animal is rarely alone in a habitat; each shares the resources with its neighbors. To do this with greatest effectiveness all the members of a community must shift the sites of their homes toward each other. In terms of Figure 28.1, the situation may be visualized as follows: suppose you had a number of clear plastic discs of the size of the outer circle of that figure, and on each there was a comparable number of dots (about 325) similarly distributed. First you place the discs so that their outer edges just touch. A photograph of this array would reveal as many clusters of dots as there were discs. Then if you begin to push the discs together so that each overlaps its neighbors by comparable amounts, successive photographs will gradually reveal a distribution of dots with even more nearly the same number in each smaller area examined. At this point in the process we have the situation where home sites are as far apart as possible and yet there is equal impact exerted by the animals together on every part of their habitat. In fact the distance between home sites of any two neighbors is the same as that of the radius from the home site shown in Figure 28.1 out to the second circle about it. Thus there is considerable overlap of the ranges of adjoining animals, and thus also meetings between neighbors must take place if only as chance encounters.

Homes sites are distributed through the environment by the forces of mutual antagonism interacting with that of natural selection. This tends to foster the evolution of forms capable of making the most effective use of resources available to them. When this distribution is established, we can turn our attention to the consequences of neighbors getting to know each other. In Figure 28.2 we see dots again, or tiny circles, but this time each

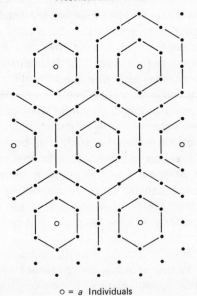

Preconstellation Phase

o = a Individuals

FIGURE 28.2
Spatial distribution of home range centers during the preconstellation phase. Small open circles represent centers for individuals destined to become alpha members. Dots represent home range centers for all other individuals. Home range centers are uniformly distributed. (Reproduced by permission of Academic Press. See Calhoun.[12])

represents a home site once the process described above has been completed. If we focus on some one of these, for example the central one where the dot is enlarged to a small circle, and now think of the dots as also representing individuals, it can be seen that this one has six nearest neighbors, indicated by the hexagon formed by connecting their home sites. Let us call the central member of this group of seven an alpha individual. We may now ask: What will be the distribution of the homes of other alpha individuals in which no alpha individual during its wanderings is ever likely to encounter the nearest neighbors of any other alpha individual? These are shown in Figure 28.2 by additional small circles, each with its surrounding group of six nearest neighbors. At this stage we have the conditions for the beginnings of a social knowing or neighborliness existing be-

[12]John B. Calhoun, "The Social Use of Space," pp. 1–187 of William Mayer and R. van Gelder (eds.), *Physiological Mammalogy, Vol. 1* (New York: Academic Press, 1964)

tween alpha individuals and the six nearest neighbors each has. These latter we may call beta individuals.

If we look at this whole system of home sites, and if we connect the home sites of those not involved in the above primordial clusters, it will be noted that these lines form larger hexagons about each alpha individual. We may designate as gamma individuals these whose home sites are farthest from alphas. Each gamma becomes a next nearest neighbor to two or three alphas.

Then there sets in a process of further clustering in which beta and gamma individuals are attracted toward alphas. Every alpha will have attracted to him his six nearest beta neighbors. But the gamma individuals are in a real quandary, if only in a probabilistic sense. Six gammas which are next-nearest neighbors to any one alpha are each also the next-nearest neighbor to some other alpha. Thus each has a fifty-fifty chance of shifting toward either one of his neighboring alphas. By this process each alpha on the average acquires three gamma associates. Likewise, the remaining six gammas (on the corners of the larger hexagons in Figure 28.2) in their original state have their homes equidistant from three different alphas. Thus any one alpha has only one chance in three of having attracted to him each of these six gamma individuals with the consequence that on the average he attracts towards himself only two of them.

The end consequence of this process is shown in Figure 28.3 in which a small circle, equal to one third the radius of each animal's range, is shown about each one's home. The betas have slightly reduced the size of their ranges as they shifted toward their alpha colleague, while more marked reduction in range is exhibited by the gamma individuals. With this shifting and concentration of home ranges there now arise clusters of individuals with a much reduced contact between members of adjoining clusters. Of course these changes are never seen with such precision in nature. What I have shown to you is an idealized model given confirmation[12] from studies of mice in their natural habitat, the mirror to the earlier garden.

Conditions of that garden fostered a way of life in which each individual on the average became a member of a dispersed network of twelve of his kind. Among the many species of mammals surviving to the present with their members forming groups of about twelve adults there are two major patterns. The first, and more primitive pattern, is that where the members form a dispersed group or constellation as described above. The second is where the twelve or so members form a compact group, whose residence is at the same place or which roam together through their habitat. In every case where a species is characterized by such compact groups the evolutionary transition from the dispersed state must have been a rapid one. Judging from existing species the transition to a compact way of life most frequently takes place when a body size of about 500 grams, a little over one pound, has been attained. From this I suspect that this group way of life must have characterized the human lineage for quite some millions of years.

Not an "Adam and Eve" alone, but a close association among a group of others is the legacy from this far distant garden. Let us now look at some of the clauses in this legacy for some of the limitations with which it has straddled us. We should find these limitations revealed in any species now living in groups of about twelve adults. First we will look at some theoretical implications of group life and then turn to some more empirical results.

Among all species which live in groups, including man, each individual appears to gain some satisfaction from some of its associations with its fellows. This is most clearly observable in the generally rather intense sexual behavior. For example, take a female rat: At the beginning of her period of receptivity she seeks out males, but after a few copulations her attitude changes and she attempts to repel their advances; she frustrates their attempts at seeking satisfaction from social interaction. Such frustrated males then alter their behavior toward others, they become more aggressive. We may extract from such observations a general model of social interaction. When two individuals, who are both in need of social interaction, encounter each other, each responds appro-

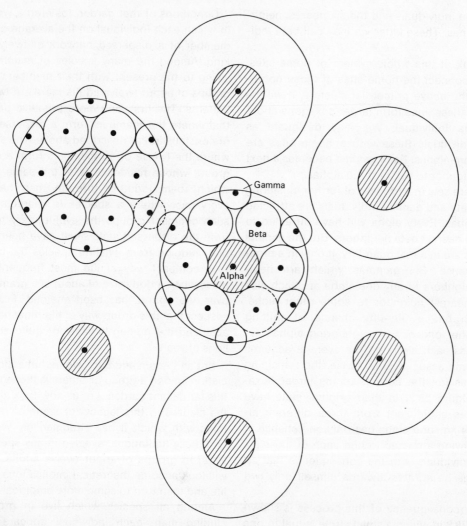

FIGURE 28.3
The theoretical constellation phase of intraspecific community organization of dominant species. A 3-sigma radius home range for alpha individuals is represented by the large circle. Small circles represent 1-sigma radius portions of the ranges of all members of a constellation. Contraction of home range by beta and alpha members permits the more intensively used portion of the home ranges of all individuals to fall mostly within the 3-sigma radius home range of the dominant alpha members. Cross-hatched circles represent the 1-sigma portion of the home range of alpha individuals. (Reproduced by permission of Academic Press. See Calhoun.[12])

priately to the other's needs; as a result each for a period of time enters a state of gratification during which it will no longer behave completely appropriately to the advances of other associates who feel the need for social interaction. Such individuals are then thrown for a while into a state of frustration during which they also will not behave appropriately to the advances of associates who are seeking gratification.

Examining the implications of such a system of social interaction with respect to the number of individuals in the group we come up with a very interesting picture as depicted in Figure 28.4. First look at what happens within the context of an optimum sized group, here indicated as $N_b = 12$. For each unit of gratification each individual experiences an equal amount of frustration. This is the best of all possible worlds, life in the garden. The

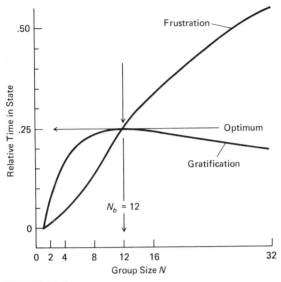

FIGURE 28.4

The influence of group size on the relative amount of time an individual is in either a state of gratification or a state of frustration. N_b stands for the basic (or optimum) group size. The example shown here is for a species with an optimum group size of 12 adults. (Reprinted by permission of Grune and Stratton from the chapter by John B. Calhoun titled "Ecological Factors in the Development of Behavioral Anomaly" in Comparative Psychopathology *Joseph Zubin [ed.] to be published in 1966.)*

physiology of our earlier ancestors as well as ourselves must be attuned to the need of experiencing equal amounts of gratification and frustration. The hitch comes in when animals develop an acute awareness of their actions and those of their associates without understanding that these actions produce effects which are unavoidable consequences of social life—this is the human condition. In our awareness of the effects of our actions, and those of our fellows, we develop guilt from the knowledge that these actions do not always accord with felt desires; we have gone so far as to codify this remorse into the concept of original sin. This has led us into the search for universal love while the Grail should instead be compassionate understanding.

From Figure 28.4 we can also see the consequences of life within groups larger or smaller than that to which the genetic constitution permits optimum adjustment. As groups get too small both the amount of gratification and of frustration de-

creases. For all practical purposes, when the group size becomes the square of the optimum every individual is frustrated all the time.

The above comments relating to Figure 28.4 assume that in any group each individual experiences exactly the same amount of gratification and frustration as every other one. Life in a group just doesn't work this way; some individuals experience more frustration that others. Each frustration increases the likelihood that an individual will deviate from appropriate behavior in his next encounter with an associate. To the extent of this deviation he will be rejected by his associates. As these rejections lead to further frustrations and begin to pile up, the individual begins to avoid his associates; he withdraws both physically and psychologically; he seeks every avenue to block out awareness and contact with the world about him.

All of this process can be placed into an elaborate mathematical model.[12] The observed behavior of animals conforms remarkably to this model, which predicts that the several members of the group will withdraw in different amounts. The degree of withdrawal may be measured by the amount of time spent in that part of the environment where contact with others is most likely to take place. I have called this measure of social engagement or withdrawal, "social velocity" or just simply "velocity." We can then rank the members of a group according to their measured velocity. The dots in Figure 28.5 are such measured values, while the line is that of predictions based upon the model. In terms of social withdrawal alone, remarkable differences exist between members of the group. This is life in the garden. The lowest point on the theoretical line represents the maximum amount of withdrawal, or the lowest velocity, compatible with physical survival. Individuals with such reduced velocity appear to be unaware of their companions even when in close proximity to them. Increasing the group size, which really amounts to increasing the number of social contacts per unit of time, has the consequence of decreasing the velocity, that is increasing the amount of social withdrawal, of every member of the group.

My studies of rodents have revealed regular

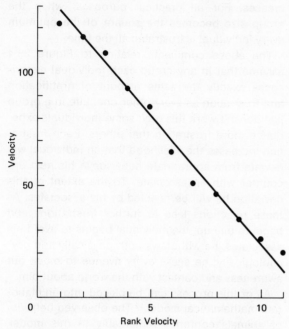

FIGURE 28.5
Degree of social withdrawal as reflected by velocity measurements of eleven male mice which formed an organized social group. (Reproduced by permission of Grune and Stratton from source indicated in legend to Figure 28.4.)

changes in behavior which accompany changes in velocity. The most socially active ones include the territorial males, those males which are quite dominant but not territorial, and the females who are the best mothers. These rats are the most conformist in two senses: Their behavior is most predictable and it follows most precisely along those patterns which give greater assurance to the reproductive survival of the species. As one goes down the scale toward more social withdrawal, or reduced velocity, behavior becomes more deviant. The whole repertoire of maternal behavior becomes impaired; nest building and care of young become disrupted, disorganized, and reduced in frequency of expression. On the male side this trend is most apparent in sexual behavior. As velocity declines the objects of sexual advances encompass a wider range of the associates present, until finally any associate regardless of age, sex, or receptivity will be mounted. There is obvious impairment in the ability to respond with rel-

evance to stimuli in the environment; at the very bottom of the scale of social withdrawal individuals are found who behave as if they are totally unaware of most of their environment. Such males essentially never engage in interaction with their associates, and their associates seem even to be unaware of them to the extent that they ignore them as appropriate targets for social action.

This social structuring of the group is a part of the garden as it has been for a long, long time, and I believe that it is an inherent aspect of any garden now experienced by man or which may be realized in the future. True, the expressions of this process on the human level will be different from those among lower mammals, but it is my belief that the general consequences of such a process are ultimately unavoidable. We can attempt to prevent the average velocity from dropping below that which the optimum circumstances of the system permit, and to increase the benefit any individual derives from membership in it.

You may think that I thus join ranks with the dystopian prophets who see man as basically unable to draw himself up onto and out upon a higher plain of existence and into a more evolved garden. This judgment is true with reservations. In any vision of the future we write about and work toward, there must be a fusion of utopian and dystopian thought to produce "syntopias" whose hopes weave strength out of obvious weaknesses. When one examines a wide range of current literature concerning the relationship between the growth of the human population and the rapid pace of technological and cultural change affecting man, one becomes immediately struck with the emphasis placed upon creativity, communication, and compassionate understanding. They are the key processes in our attempt to pass through that great transformation which faces the human species during the coming century. They are the three forces which can give strength to any syntopia. Let me conclude with a few brief remarks about each.

Creativity requires the incorporation of some new image of reality within the context of a rearrangement of one's existing images. My studies of rats have revealed that the most random sequences of behavior are found in individuals with lowest velocity, the most withdrawn ones. Much of the literature on human creativity indicates a need for both temporary social withdrawal and solitude, a combination of the effects of social inhibitions and respite from them. In brief I suspect that forced social withdrawal has the effect of breaking the sequential patterns of behaving and thinking which characterize high velocity individuals and thus permits the incorporation of new images and new ways of behavior, provided that a release from social pressures then permits persisting entrainment of such new combinations of behavioral states or images. That is to say, once new behavioral states become incorporated into a rearrangement of prior ones, this whole new sequence must remain stable for some time, must thus become a persisting entrainment. For only then may its consequences on the individual and his associates have any opportunity of producing lasting effects. By the present formulations this stability can only come after a reduction of the prior inhibitory actions toward the individual by his companions. Inherent in the creative process is the prior opportunity to have been exposed to new experiences and to new relationships. But to maximize his potential contribution to the creative process the individual must "flow" up and down the velocity gradient from minimal to enhanced velocity with all the accompanying alterations in awareness and randomness of thought and action. If we are to maximize creativity, to increase the prevalence of "suffering servants"[13,14] in our midst, all social groups must be in a frequent state of flux in which the social relationships among its members rarely remain constant over any appreciable period of time. Syntopian flux replaces utopian bliss and dystopian lethargy and despondency. Such flux means that the life of each of us must fluctuate continually between two cocoons; one is what Royce[15] refers to as encapsulation in the certainty of, and conformity to, fixed images of reality; the other is that protective state of unawareness and unconsciousness of self and larger world. It is the

entrance into, emergence from, and passage between these two cocoons that forms the process of continual self-renewal advanced by John Gardner.[16]

Communication becomes critical in the formation and acceptance of values as world society faces entry into a continuing state of flux, bordering on that between chaos and conformity. Karl Jaspers[17] grasps the nature of this communication when he argues for untrammeled dialogue within and between all levels of society, for a dialogue carried on with compassionate understanding and a striving for what Warren Wager[18] calls a "will to agree," even though agreement will always be fleeting as visions of reality shift. But dialogue sensitive to the diverse needs of a variable world requires structuring of the communication to make it effective over the shortening intervals of time accompanying increasing rates of change. Sir Geoffrey Vickers[19] describes such an organization of dialogue as an "appreciative system." By an appreciative system he means a network of communication so structured as to enhance the likelihood of its rapidly leading to a consensus of opinion among its members regarding goals for human action despite initial divergence of viewpoints. Vickers emphasizes that such a system, which will permit us to decide more readily what to do, and why, is much less evolved, even hardly present, in comparison with the highly evolved cybernetic-type regulatory systems we utilize so effectively in the "doing" operations in many areas of management and manufacturing. However, even these regulatory systems give us some guide lines for the structure of appreciative systems. Muller-Thyme[20] describes the modern industrial

[13]Isaiah 52:13 to 53:12

[14]Gerald Sykes, *The Hidden Remnant* (New York: Harper, 1962) 241 pp.

[15]Joseph R. Royce, *The Encapsulated Man* (Princeton, N.J.: D. Van Nostrand, 1964) 206 pp.

[16]John W. Gardner, *Self-Renewal: The Individual and the Innovative Society* (New York: Harper and Row, 1963) 142 pp.

[17]Karl Jaspers, *The Future of Mankind* (Chicago: University of Chicago Press, 1961) 342 pp.
and comments in:
James L. Titchner, "Fear and the Long Struggle: A Commentary on Karl Jasper's *The Future of Mankind*," *Comprehensive Psychiatry*, 2(6):311–316 (1961) and:
W. Warren Wager, *The City of Man* (18) below:

[18]W. Warren Wager, *The City of Man* (Boston: Houghton Mifflin, 1963) 310 pp.

[19]Geoffrey Vickers, "The Psychology of Policy Making and Social Change," *British Journal of Psychiatry*, 110(467):465–477 (1964)

[20]Bernard J. Muller-Thym, "Comments on the Conference Subtopic: The Management of Business," pp. 148–153 of *The Environment of Change* (New York: Time, the weekly news-magazine, 1964) (Proceedings of a Conference at Sterling Forest, New York, June 14–17, 1964)

concern as a network of centers in which there is free communication between any two centers. As he says, this complex is like a brain in that the more dependent industry becomes upon an increasing number of relationships among its contained centers the greater will be its freedom of choice of action. My studies on rodents have suggested a means for developing appreciative systems capable of circling the globe and of evolving new images of destiny without coercion. In essence this involves a network of "invisible colleges." Such invisible colleges have operated effectively behind the scenes for three centuries.[21] Formalizing their structure from insights developed from lower animals we can say that each should consist of twelve groups of twelve individuals, and that a representative from each such smaller assembly should form a coordinating assembly. If each of the twelve basic assemblies in each invisible college is at the same time a coordinating assembly for another invisible college we have the basis for a network of communication that can enlarge to 12^n. This is of course a too brief presentation of the concept here, but it is my firm conviction that we may logically organize such an appreciative system capable of generating new values consonant with the world that is coming into being.

Compassionate understanding connotes both rational and emotional or empathetic reactions which must come to characterize our relations with our fellow man. Through rational processes we must come to know both the limitations and potentialities of our being and our action. It is here that studies on animals open our eyes to processes which otherwise we might ignore. Compassion is that essence of empathy coming from understanding that in a dynamic and variable world every other person is but a "might have been I," a "has been I" or a "might become I." Compassion must become the dominant attribute of the man of the future, as it has been of a few in the past.

Such are my syntopian views into the garden. We have never been out of it, although there have been nooks and crannies in it we have ignored or hardly been aware of. And from time to time the garden has become enriched enabling us to live on a higher plane. Each of these enrichments has been a conception of a new opportunity for living. These have been few. Some we can recognize for certain.

Prior revolutions have involved understanding, creativity and communication in their completion, but compassion as a universal characteristic has been sadly missing. For this reason I wish to designate the coming transformation as the "compassionate revolution," the last revolution until the human race as a society makes more than a quantum jump as expressed in the past revolutions. To see why I say the compassionate revolution must be the last one, the garden achieved, we must look over the course of past revolutions.

In this last paragraph I have introduced three concepts which require clarification. First is "quantum jumps." They represent changes in organization, along with a greater variety of subtypes of organization and relationships among them. Marney and Smith[22] elaborate this idea. Emergence of new biological taxonomic groups such as the replacement of *Homo erectus* by *Homo sapiens* with the presumed greater capacity of developing culture by the latter, or the change from discursive thinking to that of the paradigm of structured organization of theory[23] introduced by Newton which ushered in the scientific era, both these represent quantum jumps. All the throes of competition and change involved in such a transition from one level of organization to another represent the revolution. The human lineage, possibly even beginning with the emergence of that preman, *Australopithecus,* and extending through the revolution of compassionate understanding, forms a domain or progression of revolutions. After it there is the opportunity for a similar succession of revolutions forming another domain, which may well last for an equal period of time. I hesitate to

[21]Derek J. De Solla Price, "The Scientific Foundations of Science Policy," *Nature,* 206(4981):233–238 (1965)

[22]Milton C. Marney and Nicholas N. Smith, "The Domain of Adaptive Systems: A Rudimentary Taxonomy," *General Systems. Yearbook,* 9:107–133 (1964)

[23]Thomas S. Kuhn, *The Structure of Scientific Revolutions* (Chicago: University of Chicago Press, 1962) 172 pp.

TABLE 28.2
Man's revolutionary course

Revolution	Years to next revolution	Years before 2027 A.D.	Date
Homo habilis	1,682,616	2,044,850	—
Homo habilis	1,682,616	2,044,850	—
Homo erectus	298,072	362,234	—
Homo sapiens	52,803	64,162	—
Agricultural	9,356	11,359	(9332 B.C.)
Axial (Religious)	1,657	2,003	(24 A.D.)
Scientific	294	346	(1671 A.D.)
Electronic	52	52 (1975 A.D.)	(1975 A.D.)
Compassionate	No more (?)		(2027 A.D.)

make any speculations about the possible course of change through this emerging domain.

Biological evolutionists have established the first three revolutions as being represented by the three major species of man. *Homo habilis,* the earliest form of man recently discovered by Professor Leakey, is known to have lived at least back to 1.75 million years ago.[24] He was replaced by *Homo erectus* by about the beginning of the middle Pleistocene. As a first rough figure I have taken this to be about 350 thousand years ago. This middle man in turn too was replaced by *Homo sapiens.* I have taken the carbon dating of the first known use of fire in Africa at Kalambo Falls some 57,300 years ago as the time of this final man's establishment. Karl Jaspers[17] includes this transition into present biological man among his four great historical breakthroughs. His four revolutions are the emergence of man, the beginning of settled agricultural life, the establishment of the major religious philosophies (the Axial period), and the scientific revolution.

I have taken the time of the establishment of the agricultural revolution as 8,800 years ago, the dating of the village of Jarmo in Iraq studied by R.J. Braidwood,[25] although evidence of agriculture in the near east extends back for some 2,000 years

earlier.[26,27] This was followed by the Axial Period of 800 to 200 B.C., the period of formation of the major religious and spiritual traditions. I have taken 200 B.C. as the establishment of this revolution. Then comes the scientific-technological revolution which can be taken as being established about 1650 A.D. Since the time Jasper recognized these four revolutions it is quite clear that we are now in the throes of the establishment of the electronic-communication revolution, which judged by current opinions can be expected to be well established by 1975. In the absence of any other fixed date I will take von Foerster's 2026 A.D. as the establishment of the "compassionate revolution."

It will be noted that, just as each successive doubling of the human population on earth has taken a shorter time, so it is here we find a shortening of time between successive revolutions. On the basis of the above dates the time intervening between any two revolutions is on the average 5.645 times as long as between the latter of these and the one which follows it. Then assuming that 52 years is a good estimate of the interval between the last of these revolutions, we can use this estimated common factor of 5.645 to make another, and perhaps more accurate, guess as to how long ago each revolution started as given in Table 28.2.

This table leads to the conclusion that we are

[24]Phillip V. Tobias, "Early Man in East Africa," *Science,* 149:22–23 (1965)
[25]Robert J. Braidwood and Charles A. Reed, "The Achievement and Early Consequences of Food-Production: A Consideration of the Archeological and Natural-Historical Evidence," *Cold Spring Harbor Symposia on Quantitative Biology,* 22:19–31 (1957)

[26]Kent V. Flannery, "The Ecology of Early Food Production in Mesopotamia," *Science,* 147:1247–1256 (1965)
[27]Karl W. Butzer, *Environment and Archaeology* (Chicago: Aldine, 1964) 524 pp.

fast approaching the termination of a long historical course of revolution by quantum jumps initiated two million years ago by *Homo habilis*. Three such comparable revolutions before *Homo habilis* would take us back through the dawn of mammalian evolution. This first backward step would take the Australopithecine revolution to eleven million years ago. Even slight refinements of this picture will alter little the anticipation of the termination of this age-long process of accelerating revolutions. We here now, we and our children, are blessed with the opportunity of participating in the conception of the compassionate revolution. Beyond that, who knows what may be the character of a new course of revolutions. Even Teilhard de Chardin[28] with his vision of a Noosphere circling the earth (the compassionate revolution perhaps) has peered only a slight distance into the future. I agree with Warren Wager[18] that our present gropings toward the moon and beyond, form the first necessary glimmer of our participation in a cosmic revolution, and this too may encompass a set of revolutions over a time course comparable to the evolutionary course we are now completing.

[28]Pierre Teilhard de Chardin, *The Phenomenon of Man* (New York: Harper, 1959) 318 pp.

Research on the social psychology of the experiment such as that described in the text has led investigators to re-examine many hitherto unquestioned findings in behavioral science. This final section begins with Martin T. Orne's paper which reinterprets classical hypnotic phenomena from the standpoint of a role theory explanation and in light of the author's impressive discoveries in this area.

We conclude the volume with a chapter from Eugene Burdick's novel of the late 1950s, *The Ninth Wave*—an account of the experiences of the book's hero, Mike Freesmith, as a research subject in a psychology study. Several of the mediating influences discussed in the text appear to have been intuitively grasped by Burdick. This may not be a surprise, but what *is* surprising, as Irwin Silverman has recently noted,[1] is that psychologists have taken so long to grasp the same ideas, to realize the implications of these factors for the interpersonal situation between experimenter and subject that comprises the psychological experiment.

[1] Paper represented by Irwin Silverman at the Southeastern Psychological Association meeting in the symposium, Methodological Problems and Research in Social Influence, New Orleans, Louisiana, February 1969.

Part XIV
THE "GOOD SUBJECT" IN PSYCHOLOGICAL RESEARCH

Recent research findings have indicated the need to reconsider what had appeared to be reasonable assumptions about the nature of hypnosis. At first sight, the implications of these studies seem to be at variance with clinical experience and common sense, but careful consideration actually allows us to reconcile clinical and experimental findings in a more satisfactory way than has been possible in the past.

It has been widely held that hypnosis alters the relationship between subject and hypnotist by changing the subject's motivation. One of the more extreme statements of this position was made by the present author (8, 9) in an extrapolation of the views of White (17, 18). It was assumed that the hypnotic state increases the subject's motivation to please the hypnotist; in other words, that it makes him unusually compliant. This assumption seems soundly based on the behavior of hypnotized individuals who certainly *appear* to do things that they would not do ordinarily. Nevertheless, a careful evaluation has failed to uncover any valid evidence for increased compliance in hypnosis, as the hypnotic state has usually been defined. To reconcile this finding with the effectiveness of hypnosis in clinical practice, it has been necessary to clarify the definition of hypnosis itself.

This paper will begin by reviewing the experimental evidence that has made it necessary to reject the usual concept of hypnosis in terms of motivation and compliance. This evidence suggests that hypnosis is not a change in the degree of compliance but rather, a change in the subjective experience of hypnotized individuals. The kinds of phenomena that are subsumed under the concept of hypnosis will be discussed in order to show that a definition in terms of subjective expe-

29
Hypnosis, Motivation and Compliance

Martin T. Orne

Read at the 121st annual meeting of the American Psychiatric Association, New York, N.Y., May 3–7, 1965, under the title "Empirical Research on Hypnotic Phenomena."
This work was supported in part by Public Health Service grant MH-11028 from the National Institute of Mental Health.
The author wishes to thank the following associates for their comments in the preparation of this paper: Drs. Frederick J. Evans, Lawrence A. Gustafson, Ulric Neisser, Donald N. O'Connell and Ronald E. Shor.

This article was printed in its original form in *The American Journal of Psychiatry*, vol. 122, 1966, pp. 721–726. Copyright 1966, the American Psychiatric Association. A more extensive statement of the author's positions is available in the 1970 Nebraska Symposium on Motivation (Lincoln: University of Nebraska Press).

rience can encompass these adequately. Such a definition suggests that the observed compliance of hypnotized subjects and especially their responsiveness to therapeutic suggestions may not be an intrinsic part of hypnosis itself. From this point of view, the therapeutic effectiveness of hypnosis can be seen in a new light, and some previously puzzling clinical phenomena can be understood.

The motivational view of hypnosis seems compelling because hypnotized subjects are quick to comply with the hypnotist's requests even when unusual or bizarre behavior is suggested. However, the source of the subject's motivation in such cases need not be the hypnotic state itself. In lecturing to college students about hypnosis, I often illustrate this point with a simple demonstration. I ask a number of students to carry out certain actions—one will be asked to take off his right shoe, another to exchange his necktie with his neighbor, a third to give me his wallet and so on. After these things have been done, I point out that if the same behavior had been carried out after a hypnotic induction, it would have seemed that the students were under hypnotic control. The point is that while all the behaviors fell within the range of admissible requests in this situation, it is not common for lecturers to make such "unreasonable" requests. Therefore, one is tempted to assume, incorrectly, that only hypnotized persons would comply with them.

An experimental demonstration of this point is provided by Orne and Evans' (11) replication of the work of Rowland (14) and Young (19), which appeared to prove that subjects can be compelled to carry out antisocial and self-destructive actions under hypnosis. The earlier investigations had shown that deeply hypnotized subjects can be compelled to pick up a rattlesnake, lift a penny out of fuming nitric acid and throw the acid at an assistant. We found that their results are indeed replicable but that this behavior could be obtained equally well from nonhypnotized individuals in the waking state. The waking subjects were fully aware that the behavior they were being asked to carry out would normally be highly self-destructive, antisocial and dangerous. However, in a post-

experimental interview we learned that they were convinced (correctly) that appropriate safeguards would be taken to protect them and the assistant from any real harm.

In short, so far it has not been possible to find an aspect of behavior which subjects will perform in hypnosis but will not perform in the waking state. This does not entirely eliminate the possibility that hypnosis may actually increase the range of behaviors that people are willing to carry out. It merely demonstrates that subjects tend to do anything that might conceivably be required of them in an experimental setting. Any behavior that subjects might *not* carry out is well beyond the range that an experimenter could afford to request. Milgram's (7) recent studies with shock underline this point; he has shown that subjects continue to administer what seem to be extremely high and dangerous levels of electric shock to another person in the context of a learning experiment.

EFFECT ON PERFORMANCE OF DIFFICULT TASKS

Rather than examining the range of tasks that subjects will perform, one can study the effect of hypnosis on performance quantitatively by using difficult, fatiguing tasks. Such an approach requires considerable caution. If the subject is used as his own control, he may indeed perform much better in hypnosis than when awake. However, one must bear in mind that experimental subjects are extremely compliant even without being hypnotized. If they think the experimenter is attempting to prove that hypnosis increases performance, they may easily provide him with supporting data—not necessarily by *increasing* their hypnotic performance, but by *decreasing* their waking performance (4, 9). Moreover, studies by Orne (8, 9), Barber and Calverley (1) and Levitt and Brady (5) have shown that with proper motivation, waking subjects can surpass their own hypnosis performance. In these studies, however, no attempt was made to equate instructions in the two conditions, so that subjects were motivated very differently during waking and hypnosis. While the findings demonstrate that hypnosis does not lead to a transcendence of normal volitional capabilities, they shed no light on whether hypnosis alone increases the motivation of the subject to comply with requests of the hypnotist.

To investigate this question, one would need to give *identical instructions* in the waking state and in hypnosis; for example, asking the subject to hold a kilogram weight at arm's length as long as possible. Performance in such an experiment would be a measure of the degree of willingness to comply which is induced by identical instructions in different states. While some studies have used this approach, they have inevitably encountered a serious methodological problem. It is difficult, if not impossible, to give instructions to a hypnotized subject in the same way as to a waking subject. While the "lyrics" may remain constant, the "melody" is usually drastically altered and therefore the total communication is quite different. Consequent differences in performance are not surprising, but in this paradigm we cannot determine whether they are due to the way in which the instructions are given or to the presence of hypnosis.

A rather ingenious experimental design by London and Fuhrer (6) gets around this difficulty. A large number of subjects are given an initial test of susceptibility to hypnosis. From this sample, the extreme responders and nonresponders are selected. All selected subjects are told that they are sufficiently deeply hypnotizable for the purposes of the experiment. In the main part of the experiment a very neutral, relaxing form of trance induction is used and subjects are tested on a motor task. A comparison is then made between performance of good hypnotic subjects and individuals who are relatively insusceptible to hypnosis. If hypnosis makes subjects more compliant, the performance by the hypnotizable group should be greater than that by the insusceptible group. However, in several studies, London and Fuhrer (6) and Rosenhan and London (12, 13) did not find this result. If anything, *insusceptible* subjects perform better under hypnotic conditions than susceptible ones. In a detailed replication of this work, Evans and Orne (4) found *no* difference in performance between susceptible and insusceptible subjects. Nevertheless, their findings, while not confirming all of the earlier results, certainly do not suggest that the hypnotizable subjects were more motivated to comply with the wishes of the hypnotist than the others.

In another study in a different context, we tried to measure compliance by giving subjects a large stack of postcards and asking them to mail one back to the laboratory every day. The request was made while the subject was awake, but the experimenter had previously hypnotized each one to determine his degree of hypnotizability. If hypnosis significantly alters the hypnotist-subject relationship, one might expect that the good hypnotic subjects would send more postcards than those who were unable to enter hypnosis, even though the request itself was not given hypnotically. However, the correlation between the number of postcards sent and depth of hypnosis achieved on the test was essentially nil.

It is possible that the criterion used in the postcard study is inappropriate to the problem. We have also examined a less contrived measure which may well reflect level of motivation. Much of our experimental work has involved not only excellent hypnotic subjects but also essentially unhypnotizable individuals used as controls. Retrospectively, it occurred to us that the number of cancelled appointments and actual drop-outs in the highly hypnotizable group was greater than in the nonhypnotizable individuals. Therefore, we began recording subjects' time of arrival for experimental sessions and correlated their punctuality with their hypnotic performance. We found a modest but significant *negative* relationship— the good subjects tended to arrive late for the experiment, while the relatively insusceptible subjects tended to arrive early. Undoubtedly there are many ways of explaining this finding, but it is certainly not what would be expected if good hypnotic subjects are especially motivated to please the hypnotist.

A further relevant finding emerged in a study conducted in our laboratory by Shor (15). Prior to an experiment involving electric shock, subjects were asked to choose the highest level of shock they would be willing to tolerate. The relatively insusceptible subjects chose to tolerate significantly higher levels of shock than the good somnambulists.

All these findings argue against the hypothesis that being found susceptible to hypnosis leads to a generalized tendency to comply with requests from the hypnotist. No such tendency appears when the requests are not directly relevant to the hypnotic situation. In other words, a subject who carries out hypnotic suggestions may not necessarily be more inclined to carry out other requests.

CRITERIA FOR HYPNOSIS

In order to understand these results, it is necessary to examine the definition of hypnosis itself. What criteria do we have in mind when we say that someone is hypnotized? It is true that observers watching a subject respond to suggestions usually agree on whether he is hypnotized, and how deeply. Moreover, an objective scale of hypnotic depth is employed in most of the empirical work done today. The Stanford Hypnotic Susceptibility Scale, Form C (16) is probably the most widely used. The scale scores agree very well with the judgment of trained observers.

Nevertheless, it is appropriate to ask what criterion the observers are actually using, or, conversely, what a subject must do to achieve a high score on a scale of hypnotic depth. It is clear that the critical variable is the subject's ability to respond to suggestions. The hypnotic suggestions, however, are not all of the same kind. They can be classified into four groups: 1) ideomotor suggestions, 2) challenge suggestions, 3) hallucinations and memory distortions (of which amnesia is a special example) and 4) posthypnotic behavior. Such a classification has received recent empirical support by the factor analytic results of Evans (3).

In a classic ideomotor suggestion such as the sway test, the subject is told that he is falling backward. He is told what to experience: "You are falling backward...you feel yourself falling further and further backward." The response is defined as

positive by the extent to which the subject actually falls, but it is implicitly assumed that he is to fall *because he feels himself drawn backward* rather than because of the conscious volitional decision: "I will fall backward." To the degree that the actual falling depends on a volitional decision, it has failed to measure an ideomotor response. The experimenter is not attempting to measure behavioral compliance per se but rather the behavioral manifestations of a subjective experience. If one were measuring only behavioral compliance, one would use the simple instruction, "Fall backward now." In an experimental context at least, compliance would be almost total.

The challenge suggestion (exemplified by: "Your eyes are tightly glued together; you cannot open them. Try to open them. You cannot.") is also scored behaviorally, on the basis of the subject's failure to open his eyes. Here too, however, it is hoped that this behavior accurately reflects a subjective inability to open the eyes, rather than mere compliance with the hypnotist's wish. While these two possibilities are difficult to distinguish operationally, the response measures "depth of hypnosis" only insofar as it reflects an *experienced* inability on the part of the subject to open his eyes, i.e., the extent to which a subject *cannot* comply even when he is challenged to do so.

Items dealing with hallucination, amnesia or other memory distortions are also designed to produce responses which reflect a presumed change in the subjective experience. A subject is genuinely hypnotized not because he is willing to report certain things, but because his report really describes his personal subjective experience.

POSTHYPNOTIC PHENOMENON

The posthypnotic phenomenon is most difficult to deal with in this context because the usual criterion is purely behavioral: does the subject carry out the suggestion? Nevertheless, the response to posthypnotic suggestion is subjectively quite different from simple compliance. It is presumed that subjects experience a *compulsion* to carry out the suggested behavior, regardless of whether they actually recall the suggestion. In fact, Evans (3) has attempted to measure separately the compulsion and recall elements of typical posthypnotic suggestions and found them to be only moderately correlated. Elsewhere the author has summarized data on posthypnotic behavior (10, see also 2) showing that, despite this subjective compulsion, a posthypnotic suggestion is apt to be less effective than a simple request to carry out experimental behavior. These quantitative and qualitative differences provide convincing evidence that posthypnotic suggestion is not merely a matter of behavioral compliance.

In short, the criteria used to determine whether a subject is hypnotized do not focus primarily on whether he does what he is told. Rather, they are attempts to measure the extent to which distortions in his perception or memory can be induced by appropriate cues. If a wide range of distortions can easily be caused to appear, the subject is said to be deeply hypnotized; individuals in whom few, if any, distortions can be produced are considered not hypnotized. Thus the essence of hypnosis as it is often described in popular literature and patients' fantasy does not correspond to its actual definiton. Hypnosis is not so much a way of manipulating behavior as of creating distortions of perception and memory. Thus we can understand why it does not necessarily increase compliance or obedience per se, especially in experimental contexts which already predispose subjects to a very high degree of compliance.

If we adhere to the experiential definition that is actually employed by trained observers and objective scales alike, performance and behavior are not the criteria of hypnosis. It is for this reason that a simple motivational theory of hypnosis cannot be sustained and has been repeatedly contradicted by experimental findings. Tasks which could, in principle, be carried out by nonhypnotized individuals are not carried out better under hypnosis. The hypothetical "increased motivation to please the hypnotist," which ought to manifest itself in performance on such tasks, apparently does not occur.

In a clinical context, the therapist is often more interested in altering the patient's behavior than in studying his experience. So-called "hypnotic" therapy has been reported useful in altering habit patterns and in the suppression of a wide range of neurotic symptoms. Understandably, those using this method have often decided that a patient was successfully hypnotized whenever his behavior was altered by the therapist's suggestion. By this definition, a suggestion is "hypnotic" if it follows a trance induction procedure and has successful results, even without any attempt to evaluate depth of hypnosis by the usual means. It should be clear that this definition of "hypnosis" is quite different from the subjective criterion we have discussed here. It is entirely possible that patients fail to enter hypnosis in the experiential sense, and yet respond to a therapeutic suggestion. Conversely, other patients may be deeply hypnotized and fail to respond to such a suggestion. The clinical procedure which defines "hypnosis" post hoc would, by its nature, fail to recognize such a situation.

It is highly probable that hypnotizability in our sense does not correlate highly with response to therapeutic suggestion. This is indicated by a phenomenon that has long been recognized as puzzling: namely, that even a "light hypnotic trance" may be sufficient to produce therapeutically marked changes in behavior. I have been struck particularly by two recent patients who were totally unable to manifest hypnotic phenomena and did nothing more than close their eyes in response to a request to do so. By any of the usual criteria, one would have to conclude that they were not hypnotized at all. Nonetheless, therapeutic suggestions produced dramatic positive responses.

If we are to be consistent in our definitions, we must recognize the possibility that a hypnotic trance-induction procedure may fail to induce hypnosis itself and yet make the patient more responsive to therapeutic suggestions designed to alter his behavior. Two aspects of the therapeutic situation utilizing trance induction can be separated: 1) the effect of suggestions made during a situation defined by doctor and patient as "hypnosis" and 2) the classic state of hypnosis in which the patient responds to appropriate suggestions from the hypnotist by distorting reality. Susceptibility to hypnosis itself may be different from susceptibility to therapeutically oriented requests which often involve no cognitive distortion.

The necessary and sufficient conditions for the classic subjective phenomena of hypnosis are as yet unclear, but the hypothesis that hypnosis is essentially a matter of compliance seems untenable. Even the more plausible hypothesis that hypnosis depends on an increased motivation to carry out any tasks requested by the hypnotist must be rejected, or at least restricted to apply only to tasks involving cognitive distortions. If this is true, how can we understand the clinical effectiveness of the hypnotic induction procedure? This procedure does appear to change the existing transference relationship, and "hypnotic" suggestions do often alter symptoms which resisted other forms of suggestion.

EFFECT ON ROLE RELATIONSHIP

In terms of the present formulation, these effects may not be primarily a function of hypnosis itself. Rather, they may result from the altered relationship which exists when a therapist assumes the role of "hypnotist" and shares with his patient the expectation that hypnosis involves unlimited compliance. This is certainly a different role relationship than the usual therapeutic one. Not only are magical powers ascribed to the therapist by the patient, but the therapist's behavior tends to reinforce these fantasies. Furthermore, therapists allow (in fact encourage) regressive behavior and permit an intense closeness which they might otherwise be unwilling to tolerate. These changes in the relationship between doctor and patient do not in themselves constitute the real hypnotic state, although they may indeed be among the sufficient conditions to evoke it. If one could devise a relationship where these accoutrements of the hypnotic relationship exist without hypnosis itself, there would be hope of separating the two empirically.

Perhaps the augmented response to suggestions usually ascribed to hypnosis relates more to

these changes in doctor-patient relationship than to the hypnotic potentiality for distorted perceptions. This relationship helps to evoke hypnosis in some individuals. However, even if in other individuals it fails to do so, the relationship per se may still alter the motivation of the patient and dramatically affect his response to certain types of suggestion. If this were the case, it would help to explain many of the apparent contradictions about hypnosis, including not only the vastly differing reports by different hypnotists about the percentage of hypnotizable individuals in the population, but also the lack of correlation between hypnotizability and compliance.

REFERENCES

1. Barber, T.X., and Calverley, D.S.: Toward a Theory of "Hypnotic" Behaviour: Enhancement of Strength and Endurance, Canad. J. Psychol. 18:156–167, 1964.

2. Damaser, E.: Experimental Study of Long-Term Post-Hypnotic Suggestion, unpublished doctoral dissertation. Department of Social Relations, Harvard University, 1964.

3. Evans, F.J.: The Structure of Hypnosis: A Factor Analytic Investigation, unpublished doctoral dissertation. University of Sydney, Australia, 1965.

4. Evans, F.J., and Orne, M.T.: Motivation, Performance, and Hypnosis, Int. J. Clin. Exp. Hypn. 13:103–116, 1965.

5. Levitt, E.E., and Brady, J.P.: Muscular Endurance under Hypnosis and in the Motivated Waking State, Int. J. Clin. Exp. Hypn. 12:21–27, 1964.

6. London, P., and Fuhrer, M.: Hypnosis, Motivation, and Performance, J. Personality 29:321–333, 1961.

7. Milgram, S.: Behavioral Study of Obedience, J. Abnorm. Soc. Psychol. 67:371–378, 1963.

8. Orne, M.T.: Die Leistungsfähigkeit in Hypnose und im Wachzustand, Psychol. Rdsch. 5:291–297, 1954.

9. Orne, M.T.: The Nature of Hypnosis: Artifact and Essence, J. Abnorm. Soc. Psychol. 58:277–299, 1959.

10. Orne, M.T.: "Psychological Factors Maximizing Resistance to Stress: With Special Reference to Hypnosis," in Klausner, S.Z., ed.: The Quest for Self-Control. New York: The Free Press, 1965.

11. Orne, M.T., and Evans, F.J.: Social Control in the Psychological Experiment: Antisocial Behavior and Hypnosis, J. Pers. Soc. Psychol. 1:189–200, 1965.

12. Rosenhan, D., and London, P.: Hypnosis: Expectation, Susceptibility, and Performance, J. Abnorm. Soc. Psychol. 66:77–81, 1963.

13. Rosenhan, D., and London, P.: Hypnosis in the Unhypnotizable: A Study in Rote Learning. J. Exp. Psychol. 65:30–34, 1963.

14. Rowland, L.W.: Will Hypnotized Persons Try to Harm Themselves or Others? J. Abnorm. Soc. Psychol. 34:114–117, 1939.

15. Shor, R.E.: A Note on Shock Tolerances of Real and Simulating Hypnotic Subjects, Int. J. Clin. Exp. Hypn. 12:258–262, 1964.

16. Weitzenhoffer, A.M., and Hilgard, E.R.: Stanford Hypnotic Susceptibility Scale, Form C. Palo Alto, Calif.: Consulting Psychologists Press, 1962.

17. White, R.W.: A Preface to a Theory of Hypnotism, J. Abnorm. Soc. Psychol. 36:477–505, 1941.

18. White, R.W.: An Analysis of Motivation in Hypnosis, J. Gen. Psychol. 24: 204–224, 1941.

19. Young, P.C.: "Antisocial Uses of Hypnosis," in LeCron, L.M., ed.: Experimental Hypnosis. New York: Macmillan Co., 1952

Mike got a job as a guinea pig the second month he was at Stanford. On the bulletin board on the English Corner there was a sign that stated that subjects for an important psychological experiment were wanted. The pay was fifty cents an hour. The sign directed applicants to see Miss Bird in the Psychology Department.

Mike saw Miss Bird and was hired. She told him where to report for the experiment and the next afternoon he climbed to the top floor of the Psychology Building. He walked down a long corridor lined with rat cages. He could see hundreds of pink eyes glittering in the semi-darkness and a wave of sound preceded him. It was the scurrying of thousands of horny feet. The smell of the rats was thick and hot; like rotted cereal. In one cage there were six rats with neat scars down their skulls. Something had been cut out of their brains for they stayed frozen in one position, unable to move, although their eyes glittered wildly when Mike put his face close to their cage. One rat had been placed with its forepaws tucked under its chin and it squatted on its hind legs. Once it shivered as it tried to move and its eyes rolled, but it remained motionless...only its hair rippled.

Mike turned away and walked down to the room where the experiment was being conducted. Two people were in the room and they were both wearing long white coats. One was a middle-aged woman, the other was a young man with protruding eyes.

"Are you Mr. Freesmith?" the man asked. "I'm Dr. Sutliff. This is Dr. Urich."

Mike shook hands with both of them.

"Could you for the next week every afternoon be available?" Dr. Urich said. She had a foreign accent and spoke very slowly. "Two hours every afternoon?"

"Sure," Mike said.

They led him over to a large table at the end of the room. On the table was a large black box with a naked electric light bulb protruding from the top. There were two windows in the front of the box, one covered with a red card, the other with a blue

30
The Experiment

Eugene Burdick

Reprinted by permission from Eugene Burdick, *The Ninth Wave*, Chapter 4, Houghton Mifflin Company, 1956.

card. In the center of the machine was a small funnel. Mike sat down at the chair in front of the apparatus.

"The object of the experiment is to see how many times you can cause the light to go on," Dr. Urich said in a slow precise voice. Mike sensed that this was a special voice, developed just for giving instructions to subjects. "The light can be illuminated by pressing one or the other of the two cards. Every five seconds a machine within the box automatically changes the cards, giving you cards of different colors. It also changes the window, which will close the circuit and cause the light to go on. So every five seconds you will have a fresh choice. Each time you illuminate the light a penny will drop out of the funnel. You may keep all the pennies you earn. If they do not equal fifty cents an hour we will make up the difference. Do you have any questions?"

"No."

"You may begin."

Mike pressed the red card in the left-hand window. The light did not go on. The machine whirred, two new cards, orange and yellow, dropped down into the windows. Mike pressed the yellow card. The light did not go on. The mechanism whirred again and the cards were changed.

Mike hesitated. Something was wrong. He pressed the right-hand card again. A penny dropped down the funnel, rolled slowly on the table and slowly spun to the surface between his hands. Mike looked down at the penny. The mechanism whirred. He pressed the right-hand card which was black. Again a penny came down the funnel and the light briefly glowed on top of the box.

Forget the cards, he told himself. They're not important. What is important is the mechanism. Forget the cards.

Then, quite intuitively, he was playing the two people in white coats. They must have set the mechanism to work in a certain pattern. The thing to do was to find the pattern. Hell with the cards, Mike thought. Play the people.

Mike pressed the right-hand window two more times and the light did not glow. Then three times it did glow and the pennies rolled down the funnel. Then three times he failed.

That's it, he thought. The pattern is once right, once left; then twice right and twice left, then three times right and three times left and so on.

He pressed the right-hand window four times running and each time he won a penny. Then he switched to the left-hand window and pressed it four times and each time a penny rolled on the table. Then the right-hand window five times. Then the left-hand window five times. The pennies jingled on the table, grew in a heap between his hands. Once a penny rolled out on the floor, but Mike did not notice it. Also he did not notice the color of the cards and he did not look up to see if the light went on. He only watched the funnel to see the little jump that the pennies made when they were ejected onto the slippery metal slide.

He pressed the right-hand window six times, but the fifth and sixth time the penny did not drop down. Mike hesitated. Something had changed. He switched to the left-hand window. It paid twice and then twice it did not. The mechanism had switched to four times on each side. Instantly Mike had it. The mechanism was set to alternate from side to side until it reached five times on each side and then it went down again; four, three, two, one. When it reached one he guessed that it would start up again.

Mike played that pattern and he was correct. Each time the penny jumped onto the funnel, slid down onto the table and rolled to a halt between his fingers. Mike chuckled and played the pattern and each time he pressed the windows he felt he was defeating the two people standing behind him.

For twenty minutes he played without an error. Dr. Urich spoke to Dr. Sutliff. Mike did not listen, but he could tell they were arguing. The stack of pennies grew in front of Mike. The light glowed regularly on top of the black box. Dr. Urich's voice grew slightly shrill.

Dr. Sutliff coughed. He had moved directly behind Mike. Mike looked over his shoulder.

"That will be enough for today, Mr. Freesmith," Dr. Sutliff said.

"I thought you wanted me for two hours," Mike said.

"For our purposes that will be enough today. Tomorrow we will want you again. The apparatus will be the same, but the circumstances will be different."

Mike pushed back his chair and started to stuff the pennies in his pocket. Once he looked up and Dr. Urich was watching him closely, antagonism in her eyes. She smiled over the antagonism. The pennies filled one pocket and half of another. Mike walked lopsided out of the room.

When he was outside the door he paused. He looked at the rats with the thin red wounds in their heads. Through the thin plywood wall he heard Dr. Urich talk.

"He does not play the colors at all," she said. Her voice was full of complaint. "It was exactly as if the colors he did not notice."

"He figured out the pattern we set in the mechanism," Dr. Sutliff said.

"But he is the only one. All else choose by the colors. This will the figures badly skew. How do we explain?"

"We'll alter the mechanism tomorrow and then see how he does," Dr. Sutliff said.

"Why would he not do as the others?" Dr. Urich said. "It was plain that he should choose by colors."

"It's a stress situation. The pennies are positive motivation to take the pattern rather than respond by colors. It's just funny that he is the only one that concentrated on the pattern."

Mike put his finger through the wire of the cage and pushed gently against the rat standing on its hind legs. The rat's eyes bulged, its fur bent away from his finger, but the rat's body moved like putty. Mike pushed it to one side and the rat stayed in that position, bent at an impossible angle, its tiny claws tucked under its chin. Mike turned and hurried off down the corridor.

The next day when Mike reported for the experiment there were two more subjects in the room. One was a girl named Connie Burton and the other was a boy named Bill Evans. The girl was attractive and she was wearing a cashmere sweater and Mike guessed she was doing the ex-

periment for some other reason than money. The boy was skinny and very embarrassed.

Dr. Urich gave the instructions again.

"Each of you has operated this apparatus before. Today the mechanism has been altered so that a new pattern is operating. You will decide among yourselves which window you will choose on each try. You may choose the window on whatever basis you wish. But you must all agree on the decision. If you are not agreed you can make no choice. None of you may press the window until the other two have agreed to your choice. You will share the pennies that you earn. Please make your discussion audible for what you say will be recorded on a wire recorder."

A paper in her hand rustled, she coughed and the room was quiet. Bill Evans looked at her with agony.

"Do we start now?" Mike asked.

"You may start now," Dr. Urich said. She walked to the back of the room and joined Dr. Sutliff.

The three students looked down at the windows. There was a pink card in the left window and a blue card in the right window.

"Let's start with the pink card," Connie said.

"Why?" Mike asked.

"Well, we have to start somewhere. Also I noticed when I did the test alone that pastel-colored cards turned on the light more often than darker colors."

"What about you?" Mike asked Bill.

"I don't remember," Bill said. "I just picked the color I liked each time. It's supposed to be a test in color perception so I tried to wipe my mind clean and pick the color I liked best between the two cards."

"Who said it was supposed to be a test in color perception?" Mike said.

"Nobody." Connie said. "But you can see that it is. That's why the cards change. What else could be the point of having the cards change?"

Mike looked slowly from the boy to the girl.

"Look, isn't the point to illuminate the light, to make the pennies come down the slide?" he asked.

"Sure, but we ought to do it the way they want us to do it," Bill said. "They're trying to learn something about colors and we ought to decide on the basis of the colors we like or something like that."

He looked over his shoulder. Dr. Sutliff and Dr. Urich were in a shadow and he could not see their faces.

"He's right," Connie said. "We ought to do what they want. We really should co-operate. It's an important experiment."

"The important thing is to illuminate the light as often as you can," Mike said. "That's all they've told us. Let's do that. O.K., you can disregard the cards then. They're not important. What is important is the mechanism inside the box. Every time it changes it makes one or the other window the right choice."

"What about the cards?" Bill asked.

"Forget the damned cards," Mike said. "Use your head. Someone had to fix the mechanism, put a pattern into it. If you discover that pattern you can make the light go on every time and you'll get a penny every time. Right?"

He could see that it had never occurred to either of them before. The girl saw it first and she started to smile, but almost at once she looked over her shoulder at the rear of the room.

"What if there isn't any pattern in the mechanism?" she said. "What if it's just a random choice?"

"That's probably what they think it is," Mike said. "But making things random is hard. Whoever set the mechanism probably did it a certain way just out of laziness. Or because he thought we would concentrate on the colors of the cards. Do you agree that if there is a pattern in the mechanism and we can find it out that is the quickest way to earn the pennies?"

Faintly, like the sound of a machine heard through a thick wall, Dr. Urich was talking urgently to Dr. Sutliff.

"Well, logically I think you're right," Connie said. "But I don't think that's what they want us to do. The cards are there for a reason."

"Who cares what they want us to do?" Mike asked. "Let's do the best thing. We could have pressed the window twenty times by now. We're just wasting time. Look, I'll start to press the windows and find out the pattern of the machine. If I don't find it in a few minutes we'll try another method."

He leaned forward.

"Remember, Mr. Freesmith," Dr. Urich's voice said softly, "every one of the subjects must agree to letting you proceed."

Mike looked first at Connie and then at Bill.

"How about it?" Mike said. "Are we just going to sit here or are we going to do something? They don't care what we do. They said we can do anything we want." Bill was sweating in the dull yellow light. "Anything is better than nothing. Is it all right for me to go ahead? Do you agree?"

Bill glanced once more over his shoulder and then his face dissolved in confusion. He nodded agreement at Mike. Mike turned to Connie. She nodded.

Mike began to push the left-hand door. He pushed it twenty times in a row. It only paid off six times, but at the end of that time he had found the pattern. He pulled his chair closer and began to play his system. Once he had to alter it when a slight change was made in the pattern.

Behind him he could hear Dr. Urich arguing with Dr. Sutliff.

Mike pushed one window after another and every time a penny rolled down the slide. The heap of pennies grew between his hands. At the end of twenty minutes he pushed the heap of pennies aside and Connie and Bill began to stack them. He did not take time to explain the pattern which he was playing to them. They became bored and once he heard Connie yawn. Bill stood rigidly beside him, stiffly stacking pennies into little piles of ten.

At the end of the hour the table was almost covered with the little piles of pennies. Dr. Urich and Dr. Sutliff came up from the back of the room and thanked them. Dr. Sutliff put his open notebook down on the table.

"Thank you very much for your co-operation," Dr. Sutliff said. "It was very good of you to give us your time. I think you will discover that you have earned a good deal more than fifty cents for your hour's work." He smiled thinly. "Your co-operation was very helpful."

Dr. Urich was standing to one side. She looked

steadily at Mike and her face was strained with anger. When Mike caught her eye she flushed and looked down at her hands.

"Will you want us tomorrow?" Mike said.

"No. Not tomorrow," Dr. Urich cut in. "Not ever again, I think. We must revise the experiment on the basis of today's results."

Mike edged over to the table and he glanced down at Dr. Sutliff's notebook. On the top of the page was the title of the experiment: "Color Apperception: The Latent Tendency to Overselect Dark Colors." There was a notation of the scores that Connie and Bill had made on previous attempts. Connie had guessed right forty-two per cent of the time. Bill had guessed right thirty-eight per cent of the time. Mike glanced down the page to a section of notes written in ink and bearing the date of that day. He read it quickly:

> The three subjects did not make the selection on the basis of color preference, but seemed to make what might be called a political selection. Subject 34 dominated the group and insisted that the choices be made on a basis other than the color of the cards. For this reason today's results are being discarded as being atypical and aberrant. Subject 34 will not be used again in the experiments.

Mike turned away. The pennies had been divided and each of them received 205 pennies. Mike took his, put them in his pocket. He grinned at Dr. Urich and walked out of the door. In the corridor he stopped for a moment to look at the catatonic rats. The rat with its paws under its chin was still slanted sideways. Mike gently bent the rat forward until it was on all fours. Then he pushed it over to the water spout at the end of the cage. The rat's tongue shot out, licked at the water and Mike left after it had consumed a half dozen drops.

Mike was almost at the foot of the stairs before Bill Evans caught up with him. Bill was breathing hard, but his face was bright with excitement.

"I wanted to thank you," he said hurriedly, not looking at Mike's face. "I hate both of them; Dr. Urich and Dr. Sutliff. I hate them and that damned

test. It made me nervous. I've been doing it for weeks. I always get about the same number of pennies. Never over fifty an hour. They always acted so damned superior. I'm glad we did it the way you wanted. Did you see how mad Dr. Urich was? Serves her right. I'm glad. Really glad."

He jingled the pennies in his pocket and smiled quickly at Mike and then looked away.

"Anyway thanks," Bill said. "I'm glad we did it. I got so I was hating the two of them. I feel better now."

He turned quickly and trotted away. Mike never saw him again at Stanford.

Mike walked slowly across the Quad. Something is wrong with the two professors, he thought. There was something important they were missing. They were testing for something little, something screwy, unimportant. And something big was involved.

He turned the experiment over in his mind, tried to find the correct words. They slipped away from him, remained just at the edge of his mind. He walked by the chapel, past the clumps of palm trees and around the tall thin hulk of the Hoover Library.

Then it came to him. He stopped. A girl drove by on a bicycle and he was only aware of the spinning wheels, the clank of the chain, the flash of her plaid skirt.

The important part of the afternoon's experiment was this, Mike thought, and the words went like a written sentence across his mind: one person can make a decision faster than a group.

That's it, he thought. That's Freesmith's First Principle of Human Behavior: One person can make a decision faster than a group. That's exactly, perfectly, precisely, absolutely it.

He walked on toward Encina Hall. He was almost there when he thought of Bill Evans and another principle crossed his mind. Freesmith's Second Principle of Human Behavior: The weak person wants to be delivered from the superior person.

Delivered to what? he asked, as if the principle had been stated by another person.

It doesn't matter, he said. Deliverance is enough.

Name Index

White, R.W., 321, 327
White, T.H., 226
Whitehead, A., 3
Wicker, R., 199
Wike, E.L., 110, 116
Wilbur, C.B., 205
Wilkins, R., 218, 223
Willet, Mrs., 57
Williams, C.L., 162
Williams, J.T., 273
Williams, L., 265
Williams, R.M., 239, 245, 248, 252, 256, 260, 265, 266
Willis, R.H., 265
Wilner, D.M., 252, 256, 266
Wilson, R.H.L., 309
Wilson, W., 111, 116
Winokur, G., 72
Winston, H.D., 189
Wolf, S., 72
Wolff, H.G., 65, 70, 71

Wolfgang, M.E., 305
Wolpe, J., 199, 206
Works, E., 252, 256, 266
Wyatt, G.L., 117, 119

Yarrow, M.R., 252, 266
Yaryan, R., 106
Yerkes, R.M., 134, 142, 143
York, R.L., 264
Young, P.C., 322, 327
Young, W.C., 189

Zahn, G.C., 242, 248
Zajonc, R.B., 97
Zangwill, O.L., 189
Ziferstein, I., 306
Zimmerman, R.R., 188
Zimring, F., 306
Zinberg, N.E., 21, 30
Zubin, J., 313